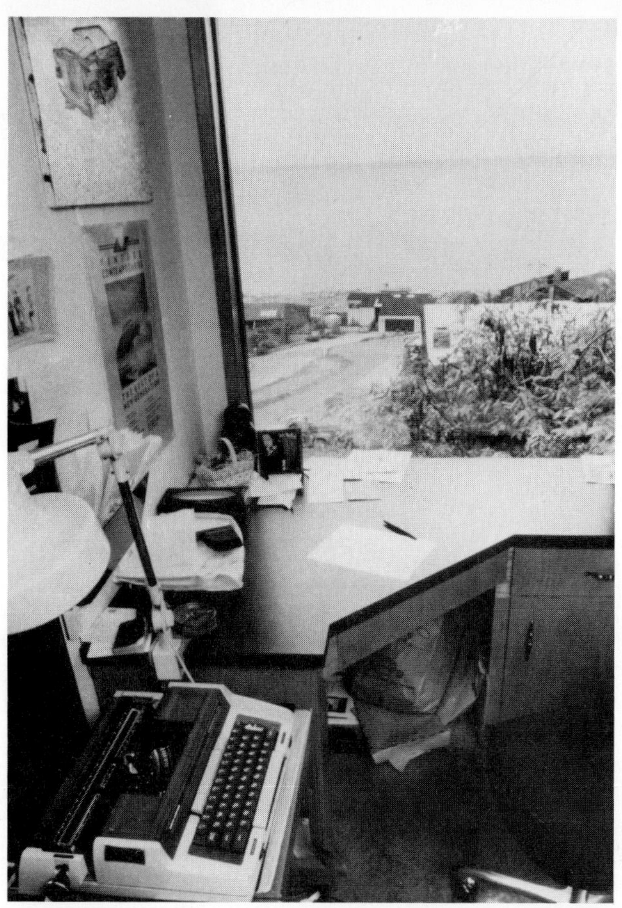

MACMILLAN ENGLISH

the program with the most choices for students and teachers

- Sequenced instruction in the Writing Process with writing choices for different-ability students.
- Thorough development of Grammar, Usage, and Mechanics with extensive practice options.
- Complete coverage of Skills and Resources with built-in flexibility for use all year long.
- Convenient and abundant teaching materials for more teaching choices and easier lesson planning.

Macmillan English – The best choice!

PART ONE •

COMPOSITION *Sequenced instruction in the Writing Process leads to independence in writing.*

Prewriting Skills

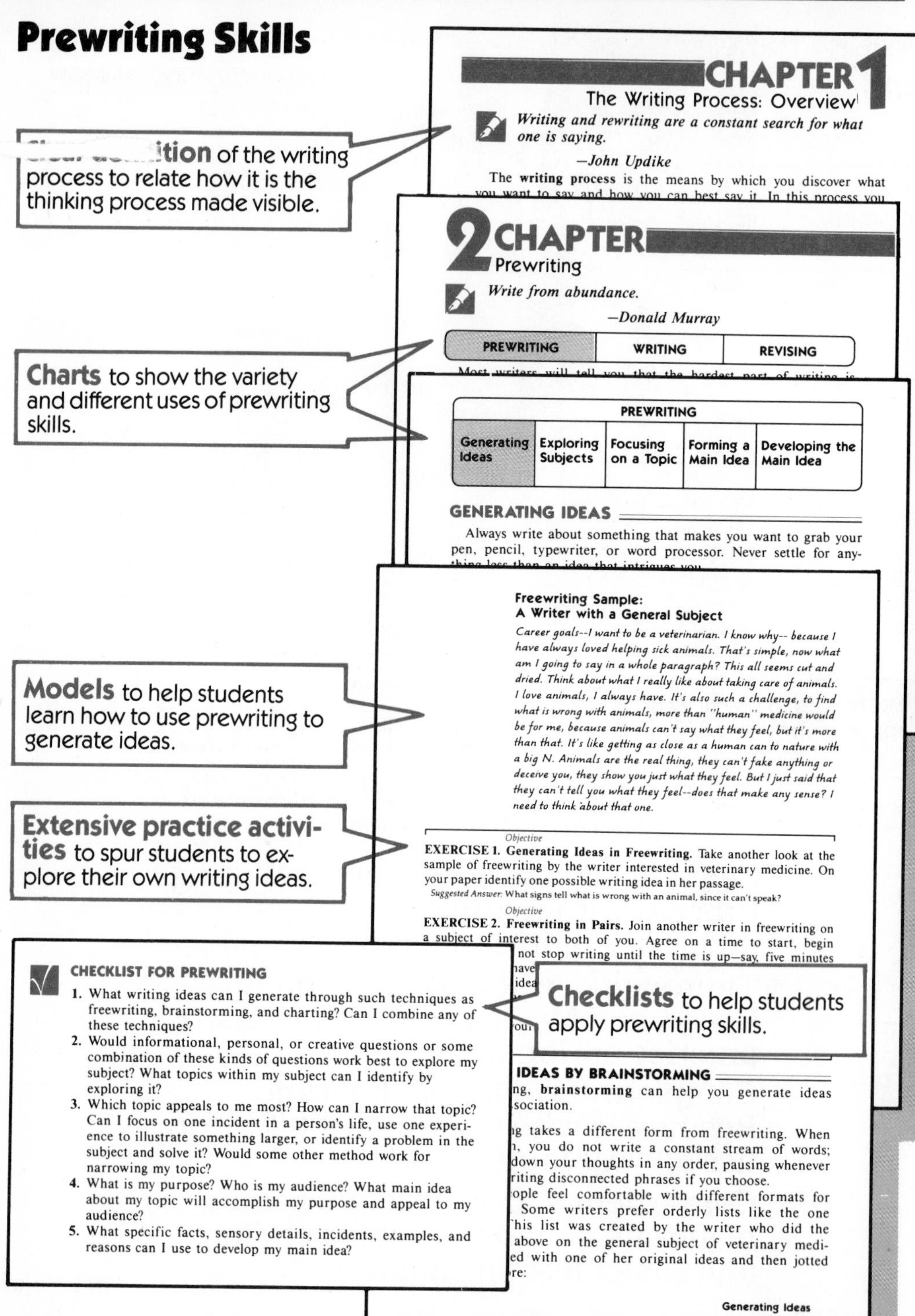

...ition of the writing process to relate how it is the thinking process made visible.
CHAPTER 1
The Writing Process: Overview
Writing and rewriting are a constant search for what one is saying.
—John Updike
The writing process is the means by which you discover what
2 CHAPTER
Prewriting
Write from abundance.
—Donald Murray
PREWRITING
WRITING
REVISING
Charts to show the variety and different uses of prewriting skills.
PREWRITING
Generating Ideas
Exploring Subjects
Focusing on a Topic
Forming a Main Idea
Developing the Main Idea
GENERATING IDEAS
Always write about something that makes you want to grab your pen, pencil, typewriter, or word processor. Never settle for any-
Freewriting Sample:
A Writer with a General Subject
Career goals--I want to be a veterinarian. I know why-- because I have always loved helping sick animals. That's simple, now what am I going to say in a whole paragraph? This all seems cut and dried. Think about what I really like about taking care of animals. I love animals, I always have. It's also such a challenge, to find what is wrong with animals, more than "human" medicine would be for me, because animals can't say what they feel, but it's more than that. It's like getting as close as a human can to nature with a big N. Animals are the real thing, they can't fake anything or deceive you, they show you just what they feel. But I just said that they can't tell you what they feel--does that make any sense? I need to think about that one.
Models to help students learn how to use prewriting to generate ideas.
Extensive practice activities to spur students to explore their own writing ideas.
Objective
EXERCISE 1. Generating Ideas in Freewriting. Take another look at the sample of freewriting by the writer interested in veterinary medicine. On your paper identify one possible writing idea in her passage.
Suggested Answer: What signs tell what is wrong with an animal, since it can't speak?
Objective
EXERCISE 2. Freewriting in Pairs. Join another writer in freewriting on a subject of interest to both of you. Agree on a time to start, begin
not stop writing until the time is up—say, five minutes
CHECKLIST FOR PREWRITING
1. What writing ideas can I generate through such techniques as freewriting, brainstorming, and charting? Can I combine any of these techniques?
2. Would informational, personal, or creative questions or some combination of these kinds of questions work best to explore my subject? What topics within my subject can I identify by exploring it?
3. Which topic appeals to me most? How can I narrow that topic? Can I focus on one incident in a person's life, use one experience to illustrate something larger, or identify a problem in the subject and solve it? Would some other method work for narrowing my topic?
4. What is my purpose? Who is my audience? What main idea about my topic will accomplish my purpose and appeal to my audience?
5. What specific facts, sensory details, incidents, examples, and reasons can I use to develop my main idea?
Checklists to help students apply prewriting skills.
IDEAS BY BRAINSTORMING
ng, brainstorming can help you generate ideas
sociation.
Generating Ideas

Writing Paragraphs and Forms

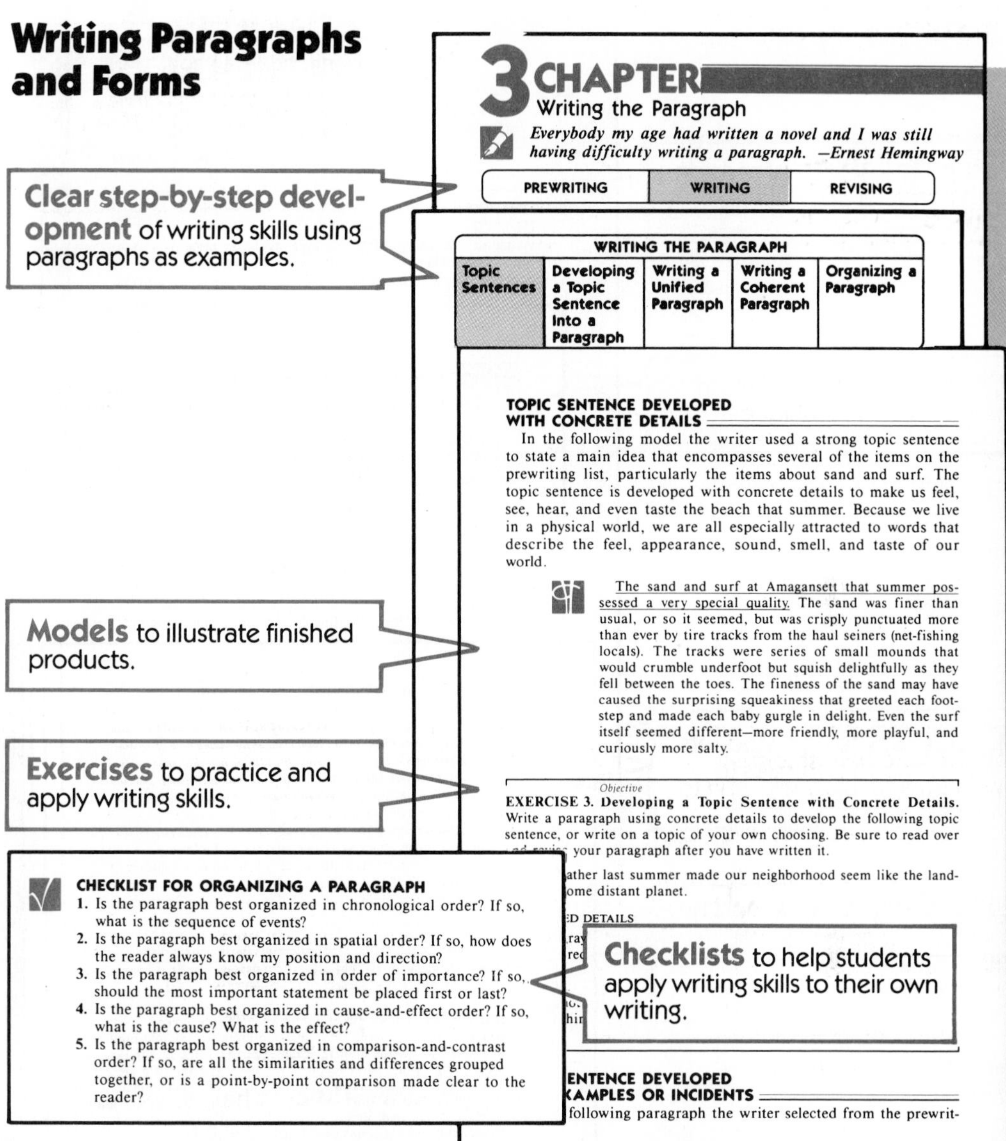

Clear step-by-step development of writing skills using paragraphs as examples.

Models to illustrate finished products.

Exercises to practice and apply writing skills.

Checklists to help students apply writing skills to their own writing.

3 CHAPTER

Writing the Paragraph

Everybody my age had written a novel and I was still having difficulty writing a paragraph. —*Ernest Hemingway*

PREWRITING	WRITING	REVISING

WRITING THE PARAGRAPH				
Topic Sentences	Developing a Topic Sentence Into a Paragraph	Writing a Unified Paragraph	Writing a Coherent Paragraph	Organizing a Paragraph

TOPIC SENTENCE DEVELOPED WITH CONCRETE DETAILS

In the following model the writer used a strong topic sentence to state a main idea that encompasses several of the items on the prewriting list, particularly the items about sand and surf. The topic sentence is developed with concrete details to make us feel, see, hear, and even taste the beach that summer. Because we live in a physical world, we are all especially attracted to words that describe the feel, appearance, sound, smell, and taste of our world.

The sand and surf at Amagansett that summer possessed a very special quality. The sand was finer than usual, or so it seemed, but was crisply punctuated more than ever by tire tracks from the haul seiners (net-fishing locals). The tracks were series of small mounds that would crumble underfoot but squish delightfully as they fell between the toes. The fineness of the sand may have caused the surprising squeakiness that greeted each footstep and made each baby gurgle in delight. Even the surf itself seemed different—more friendly, more playful, and curiously more salty.

Objective

EXERCISE 3. Developing a Topic Sentence with Concrete Details. Write a paragraph using concrete details to develop the following topic sentence, or write on a topic of your own choosing. Be sure to read over and revise your paragraph after you have written it.

...ather last summer made our neighborhood seem like the land-...ome distant planet.

...D DETAILS

...ENTENCE DEVELOPED ...AMPLES OR INCIDENTS

...following paragraph the writer selected from the prewrit-

CHECKLIST FOR ORGANIZING A PARAGRAPH

1. Is the paragraph best organized in chronological order? If so, what is the sequence of events?
2. Is the paragraph best organized in spatial order? If so, how does the reader always know my position and direction?
3. Is the paragraph best organized in order of importance? If so, should the most important statement be placed first or last?
4. Is the paragraph best organized in cause-and-effect order? If so, what is the cause? What is the effect?
5. Is the paragraph best organized in comparison-and-contrast order? If so, are all the similarities and differences grouped together, or is a point-by-point comparison made clear to the reader?

Extensive instruction and practice in using the writing process with longer forms of writing

- Descriptive Writing
- Narrative Writing
- Expository Writing
- Critical Thinking and Persuasive Writing
- The Essay
- The Research Paper

COMPOSITION

Revising Strategies

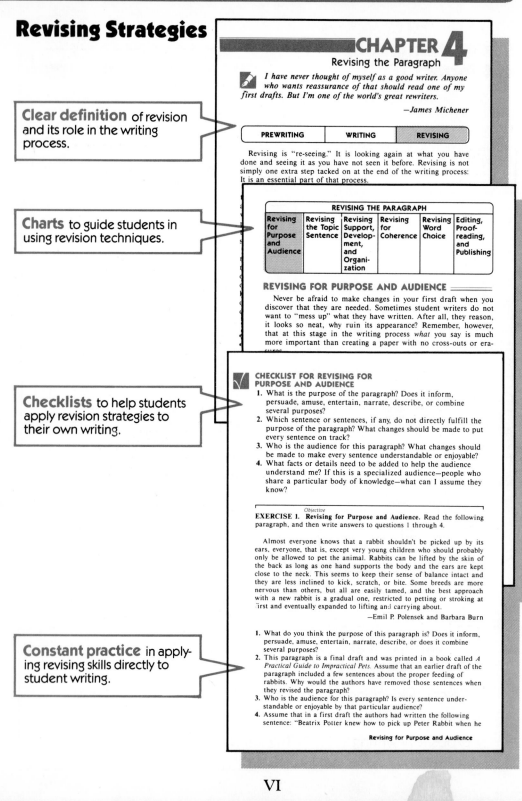

Clear definition of revision and its role in the writing process.

Charts to guide students in using revision techniques.

Checklists to help students apply revision strategies to their own writing.

Constant practice in applying revising skills directly to student writing.

CHAPTER 4

Revising the Paragraph

I have never thought of myself as a good writer. Anyone who wants reassurance of that should read one of my first drafts. But I'm one of the world's great rewriters.

—*James Michener*

PREWRITING	WRITING	REVISING

Revising is "re-seeing." It is looking again at what you have done and seeing it as you have not seen it before. Revising is not simply one extra step tacked on at the end of the writing process: It is an essential part of that process.

REVISING THE PARAGRAPH					
Revising for Purpose and Audience	Revising the Topic Sentence	Revising Support, Development, and Organization	Revising for Coherence	Revising Word Choice	Editing, Proofreading, and Publishing

REVISING FOR PURPOSE AND AUDIENCE

Never be afraid to make changes in your first draft when you discover that they are needed. Sometimes student writers do not want to "mess up" what they have written. After all, they reason, it looks so neat, why ruin its appearance? Remember, however, that at this stage in the writing process *what* you say is much more important than creating a paper with no cross-outs or erasures.

CHECKLIST FOR REVISING FOR PURPOSE AND AUDIENCE

1. What is the purpose of the paragraph? Does it inform, persuade, amuse, entertain, narrate, describe, or combine several purposes?
2. Which sentence or sentences, if any, do not directly fulfill the purpose of the paragraph? What changes should be made to put every sentence on track?
3. Who is the audience for this paragraph? What changes should be made to make every sentence understandable or enjoyable?
4. What facts or details need to be added to help the audience understand me? If this is a specialized audience—people who share a particular body of knowledge—what can I assume they know?

Objective

EXERCISE 1. Revising for Purpose and Audience. Read the following paragraph, and then write answers to questions 1 through 4.

Almost everyone knows that a rabbit shouldn't be picked up by its ears, everyone, that is, except very young children who should probably only be allowed to pet the animal. Rabbits can be lifted by the skin of the back as long as one hand supports the body and the ears are kept close to the neck. This seems to keep their sense of balance intact and they are less inclined to kick, scratch, or bite. Some breeds are more nervous than others, but all are easily tamed, and the best approach with a new rabbit is a gradual one, restricted to petting or stroking at first and eventually expanded to lifting and carrying about.

—Emil P. Polensek and Barbara Burn

1. What do you think the purpose of this paragraph is? Does it inform, persuade, amuse, entertain, narrate, describe, or does it combine several purposes?
2. This paragraph is a final draft and was printed in a book called *A Practical Guide to Impractical Pets.* Assume that an earlier draft of the paragraph included a few sentences about the proper feeding of rabbits. Why would the authors have removed those sentences when they revised the paragraph?
3. Who is the audience for this paragraph? Is every sentence understandable or enjoyable by that particular audience?
4. Assume that in a first draft the authors had written the following sentence: "Beatrix Potter knew how to pick up Peter Rabbit when he

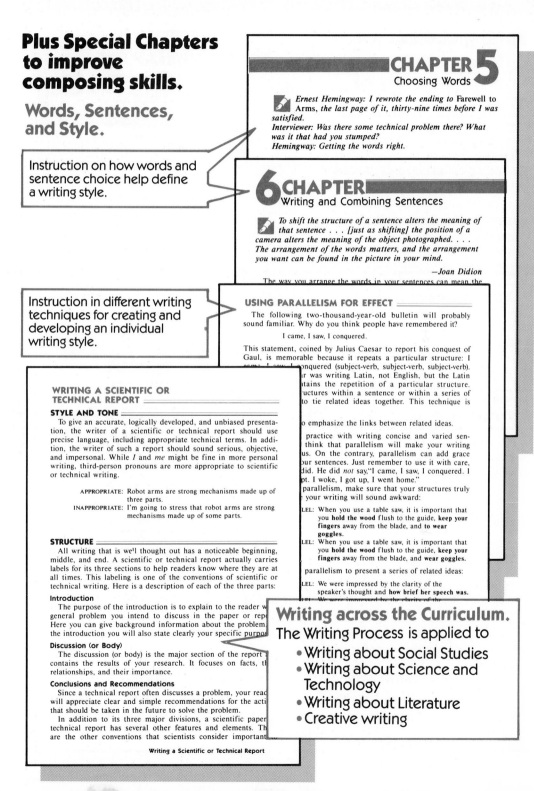

Plus Special Chapters to improve composing skills.

Words, Sentences, and Style.

Instruction on how words and sentence choice help define a writing style.

CHAPTER 5
Choosing Words

Ernest Hemingway: I rewrote the ending to Farewell to Arms, *the last page of it, thirty-nine times before I was satisfied.*
Interviewer: Was there some technical problem there? What was it that had you stumped?
Hemingway: Getting the words right.

6 CHAPTER
Writing and Combining Sentences

To shift the structure of a sentence alters the meaning of that sentence . . . [just as shifting] the position of a camera alters the meaning of the object photographed. . . . The arrangement of the words matters, and the arrangement you want can be found in the picture in your mind.

—Joan Didion

The way you arrange the words in your sentences can mean the

Instruction in different writing techniques for creating and developing an individual writing style.

USING PARALLELISM FOR EFFECT

The following two-thousand-year-old bulletin will probably sound familiar. Why do you think people have remembered it?

I came, I saw, I conquered.

This statement, coined by Julius Caesar to report his conquest of Gaul, is memorable because it repeats a particular structure: I came, I saw, I conquered (subject-verb, subject-verb, subject-verb). ...r was writing Latin, not English, but the Latin ...tains the repetition of a particular structure. ...uctures within a sentence or within a series of ...to tie related ideas together. This technique is

...o emphasize the links between related ideas.

... practice with writing concise and varied sen... think that parallelism will make your writing ...us. On the contrary, parallelism can add grace ...our sentences. Just remember to use it with care, ...did. He did *not* say, "I came, I saw, I conquered. I ...pt. I woke, I got up, I went home."

... parallelism, make sure that your structures truly ... your writing will sound awkward:

...LEL: When you use a table saw, it is important that you **hold the wood** flush to the guide, **keep your fingers** away from the blade, and **to wear goggles.**

...LEL: When you use a table saw, it is important that you **hold the wood** flush to the guide, **keep your fingers** away from the blade, and **wear goggles.**

... parallelism to present a series of related ideas:

...LEL: We were impressed by the clarity of the speaker's thought and **how brief her speech was.**

WRITING A SCIENTIFIC OR TECHNICAL REPORT

STYLE AND TONE

To give an accurate, logically developed, and unbiased presentation, the writer of a scientific or technical report should use precise language, including appropriate technical terms. In addition, the writer of such a report should sound serious, objective, and impersonal. While *I* and *me* might be fine in more personal writing, third-person pronouns are more appropriate to scientific or technical writing.

APPROPRIATE: Robot arms are strong mechanisms made up of three parts.
INAPPROPRIATE: I'm going to stress that robot arms are strong mechanisms made up of some parts.

STRUCTURE

All writing that is well thought out has a noticeable beginning, middle, and end. A scientific or technical report actually carries labels for its three sections to help readers know where they are at all times. This labeling is one of the conventions of scientific or technical writing. Here is a description of each of the three parts:

Introduction

The purpose of the introduction is to explain to the reader w... general problem you intend to discuss in the paper or rep... Here you can give background information about the problem. ... the introduction you will also state clearly your specific purpos...

Discussion (or Body)

The discussion (or body) is the major section of the report ... contains the results of your research. It focuses on facts, t... relationships, and their importance.

Conclusions and Recommendations

Since a technical report often discusses a problem, your reac... will appreciate clear and simple recommendations for the acti... that should be taken in the future to solve the problem.

In addition to its three major divisions, a scientific paper ... technical report has several other features and elements. Th... are the other conventions that scientists consider important ...

Writing a Scientific or Technical Report

Writing across the Curriculum.

The Writing Process is applied to

- Writing about Social Studies
- Writing about Science and Technology
- Writing about Literature
- Creative writing

Writing Choices for different-ability students and for a variety of interests.

End of chapter writing assignments to provide a sequence of writing opportunities and choices.

Structured assignments to enable students to apply the focus of each chapter to their own writing.

Other assignments to allow for more flexibility of choices.

Unstructured Final assignment for student and teacher choice. This choice often sends the student to the **Writer's Sourcebook** for motivation and ideas.

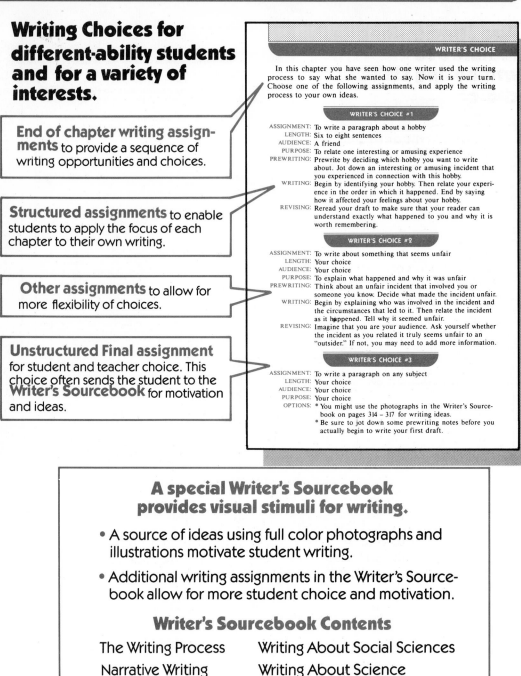

WRITER'S CHOICE

In this chapter you have seen how one writer used the writing process to say what she wanted to say. Now it is your turn. Choose one of the following assignments, and apply the writing process to your own ideas.

WRITER'S CHOICE #1

ASSIGNMENT: To write a paragraph about a hobby
LENGTH: Six to eight sentences
AUDIENCE: A friend
PURPOSE: To relate one interesting or amusing experience
PREWRITING: Prewrite by deciding which hobby you want to write about. Jot down an interesting or amusing incident that you experienced in connection with this hobby.
WRITING: Begin by identifying your hobby. Then relate your experience in the order in which it happened. End by saying how it affected your feelings about your hobby.
REVISING: Reread your draft to make sure that your reader can understand exactly what happened to you and why it is worth remembering.

WRITER'S CHOICE #2

ASSIGNMENT: To write about something that seems unfair
LENGTH: Your choice
AUDIENCE: Your choice
PURPOSE: To explain what happened and why it was unfair
PREWRITING: Think about an unfair incident that involved you or someone you know. Decide what made the incident unfair.
WRITING: Begin by explaining who was involved in the incident and the circumstances that led to it. Then relate the incident as it happened. Tell why it seemed unfair.
REVISING: Imagine that you are your audience. Ask yourself whether the incident as you related it truly seems unfair to an "outsider." If not, you may need to add more information.

WRITER'S CHOICE #3

ASSIGNMENT: To write a paragraph on any subject
LENGTH: Your choice
AUDIENCE: Your choice
PURPOSE: Your choice
OPTIONS:
- You might use the photographs in the Writer's Sourcebook on pages 314 – 317 for writing ideas.
- Be sure to jot down some prewriting notes before you actually begin to write your first draft.

A special Writer's Sourcebook provides visual stimuli for writing.

- A source of ideas using full color photographs and illustrations motivate student writing.
- Additional writing assignments in the Writer's Sourcebook allow for more student choice and motivation.

Writer's Sourcebook Contents

The Writing Process
Narrative Writing
Expository Writing
Persuasive Writing
The Essay
Writing About Social Sciences
Writing About Science
Writing About Literature
Creative Writing

And More Unique Features to encourage writing and student choice

A student model as a writing example.

Explanation by the student about the process of creating the written product.

Immediate opportunity for writing by students.

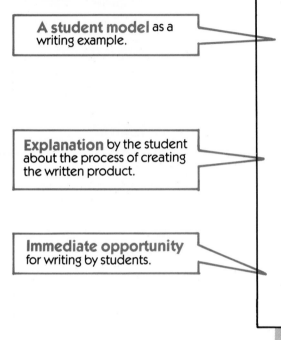

WRITERS ON WRITING

THE WRITER

Roselle Graskey wrote the following story opener and commentary as a student at Eastwood High School in El Paso, Texas. She plans to major in drama and writing at Trinity College in Ireland.

THE FINISHED PRODUCT

Pessimism plays an important role in the tone George Orwell creates in his novel *1984*. Winston, the main character, is constantly complaining about things he cannot change. Nothing is good in his eyes; everything is described in pessimistic terms. Even normally pleasant-sounding phrases are qualified to express an extremely pessimistic attitude, as in this example: "Outside, even through the shut window pane, the world looked cold. . . . Though the sun was shining and the sky a harsh blue, there seemed to be no color in anything except the posters. . . . "Orwell does not make this word choice by accident but for a purpose. He wishes the reader to detect this bleak attitude and equate it with the attitude of societies like Oceania. Another example is the moment when Winston resigns himself to the fact that he will be killed: "Mrs. Parsons would be vaporized. Syme would be vaporized. Winston would be vaporized." Again, Orwell is using tone very effectively to make a point.

THE WRITER AT WORK

When I start writing, I get a piece of paper and just jot down anything that pops into my head. If I think of something better, I add it. Once I run out of ideas, I do something else and return to writing later, or I try to arrange my ideas into some kind of order.

Usually by this time I have written a topic sentence. Next, I include more specific information. I might add an example to illustrate the point I am making. In my paragraph on *1984* I used quotations from the novel as examples. When I can, I try to use several short examples and follow each one with an explanation.

I usually go through a piece of writing several times before it sounds the way I want it to. I use a word processor so that I can easily change any words I do not like.

YOUR TURN **Writing a Paragraph**

Write a paragraph about a topic that is genuinely interesting to you. Pay special attention to the topic sentence: As Mariano Fernandez writes, the topic sentence cannot be vague or confusing or too limited. Develop your topic sentence with concrete details, examples or incidents, facts or statistics, or reasons.

WRITERS ON WRITING

to offer good examples of student writing for encouragement and for opportunities to analyze the writing process.

PART TWO

GRAMMAR, USAGE, AND MECHANICS

Thorough development of the structure of language and its application.

Exercise options for different purposes and practice.

Highlighted Terms for easy student use.

Abundant exercises for practice of grammar, usage, and mechanics.

Application exercises to apply language skills to writing.

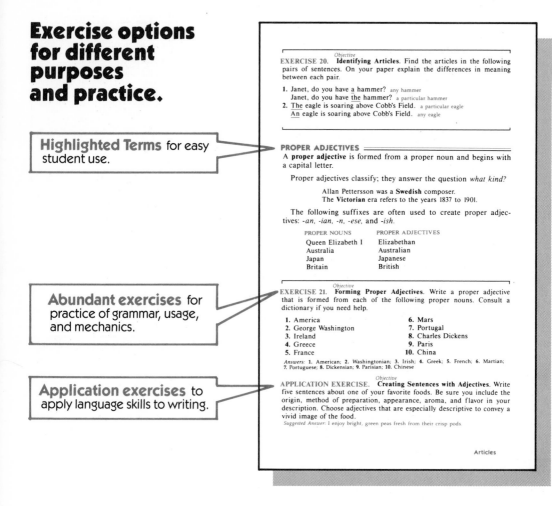

Objective

EXERCISE 20. **Identifying Articles.** Find the articles in the following pairs of sentences. On your paper explain the differences in meaning between each pair.

1. Janet, do you have a hammer? any hammer
   Janet, do you have the hammer? a particular hammer
2. The eagle is soaring above Cobb's Field. a particular eagle
   An eagle is soaring above Cobb's Field. any eagle

PROPER ADJECTIVES

A **proper adjective** is formed from a proper noun and begins with a capital letter.

Proper adjectives classify; they answer the question *what kind?*

Allan Pettersson was a **Swedish** composer.
The **Victorian** era refers to the years 1837 to 1901.

The following suffixes are often used to create proper adjectives: *-an, -ian, -n, -ese,* and *-ish.*

PROPER NOUNS	PROPER ADJECTIVES
Queen Elizabeth I	Elizabethan
Australia	Australian
Japan	Japanese
Britain	British

Objective

EXERCISE 21. **Forming Proper Adjectives.** Write a proper adjective that is formed from each of the following proper nouns. Consult a dictionary if you need help.

1. America
2. George Washington
3. Ireland
4. Greece
5. France
6. Mars
7. Portugal
8. Charles Dickens
9. Paris
10. China

Answers: **1.** American; **2.** Washingtonian; **3.** Irish; **4.** Greek; **5.** French; **6.** Martian; **7.** Portuguese; **8.** Dickensian; **9.** Parisian; **10.** Chinese

Objective

APPLICATION EXERCISE. **Creating Sentences with Adjectives.** Write five sentences about one of your favorite foods. Be sure you include the origin, method of preparation, appearance, aroma, and flavor in your description. Choose adjectives that are especially descriptive to convey a vivid image of the food.

Suggested Answer: I enjoy bright, green peas fresh from their crisp pods.

Articles

REVIEW EXERCISE. **Adjectives.** On your paper write the twenty adjectives, including articles, that appear in the following paragraph. Next to each adjective listed, write the word that it modifies.

(1) Hawaii consists of a chain of 132 islands. **(2)** These islands extend northwest for 1,523 miles. **(3)** Main islands of Hawaii include Maui, Lanai, Kahoolawe, Molokai, Oahu, Kauai, Niihau, and Hawaii, an island that is quite large and famous for active volcanoes. **(4)** Although there are a number of islands, Hawaiian people live only on major ones. **(5)** Kahoolawe, for example, has no inhabitants and is used only for naval purposes. **(6)** Minor islands, only as big as great rocks, are too small and infertile to support human life.

chain islands islands miles islands island island island volcanoes number people ones inhabitants purposes islands islands rocks islands islands life

REVISION EXERCISE. **Adjectives.** Examine the following description of the Mississippi River written by Mark Twain. Notice especially the effective use of the italicized adjectives.

Objective

A *broad* expanse of the river was turned to blood; in the middle distance the *red* hue brightened into gold, through which a *solitary* log came floating, *black* and *conspicuous;* in one place a *long, slanting* mark lay *sparkling* upon the water; in another the surface was broken by *boiling, tumbling* rings, that were as *many-tinted* as an opal; where the *ruddy* flush was *faintest,* was a *smooth* spot that was covered with *graceful* circles and *radiating* lines, ever so delicately traced. . . .

Here are some of Twain's techniques that you can apply when you write and revise your work:

1. Try to use adjectives that will make nouns more specific. Twain makes his nouns more specific by using vivid adjectives that describe color (*red, black, many-tinted, ruddy*), shape or position (*broad, middle, solitary, conspicuous, long, slanting*), and other visual characteristics (*faintest, smooth, graceful*). These adjectives appeal to our senses.
2. Try to use adjectives that suggest action. Notice Twain's lively *-ing* words: *sparkling, boiling, tumbling, radiating.* All of these give us the picture of a river in motion.
3. Try to determine where adjectives are helpful and where they are not needed. Notice the beginning of Twain's description. Twain uses *broad* to specify the size of the expanse, but he leaves the nouns *river* and *blood* unmodified. Do not feel that every noun needs an adjective.

Here is the rest of Twain's description, but without his adjectives. Revise the passage, adding your own adjectives in the places indicated by the carets (∧).

CHAPTER 17 Parts of Speech

Review exercises to maintain language skills.

Revision exercises that asks students to interact with leading authors to learn revision techniques using the parts of speech.

PART THREE

SKILLS AND RESOURCES *Complete coverage with built-in flexibility for use all year long.*

Self-contained SKILLS UNITS to use as students need them.

CHAPTER 28
Vocabulary Skills

A good vocabulary is an important tool of effective communication. The more words you know, the more clearly you will be able to express yourself. This chapter looks at ways to build your vocabulary. It focuses especially on helping you to improve the vocabulary you use in your writing.

CHAPTER 29
Spelling Skills

Spelling is a vital element in writing. Correct spelling is never noticed, but even one spelling error jars a reader and spoils a sentence. This chapter looks at some of the ways in which you can improve your spelling.

31 CHAPTER
Listening and Speaking Skills

All spoken communication involves three separate elements:

- the sender—the human voice
- the message—the spoken words
- the receiver—one or more listeners

32 CHAPTER
Study and Test-Taking Skills

This chapter will help you learn two skills that are very important to you as a student: how to study and how to take standardized tests. In the first section you will learn ways to become a better listener, reader, and note-taker. In the second section you will examine multiple-choice questions, essay questions, and strategies for answering these questions. You will also answer sample questions from the Preliminary Scholastic Aptitude Test (PSAT), a standardized test that many high school students take in October of their junior year.

STUDY SKILLS

Why do some students understand and remember more information than other students? Part of the reason may be that they have a better understanding of how to listen, to read textbooks, and to take notes.

LISTENING SKILLS

A great deal of information that you learn in school is imparted orally. Teachers speak, and you must listen and learn. To be a good listener, you must be an *active listener.* That is, you must completely fill your mind by thinking about what you hear as you hear it. The following five suggestions will help you become an active listener:

1. As you listen, think from time to time about the main points that the speaker has already made.
2. Try to think ahead of the speaker and to figure out the direction his or her speech is taking.
3. Consider what the speaker may be suggesting but not actually saying. In other words, listen "between the lines."
4. Try not to react emotionally to what the speaker is saying until you have heard all of it. If you start to think about how you feel about a particular statement, you may miss what the speaker is saying next.

CHAPTER 32 Study and Test-Taking Skills

30 CHAPTER
Business Communication Skills

BUSINESS LETTERS

A **business letter** is a formal letter written to communicate information or request action.

A letter is often far more effective than a telephone conversation because it gives you an opportunity to organize your thoughts and to state them in specific, unmistakable terms. A letter also provides a dated written record that you can use for further reference or, occasionally, for legal proof of your communication. For these reasons, you should always keep a copy of each business letter you write, at least until the matter under consideration has been resolved or concluded.

APPEARANCE AND FORMAT OF BUSINESS LETTERS

Every business letter follows certain conventions of format and style. Generally, business letters should be neat, clear, courteous, brief, and easy to read. It is therefore advisable to *type* business letters whenever possible. Use single spacing, and leave an extra space between paragraphs and between the different parts of the letter. To make the letter visually pleasing to the reader, use wide margins and center the letter vertically on the page.

Model Business Letter (Modified Block Style)

heading

835 Salem Lane
Lake Worth, FL 33463
January 15, 19—

inside address

Ms. Catherine Reilly, Director
Public Relations Department
Chrysler Corporation of America
12000 Lynn Townsend Drive
Detroit, MI 48288

salutation

Dear Ms. Reilly:

body

I am a high school sophomore currently preparing a school report about employee-management relations in America. I am planning to include a section about the landmark agreements made between employees and management of the Chrysler Corporation after Lee Iacocca became chairman of the corporation in 1979. I would therefore like to obtain any available printed material on these agreements.

I appreciate your assistance very much and look forward to hearing from you.

closing

Very truly yours,

signature

Susan Fenton

Susan Fenton

CHAPTER 33
The Dictionary and the Thesaurus

A dictionary and a thesaurus are two kinds of reference books providing important information that you will find e
helpful when you are writing. This chapter examines dict
thesauruses, and the important information that they pro

THE DICTIONARY

A **dictionary of the English language** is an alphabetica
words, their meanings, and other useful information ab
words.

An **unabridged dictionary** is the largest and most compl
of dictionary. It lists over 400,000 words and gives detaile
mation about their histories and usage. Two of the bes
unabridged dictionaries are the *Oxford English Dictio*
OED, and *Webster's Third New International Dictionar*
bridged. Because most unabridged dictionaries consist
volumes and are quite expensive, people usually consult th

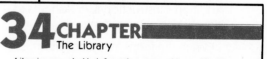

RESOURCES for research skills used in writing.

34 CHAPTER
The Library

Libraries are valuable information centers. Most **public libraries** and **school libraries** (sometimes called **learning resource centers** or **media centers**) contain a wide variety of materials that can help you with your research and writing. This chapter looks at the different types of materials available at libraries and explains how to find and use these materials.

FICTION AND NONFICTION BOOKS

Libraries have a wide selection of **nonfiction** (fact-based) books

Teacher's Resource Book *Abundant materials for more teaching choices.*

Practice Book Blackline Masters
Additional reinforcement and practice for students needing more practice.

Practice Book Teachers Edition
All answers in place on the student page.

Test Blackline Masters
A comprehensive testing program in a standardized test format that includes writing samples.

Test Book Teachers Edition
All answers in place on the student page.

Study and Composition Blackline Masters
Additional instructional worksheets to aid you and your students.

- Evaluation forms for composition, speaking and listening.
- Checklists for prewriting, writing a paragraph and longer forms, and revising.
- Forms for outlining, note cards, and bibliography cards.
- Business communication forms, letters, and applications.

Plus

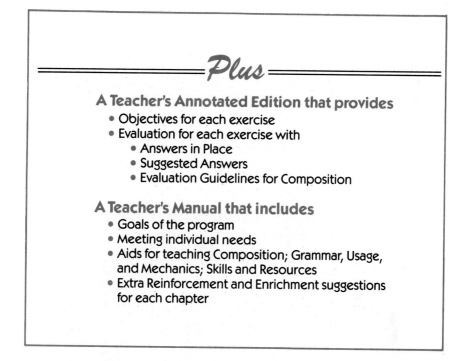

A Teacher's Annotated Edition that provides

- Objectives for each exercise
- Evaluation for each exercise with
  - Answers in Place
  - Suggested Answers
  - Evaluation Guidelines for Composition

A Teacher's Manual that includes

- Goals of the program
- Meeting individual needs
- Aids for teaching Composition; Grammar, Usage, and Mechanics; Skills and Resources
- Extra Reinforcement and Enrichment suggestions for each chapter

Components of Macmillan English

GRADE	9	10	11	12
Student Text	●	●	●	●
Teacher's Annotated Edition	●	●	●	●
Teacher's Resource Book	●	●	●	●
Practice Book Blackline Masters	●	●	●	●
Practice Book Teacher's Edition	●	●	●	●
Test Blackline Masters	●	●	●	●
Test Book Teacher's Edition	●	●	●	●
Study and Composition Blackline Masters	●	●	●	●
Practice Book	●	●	●	●
Test Book	●	●	●	●
Student Writing Folder	●	●	●	●

MACMILLAN ENGLISH

the program with the most choices for students and teachers

Writer's Choice to encourage independence in writing by allowing decision-making choices at each step in the writing process.

Writers on Writing to offer good examples of student writing for encouragement and for opportunities to analyze the writing process.

Writer's Sourcebook to provide visual stimuli as a source of ideas for writing.

A Variety of Language Exercises to allow for different practice options.

A Teacher's Annotated Edition with answers in place for ease of daily use that includes a Teacher's Manual for more help with lesson planning.

A Teacher's Resource Book for more teaching choices.

Macmillan English – the best choice!

CONTENTS OF TEACHER'S MANUAL

GOALS OF *MACMILLAN ENGLISH 9–12*

The purpose of *Macmillan English* is to teach students to use language effectively in written and oral communication. Correlated with national and state guidelines and curricula, the goals of *Macmillan English* are divided into three main skill areas: composition; grammar, usage, and mechanics; and skills and resources.

COMPOSITION

- to develop positive attitudes toward writing
- to recognize that writing is a process made up of recursive steps—prewriting, writing, revising (including editing, proofreading, and publishing)
- to generate ideas about which to write
- to write appropriately for given audiences and purposes
- to write works of various lengths and of various modes
- to prepare personal, creative, business, and academic writing, including researched written products with accurate documentation
- to use sentence variety in writing
- to develop a voice of one's own
- to write persuasively using critical-thinking skills
- to evaluate one's own written products and those of others
- to apply all the foregoing skills when writing not only in the English classroom but also in other subject areas

GRAMMAR, USAGE, AND MECHANICS

- to analyze and apply the grammar and usage of the English language
- to understand and practice the principles of the English language including the language's tendency to change, its several levels of usage, and its many dialects
- to use competently the conventions of standard English including punctuation and capitalization

SKILLS AND RESOURCES

- to interact with others in a constructive manner during class discussions
- to summarize the main and subordinate ideas in spoken presentations
- to generate ideas about which to speak
- to use competently the conventions of standard English in speaking
- to speak appropriately for given audiences and purposes
- to present an opinion persuasively
- to expand both general and specialized vocabularies
- to understand the origins of the English language
- to find and use library and other resources and then to incorporate findings from such sources in both written and spoken presentations
- to prepare for standardized examinations and essay examinations

DIFFERENT ABILITY LEVELS AND *MACMILLAN ENGLISH 9–12*

The creators of *Macmillan English 9–12* realize that any given classroom may have students of varying abilities. To guarantee that *Macmillan English* can function as the sole textbook in the classroom, we have built in several features for meeting the needs of both less-advanced students and advanced students:

1. *Options Within Exercises:* Whenever an exercise asks students to generate a piece of writing, the exercise (a) suggests topics that students may explore or write about and (b) gives the students the option to work on topics of their own choosing. Thus students who need prompts have them, and those who are more independent can follow through on personal interests.

2. *Application Exercises:* These activities ask students to apply what they have just learned about grammar by generating sentences of their own. These exercises may be more appropriate for some students than for others.
3. *Revision Exercises:* These exercises ask students to engage in higher level work by interacting with writing by leading fiction and nonfiction authors.
4. *Reinforcement and Enrichment Activities:* Suggestions for reinforcement and for enrichment appear on a chapter-by-chapter basis within this teacher's manual. These suggestions will help teachers generate yet additional activities to help less-advanced students fully grasp a given concept and to help advanced students gain further insights.
5. *Writer's Choice:* Each chapter in Part One: Composition has one or more pages devoted to the Writer's Choice feature. Here students will find a series of assignments based on the preceding instruction, which move from highly structured to open ended.
6. *Writers on Writing:* Many of the chapters within Part One: Composition have a Writers on Writing feature. Here students will find the work of other students, who have prepared pieces of writing and commentaries on those pieces expressly for *Macmillan English.* For less-advanced students this feature may serve an important cheerleading function: "If they've done it, I can do it!" For advanced students this feature will provide opportunities to analyze in greater detail all aspects of the writing process.
7. *Writer's Sourcebook:* This unique four-color section provides visual stimuli to encourage writing in a variety of modes and in a variety of subject areas. The groupings of illustrations are sequenced to follow the order of the chapters within Part One: Composition. Students of different abilities will use the stimuli in different ways. For example, some students will use the visuals to spur their own thinking about topics for writing; other students will work with the visuals along with the optional assignments that are keyed to them.

LESSON PLANNING FOR *MACMILLAN ENGLISH 9–12*

FLEXIBILITY OF USE

Macmillan English at every grade level offers flexibility in teaching different ability students and in teaching to different curriculum needs. The three content parts—Composition; Grammar, Usage, Mechanics; and Skills and Resources—can be taught in the order that best meets the needs of your students. The chapters provide self-contained instruction and practice with Reviews and accompanying Tests that allow you to teach the chapters in the sequence you chose.

INSTRUCTIONAL STRATEGY

Here we would like to present a summary of a basic lesson design as developed by successful English teachers. This basic structure can be adapted to teaching composition, grammar, or study and reference skills.

SET THE OBJECTIVE — The Chapter Objectives are included in the Teacher's Manual, and objectives for each exercise are set above the exercise title in the Teacher's Annotated Edition. The teacher may want also to prepare students at this time with an *informal review* of what they have already studied or set the stage with a *motivational activity.*

DEVELOP — Students learn the skill, concept, or process that reviews or provides new information through questioning, reading, or discovery methods.

MODEL — Each concept is illustrated with examples to strengthen student comprehension. Models with every step of the writing process—prewriting, writing, revising—offer examples of writing types to be mastered.

PRACTICE — Frequent, extensive practice is provided to reinforce concepts or skills. The many practice options include Exercises, Application Exercises, Review Exercises, and Revision Exercises. Part One: Composition offers exercises from first draft to the final product and allows many choices in assignments for teachers and students. Practice opportunities also encourage *discussion* led by the teacher and *guided practice* to check for understanding. *Independent practice* can also be assigned by teachers who are reasonably sure that students are ready for unsupervised practice. Also available for extra practice for all students is the *Macmillan English Practice Book* (one each for Grades 9–12). This product appears as blackline masters in the *Macmillan English Teacher's Resource Book* and as a separate, consumable component.

APPLY

The final step is the opportunity for students to apply their understanding. *Macmillan English* features such as Application Exercises, Writer's Choice, Writers on Writing, and the Writer's Sourcebook all offer opportunites for students to apply their knowledge to meaningful experiences with language and writing.

EVALUATE

Review Exercises and Chapter or Unit Reviews allow for constant evaluation opportunities. A complete testing program with writing samples is also available as a separate component and as part of the *Macmillan English Teacher's Resource Book.*

TEACHING PART ONE: COMPOSITION

We would like your students to understand from the outset that they are *writers.* They may not all be very good writers yet, but they are still writers. The purpose of *Macmillan English* is to help your students understand the way our language works—its grammar, its usage, its conventions of punctuation and capitalization—so that they will be able to write it as well as possible. Students can improve their ability to write by focusing on writing at all times—while learning grammar, increasing their vocabulary, using the dictionary, and improving their spelling.

THE WRITING PROCESS AND THE THINKING PROCESS

The writing process is the thinking process made visible. All writers think about a series of increasingly specific problems: What shall I write about? What part of this subject should I cover in this space? How shall I begin? The *real* question is, What does "thinking about" these problems actually mean? "Thinking" may mean consciously formulating a problem and listing alternative solutions. "Thinking" may also mean feeling frustrated, getting up for a snack, and then suddenly stumbling upon a solution. "Thinking" means doing whatever the mind does; it is a sometimes orderly, sometimes disorderly, sometimes deliberate, sometimes unpredictable activity. If the writing process is the thinking process made visible, how can it be taught?

Writing can be taught successfully if the writing program accomplishes two objectives simultaneously. First, a successful writing program must create room for the disorderly, spontaneous nature of the writing/thinking process; without spontaneity, writing is dry, formulaic, and dead. At the same time, the successful writing program needs to instill in students the sense that they are making real progress as they engage in this process. A writing program needs to supply students with signposts, objective criteria that will help them find their way through the writing/thinking process. In short, a successful writing program needs to combine *process* and *structure.*

THE MACMILLAN APPROACH

Throughout *Macmillan English* varied and exciting activities, open-ended questions, and evolving models reinforce the idea that writing is a *process,* one that every writer works out for himself or herself. At the same time, the chapter-by-chapter organization and numerous checklists, annotated models, and detailed exercise instructions provide the structure that young writers need as they discover what it is they want to say and how they can best say it. Here are only a few examples of the approach developed in *Macmillan English:*

PROCESS +	In the chapter focusing on *Prewriting,* students engage in prewriting activities that spur them to generate and explore writing ideas of their own. Students are also encouraged to experiment with and adapt these prewriting activities to their own styles of thinking and writing.
STRUCTURE	At the same time these prewriting activities are constructed and sequenced in such a way that students can recognize a beginning and an ending point to each activity and learn to make good use of what they produce in between.
PROCESS +	In the chapter focusing on *The Essay,* students follow the evolution of an essay from first idea to finished product. At each step in this process, students practice with techniques like those used by the essay writer as they develop ideas of their own into finished essays.
STRUCTURE	At the same time students acquire skills necessary to a successful essay writer: They learn how to formulate a cogent thesis statement and how to organize and maintain the coherence of an extended piece of writing.

PROCESS +	In the chapter focusing on *Creative Writing,* students adapt the writing process to the creation of original stories, scenes, and poems. They experiment with creative-writing techniques demonstrated in the text, which presents from start to finish the evolution of an original story, scene, and poem.
STRUCTURE	At the same time the sequencing of the activities gives students the sense that they are progressing steadily toward finished stories, scenes, and poems. In addition, students review the formal literary elements that contribute to the effects of fiction, drama, and poetry.

PUBLISHING

As we see it, presenting writing to an audience is the crowning phase of the writing process. *Macmillan English* has taken the idea of "publishing" literally by including student writing throughout this text. In particular, in the Writers on Writing feature, eleven student writers share with their peers both their finished products and their thoughts about the writing processes that led to these products.

In addition, the checklists that appear in each chapter suggest different forums in which students might share their work with an audience. The most accessible of these forums is, of course, the classroom, where this sharing can take the form of peer editing. (For more information about peer editing, see page 8 in this teacher's manual).

GUIDELINES FOR DEVELOPING WRITING ASSIGNMENTS

The following suggestions may help in the development of writing assignments, particularly for timed, in-class compositions.

1. If the writing is being done in class, the writing situation is obviously different from an assignment that allows time for students to develop an outline. Furthermore, in the classroom students usually have no dictionaries, notes, or texts to use as they write. Therefore, the in-class writing assignment should contain all the direction and information the student needs in order to write well.
2. Students should be told directly that *how* they write is an important factor in the score or grade given to their answer. That is, quantity of prose is not the same as quality of writing.
3. Every assignment should include some suggestion for organizing the response. That is, no question should simply ask students just to "discuss" or to "tell" or to "analyze" an idea or statement. An organizing principle should be given: *Compare and contrast . . ., Agree or disagree with . . ., Develop an argument and support it with evidence from your reading and study . . .,* etc.
4. A good test of the usefulness and quality of a writing assignment is for the teacher to write an answer to the question. This experience will immediately reveal to the teacher any weakness, vagueness, or ambiguity of the question.
5. The best assignments usually have three distinct parts:

   a. a clearly phrased and succinctly stated question
   b. a suggestion about how to structure the response (see Number 3 above)
   c. an injunction that grammar, diction, correctness of mechanics, and legible handwriting are important factors in good writing

The assignment below is an obvious example of a weak, diffuse question, one that almost invites the students to wander off in many directions and to discover too late that their essays lack point and structure:

Weak Assignment (20 minutes): Discuss the importance of the boys' and girls' sports programs in your school.

The next question is a good example of a directed exercise that permits students to focus immediately on the problem presented and to think in terms of a structured response before they start writing.

Strong Assignment (20 minutes): Write an essay that compares the boys' sports program with the girls' sports program in your school. For example, do both programs have equal opportunity to use the gym, the athletic facilities, and the athletic faculty? Be specific and give facts and examples from your personal experience. Finally, end your essay with suggestions about ways to improve both sports programs.

EVALUATION OF STUDENT WRITING

TEACHER EVALUATION

Holistic Evaluation

Holistic evaluation is a method based on the concept that the reader reacts to a piece of writing as a whole—i.e., that the whole of a piece of writing is greater than the sum of its parts. The total composition, whether it is a paragraph or a research paper, should be looked at as a whole. In other words, although students make various errors, their work must be reacted to for its overall strengths and its overall weaknesses. The Educational Testing Service, which publishes procedures for this evaluation method, states, "The basic assumptions of holistic reading are that each of the factors involved in writing skills is related to all the others and that no one factor can be separated from the others. Readers must judge each essay as a whole; they must read each paper for the impression its totality makes."

Holistic evaluation can be used with any writing assignment in *Macmillan English.* However, an effective use of this method would be a systematic program that assesses writing ability at three times: the beginning of the year, the middle of the year, and the end of the year.

The holistic method includes certain *standards:* (a) papers are not judged against an ideal but against what is--what students have written on this topic at this time; (b) a group of papers is read by a group of readers, not just by an individual teacher; (c) standards are not imposed upon readers as with analytic criteria; the readers themselves determine standards according to the assignment and group of students. Minimal competency writing tests often have a fixed standard that is used to train readers.

Judgments using the holistic method have these characteristics: (a) judgments are made on anonymous papers and must be quick, immediate, and independent; (b) at least two judgments on each paper are mandatory; (c) judgments must be definite; usually a ranking system of 1–4 (with 4 being high) is used so that there are no middle points; (d) all papers must be read once before any are read twice. Judgments that vary will need a mediator.

Holistic *scoring* includes these criteria: (a) the score is the sum of all readers' judgments; (b) when the papers are read, the first reader's score must remain unknown to other readers; (c) regular divergence from the standards on the part of any reader must be corrected.

Good *topics* are important if holistic scoring is to be effective. The topic must interest the students, interest the readers, produce a range of writing, and be able to be scored with relative objectivity.

Holistic evaluation offers the following advantages:

- Teachers can give a quick response to student writing, emphasizing a student's successes.
- Teachers as a group can determine standards for writing and can evaluate the entire writing curriculum in the school.
- The scoring shows how an individual student's writing compares to the group and how well the group as a whole writes.

Holistic scoring can take many forms. A blank piece of paper, form #4 in the *Macmillan English Study and Composition Worksheets,* or the following checklists can be used effectively. Three main areas are evaluated according to four categories. Circle the appropriate response number.

Content and Ideas

1	Excellent
2	Very Good
3	Satisfactory
4	Poor

Organization and Paragraph Structure

1	Excellent
2	Very Good
3	Satisfactory
4	Poor

Grammar, Usage, Mechanics, Spelling

1	Excellent
2	Very Good
3	Satisfactory
4	Poor

Analytical Evaluation

Analytical evaluation is a method that relies on assessment of particular features associated with a skill. Specific characteristics or elements—such as content, organization, or mechanics—are evaluated against a general ideal, rather than a group of specific papers as in holistic writing evaluation. Analytical scoring takes the various elements of writing, assigns weights to each element, and then sums up the weighted scores. Analytical evaluation can be used with any writing assignment in *Macmillan English.* The checklists for revising, editing, and publishing that appear throughout the composition chapters will be useful for this type of evaluation.

Analytical evaluation offers the following advantages:

- Analytical evaluation can be tied to editing guidelines. Revision questions can form the criteria for scoring so that students can become involved in the evaluation process.
- The editing guidelines can form the basis for peer-editing when students work in pairs or groups.
- Analytical evaluation reinforces the correct use of language in writing because it emphasizes specific elements. Teachers can relate grammar, usage, mechanics, and vocabulary lessons to the writing assignment by focusing on specific elements of writing.
- When combined with peer-editing, analytical evaluation develops students' ability to assess specific characteristics of writing. Objective testing of writing depends upon multiple-choice questions based on specific units, such as usage or sequencing of sentences in paragraphs. Therefore, this method helps students with many questions on standardized tests.

STUDENT EVALUATION

Self-Editing

Editing is an integral part of the writing process in *Macmillan English.* The first unit in the textbook explains the importance of revision and introduces editing symbols. In addition, each chapter includes at least one and usually several checklists for revising, editing, and publishing.

Peer-Editing

Students can benefit from reading and listening to each other's writing. The process helps to develop a sense of audience, allows students to see how their writing affects others, and leads to good self-editing practices. In a peer-editing program, students will have to address themselves both to holistic and analytic concerns.

Holistic Questions:

1. What is the best part of the composition? What makes it good?
2. What is the topic sentence? How is the paragraph developed?
3. Are there any questions the writer has not answered?

4. What are one or two ways in which the writer can improve the next piece of writing? What would be your advice?

Analytical Procedures:

1. Students need to be directed to look for specific errors in usage, mechanics, and spelling. Criteria need to be established in the beginning.
2. The method will be enhanced if students work with short units of writing such as sentences.

USING WORD PROCESSORS TO EXTEND WRITING INSTRUCTION

We present here some supplemental activities for those students with access to word processors. The activities are keyed to specific writing skills as taught in *Macmillan English;* the relevant skills are noted in the left margin. These activities extend the writing instruction presented in the textbook and provide students who use word processors with special opportunities to develop and refine their writing skills. These suggested activities do not involve special computer programs and can be used with most word processors.

PREWRITING *Invisible Writing.* This prewriting technique, developed by Stephen Marcus of the University of California at Santa Barbara,[1] will help students to generate words and thoughts more fluently. Invisible writing is simply freewriting done with a word processor whose screen is dimmed. Because students cannot see what is on the screen, they can then record their thoughts uncritically, without pausing to rewrite. Used for very limited periods of time, invisible writing helps students concentrate on their ideas without being distracted by the quality of their expression.

Exploring Ideas with a Partner. For this prewriting activity students work in pairs, adapting and extending the exploring questions presented in Chapter 2 of *Macmillan English.* Student writers can tell their partners what subject they want to write about, and the partners should then quickly choose and list on screen the exploring questions they think the writers should answer. The writers then insert their answers; the partners could add new questions based on these answers, and so on. This activity turns informal oral brainstorming into a written dialogue, giving it an interesting twist and also providing student writers with a useful record of the evolution of the session.

WRITING THE PARAGRAPH *Jumbled Paragraphs.* This class activity reinforces students' sense of the logic of a paragraph. Someone (you or a member of the class) selects a paragraph with which the students are not familiar and then "jumbles" the sentences in that paragraph, deliberately rewriting them out of order. Students type the jumbled paragraph and then use the "move" command to rearrange the sentences in what they believe to be the correct order. A variation on this activity involves students working in pairs. Each student types on screen a jumbled paragraph for his or her partner; the partners then switch terminals and rewrite the paragraphs.

REVISING *Search and Replace.* Students identifying characteristic errors in usage, spelling, or punctuation can find and correct every instance of such errors within a paper by using the search-and-replace option available in most word-processing programs. Students who want to change a name or term that they use many times in a paper can also use this option profitably.

---

[1] Stephen Marcus describes invisible writing in "Real-Time Gadgets with Feedback: Special Effects in Computer-Assisted Writing," in *The Computer in Composition Instruction,* edited by William Wresch (NCTE, 1984).

Peer-Editing. In classes with access to word processors, students "exchange" papers electronically. The editing partner puts on screen notes, questions, suggestions, or even examples of revisions for the benefit of the writing partner.

WORD CHOICE

Changing Tone or Mood. Students practice altering the tone of a piece of writing (one of their own or one by a professional writer) by consistently changing one type of word throughout—for example, all the verbs or all the adjectives. They may take a passage portraying a subject in positive terms and make that passage negative in its tone. They can make something with a chatty, conversational tone into something very weighty (or vice versa). They can do the same for mood, rewriting a passage with a cheerful atmosphere to make it gloomy. (Of course, this activity can also be performed with conventional writing tools, but word processors make recopying less laborious, allowing students to concentrate instead on aspects of writing.)

WRITING AND COMBINING SENTENCES

Combining Sentences. A word processor enables students to experiment with different responses to any of the sentence-combining exercises in Chapter 6. Students use the copying command on the word processor and create a new version of a paragraph largely by changing sentence structure. You may give students some guidance by suggesting that they appeal to a specific audience (say, a group of children) or try to create a specific effect (say, to emphasize a different detail in the paragraph).

STYLE

Experimenting with Style. Students using word processors may enjoy changing the level of diction of a piece of writing—either their own writing or a passage by a professional writer. For instance, they may have fun rewriting a passage from Charles Dickens or George Eliot in a slangy, contemporary style.

NARRATIVE WRITING

Changing a Narrative's Point of View. Students rewrite one of their own narrative paragraphs or one by a professional writer, altering it by changing the point of view. They start out by making simple changes in pronouns (first to third person, or vice versa). However, they may find that they need to make other changes as well—for example, adding or removing certain details or altering the tone.

RESEARCH PAPER

Using a Word Processor as Research Tool. Students with unlimited access to word processors can use them as aids in gathering and sorting information for a research paper. Students who use their word processors for taking notes will probably find themselves taking fuller notes, including longer quotations. In addition, students can use the "search" command to keep track of where certain key concepts are covered in their notes; students can also arrange and rearrange their notes electronically. A word processor also expedites the preparation of footnotes and bibliography.

CREATIVE WRITING

Prose into Free Verse. Students create "found" poems by typing a prose passage from a book, newspaper, or magazine (or even a sentence, such as an advertising slogan) and putting in line breaks to create new emphases.

Electronic Collaboration. Students work together to write two-character scenes. Student 1 takes the role of one character in the scene and writes a line of dialogue; student 2 reads the line on his or her screen and responds as the second character in the scene; and so forth.

Screen Scenes. This activity, devised by the UCLA Writing Project, presents students with two seemingly unconnected sentences. The example cited by Stephen Marcus in his description of this activity is made up of these two sentences:

He checked his schedule to see what he planned to ruin today. They left him wondering whether the door would close in time.

The students are then asked to write a series of sentences connecting the original two sentences, usually in a narrative. Students see the narrative progressing as they insert their own sentences between the first sentence and the final sentence.[2]

The Group Story. The entire class composes an original story. You may make this activity a week-long adjunct to your regular writing class. Begin the story with an interesting sentence or two. Each student adds a few sentences at a time to this story. No student should add more than (say) five sentences at one time to the story, but students may return to the story outside class and add a few more sentences to it. No student may alter anything that precedes his or her contribution. At the end of the week, you write an appropriate ending to the story and print it out for the whole class to read.

PART ONE: OBJECTIVES, ANSWERS, REINFORCEMENT AND ENRICHMENT

Part One: Composition is made up of five units, each of which contains two or more chapters. Here on a chapter-by-chapter basis you will find

- Chapter Objectives
- Answers and Guidelines for Evaluation that did not fit in the space allotted for teacher's annotations in the book proper
- Reinforcement and Enrichment activities: the former designed for students who need additional help in understanding the basic concepts of the chapter, the latter designed for students who are ready to go beyond the textbook into more advanced territory

CHAPTER 1 THE WRITING PROCESS: OVERVIEW

CHAPTER OBJECTIVES

In this chapter the student will

- discover the three types of activities that make up the writing process
- identify and discuss an example of prewriting
- identify and discuss an example of writing a first draft of a paragraph
- identify and discuss an example of revising a paragraph

SUGGESTED ANSWERS AND GUIDELINES FOR EVALUATION

PAGE 7, EXERCISE 3

1. The writer decided to develop the idea that some people buy computers when they know nothing about them. The writer added some details about the student who has a legitimate need for a computer's word processing capability and also noted other legitimate needs: small businesses, education, entertainment.
2. The writer's main purpose is to inform readers that some people purchase computers although they know very little about them. The writer wanted to reach the general reader.

---

[2] Stephen Marcus describes screen scenes in "Real-Time Gadgets with Feedback: Special Effects in Computer-Assisted Writing."

PAGE 8, EXERCISE 4

1. The writer underscored the word *think* to emphasize its meaning. The writer referred to Alex as "a man whom I shall call Alex," thereby depersonalizing the individual and making him better stand for the unknowledgeable buyer. The writer uses the word *contraptions* to suggest the possible limited use of computers for most people.
2. The writer cut down the attention paid to a student's use of word processing in order to devote more space to the paragraph's main point. The writer expanded his treatment of Alex—the unknowledgeable buyer—in order to devote more space to the paragraph's main point.

PAGE 9, WRITER'S CHOICE #1
Objective: Writing a Paragraph
Type of Writing: An expository paragraph
Length: Eight to ten sentences
Guidelines for Evaluation: The paragraph should
- explain how important a selected invention has become to modern life
- use the student's classmates as an audience
- derive from prewriting notes
- end with statements that tell what modern life would be like without the invention

PAGE 9, WRITER'S CHOICE #2
Objective: Writing a composition of any length
Type of Writing: An expository composition
Length: Variable
Guidelines for Evaluation: The composition should
- be about the best movie the student has ever seen
- imply a clear audience and purpose
- derive from prewriting notes
- end by stating whether or not the student would recommend the movie to others

PAGE 9, WRITER'S CHOICE #3
Objective: Writing a paragraph
Type of Writing: A paragraph of any kind
Length: Variable
Guidelines for Evaluation: The student should
- consider using an idea from the Writer's Sourcebook
- begin by making prewriting notes
- imply a clear audience and purpose
- revise the first draft

REINFORCEMENT

Recognizing the Process To give students support as they begin the writing process, have students work in pairs. Each pair of students should agree on a topic and work on the prewriting activities in the chapter. Make sure that students understand each assignment. Then have students write a rough draft and trade papers with another pair. Students should edit one another's papers for content, sentence structure, and mechanical errors and make suggestions for improvement. When their papers are returned, the pair should make needed changes and write the final draft.

ENRICHMENT

Understanding the Process To help students better understand the writing process and retain the concepts, tell them that you want them to analyze what they have just done and explain the purpose of each stage—prewriting, writing, and revising—to themselves and their classmates.

CHAPTER 2 PREWRITING

CHAPTER OBJECTIVES

In this chapter the student will

- generate writing ideas by freewriting, brainstorming, charting, and observing
- explore writing ideas with informational, personal, creative, and analytical questions
- narrow and focus writing topics
- determine purpose and audience
- form a main idea
- develop a main idea with specific support

SUGGESTED ANSWERS AND GUIDELINES FOR EVALUATION

PAGE 12, EXERCISE 2
Objective: Freewriting in pairs
Type of Writing: Freewriting notes
Length: Depends on the time spent freewriting; suggested time is five minutes
Guidelines for Evaluation: Students should
- demonstrate full commitment to freewriting
- identify several writing ideas among their notes
- see that they and their partners have come up with similar or different ideas

PAGE 13, EXERCISE 4
Objective: Brainstorming from another source
Type of Writing: Notes in list or clustering format
Length: About one page
Guidelines for Evaluation: Brainstorming notes should
- derive from a book or a magazine or from material in the Writer's Sourcebook
- include a variety of thoughts
- show connections between thoughts
- follow a format similar to (but not necessarily identical to) the notes in the text

PAGE 15, EXERCISE 5
Objective: Generating ideas by charting
Type of Writing: Chart with three columns
Length: The sample chart contains seven categories with multiple entries in some categories
Guidelines for Evaluation: The chart should
- contain in the left-hand column seven to fifteen general areas of experience
- contain in the middle column specific experiences from the student's life
- contain in the right-hand column writing ideas based on these experiences

PAGE 16, EXERCISE 6
Objective: Generating ideas by observing
Type of Writing: Prewriting list
Length: About one page
Guidelines for Evaluation: The list should include
- a scene or object to be observed, chosen perhaps from the Writer's Sourcebook
- identification of sensory details

PAGE 16, EXERCISE 7
Objective: Compiling writing ideas
Type of Writing: Prewriting list
Length: More than five ideas
Guidelines for Evaluation: The list should
- derive from the student's responses to Exercises 2–6
- include at least five promising ideas starred by the student

PAGE 17, EXERCISE 8
Objective: Exploring a subject with informational questions
Type of Writing: Prewriting notes
Length: About one page
Guidelines for Evaluation: The notes should
- focus on the subject areas starred in Exercise 7
- adapt the informational questions to this subject
- include the student's own answers to these questions

PAGE 20, EXERCISE 11
Objective: Exploring a subject through analytical questions
Type of Writing: Prewriting notes
Length: About one page
Guidelines for Evaluation: The notes should
- focus on one of the subject areas starred for Exercise 7
- adapt the analytical questions to this subject
- include the student's own answers to these questions

PAGE 21, EXERCISE 13
Objective: Focusing on a topic for a paragraph
Type of Writing: Notes showing one topic being narrowed
Length: About half a page
Guidelines for Evaluation: The notes should
- show a clear progression from a broad subject to successively narrower topics
- end with a topic narrow enough to be developed in one paragraph

PAGE 25, EXERCISE 16
Objective: Forming a main idea for a paragraph
Type of Writing: Prewriting notes
Length: Two main ideas, expressed as sentences, each with a purpose and audience
Guidelines for Evaluation: The notes should
- identify two different but appropriate purposes and audiences for the topic narrowed in Exercise 13
- include for each a purpose/audience combination a main idea stated in a sentence

PAGE 26, EXERCISE 18
Objective: Developing a main idea with specific support
Type of Writing: List of supporting items
Length: At least five items
Guidelines for Evaluation: The list should
- include specific items supporting a main idea stated in Exercise 16
- include some combination of facts, incidents, sensory details, examples, and reasons

PAGE 29, WRITER'S CHOICE #1
Objective: Writing a paragraph
Type of Writing: A paragraph of any type
Length: Ten to twelve sentences
Guidelines for Evaluation: The paragraph should
- clearly derive from the student's prewriting notes in Exercises 7–11, 13, 16, and 18
- reflect the purpose, audience, main idea, and support chosen by the student
- state the main idea in the first sentence
- end with an observation or a conclusion

PAGE 29, WRITER'S CHOICE #2
Objective: Writing a paragraph
Type of Writing: A paragraph that informs and persuades

Length: Ten to twelve sentences
Guidelines for Evaluation: The paragraph should
- tell about how one invention often opens the way to a series of related inventions
- clearly derive from freewriting and brainstorming notes
- state the main idea in the first sentence
- include supporting details derived from answers to informational and analytical questions

PAGE 29, WRITER'S CHOICE #3
Objective: Writing a composition
Type of Writing: A composition of any type
Length: Variable
Guidelines for Evaluation: The student should
- consider using an idea from the Writer's Sourcebook
- use prewriting activities like those practiced in this chapter
- develop one main idea
- imply a clear purpose and audience

PAGE 31, WRITERS ON WRITING, YOUR TURN
Objective: Prewriting about a special interest
Type of Writing: Prewriting notes and first draft
Length: A page of notes and a first draft of one paragraph
Guidelines for Evaluation: Students should
- use any prewriting technique or combination of techniques to generate ideas about a special interest or hobby of their own
- use informational, personal, and/or creative questions to explore the ideas they generated
- focus on one unusual aspect of their special interest
- decide on a purpose, audience, and main idea
- write a first draft of a paragraph based on these prewriting notes

REINFORCEMENT

Weekly Observer Each Friday suggest a different place that students might visit in order to observe and study the people or patterns of activity there. Students should note the writing ideas that strike them. You may want to specify a certain kind of information to record; for example, you might tell them to go to a local department store and spend some time "experiencing" the atmosphere. Students might want to go more than once to observe the difference between busy and slack times. Tell them to record their sensory impressions on a chart with columns for each of the senses. Give students time in class to share their ideas, and then have them store their notes in a folder for use with future writing assignments.

ENRICHMENT

Research Files Before students begin to write papers that require various kinds of research, give them some limited practice with each type. For example, suggest a topic that requires the use of specialized reference books, the vertical file, periodicals or newspapers, or other library references. Later you might want to suggest topics that have students branch out into the community to interview people, look up public records, find primary source material, or make personal observations. Allow time in class for them to share their findings. Have students keep their notes in a folder for future writing assignments.

CHAPTER 3 WRITING THE PARAGRAPH

CHAPTER OBJECTIVES

In this chapter the student will

- write a variety of topic sentences, appropriate to audience and purpose
- vary the placement of a topic sentence within a paragraph

- develop a topic sentence with concrete details, examples or incidents, facts or statistics, reasons, and mixed support
- identify good closing sentences
- write a unified paragraph
- write a coherent paragraph by using repeated words or synonyms, pronoun references, and transitions
- organize a paragraph by using chronological order, spatial order, order of importance, order based on cause and effect, and order based on comparison and contrast, or a combination of methods of development

SUGGESTED ANSWERS AND GUIDELINES FOR EVALUATION

PAGE 38, EXERCISE 2

Objective: Placing topic sentences

Type of Writing: Moving topic sentences to various positions in a paragraph

Guidelines for Evaluation: Students should be able to explain that

- the topic sentence at the beginning makes the paragraph begin with a general statement that is proved by the supporting details that follow
- the topic sentence in the middle acts as a bridge between the two groups of details
- the topic sentence at the end lets the paragraph provide details that are then drawn together or summarized by the topic sentence

PAGE 39, EXERCISE 3

Objective: Developing a topic sentence with concrete details

Type of Writing: A paragraph

Length: Six to eight sentences

Guidelines for Evaluation: The paragraph should

- include a clear topic sentence
- develop the topic sentence with sensory details
- clearly take direction and focus from the topic sentence

PAGE 40, EXERCISE 4

Objective: Developing a topic sentence with examples or incidents

Type of Writing: A paragraph

Length: Six to eight sentences

Guidelines for Evaluation: The paragraph should

- include a clear topic sentence
- develop the topic sentence with one or more examples or incidents
- clearly take direction and focus from the topic sentence

PAGE 41, EXERCISE 5

Objective: Developing a topic sentence with facts or statistics

Type of Writing: A paragraph

Length: Six to eight sentences

Guidelines for Evaluation: The paragraph should

- include a clear topic sentence
- develop the topic sentence with several facts or statistics
- clearly take direction and focus from the topic sentence

PAGE 42, EXERCISE 6

Objective: Developing a topic sentence with reasons

Type of Writing: A paragraph

Length: Six to eight sentences

Guidelines for Evaluation: The paragraph should

- include a clear topic sentence
- develop and support the topic sentence with several reasons
- clearly take their direction and focus from the topic sentence

PAGE 42, EXERCISE 7
Objective: Developing a topic sentence with mixed support
Type of Writing: A paragraph
Length: Six to eight sentences
Guidelines for Evaluation: The paragraph should
- include a clear topic sentence
- develop and support the topic sentence with an appropriate combination of supporting details
- clearly take direction and focus from the topic sentence

PAGE 44, EXERCISE 8
Objective: Writing closing sentences
Type of Writing: Closing a paragraph
Length: One sentence
Guidelines for Evaluation: The closing sentence should either
- restate the topic sentence (*American cities had risen from the dead.*)
- summarize the main points (*Building boomed, people were attracted, and services were restored.*)
- draw a logical conclusion (*Because cities were made liveable, they once again prospered.*)
- clinch an argument (*Young people brought up in the suburbs returned to the cities their parents once fled.*)

PAGE 46, EXERCISE 9
Objective: Writing a unified paragraph
Type of Writing: A paragraph
Length: No less than seven sentences
Guidelines for Evaluation: The paragraph should
- include a clear topic sentence
- develop the topic sentence with concrete details based on the senses, with examples or incidents, with facts or statistics, with reasons, or with mixed support
- maintain consistency in the method of development used
- demonstrate special attention paid to unity

PAGE 48, EXERCISE 10
Objective: Writing a coherent paragraph
Type of Writing: A paragraph
Length: Variable
Guidelines for Evaluation: The paragraph should
- present information coherently
- use at least one example of repeated words or synonyms
- use at least one example of pronoun reference
- use at least two transitions

PAGE 49, EXERCISE 11
Objective: Using chronological order
Type of Writing: A paragraph
Length: Variable
Guidelines for Evaluation: The paragraph should
- use chronological order, clearly indicating the sequence of events
- maintain unity by excluding all irrelevant sentences
- maintain coherence, using transitions that show time

PAGE 50, EXERCISE 12
Objective: Using spatial order
Type of Writing: A paragraph

Length: Variable
Guidelines for Evaluation: The paragraph should
- use special order, clearly indicating position and direction
- maintain unity by excluding all irrevelant sentences
- maintain coherence, using transitions that show place

PAGE 52, EXERCISE 13
Objective: Using order of importance
Type of Writing: A paragraph
Length: Variable
Guidelines for Evaluation: The paragraph should
- use order of either increasing or decreasing importance
- maintain unity by excluding all irrelevant sentences
- maintain coherence, using transitions that show order of importance

PAGE 52, EXERCISE 14
Objective: Using order based on cause and effect
Type of Writing: A paragraph
Length: Variable
Guidelines for Evaluation: The writer should
- use order based on cause and effect
- develop a genuine cause-and-effect relationship
- maintain unity by excluding all irrelevant sentences
- maintain coherence, using transitions that show cause and effect

PAGE 54, EXERCISE 15
Objective: Using order based on comparison and contrast
Type of Writing: A paragraph
Length: Variable
Guidelines for Evaluation: The writer should
- use order based on comparison and contrast
- clearly indicate the specific points of comparison and contrast
- maintain unity be excluding all irrelevant sentences
- maintain coherence, using transitions that show comparison and contrast

PAGE 55, WRITER'S CHOICE #1
Objective: Writing a paragraph for a news story
Type of Writing: A paragraph that relates an event
Length: Ten to twelve sentences
Guidelines for Evaluation: The paragraph should
- begin with a statement that identifies the event and tells why it is important
- describe the event in chronological order, using sentences that contain concrete details, examples, or facts
- maintain unity by excluding all irrelevant details
- maintain coherence by using transitions
- close, if appropriate, with a clincher sentence

PAGE 55, WRITER'S CHOICE #2
Objective: Writing a paragraph to a school newspaper editor
Type of Writing: A persuasive paragraph
Length: Variable
Guidelines for Evaluation: The paragraph should
- begin with a topic sentence that states the writer's opinion
- develop the topic sentence by offering reasons and examples that support the writer's opinion

- conclude with a sentence that identifies the most important effect that would occur if the writer's suggestion were taken
- maintain unity by excluding all irrelevant details
- maintain coherence by using transitions

PAGE 55, WRITER'S CHOICE #3
Objective: Writing a paragraph
Type of Writing: A paragraph of any kind
Length: Variable
Guidelines for Evaluation: The writer should
- write on any subject
- consider consulting the Writer's Sourcebook (pages 346–347) for a writing idea
- state the topic sentence at the beginning, in the middle, or at the end of the paragraph
- omit the topic sentence if all supporting details strongly imply the paragraph's main idea
- use an appropriate method of organization
- maintain unity by excluding all irrelevant details
- maintain coherence by using transitions

PAGE 56, WRITERS ON WRITING, YOUR TURN
Objective: Writing a paragraph
Type of Writing: A paragraph of any kind
Length: Five to ten sentences
Guidelines for Evaluation: Students should
- choose subject matter for which they feel a strong interest
- use prewriting techniques like those practiced in Chapter 2 to generate and explore ideas, narrow a topic, and formulate a main idea about that topic
- state the main idea in a well focused topic sentence
- develop the topic sentence with facts, details, incidents, or reasons
- use transitions to add coherence to the paragraph
- follow an appropriate method of organization

REINFORCEMENT

Grouping Ideas Give students a broad topic and have them brainstorm to produce a list of writing ideas related to that topic. Then have students group the ideas into categories that they can use as the basis for a paragraph. Then they are to take each category and write a topic sentence and a conclusion that seem appropriate for the ideas in that category.

ENRICHMENT

The End Have students bring to class a number of well developed expository paragraphs from which they have omitted the closing sentences. Have students trade paragraphs and write two different concluding sentences for the paragraph. Then have students discuss with their partners the concluding sentences each has written and compare them to the concluding sentences the writers of the paragraphs actually wrote.

CHAPTER 4 REVISING THE PARAGRAPH

CHAPTER OBJECTIVES

In this chapter the student will

- revise a paragraph for purpose and audience
- revise a variety of topic sentences and vary their positions in paragraphs
- revise a paragraph for correct support, sufficient development, logical organization, and strong conclusion
- revise a paragraph for coherence

- revise a paragraph for appropriateness and consistency of word choice
- edit, proofread, and publish a variety of paragraphs

SUGGESTED ANSWERS AND GUIDELINES FOR EVALUATION

Note: Throughout this chapter, most of the writing assignments call for students to hand in *revised* writing. However, in order to assess specific revising skills, you may want to ask students to hand in *both* the first draft and the revision of a particular writing assignment.

PAGE 64, EXERCISE 3
Objective: Revising support, development, and organization
Type of Writing: A revised paragraph
Length: Variable
Guidelines for Evaluation: The revised paragraph should
- state the main idea in a clear topic sentence
- support the topic sentence with the strongest possible details, facts, examples, or reasons
- develop the topic sentence sufficiently
- organize the supporting sentences logically

PAGE 65, WRITER'S CHOICE #1
Objective: Writing and revising a paragraph
Type of Writing: A paragraph
Length: Eight to ten sentences
Guidelines for Evaluation: The revised paragraph should
- demonstrate clarity of purpose and awareness of audience
- organize supporting sentences in a manner appropriate to the purpose
- include details, facts, examples, or reasons in support sentences
- demonstrate careful revision

PAGE 65, WRITER'S CHOICE #2
Objective: Writing and revising a paragraph
Type of Writing: A paragraph
Length: Variable
Guidelines for Evaluation: The revised paragraph should
- state the main idea in a clear topic sentence
- demonstrate clarity of purpose and awareness of audience
- develop the topic sentence with relevant, well-organized supporting sentences
- follow a method of organization appropriate to the topic
- demonstrate careful revision

PAGE 65, WRITER'S CHOICE #3
Objective: Writing and revising a paragraph
Type of Writing: A paragraph on any appropriate topic
Length: Variable
Guidelines for Evaluation: The revised paragraph should
- demonstrate clarity of purpose and awareness of audience
- state the main idea in a clear topic sentence
- develop the topic sentence with relevant, well-organized supporting sentences
- demonstrate careful revision

PAGE 67, EXERCISE 4
Objective: Revising for coherence
Type of Writing: A revised paragraph
Length: Variable
Guidelines for Evaluation: The revised paragraph should

- be a revision of the paragraph on nuclear and solar energy
- achieve coherence by using repeated words and synonyms, pronoun references and transitions

PAGE 68, EXERCISE 5
Objective: Revising word choice
Type of Writing: Two revised paragraphs
Length: Variable
Guidelines for Evaluation: The revised paragraphs should
- be revisions of the paragraphs provided in the exercise
- eliminate the inappropriate use of informal diction and slang (such as *bunch* and *bucks*), and formal diction (such as *perceptions* and *domination*)
- create consistency of word choice by revising sentences to attain a middle level of diction

PAGE 70, EXERCISE 6
Objective: Revising sentence structure
Type of Writing: A revised paragraph
Length: Variable
Guidelines for Evaluation: The revised paragraph should
- contain a number of sentences that do not begin with the subject
- contain a number of sentences that begin with modifiers
- contain a pleasing balance of sentence openings

PAGE 74, EXERCISE 7
Objective: Editing and proofreading
Type of Writing: Revised paragraphs
Length: Variable
Guidelines for Evaluation: The revised paragraph should eliminate all problems with the topic sentence, support, organization, coherence, and word choice

PAGE 76, WRITER'S CHOICE #1
Objective: Writing and revising a paragraph
Type of Writing: A paragraph that will appear on a local newspaper's editorial page
Length: Eight to ten sentences
Guidelines for Evaluation: The revised paragraph should
- demonstrate clarity of purpose and awareness of audience
- state the main idea in a clear topic sentence
- include details, facts, statistics, examples, or reasons in supporting sentences
- conclude with a sentence that summarizes the main idea
- demonstrate careful revision

PAGE 76, WRITER'S CHOICE #2
Objective: Writing and revising a paragraph
Type of Writing: A paragraph on a topic for young readers
Length: Eight to ten sentences
Guidelines for Evaluation: The revised paragraph should
- demonstrate clarity of purpose and awareness of the specific audience
- include a topic sentence that states the main idea clearly
- develop the topic sentence by using examples, details, facts, and reasons
- demonstrate careful revision

PAGE 76, WRITER'S CHOICE #3
Objective: Writing and revising a paragraph
Type of Writing: A paragraph on an appropriate topic
Length: Variable

Guidelines for Evaluation: The revised paragraph should
- develop a topic of the writer's own choice—possibly using the Writer's Sourcebook
- clearly imply a purpose and an audience
- state the main idea in a clear topic sentence
- develop the topic sentence with relevant, well-organized supporting sentences
- demonstrate careful revision, including revision of the topic sentence, of the supporting sentences, of organization, of coherence, and of word choice

PAGE 77, WRITERS ON WRITING, YOUR TURN
Objective: Revising a paragraph
Type of Writing: A paragraph
Length: Variable; will depend on the length of the original draft
Guidelines for Evaluation: Students should
- choose something that they have written that they feel needs improvement
- revise that draft using the questions and techniques taught in the chapter
- try to sharpen the paragraph's topic sentence
- strengthen the paragraph's development by adding or eliminating supporting items
- improve coherence by using transitions
- edit the draft for word choice, sentence structure, and grammatical and mechanical correctness
- proofread the final copy

REINFORCEMENT

Peer Editing Because it is often easier to spot flaws in organization, unity, or coherence in other people's writing than in one's own, peer editing is a good technique to use when you teach the revision process. Place students in groups of three or four and tell them to read and revise the papers written by the other members of the group. As guides, have students use the checklists in the book. Divide the class into small groups in such a way that a mixture of ability levels is represented in each group. Limit the groups to four students in each; otherwise students will have too many papers to edit and will not give each one the proper amount of attention.

ENRICHMENT

Rewrite Desk Collect several poorly written paragraphs printed in newspapers or magazines, and have students edit them. Students should refer to the checklists in the chapter to help them identify the likely sources of problems. Students should then rewrite the paragraphs to correct the problems they have identified.

CHAPTER 5 CHOOSING WORDS

CHAPTER OBJECTIVES

In this chapter the student will

- identify and select words by denotation and connotation
- order words from general to specific
- distinguish between concrete and abstract words
- determine levels of diction
- identify and write with idioms
- revise inflated diction, clichés, and jargon
- identify and write with similes, metaphors, and personification

SUGGESTED ANSWERS AND GUIDELINES FOR EVALUATION

PAGE 82, EXERCISE 1

1. Olympics: *Denotation*—game held once every four years; made up of international athletic contests. *Connotation*—the highest level of competition; of great importance; of championship status

2. Literature: *Denotation*—writings having excellence of form or expression that present ideas of universal importance. *Connotation*—something classical; beyond the reach of ordinary people; requiring great powers of understanding
3. Texas: *Denotation*—in area, the second-largest state in the United States; located in the southwest. *Connotation*—larger than life; where cowboys roam; oil-rich and affluent
4. mansion: *Denotation*—a large imposing residence. *Connotation*—where the rich live; a large, fancy house
5. jungle: *Denotation*—an impenetrable mass of tropical vegetation. *Connotation*—a place of dark mystery and strange sounds; a place where animals and birds abound
6. Mississippi River: *Denotation*—a 2740 mile river flowing from northern Minnesota to the Gulf of Mexico. *Connotation*—where steamboats roam; great and powerful; overflowing and dangerous

PAGE 85, EXERCISE 3

Abstract	*Concrete*	
nostalgia	autumn: sight, touch	boy: sight
sadness	bluejay: sight, hearing	wind: touch, hearing
	enameled: sight, touch	warm: touch
	wings: sight	garden: sight, smell

PAGE 86, EXERCISE 5

Many elegant restaurants take advantage of customers. First of all, these places serve small portions of meat and fish. They spice their entrees and embellish them with sauces. The salads are always ordinary—a lone lettuce leaf supporting a skimpy slice of tomato. The waiters are stiff and remote. The final act is inevitable: the itemized bill for food and services. We never leave one of these restaurants with any money.

PAGE 87, EXERCISE 6

1. bite the dust (informal)
2. cross a bridge when one comes to it (middle)
3. discharge an obligation (formal)
4. drop in (middle)
5. mind one's manners (middle)
6. cool off (middle)
7. run a temperature (middle)
8. fall into line (middle)
9. capture attention (middle)
10. make a mountain out of a mole hill (informal)

PAGE 90, EXERCISE 10

1. Even at the advanced age of 70, Benjamin Franklin sought new inventions.
2. It is obvious that excessive taxation will eliminate your financial reserves.
3. Carol is brilliant in the chemistry lab.
4. We were marooned as our boat drifted hopelessly across the bay.
5. As the sun rose, we waited expectantly for the unreliable school bus.

PAGE 94, WRITER'S CHOICE #1

Objective: Writing a paragraph about a busy place
Type of Writing: A descriptive paragraph
Length: Eight to ten sentences
Guidelines for Evaluation: The paragraph should

- use vivid, sensory language to describe the scene
- tell what the scene is and where it is located
- clearly show the results of revision

PAGE 94, WRITER'S CHOICE #2
Objective: Writing a paragraph about the names of professional sports teams
Type of Writing: A paragraph
Length: Eight to ten sentences
Guidelines for Evaluation: The paragraph should
- discuss how the connotations of sports teams names imply certain team characteristics
- include a topic sentence that explains the paragraph's purpose
- conclude with a clincher sentence that identifies the image that the names of the teams conveys

PAGE 94, WRITER'S CHOICE #3
Objective: Writing a paragraph
Type of Writing: A descriptive paragraph of any kind
Length: Variable
Guidelines for Evaluation: The student should
- describe exactly what he or she sees
- consider describing a view from the vantage point inside a moving vehicle
- use carefully chosen words and figures of speech

PAGE 95, WRITERS ON WRITING, YOUR TURN
Objective: Using vivid language
Type of Writing: A paragraph describing a scene
Length: Five to ten sentences
Guidelines for Evaluation: Students should
- describe a scene of their choice, either indoors or outdoors
- choose vivid language to present a series of sensory details evoking the scene

REINFORCEMENT

Sensory Awareness Give the students a list of six to ten words, most of which name things. Include a few abstract words, such as *fear* or *joy.* Have the students make a five-column chart with the names of five senses written across the top. For each object on the list, have students write several words that describe how the object appeals to each of the senses. Some of the items will appeal to the senses directly, but others will have a less obvious association. Encourage the students to think of figurative associations for the abstract words.

ENRICHMENT

Figures of Speech Give the students a list of ten items and ask them to describe each with (1) a simile, (2) a metaphor, and (3) an example of personification. Have students share their answers and discuss how effectively the figurative language describes each item.

CHAPTER 6 WRITING AND COMBINING SENTENCES

CHAPTER OBJECTIVES

In this chapter the student will

- expand sentences by adding details
- combine sentences through coordination
- combine sentences through subordinating information about nouns and verbs and subordinating to create noun substitutes
- combine sentences through both coordination and subordination
- combine sentences by using appositives
- combine sentences by using participles and participial phrases
- combine sentences by using absolute phrases
- revise paragraphs by means of a variety of methods

- write concise sentences and paragraphs
- create variety by varying sentence lengths and structures, varying sentence beginnings, and varying sentence types
- create parallelism within sentences and within paragraphs

SUGGESTED ANSWERS AND GUIDELINES FOR EVALUATION

PAGE 100, REVIEW EXERCISE
Students may automatically use subordination rather than coordination in their response. You might commend their mature sentence structure but remind them that this exercise was devised to have them practice the various kinds of coordination.

PAGE 109, EXERCISE 8
Encourage students to use as many different subordinating techniques as possible. You might have students rework each of the sentence groupings a second time after they have studied participles, appositives, and absolute phrases, since many opportunities for using those structures appear in this exercise.

PAGE 110, REVIEW EXERCISE
Encourage students to use as many different coordinating and subordinating techniques as possible. You might have students revise the paragraph a second time after they have studied participles, appositives, and absolute phrases, since many opportunities for using these structures also exist in this exercise.

PAGE 116, EXERCISE 12
A number of different methods can be used to make the paragraph more concise. Be sure that students have eliminated all repetitious language and that all overly long sentences have been simplified.

PAGE 117, EXERCISE 13
Encourage students not only to vary their sentence lengths and structure but also to choose the length and structure that will best express each idea.

PAGE 118, EXERCISE 14
Students will find a number of different ways to combine the sentences and rearrange the structures. Each sentence beginning should be different from the ones that precede and follow it.

PAGE 119, EXERCISE 15
The passage can be revised in a variety of ways. Students may form a question and command from existing sentences, or they might create their own.

PAGE 120, EXERCISE 17
The paragraph can be revised in variety of ways, but be sure that students use parallel structures in their versions. You might have students read their revised paragraphs aloud and discuss the relative effectiveness of various revisions.

PAGE 121, WRITER'S CHOICE #1
Objective: To revise a passage from a lower grade-level textbook or a junior book
Type of Writing: Revising paragraphs
Length: Two or three paragraphs
Guidelines for Evaluation: The revised passage should
- consist of a variety of expanded, coordinated, and subordinated sentences
- consist of sentences of varying lengths and structures
- communicate clearly to a general, adult audience

PAGE 121, WRITER'S CHOICE #2
Objective: Revising sentences in a sample of the student's own writing
Type of Writing: Revising

Length: Variable
Guidelines for Evaluation: The revised paragraph should
- contain sentence structures and lengths different from those in the original piece of writing
- use a variety of sentence beginnings
- include some of the sentence options taught in this chapter

PAGE 121, WRITER'S CHOICE #3
Objective: Writing a campaign speech
Type of Writing: A speech on any appropriate topic
Length: Variable
Guidelines for Evaluation: The student should
- prepare by using prewriting and writing steps like those practiced in Chapters 1–4
- revise by using a variety of sentence options
- present the speech to an audience
- consider finding an idea in the Writer's Sourcebook, pages 346–347

REINFORCEMENT
Imitating Model Sentences To help students use more complex and sophisticated structures in the sentences that they write, give them eight to ten examples of the sentence varieties taught in this chapter. Use professional models if possible. Discuss the sentence structure of each model with the students. Then have the students write five setences for each model, imitating exactly the structure and length of the original.

ENRICHMENT
Imitating Speeches Parallelism is a device used frequently in speeches. Provide students with copies of a well-known speech that effectively uses parallelism. Read the speech aloud so that the students can hear the rhythms that the parallel structures create. Then have students write their own speeches, closely imitating the sentence structures, parallel patterns, and rhythms of the model.

CHAPTER 7 WRITING STYLE

CHAPTER OBJECTIVES
In this chapter the student will

- prewrite to choose an appropriate voice for subject and audience
- prewrite to find his or her own distinctive voice as a writer
- write to develop grace, clarity, and precision in a personal style by using rhythm, parallelism, sentence variety, precise nouns, and action verbs
- revise for style, voice, and tone by avoiding ambiguity and empty superlatives
- revise by participating in writing conferences

SUGGESTED ANSWERS AND GUIDELINES FOR EVALUATION
PAGE 126, EXERCISE 2
Objective: Selecting an appropriate voice in writing
Type of Writing: Prewriting notes
Length: About one page
Guidelines for Evaluation: The notes should
- clearly identify a purpose and audience
- derive from brainstorming about the topic
- describe an appropriate tone—formal, informal, humorous, and so forth

PAGE 127, EXERCISE 3
Objective: Identifying rhythmic elements in prose
Type of Writing: List

Length: Six to eight sentences
Guidelines for Evaluation: The list should
- point out the variety in sentence beginnings
- point out the use of parallelism in repeated constructions (for example, "mortician for undertaker" to the end of the passage)
- point to the basic musicality of such sentences as "Here we glimpse the origin of a multitude of characteristic American euphemisms. . . ."

PAGE 128, EXERCISE 4
Students may rewrite the passage in a variety of ways and add details to make the passage more rhythmic.

PAGE 130, EXERCISE 6
Objective: Writing with grace, clarity, and precision
Type of Writing: A paragraph
Length: Variable
Guidelines for Evaluation: The paragraph should
- derive clearly from prewriting notes prepared in Exercise 2
- begin with a clear topic sentence
- contain supporting sentences of varied rhythm and structure
- contain precise, specific, and vivid language

PAGE 133, EXERCISE 9
Objective: Revising writing on the basis of readers' reactions
Type of Writing: A revised paragraph
Length: Variable
Guidelines for Evaluation: The student should
- share with another the paragraph prepared in Exercises 2 and 6
- use the reactions received to revise the paragraph
- edit and proofread the paragraph

PAGE 134, WRITER'S CHOICE #1
Objective: Revise a paragraph written earlier
Type of Writing: A paragraph of any kind
Length: Variable
Guidelines for Evaluation: The paragraph should
- imply a clear purpose and audience
- contain language that discloses the writer's voice
- contain language that is straightforward and direct
- contain sentences that are varied, clear, and unambiguous
- contain precise nouns and verbs

PAGE 134, WRITER'S CHOICE #2
Objective: Writing a paragraph about something that means a great deal to the writer
Type of Writing: A paragraph
Length: Six to ten sentences
Guidelines for Evaluation: The paragraph should
- imply a clear purpose and audience
- begin with a topic sentence
- communicate with authority and conviction and with clarity and directness
- be revised on the basis of a reader's reaction

PAGE 134, WRITER'S CHOICE #3
Objective: Writing a short paragraph on any subject
Type of Writing: A paragraph

Length: Variable
Guidelines for Evaluation: The student should
- consider raising a paragraph written earlier
- consider basing the paragraph on one or more of the items in the Writer's Sourcebook, pages 346–347
- be sure his or her voice is clearly evident behind the words

PAGE 136, WRITERS ON WRITING, YOUR TURN
Objective: Writing with contrasting styles
Type of Writing: Two paragraphs
Length: Fifteen to thirty sentences
Guidelines for Evaluation: Student should
- choose a topic on which they can write two connected but contrasting paragraphs
- decide on a purpose for each paragraph
- write each paragraph in a style suited to its purpose—for example, write one action-packed narrative paragraph, followed by a more analytical paragraph giving background information
- choose words and write sentences suited to the purpose of each paragraph

REINFORCEMENT

Rhythm in Writing It is important that students analyze the rhythm of their own writing. To help them, tell them to think about something that happened to them that was exciting and that made them very happy. They should try to relive this event in their minds, remembering how people looked, what noises and smells existed there, and how they felt at that moment. Then they should write a short description of this event. Tell them to write rapidly and with a minimum of pauses. When they have finished, ask them to read aloud what they have written, listening for the basic rhythms that should characterize their writing. Then have them go to the chapter to improve and refine that rhythm.

ENRICHMENT

Imitating the Masters To help students understand differences in writing style, have them try their hand at imitating notable writers. Select short passages from the works of authors who have a distinctive writing style. Have students read each passage and discuss the characteristics of the writer's style. Then ask the students to write an imitation of each passage. Students should use a different topic from the author's, but imitate the sentence lengths, sentence structures, literary devices, diction, tone, and voice of the original.

CHAPTER 8 DESCRIPTIVE WRITING

CHAPTER OBJECTIVES

In this chapter the student will

- prewrite to determine purpose and audience for a description
- prewrite to identify and collect sensory details
- prewrite to create and maintain an overall impression
- write descriptions using chronological and spatial order and order of importance
- write with descriptive language and figures of speech
- write a descriptive paragraph to create a mood
- write a character sketch
- revise, edit, and publish descriptive writing

SUGGESTED ANSWERS AND GUIDELINES FOR EVALUATION

PAGE 143, EXERCISE 2

1. *Expert audience*—teenagers who listen to popular music; *nonexpert audience*—adults who do not listen to popular music. The expert audience would need only a straightforward

description. The nonexpert would require background information and would need to have basic terms defined.

2. *Expert audience*—experienced mechanics; *nonexpert audience*—adults who do not follow automobiles. The expert audience would understand references to previous models and to other cars. The nonexpert audience would need a straightforward description of the car.
3. *Expert audience*—experienced gardeners; *nonexpert audience*—people with no gardening experience. The expert audience would understand gardening terms and the common names of flowers or vegetables. Gardening terms would have to be explained to the nonexpert audience, and the plants would have to be described.

PAGE 144, EXERCISE 3
high grass that stretches for miles—sight
very hot and still—touch, hearing
black water of the channels—sight
pungent odor—smell
taste of the anchovies—taste
smooth as glass—sight

PAGE 147, EXERCISE 5
Objective: Prewriting to create an overall impression
Type of Writing: Prewriting notes
Length: Two sentences, each supported by a list of details
Guidelines for Evaluation: The notes should
- derive clearly from the observation table
- state two alternative overall impressions of a baseball park during a game
- list supporting details for each impression

PAGE 147, EXERCISE 6
Objective: Prewriting to create an overall impression
Type of Writing: Prewriting notes
Length: One or two sentences
Guidelines for Evaluation: The notes should
- derive clearly from details listed in responses to Exercise 4
- state an overall impression based on these details

PAGE 149, EXERCISE 8
Objective: Writing a description by using spatial order
Type of Writing: A descriptive paragraph
Length: Variable
Guidelines for Evaluation: The paragraph should
- describe a baseball park during a game
- develop one of the overall impressions stated in Exercise 5
- support the impression with details arranged in spatial order

PAGE 149, EXERCISE 9
Objective: Writing a description by using chronological order
Type of Writing: A descriptive paragraph
Length: Variable
Guidelines for Evaluation: The paragraph should
- describe a panoramic scene
- be written from the vantage point of a rider in a moving vehicle
- indicate an overall impression based on details generated by freewriting
- present these details in chronological order
- use transitions that clearly indicate time order

PAGE 150, EXERCISE 10
Objective: Writing a description by using order of importance
Type of Writing: A descriptive paragraph
Length: Variable
Guidelines for Evaluation: The paragraph should
- describe the set for a science-fiction film
- indicate an overall impression based on details selected from the exercise
- support this impression with at least four details
- present these details in the order of their importance
- use transitions that indicate order of importance

PAGE 151, EXERCISE 11
Objective: Using descriptive language
Type of Writing: Revising
Length: Four to six sentences
Guidelines for Evaluation: The writer should replace clichés and general, bland language with more vivid expressions.

PAGE 152, WRITER'S CHOICE #1
Objective: Describing an important local structure
Type of Writing: A descriptive paragraph
Length: Six to eight sentences
Guidelines for Evaluation: The paragraph should
- be directed at someone who has never seen the structure
- derive from details on an observation table, such as the one in the student text
- emphasize the structure's most important feature
- use special order to organize the landmark's other important features

PAGE 152, WRITER'S CHOICE #2
Objective: Describing an abstract idea or feeling
Type of Writing: A descriptive paragraph
Length: Eight to ten sentences
Guidelines for Evaluation: The paragraph should
- describe an abstract idea or feeling such as freedom
- begin with a statement of what the abstract idea is and how it will be made concrete in the paragraph
- be developed by specific and concrete examples or details that precisely describe the idea
- be organized according to order of importance

PAGE 152, WRITER'S CHOICE #3
Objective: Writing description
Type of Writing: A descriptive composition
Length: Variable
Guidelines for Evaluation: The composition should
- clearly imply a purpose and an audience
- possibly be based on prewriting notes from Exercises 4 and 6
- state an overall impression supported by sensory details
- be organized by spatial or chronological order or order of importance

PAGE 154, EXERCISE 12
Objective: Creating a mood with descriptive details
Type of Writing: Descriptive writing
Length: Two paragraphs of variable length
Guidelines for Evaluation: The paragraphs should
- describe the same place at two different times, such as during summer and fall or when the place is empty and when it is inhabited by many people

- begin with topic sentences that convey an overall impression
- be supported by details that convey a mood appropriate to the overall impression

PAGE 156, EXERCISE 13
Objective: Writing a character sketch
Type of Writing: A descriptive paragraph
Length: Variable
Guidelines for Evaluation: The paragraph should
- derive from prewriting activities like those in the chapter
- begin with a topic sentence that expresses the writer's overall impression of the person
- be supported by details first about the subject's physical appearance and then about the subject's character traits

PAGE 157, WRITER'S CHOICE #1
Objective: Writing a character sketch
Type of Writing: A character sketch
Length: Eight to ten sentences
Guidelines for Evaluation: The paragraph should
- have as its subject a famous historical figure
- derive from prewriting notes
- begin with a sentence that identifies the subject and then describes the feature selected for emphasis
- be developed by a brief anecdote or a series of anecdotes that illustrate the subject's personality

PAGE 157, WRITER'S CHOICE #2
Objective: Describing an inanimate object
Type of Writing: A descriptive composition
Length: Variable
Guidelines for Evaluation: The composition should
- imply a clear audience and purpose
- describe the physical characteristics of the object in such a way that the object's "personality" is revealed
- derive from a list of prewriting notes
- use vivid language, including possibly similes, metaphors, and personification
- be organized by spatial order or order of importance

PAGE 157, WRITER'S CHOICE #3
Objective: Writing a description
Type of Writing: A descriptive composition
Length: Variable
Guideline for Evaluation: The student should
- consider basing the description on a subject in the Writer's Sourcebook

PAGE 158, WRITERS ON WRITING, YOUR TURN
Objective: Describing a disturbing experience
Type of Writing: A descriptive paragraph
Length: Five to ten sentences
Guidelines for Evaluation: Students should
- choose a disturbing experience such as trying to sleep through a thunderstorm and describe the experience in vivid terms
- use sensory details associated with that experience
- present an overall impression of the experience

REINFORCEMENT

Describing an Unfamiliar Object Bring to class several objects with which the students are unfamiliar. These objects could be tools, pieces of machinery, or specialized equipment.

Have students look at and handle the objects without discussing them. Then ask the students to write a one-paragraph description of one of the objects, following the prewriting activities outlined in the chapter. The students' descriptions should appeal to the senses and be detailed descriptions of the object itself, with no conjecture about the function of the object.

ENRICHMENT

A Prewriting Collage Have students select a place to describe. Ask them to plan a slide-show presentation about the place they have chosen. They are to determine an overall impression, and then list and describe in specific detail no more than twenty slides that would develop that impression. (An alternative would be to have students make collages of pictures clipped from magazines.) After this activity is completed, have students write a description of the place, using sensory language and organizing details within a spatial organizational pattern.

CHAPTER 9 NARRATIVE WRITING

CHAPTER OBJECTIVES

In this chapter the student will

- identify the elements of a narrative
- prewrite to determine subject, purpose, and audience
- prewrite to determine the necessary events and details of a narrative
- prepare and write from a narrative outline
- write a narrative in chronological order, using transitions
- write a narrative, changing indirect quotation to dialogue
- write a narrative with vivid verbs and narrative details
- revise, edit, and publish a narrative

SUGGESTED ANSWERS AND GUIDELINES FOR EVALUATION

PAGE 163, EXERCISE 1

1. This narrative is a nonfiction narrative because it tells a true story.
2. The narrative tells how the author's dog would refuse to come inside the house, preferring instead to remain outside threatening tradesmen. The problem was that the dog's behavior destroyed the family's artificial thunder, since thunder was the only thing that would drive the dog indoors.
3. The setting is the writer's home. The mood is humorous.
4. The narrative is told from the first-person point of view.

PAGE 164, EXERCISE 2
Objective: Prewriting
Type of Writing: Prewriting notes
Length: Determined by time spent prewriting; suggested time is ten minutes
Guidelines for Evaluation: The notes should

- generate a variety of ideas for writing
- explore ideas by answering the questions *who?, what?, when?, where?,* and *how?*

PAGE 164, EXERCISE 3
Objective: Defining purpose and audience
Type of Writing: Prewriting
Length: Two or three sentences
Guidelines for Evaluation: The answers should

- clearly state the goal or goals of the narrative
- identify the audience of the narrative
- list any terms with which the audience might be unfamiliar

PAGE 165, EXERCISE 4
Objective: Choosing events for a narrative
Type of Writing: Chart
Guidelines for Evaluation: The answers should
- cover the experience or incident from beginning to end, focusing on the most important events
- include a conflict and its resolution, as well as information about important characters

PAGE 166, EXERCISE 5
Objective: Eliminating unnecessary events
Type of Writing: Prewriting
Guideline for Evaluation: The student should
- eliminate events not directly related to the purpose of the narrative

PAGE 168, EXERCISE 6
Objective: Collecting narrative details
Type of Writing: Charts modeled on charts in the text
Guidelines for Evaluation: The first chart (*Characters in a Narrative*) should
- list details about the narrator and other characters relevant to the narrative, focusing on significant character traits and behavior

The second chart (*Setting for a Narrative*) should
- set the narrative in terms of time, place, and general environment

The third chart (*Mood for a Narrative*) should
- establish the mood of the narrative in terms of sense words and descriptive details

PAGE 169, EXERCISE 7
Objective: Preparing a narrative outline
Type of Writing: Outline
Length: About a page
Guidelines for Evaluation: The narrative outline should
- organize the prewriting done in the first six exercises
- be modeled on the outline in the student text
- preesent the events in chronological order

PAGE 171, EXERCISE 9
Objective: Writing from a narrative outline
Type of Writing: Narration
Length: One to several paragraphs
Guidelines for Evaluation: The narrative should
- present all of the events of the experience or incident
- include details of character and setting, presented with descriptive language
- follow chronological order, using transitions to make the sequence of events clear

PAGE 172, EXERCISE 10
Objective: Changing indirect quotation to dialogue
Guidelines for Evaluation: Student's versions should contain eight paragraphs and use dialogue five times

PAGE 174, WRITER'S CHOICE #1
Objective: Writing a narrative
Type of Writing: A narrative paragraph
Length: Eight to ten sentences

Guidelines for Evaluation: The paragraph should
- present an experience that led to an understanding or an appreciation of someone or something
- imply a clear audience and purpose
- be told from a first-person point of view
- conclude with a comment about what the writer learned or came to appreciate

PAGE 174, WRITER'S CHOICE #2
Objective: Writing a historical narrative
Type of Writing: Narration
Length: Variable
Guidelines for Evaluation: The composition should
- recount an important historical event as if the writer were a participant in the event
- clearly derive from charts containing details about character, setting, and mood
- use first-person point of view throughout
- begin with a description of the setting, followed by the presentation of events in chronological order
- use vivid language to describe the events and the characters

PAGE 174, WRITER'S CHOICE #3
Objective: Writing a narrative
Type of Writing: Narration
Length: Variable
Guidelines for Evaluation: The student should
- prepare by using prewriting activities practiced in the exercises
- consider using a subject suggested by the Writer's Sourcebook
- clearly imply a purpose and audience
- present the setting, plot, characters, and mood of their narratives in vivid and precise language

PAGE 176, WRITERS ON WRITING, YOUR TURN
Objective: Writing a personal narrative
Type of Writing: A narrative paragraph or essay
Length: Variable
Guidelines for Evaluation: Students should
- relate an experience that they feel represents a turning point in their lives
- present the experience in chronological order
- include details describing setting and characters
- indicate how the experience changed their lives

REINFORCEMENT

Fables Read and discuss fables. Note especially the types of characters, setting, action, and tone commonly used. Then give students a list of maxims. Ask students to select one of the maxims and to write a fable to illustrate it. The maxim will be the moral of each student's story.

ENRICHMENT

Historical Narrative Have students choose an interesting event in history. As a part of prewriting, they should research the topic, noting all of the available details. Then, following the prewriting activities outlined in the chapter, have them write a narrative account of the event from the viewpoint of one of the participants. The students should tell what took place during the event and also make a point for the reader. This point could be an opinion about the people involved, the causes of the event, or a commentary on the lessons to be learned from the event.

CHAPTER 10 EXPOSITORY WRITING

CHAPTER OBJECTIVES

In this chapter the student will

- prewrite to determine purpose and audience for expository writing
- prewrite, write, and revise an explanation of a process
- prewrite to identify and explore cause-and-effect relationships
- write, revise, edit, and publish a paragraph about a cause-and-effect relationship
- prewrite to divide and to classify subjects
- write, revise, edit, and publish paragraphs using division and classification
- prewrite, write, revise, edit, and publish definitions of familiar and unfamiliar terms
- prewrite to compare and contrast items
- write, revise, edit, and publish a paragraph using comparison and contrast
- prewrite to explain by analogy
- write, revise, edit, and publish a paragraph that uses analogy

SUGGESTED ANSWERS AND GUIDELINES FOR EVALUATION

PAGE 185, EXERCISE 5
Objective: Writing and revising an explanation of a process
Type of Writing: An expository paragraph
Length: Five to ten sentences
Guidelines for Evaluation: The paragraph should
- derive from the student's response to Exercise 4
- follow chronological order with appropriate transitions

PAGE 186, EXERCISE 7
Objective: Prewriting to explain a cause-and-effect relationship
Type of Writing: Prewriting notes
Length: About one page
Guidelines for Evaluation: The notes should
- indicate whether the student will focus on causes or effects
- designate the central event
- list in logical sequence either the causes that led up to the event or the effects that it produced
- indicate any links between the events

PAGE 188, EXERCISE 8
Objective: Writing and revising a paragraph about a cause-and-effect relationship
Type of Writing: An expository paragraph
Length: Five to ten sentences
Guidelines for Evaluation: The paragraph should
- explain the cause-and-effect relationship for which the student made notes in Exercise 7
- set forth causes and effects in chronological order, using appropriate transitions
- imply a clear purpose and audience

PAGE 190, EXERCISE 10
Objective: Writing and revising a paragraph based on division
Type of Writing: An expository paragraph
Length: Five to ten sentences
Guidelines for Evaluation: The paragraph should
- divide a subject into at least two overlapping parts
- derive from the prewriting activities in Exercise 9
- imply a clear purpose and audience

PAGE 192, EXERCISE 12
Objective: Writing and revising a paragraph based on classification
Type of Writing: An expository paragraph
Length: Five to ten sentences
Guidelines for Evaluation: The paragraph should
- create meaningful, nonoverlapping classes within a large group of related items
- derive from the prewriting activities in Exercise 11
- imply a clear purpose and audience

PAGE 194, EXERCISE 13
Objective: Prewriting to define an unfamiliar term
Type of Writing: Prewriting notes
Length: About one page
Guidelines for Evaluation: The notes should
- prepare the student to define a specialized or unfamiliar term
- include a wider frame of reference in which to place the term
- include specific distinguishing characteristics of the item

PAGE 194, EXERCISE 14
Objective : Writing and revising a definition of an unfamiliar term
Type of Writing: An expository paragraph
Length: Five to ten sentences
Guidelines for Evaluation: The paragraph should
- address an audience unfamiliar with the term
- derive from the notes taken during Exercise 13
- identify the term to be defined
- indicate the general class to which the term belongs
- differentiate the term from other members of its class
- include examples to clarify the definition

PAGE 195, EXERCISE 15
Objective: Prewriting to define a familiar term
Type of Writing: Prewriting notes
Length: About one page
Guidelines for Evaluation: The notes should
- prepare the student to define a generally familiar term
- lead to an explanation of how the writer's definition differs from the common one

PAGE 196, EXERCISE 16
Objective: Writing and revising a definition of a familiar term
Type of Writing: An expository paragraph
Length: Five to ten sentences
Guidelines for Evaluation: The paragraph should
- show how the student's definition of the term differs from the commonly accepted one
- include examples or anecdotes to clarify the writer's definition

PAGE 197, EXERCISE 17
Objective: Prewriting by making a comparison frame
Type of Writing: A list in chart form
Length: Five points of comparison
Guidelines for Evaluation: The comparison frame should
- follow the format presented in the text
- identify two specific items to be compared and contrasted
- include reasonable categories on which to base the comparison
- indicate at least four specific points of comparison

PAGE 198, EXERCISE 18
Objective: Writing and revising a comparison and contrast
Type of Writing: An expository paragraph
Length: Ten to twelve sentences
Guidelines for Evaluation: The paragraph should
- clearly derive from the comparison frame created for Exercise 17
- state or imply the reason for the comparison
- present the similarities and differences between the two items
- follow either the AAABBB or the ABABAB pattern of organization

PAGE 200, EXERCISE 19
Objective: Prewriting by making an analogy frame
Type of Writing: A chart like the one shown in the student text
Length: About half a page
Guidelines for Evaluation: The chart should
- identify both the unfamiliar item and the familiar item
- list similarities between the pair of items

PAGE 201, EXERCISE 20
Objective: Writing an analogy
Type of Writing: An expository paragraph
Length: Eight to ten sentences
Guidelines for Evaluation: The paragraph should
- derive directly from the analogy frame prepared in Exercise 19
- imply a clear purpose to explain the unfamiliar item
- begin with a clearly stated topic sentence
- support the topic sentence with specific details
- include transitions
- be organized according to the ABABAB pattern of development

PAGE 202, WRITER'S CHOICE #1
Objective: Explaining how to perform a simple task
Type of Writing: An expository paragraph
Length: Six to eight sentences
Guidelines for Evaluation: The paragraph should
- be directed at an audience unfamiliar with the process or task
- derive obviously from prewriting notes
- begin with a clearly stated topic sentence that explains the paragraph's purpose
- include supporting sentences presented in chronological order

PAGE 202, WRITER'S CHOICE #2
Objective: Writing a paragraph
Type of Writing: An expository paragraph
Length: Six to ten sentences
Guidelines for Evaluation: The paragraph should
- have a clearly stated purpose
- derive obviously from prewriting
- be developed according to an appropriate method of organization
- use transitional words to assure coherence

PAGE 202, WRITER'S CHOICE #3
Objective: To define a term
Type of Writing: An expository essay
Length: Variable

Guidelines for Evaluation: The student should
- follow appropriate prewriting, writing, and revising steps
- indicate the wider category to which the term belongs
- explain what sets the term apart from other terms in its same general category
- use examples or comparisons to help readers understand the term defined

PAGE 203, WRITER'S CHOICE #4
Objective: To compare and contrast two school subjects
Type of Writing: An expository essay
Length: Variable
Guidelines for Evaluation: The student should
- follow appropriate prewriting, writing, and revising steps
- point out both similarities and differences between the subjects
- use either an AAABBB or an ABABAB pattern of organization

PAGE 203, WRITER'S CHOICE #5
Objective: To explain an unfamiliar term by means of an analogy
Type of Writing: An expository essay
Length: Variable
Guidelines for Evaluation: The student should
- follow appropriate prewriting, writing, and revising steps
- make an analogy frame showing the similarities between the term and the item with which it is being compared
- use an ABABAB pattern of organization
- make the analogy clear

PAGE 203, WRITER'S CHOICE #6
Objective: Writing a short expository paper
Type of Writing: An expository composition
Length: Variable
Guidelines for Evaluation: The student should
- choose an appropriate topic
- consider using the Writer's Sourcebook to find a topic
- follow appropriate prewriting, writing, and revising steps

PAGE 205, WRITERS ON WRITING, YOUR TURN
Objective: Writing a comparison
Type of Writing: An expository composition
Length: Three to five paragraphs
Guidelines for Evaluation: Students should
- choose two subjects to compare
- prewrite by listing the points on which the subjects can be compared, noting similarities and differences
- decide on a main idea, and state it in a topic sentence
- write the composition, using either the AAABBB or the ABABAB patterns
- include appropriate transitions to add coherence

REINFORCEMENT

Explain a Process Give the students a list of tasks that involve a fairly complicated process; for example; how to tune an engine, assemble a piece of telephone equipment, make plastic, and so forth. The tasks should be ones that the students do not know firsthand but can research easily. Local industries and repair businesses are ideal subjects. Have students choose and research a task that interests them. Encourage them to make arrangements to observe how the task is performed. Then ask students to write a process paper that explains the task. Share and discuss the finished papers.

ENRICHMENT

Cause and Effect Give students a list of situations, such as a solar eclipse, an increase or decrease in school enrollment, or the growth of women's sports. Once the students have chosen a situation from your list, have them follow the prewriting activities in the chapter and write an outline that organizes the paper from cause to effect. Then have them write an outline for the same paper and organize the paper from the effect to the cause. Ask students to decide which organizational pattern will be more effective for their situation, and then have them write the paper.

CHAPTER 11 CRITICAL THINKING AND PERSUASIVE WRITING

CHAPTER OBJECTIVES

In this chapter the student will

- prewrite to determine appropriate propositions for persuasive writing
- prewrite to suit topic to audience
- prewrite to identify facts and opinions
- prewrite to distinguish between inductive and deductive reasoning
- prewrite to limit generalizations for persuasive writing
- write a persuasive argument
- revise to avoid stereotypes, bandwagon persuasion, name-calling, testimonials, and red herrings
- revise to avoid either-or thinking and faulty cause-and-effect thinking
- edit, proofread, and publish persuasive writing

SUGGESTED ANSWERS AND GUIDELINES FOR EVALUATION

PAGE 212, EXERCISE 4

Answers: 1. fact; 2. unsound opinion; 3. unreliable authoritive opinion; 4. sound opinion; 5. sound authoritative opinion

PAGE 217, EXERCISE 8

1. In order for the conclusion to be acceptable, it would be necessary to show that all state colleges should indeed be tuition-free. Audience—college-bound students
2. The conclusion would be acceptable only if it could be shown that all good students should have to attend school for only four days a week. It would also have to be established that the person in question is indeed a good student. Audience—good students.
3. The validity of the conclusion would depend upon establishing that all lazy students should receive extra homework. It would also have to be shown that the students in a particular class are indeed lazy. Audience—students who are not lazy

PAGE 220, EXERCISE 9

Objective: Writing an argument
Type of Writing: A persuasive essay
Length: Four to six paragraphs
Guidelines for Evaluation: The argument should

- imply a clear purpose and audience
- derive obviously from prewriting
- state a position clearly at the beginning
- include necessary background information
- support the position with reasons or facts
- use transition words effectively
- conclude by calling for either a move to action or a change in belief or attitude

PAGE 226, WRITER'S CHOICE #1

Objective: Writing persuasively
Type of Writing: An essay

Length: Four to five paragraphs
Guidelines for Evaluation: The persuasive essay should
- be based upon the position statement: The age for obtaining a driver's license should be raised to twenty-one.
- be aimed at a specific audience identified by an audience profile
- derive from brainstorming
- include the position statement in the first paragraph along with whatever background information the reader might need to follow the argument
- present in the body paragraphs reliable evidence in support of the writer's opinion
- if the writer wishes, include a paragraph in which an opposing view is stated and then answered
- include a final paragraph that urges readers to adopt the position presented

PAGE 226, WRITER'S CHOICE #2
Objective: Writing an endorsement
Type of Writing: Persuasive essay
Length: Four to five paragraphs
Guidelines for Evaluation: The endorsement should
- be for something that the student likes or repsects (a product, an event, a group, a person in a political campaign)
- be aimed at a specific audience
- derive from prewriting through brainstorming or charting
- follow the procedures for organizing and presenting a convincing argument
- begin with a position statement, followed by paragraphs in the main section that present reliable evidence developed deductively and/or inductively
- avoid fallacies

PAGE 226, WRITER'S CHOICE #3
Objective: Writing persuasively on a topic of the student's choice
Type of Writing: An essay
Length: Four to five paragraphs
Guidelines for Evaluation: The student should
- clearly identify a topic and audience and prepare a statement of purpose
- write a position statement and provide any necessary background information
- use deductive and/or inductive reasoning to present the argument
- organize facts and opinions logically
- consider developing a rebuttal to an opposing viewpoint
- state a conclusion and urge the reader to take certain action or to support the writer's position

PAGE 228, WRITERS ON WRITING, YOUR TURN
Objective: Writing persuasively
Type of Writing: A persuasive paragraph
Length: Eight to fifteen sentences
Guidelines for Evaluation: Students should
- choose a subject about which they have strong opinions—perhaps a pet peeve
- state a purpose and identify an audience
- clearly express the opinion to be defended
- present valid evidence—facts, examples, cogent reasons—in support of this opinion
- end with a strong restatement of their position, perhaps calling upon the readers to take action of some kind. Students may also use a humorous approach to the subject.

REINFORCEMENT

Advertising Collect several advertisements from magazines and bring them to class. Have students discuss the emotions that are being appealed to by means of words and pictures. Videotape several television commercials, show them in class, and discuss the emotional appeals. Then tell students that you want them to decide how they react to being the audience for such advertising. Do they think that commercials are clever manipulations of language and images and that the audiences should be responsible for being careful readers and watchers, or do they think that the public is being insulted or victimized and should demand an end to the practice? Ask students to follow the prewriting in the chapter to develop their ideas and then write the papers as "letters to the editor."

ENRICHMENT

Propaganda Bring to class several examples of political propaganda. These examples should come from the U.S. and other countries and should represent both positive and negative propaganda. Include both contemporary examples of propaganda and historical ones (Thomas Paine's *Common Sense,* for example). Have students analyze each example for effectiveness and discuss the techniques used by the author. Choose several topics from current political issues, and have students write a pamphlet about one of the issues. Remind students that when they are writing arguments, they must take a stand and not present both sides of an issue.

CHAPTER 12 THE ESSAY

CHAPTER OBJECTIVES

In this chapter the student will

- prewrite to generate essay ideas by freewriting, brainstorming, and clustering
- prewrite to explore essay ideas by asking informational, personal, analytical, or creative questions
- prewrite to focus and limit essay ideas
- prewrite to determine purpose and audience for an essay
- prewrite to prepare a working outline for an essay
- write a first draft of an essay
- revise a first draft and prepare a formal outline of an essay
- revise an essay by editing, proofreading, and publishing the finished product

SUGGESTED ANSWERS AND GUIDELINES FOR EVALUATION

PAGE 238, EXERCISE 8
Objective: Writing a working outline
Type of Writing: Outlining
Length: About a page
Guidelines for Evaluation: The working outline should

- logically present all the main ideas to be covered in the essay
- list at least three main ideas, identified by Roman numerals, as well as numerous supporting details, identified by capital letters

PAGE 241, EXERCISE 10
Objective: Writing introductory paragraphs
Type of Writing: Writing an essay
Length: Six to ten sentences
Guidelines for Evaluation: The students should

- Write two different introductions based on the thesis statement written for Exercise 9
- write an introductory paragraph that captures the reader's interest and sets the tone of the essay
- consider using one of the following techniques in their introductions: asking a question, addressing the reader directly, stating an interesting fact or statistic, telling an anecdote, taking a strong stand, or quoting from a book, poem, or song
- explain in writing which of the two introductory paragraphs the writer prefers

PAGE 242, EXERCISE 11
Objective: Writing a first draft
Type of Writing: Prewriting
Length: Four or five paragraphs
Guidelines for Evaluation: The first draft should
- cover all the main points and supporting details on the working outline
- begin with the preferred introduction written for Exercise 10
- contain at least three body paragraphs

PAGE 243, EXERCISE 12
Objective: Revising a first draft
Type of Writing: Revising
Length: Four or five paragraphs
Guidelines for Evaluation: Students should
- base their revisions on the Checklist for Revising an Essay
- consider purpose, audience, organization, sentence structure, and sentence length as likely candidates for revision
- carefully proofread their draft

PAGE 246, EXERCISE 13

I. The causes of volcanoes
  A. Location of the volcanic zones
    1. Area surrounding the Pacific Ocean
    2. The Mediterranean region eastward into Indonesia
  B. The contents of a volcanic eruption
    1. Lava
    2. Hot gases
    3. Ash

II. Kinds of volcanoes
  A. Shield volcanoes
  B. Cone volcanoes
  C. Composite volcanoes

III. Active volcanoes
  A. Mt. St. Helens, Washington (May, 1980)
  B. Kilauea, Hawaii (May, 1980)

PAGE 249, WRITER'S CHOICE #1
Objective: Writing a formal outline and a final version
Type of Writing: Formal outline and essay
Length: Five to seven paragraphs
Guidelines for Evaluation: Writing the formal outline, the student should
- prepare an outline that reflects any organizational changes the writer made in Exercise 12
- place his or her topic at the top of the outline
- follow correct outline form

Writing the final version, the student should
- make sure that content of the essay reflects organization of the final outline
- incorporate all revisions made in Exercise 12
- edit and proofread carefully

PAGE 249, WRITER'S CHOICE #2
Objective: Writing an entry for an essay contest
Type of Writing: Formal essay
Length: Five to seven paragraphs
Guidelines for Evaluation: The student should
- write about one of two topics: the value of work or a significant discovery
- address the essay to a general audience
- include an introductory paragraph with thesis clearly stated, body, and a concluding paragraph
- revise, edit, and proofread before handing in the final version

PAGE 250, WRITER'S CHOICE #3
Objective: Writing a formal essay for a national essay-writing contest
Kind of Writing: Formal essay
Length: Five to seven paragraphs
Guidelines for Evaluation: The essay should
- imply a clear purpose and audience
- derive obviously from prewriting
- have as its subject a suitably narowed topic
- follow these writing stages: working outline, first draft, formal outline, final draft
- be revised according to the Checklist for Revising on page 243

PAGE 250, WRITER'S CHOICE #4
Objective: Writing a formal essay
Kind of Writing: Formal essay
Length: Variable
Guidelines for Evaluation: The essay should
- imply a clear purpose and audience
- develop a writing idea possibly found in the Writer's Sourcebook
- follow these writing stages: working outline, first draft, formal outline, final draft
- be carefully edited and proofread

PAGE 250, WRITER'S CHOICE #5
Objective: Writing an informal essay
Kind of Writing: Informal essay
Length: Variable
Guidelines for Evaluation: The essay should
- imply a clear purpose and audience
- maintain a light tone throughout
- use descriptive and narrative elements, as appropriate, in its development
- follow these writing stages: prewriting, working outline, first draft, formal outline, final draft
- be carefully edited and proofread

REINFORCEMENT

Essay About a Place Bring to class several travel articles that describe places to visit. Have students read and discuss each article. Next have students select a place that they know or can visit. Ask them to write an essay that could be used in a travel guide to your city, state, or geographic area. The descriptions should be factual and informative in such a way that people will want to visit it.

ENRICHMENT

A Personal Essay Bring to class several examples of personal essays, such as those written by Virginia Woolf, E. B. White, and Russell Baker. Read and discuss these essays with the students. Then ask them to write an essay, using the first-person point of view. Have them use a personal experience to introduce and develop their main idea. They should use as their models the essays discussed in class and follow the prewriting activities outlined in the chapter.

CHAPTER 13 THE RESEARCH PAPER

CHAPTER OBJECTIVES

In this chapter the student will

- prewrite to select and limit a research topic
- identify library sources for a research topic

- use the library to gather general information on a research topic
- prewrite to determine purpose, audience, and controlling idea
- prepare a working outline for a research paper
- use the library to find sources and gather detailed information
- keep a working bibliography, correctly identifying sources on bibliography cards
- take useful notes and avoid plagiarism
- prepare a formal outline
- write a first draft, using an outline and note cards
- revise a first draft
- use correct footnote and bibliography style
- edit, proofread, and publish a finished research paper

SUGGESTED ANSWERS AND GUIDELINES FOR EVALUATION

PAGE 254, EXERCISE 2
Objectives: Checking the library for sources
Type of Writing: Prewriting
Length: About half a page
Guidelines for Evaluation: Students should
- list at least eight suitable sources
- consider periodicals as well as books

PAGE 255, EXERCISE 3
Objective: Finding general information on a topic
Type of Writing: Prewriting
Length: About a page
Guidelines for Evaluation: Students should
- read several encyclopedia articles or a magazine article
- list at least five important aspects of their topics

PAGE 256, EXERCISE 4
Objective: Determining purpose, audience, and controlling idea
Type of Writing: Prewriting
Length: About a page
Guidelines for Evaluation: The student should
- clearly explain his or her reasons for writing the paper
- state who the audience is to be
- develop a controlling idea that states the main point of the paper, explains the student's attitude toward the topic, and suggests the path the paper will follow

PAGE 257, EXERCISE 5
Objective: Preparing a working outline
Type of Writing: Outlining
Length: About a page
Guidelines for Evaluation: The working outline should
- be generated by answering specific questions about aspects of the topic
- include major headings and as many subheadings as possible
- indicate the modes of writing the student plans to use in the report

PAGE 259, EXERCISE 6
Objective: Finding Sources
Type of Writing: Prewriting
Length: About half a page
Guidelines for Evaluation: The student should

• review the sources located for Exercise 2
• after skimming the material to make sure it is useful, fill out bibliography cards, according to the forms shown in the student text

PAGE 261, EXERCISE 7
Objective: Taking notes
Type of Writing: Notes
Length: A sufficient amount to cover the topic thoroughly
Guidelines for Evaluation: The notes should
• be written on large index cards following the forms shown in the student book
• be in the student's own words
• use quotation marks around direct quotations
• be written on the front of the cards and should never continue onto the back

PAGE 262, EXERCISE 8
Objective: Writing a formal outline
Type of Writing: Outlining
Length: About a page
Guidelines for Evaluation: The student should
• present his or her ideas in a logical order
• use note cards and working outline to prepare the formal outline
• use the outlining questions in the student text as a guide

PAGE 264, EXERCISE 9
Objective: Evaluating progress
Type of Writing: Prewriting
Length: Variable
Guidelines for Evaluation: The students should
• use the questions in this exercise to double-check all the work done on the paper thus far
• make any revisions called for by their responses to the questions
• be ready to write their first drafts after completing this exercise

PAGE 266, EXERCISE 10

[1]Christopher Bird, and Peter Tompkins, *The Secret Life of Plants* (New York: Avon Books, 1973), p. 10

[2]Winston Churchill, *Blood, Sweat, and Tears* (New York: G. P. Putnam's Sons, 1941), p. 23.

[3]Simone de Beauvoir, *The Coming of Age* (New York: Warner Paperbacks, 1973), p. 375.

[4]Norman Podhoretz, "How the West Was Won," *New York Times Magazine,* September 30, 1979, p. 17.

[5]Edna St. Vincent Millay, "When the Year Grows Old," in *Yesterday and Today,* ed. Louis Untermeyer (New York: Harcourt Brace Jovanovich, 1926), p. 197.

PAGE 267, EXERCISE 11

Bird, Christopher and Peter Tompkins. *The Secret Life of Plants.* New York: Avon Books, 1973.

Churchill, Winston. *Blood, Sweat, and Tears.* New York: G. P. Putnam's Sons, 1941.

de Beauvoir, Simone. *The Coming of Age.* New York: Warner Paperbacks, 1973.

Millay, Edna St. Vincent. "When the Year Grows Old," in *Yesterday and Today.* Ed. Louis Untermeyer. New York: Harcourt Brace Jovanovich, 1926.

Podhoretz, Norman. "How the West Was Won." *New York Times Magazine,* September 30, 1979.

PAGE 274, WRITER'S CHOICE #1
Objective: Writing a research paper
Type of Writing: Research paper

Length: Five to eight pages
Guidelines for Evaluation: The research report should
- represent the culmination of the work the student has done in Exercises 1–11
- be prepared from a formal outline
- have these components: introduction, thesis statement, body, and conclusion
- include footnotes and bibliography following the formats in the student text
- have been carefully proofread

PAGE 274, WRITER'S CHOICE #2
Objective: Writing a research paper on the use of computers in American schools
Type of Writing: Research paper
Length: Eight to fifteen pages
Guidelines for Evaluation: The paper should
- be preapred for the members of your local school board and school administrators
- be based upon information from articles located by using the *Readers' Guide to Periodical Literature* and the *New York Times Index*
- be prepared from a formal outline
- include an introduction, thesis statement, body, and conclusion
- be carefully proofread

PAGE 274, WRITER'S CHOICE #3
Objective: Writing a research paper on any topic
Type of Writing: Research paper
Length: Variable
Guidelines for Evaluation: The research paper
- imply a clear purpose and audience
- discuss a suitably limited topic, perhaps one suggested by the Writer's Sourcebook
- should include all the basic parts of a research paper: introduction, thesis statement, body, conclusion
- be carefully proofread

REINFORCEMENT

The Controlled Paper If you feel some of your students will have difficulty writing an independent research paper, use the controlled paper. These students will follow the same process as those writing a regular paper, but you must carefully direct and monitor their progress. First, through class discussions, have all the students agree upon a single, appropriately narrowed topic and then have students go to the library to look for sources on the topic. Prearrange with the librarian to allow the students to take all the materials they find back to the classroom for two weeks. Then, using these materials in class, have students follow the steps outlined in the chapter to develop their papers. Have students work through every stage as a class or in groups before allowing them to work independently. Be particularly careful as you monitor their notetaking; help them take notes that are useful and relevant. When they finish their notes, have students organize the cards into an outline for the paper. Direct them as they write their introductions and rough drafts. After their drafts have undergone peer-editing and when all necessary corrections and changes have been made, have students produce the final outline and draft.

ENRICHMENT

Special Research Sources In addition to the commonly recommended sources that students use to develop their research papers, require them to use some less common sources: brochures, pamphlets, and other materials from the library's vertical file. Have them also contact individuals within the community who can provide useful information. To help them prepare for this type of research, have them generate a list of questions to ask in an interview and role-play the interview so that they will know how to conduct it properly and efficiently.

CHAPTER 14 WRITING ABOUT SOCIAL STUDIES

CHAPTER OBJECTIVES

In this chapter the student will

- prewrite to focus a social studies topic and determine audience and purpose
- prewrite to identify types of social studies evidence
- prewrite to form a generalization from social studies facts
- write objectively about a social studies topic
- write about social studies events in chronological order
- write about the causes and effects of a social studies event
- write about a social studies topic by using comparison and contrast
- revise, edit, proofread, and publish a social studies report

SUGGESTED ANSWERS AND GUIDELINES FOR EVALUATION

PAGE 281, EXERCISE 3

1. autobiography—useful because it could shed direct light on the stock market crash
2. Novel—not useful because it is basically fiction
3. article—useful because it would contain information from reliable sources
4. letters—useful because they would contain the insights of participant in the events

PAGE 281, EXERCISE 4

Objective: Making generalizations
Type of Writing: A list of five items followed by a general statement
Length: Variable
Guidelines for Evaluation: The list should

- include enough information to lead to a generalization

The generalization should

- be based on the list of facts
- contain limiting words to make the statement more precise

PAGE 281, EXERCISE 5

Objective: Writing objectively
Type of Writing: Revising
Length: Variable
Guidelines for Evaluation: The social studies paragraph should

- be a revision of the paragraph about the purchase of Alaska
- avoid all biased or prejudiced statements such as "such opposition was grounded in the foolish fear that a country . . . could not afford such extravagance."
- state the facts in clear, straightforward language
- quote sources exactly, avoiding conjecture such as "Seward probably saw the real value. . . ."
- label opinions as opinions
- use adverbs sparingly
- be carefully edited and proofread

PAGE 282, EXERCISE 6

at the very start—designates the point in time that the paragraph will deal with
For a century or more—designates events that came before
First . . . then—specify a sequence of events
As early as 1849—specifies an exact point
then—designates a sequential point
After—designates a sequential event
And in 1859—designates a final event

PAGE 282, EXERCISE 7
Objective: Writing chronologically
Type of Writing: A social studies paragraph
Length: Variable
Guidelines for Evaluation: The paragraph should
- be based on a series of social studies events selected by the writer
- describe the selected events in clear chronological order
- use appropriate transitions
- be carefully edited and proofread

PAGE 283, EXERCISE 8
Objective: Writing about causes and effects
Type of Writing: A social studies paragraph about causes or effects of a cultural or historical event
Length: Variable
Guidelines for Evaluation: The paragraph should
- identify clearly and relate the causes or effects of a particular event
- demonstrate awareness of a wide variety of possible causes or effects, including short-term and long-term causes or effects
- avoid all biased or prejudiced statements
- state the facts in clear, straightforward language
- quote sources exactly and label opinions as opinions
- be carefully edited and proofread

PAGE 285, EXERCISE 9
Objective: Writing with comparison and contrast
Type of Writing: A paragraph comparing or contrasting two social studies subjects
Length: Variable
Guidelines for Evaluation: The social studies paragraph should
- demonstrate awareness of a specific audience and purpose
- identify clearly the subjects being compared or contrasted
- be organized by either the AAABBB or the ABABAB pattern
- conclude with a general statement
- avoid all biased or prejudiced statements
- state the facts in clear, straightforward language
- quote sources exactly and label opinions as opinions
- be carefully edited and proofread

PAGE 287, WRITER'S CHOICE #1
Objective: A paragraph comparing two historical figures
Type of Writing: A paragraph that compares and contrasts
Length: Variable
Guidelines for Evaluation: The paragraph should
- be a comparative biographical sketch of any two of the historical figures named
- demonstrate awareness of a specific audience and purpose
- derive from a prewriting chart listing the characters' similarities and differences
- be organized in one of two ways—AAABBB or ABABAB
- conclude with a general statement about the two figures
- contain appropriate qualifying words and phrases
- be carefully edited and proofread

PAGE 287, WRITER'S CHOICE #2
Objective: Writing about causes and effects
Type of Writing: A composition about the causes or effects of a historical event

Length: Variable
Guidelines for Evaluation: The composition should
- derive from answers to the personal, social, and economic questions listed in the text
- demonstrate an awareness of a wide variety of possible causes and effects
- include supporting details that are clear and relevant
- state the facts in straightforward unbiased language
- quote sources exactly and label opinions as opinions
- be carefully edited and proofread

PAGE 287, WRITER'S CHOICE #3
Objective: Writing about social studies
Type of Writing: A paragraph or brief essay about an appropriate social studies topic
Length: Variable
Guidelines for Evaluation: The student's writing should
- demonstrate a clear awareness of audience and purpose
- begin with a clear statement identifying the topic
- present the supporting statements in a clear, logical, and unbiased fashion
- use appropriate qualifying words
- be carefully edited and proofread

REINFORCEMENT

Geography Have students discuss the study of geography, specifically the aspect of the discipline devoted to studying people and the land. Give students a list of different land formations, and have them choose one to explore. Then have them write a paper in which they discuss the effect caused by boundary disputes, drought, or other factors on the lives of people. Have students share finished papers and check for clear organization.

ENRICHMENT

Economics Discuss the study of economics and the economic principles which govern money and society. Give students a list of basic economic principles and have them choose one to research. When they have researched the principle and understand how it works, have them write a paper in which they demonstrate the principles as exemplified by a cause-and-effect analysis of events they select as part of prewriting. The paper should include both the short- and long-term effects. Have students trade finished papers and check for proper organization.

CHAPTER 15 WRITING ABOUT SCIENCE AND TECHNOLOGY

CHAPTER OBJECTIVES

In this chapter the student will

- prewrite to identify and select a suitable scientific or technical topic
- prewrite to determine audience and purpose
- prewrite to gather information and prepare a working outline
- write about a scientific or technical subject in an appropriately objective tone and impersonal style
- write a scientific or technical paper with a clearly defined introduction, discussion (or body), and conclusion
- write about a scientific or technical subject using the standard conventions of scientific writing
- revise, edit, proofread, and publish a scientific or technical report

SUGGESTED ANSWERS AND GUIDELINES FOR EVALUATION

PAGE 290, EXERCISE 2
Objective: Selecting a topic
Type of Writing: Prewriting notes

Length: Variable
Guidelines for Evaluation: Using the prospects of future space colonization as an example, the notes should
- help students develop this topic into a scientific or technical report
- explore ideas associated with space colonization such as how these colonies will be established and operate
- compare the advantages and risks of space colonization

PAGE 291, EXERCISE 3
Objective: Determining a purpose
Type of Writing: Prewriting notes
Length: One sentence
Guidelines for Evaluation: Students should
- try to form an idea of the kind of report they will write
- narrow their topics sufficiently
- state their purpose clearly

PAGE 291, EXERCISE 5
Objective: Identifying your audience
Type of Writing: Prewriting
Length: One or two sentences
Guidelines for Evaluation: The sentence should
- derive from the student's responses to Exercises 2 and 3
- describe the audience, indicating whether it is comprised of experts or nonexperts
- consider the audience's knowledge of and interest in the topic

PAGE 293, EXERCISE 6
Objective: Gathering information
Type of Writing: Prewriting notes
Length: Variable
Guidelines for Evaluation: Students should
- prepare a list of questions about their topic
- consult general reference works on their topic
- prepare a working outline
- locate specific reference books
- take notes on the assembled materials
- prepare a formal outline

PAGE 295, EXERCISE 7
Objective: Revising for style and tone
Type of Writing: A revised paragraph
Length: Four sentences
Guidelines for Evaluation: The revised paragraph should
- use precise language
- adopt a serious and objective tone
- avoid the first-person pronoun

PAGE 297, EXERCISE 8
1. The introduction differs from the discussion in that it presents the general problem that will be expanded in the discussion. The conclusions and recommendations section differs from the discussion section in that it makes conclusions based on the problem that was presented in detail in the discussion section and recommends the actions that should be taken in the future to solve the problem.
2. The first acknowledgement of the Shapiro source differs from the other acknowledgements of that source because it cites the year of publication.

3. The formation process of high-level wastes is attributed to Johansson's book, although no direct quotation is made from the work.
4. The purpose of Figure 1 is to aid the complex explanation of how spent nuclear fuel could be recycled in the fission process.

PAGE 304, WRITER'S CHOICE #1
Objective: Writing a scientific or technical report
Type of Writing: Scientific or technical
Length: 1,000 to 2,000 words
Guidelines for Evaluation: The report should
- derive from the student's responses to Exercises 2, 3, 5, and 6
- imply a clear purpose and audience
- follow the conventions of scientific or technical writing

PAGE 304, WRITER'S CHOICE #2
Objective: Writing a report comparing two or more similar technical products
Type of Writing: A technical report
Length: At least four pages
Guidelines for Evaluation: The report should
- be written for an audience unfamiliar with the products
- compare and contrast the products
- derive from a working outline that will guide research
- follow the conventions of scientific or technical writing

PAGE 304, WRITER'S CHOICE #3
Objective: Writing a pamphlet for fellow classmates
Type of Writing: A brief discussion of how TV signals are transmitted
Length: Two or more pages
Guidelines for Evaluation: The discussion should
- reflect clearly the prewriting process
- be on a level appropriate to subject, audience, and purpose
- reflect the extent of research through footnote citations and bibliography
- use an impersonal tone
- contain all the formal apparatus called for by the assignment

PAGE 305, WRITER'S CHOICE #4
Objective: To prepare a report about the results of one's own experiment
Type of Writing: Scientific or technical report
Length: Variable
Guidelines for Evaluation: The discussion should
- report the results of a scientific experiment performed in science class under the supervision of the student's science teacher
- follow the standard conventions of scientific or technical writing with regard to format, tone, and objectivity of language
- include visual aids, if needed

PAGE 305, WRITER'S CHOICE #5
Objective: Writing a scientific or technical report
Type of Writing: A scientific or technical report
Length: Variable
Guidelines for Evaluation: The student should
- report on any appropriate topic
- consider finding a writing idea in the Writer's Sourcebook, pages 362–365

- consider discussing the topic with a science teacher
- follow the conventions of scientific or technical writing

REINFORCEMENT

Ecology Provide students with a list of conditions that have been identified as damaging to some aspect of the environment. Have students choose a topic that is of interest to them and research the long- and short-term effects on the environment. Then have students write a paper, reminding them to be sure to maintain an objective point of view. Share completed papers and check for organization and objectivity.

ENRICHMENT

Normal vs. Abnormal Provide students with a list of health-related topics. Have them choose a topic of interest and research both the normal and abnormal functioning of, for example, white blood cells. Students would discover that when these act abnormally, the condition is called leukemia. After students have completed their research, students are to write a comparison and contrast paper discussing the normal and abnormal operations of the given biological function. Share completed papers, and check for organization and clarity.

CHAPTER 16 WRITING ABOUT LITERATURE

CHAPTER OBJECTIVES

In this chapter the student will

- prewrite to identify first responses to a short story or novel
- prewrite to explore the elements of a short story or novel
- prewrite to determine the main idea and support for a paper about a short story or novel
- write and revise a first draft of an essay about a short story or novel
- prewrite to identify first responses to a dramatic scene
- prewrite to explore the elements of a dramatic scene
- prewrite to determine the main idea and support for a paper about a dramatic scene
- write and revise a first draft of a paper about a dramatic scene
- prewrite to compare and contrast two poems
- prewrite to explore the elements that contribute to the meaning of a poem
- prewrite to determine the main idea and support for a paper about a poem
- write and revise a first draft of a paper about a poem

SUGGESTED ANSWERS AND GUIDELINES FOR EVALUATION

PAGE 309, EXERCISE 1
Objective: Prewriting for an essay about a short story or novel
Type of Writing: Prewriting notes
Length: About one page
Guidelines for Evaluation: The notes should

- derive from a careful reading and rereading of the work
- derive from either freewriting or brainstorming
- include answers to exploratory questions
- end with a statement of the writer's main idea about the short story or novel

PAGE 311, EXERCISE 2
Objective: Writing and revising a paper about a short story or novel
Type of Writing: Expository composition
Length: Three to five paragraphs
Guidelines for Evaluation: The composition should

- clearly derive from prewriting activities
- begin with an introduction that includes a thesis statement about the story's or novel's theme and the elements contributing to that theme

- include several body paragraphs, each of which discusses how one element contributes to the theme
- support the thesis statement with specific examples from the story or novel
- end with a paragraph that restates the main idea about the theme in an interesting way

PAGE 313, EXERCISE 3
Objective: Prewriting for a paper about a dramatic scene
Type of Writing: Prewriting notes
Length: About one page
Guidelines for Evaluation: The notes should
- derive from a careful reading and rereading of the scene
- derive from either freewriting or brainstorming
- include answers to exploratory questions
- end with a statement of the writer's main idea about the scene

PAGE 315, EXERCISE 4
Objective: Writing and revising a paper about a dramatic scene
Type of Writing: Expository composition
Length: Three to five paragraphs
Guidelines for Evaluation: The composition should
- clearly derive from prewriting
- begin with an introduction that includes the writer's thesis statement about how the scene fits into the play
- summarize the action and discuss the characters, quoting their significant statements
- end with a paragraph that restates the main idea in an interesting way

PAGE 318, EXERCISE 5
Objective: Prewriting for a paper about two poems
Type of Writing: Prewriting notes
Length: About one page
Guidelines for Evaluation: The notes should
- derive from a careful reading and rereading of the two poems chosen
- derive from brainstorming about the similarities and differences between the two poems
- include answers to exploratory questions
- end with a statement of the student's main idea about a major similarity or difference between the poems

PAGE 320, EXERCISE 6
Objective: Writing and revising a paper about two poems
Type of Writing: Expository composition
Length: Three to five paragraphs
Guidelines for Evaluation: The composition should
- clearly derive from prewriting activities
- begin with an introduction that includes a thesis statement expressing the major similarities or differences between the poems
- include several body paragraphs that discuss each point raised, either by separately or alternately citing specific examples from the poems
- end with a paragraph that restates the student's main idea in an interesting way

PAGE 321, WRITER'S CHOICE #1
Objective: Writing a review of a play
Type of Writing: Expository composition
Length: Variable

Guidelines for Evaluation: The composition should
- clearly imply a purpose and an audience
- concentrate upon a scene that reflects the major theme(s), action, characters, and conflict
- include body paragraphs that explain the writer's interpretation, relating it to modern life and presenting a favorable impression of the play
- conclude with a paragraph that ends with a clincher sentence

PAGE 321, WRITER'S CHOICE #2
Objective: Writing about a short story or novel
Type of Writing: A letter
Length: Variable
Guidelines for Evaluation: The letter should
- clearly imply a purpose and an audience
- identify the work, offer an interpretation of it, and explain why it should be studied

PAGE 321, WRITER'S CHOICE #3
Objective: Comparing two stories, scenes, or poems
Type of Writing: An expository composition
Length: Variable
Guidelines for Evaluation: The composition should
- have as its subject two literary works with something important in common
- identify the two works and the points on which they will be compared
- present a point-by-point comparison of the two works

REINFORCEMENT

Short Story News Assign the students a short story to read and discuss. Tell them that you want them to turn the story into a news story for the local paper. They are to use a brief and concise journalistic style of writing. Discuss journalistic style, and read some examples, if the students need this type of background before beginning their papers.

ENRICHMENT

Persuasion Assign the students a short story to read in which the theme clearly reflects the author's philosophy or opinion. Discuss the theme from this angle, and tell the students that you want them to take the opposing viewpoint. Have them write a persuasive essay disagreeing with the author. Remind them to use examples from the story to rebut its own theme. You may want to review persuasive writing and refer the students to Chapter 11 for prewriting activities. Have students share their finished papers to check for clarity of organization.

CHAPTER 17 CREATIVE WRITING

CHAPTER OBJECTIVES

In this chapter the student will

- prewrite to determine purpose and audience
- prewrite to generate and explore ideas for a short story
- prewrite to develop a short story outline
- write the first draft of a short story
- revise, edit, proofread, and publish a short story
- prewrite to generate and explore ideas for a scene
- prewrite to develop a scene outline
- write the first draft of a scene
- revise, edit, proofread, and publish a scene
- prewrite to generate and explore ideas for a poem by charting
- writing the first draft of a poem
- revise, edit, proofread, and publish a poem

SUGGESTED ANSWERS AND GUIDELINES FOR EVALUATION

PAGE 323, EXERCISE 1
Objective: Exploring a purpose and audience
Type of Writing: Prewriting
Length: About a page
Guidelines for Evaluation: The writer should
- identify a subject for a story
- brainstorm for ten minutes about the aspects of the story that might interest three different audiences: second graders, teenagers, and adults
- generate ideas for each of the three audiences
- write a specific story for each set of ideas

PAGE 324, EXERCISE 2
Objective: Generating ideas for a story
Type of Writing: Prewriting chart
Lenth: At least four story ideas
Guidelines for Evaluation: The chart should
- list several situations, characters, and settings that can be developed into stories
- include a variety of story ideas
- at the student's option, draw upon the Writer's Sourcebook for ideas

PAGE 326, EXERCISE 3
Objective: Exploring and outlining a story idea
Type of Writing: Prewriting notes
Length: About two pages
Guidelines for Evaluation: The notes should
- explore one idea of the list generated in Exercise 2
- answer questions like those shown in the student text
- include an outline listing in chronological order the main events of the plot

PAGE 329, EXERCISE 4
Objective: Writing, revising, and publishing a story
Type of Writing: An original short story
Length: Variable
Guidelines for Evaluation: The story should
- clearly derive from prewriting notes generated in Exercises 2 and 3
- maintain a consistent point of view
- introduce one or several characters and place them in a setting
- relate a series of events involving a conflict or problem of some kind
- lead up to a climax and end by presenting the resolution

PAGE 330, EXERCISE 5
Objective: Generating ideas for a scene
Type of Writing: Prewriting chart
Length: At least four different scene ideas
Guidelines for Evaluation: The chart should
- list two contrasting characters for each scene idea
- clearly indicate the conflict

PAGE 332, EXERCISE 6
Objective: Exploring and outlining a scene idea
Type of Writing: Prewriting notes
Length: About two pages
Guidelines for Evaluation: The notes should

- explore one idea on the list generated in Exercise 5
- answer questions like those shown in the student text
- include an outline listing in chronological order the principal action of the scene

PAGE 335, EXERCISE 7
Objective: Writing, revising, and publishing a scene
Type of Writing: An original dramatic scene
Length: Variable
Guidelines for Evaluation: The scene should
- clearly derive from the prewriting notes generated in Exercises 5 and 6
- follow the format for a scene shown in the text
- list and describe the characters
- describe the setting in stage directions
- use dialogue and action to present a conflict between the characters
- lead up to a climax and end by presenting the resolution

PAGE 337, EXERCISE 8
Objective: Charting to generate ideas for a poem
Type of Writing: A prewriting chart
Length: At least six entries
Guidelines for Evaluation: The chart should
- list in the left-hand column the general categories shown in the chart in the text
- list in the right-hand column specific subjects for a poem based on these categories

PAGE 338, EXERCISE 9
Objective: Exploring an idea for a poem
Type of Writing: Prewriting notes
Length: About one page
Guidelines for Evaluation: The notes should
- indicate the students' choice of one idea for a poem
- answer questions like those in the student text

PAGE 339, EXERCISE 10
Objective: Writing, revising, and publishing a poem
Type of Writing: An original poem
Length: Variable
Guidelines for Evaluation: The poem should
- clearly derive from prewriting notes
- include sensory images and possibly figurative language and various sound effects

PAGE 340, WRITER'S CHOICE #1
Objective: Writing a story or a dramatic scene
Type of Writing: Original story or scene
Length: Variable
Guidelines for Evaluation: The story or scene should
- recreate and fictionalize a historical event
- clearly identify and present an actual event that the writer can alter as he or she chooses
- present several characters within a particular setting
- include a plot that pivots on a conflict of some kind
- bring the conflict to a climax and then resolve it
- follow the appropriate format for a story or scene

PAGE 340, WRITER'S CHOICE #2
Objective: Writing a poem
Type of Writing: An original poem

Length: Two to four stanzas
Guidelines for Evaluation: The poem should
- reveal unusual qualities in a very common object
- express an emotion of some kind
- derive from brainstorming about an interesting object
- include sensory images, figures of speech, and sound effects

PAGE 340, WRITER'S CHOICE #3
Objective: Writing a story, scene, or poem
Type of Writing: Any original piece of writing
Length: Variable
Guidelines for Evaluation: Students should
- follow the appropriate format for a story, scene, or poem
- prepare to write by prewriting
- consider basing their creative writing on material in the Writer's Sourcebook

PAGE 342, WRITERS ON WRITING, YOUR TURN
Objective: Writing a poem with a persona
Type of Writing: An unrhymed poem
Length: Variable
Guidelines for Evaluation: Students should
- write a poem about a well-known historical event
- using as a speaker a minor participant in that event
- relate the event from the point of view of that minor participant
- include the speaker's reaction to the event

PAGE 343, WRITERS ON WRITING, YOUR TURN
Objective: Writing a story
Type of Writing: A short story
Length: Variable
Guidelines for Evaluation: Students should
- plan and write a short story based on one concrete item, natural or artificial; for example, rock, a painting, a sneaker, a chewed-down pencil
- use the item as a springboard for a series of events involving a conflict of some kind
- build to a climax and resolve the conflict
- include a character or several characters involved in some way with the item
- create an appropriate setting for the item

REINFORCEMENT

Scripts for Commercials Tell students that for one week you want them to observe and analyze television commercials that contain scenes with some type of narrative action. Design a chart for students to use to record information about the commercials. The chart should include items such as dialogue, sets and props, movement of the actors, and the tone or mood of the scene. At the end of the week, have students bring their charts to class and discuss the content, form, and effectiveness of the commercials. Then have students choose a product and write a script for a television commercial. The scripts should include the same elements students identified while analyzing commercials. Share the scripts in class.

ENRICHMENT

Poetry Have students read several short poems and then discuss the poems in class. Analyze the poets' word choice, rhythm, types of images, figurative language, and so forth. Students should then select a topic for a poem and use language and images in ways similar to those of the poems discussed in class. Have students read aloud and discuss the poems they have written.

TEACHING PART TWO: GRAMMAR, USAGE, AND MECHANICS

You may want to begin with Part Two before going on to the writing program presented in Part One of this textbook, depending on your students' needs. We are aware that some high school students can distinguish betwen a subordinate conjunction and coordinate conjunction, while others cannot make this distinction and may in fact be virtually oblivious to all parts of speech. Therefore, *Macmillan English* presents grammar, usage, and mechanics with the understanding that you may want to use the text either as a review or as an introduction to these matters.

We would encourage you to dip into Part Two flexibly, as you identify particular sentence-level problems in your students' writing. For example, you may not need to teach all the parts of speech but may need to devote some time to verbs. You may also want to teach the parts of a sentence in Part Two in conjunction with the material on writing and combining sentences in Part One.

Throughout Part Two, interesting, creative exercises help students remember that they are studying grammar, usage, and mechanics not as ends in themselves but as means of improving their writing.

PART TWO: OBJECTIVES, ANSWERS, REINFORCEMENT AND ENRICHMENT

Part Two; Grammar, Usage, and Mechanics is made up of three units, each of which contains two or more chapters. Here on a chapter-by-chapter basis you will find

- Chapter Objectives
- Answers and Guidelines for Evaluation that did not fit in the space allotted for teacher's annotations in the book proper
- Reinforcement and Enrichment activities: the former designed for students who need additional help in understanding the basic concepts of the chapter, the latter designed for students who are ready to go beyond the textbook into more advanced territory.

CHAPTER 18 PARTS OF SPEECH

CHAPTER OBJECTIVES

In this chapter the student will

- identify nouns
- identify noun phrases
- write and revise with special attention to nouns
- identify pronouns and use pronouns in sentences
- write and revise with special attention to pronouns
- identify verbs and distinguish between action verbs and linking verbs
- identify verb phrases and auxiliary verbs
- write and revise with special attention to verbs
- identify adjectives—degrees of comparison, articles, and proper adjectives
- write and revise with special attention to adjectives
- identify adverbs and recognize degrees of comparison
- write and revise with special attention to adverbs
- identify prepositions and use prepositions in sentences
- write and revise with special attention to prepositions
- identify conjunctions and use conjunctions in sentences
- write and revise with special attention to conjunctions
- identify and supply interjections
- identify and distinguish between words that may be used as more than one part of speech

SUGGESTED ANSWERS AND GUIDELINES FOR EVALUATION

PAGE 381, EXERCISE 7

1. the twentieth century; American drama; little impact on American literature as a whole
2. the reasons for the lack of American drama
3. theaters such as the elitist European institutions of the eighteenth century; our infant democracy
4. the melodrama that became so popular in Victorian times; serious American writers
5. the early twentieth century; American playwrights; tragedies and psychological dramas that revolutionized American theater

PAGE 382, REVISION: NOUNS

Objective: Revising to improve the nouns in a passage
Type of Writing: A descriptive paragraph
Length: Four sentences
Guidelines for Evaluatin: The student should

- rewrite the passagge
- retain the basic ideas and as much of the original as he or she wants
- balance concrete nouns with abstract nouns
- make the sound an echo of the sense
- imaginatively generate new details to create vivid noun phrases from single nouns

PAGE 397, REVISION: VERBS

Objective: Revising to improve the verbs in a passage
Type of Writing: A descriptive paragraph
Length: Nine sentences
Guidelines for Evaluation: The student should

- rewrite the passage
- retain the basic ideas and as much of the original as he or she wishes
- substitute livelier, more precise verbs for the terms italicized in the original
- substitute single action verbs for wordy constructions
- replace linking verbs with action verbs wherever possible
- avoid *there is* or *there are* constructions
- imaginatively generate new action verbs to be added to the passage

PAGE 416, REVISION: CONJUNCTIONS

Objective: Revising to improve the conjunctions in a passage
Type of Writing: A narrative paragraph
Length: Five or six sentences
Guidelines for Evaluation: The student should

- rewrite the passage
- retain the basic ideas and as much of the original as he or she wants
- replace coordinating conjunctions with more precise correlative conjunctions, conjunctive adverbs, and subordinating conjunctions

REINFORCEMENT

Parts of Speech Have students write a short paragraph of five to seven sentences or use a short corrected and revised paragraph they have written recently. Have them trade papers with other students and analyze the sentences in the paragraphs. They should identify the part of speech of each word in the sentences and be ready to explain the sentences to the class.

ENRICHMENT

Parts of Speech Give the students three or four interesting topics and have them write five good sentences about each. Tell them you want fully developed sentences that use as many of the different parts of speech as possible without making the sentences awkward.

When they have finished, have them share their sentences and explain each part of speech they used. It helps to see the sentence as it is discussed, so have them use the chalkboard or an overhead projector.

CHAPTER 19 PARTS OF THE SENTENCE

CHAPTER OBJECTIVES

In this chapter the student will

- identify simple subjects and simple predicates
- identify compound subjects and compound predicates
- write sentences with simple and compound subjects and predicates
- recognize normal and inverted order of subjects and predicates
- identify complements and write sentences with complements
- identify and write basic sentence patterns
- diagram basic sentence patterns

ANSWERS

PAGE 438, EXERCISE 13

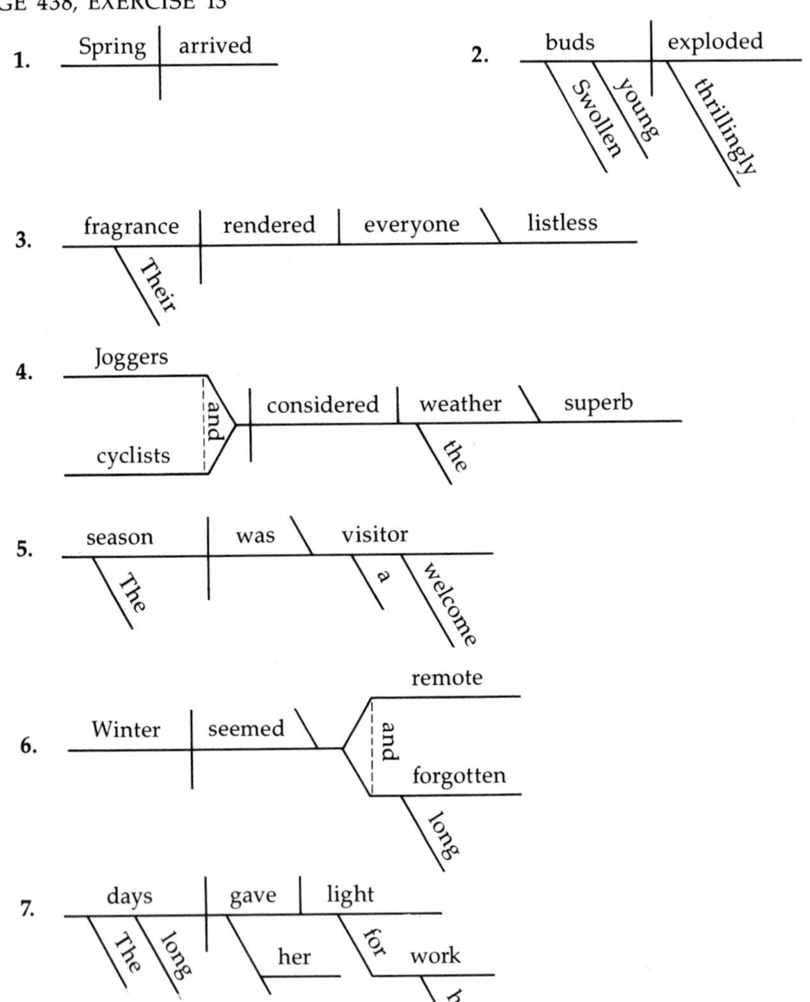

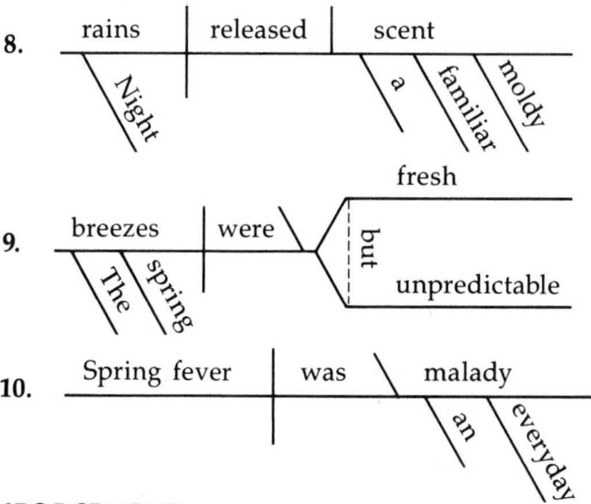

REINFORCEMENT

Sentence Puzzle Create a crossword puzzle that will reinforce the information in the chapter. The "across" and "down" clues should be sentences with words underlined; the names for the parts of the sentence will be the answers.

ENRICHMENT

News Rewrites Many of the "fast-breaking" news reports in newspapers are composed in haste and written to fit limited space. As a result the sentences tend to be short and choppy, and the same sentence patterns are repeated frequently. These reports provide good sources for sentences on which to practice the skills of sentence combining. Bring several articles from the newspaper to class, and have students rewrite them, combining and extending sentences where possible. Share the finished rewrites in class in order to show that thoughts can be expressed in several ways through a variety of sentence patterns.

CHAPTER 20 PHRASES

CHAPTER OBJECTIVES

In this chapter the student will

- identify and write prepositional phrases used as adjectives and as adverbs
- identify and write appositives and appositive phrases
- identify and write participles and participial phrases
- identify and write gerunds and gerund phrases
- identify and write infinitives and infinitive phrases
- recognize subjects of infinitives
- identify absolute phrases
- diagram all types of phrases

ANSWERS

PAGE 442, EXERCISE 2

1. alive—adverbial
2. seem—adverbial
3. result—adverbial
4. rectangular, square—adverbial
5. plow—adverbial; contours—adjectival
6. patterns—adjectival; variety—adjectival; result—adverbial
7. pivots—adverbial
8. disks—adjectival
9. No one—adjectival
10. bonus—adjectival; collaboration—adjectival

PAGE 453, EXERCISE 11

1. (Ex. 1, sentence 2)

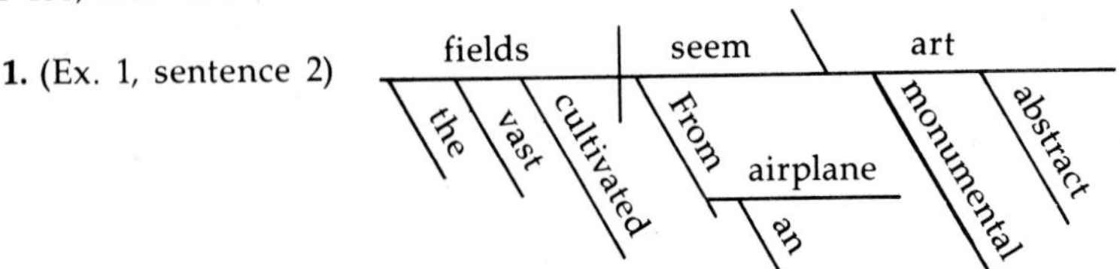

2. (Ex. 1, sentence 4)

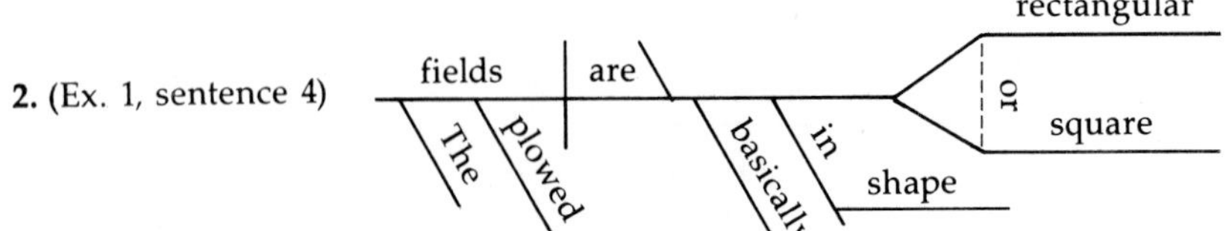

3. (Ex. 1, sentence 6)

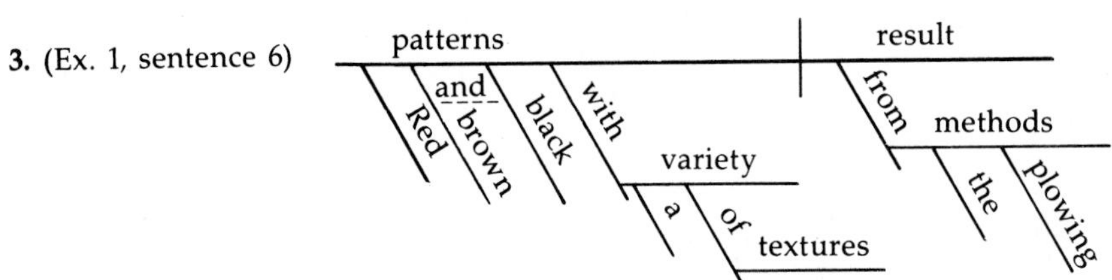

4. (Ex. 1, sentence 7)

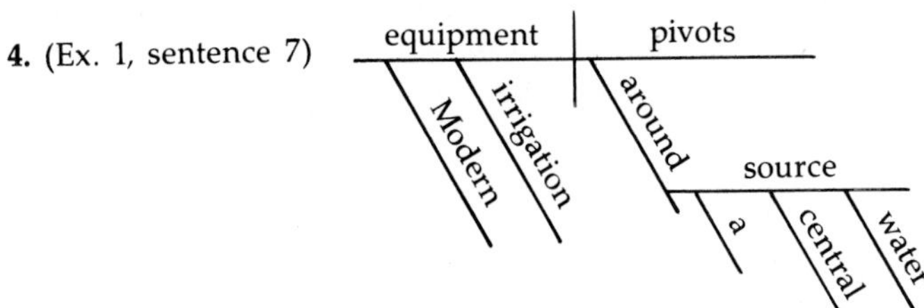

PAGE 453, EXERCISE 12

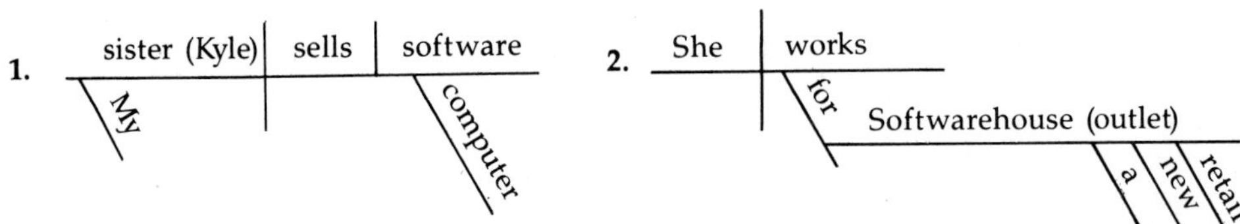

PAGE 453, EXERCISE 13

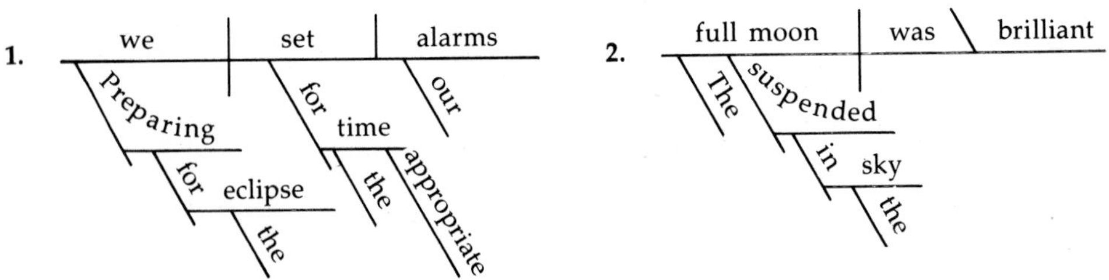

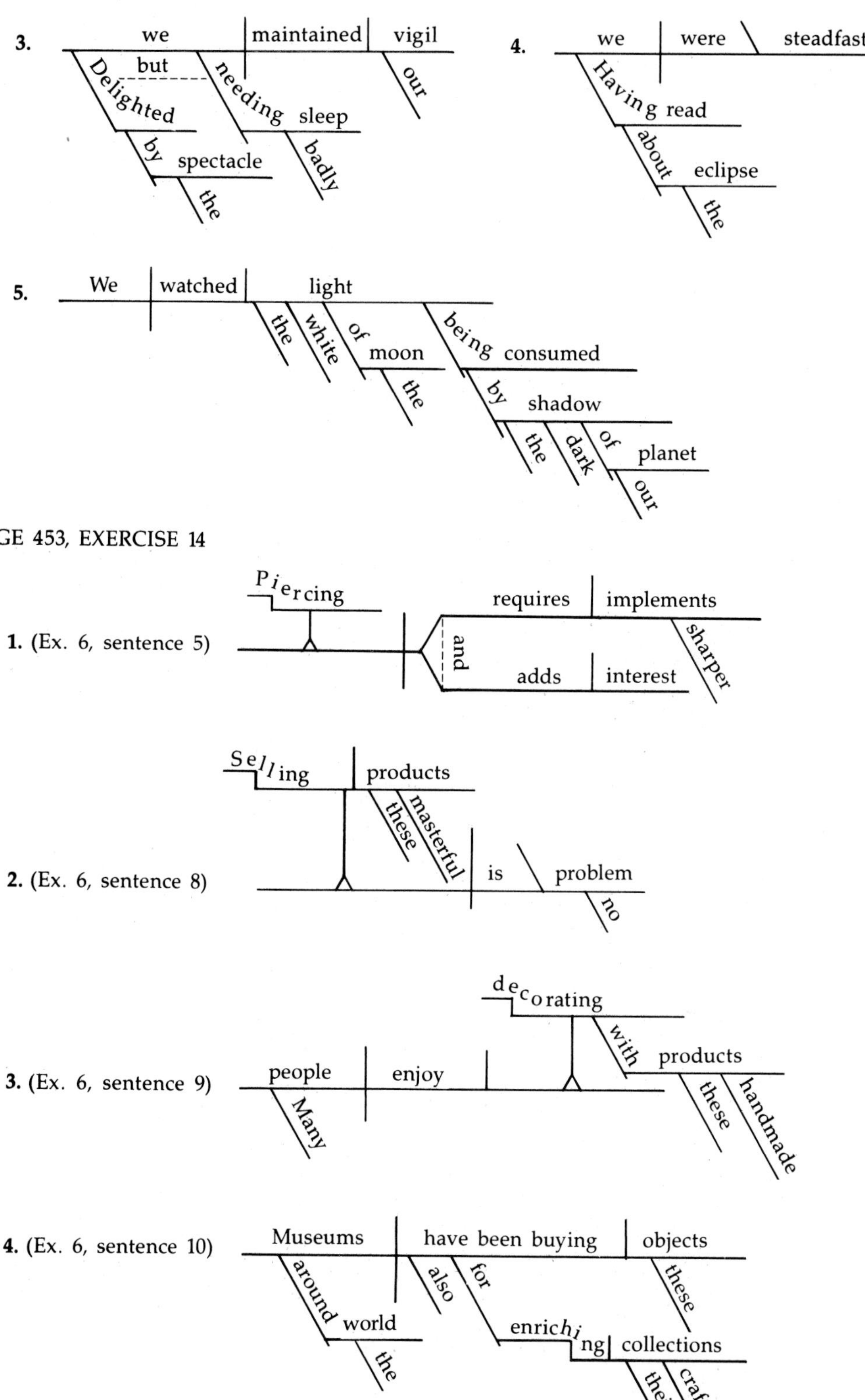
3.
we
maintained
vigil
our
but
Delighted
by
spectacle
the
needing
sleep
badly
4.
we
were
steadfast
Having read
about
eclipse
the
5.
We
watched
light
the
white
of
moon
the
being consumed
by
shadow
the
dark
of
planet
our
PAGE 453, EXERCISE 14
1. (Ex. 6, sentence 5)
Piercing
requires
implements
sharper
and
adds
interest
2. (Ex. 6, sentence 8)
Selling
products
these
masterful
is
problem
no
3. (Ex. 6, sentence 9)
people
Many
enjoy
decorating
with
products
these
handmade
4. (Ex. 6, sentence 10)
Museums
around
world
the
have been buying
also
for
enriching
collections
their
craft
objects
these

PAGE 453, EXERCISE 15

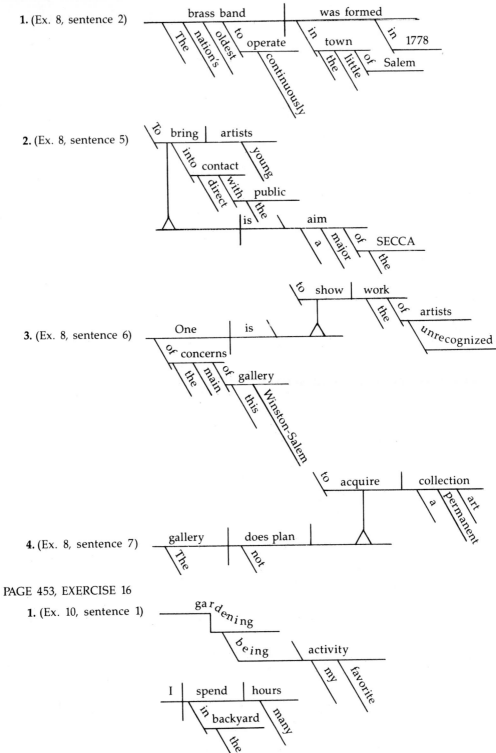

1. (Ex. 8, sentence 2)

brass band | was formed
The
nation's
oldest
to operate
continuously
in town
the
little
of Salem
in 1778

2. (Ex. 8, sentence 5)

To bring | artists
young
into contact
direct
with public
the
is
aim
a
major
of SECCA
the

3. (Ex. 8, sentence 6)

to show | work
the
of artists
unrecognized
One | is
of concerns
the
main
of gallery
this
Winston-Salem

4. (Ex. 8, sentence 7)

to acquire | collection
a
permanent
art
gallery | does plan
The
not

PAGE 453, EXERCISE 16

1. (Ex. 10, sentence 1)

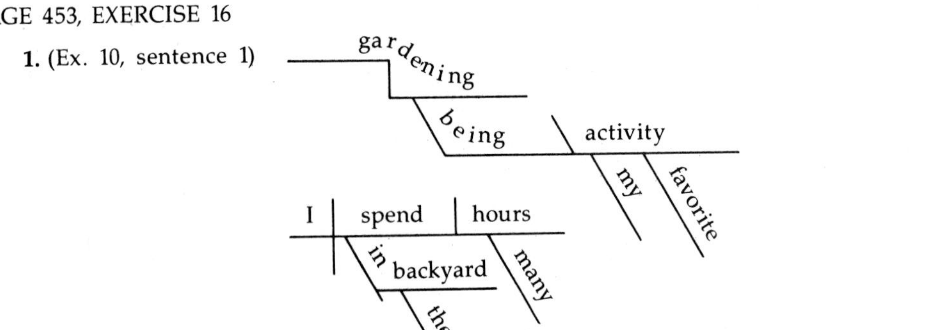

2. (Ex. 10, sentence 3)

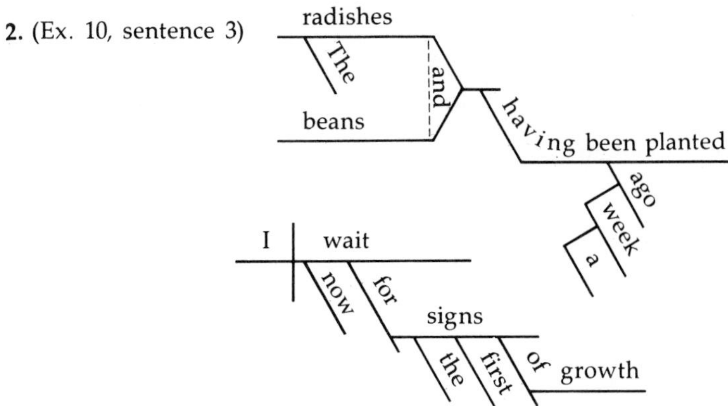

REINFORCEMENT

Creative Phrases Tell the students that they are to write sentences that include specific types of phrases. They may place the phrases in any order they choose to create interesting sentences. For example, have students write a sentence containing two prepositional and one participial phrase or a sentence with one prepositional, one appositive, and one gerund phrase. Have students share their sentences and discuss the different ways they used the phrases to build their sentences.

ENRICHMENT

Phrases in Poetry Bring some examples of poetry to class, and have the students read the poems. Then, tell them to identify and label all of the phrases used in the poems. Have students read their answers aloud; correct any missed or mislabeled phrases.

CHAPTER 21 CLAUSES AND SENTENCE STRUCTURE

CHAPTER OBJECTIVES

In this chapter the student will

- identify main and subordinate clauses
- identify and write simple sentences and compound sentences
- identify and write complex and compound-complex sentences
- identify and write essential and nonessential adjective clauses
- identify and write adverb clauses
- identify and write noun clauses
- identify and write the four types of sentence structures—declarative, imperative, interrogative, and exclamatory
- identify and correct sentence fragments and run-on sentences
- diagram compound sentences, and sentences with adjective clauses, adverb clauses, and noun clauses

SUGGESTED ANSWERS AND GUIDELINES FOR EVALUATION

PAGE 468, REVISION: SENTENCE FRAGMENTS

Revisions may vary in the methods used to turn the fragments into complete sentences. Because students have been asked to combine sentences, the revised paragraphs should be shorter than the one in the student text.

PAGE 469, REVIEW: SENTENCE COMPLETENESS

Revisions may vary in the methods used to correct the fragments and run-ons. Acceptable revisions may contain fewer or more sentences than in the original paragraph because some of the original fragments and run-ons can be corrected by being combined or broken up in a variety of ways.

PAGE 472, EXERCISE 11

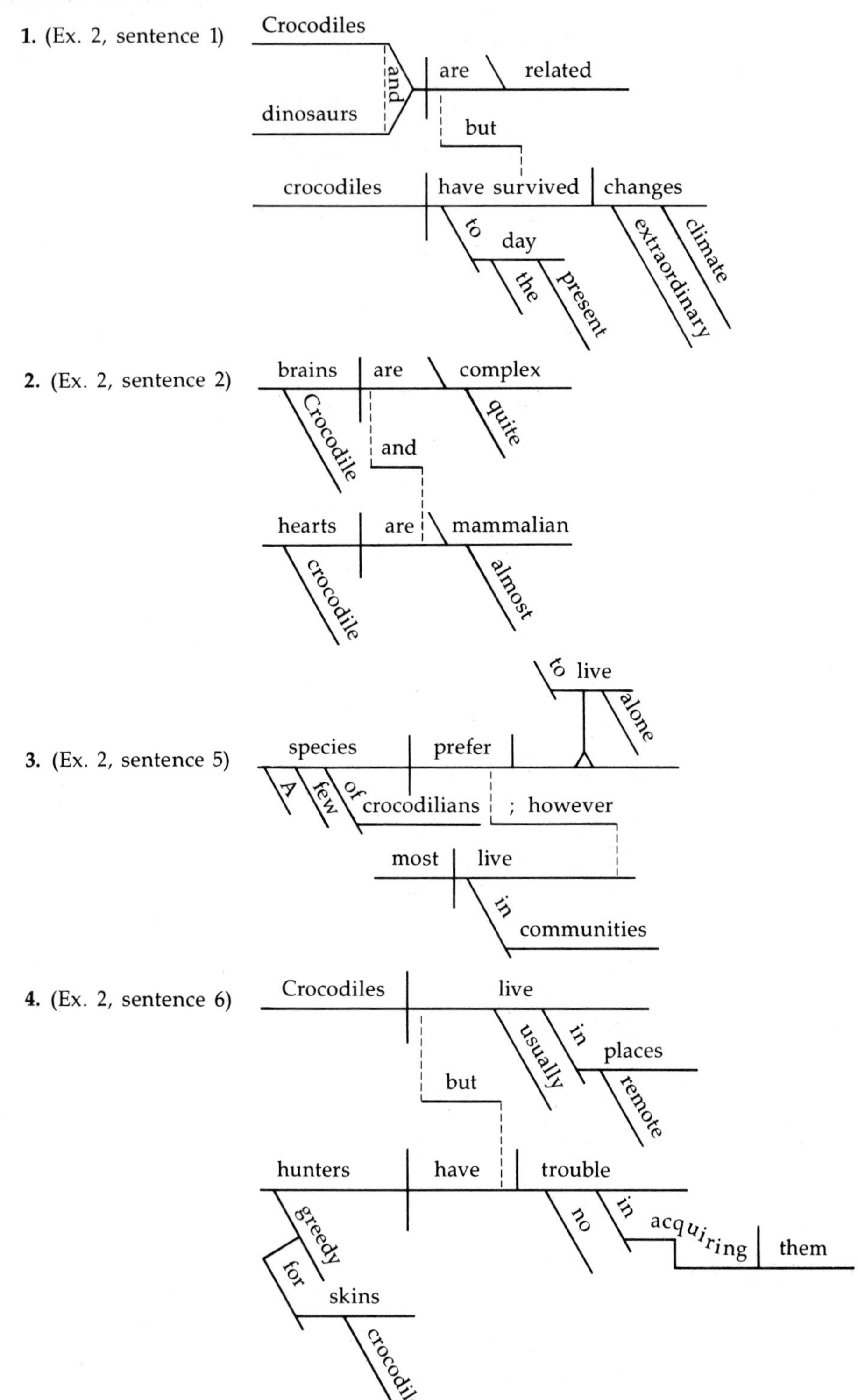

PAGE 472, EXERCISE 12

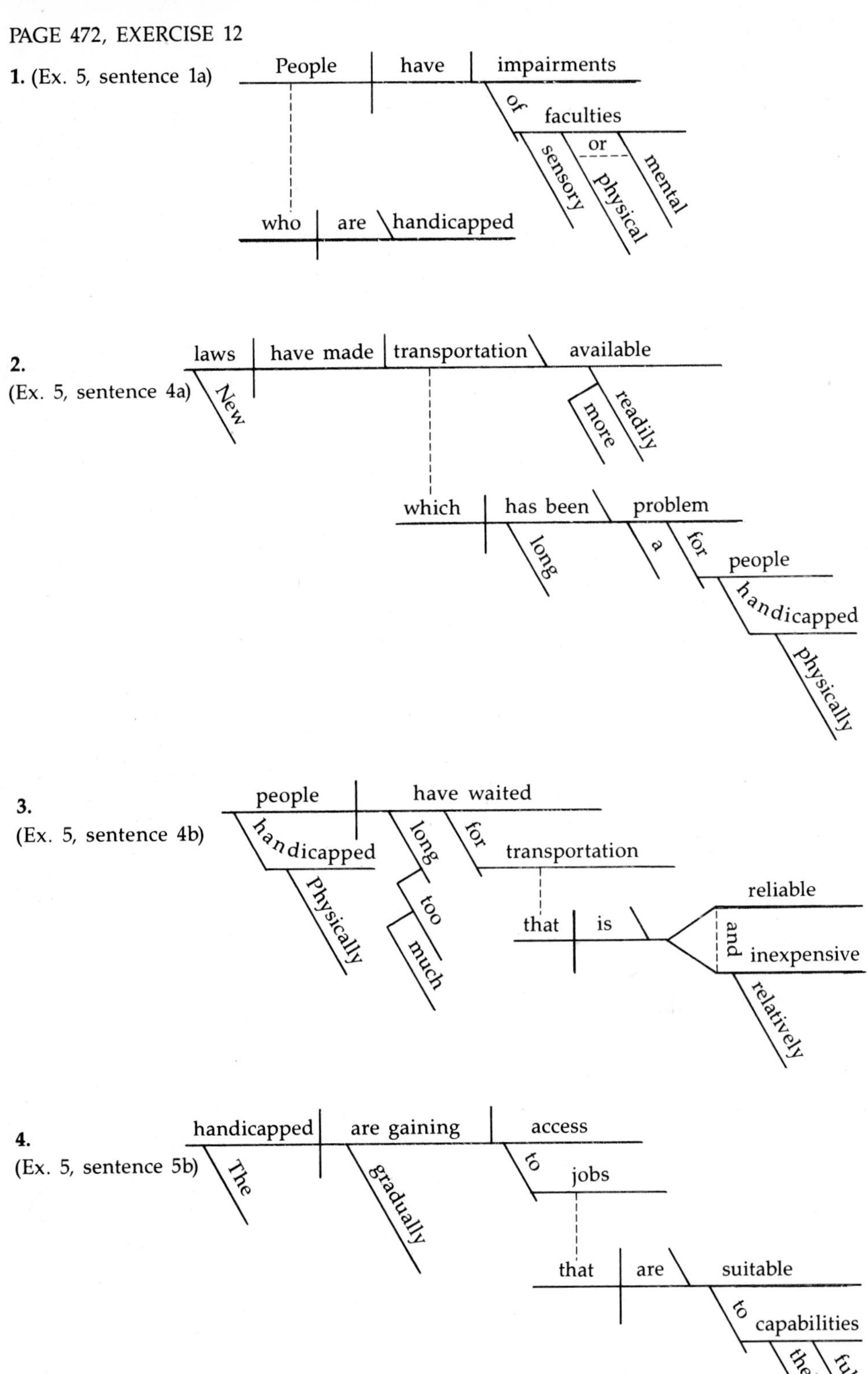

PAGE 472, EXERCISE 13

1. (Ex. 6, sentence 1)

2. (Ex. 6, sentence 4)

3. (Ex. 6, sentence 5)

4. (Ex. 6, sentence 10)

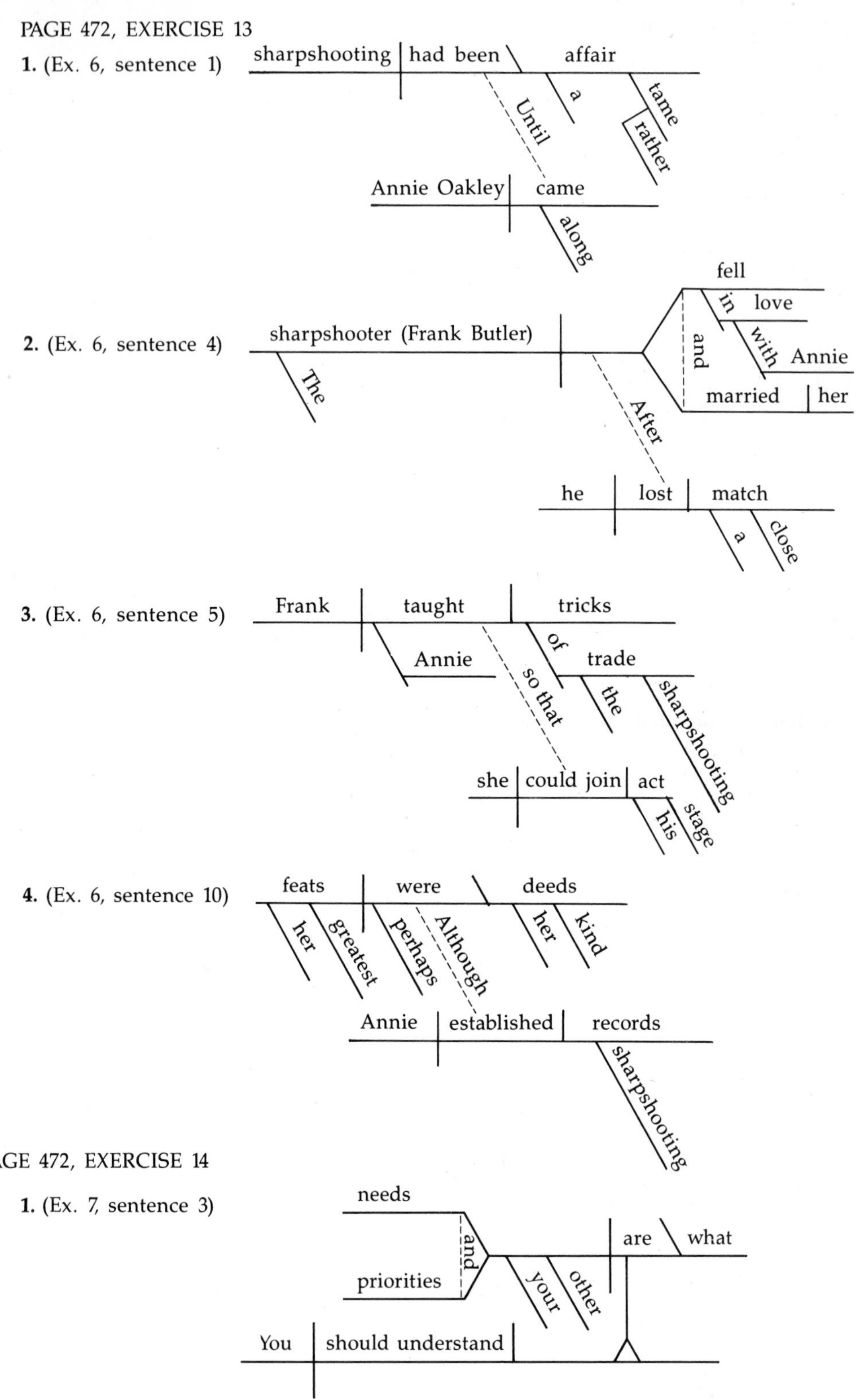

PAGE 472, EXERCISE 14

1. (Ex. 7, sentence 3)

2. (Ex. 7, sentence 8)

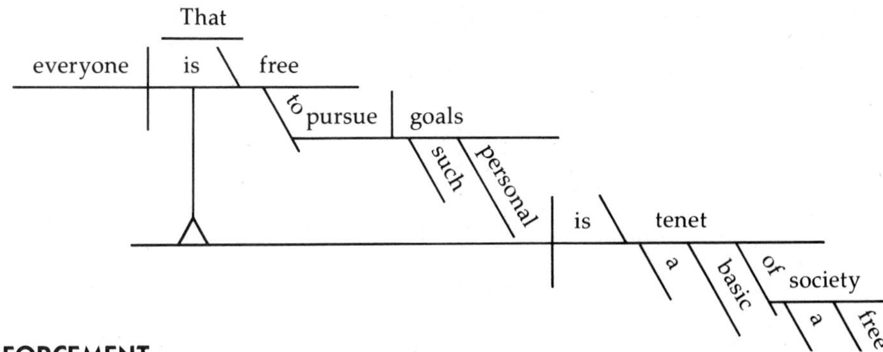

REINFORCEMENT

Sentence Combining Use sentence combining techniques to encourage students to write sentences with more sophisticated structures. Give students a set of short sentences and have them combine them into one sentence; for example, these two sentences—*We left the house early.* and *We wanted to be on time.*—could be combined as *We left the house early because we wanted to be on time.* Now may be a useful time to begin or review Chapter 6, Writing and Combining Sentences

ENRICHMENT

Sentence Rewrites Look ahead to the literature that the students will be reading as they study this chapter. Select passages that contain examples of complex and compound-complex sentences. Rewrite these passages in simple, short sentences. After students have read the selection, give them the rewritten passages and have them discuss what makes the rewritten passages different from the original passages they have just read. The students should notice that the rewritten passages are choppy, boring, and more difficult to read because they do not flow smoothly. Have students revise the passages by using the sentence structures learned in the chapter.

CHAPTER 22 VERB TENSES, VOICE, AND MOOD

CHAPTER OBJECTIVES

In this chapter the student will

- identify and supply the principal parts of regular and irregular verbs—basic form, present participle, simple past, and past participle
- identify and write the six tenses of verbs—present, past, future, present perfect, past perfect, and future perfect
- identify and write the progressive and emphatic forms of verbs
- identify and correct incompatible tense forms in sentences
- identify and write sentences in the active and the passive voice
- identify mood and correct errors in the use of the subjunctive mood

SUGGESTED ANSWERS AND GUIDELINES FOR EVALUATION

PAGE 486, APPLICATION EXERCISE

Objective: Expressing past time in a paragraph

Type of Writing: Narrative paragraph

Length: At least five sentences

Guidelines for Evaluation: The student should

- write a short autobiographical narrative
- correctly use verb tenses to express past time, including the perfect tenses as well as the simple past tense
- identify the tenses of the verbs used in the paragraph

REINFORCEMENT

Compatible Tenses Choose several short passages from the literature book, and when you retype them, mix up the tenses of the verbs. Have students read the passages and discuss the confusion caused by the incompatible tenses. Give students the tense or tenses that the author originally used, and have students rewrite the passages making the tenses compatible. Share the finished passages in class, and discuss any problems students experienced as they rewrote.

ENRICHMENT

Vivid Verbs Give the students a group of short, simple sentences that list a series of actions in sequence; for example, *The dog jumped the fence. The dog ran away. The children chased the dog. The dog hid in the alley behind the store. The children looked up and down the street for the dog. They looked in the alley. They saw the dog. They caught the dog. They took the dog home. The dog ate supper and went to sleep.* First have students brainstorm all of the vivid verbs they could use to describe the action in each of the sentences. List the verbs they suggest on the chalkboard. Then have students write the paragraph by making the verbs more vivid and by varying sentence length and structure.

CHAPTER 23 SUBJECT-VERB AGREEMENT

CHAPTER OBJECTIVES

In this chapter the student will

- identify correct subject-verb agreement
- make subjects and verbs agree when prepositional phrases intervene
- make subjects and linking verbs agree
- make subjects and verbs in inverted sentences agree
- make verbs agree with special subjects
- make verbs agree with compound subjects
- make verbs agree with indefinite pronoun subjects
- make subjects and verbs in adjective clauses agree

REINFORCEMENT

Subject-Verb Agreement Select three or four newspaper or magazine articles and rewrite them so that the subjects and verbs do not agree. In order to represent all of the points in the chapter, you may need to rewrite some of the sentences completely. Give the articles to the students to read, and discuss the problems caused by nonagreement of the subjects and the verbs. Have them rewrite the articles, correcting the agreement problems. Have them share their sentences with the class and discuss any problems.

ENRICHMENT

Directed Sentences Have the students write sentences that incorporate the specific directions you give for each. For example, tell them to write a sentence that begins with *there* or one with a relative pronoun as the subject or one with a collective noun as the subject. Be sure to include at least two examples of each point in the chapter, even though the second example may be in a clause in the same sentence. Have students share their sentences and correct any mistakes they may have made.

CHAPTER 24 USING PRONOUNS CORRECTLY

CHAPTER OBJECTIVES

In this chapter the student will

- identify and write the correct case forms of pronouns—nominative, objective, and possessive
- identify and write the correct pronoun in appositive phrases

- identify and write the correct pronoun in elliptical adverb clauses
- choose the correct pronoun form—*who* or *whom* and *whoever* or *whomever*—in sentences
- make pronouns and antecedents agree in number, gender, and person
- make pronouns agree with collective noun antecedents
- make pronouns agree with indefinite pronoun antecedents
- make pronoun reference clear

SUGGESTED ANSWERS AND GUIDELINES FOR EVALUATION

PAGE 510, EXERCISE 9

Revisions may vary somewhat. The student's new version should make the pronoun references as clear as they are in these suggested answers:

1. William Blake's apprenticeship to an engraver was useful when Blake decided to publish his poems together with his own illustrations.
2. Blake told his father that he, the son, had little interest in being a tradesman.
3. Blake's first major poems, which were pivotally important, appeared during the early years of the French Revolution.
4. A key Romantic idea in Blake's poetry is his comparison of the effects of the Industrial Revolution to an individual's loss of innocence.

REINFORCEMENT

Nouns to Pronouns Select a passage and rewrite it so that there are no pronouns. (Make sure that all of the pronouns studied in the chapter are represented in the paragraph at least twice, even if it means restructuring some of the sentences.) Have students read the paragraph and discuss how awkward it is to read. Then have them rewrite the passage by substituting pronouns where possible. Warn them not to forget that each pronoun must have a clear antecedent. Share the finished paragraphs in class, and discuss any problems or errors made in the rewriting.

ENRICHMENT

Name the Pronoun Have students write sentences with specified types of pronouns. For example, have students write a sentence with one pronoun in the nominative case, two in the objective case, and one in an adverb clause. Then have students write a short paragraph with two pronouns in the nominative case, four in the objective case, one in the possessive case, two in elliptical adverb clauses, and three uses of *who* or *whom.* Remind them to be sure all pronouns agree with their antecedents and that the pronoun reference is clear.

CHAPTER 25 USING MODIFIERS CORRECTLY

CHAPTER OBJECTIVES

In this chapter the student will

- identify and write the three degrees of comparison of modifiers
- identify and correct double comparisons
- identify and correct incomplete comparisons
- choose the correct modifier—*good* or *well, bad* or *badly*—in sentences
- identify and correct double negatives
- identify and correct misplaced and dangling modifiers

SUGGESTED ANSWERS AND GUIDELINES FOR EVALUATION

PAGE 519, EXERCISE 7

1. Created in California during the Gold Rush, blue jeans are now worn by people all over the world.
2. Gold prospectors liked to wear jeans because they were guaranteed not to rip.
3. Designed originally for rough conditions, denim pants were at first worn only by prospectors and laborers.

4. Jeans first gained popularity in the West, where cowboys wore them for work and for dress wear.
5. No longer associated with bucking broncos, jeans are now considered to be high fashion by men and women alike.

REINFORCEMENT

Misplaced Modifiers Give the students a set of sentences that contain misplaced and dangling modifiers. Show them some additional examples that can be corrected in more than one way, with the meaning altered depending on how the sentence is rewritten. Then have students rewrite the sentences in the original set. Then have them trade papers and discuss the results of their revisions, especially noting the sentences where it was not clear what the writer wanted to say, depending on how the sentence was rewritten.

ENRICHMENT

Using Adjectives and Adverbs Give the students a list of adjectives and adverbs, including several comparative and superlative forms. Have the students write sentences using each word on the list. Discuss the finished sentences in class, and correct any of the sentences that seem to give the students problems. To make the exercise more interesting, give them a topic to which the sentences can relate.

CHAPTER 26 GLOSSARY OF SPECIFIC USAGE ITEMS

CHAPTER OBJECTIVES

In this chapter the student will make correct choices to solve a variety of specific usage problems, including the following:

- correct use of verb forms, modifiers, and other parts of speech
- formal and informal language situations
- standard and nonstandard expressions
- words frequently misused
- words frequently confused

REINFORCEMENT

Words Frequently Misused Have students review the paragraphs and compositions they have written this semester to compile a personal list of the frequently misused words from the chapter that appear in their own writing. Have students place this list in their writing folders and consult their lists each time they revise a piece of writing. Encourage students to update their lists by deleting words they use correctly in more than two pieces of writing and adding new words that cause them difficulties.

ENRICHMENT

Malapropisms Have students research the meaning and derivation of the term *malapropism.* Then have students use the words and expressions taught in this chapter to help them write a brief humorous essay that contains several malapropisms.

CHAPTER 27 CAPITALIZATION

CHAPTER OBJECTIVES

In this chapter the student will use capitalization correctly when writing

- the pronoun *I*
- sentence beginnings
- sentences in parentheses
- quotations
- proper nouns
- proper adjectives

REINFORCEMENT

Capitalization Find an interesting magazine article and retype it, making numerous errors in capitalization. Have the students read the article and correct all of the errors. To make this a game, put them into competition with the clock.

ENRICHMENT

Sentence Patterns Have students write sentences that include specific kinds of words that should be capitalized. For example, have students write a sentence which includes the names of three famous people, someone with a title, and the name of a city. Have students share their sentences and discuss the words they capitalized, giving the reasons for each.

CHAPTER 28 PUNCTUATION, ABBREVIATIONS, AND NUMBERS

CHAPTER OBJECTIVES

In this chapter the student will

- use end punctuation correctly
- use the colon and semicolon correctly
- use the comma correctly
- use the dash and parentheses correctly
- use brackets correctly
- use ellipsis points correctly
- use quotation marks correctly
- use italics correctly
- use the apostrophe correctly
- use the hyphen correctly
- use abbreviations correctly
- use numbers and numerals correctly

REINFORCEMENT

Punctuation Puzzle Develop a crossword puzzle as a review of the rules about punctuation, abbreviations, and numbers. The squares are to be filled with the names of the punctuation marks, the reasons for the punctuation, or the abbreviations of given words. The clues can be direct questions, sentences with an underlined mark of punctuation which must be named or about which a question must be answered, or simply a word for which an abbreviation exists.

ENRICHMENT

Sneaky Sentences Give students specific sentence structures that require certain kinds of punctuation. For example, have students write a sentence that contains three commas, one use of quotation marks, two abbreviations, and one semicolon. Have them share their sentences and discuss how they used each type of punctuation.

TEACHING PART THREE: SKILLS AND RESOURCES

Part Three contains two kinds of chapters: (1) those that make special applications of the skills taught in the earlier chapters and (2) those that supplement these skills with technical information. Therefore, you may want to vary your teaching of the chapters in Part Three to suit the material in each chapter. For example, you may want to teach the chapters on business writing and speaking and listening after teaching the writing, usage, and mechanics skills taught in Parts One and Two, since the skills in Part Three draw on those taught in Parts One and Two. On the other hand, you may, in teaching word choice in Part One, want to refer students to Part Three's chapters on vocabulary building, spelling, and using the dictionary and thesaurus, since these chapters provide specialized, technical information that supplements the material taught in Part One.

PART THREE: OBJECTIVES, ANSWERS, REINFORCEMENT, AND ENRICHMENT

"Part Three: Skills and Resources" is made up seven chapters divided into two units. Here on a chapter-by-chapter basis you will find

- Chapter Objectives
- Answers and Guidelines for Evaluation that did not fit in the space allotted for teacher's annotations in the book proper

- Reinforcement and Enrichment activities: the former designed for students who need additional help in understanding the basic concepts of the chapter, the latter designed for students who are ready to go beyond the textbook into more advanced territory

CHAPTER 29 VOCABULARY SKILLS

CHAPTER OBJECTIVES

In this chapter the student will

- determine word meanings from context
- identify and use prefixes, suffixes, and roots
- examine and use Americanisms and regional dialects
- revise sentences using synonyms and antonyms
- experiment with new words by using a writer's word list

SUGGESTED ANSWERS AND GUIDELINES FOR EVALUATION

PAGE 591, EXERCISE 4

Students will not always be able to determine the precise definition of a word from their knowledge of its parts, but they should get an idea of what the word means.

1. to make right
2. not characterized by dying
3. (an animal having) two feet
4. (spoken with) one sound
5. the state of being the opposite of placed; the state of being out of place
6. relating to or characteristic of water
7. (an insect with) a hundred feet
8. something that leads water; a water conveyor
9. marked by being with knowledge; aware
10. capable of being equal; fair
11. the action of sending across
12. one who does good (for another)
13. tending to be broken; incomplete
14. full of the opposite of belief; not believing
15. able to like or be liked; friendly; pleasant

PAGE 592, EXERCISE 5

1. self-writing; a signature; to sign one's name
2. one who loves knowledge; a profound thinker
3. (a word that has) the same sound (as that of another word)
4. to cause to be together in time
5. characteristic of the stars
6. fear of water; rabies
7. the action of writing (and deciphering) secret codes
8. the action of studying (the nature and causes of) suffering (from disease)
9. characteristic of heat (obtained naturally) from the earth
10. a sailor in the air; a pilot (of a lighter-than-air vehicle)
11. (a person) suffering in the mind
12. characteristic of ships or sailing
13. not marked by a (definite) shape; shapeless
14. to make one kind
15. the action of studying the stars

PAGE 593, EXERCISE 6

1. a marshy area; from Louisiana French *bayou,* from Chocktaw *bayuk,* "stream."
2. a backwoods area; from Tagalog (Philippine) *bundok,* "mountain."
3. a small fried cake of twisted dough; a twisted doughnut; from Dutch *krulle,* "curled cake," from *krullen,* "to curl."
4. a railroad station; a storehouse; from French *dépôt,* "a deposit, a warehouse," from Latin *depositum,* "a deposit, something put down."
5. the delaying of legislative action by means of long speeches; a pirate; from Spanish

filibustero, "buccaneer," from French *filibustier,* "buccaneer, robber," from Dutch *vrijbuiter,* "freebooter," going back to *vrij,* "free," and *buit,* "booty."

6. okra; a thick, spicy soup made with okra; from Bantu (African).
7. to bewitch; an evil spell; from Pennsylvania German *hexe,* from German *Hexe,* "witch."
8. Eskimo canoe made of animal skins; from Eskimo *qajaq.*
9. a wild horse of the American plains; from (Mexican) Spanish *mestengo,* "stray," going back to Middle Latin (*animalia*) *mixta,* "mixed animals."
10. smoked and highly seasoned beef usually from shoulder cuts; from Yiddish *pastrami,* from Romanian *pastrama.*
11. a yellow turnip; from Swedish dialect *rotabagge,* from *rot,* "root," + *bagge,* "bag."
12. a person who explores caves; from Latin *spelunca,* "cave," from Greek *spelynx.*
13. a natural object taken as the emblem of a clan or a tribe; a representation of such an object; from Ojibwa *ototeman,* "his brother–sister kin."
14. a small guitar traditionally played in Hawaii; from Hawaiian *ukulele,* from *uku,* "flea," + *lele,* "jumping."
15. a long green summer squash, also called an Italian squash; from Italian *zucchino,* diminutive of *zucca,* "gourd."

PAGE 594, EXERCISE 7

1. horse chestnut
2. creek, run, kill, branch
3. pancake, hotcake, griddlecake
4. doughnut, fatcake, cruller
5. firefly, June bug, lightning bug
6. peanut, pinder, groundnut
7. whip, flog, wallop; *also,* trounce
8. harmonica, French harp
9. earthworm, angleworm, fishworm, redworm, dew worm
10. tadpole
11. frying pan, spider
12. cottage cheese, pot cheese, Dutch cheese, sourmilk cheese
13. porch
14. seesaw, dandle, totterboard
15. pinwheel (toy); *also,* merry-go-round, carousel

REINFORCEMENT

Prefixes and Suffixes Give the students a list of prefixes, suffixes, and root words, each in a column appropriately labeled. Have the students work in groups that will compete with other groups in class to determine how many different words they can make from the lists in five to ten minutes. At the end of the stated time, have the groups share their words and chart how many were repeats and how many were on only one group's list.

ENRICHMENT

Hidden Words To challenge the students and give them some exposure to words in a different way, try the hidden word puzzle. In this puzzle you use parts of other words put together to form a new word. Example: Add *a great bulk* to *a plot of land* and get *a terrible slaughter* (*Answer:* mass + acre = massacre). Give the students six or eight such examples, and then put the students into groups of three or four. Ask them to make up their own examples. Then have them trade with another group to see if they can solve their classmates' word puzzles.

CHAPTER 30 SPELLING SKILLS

CHAPTER OBJECTIVES

In this chapter the student will

- apply rules for adding prefixes and suffixes; form plurals; and spell words containing *ie* or *ei, sede, ceed,* or *cede,* and unstressed vowels (*schwa*)
- examine and practice the correct use of homophones and words with similar sounds
- practice mastering the spelling of frequently misspelled words

REINFORCEMENT

Spelling Method Using the word list in the chapter, follow these steps to teach each word. (1) Introduce the word with a story or fact, if possible, so that you give students some idea of the meaning. (2) Read the word in context, using several different sentences. (3) Have students use the words in original sentences and share with the class to check spelling and meaning. (4) Drill students on the words for the next two or three weeks or until you are sure they can spell them correctly. One efficient way to conduct this drill is by making a set of flash cards with the word on one side and the definition on the other.

ENRICHMENT

Spelling Notebooks As students continue to write and study language as well as build their vocabulary, they will encounter words that cause spelling problems. To help them learn the correct spellings and meanings of these new words, have them keep a spelling notebook. They are to use a looseleaf binder so that pages can be added in alphabetical order as words are entered. Students should put two words on a page, one at the top and one in the middle. For each word they should supply a definition in their own words, the pronunciation, and an example of the word used in a sentence.

CHAPTER 31 BUSINESS COMMUNICATION SKILLS

CHAPTER OBJECTIVES

In this chapter the student will

- examine and practice the correct format for business letters and envelopes
- examine and practice writing a letter of application, a letter of request, an order letter, a letter of adjustment or complaint, and a letter of inquiry
- apply guidlines for filling out a college application and for writing a college-application essay

REINFORCEMENT

Dear Store Have the students bring a mail-order catalogue to school. Have them find an item that they would like to order, and ask them to write an order letter to the store or company. Remind them to include all necessary information, including color, size, order number, etc. At the next class have them suppose that an incorrect order arrived. Ask them to write a letter of complaint, giving all the details of the original letter and the details of the wrong item. Have them state how they would like the store to compensate them.

ENRICHMENT

Jobs, Jobs, Jobs Bring to class several copies of the want ads from the newspaper. Have the students find a job that they would like to investigate. First have them go to the library and research the occupation in question to determine the qualifications and educational background required. Next have them assume that they are qualified to apply for the job. Have them write a letter of application to accompany a résumé. The letter should identify the job in question, give a brief overview of the applicant's qualifications, and supply some positive statements about the applicant's suitability for the position.

CHAPTER 32 LISTENING AND SPEAKING SKILLS

CHAPTER OBJECTIVES

In this chapter the student will

- explore and practice responsive listening, listening for main ideas and details, and critical listening
- improve speaking skills through the effective use of voice and body language
- apply guidelines for reading aloud and reciting

- prepare, deliver, and evaluate a persuasive speech
- apply procedures for conducting a debate
- make effective announcements
- observe group behavior and participate in a group discussion

SUGGESTED ANSWERS AND GUIDELINES FOR EVALUATION

PAGE 627, EXERCISE 2

Students' notes should include the main ideas and supporting details of the passage and be organized to show the relationships between those, as in this example:

Communication essential as ancient world expanded
  first postal system—Egypt, 2000 B.C.
  used to convey orders throughout empire
Roman postal system
  most complex
  could transport mail 170 miles in a day

Modern system—Roland Hill treatise
  began in England 150 years ago
  established practice of pricing mail
    by weight and distance
  introduced postage stamp

PAGE 629, EXERCISE 3

Guidelines for Evaluation: Students' examples should include the following:

- a description of the visual presentation or sound effects
- the apparent market or audience
- the text
- whether the fallacy is contained entirely in the words or whether the pictures or sound effects contribute

PAGE 631, EXERCISE 7

Guidelines for Evaluation: Evaluate students' performances on the basis of

- how appropriate their gestures and facial expressions are
- how convincing their gestures and facial expressions are
- the degree of contact they are able to establish and maintain with the audience

PAGE 632, EXERCISE 8

Guidelines for Evaluation: Evaluate students' performances on the basis of

- how well they convey the meaning of the poem
- how well they convey their own feelings about the poem
- the quality of their voice production
- how expressively they use their voices and bodies
- the degree of contact they are able to establish and maintain with the audience

PAGE 634, EXERCISES 9 AND 10

Guidelines for Evaluation: Use the guidelines in the student text to evaluate students' speeches and to help students evaluate their own and each other's speeches. You may want to use the *Macmillan English Study and Composition Blackline Masters,* numbers 41–42.

PAGE 636, EXERCISE 11

Guidelines for Evaluation: Possible propositions for debate are

1. Resolved: The highway speed limit should be reduced to 50 miles an hour.
2. Resolved: A nonsmoking section should be established in every public building.
3. Resolved: The voting age should be raised to 21.
4. Resolved: The driving age nationwide should be raised to 19.
5. Resolved: The use of animals in laboratory research should be abolished.

PAGE 638, EXERCISE 13

Guidelines for Evaluation: The student should

- attract the attention of the audience
- speak in a clear and audible voice
- organize the announcement to emphasize important information

REINFORCEMENT

Critical Listening Discuss the propaganda techniques that speakers use when they are giving speeches. Include a discussion of fact versus opinion, faulty generalizations, half-truths, misleading comparisons, personal attacks, and faulty cause-effect relationships. Give several examples as the discussion progresses, so that students understand the concepts.

ENRICHMENT

Group Discussions Review the information in the chapter about group discussions, and have students divide into groups to practice. Give them a choice of situations requiring them to be a member of a committee that has a stated problem to solve. Tell them to follow the five steps in the "problem-solving process": **(1)** Define the problem with all of its facets. **(2)** Determine the causes and decide what the solutions must accomplish. **(3)** List several possible solutions, giving advantages and disadvantages of each. **(4)** Choose the solution that is most workable. **(5)** List the steps that should be followed to reach the chosen solution. Have them report their committee's work on a form that uses the five steps above.

CHAPTER 33 TEST-TAKING SKILLS

CHAPTER OBJECTIVES

In this chapter the student will

- explore guidelines for taking standardized tests
- practice answering SAT/PSAT antonym questions, analogy questions, and sentence-completion questions
- examine reading-comprehension questions
- practice answering ECT grammar-and-usage questions, sentence-correction questions, and construction-shift questions
- explore strategies for answering essay questions and practice answering an essay question from the ECT

REINFORCEMENT

Note Taking Many students have problems taking notes in an organized way. They either take notes in a random manner that is difficult to understand later, or they try to use an outline and have difficulty making the information fit the rigid structure. As an alternative, have them learn to use the mapping technique. They start with a circle and write in it the main idea. Then they write the supporting details on lines around the circle. After the notes are complete, they can go back and number the details, if sequence is important to remember. Also, if the supporting details have points that must be noted, they are written on lines below the main detail line. (See the diagram.) This visual image of the information aids students in remembering the important points from their reading or lectures.

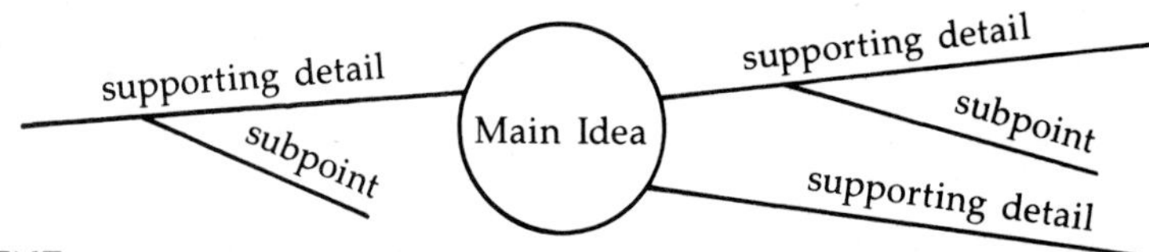

ENRICHMENT

Types of Test Questions All test questions fall into one of four categories. Teach students how to read a question and classify it. Then they will know how to answer it. The four types are: (1) Main idea questions—asking for the main point of the problem or selection. (2) Detail questions—asking for specific pieces of information. (3) Vocabulary questions—giving multiple-choice responses dependent on understanding a specific term.

(4) Inference questions—Information is not found in the test item but can be deduced from what is given, with responses qualified with a word such as "probably," "might" or "apparently." Give students frequent practice in identifying question types and in knowing how to answer them.

CHAPTER 34 THE DICTIONARY AND THE THESAURUS

CHAPTER OBJECTIVES

In this chapter the student will

- identify different types of dictionaries and thesauruses
- examine dictionary entries
- practice using a dictionary and a thesaurus

ANSWERS

PAGE 664, EXERCISE 1

Answers may vary, depending on the dictionary consulted.

1. **(a)** affidavit, **(b)** correct, **(c)** rainstorm, **(d)** correct
2. traveler; after the *v* or the *l*
3. "relating to the American Revolution"
4. the *g* in *gesture;* "leadership or dominance, especially of one nation over others"; Greek *hēgemonia,* "leadership," from *hēgemōn,* "leader"
5. the second
6. worse, worst
7. Scottish dialect; "a sloping bank or a hillside"
8. "to talk bluntly and directly"
9. Possible synonyms include *peak, acme, apex, pinnacle, zenith,* and *climax.*
10. Most dictionaries will list the adverb form *belligerently;* a possible definition is "in a warlike or quarrelsome manner."

REINFORCEMENT

Jazz It Up Give the students a dull, colorless paragraph, and have them use the thesaurus to find words that would improve the interest level of the piece. Students will have a tendency to go overboard and replace every word with a synonym. Warn them not to use words that cause the sentences to become stilted. The object of this exercise is not to replace every word with one that is longer or more flowery but to be selective in using words that enhance the message.

ENRICHMENT

Special Dictionaries Have the students go to the library and find several dictionaries that deal with a particular subject. Give them a list of words from one of these dictionaries, and have them define each. Also, have them answer questions such as the ones in the chapter that will lead them into using all the features of the dictionary. Next, working in groups, have them select one of the other specialized dictionaries and study its organization and features. Have them select some sample words to be defined, and have them design a set of questions that correlate with the specific features they have found. Then have the groups trade words and questions and proceed as they did with your list.

CHAPTER 35 THE LIBRARY

CHAPTER OBJECTIVES

In this chapter the student will

- examine and practice using catalog cards
- explore the classification and arrangement of library books and practice locating books in a library

- identify the parts of a book
- locate newspapers and periodicals and practice using the *Readers' Guide to Periodical Literature* and other indexes to newspapers and periodicals
- explore and practice using encyclopedias, almanacs, atlases, and other reference works
- examine microforms, the vertical file, and nonprint material

ANSWERS

PAGE 672, EXERCISE 2

Specific information will vary. Of the ten books listed, items 1, 3, 4, 6, and 9, are unsuitable because they cover periods in American history or literature later than the colonial period before 1700. Students should list the requested information for some or all of the remaining five books and should substitute other books on colonial America for any of the remaining books not available at the library.

PAGE 679, EXERCISE 8

1. a freed slave and an American Abolitionist; the "Ain't I a Woman?" speech
2. Germany, 1900; *Maggie: A Girl of the Streets* and *The Red Badge of Courage*
3. a figure of speech in which one thing is used to indicate something else with which it is associated; for example, using "the crown" to mean "the monarchy" or "the royal government"
4. The quotation is from Emerson's "Concord Hymn"; anthologies will vary. After finding the source of the quotation in a book of quotations, students should look up the poem in *Granger's* to find out the anthologies in which it appears and should then check a current *Books in Print* to find out which of the anthologies are currently in print.
5. an edict issued in 1598 by Henry IV of France to define the rights of French Protestants, or Huguenots; Louis XIV of France; they were forced to flee France in order to practice their religion, and some eventually settled in the New World
6. the hydrogen–ion concentration of a solution and thus its acidity or alkalinity; neither acid nor alkali—that is, neutral
7. French Impressionism; the United States
8. Examples include the ballets *Appalachian Spring* and *Billy the Kid*
9. Examples include Louis J. M. Daguerre, who developed the first direct positive image on silver plate, called a *daguerreotype;* and William H. F. Talbot, who developed the first paper negative from which a number of positive prints could be made.

REINFORCEMENT

Using the Library Students need to learn to use all the resources in the library to research a single topic. Have them choose a topic and compile a working bibliography, using the bibliography forms you give them. They are to locate reference books and periodicals, as well as information in the vertical file and on microforms. Finally, they are to ask the librarian if there are any nonprint materials available. When you return to class have students share their topics and the resources they have found.

ENRICHMENT

Annotated Bibliographies All libraries have different procedures and contain different types of material and equipment, so students need the experience of using a variety of libraries. Have them choose a topic to research, and tell them you want an annotated bibliography on their topic compiled from the resources of at least three different libraries (if possible, one should be a university library). The annotations should be brief, since the purpose is to learn to use the library and not actually to research the topic in depth. When they finish, have them share their experiences at the various libraries. If a large number of libraries is available, you may want to specify certain ones to different students so that the class can visit a wide variety of libraries.

MACMILLAN ENGLISH

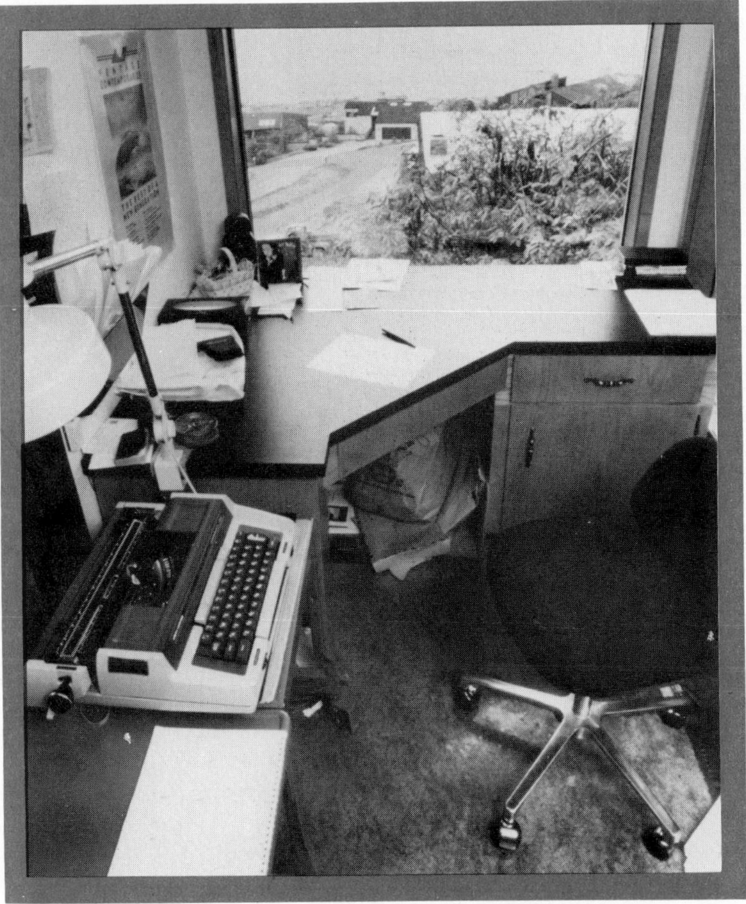

About the Cover RAYMOND CARVER (born 1939) is an award-winning poet and short story writer. Carver does most of his writing in the morning at this desk in his home in Port Angeles, Washington. The view of the bay is part of Carver's writing process, serving as inspiration for nearly a hundred poems. Just as Carver's view expanded his writing, *Macmillan English* will expand your language and writing skills.

AUTHORS AND ADVISORS

Elizabeth Ackley
English Teacher
Indian Hill High School
Cincinnati, Ohio

Paula A. Calabrese
Assistant Principal
Ingomar Middle School
North Allegheny School District
Pittsburgh, Pennsylvania

Sandra A. Cavender
English Teacher
Nathan Hale High School
West Allis, Wisconsin

Sylvia Collins-Kimbell
Supervisor of Language Arts
Hillsborough County Schools
Tampa, Florida

Sonya Pohlman
English Teacher
Rangeview High School
Aurora, Colorado

Judi Purvis
Department Head
Irving High School
Irving, Texas

Robert Ranta
Department Head
Lacey Township High School
Lanoka Harbor, New Jersey

Marjory Carter Willis
English Teacher
Midlothian High School
Midlothian Virginia

Gail Witt
Educational Consultant
Region XIII, Education Service Center
Austin, Texas

Part One materials prepared by Intentional Educations, Watertown, Massachusetts

SPECIAL CONSULTANT

Franklin E. Horowitz, Adjunct Assistant Professor of Education
Teachers College, Columbia University
New York, New York

CONTRIBUTING WRITERS

Harrison B. Bell, Robert A. Bell, Sally R. Bell, Sheila C. Crowell, Richard Foerster, Eleanor Franklin, Carol Goldman, Joan C. Gregory, Florence W. Harris, Paula R. Hartz, Barbara Klinger, Ellen D. Kolba, Christopher T. McMillan, William Maxey III, Cynthia Miller, Carroll Moulton, Eileen Hillary Oshinsky, Milton Polsky, John David Richardson, Gail Schiller Tuchman, Sidney Zimmerman

STUDENT CONTRIBUTORS
TO "WRITERS ON WRITING" FEATURE

Tracy Anderson
Kentridge High School
Kent, Washington

Sharon Anich
Nathan Hale High School
West Allis, Wisconsin

Susan Appel
Indian Hill High School
Cincinnati, Ohio

Leemon Baird
Brandon High School
Brandon, Florida

Michelle Calantine
Eastwood High School
El Paso, Texas

Chris Canitz
Nathan Hale High School
West Allis, Wisconsin

Carin Chabut
Indian Hill High School
Cincinnati, Ohio

Juhee Choi
Rangeview High School
Aurora, Colorado

Brad Denton
Rangeview High School
Aurora, Colorado

Ghia Euskirchen
Indian Hill High School
Cincinnati, Ohio

Chris Faigle
Midlothian High School
Midlothian, Virginia

Mariano Fernandez
Indian Hill High School
Cincinnati, Ohio

Steve Francis
Eastwood High School
El Paso, Texas

Hugh Geier
Indian Hill High School
Cincinnati, Ohio

Roselle Graskey
Eastwood High School
El Paso, Texas

Gina Griffin
Brandon High School
Brandon, Florida

Kris Hansen
Eastwood High School
El Paso, Texas

Ken Jones
Indian Hill High School
Cincinnati, Ohio

Paul Kalomeres
Indian Hill High School
Cincinnati, Ohio

David Kilday
Indian Hill High School
Cincinnati, Ohio

Chris Kolkhurst
Midlothian High School
Midlothian, Virginia

Ed Leman
Rangeview High School
Aurora, Colorado

Susan Lynch
Lacey Township High School
Lacey, New Jersey

Susan Maas
North Allegheny Senior High School
Wexford, Pennsylvania

Paul Monarch
Indian Hill High School
Cincinnati, Ohio

Minda Morgan
Midlothian High School
Midlothian, Virginia

Robert Nichols
Indian Hill High School
Cincinnati, Ohio

Paige Orchard
Rangeview High School
Aurora, Colorado

Stephanie Pallo
Midlothian High School
Midlothian, Virginia

Jeff Partin
Nathan Hale High School
West Allis, Wisconsin

Brian Rowe
Indian Hill High School
Cincinnati, Ohio

Ken Sachar
Rockland Country Day School
Congers, New York

Robert Seal
Indian Hill High School
Cincinnati, Ohio

Michelle Siqueiros
Eastwood High School
El Paso, Texas

Krystal Starling
Brandon High School
Brandon, Florida

Liza Steele
Midlothian High School
Midlothian, Virginia

Aric Swaney
Eastwood High School
El Paso, Texas

Richard Turner
Midlothian High School
Midlothian, Virginia

Eric White
Rangeview High School
Aurora, Colorado

Peter Wilke
Indian Hill High School
Cincinnati, Ohio

Rachel Wright
Rangeview High School
Aurora, Colorado

Steve Zinck
Rangeview High School
Aurora, Colorado

MACMILLAN
ENGLISH

Scribner Educational Publishers
New York
Macmillan Publishing Company
New York
Collier Macmillan Publishers
London

ACKNOWLEDGMENTS

Grateful acknowledgment is given authors, publishers, and agents for permission to reprint the following copyrighted material. In the case of any omissions, the Publisher will be pleased to make suitable acknowledgments in future editions.

William Heinemann Ltd.
"The Far and the Near" from *From Death to Morning* by Thomas Wolfe. Reprinted by permission of William Heinemann Limited.

Liveright Publishing Co.
"Those Winter Sundays" from *Angle of Ascent, New and Selected Poems* by Robert Hayden. Copyright © 1975, 1972, 1970, 1966 by Robert Hayden. Reprinted by permission of Liveright Publishing Co.

Macmillan Publishing Company
"The Secret Heart" from *Collected Poems* by Robert P. Tristram Coffin. Copyright © 1935 by Macmillan Publishing Company; copyright renewed © 1963 by Margaret Coffin Halvosa.

Charles Scribner's Sons
"The Far and the Near" from *From Death to Morning* by Thomas Wolfe. Copyright © 1935 Charles Scribner's Sons; copyright renewed © 1963 Paul Gitlin. Reprinted with permission of Charles Scribner's Sons.

Photo Credits © *America Hurrah Antiques, N.Y.C.:* pp. 348–349 T. © *Orville Andrews:* p. 346 BL. *Animals Animals:* © C.W. Perkins, p. 352 BL; © Marty Stouffer, p. 352 BR; © Stouffer Productions, p. 353 BL. © *The Bettmann Archive:* p. 359 TL. © *Brown Bros.:* p. 349 CR. *Bruce Coleman, Inc.:* © E. R. Degginger, p. 365 R, T, CL, and CR; © J. Fennel, p. 365 R and B. © *Colour Library International:* p. 375 TR. © *Leo de Wys:* p. 371 B; © Everett C. Johnson, p. 356 BR. *Earth Scenes:* © John Gerlach, p. 347 TR. © *Walker Evans:* courtesy John T. Hill, executor, pp. 354–355 B. *The Image Bank:* © Steve Dunwell, p. 356 TR; © W. Weismeier, pp. 350 TR, 351 TL and TR; © Von Baich, pp. 372–373 T. *Courtesy Jay Johnson Gallery:* © Kathy Jacobson, p. 349 B. *Metropolitan Museum of Art:* George A. Hearn Fund, 1931, p. 373 T; Gift of Mrs. William F. Milton, 1923, p. 374 TL. *Monkmeyer Press Photo:* © Mimi Forsyth, 356 BL; © Freda Leinwand, pp. 353 BR, 357 TR and TL; © Renate Hiller, pp. 350 BL and BR, 351 BL and BR; © George Zimbel, pp. 346–347. *Museum of Modern Art: New York,* p. 373 BR. *Courtesy Rainbird Publishing Group, Ltd.:* © Paul Dohertz, p. 372 BL. *Rainbow:* © Linda K. Moore, pp. 372–373 B. Shostal Associates: © Eric Carle, pp. 346–347 T. *Taurus Photos:* © Pam Hasagawa, pp. 374–375 B; © Frank Siteman, p. 357 BL. *Whitney Museum of American Art:* p. 348 B. *Woodfin Camp & Assoc.:* © Jonathon Blair, p. 347 BR; © Michal Heron, p. 357 R; © William Strode, pp. 374–375 T.

Design and Art Production
Canard Design, Inc.

Scribner Educational Publishers
Macmillan Publishing Company
866 Third Avenue
New York, NY 10022
Collier Macmillan Canada, Inc.

Printed in the United States of America

ISBN 0-02-214420-X
9 8 7 6 5 4 3 2 1

CONTENTS

PART ONE: COMPOSITION

UNIT I The Paragraph and the Writing Process 2

UNIT II Words, Sentences, and Style 80

CHAPTER 19: PARTS OF THE SENTENCE 424

CHAPTER 20: PHRASES 441

CHAPTER 21: CLAUSES AND SENTENCE STRUCTURE 455

UNIT VII Usage 474

CHAPTER 22: VERB TENSES, VOICE, AND MOOD 475

CHAPTER 23: SUBJECT–VERB AGREEMENT 491

CHAPTER 24: USING PRONOUNS CORRECTLY 500

CHAPTER 25: USING MODIFIERS CORRECTLY 512

CHAPTER 26: GLOSSARY OF SPECIFIC USAGE ITEMS 520

UNIT VIII Mechanics 540

PART THREE: SKILLS AND RESOURCES

UNIT IX Skills 582

UNIT X Resources 658

PART ONE: COMPOSITION

UNIT I

The Paragraph and the Writing Process

Some people develop careers with their writing skills—the poet, the novelist, the newspaper reporter, the technical writer, and the historian, for example. Not all people are professional writers; however, we *all* use writing. When you compose a business or a personal letter, answer an essay exam question, or write a list of reminder notes for shopping, you are a writer. You may prepare a fifteen-page research paper about Renaissance art, create a five-line poem about a buzzing fly, or fashion a persuasive paragraph arguing the benefits of a shorter or longer school week. In each case, you are a writer actively engaged in the writing process—a writer who has developed a purpose for a particular piece of writing and who is directing that writing to an audience.

In the next few chapters you will work through the three specific stages of the writing process—prewriting, writing, and revising. By developing various writing skills appropriate to each of these stages, you will learn to express your ideas clearly and vividly. Regardless of your purpose—to narrate a personal experience, to explain the inner mechanics of a machine, to describe a brilliant sunrise, or to persuade someone of your opinion about a political issue—when you write clearly and vividly, both you and your audience become interested in what you write.

The most practical way to master the skills of paragraph writing is to write paragraphs. By learning to write effective paragraphs, you will develop writing strategies and techniques that you can later apply with confidence to longer kinds of writing, such as essays and reports, that draw upon many of the same writing skills.

No one is born an accomplished writer, nor is the skill of writing easily or mysteriously acquired. All writers learn their craft by writing—by experimenting with and exploring the process of writing.

In this unit you will learn to generate, explore, and develop writing ideas. You will learn how to organize those ideas and express them clearly in paragraphs. You will also learn how to question, evaluate, and revise your writing so that it expresses what you want it to express before you present it to an audience.

The writing process takes you on a journey of exploration and discovery. As you write, you will discover and explore *what* you want to say and *how* to say it. The chapters that follow will take you into that discovery process and help you also to discover the writer in you.

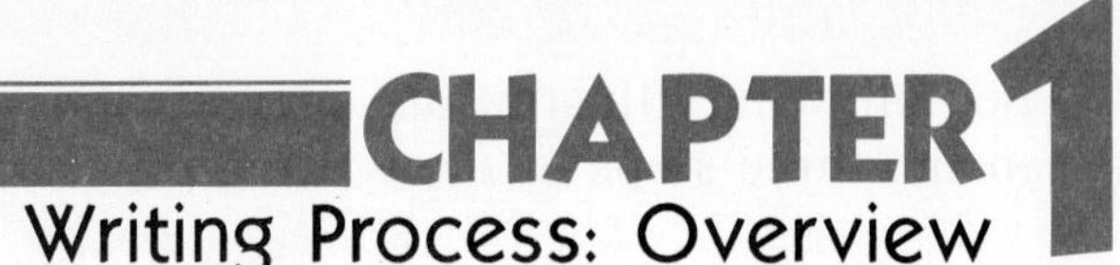

CHAPTER 1
The Writing Process: Overview

In one sense, my whole effort for years might be described as an effort to fathom my own design, to explore my own channels, to discover my own ways. . . . I believe I have found my own language, I think I know my way.

–Thomas Wolfe

A writer's search–what Thomas Wolfe called the effort "to discover my own ways"–is the actual process of writing. It is during the **writing process** that a writer discovers what to say about a subject and how best to say it. During this process a writer constantly tests his or her imagination against the real world, all the while translating thoughts into language that readers can understand. Writers use this process whether they are involved in personal, creative writing–fiction or poetry–or more formal, functional writing, such as research, reports, essays, and letters.

In this chapter you will receive an overview of the writing process. The next three chapters will present in detail the three types of activities that make up the writing process:

- **prewriting**–generating ideas and preparing to write
- **writing a first draft**–or a **discovery draft**
- **revising**, also called **postwriting**–questioning, rethinking, and editing your draft until it best says what you want it to say; preparing a final copy, proofreading it, and publishing it so that you can share it with an audience.

The three steps of the writing process–prewriting, writing, and revising–are described in a logical sequence here. However, you may find yourself alternating between these steps as you write. For example, when revising you may change the wording of a sentence and suddenly discover a new thought worth exploring. At that point you may decide to do additional prewriting activities to expand the new thought. You may even decide to change the focus of your draft after completing your new prewriting. When you write, your mind is in a state of perpetual motion, constantly shifting between the various steps or stages of writing. That perpetual motion is absolutely necessary; after all, you are involved in an exploration of discovery.

The following illustration suggests how you might move between the three steps of the writing process.

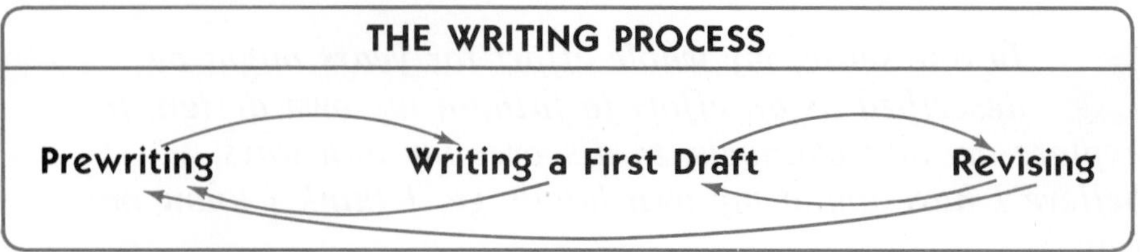

PREWRITING

Prewriting prepares you to write. It is the first and perhaps most important step in the writing process. The decisions that you make when you prewrite are likely to determine what you write about, how you organize your writing, why you are writing, and for whom you are writing.

When you spend time prewriting, you save time at the writing and rewriting, or revision, stages. The more time and serious effort you put into prewriting, the more likely it is that your writing will be informative, interesting, and organized. Good writing grows from thoughtful prewriting. On the other hand, writing that does not grow from prewriting is likely to be skimpy, repetitive, rambling and dull. For example, read the following paragraph, which was written without any prewriting effort.

[1]I think that I have always been interested in computers. [2]Many people are interested in computers, but most people do not know a byte from a bunion. [3]I never dreamed that the personal computer would become so popular. [4]Computers have a wide variety of uses. [5]The personal computers of today are very versatile and can perform many tasks. [6]Everyone today seems interested in computers, but not many people can tell you the difference between software and hardware. [7]The computer industry's goal is to install a computer in every home by the year 2000.

Objective

EXERCISE 1. Thinking About Prewriting. Reread the preceding paragraph, and write answers to the following questions.

1. What information about computers does the writer give you? What do you think his purpose is in this paragraph?
2. Do you think the writer has effectively communicated his ideas? Why or why not?

Suggested Answers: 1. the past, present, and future of the computer industry; to inform; 2. no; too repetitious

The writer of the paragraph about computers sounds confused. He has obviously been involved with computers for some time and has knowledge of the computer industry; yet he fails to communicate his ideas in an interesting or logical manner. His lack of prewriting makes the paragraph hard to follow.

After being told why his paragraph was unsuccessful, he put it aside and began a prewriting exercise. First he listed a variety of topics, questions, and statements that interested him as he thought about computers. Here are some of his prewriting notes:

First Set of Prewriting Notes

- *Why have I always been fascinated by computers?*
- *the many uses of computers*
- *limitations of computers: garbage in, garbage out*
- *Why did personal computers become so popular so quickly?*
- *the computer's influence on life by the year 2000*
- *Why people buy computers when they don't know anything about them?*
- *computer jargon, a very weird language*
- *possible careers in the computer industry*
- *how computers work*

The writer then began to review, evaluate, and explore some of the ideas in his notes. He realized that some of the ideas would be either uninteresting or difficult to write about in a single paragraph. So he eliminated those notes. He took the remaining notes and formed a second list. He added details to some of the ideas, combined other ideas, and narrowed the focus of the more promising ideas so that he might cover them in a single paragraph.

Second Set of Prewriting Notes

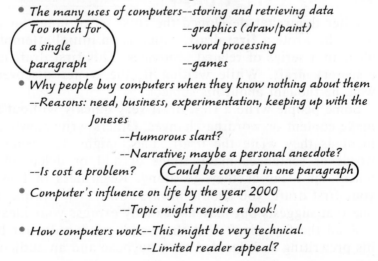

- *The many uses of computers--storing and retrieving data*
  --graphics (draw/paint)
  --word processing
  --games
  (Too much for a single paragraph)
- *Why people buy computers when they know nothing about them*
  --Reasons: need, business, experimentation, keeping up with the Joneses
  --Humorous slant?
  --Narrative; maybe a personal anecdote?
  --Is cost a problem?
  (Could be covered in one paragraph)
- *Computer's influence on life by the year 2000*
  --Topic might require a book!
- *How computers work--This might be very technical.*
  --Limited reader appeal?

At this stage of prewriting, the writer reviewed his second set of notes and began the process of choosing one of the topics for writing a single paragraph. While making this choice, he had to consider his audience. If his intended audience knows very little about computers, he would not want to write a highly technical explanation of how computers work. He also had to think about his purpose for writing to the audience. Did he want to entertain them, for example, with his opinions about why people buy computers they know little about? Did he want to inform them about the many uses of computers or perhaps persuade them of the importance of computers by the year 2000? These are the kinds of decisions that any writer must make at this point of the writing process. Such decisions, however, are never irreversible; you can always stop, change your mind, pursue a different topic, audience, or purpose, and then continue your prewriting.

Objective

EXERCISE 2. Thinking About Prewriting. Review the writer's two sets of prewriting notes on page 5. Then write your answers to the following questions.

1. Compare the two sets of notes. Which items on the first set did the writer eliminate when he wrote a detailed second set of notes? Why do you think he eliminated those items? Would you have? Why?

2. From the second set of notes, pick two topics that you think are promising writing ideas. Explain why you think each is promising, what you would choose as a writing purpose, and who you would choose as an intended audience.

Answers: **1.** items 1, 3, 7, 8; **2.** Students should choose topics on the basis of personal and audience interests.

WRITING A FIRST DRAFT

After the writer developed the final set of notes for his selected topic, he wrote a **first draft**, which is an initial attempt to express ideas in a series of related sentences. This first draft is actually a **discovery draft**. While writing it, the writer discovered exactly what he thought about his subject.

Some people write a first draft very quickly without stopping to make content or wording changes. Others write slowly and experiment as they write the draft. They might, for example, change words or sentences many times or add or delete phrases, sentences, or ideas as they go along. Regardless of how you write your first draft, you should always consider it a work in progress, one that suggests but may not exactly express your ideas.

Read the first draft that the writer produced after he reviewed his prewriting and decided on a purpose and an audience.

First Draft

Would you buy a car if you lacked the foggiest notion of what it was, how it worked, and how to use it? Of course not! You might, however, buy a computer even if you do not know the difference between a byte and a bunion. This year people will spend between two thousand and five thousand dollars for a personal "computer system," ~~and most of them won't know whether they bought software or hardware.~~ Why do so many buy computers when they don't know little ~~anything~~ about the contraptions? ~~Well,~~ some people have, or think that they have, ~~legitimat~~ (legitimate?) computer needs. However I suspect that most people purchase computers out ~~because~~ of fear or ~~and~~ guilt. A man named Alex recently bought a five-thousand-dollar personal computer because he ~~Alex~~ was not about to be left behind in the fast-paced information-processing age. This man admitted in the newspaper that he had wasted his money.

Objective

EXERCISE 3. Thinking About the First Draft. Reread the first draft, review the second set of prewriting notes on page 5, and then write your answers to the following questions.

1. Which item or items in his prewriting notes did the writer develop in this draft? Find at least two new details that the writer added.
2. What do you think the writer's purpose was?
3. What audience do you think the writer intended to reach?

REVISING

You can **revise,** or improve your draft, on both a large scale and a small scale. On a large scale, you may add an entirely new portion of text or delete a part of your draft or both add and delete. For example, you may find that you left out an important point when developing an idea, and you need to insert that point. On the other hand, you may find that pruning your original draft often improves it.

When you revise on a small scale, you **edit** your draft; you may decide to change the wording and the structure of some sentences. You may add or delete phrases. You should also edit your paper by checking for any errors in grammar, usage, capitalization, punctuation, and spelling.

When you have finished revising and editing your draft and you are satisfied with its overall quality, you need to prepare a final version of it, a copy that incorporates all of your revising and editing changes. After you prepare your final version, spend some time **proofreading** it, checking again for any mistakes in spelling or punctuation.

The writer who wrote a first draft about why people buy computers reread his discovery draft and spotted several small-scale problems of grammar, punctuation, and spelling. He also saw some phrases and sentences that needed restructuring. More importantly, he realized that he needed to make one large-scale revision. He wanted his paragraph to emphasize the story about Alex. So he revised his first draft to focus on that story.

Final Version

Would you buy a car if you lacked the foggiest notion of what it was, how it worked, and how to use it? Of course not! You might, however, buy a computer even if you do not know the difference between a byte and a bunion. This year thousands of people will spend between two thousand and five thousand dollars for a personal computer system. Why do so many people buy computers when they know little about the contraptions? Some people have or *think* that they have legitimate computer needs. However, most people purchase computers out of fear or guilt. A man whom I shall call Alex is a good example. For months Alex has been subjected to a barrage of media propaganda about the miracles that computers perform. So Alex now owns a five-thousand-dollar personal computer. Alex was not about to be left behind in the fast-paced information-processing age. Alex has not yet figured out how to hook up the keyboard, monitor, and disk drives, but someday he will. In the meantime Alex has been relieved of all fear and guilt. He has also been relieved of five thousand dollars. Everything has its price.

Objective

EXERCISE 4. Thinking About Revision. Compare the final version with the first draft on page 7. Then answer the following questions.

1. Find at least three small-scale changes in the final revised version. Why do you think the writer made these changes?
2. What two large-scale revisions did the writer make? What is the effect of each large-scale revision?

WRITER'S CHOICE #1

ASSIGNMENT: To write a paragraph about a modern invention
LENGTH: Eight to ten sentences
AUDIENCE: Your classmates
PURPOSE: To explain how important this invention has become
PREWRITING: Decide which invention you want to write about. Write notes about what the invention is, how it is used, and what modern life would be like without the invention.
WRITING: First, identify the invention and tell something significant about it. Next give several details about the importance of the invention and its effect on modern life. End with one or two statements about what modern life would be like without the invention.
REVISING: Reread your draft to make sure that a reader will understand what the invention is and how important it has become. Then edit your draft, copy it, proofread it, and share it with an audience.

WRITER'S CHOICE #2

ASSIGNMENT: To write about the best movie that you have ever seen
LENGTH: Your choice
AUDIENCE: Your choice
PURPOSE: To make a reader share your opinion of the movie
PREWRITING: Jot down the general aspects of the movie that impressed you, such as plot, characters, acting, film technique. For each aspect list some specific details or examples.
WRITING: Begin by identifying the movie, briefly describing it. Then state what aspects of the movie impressed you. Provide specific details for each aspect you discuss. End by indicating whether or not you would recommend that others see the movie.
REVISING: Imagine that you are your audience. Read the draft, and ask yourself if it is persuasive. Then edit your draft, copy it, proofread it, and share it with an audience.

WRITER'S CHOICE #3

ASSIGNMENT: To write a paragraph on any subject
LENGTH: Your choice
AUDIENCE: Your choice
PURPOSE: Your choice
OPTIONS:
- You might use the photographs in the Writer's Sourcebook on pages 346–347 for writing ideas.
- Remember to write some prewriting notes before you actually begin to write your first draft.

2 CHAPTER Prewriting

Get it down. Take chances. It may be bad, but it's the only way you can do anything really good.

—William Faulkner

PREWRITING	WRITING THE PARAGRAPH	REVISING

Starting to write need not be such a trying experience. Faulkner's advice, "Get it down. Take chances," is solid. As he indicates, you cannot do anything really good until you start, and the way to get started is through prewriting.

Prewriting is that part of the writing process in which you find a writing idea that interests and appeals to you, and you prepare to write about that idea.

Prewriting is more open, freewheeling, and experimental than any other stage of the writing process. When you prewrite, you concentrate on motivating your imagination to search for, create, and explore ideas.

This chapter divides prewriting into the following stages:

- generating ideas
- exploring subjects
- focusing on a topic
- forming a main idea
- developing the main idea

PREWRITING				
Generating Ideas	Exploring Subjects	Focusing on a Topic	Forming a Main Idea	Developing the Main Idea

GENERATING IDEAS

Probably the most important decision that a writer makes involves the writing idea. Remember this: Choose an idea that stimulates, intrigues, and interests you. If your idea really interests you, you will write honestly, persuasively, and confidently about it.

Where are all these interesting writing ideas? The techniques of **freewriting, brainstorming, charting,** and **observing** can help stimulate your imagination. In the next few pages you will experiment with each of these techniques to find out which ones work best for you. As you work with them, you may even invent other techniques to help you find ideas for writing.

- You can work by yourself in a personal journal, notebook, or on scraps of paper.
- You can work with another person or several people in a small group or conference.

GENERATING IDEAS BY FREEWRITING

Freewriting is continuous writing done within a specific but brief period of time.

Freewriting is like a warmup session before a race. Instead of loosening your muscles, however, you are exercising your mind and starting the flow of ideas. Someone gives a signal and you start writing. You do not have to worry about grammar, style, or logic. During freewriting you set your mind free and record all thoughts and free associations as they flow. The following is a piece of freewriting. It rambles and contains errors but has a flow of associated ideas throughout.

Freewriting Sample: A Writer Looking for a Subject

I'm supposed to start writing now. Could write about who invented space flight, rockets? I think his name was Goddard (?), but not sure. Rockets became very important, very quickly. Unbelievable invention. The car was a fantastic invention also, so were the wheel, forks, pencil, paper. Eyeglasses for chickens never really caught on. Wonder what the future holds in the realm of inventions? Silicon-encapsulated cities? Opportunities for inventions are limited only by people's imaginations. That's three minutes. Done.

Likewise, if you are assigned a subject or writing topic, you can use the freewriting technique to discover other approaches to the assigned topic. For example, a student who was assigned the general topic *conservation* used a few minutes of freewriting to unlock several other specific writing ideas related to the general subject. Her freewriting contains some grammatical and mechanical imperfections, but it also contains ideas.

Freewriting Sample:
A Writer with a General Subject

Conservation--the act of conserving, saving. But conserving what?! Peanut butter, gasoline, energy, time, wildlife, nature?? Pick one! How about wildlife conservation--that's such a broad topic. I could write twenty research papers about it and yet only scratch the surface. What happens if we don't conserve our wildlife, our natural woodlands? We lose them. But more than that happens. Think about Thoreau. Why did he go to live in the woods at Walden? Not just for pleasure, for nature--but to discover something about himself. Lessons from nature? life, death, survival, simplicity. What has this to do with conservation?

Objective

EXERCISE 1. Generating Ideas in Freewriting. Look at both examples of freewriting on pages 11 and 12. Note a possible writing idea that you see generated in each piece of freewriting.

Suggested Answers: For page 11: the inventor of the rocket engine; For page 12: the self-instructive aspect of nature

Objective

EXERCISE 2. Freewriting in Pairs. Join with another writer in freewriting on a subject of interest to both of you. Then agree on a time limitation—say, five minutes. Each of you should begin freewriting your own thoughts and continue until the time limit is reached. Then separately reread your freewriting, and compile a list of writing ideas that can provide the basis for a paragraph. Compare your ideas with those of the other writer. Save your notes for a later exercise.

GENERATING IDEAS BY BRAINSTORMING

Brainstorming is another prewriting activity that can help you generate ideas through free association.

Brainstorming notes can take different forms. The writer who did freewriting on conservation felt comfortable with the orderly list format. She began with some of her original ideas and then added a few more.

Brainstorming Sample: List Format

1. *Wildlife conservation--the act of conserving, saving, protecting.*
2. *Why conserve nature? What would Thoreau answer? He discovered simple truths about himself at Walden.*
3. *What other "observers" of nature have I read? Loren Eisley's The Night Country. What did I learn from him?*
4. *My own experiences with nature: camping, fishing, hiking, etc. My favorite is probably fishing. Why do I like it so much?*
5. *List specific fishing experiences; what did I learn or what part of myself did they put me in touch with? Think about.*

Other writers are more comfortable with a brainstorming format less rigid than listing. They like the open, graphic format in which they can connect ideas with circles and lines. This open, graphic format is called **clustering.** The writer who did the freewriting on page 11 used the clustering format to brainstorm on the subject of *inventions.*

Clustering

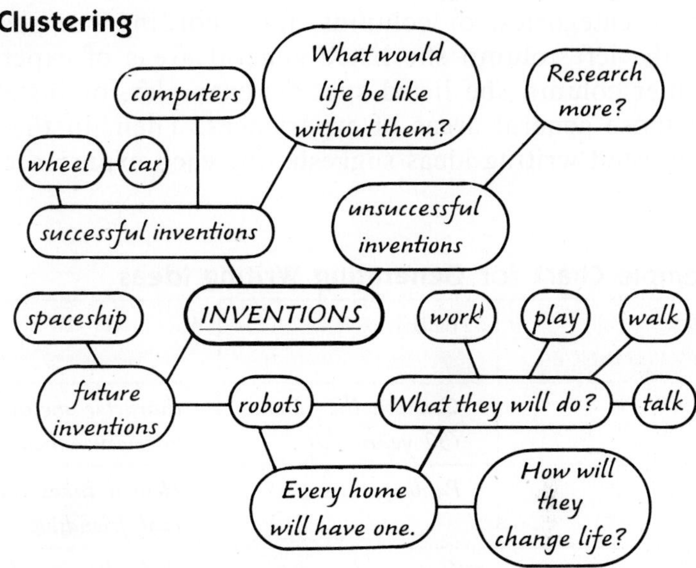

Like each of these writers, you can try freewriting first, then choose an idea from your freewriting and brainstorm about that idea, or you may reverse the process. You may prefer one method to another, or use different methods for different situations. There are a number of ways to use these techniques to generate ideas. Experiment with them, and use what works best for you.

Objective

EXERCISE 3. Generating Ideas by Brainstorming. Choose one of the following general subjects or one idea that interests you from your freewriting in Exercise 2. Choose one of the brainstorming formats—listing or clustering—and brainstorm for ten minutes on the idea. Save your notes.

1. money	**3.** dreams	**5.** heroes/heroines
2. careers in science	**4.** favorite sport	**6.** nuclear energy

Suggested Answer: For example, for *acid-rain pollution* students might list dangers and then react to each.

Objective

EXERCISE 4. Brainstorming from Another Source. Page through a book, a magazine, or the Writer's Sourcebook (pages 346–347). Choose an illustration that interests you, and then brainstorm about it for ten minutes. Use whichever format is useful to you. Save your notes.

GENERATING IDEAS BY CHARTING

Charting helps you focus on specific life experiences in order to generate writing ideas.

When you are given a choice of subjects as a writing assignment, you can review your past experiences for writing ideas by charting. For example, in the following chart the writer developed three categories, or columns, for recording her past experiences. In the left column she listed general areas of experiences. In the center column she listed specific examples, or instances, for each of those general areas of experiences. Then, in the right column, she listed writing ideas suggested by each experience.

Sample Chart for Generating Writing Ideas

AREA OF EXPERIENCE	SPECIFIC INSTANCE	WRITING IDEA
FAMILY	• *Grandmother Stone (90 years old)*	• *character sketch* • *interview--then and now*
FRIENDS	• *Pauline*	• *How it takes time to develop a real friendship*
MEMORIES OF EARLY CHILDHOOD	• *first camping trip in the woods*	• *difficulties involved in family camping*
HOBBIES, FAVORITE SPORTS, INTERESTS	• *basketball* • *golf*	• *team competition vs. individual competition* • *mastering a difficult game--golf (see Nicklaus book)*
INTERESTING (FUNNY OR INFURIATING) EXPERIENCES	• *Losing my work inside the computer's memory*	• *computer frustrations and triumphs*
CURRENT EVENTS	• *starvation in Africa*	• *causes* • *What can I do about it?*
ASSIGNED READING, CLASSWORK	• *The Pearl* • *history--early explorers*	• *general truths that apply to us* • *mini-biography: Polo, Columbus, Magellan*
LEISURE READING, TELEVISION, FILMS	• *article on solar energy* • *Marco Polo feature in newspaper*	• *benefits/drawbacks* • *Polo's explorations of Asia*

Objective

EXERCISE 5. Generating Ideas by Charting. Create a chart for recording your own personal experiences. Use the three-column format on page 14. Copy the headings at the top of each column. In the left column you can copy the same general areas of experience or create your own. In the middle column write specific instances or personal examples for each general area you list. In the right column list writing ideas suggested by each personal experience. Save your notes for a later exercise.

GENERATING IDEAS BY OBSERVING

Observing helps you focus on specific details about persons, places, or events for an extended period of time in order to generate writing ideas.

You can use a concentrated, systematic method of observation to generate writing ideas. You simply have to train yourself to record details of what you see. Many of those details will be of a sensory nature related to sight, sound, smell, taste, and touch or feel.

Following is an example of how one writer used observation to generate a number of writing ideas. He had just seen a very exciting overtime basketball game, in which his school had won the state championship. As he was preparing to leave the gym, he was struck by the sudden silence. He began to list some details about the scene.

Observation Sample: List Format

1. *School gym*—fifteen minutes ago packed with cheering, jostling, frenzied fans and fast-paced, hectic action on the basketball floor—now empty and silent
2. *Sights*—candy wrappers, soft-drink cups, punctured balloons, ripped banners, torn program sheets; half-darkened gym, empty bleachers, an abandoned basketball in the remote corner of the gym
3. *Sounds*—the silent whir of the heating system clicking on and off, a fizzling from an overhead light, no other sounds—just the steady beat of silence

In the preceding observation list, the writer recorded specific details of the scene, mostly details that related to sight and sound. Another option is to sketch your scene, person, or object. In either method, listing or sketching, you should concentrate on capturing a dominant impression or a mood. If you wish, you can then use other prewriting techniques, particularly brainstorming, to generate additional writing ideas related to that dominant impression or mood.

Objective

EXERCISE 6. Generating Ideas by Observation. Choose a scene or a place, or choose one of the photographs from the Writer's Sourcebook (pages 346-347). Study it closely, concentrating on details, especially sensory details. Then record and list those details, as in the example on page 15. Make sure that your list includes the specific details of the scene and whatever other thoughts or writing ideas this impression suggests. Save your notes for a later exercise.

Objective

EXERCISE 7. Compiling Your Writing Ideas. Review the prewriting notes and writing ideas that you generated in Exercises 2–6 when you practiced freewriting, brainstorming, charting, and observing techniques. Evaluate your ideas and star at least five that really interest you and that you may want to write about later. Save your ideas and notes for a later exercise.

PREWRITING				
Generating Ideas	**Exploring Subjects**	Focusing on a Topic	Forming a Main Idea	Developing the Main Idea

EXPLORING SUBJECTS

Thus far you have experimented with a variety of techniques for generating writing ideas. At this point, however, you may not know the exact focus of your writing. In this section you will explore the writing ideas that most interest you. Through exploration you will begin to focus on a topic—one specific aspect of your subject or writing idea.

The following pages offer examples of the kinds of questions you can ask. You can use these questions or you can invent other questions that seem more appropriate to your subject.

EXPLORING A SUBJECT WITH INFORMATIONAL QUESTIONS

Reporters use some very basic questions when they gather information for a news story: *who? what? when? where? how?* and *why?* Then they use the answers to these five *W*s and *H* questions to write the lead paragraph for a story. You, too, can use or adapt the five *W*s and *H* questions to explore a subject. For example, the writer of the following chart used these informational questions to explore the subject of Marco Polo.

INFORMATIONAL QUESTIONS TO EXPLORE A SUBJECT	SAMPLE ANSWERS
1. Who or what is my subject? For human subjects: What kind of person is my subject?	*Marco Polo--thirteenth century Venetian trader, explorer, traveler, and "author" of The Description of the World; very little is known about him, only what is recorded in his book.*
2. What happened regarding my subject? What memorable incident(s) can I relate about my subject?	*Spent 24 years in China at court of Kublai Khan; returned to Venice rich; later captured during war between Venice and Genoa; imprisoned for several years (records spotty); dictated his travel adventures to the romance writer and fellow prisoner Rustichello; later published--Polo often criticized as a masterful liar and spinner of tall tales.*
3. When did these events occur? In what ways did my subject change over time?	*He lived from 1254 to 1324. Traveled in China from 1271–1295; then returned to Venice; captured and imprisoned in 1296(?) Wrote Description of the World, released in 1299.*
4. Where did all this happen?	*Venice, China, Genoa*
5. How did one or more of the events happen? (Is the information reliable?)	*No recorded biographical data about Marco Polo other than his book; was taken on the trip to China by his father and uncle, at age of 17; became the favorite of the Great Kublai Khan.*
6. Why did the event happen?	*Khan very inquisitive about the world outside his realm, used Polo as his "eyes."*
7. With whom can I compare my subject?	*Columbus, Magellan (roughly contemporary); more known about them*

Objective

EXERCISE 8. Exploring a Subject with Informational Questions. Choose one of the writing ideas or subjects that you starred in Exercise 7. Then explore the subject by adapting and answering the informational questions from the preceding chart. Save your notes.

EXPLORING A SUBJECT WITH PERSONAL QUESTIONS

If your subject is of a personal nature—for example, an experience you have had—then you can explore it with questions like the ones in the following chart.

PERSONAL QUESTIONS TO EXPLORE A SUBJECT	SAMPLE ANSWERS
1. What are my own experiences with the subject? my most memorable experience?	*Many camping, hiking, fishing experiences, too many to list; most memorable: the day I caught and released a four-pound rainbow trout*
2. Where and when did the experience take place?	*Late October, end of fishing season, had just turned seventeen; on the Russian River, redwood territory in northern California*
3. Why was the experience so memorable to me?	*Had caught hundreds of trout in ten years of fishing, but that was the first one I ever released*
4. What were my emotions during the experience?	*Three emotions really: 1) had never caught a trout that large before, was ecstatic; 2) confusion, something inside told me to release it, but didn't want to, had to; 3) felt older, wiser as I released it and watched it swim off*
5. What did I learn from the experience?	*Learned or understood for the first time the principle of conservation: If you want to continue to fish, learn to conserve, protect, and set wildlife free.*

Objective

EXERCISE 9. Exploring a Subject Through Personal Questions. Choose one subject, either from the list you made in Exercise 7 or from the list that follows. On a separate sheet of paper, explore the subject by asking and answering personal questions like those in the chart above. Save your notes.

1. a person whom you admire
2. the most important lesson you have learned as a teen-ager
3. a hobby, sport, or activity that you consider exciting and valuable
4. something which is absolutely essential to modern living

Suggested Answer: For example, for *a person whom you admire,* students might make notes about the person's appearance or accomplishments.

EXPLORING A SUBJECT WITH CREATIVE QUESTIONS

Another way to explore a subject is to look at it from an unusual angle or unconventional viewpoint. Here is an example of how a writer used creative questions to explore the subject of future inventions and their effect on life, a subject he found while freewriting and brainstorming.

CREATIVE QUESTIONS TO EXPLORE A SUBJECT	SAMPLE ANSWERS
1. What might be an unusual way of looking at my subject? (For example, how might someone from the 18th Century view it?)	• *What would George Washington say about galactic cruisers or interstellar bikes?* • *Could Ben Franklin improve hearing-aid-type computers?*
2. What story, real or imagined, could revolve around my subject?	• *Star Wars/Star Trek type stories* • *Success stories--first person to establish an intergallactic chain of fast-food/energy-refill stations*
3. How would life be changed by my subject?	• *Robots would perform many laborious tasks we humans now do.*
4. What might be humorous about my subject?	• *How some future inventions become outmoded--for example, winged shoes replace spaceships.*
5. How might my subject be represented in music? painting? film?	• *Painting--a painting equipped with a computerized brain that constantly transforms the painting.*

Objective

EXERCISE 10. Exploring a Subject Through Creative Questions. Choose one of the following subjects or one that you listed for Exercise 7. Use a separate sheet of paper, and explore your subject by posing and answering creative questions like those above or others that you have made up. Save your notes.

1. a pencil
2. Kennedy Space Center
3. radio
4. Halley's comet
5. the White House
6. a rock band or singer
7. sports event
8. airplanes
9. dinosaurs
10. the sun

Suggested Answers: For example, the answers to *Halley's Comet* might include the following: story—scientists attach a satellite to the comet's tail.

EXPLORING SUBJECTS WITH ANALYTICAL QUESTIONS

Another way to explore a subject is to examine it analytically. Analytical questions usually asked about a subject's structure or its relationships. When exploring a subject, you can use some of the analytical questions shown here, or you can invent your own questions.

ANALYTICAL QUESTIONS TO EXPLORE A SUBJECT	SAMPLE ANSWERS
1. What are some of the most important features of my subject? What parts can I divide it into?	• *features depend upon the invention and upon its success or failure, its acceptance or rejection* • *a number of possible divisions: past/present/future inventions; successful and unsuccessful inventions*
2. What can I compare or contrast my subject to?	• *why an invention becomes successful vs. why one is unsuccessful; past inventions that changed the course of life (auto) vs. future inventions that will likely change life (robot)*
3. What does my subject cause? What *could* it cause?	• *could trace the influence of one invention, such as the car and how it led to a series of changes in environment, in lifestyle, and in personal attitudes or perceptions*
4. What larger whole or bigger picture is my subject a part of?	• *the quality of life; how civilizations change over time, culturally, physically, and philosophically*

Remember that these analytical questions are only examples. Always ask yourself analytical questions that fit the nature of your subject and that will help you analyze specific aspects of your subject.

Objective

EXERCISE 11. Exploring a Subject Through Analytical Questions. Choose one subject from the list you made in Exercise 7. Use a separate sheet of paper, and explore that subject through analytic questions like those listed above. Save your notes.

PREWRITING				
Generating Ideas	Exploring Subjects	Focusing on a Topic	Forming a Main Idea	Developing the Main Idea

FOCUSING ON A TOPIC

In this section you will begin to focus on a writing topic and will learn to narrow its scope so that you can write about it in a single paragraph.

CHOOSING AND NARROWING A TOPIC

You can narrow a topic in many ways. The writer whose original subject was Marco Polo reviewed her exploring notes (page 17) and found a number of possible writing topics. She was particularly interested in whether she could determine the nature of Polo's book—was it fact or fiction? She knew, however, that many scholars had spent years working on that issue and that the topic was too broad for a single paragraph treatment. Her topic needed to be narrower. So she focused on only one aspect of the book, the collaborative writing of the book by Marco Polo and Rustichello. She further narrowed her topic to focus on how Rustichello, the writer of many romances, influenced the factual quality of Polo's narrative. The process of narrowing her topic looks like this:

GENERAL SUBJECT: the life of Marco Polo
NARROWER TOPIC: Polo's book—fact or fiction?
NARROWER TOPIC: how it was written
STILL NARROWER: Rustichello's influence

Objective
EXERCISE 12. Narrowing Topics. For each of the following groups indicate in writing which is the narrowest.

1. **a.** how a canal lock operates
   b. the Erie Canal
   c. inland water transportation in the United States
2. **a.** American coins
   b. money through the ages
   c. New England's pine tree shilling

Answers: **1.** a; **2.** c.

Objective
EXERCISE 13. Focusing on Your Topic. Choose a subject that you explored in Exercises 8–11. Narrow it so that it can be covered in a single written paragraph. Save a copy of your narrowed topic.

PREWRITING				
Generating Ideas	Exploring Subjects	Focusing on a Topic	**Forming a Main Idea**	Developing the Main Idea

FORMING A MAIN IDEA

After generating and exploring a writing idea and then narrowing the scope of the idea, the next step is to form a **main idea** about the narrowed topic. Before you actually state a main idea, you need to consider:

- your **purpose**—what you hope to accomplish in your writing
- your **audience**—the person or people who will read your writing

THINKING ABOUT PURPOSE

At this point you should identify and clarify that purpose by asking and answering the following questions:

1. Why do I want to write about this specific topic?
2. Is my purpose to **inform** my readers about something or to **explain** something to them?
3. Is my purpose to **persuade** them of my opinion, to change their minds about an issue, or to urge them to take some action?
4. Is my purpose to **amuse** or **entertain** them?
5. Is my purpose to **narrate** a story or an anecdote?
6. Is my purpose to **describe** a person, place, or thing?
7. Is my purpose some **combination** of these different goals? For example, do I want to persuade my readers by informing them of some startling facts about an issue?

The writer who worked on the topic of future inventions clarified his purpose and listed several alternative purposes.

SUBJECT	NARROWED TOPIC	ALTERNATIVE PURPOSES
future inventions	*robots--influence on life*	• *to explain how robots will change human activities in the future* • *describe a personal home robot* • *to persuade readers that robots will radically change our lifestyles that we should prepare for such change now*

Objective

EXERCISE 14. Thinking About Purpose. Read each of the following writing topics. Then write at least two possible writing purposes for each topic.

1. the invention of paper
2. learning how to drive a car
3. nuclear waste disposal
4. the importance of a balanced diet

Suggested Answers: For example, for *the invention of paper,* answers could include explaining the importance of the invention.

BECOMING AWARE OF AN AUDIENCE

In addition to a writing purpose, you also should be attentive to your **audience**—your intended reader or readers. You address a wide variety of audiences: a teacher, friends, family, and various people business or social contexts. In each writing situation, you need to adjust what you say to suit your particular audience.

You can begin to develop an awareness of your audience by studying the following questions and using them at the prewriting stage of any writing project. Note that the sample answers are by the writer who is planning to write on the subject of conservation.

QUESTIONS ABOUT AUDIENCE	SAMPLE ANSWERS
1. Am I writing for a general audience or a special audience, such as my peers or young children?	*For a class assignment. Therefore, I have to assume my audience is my fellow students.*
2. What do I want to say to this audience specifically?	*I want to share a single experience I had while fishing. I want them to be able to understand what I learned about conservation and how I felt when I released the trout.*
3. How much do my readers already know about my topic? What information will they need?	*My peers probably vary in their knowledge of fishing. I will try to avoid any technical or fishing jargon.*
4. What areas of my topic are likely to interest them most?	*Because they are my peers, they may be very interested in how I matured during this experience.*
5. What firm ideas about my topic might they already have? What preconceptions, objections, or prejudices do I need to counteract?	*Probably only one--the same one I had before I released the fish. I'll have to emphasize, somehow, that preserving is more important than killing--hence, "conservation."*

QUESTIONS ABOUT AUDIENCE	SAMPLE ANSWERS
6. What particular techniques would help accomplish my purpose with this audience? Would a humorous tone, for example, be effective or inappropriate?	*Should be a serious tone, not aloof but serious. Telling the sequences of events as they happened should do it.*

Objective

EXERCISE 15. Thinking About Audience. For each of the following topics, identify in writing a specific, intended audience.

1. how to prepare for the SAT exam
2. the dangers of smoking
3. why your school needs a new gym
4. changes in the tax laws that will affect large corporations

Suggested Answers: 1. high school students; 2. teen-agers; 3. the town council; 4. corporate officials

STATING THE MAIN IDEA

After narrowing your topic and focusing on an audience and a purpose, you should write your **main idea**—the main thought that you will develop in your paragraph. This is a very important step because the main idea directs the remainder of the paragraph. It indicates what kind of information and details will follow. Thus it helps direct you when you write your paragraph.

Your main idea should be stated in sentence form. As you form a main idea about your topic, consider these points:

1. Your main idea should interest both you and your audience.
2. Your main idea should convey some key point about your topic.
3. You should be able to develop your main idea adequately in a single paragraph.
4. Your main idea should clearly convey your purpose.

Throughout this chapter we have followed several writers through various prewriting stages. The writer who chose conservation as his topic developed the following main ideas.

ORIGINAL SUBJECT: Conservation
FINAL, NARROWED TOPIC: My first release of a fish
PURPOSE: To narrate
AUDIENCE: Peer group
MAIN IDEA: The first time I released a prize fish, I discovered the real meaning of conservation.

Objective

EXERCISE 16. Forming Your Main Idea. Reread the topic that you narrowed in Exercise 13 on page 21. Write two possible purposes and audiences for your topic. Then, for each purpose-audience pair, write a main idea that could be developed in a single paragraph. Save your notes for a later exercise.

PREWRITING				
Generating Ideas	Exploring Subjects	Focusing on a Topic	Forming a Main Idea	Developing the Main Idea

DEVELOPING THE MAIN IDEA

When you write a paragraph, you will use your main-idea statement as the central focus of the paragraph. The remainder of the paragraph will **develop**—express, prove, clarify, and expand upon —that main idea.

You can find some of these support items in your prewriting notes. You should review your notes and select relevant and supporting facts, details, examples, incidents, and reasons. In addition, you will probably need to create more items that support your main idea. You may even have to research other sources to find additional supporting facts, details, and examples.

SPECIFIC SUPPORT: FACTS, SENSORY DETAILS, EXAMPLES, INCIDENTS, REASONS

The main idea of a paragraph needs specific support. Without that support, it is unlikely that your audience will fully understand or believe your main-idea statement. When you review your prewriting notes or search other resources for additional support items, you should concentrate on finding the following:

- **facts**—objective statements that can be proven by experience, observation, or study
- **sensory details**—concrete, specific features of an item or an experience
- **examples**—particular cases or instances of a larger pattern
- **incidents**—particular events
- **reasons**—logical arguments used to support an opinion or interpretation

Following is an example of the various kinds of specific support that one writer listed for her main idea.

MAIN IDEA: Rustichello, Marco Polo's collaborator and recorder, influenced the factual quality of Polo's book.

SUPPORT:
- Polo and Rustichello were in prison together for several years during the latter stages of the war between Venice and Genoa, 1296(?)–1299. (FACT)
- Rustichello had previously written a number of Arthurian romances. (FACT)
- They agreed to collaborate on a book about Polo's China adventures, entitling the book *Description of the World.* (FACT)
- Using his travel notes, Polo narrated the story while Rustichello recorded the narrative. (FACT)
- Rustichello's romantic style surfaces throughout Polo's book. (REASON)
- Polo's introduction to Kublai Khan is similar to Rustichello's earlier tale about King Arthur and Tristan at Camelot. (EXAMPLE)
- Descriptions of Asiatic battles resemble Knights of the Round Table combats. (EXAMPLES)

Objective

EXERCISE 17. Developing a Main Idea with Specific Support. Read the notes that follow on the subject of the meaning of conservation. First, write the *type* of support that each numbered item is: fact, sensory detail, example, incident, or reason. Then write at least two new items that could support the main idea.

MAIN IDEA: I discovered one meaning of conservation while on a recent fishing trip.

SUPPORT:
1. I was fishing for trout on the Russian River.
2. The river silently slipped and curved around my waders as I cast into pools, eddies, and ripples.
3. A fish struck, my rod bent, and the combat began.
4. I eased a silver-sided, rose-spotted trout into my net.
5. I had caught and killed hundreds of fish in the past.
6. I held the fish under the water until it revived, and then let it go.
7. At that instant, I understood a principle of conservation: If you kill a fish, it will no longer be in the river.

Suggested Answers: Facts—items **1** and **5**; sensory details—items **2** and **4**; example—item **7**; incidents—items **3** and **6**

Objective

EXERCISE 18. Developing your Main Idea with Specific Support. Choose one of the main ideas that you formed in Exercise 16. For it, list at least five supporting items. Try to use as many different kinds of support—facts, incidents, sensory details, examples, or reasons—as you can. Save your notes and list for a later exercise.

LOOKING BACK AND LOOKING AHEAD

Although you have been doing prewriting exercises throughout this chapter, you have also done a fair amount of actual writing. The work you have done has provided you with valuable raw material, which you are now ready to shape into a first draft. Your prewriting work should make writing the first draft a much easier task.

CHECKLIST FOR PREWRITING

1. What writing ideas can I generate through such techniques as freewriting, brainstorming, and charting? Can I combine any of these techniques?
2. Would informational, personal, or creative questions, or some combination of questions work best to explore my subject? What topics within my subject can I identify by exploring it?
3. Which topic most appeals to me? How can I narrow that topic? Can I focus on one incident in a person's life, use one experience to illustrate something larger, focus on a single aspect or feature of a topic, or identify a problem in the subject and solve it? Would some other method work for narrowing my topic?
4. What is my purpose? Who is my audience? What main idea about my topic will accomplish my purpose and appeal to my audience?
5. What specific facts, sensory details, incidents, examples, and reasons can I use to support and develop my main idea?

LOOKING AHEAD TO WRITING A FIRST DRAFT

Throughout this chapter you examined the prewriting work of several writers. Each writer probably spent no more than one or two hours generating ideas, exploring various subjects, narrowing a topic, and then forming, developing, and supporting a main idea. Each writer thoroughly prepared herself or himself to write a first draft. Following are two of the first-draft paragraphs that they wrote. Notice that these writers have not used all the prewriting notes they recorded. In fact, they excluded many previous thoughts, combined others, and added new ones in their first drafts.

Marco Polo and Rustichello's Book: History or Fantasy? (First Draft)

Marco Polo's book, *Description of the World,* is a highly imaginative personal narrative of his twenty-four years in thirteenth-century China. A number of people in Polo's time thought his narrative too imaginative to be real. While in prison, Polo wrote the book with a collaborator named Rustichello. The latter was an experienced writer of Arthurian romances—tales about the Knights of the Round Table. Using his travel notes, Polo dictated his experiences, and Rustichello wrote and recorded them. However, Rustichello did not simply record the narrative; he "improved" it with his distinctly romantic style. Many of the descriptions of Asiatic battles witnessed by Polo read like the glorious combats of the Knights of the Round Table. The description of Polo's introduction to the Great Kublai Kahn is very similar to Rustichello's romantic tale in which King Arthur greets the young Tristan at Camelot. In fact, the opening lines of Polo's book are almost exactly word for word from a Rustichello Round Table tale: "Lords, Emperors and Kings, Dukes and Marquesses, counts, knights. . . ." None of this means that Polo's book was pure imaginative fiction or that it was a lie. However, it does point to Rustichello's influence on the narrative and to his imaginative embellishment of Polo's facts from time to time.

What Is Conservation: (First Draft)

Wildlife conservation means different things to different people, but I discovered one meaning while on a recent fishing trip. I was fishing for trout on the Russian River in the redwoods territory of northern California. The river silently slipped and curved around my waders as I cast into pools, eddies, and ripples. Suddenly a fish struck, my rod bent like a bow, and the combat began. Twenty minutes later I carefully eased a sparkling, silver-sided, rose-spotted, four-pound rainbow trout into my nylon net. I removed the tiny artificial fly from the corner of its hook-jawed lip and stared at the tired, struggling form. I had caught and killed hundreds of trout in ten years of fishing but never one of such mammoth, almost primitive size. I do not know why I did what I did next; I had never done it before, but something inside urged me. I held the huge fish in my hands and carefully, slowly began to move it back and forth beneath the water's surface. The movement restored the fish, and so I released it. I felt confused but somehow older, wiser, as I watched the trout slowly slip into the current—alive, free. At that instant I understood a principle of conservation: If you kill a fish, it will no longer be in the river. Conservation is action—conserving, protecting, restoring, and, in this case, freeing.

WRITER'S CHOICE #1

ASSIGNMENT: To write a paragraph using the main idea and support items that you listed in Exercise 18.
LENGTH: Ten to twelve sentences
AUDIENCE: One of the audiences you selected in Exercise 16
PURPOSE: One of the purposes you selected in Exercise 16
PREWRITING: Review your prewriting notes from Exercises 7–11, 13, 16, and 18 in this chapter. If you have worked carefully through the sequence of exercises in this chapter, then your notes for exercise 18 should contain all the prewriting information you will need for writing a first draft.

WRITER'S CHOICE #2

ASSIGNMENT: To write about how one invention often opens the way to a series of related inventions
LENGTH: Ten to twelve sentences
AUDIENCE: The general public
PURPOSE: To inform and to persuade
PREWRITING: First, freewrite or brainstorm about a variety of past inventions. Concentrate on inventions that are linked in some way: wheel—*cart*—automobile—*freeways*—motels. Then choose one invention and explore it by asking informational questions like those on page 17 and analytic questions like those on page 20. Write down your main idea, and list details that support your main idea.

WRITER'S CHOICE #3

ASSIGNMENT: Your choice
LENGTH: Your choice
AUDIENCE: Your choice
PURPOSE: Your choice
OPTIONS:

- You might use one of the illustrations in the Writer's Sourcebook on pages 346–347 to give you some writing ideas.
- You might use the prewriting notes on page 19 to write a paragraph on the influence of robots on life in the future. Include the benefits and drawbacks of robots.
- Use any prewriting techniques to generate and explore writing ideas.
- Decide on a purpose and an audience, and develop one main idea.

THE WRITER

Steve Zinck divides his time among his main interests: music, sports, and schoolwork. As a student at Rangeview High school in Aurora, Colorado, he wrote the following paper about playing rock guitar. Read Steve's finished product, and then look at "The Writer at Work," in which he explains his prewriting activities.

THE FINISHED PRODUCT

To many people's surprise, rock guitar uses a wider variety of musical styles and techniques than any other type of guitar playing. In particular, rock guitar has developed its own unique—and outrageous—playing techniques.

One of the most recent and popular rock guitar techniques is two-handed fret-board playing. Instead of using the right hand to strum, as most guitarists do, the rock guitarist uses this hand to play notes on the fret board just as the left hand does. The masters of this technique can play both a bass line and a harmony at the same time, thus making the sound of two or three guitars at once. Guitarists less developed in this skill can still play more notes at a faster progression than guitarists who play in the regular way.

One especially colorful rock guitar technique is mainly a crowd pleaser, but a good guitarist can produce many sounds from it: playing the guitar with the mouth. For a more biting, stomach-wrenching effect, guitarists can slide their teeth back and forth across the strings. To get the sound of an elephant herd, they simply blow on all the strings with varying breaths.

These techniques may sound ridiculous, but true rock guitarists can and do use them effectively to produce the sounds they want. However, these techniques must be handled with skill; if overused, they can turn music into cacophony!

THE WRITER AT WORK

Choosing a subject was really quite simple for me. Since I could write about anything I wanted, I decided on something that is very familiar to me: guitar music. However, I had some trouble deciding which aspect of guitar music I wanted to write about, for I could write about the guitar's origins, its role in music, how a guitar is made, or how one is played. I settled on this last topic.

Then I had to break my topic down even more and decide which genre of guitar playing I would explain. This part was probably the most difficult for me since I am familiar with playing many kinds of guitar music. Eventually, I chose to write about rock guitar because of its more outrageous techniques. My last step in narrowing my topic was to decide which parts of rock guitar playing I would discuss. I thought it best to skip the basics and get right to the more exciting techniques of rock guitar.

Once I had all this worked out, it was quite easy for me to start writing. I just wrote the paper straight through without stopping too many times for revisions. The next day, when I could look at the paper from a fresh perspective, I reread it and changed some of the ideas around so that the paper would flow more easily.

YOUR TURN **Prewriting About a Special Interest**

Steve began with a broad subject about which he knew a great deal; he narrowed down this subject by deciding to write about one of its more "outrageous" aspects. Take a special interest of your own, and narrow it down to one particularly unusual aspect. Decide on your purpose and audience, and write a statement expressing your main idea. Then write a paragraph or two developing that main idea.

3 CHAPTER
Writing the Paragraph

I can see but one rule: to be clear.

–Stendahl

PREWRITING	WRITING	REVISING

Stendhal's single rule about effective writing is deceptively simple. However, in order for a piece of writing to be clear, a writer usually winds through a fairly long and experimental process of prewriting, writing, and revising, every step of which is aimed at accomplishing that one goal.

In any given piece of writing, you usually create paragraphs in order to group and communicate your main ideas. What would happen to the clarity of a piece of writing if its paragraphs were to become fused? For example, read the following passage about Henry Ford, whose Model T car changed the world.

The early history of Ford has been revolutionary. He had risen to unparalleled wealth and power while fighting reaction every step of the way. Early in the century he had advocated government ownership of the telephone and telegraph systems and had urged permanent federal public work programs. In 1919 he sided with strikers against the steel industry, assailing [J. P.] Morgan for dictating the labor policies of US Steel and blaming him for the violent turn the strike took. He called private ownership the curse of the railroad system and said major trunk lines should be socialized. The utilities, he said, were being operated not for the social good but for the benefit of parasites holding stocks and bonds . . .¶Ford saw himself as the benefactor of working people, helping provide them with an honest livelihood. He hired ex-convicts without a qualm and found that work reformed them. He believed, almost alone, in equal work opportunities for blacks. "I don't want any more than my share of money," Ford said, "I'm going to get rid of it–to use it all to build more and more factories, to give as many people as I can the chance to be prosperous."¶Nothing had shaken the foundations as much as his Five-Dollar Day. When he announced in 1914 that he would pay this sum to all his workers, tremors went through the industry. With a single stroke, he had doubled the wages of labor. The *Wall Street Journal* denounced the move as an economic crime. It was assailed as immoral and socialistic; it was said that the working class would be undermined and discontented by so much money. Ford's name was cursed wherever the wealthy congregated. The only consolation for them was that Ford had gone too far this time and would soon be shown for the fool he was.¶Against this opposition, however, Ford had reshaped the American economy and had created the twentieth-century consumer. He was selling a mass product and could not succeed by selling his autos only to the wealthy, so he cut prices and raised wages and produced his own customers. The move affected not only his cars but an entire economic system.

—Warren Sloat, *1929, America Before the Crash*

Obviously this passage develops a number of main ideas. The writer of this passage, news reporter Warren Sloat, originally organized the passage as four distinct paragraphs. Can you find where each of the four paragraphs actually begins and ends?

As you looked for the beginning and ending of each of the four paragraphs, you may have looked for groups of sentences that related to a main idea. If you did, your search was very similar to the writer's process in putting together each paragraph. He grouped sentences around a *main idea* or *topic sentence.* Then he refined the *development* of that topic sentence. During that development, he aimed for *unity*—each sentence relating directly to the topic sentence. He worked toward *coherence*—each sentence connecting to the other sentences. He developed a clear *organization.* By the way, Warren Sloat, the author of passage about Henry Ford, began new paragraphs at lines 13, 21, and 32.

This chapter is designed to make you even more alert to the qualities of good paragraphs. The chapter focuses on the following stages of the writing process, each of which contributes to a single purpose—to help you to write clearly:

- topic sentences
- developing a topic sentence
- writing a unified paragraph
- writing a coherent paragraph
- writing opening and closing sentences
- organizing a paragraph

WRITING THE PARAGRAPH				
Topic Sentences	Developing a Topic Sentence into a Paragraph	Writing a Unified Paragraph	Writing a Coherent Paragraph	Organizing a Paragraph

TOPIC SENTENCES

A **topic sentence** states the main idea of a paragraph and points the direction for the other sentences to follow.

A topic sentence makes the main idea of the paragraph immediately clear to the reader. It also enables the reader to follow the supporting sentences. A topic sentence somewhat resembles a summary or a generalization. Consider the underlined topic sentence in the following paragraph.

> Traveling to the moon is easy enough, but traveling to the nearest star presents some significant problems. Our present spaceships have limited speeds, and a trip to the nearest star might take 80,000 years. Star travelers would definitely have a problem with ageing. Some scientists have proposed extended hibernation, or the freezing of travelers, on star ships. However, such techniques have yet to be perfected. Of course, star trips could be speeded up by building more powerful, nuclear reactor-driven spaceships. However, nuclear reactors would have to be sanitized first—that is, made safe. Nature itself seems to present a problem for speedy star treks. At the moment, there is an absolute speed limit, the velocity of light. To shorten the length of time traveling to the nearest star may require somehow exceeding that absolute speed limit. Of course, no one knows how to accomplish that.

In the preceding paragraph, the underlined topic sentence states the main idea of the paragraph—the problematic nature of traveling to the nearest star. Then the supporting sentences that follow the topic sentence give specific examples of the main idea—specific problems associated with traveling to the nearest star.

You may find that not every paragraph needs a topic sentence. In general, most narrative paragraphs in a short story do not have a topic sentence. Some expository paragraphs in an essay or a report do not have topic sentences; the main idea in such paragraphs may be so clear that a summary statement or generalization is not needed. In this case the writer uses an **implied topic sentence**. Although many professional writers do not always use topic sentences, you should understand that topic sentences can be helpful both to your reader and to you as a writer.

Some topic sentences are more useful than others to the writer. Some can be too general and vague, giving you little direction on where to go and what main idea to develop within the paragraph. On the other hand, a clear and direct topic sentence will point the specific direction you should follow in your paragraph; it will also help you organize the informational details of your paragraph. For example, look again at the paragraph about the problem of traveling to stars. Then compare the following two topic sentences.

TOPIC SENTENCE A: Traveling to the moon is easy enough, but traveling to the nearest star presents some significant problems.

TOPIC SENTENCE B: Space travel is difficult.

Why is Sentence A a better topic sentence than Sentence B for a paragraph about the problems of star travel? Consider the questions and sample answers on the following checklist.

CHECKLIST FOR EVALUATING TOPIC SENTENCES

1. What is the one main idea presented by the topic sentence?

   Sentence A presents a comparison of space travel to the moon and space travel to the stars. Sentence B focuses on the difficulty of space travel.

2. Is the main idea of the paragraph presented as clearly and as directly as possible? If not, what elements do not belong in the topic sentence?

   Both topic sentences are clear and direct.

3. Is the topic sentence an overgeneralization; that is, does it make a statement too broad to be useful in understanding the paragraph? Or is the topic sentence too narrow in focus?

   Sentence A is a generalization that stresses the two main points being compared in the paragraph. Sentence B is too broad and unspecific to provide a solid introduction to the paragraph.

4. Do all the other sentences in the paragraph take their direction and focus from the topic sentence?

   Sentence A is sufficiently general to lead in to the variety of points in the paragraph. Sentence B is too unspecific; it does not clarify at the outset what the paragraph is about.

VARIETY OF TOPIC SENTENCES

When you write a topic sentence, keep your audience and your writing purpose in mind. Most of your topic sentences will probably be direct informational statements that convey your purpose to your audience. However, in addition to direct declarative sentences you can use other types of topic sentences to communicate your main idea. Here are some examples:

Question

Did you know that traveling to the nearest star, unlike an easy trek to the moon, presents significant problems?

Question and Answer

Is traveling to the nearest star as easy a trip as traveling to the moon? No, trips to the nearest star present some significant problems.

Two-Sentence Topic Sentence

Traveling to the moon may be an easy task. However, traveling to the nearest star presents some significant problems.

Command

Think about how easy it is to travel to the moon, and then about the significant problems of traveling to the nearest star!

Objective

EXERCISE 1. Writing a Variety of Topic Sentences. Choose a topic of your own or one of the following topics below. Write several different topic sentences for a paragraph on that topic: a statement, a question, a command, and a two sentence version. Clearly identify your purpose—to inform, persuade, entertain, narrate, or describe. Assume that your audience is the general public.

1. crazy fads
2. a major award
3. the benefits of leisure
4. traveling to other countries

Suggested Answers: Two topic sentences for #1: a) Teenagers are often victims of crazy fads. b) What is the craziest fad of all?

PLACEMENT OF TOPIC SENTENCES

Generally, you can place your topic sentence in various positions in your paragraph: at or near the beginning; in the middle; or at the end. You have already seen various topic sentences placed at the beginning of a paragraph (pages 34 and 36). When a topic sentence appears at or near the beginning of a paragraph, it immediately captures the reader's attention and alerts the reader to what will follow the main idea. When the topic sentence comes in the middle of a paragraph, it acts as a bridge between the ideas and details that come before and after it. In the middle position, the topic sentence unites the sentences, details, and ideas. A topic sentence at the end of a paragraph often summarizes the details and ideas that come before it. In the end position, it often works as a **clincher sentence** by tying together all the previous ideas and details and ensuring that your reader grasps your *main* idea.

When you write, you should experiment with the position of your topic sentence. Move it around, to see where it will be the most effective. The following two paragraphs contain essentially the same topic sentence placed in two different positions. What advantages do you see to each placement?

Topic Sentence in the Middle

Some people criticize large cities for their noise and traffic and crowded sidewalks. They do not like to hear sirens blaring at a decibel level capable of breaking eardrums. They do not like to stand in line for hours waiting to see a bank teller or to be seated in a restaurant. Have these people forgotten the benefits of living in a large city? Only large cities can afford to support museums, symphony orchestras, football teams, and other groups of cultural or social merit. Only large cities can supply the diversity of jobs and educational institutions that add to the quality of life.

Topic Sentence at the End

Some people criticize large cities for their noise and traffic and crowded sidewalks. They do not like to hear sirens blaring at a decibel level capable of breaking eardrums. They do not like to stand in line for hours waiting to see a bank teller or to be seated in a restaurant. Only large cities, though, can afford to support museums, symphony orchestras, football teams, and other groups of cultural or social merit. Only large cities can supply the diversity of jobs and educational institutions that add to the quality of life. Some people have forgotten the benefits of living in a large city.

These two paragraphs contain the same information, but the placement of the topic sentence affects how the reader sees and understands that information. The topic sentence in the middle of the paragraph links information about the negative aspects of big-city life with the benefits of living in a large city and helps to establish the contrast the writer intended. When the topic sentence appears at the end of the paragraph, it acts as a summary statement, a clincher sentence that adds a strong twist to the end of the second paragraph. The clincher sentence reinforces the writer's contention that the advantages of living in a big city outweigh the disadvantages.

Objective

EXERCISE 2. Placing Topic Sentences. Choose a factual paragraph from your history or science text or from a magazine article. Be sure that it has a topic sentence. Then move the topic sentence to different positions in the paragraph. Write a brief description of the effect the change in position has on the paragraph.

WRITING THE PARAGRAPH				
Topic Sentences	**Developing a Topic Sentence into a Paragraph**	Writing a Unified Paragraph	Writing a Coherent Paragraph	Organizing a Paragraph

DEVELOPING A TOPIC SENTENCE INTO A PARAGRAPH

When you develop a topic sentence into a complete paragraph, you use supporting sentences to prove, clarify, or expand upon your main idea. Because a topic sentence is a kind of summary statement or generalization, it needs specific support in order for a reader to believe or fully understand it. Five of the most common kinds of support—or methods of development—for a topic sentence are (1) concrete details; (2) examples or incidents; (3) facts or statistics; and (4) reasons; or (5) a combination of methods. On the next few pages, you will follow several different writers through the process of developing topic sentences into paragraphs. Each writer uses one of the preceding methods of development.

TOPIC SENTENCE DEVELOPED WITH CONCRETE DETAILS

The first writer used concrete sensory details—features that you see, feel or touch, hear, smell, or taste—to develop her paragraph. First she listed details about a favorite pond. Then she wrote a main idea related to the details.

Concrete Details

- surrounded by craggy cliffs, stately white pines
- shimmering, cold pure water
- reflects blue sky, a mirror
- other sounds—rush of nearby stream, wild geese, piercing cry of loon
- sweet smell of campfire, burning apple wood

MAIN IDEA: Camping at Jordan Pond is the ultimate escape from the hectic urban world.

Using her prewriting notes, the writer then developed the following paragraph. Notice how she supports her main idea with concrete sensory details.

Camping at Jordan Pond is the ultimate escape from the hectic urban world. It is almost like entering a timeless, primitive region. The pond itself is nestled in the palm of a valley, surrounded by craggy cliffs and stately white pine trees. The cold, pure water of the pond shimmers and reflects overhead the blue sky and passing clouds. There is a consuming silence at Jordan Pond, only occasionally punctuated by the trickling sound of a nearby stream, honking wild geese, or the piercing cry of the solitary loon. The sweet smell of burning apple wood rises from my campfire and drifts lazily, curling through the ultimate peace.

Objective

EXERCISE 3. Developing a Topic Sentence with Concrete Details. Write a paragraph using concrete details to develop the following topic sentence, or write about a topic of your own choice. Be sure to reread and revise your paragraph after writing it.

TOPIC SENTENCE: Last night's blizzard was terrifying.

CONCRETE DETAILS

- began as a light flurry of falling flakes
- quickly became a torrential, frenzied blizzard
- screeching, howling wind
- abandoned cars, trucks, buses
- blinding, furiously, whipping snow
- buried the city in a glistening white landscape
- erased the smell of the city—smoky, polluted, gaseous air driven out, purified

TOPIC SENTENCE DEVELOPED WITH EXAMPLES OR INCIDENTS

A topic sentence can also be supported by specific examples or incidents that clarify the main idea. In the following example, the writer used her prewriting notes and main idea to develop a paragraph with examples or incidents as supporting sentences.

Examples or Incidents

- 1849: the Great California Gold Rush in full bloom
- New Englanders: in schooners by way of the Horn or by sea to Panama, across the isthmus by land, then to San Francisco by ship
- Southerners: overland through Mexico or Texas

* Others: across mid-continent, 2,000 miles
* Many obstacles: desert, mountains, starvation

MAIN IDEA: In 1849 the discovery of gold threw people into a feverish pitch.

In 1849 gold fever seemed to grip a large segment of the American population. Gold had been discovered in the Sierra foothills of California, and people throughout the country rushed to claim their dreams. They came from the East and the South, by sea and land, across stormy seas, wind-swept deserts, and rocky snow-packed mountains. New Englanders packed themselves into schooners and sailed around the Horn. Some sailed down to Panama, crossed the Isthmus overland, then shipped up to San Francisco. Many Southerners took the overland route through Mexico or Texas and across the Southwest. Still others slowly struggled along the 2,000 mile mid-continent route. Many died. Most suffered through dusty, oppressive heat and freezing, bitter cold. They suffered exhaustion and starvation. Yet the fever persisted.

Objective

EXERCISE 4. Developing a Topic Sentence with Examples or Incidents. Write a paragraph using examples or incidents to develop the following topic sentence, or develop a topic sentence of your own. Reread and revise your paragraph after writing it.

TOPIC SENTENCE: Adolescents have (or do not have) too much free time.

TOPIC SENTENCE DEVELOPED WITH FACTS OR STATISTICS

Using facts or statistics is one of the most common methods of supporting a topic sentence. A **fact** is a statement that has been proved by experience, observation, or study. **Statistics** are a particular type of fact—precise numerical information. In the following example, the writer used his prewriting notes and main idea to develop a paragraph with facts and statistics as support.

Facts and Statistics

* Potato Computer Company: 2 employees in 1975; one manufacturing plant, a garage
* sold 100 computers in 1977
* from 1977 to today revenues went from $25,000 to $250,000,000
* now controls 30% of home computer market
* over 200 plants, 200,000 employees today
* produced 1,000,000 computers last year

MAIN IDEA: The Potato Computer Company experienced rapid growth.

The Potato Computer Company is one of the fastest growing companies in the history of American business. In 1975 two people started the company in an unusual manufacturing plant—a home garage. From that home garage they produced and sold 100 home computers in two years. Then something happened in the computer market—the personal home computer became a necessity for many people. Potato Computers rolled off the assembly lines. That one-garage outfit grew into more than 200 cross-country manufacturing plants with 200,000 employees. In less than seven years sales rose from 100 to one million computers per year and from $25,000 to $250,000,000 in annual revenues. Today the Potato Computer Company controls nearly 30% of a potentially multi-billion dollar home computer market—a market that did not exist seven years ago.

Objective

EXERCISE 5. Developing a Topic Sentence with Facts or Statistics. Write a paragraph using facts or statistics to develop a topic sentence of your own, or use one of the following topic sentences. You may have to do some research to find supporting facts or statistics for your topic sentence.

1. The television set has become a very important part of modern life.
2. My favorite baseball team (or some other sport) had a very fine (or poor) season last year.
3. Saturn (or some other planet) is one of the strongest (or some other descriptive feature) planets in our solar system.

TOPIC SENTENCE DEVELOPED WITH REASONS

If your topic sentence expresses an opinion, you can develop that opinion with supporting sentences that give reasons for your opinion. Notice how this writer used reasons to support his opinion about the future growth of the Potato Computer Company.

Reasons

- many new competitors building home computers
- limited market; only a certain number of people want or need home computers
- many purchasers have discovered they do not use their home computers

MAIN IDEA: Potato Computer Company may not continue its rapid growth.

Although the Potato Computer Company has experienced rapid growth, forces in the computer market may limit its future growth. For one thing, Potato's success attracted the attention of many large American, English, German, and Japanese companies that have now entered the home computer business. They are strong competitors and will undoubtably take away sales from Potato. In addition, the home computer market is a very limited market; that is, not everyone needs or wants a home computer. New customers may be very difficult to find. Finally, there is the problem of the disenchanted customer. Unlike television sets, computers are rarely used twelve hours a day. Potato is not likely to convince those customers to buy a replacement computer.

Objective

EXERCISE 6. Developing a Topic Sentence with Reasons. Write a paragraph using reasons to develop one of the following topic sentences, or use a topic sentence of your own.

1. The most beneficial form of exercise is __________.
2. The modern family would be virtually helpless if its __________. were taken away.
3. There should be a strictly-enforced law against __________.

TOPIC SENTENCE DEVELOPED WITH MIXED SUPPORT

Another option you have when developing a topic sentence is to combine several different types of supporting sentences. You can use any combination of concrete details, examples or incidents, facts or statistics, and reasons in your supporting sentences.

Objective

EXERCISE 7. Developing a Topic Sentence with Mixed Support. Choose one of the following topic sentences or write a topic sentence of your own. Make a list of supporting details—concrete details, examples or incidents, and reasons. Use those details to write a paragraph that supports your main idea. Remember to reread and revise your written paragraph.

1. Friends can provide much needed support during a time of crisis.
2. The printing press (or some other invention) changed the history of the world.
3. California (or some other state) is a great place for a vacation.
4. The Chinese (or another ethnic group) have made significant contributions to the development of this country.

WRITING OPENING AND CLOSING SENTENCES

A well-developed paragraph needs both a strong topic sentence and directly-related supporting sentences. In addition, a good closing sentence can often make the paragraph even more effective. A strong closing statement gives the reader a sense of finality and completeness. Here are examples of various types of closing sentences.

Restating the Topic Sentence

When a writer restates the topic sentence in a closing statement, the writer rewords the main idea with a slightly different slant. Read this model, paying particular attention to how the writer reworded the main idea in the underlined closing statement.

During the 1960s many major American cities were on the brink of becoming urban wastelands. Crumbling buildings, rotted waterfronts, pot-holed streets, and heavily polluted air space made the cities look physically ill. Transportation was, at best, only slightly faster and more efficient than walking. The ancient, battered buses and trains suffered the daily seizures of a patient struggling with a severe illness. The price of city rents, food and entertainment skyrocketed. Even the cities themselves could not afford to exist; many were financially bankrupt. <u>Complete and utter disaster seemed imminent for these once thriving but now debilitated metropolises.</u>

Here are two other possible closing sentences:

Summarizing the Main Points
Caught in the crippling vice of physical and financial illness, these once glorious and vibrant cities now appeared terminally ill.

Drawing a Logical Conclusion
Because of these physical and financial illnesses, the inhabitants fled in droves to the suburbs.

CLINCHER SENTENCES

Another type of closing sentence, which you have already seen earlier in this chapter, is the clincher sentence. Usually a clincher sentence brings in additional evidence to clinch an argument so that the argument appears final and irrefutable:

The last step in the process of becoming a wasteland is abandonment—and thousands of people fled the dying cities.

Objective

EXERCISE 8. Writing Closing Sentences. The closing sentence has been deleted from the following paragraph. Write a closing sentence for the paragraph. In writing tell what type of a closing sentence it is and why you chose that particular type.

During the 1970s and 1980s most major cities experienced a renaissance, or rebirth. Crumbling buildings and rotted waterfronts were either restored or replaced with new structures. As massive skyscrapers and restored town houses rose from the ashes of decay, cities attracted new businesses and inhabitants. This infusion of people led to improved transportation systems and to a steady flow of cash. Even some of those who had fled during the previous decade began to return.

CHECKLIST FOR DEVELOPING A TOPIC SENTENCE INTO A PARAGRAPH

1. What is the main idea expressed in the topic sentence?
2. Would the main idea be developed best with concrete details, examples or incidents, facts or statistics, reasons, or a mixed combination of support?
3. Which supporting items noted in my prewriting provide the strongest support for the main idea?
4. Which type of concluding sentence will be most effective?

WRITING THE PARAGRAPH				
Topic Sentences	Developing a Topic Sentence into a Paragraph	Writing a Unified Paragraph	Writing a Coherent Paragraph	Organizing a Paragraph

WRITING A UNIFIED PARAGRAPH

A writer, much like a composer of a song or a symphony, has to construct a piece of writing carefully and make sure that all of the parts fit together. The composer, of course, works toward unifying different musical instruments and the notes they produce. The writer works toward unifying sentences.

A **unified paragraph** is a paragraph in which all the sentences belong together and develop one main idea.

Each supporting sentence should *directly relate* to the main idea in the topic sentence. If some of your supporting sentences introduce irrelevant and secondary ideas, your paragraph will lack unity and will lose its focus.

Which of the following paragraphs is unified?

Paragraph A

A number of theories exist about why the pyramids were originally built. One of the most popular theories is that they were used as tombs for the Egyptian pharaohs. Some historians argue that they were merely giant sundials. Others believe that they were used as instruments to predict future events, such as floods or good crop seasons. Other people theorize that the pyramids were intended to be massive shelters during the time of the predicted great flood.

Paragraph B

A number of theories exist about why the pyramids were originally built. One of the most popular theories is that they were used as tombs for the Egyptian pharaohs. The Great Pyramid was built around 2700 B.C. during the reign of Pharaoh Khufu. Some historians argue that the pyramids were merely giant sundials. Others believe that they were used as instruments to predict future events, such as floods or good crop seasons. Some of these gigantic structures were constructed over a twenty year period. Other people theorize that the pyramids were intended to be massive shelters during the time of the predicted great flood.

With the exception of two sentences, both paragraphs contain the same topic and supporting sentences. The two additional sentences in paragraph B are underlined. Because of their inclusion, paragraph B is *not* unified. They might make good sentences in other paragraphs. However, in this paragraph, they introduce ideas and information *not directly related* to the main idea of the topic sentence. In fact, the two sentences divert the reader's attention away from the main idea—theories about why the pyramids were originally built. On the other hand, all of the supporting sentences in paragraph A directly support the main idea. Each supporting sentence introduces or explores one of the theories of pyramid construction. Therefore, paragraph A is a unified paragraph.

CHECKLIST FOR WRITING A UNIFIED PARAGRAPH

1. In what specific way does each supporting sentence relate to the topic sentence?
2. If a sentence is *not* related to the topic sentence, should I delete it, revise the topic sentence, or save the sentence for another paragraph?

EXERCISE 9. *Objective* **Writing a Unified Paragraph.** Write a unified paragraph of at least seven sentences on any topic you choose, or use one of the following:

1. the importance of laws
2. airports
3. pocket calculators
4. fame
5. bookbags
6. musical instruments

In your prewriting be sure to develop a cluster of points directly related to your main idea. When you revise, check to see that each sentence develops the main idea expressed in the topic sentence.

WRITING THE PARAGRAPH				
Topic Sentences	Developing a Topic Sentence into a Paragraph	Writing a Unified Paragraph	Writing a Coherent Paragraph	Organizing a Paragraph

WRITING A COHERENT PARAGRAPH

When you concentrate on writing a coherent paragraph, you focus on how each individual sentence is connected to the sentences around it.

A **coherent paragraph** is a paragraph in which the sentences are clearly and logically connected to one another.

Notice how, in the following model paragraph, Marchette Chute uses repeated words, pronoun references, and transitions to create a coherent paragraph.

Shakespeare came to London at a fortunate time. If he had been born twenty years earlier, he would have arrived in London when underpaid hacks were turning out childish dramas about brown-paper dragons. If he had been born twenty years later, he would have arrived when drama had begun to lose its hold on ordinary people and was succumbing to a kind of self-conscious cleverness. But his arrival in London coincided with a great wave of excitement and achievement in the theatre and he rode with it to its crest. William Shakespeare brought great gifts to London, but the city was waiting with gifts of its own to offer him. The root of his genius was Shakespeare's own but it was London that supplied him with the favoring weather.

—Marchette Chute, *Shakespeare of London*

REPEATED WORDS AND SYNONYMS

One way to create connections between sentences is to repeat either exact or similar words or phrases in two different sentences. This repetition acts like a verbal chain, linking the two sentences together, as in the following excerpt from the model.

> If he had been born twenty years earlier. . . . If he had been born twenty years later. . . .

However, you should be wary of overusing repetition as a connecting device. Use it sparingly and only when you think it might be the most effective way to link ideas in different sentences. Overuse of repetition can lead to a monotonous rhythm in your writing.

PRONOUN REFERENCES

Another connecting device is the use of pronouns to refer to a preceding word, group of words, or idea. Chute used pronouns throughout the model to create logical and clear connections, as the following sentence demonstrates.

> William Shakespeare brought great gifts to London, but the city was waiting with gifts of *its* own to offer *him*.

TRANSITIONS

You can also use transitions to create coherence within your paragraph. Transitions are words that help make the movement from one sentence to another clear, smooth, and easy to follow. Here are some of the most familiar transitions.

Transitions That Show Time

after	first	later	soon
always	following	meanwhile	then
before	immediately	now	until
finally	last	sometimes	

Transitions That Show Place

above	down	near	parallel
ahead	far	next to	there
around	here	opposite	under
below	horizontally	outside	vertically
beneath	inside	over	within

Transitions That Show Order of Importance

at first	former	latter	second
first	last	primarily	secondarily

Transitions That Show Cause and Effect

as a result	consequently	so	then
because	for that reason	so that	therefore

Transitions That Show Comparison and Contrast

but	in the same way	on the contrary
however	just as	on the other hand
in contrast	like	unlike

Transitions That Show Examples

for example	for instance	namely	that is

CHECKLIST FOR WRITING A COHERENT PARAGRAPH

1. What can I do to connect clearly and logically all the sentences to one another?
2. Which words can I repeat and still give my sentences sufficient variety? What synonyms can I use?
3. How can I use pronouns effectively to refer to preceding words, groups of words, or ideas? Are all my pronoun references absolutely clear?
4. What are the best transitions to tie the sentences together?

Objective

EXERCISE 10. Writing a Coherent Paragraph. Write a coherent paragraph on a topic of your own choice, or choose one of the following topics.

1. growing older
2. how to prepare to take a test
3. the day the water pipe burst

In your paragraph use and identify at least one example of *repeated words or synonyms* and one example of *pronoun reference.* Use at least two *transitions.* Reread and revise your paragraph.

WRITING THE PARAGRAPH				
Topic Sentences	Developing a Topic Sentence into a Paragraph	Writing a Unified Paragraph	Writing a Coherent Paragraph	Organizing a Paragraph

ORGANIZING A PARAGRAPH

To produce a unified and coherent paragraph, you must relate all the sentences to the main idea and connect each sentence to another. To produce a well-organized paragraph, you must present the sentences according to a clear, logical plan of development.

A **well-organized paragraph** is one in which the sequence of sentences is logical and orderly.

In the following pages you will learn about five of the methods that writers find most useful for organizing and presenting their thoughts.

CHRONOLOGICAL ORDER

Chronological order is time order, the order in which we say events take place in the world.

You can use chronological order to organize a variety of kinds of writing—for example, giving directions, summarizing or retelling an historical event or a personal experience, or explaining a process. Writers often use chronological order to organize a narrative and tell a story. In the following model the writer narrates an event in chronological order, and he also adds some degree of suspense as the parts of the event unfold in sequence.

The horse bolted over the pool of ice toward Peter Lake, and lowered his wide white neck. Peter Lake took possession of himself and, throwing his arms around what seemed like a swan, sprang to the horse's back. He was up again, exulting even as the pistol shots rang out in the cold air. Having become his accomplice in one graceful motion, the horse turned and skittered, leaning back slightly on his haunches to get breath and power for an explosive start. In that moment, Peter Lake faced his stunned pursuers, and laughed at them. His entire being was one light perfect laugh. He felt the horse pitch forward, and then they raced up the street, leaving Pearly Soames and some of the Short Tail Gang backed against the iron rails, firing their pistols. . . .

—Mark Helprin, *Winter's Tale*

Objective

EXERCISE 11. Using Chronological Order. Write a paragraph on a topic of your own choice, or use one of the following topics.

1. creating a super sandwich
2. the last two miles of a hotly-contested marathon race
3. the process of applying for a job
4. an imaginary adventure

Follow the process of prewriting, writing, and revising. Use chronological order to organize your paragraph. When you revise, make sure that the order of events is clear.

SPATIAL ORDER

Spatial order is order in terms of space.

Spatial order is one of the most effective ways of organizing a description. When you use spatial order, you describe features in terms of their position with regard to each other. Spatial order has a very basic rule: Always make sure that your reader can sense where you are looking during the description. Are you in one spot overlooking a scene? Are you moving through something, moving around it, or moving toward or away from it? Your writing should convey your *position* and *direction* to your reader.

Carefully read the following paragraph. Note how the writer lets you sense his position and direction as he describes the scene.

> Then, from atop a long rise, they saw the village sparkling like a group of colored candles. It was on the edge of the lake, which was crowned by the blue-and-green aurora now hanging in the sky in astounding silent ribbons. Smoke from the Coheeries chimneys crept up in intertwining white garlands and tangled on to the moon. Now skiers, countrymen, they raced in contentment, hissing down the slope, speeding toward the Christmas candle that danced before them by the frozen lake, and as they skied into the town they saw the people of the village standing on their roofs or in their bright windows.
>
> —Mark Helprin, *Winter's Tale*

The writer is positioned outside of the scene and is not an actual participant. However, the writer does allow us to imagine the scene clearly, and his description is so immediate and visual that we almost feel like participants as we ski down the slopes toward the village of Coheeries. He has clearly shown us the direction of his spatially-organized description.

Objective

EXERCISE 12. Using Spatial Order. Write a paragraph on a topic of your own choice or use one of these topics.

1. a city skyline
2. an airport
3. the view from a car while you are quickly passing through a forest
4. a familiar place, such as an ocean beach, a park, or a tennis court

Follow the process of prewriting, writing, and revising. Use spatial order to organize your paragraph. When you revise, make sure that both your position and direction are clear to a reader.

ORDER OF IMPORTANCE

Order of importance is order that indicates the value or importance of each detail.

When you write an informational or persuasive paragraph, you can organize the information in order of *decreasing* importance or in order of *increasing* importance. Order of *decreasing* importance is particularly useful when you want to attract and focus a reader's attention immediately on the most important information, as in the following model. The writer begins with what she considers Marco Polo's most important and most impressive accomplishment. She then moves to his other less important accomplishments in a gradually descending order.

Marco Polo led an absolutely fascinating life and had many accomplishments, but his most important accomplishment was the recording of his experiences in his book, *A Description of the World.* Without those written reminiscences, fourteenth-century Europeans would have remained largely ignorant of the Asian world. Compared to the writing and publication of that book, Polo's actual experiences as the personal emissary of the Great Kubla Khan and his twenty-four years in China seem secondary in importance. Even the minor details of Polo's life—his trading career, his imprisonment, the family quarrels and the details surrounding his death—are known only because his book stimulated many scholars to research his life.

You can also present information in an order of *increasing* importance. When you use this method of organization, as in the paragraph that follows, you move from ideas of lesser importance to ideas of greater importance, saving the most important idea for the end. The final sentence acts much like a clincher sentence.

Scholars have spent years researching and reporting on the minor details of Marco Polo's life—his trading career, his imprisonment, the family quarrels, and the details surrounding his death. Polo himself revealed what he thought to be his major accomplishments—his experience as the personal emissary of the Great Kubla Kahn and his twenty-four years in China. Yet none of that information would have been available had not Polo recorded his experiences in his book, *A Description of the World.* That book gave fourteenth-century Europeans a perspective of Asian culture and history they never before had. It broadened their view of the world, and it ensured Marco Polo a place in history. The book was Polo's most important single accomplishment.

Objective

EXERCISE 13. Using Order of Importance. Write a paragraph on a topic of your own choice, or use one of the following topics.

1. your goals for the next five years
2. why your school should offer a course in __________
3. important books you have read
4. how to avoid debt
5. the best bands in music today

Follow the process of prewriting, writing, and revising. Use order of either increasing or decreasing importance to organize your paragraph. When you revise, make sure that the order of importance is clear.

ORDER BASED ON CAUSE AND EFFECT

Cause and effect order indicates a casual relationship between events.

When you organize a paragraph according to cause and effect, you show the linkage between events—one event takes place *because* another event has happened. This kind of organization is particularly useful when you are writing about scientific or historical subjects or when you are attempting to persuade or convince your reader of an opinion or idea. In the following model, notice how the writer links a series of events, one causing the next, that lead to final effect—the splitting of wilderness areas.

One of the most insidious invasions of wilderness is via predator control. It works thus: wolves and lions are cleaned out of a wilderness area in the interest of big-game management. The big-game herds (usually deer or elk) then increase to the point of overbrowsing the range. Hunters must then be encouraged to harvest the surplus, but modern hunters refuse to operate far from a car; hence a road must be built to provide access to the surplus game. Again and again, wilderness areas have been split by this process, but it still continues.

—Aldo Leopold, *A Sand County Almanac*

Objective

EXERCISE 14. Using Order Based on Cause and Effect. Write a paragraph on a topic of your own choice, or use one of the following topics:

1. water pollution
2. school spirit
3. illiteracy
4. safety belts
5. freedom
6. efficiency

Follow the process of prewriting, writing, and revising. During prewriting try brainstorming both causes and effects that relate to your topic. Then choose one major effect (it could be the topic itself) and list causes that lead to that event or effect. When you revise, make sure that the relationships between the events are clear.

ORDER BASED ON COMPARISON AND CONTRAST

Comparison is writing that describes similarities; **contrast** is writing that describes differences.

When you compare and contrast something with something else, you show how the two things are both different and similar. You focus on details or characteristics that lend themselves to comparison and contrast, as in the following model.

Fishing and golf are as unlike as two outdoor sports can be. Golf is played on a lusciously groomed grass course called the links. For some, golf is the ultimate form of relaxation and the closest they will ever get to the wilderness. Golf is also a very expensive sport and involves buying forged steel clubs, a hefty bag, a cart, spiked shoes, tees, and thousands of balls, which you lose frequently in the "wilderness". Golfers also dress in outrageous, multi-colored costumes. Fishing, on the other hand, is a sport that normally takes place in the real wilderness. It too, is relaxing but can be very inexpensive. All you need is a hook, line, rod, reel, bait, and luck. Most fishermen wear plain clothes although, a few fishermen, with their heavy chest-waders, creels of flies, and weird hats, look like displaced aliens.

Notice that the writer of this paragraph first gives *all* the features or characteristics that relate to golf and then gives all the compared and contrasted characteristics of fishing. In other words, the writer uses a *consecutive* method of comparing and contrasting.

A second method of comparison and contrast organization is the alternating pattern. In this *alternating pattern* the writer compares or contrasts a specific characteristic of each subject, then moves on to a second, a third, and a fourth characteristic. Notice how the same writer reorganized the paragraph about golf and fishing into an alternating pattern.

Fishing and golf are as unlike as two outdoor sports can be. Golf is played on a lusciously groomed grass course called *the links*—hardly a wilderness area. On the other hand, fishing normally takes place in the *real wilderness.* Golf is both relaxing and expensive. Golfers must buy steel-forged clubs, a hefty bag, a cart, spiked shoes, tees, and thousands of balls, which they lose frequently in the "wilderness". However, fishing is relaxing but very inexpensive. A fisherman can get by with a hook, line, rod, reel, bait, and luck. If golfers appeared on the public streets in their outrageous, multi-colored costumes, they would be locked up. Most plainly-dressed fishermen would never be noticed in public, although a few fly fishermen, with their heavy chest-waders, creels of flies, and weird hats, look like misplaced aliens.

Objective

EXERCISE 15. Using Order Based on Comparison and Contrast. Write a paragraph on a topic of your own choice, or use one of the following topics:

1. rural and urban living
2. two sports
3. a luxury car and a compact car
4. television and radio
5. a competent sports team and an incompetent sports team

Follow the process of prewriting, writing, and revising. During prewriting, you might find it useful to list or chart the similarities and differences between your two subjects. Use an order based on consecutive or alternating patterns of comparison and contrast to organize your paragraph. When you revise, make sure that the specific points of comparison and contrast are clear.

CHECKLIST FOR ORGANIZING A PARAGRAPH

1. Is the paragraph best organized in chronological order? If so, what is the sequence of events?
2. Is the paragraph best organized in spatial order? If so, how does the reader always know my position and direction?
3. Is the paragraph best organized in order of importance? If so, should the most important statement be placed first or last?
4. Is the paragraph best organized in cause-and-effect order? If so, what is the cause? What is the effect?
5. Is the paragraph best organized in comparison-and-contrast order? Would consecutive or alternating statements be more effective?

WRITER'S CHOICE #1

ASSIGNMENT: A paragraph for a news story
LENGTH: Ten to twelve sentences
AUDIENCE: General public
PURPOSE: To inform your readers about a recent news event
PREWRITING: List or chart the details of the event in chronological order. Concentrate on details that tell *who, what, where, when, why, and how.*
WRITING: In your topic sentence, convey what the event is and why it was important. You may find that a two-sentence topic statement is effective here. Describe what happened using concrete details, examples, or facts. Close with a clincher sentence.
REVISING: Make sure that you used chronological order to narrate the event. Check to see where you can add connecting words and transitions to clarify the time order.

WRITER'S CHOICE #2

ASSIGNMENT: A paragraph for a letter-to-the-editor page of your school newspaper
LENGTH: Your choice
AUDIENCE: Students in your high school
PURPOSE: To persuade students that your school needs a better library or to persuade them about some other school-related opinion that you have
PREWRITING: Choose your own strategy.
WRITING: In your topic sentence, state your opinion. In your supporting sentences, give reasons and examples that support your opinion. Conclude with the most important effect that would occur if your proposal were accepted.
REVISING: Check your paragraph for unity. Make sure that your supporting sentences relate directly to your main idea and that they effectively support your opinion.

WRITER'S CHOICE #3

ASSIGNMENT: A paragraph of any kind
OPTIONS:
- Write on any subject you choose
- Use the Writer's Sourcebook (pages 346–347) to generate a writing idea
- Use any method of organization that suits your purpose, but be sure to check for unity and to use appropriate transitions and connecting words or phrases to give your paragraph coherence.

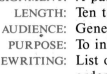

THE WRITER

Christopher Canitz, a student at Nathan Hale High School in West Allis, Wisconsin, is a member of the varsity football team and the track team. Chris plans to study medicine.

THE FINISHED PRODUCT

Sailboating and powerboating, two of the most exciting water activities, are similar in many ways, but each has a special quality that makes it unique. Sailboating, one of my favorite pastimes, sometimes can be quiet and peaceful, sometimes rough and exciting. In either case, however, it is always an adventure, one of the most difficult and strenuous activities on water. Because it requires effort, the special feeling of personal achievement that comes from sailboating cannot be matched. On the other hand, powerboating is a "free will" sport, one that makes me feel as if I can do anything on the water with ease. The feeling of sheer power I experience while making a sharp turn in a high-powered speedboat cannot be reproduced. The wind blowing across the boat while it jumps over waves creates a true sensation of speed. The feeling of achievement that comes from sailboating and the feeling of sheer power that comes from powerboating are exciting experiences that I highly recommend.

THE WRITER AT WORK

One of the more challenging aspects of writing a paragraph is maintaining a central idea. One problem that I am still working on is that I write too much. A writer can have an interesting idea but lose the reader's attention by bringing up unimportant details. I have found some ways of solving this problem. I list a few major points to cover in my first draft and write a topic sentence that I can expand with details. I also choose a purpose and audience before writing my topic sentence.

I use a few other techniques for writing efficiently. I begin with an attention-getter to hint at the content without giving everything away, thus intriguing the reader. Finally, the closing lines of a paragraph can either make or break the entire paper. I try to sum up the main ideas concisely without making the conclusion sound rushed. Otherwise, readers feel as if they missed something.

YOUR TURN **Writing a Paragraph**

Write a paragraph about a topic that is genuinely interesting to you. Pay special attention to the topic sentence and develop it with concrete details, examples or incidents, facts or reasons.

CHAPTER 4
Revising the Paragraph

Putting down on paper what you have to say is an important part of writing, but the words and ideas have to be shaped and cleaned, cleaned as severely as a dog cleans a bone, cleaned until there's not a shred of anything superfluous.
—Maya Angelou

PREWRITING	WRITING	REVISING

Professional writers like Maya Angelou know very well that writing *is* revising. During revision, a piece of writing takes on a final shape and form. The writer, much like a sculptor, arrives at that final shape by accentuating or eliminating some details and by paring, restructuring, and polishing other details. The revision process is not exactly a bone-cleaning process, but it is very close.

This chapter will provide you with some practical methods of revision. As the writer, you must decide which methods help you improve your writing. The following areas of revision are presented throughout the chapter:

- revising for purpose and audience
- revising the topic sentence
- revising support, development, and organization
- revising for coherence
- revising word choice and sentence structure
- editing, proofreading, and publishing

REVISING THE PARAGRAPH					
Revising for Purpose and Audience	Revising the Topic Sentence	Revising Support, Devel-opment, and Organi-zation	Revising for Coherence	Revising Word Choice and Sentence Structure	Editing, Proof-reading, and Publishing

REVISING FOR PURPOSE AND AUDIENCE

Always remember that a first draft is rarely a final written product. If you discover that you really need to make changes, you may revise your first draft as much as necessary. Never be afraid to "mess up" what you have written. Your corrections and revisions will lead to a better piece of written communication. At this stage of the writing process, *what* you say is more important than creating a neat paper that does not communicate your ideas.

PURPOSE

Your purpose in writing a paragraph should be clear to you and to your audience. Always try to identify your exact purpose by completing this sentence:

> The purpose of this paragraph is to ________ (*inform, persuade, entertain, narrate, describe,* or any combination of these purposes).

Then read your entire paragraph. If the *whole* paragraph really fulfills your purpose, then you do not need to revise. However, if the paragraph *as a whole* does not seem to accomplish your purpose, then you need to look closely at its *individual* sentences and identify the ones that do not fulfill your purpose. You may have to delete or revise those sentences.

AUDIENCE

In addition to fulfilling your purpose, your paragraph will also have to communicate. In order to communicate, you have to adjust your writing to the level, interests, and knowledge of your audience. After you complete a first draft, you should reread your paragraph with your audience in mind. If you identify any audience problems in your paragraph, then you should revise words, sentences, or ideas so that they communicate with your intended audience. Try not to write *at* your audience; instead, write *to* them.

CHECKLIST FOR REVISING FOR PURPOSE AND AUDIENCE

1. What is the purpose of the paragraph? Does it inform, persuade, amuse, entertain, narrate, describe, or combine several purposes?
2. Which sentence or sentences, if any, do not directly fulfill the purpose of the paragraph? What changes should be made to put every sentence on track?
3. Who is the audience for this paragraph? What changes should be made to make every sentence understandable or enjoyable?
4. What facts or details need to be added, clarified, or deleted to help the audience understand me? If this is an audience with a limited knowledge of my topic, what ideas, terms, or details should I clarify for them?

Objective

EXERCISE 1. Revising for Purpose and Audience. Read the following paragraph and then write answers to the questions.

Halley's Comet appears so infrequently that viewing it is a once-in-a-lifetime experience. Early in December of 1985, some lucky person was the first in three-quarters of a century to see Halley's Comet with the naked eye. However, the comet's brightness at that time placed it just within the limits of naked-eye viewing. People in cities could not see the comet without the use of an optical aid, such as a telescope or binoculars. Those who wanted to be the first to see this infrequent visitor took themselves far from the city lights on moonless nights late in December. Then they waited patiently.

1. What do you think the writer's purpose is?
2. Who is the audience for this paragraph? Would this have been a good paragraph for *Astronomy Theory* magazine, a publication primarily read by researchers and specialists in the field of astronomy? Why?

Suggested Answers: **1.** to inform; **2.** the general reader

REVISING THE PARAGRAPH					
Revising for Purpose and Audience	Revising the Topic Sentence	Revising Support, Development, and Organization	Revising for Coherence	Revising Word Choice and Sentence Structure	Editing, Proofreading, and Publishing

REVISING THE TOPIC SENTENCE

The topic sentence states the main idea of a paragraph and determines the scope and direction of all the supporting sentences in the paragraph. Read the following paragraph, and decide whether its underlined topic sentence really states the main idea of the paragraph.

The surface of Mars consists basically of sandy deserts, strewn boulders and rocks, huge volcanic craters, and icy cliffs and terraces. A typical summer temperature on Mars is –20°F, although temperatures do vary in a single day from near freezing to –80°F. These temperatures are too low for water to exist in liquid form, so ice cakes a large portion of the planet. In addition, raging sand and dust storms continuously race across its barren desert areas. The air on Mars is very thin and contains mostly carbon dioxide with only a trace of oxygen. <u>Mars is an interesting planet.</u>

The paragraph's topic sentence lacks both a specific scope and direction. It is too general a statement and thus fails to focus on or capture the main idea suggested by other details in the paragraph. It needs to be revised.

To revise any topic sentence, first focus on the *main idea* of the paragraph. Then try to capture that main idea by narrowing the scope and direction of your topic sentence until it specifically states your main idea. For example, the general topic sentence in the preceding model paragraph could be revised by continually refining its focus:

Mars is an interesting planet.

↓

Conditions on Mars are difficult.

↓

Conditions on Mars make survival difficult.

↓

Humans and many other Earth life forms would not survive the intolerable conditions on Mars.

What does the final revised sentence do? It *focuses* on and expresses a specific *main idea* with both defined *scope* and adequate *direction*.

Another step in revising a topic sentence is to consider its *placement* within the paragraph. Where does it work best—at the beginning, in the middle, or at the end of the paragraph? When deciding on the placement, always consider the *emphasis* that you want to develop. A topic sentence at the beginning of the paragraph will emphasize immediately the main idea that will be developed. In the middle of a paragraph, the topic sentence will emphasize the relatedness of different parts of the paragraph, and it will link those parts together. Placed at the end, as in the model paragraph on page 59, the topic sentence will act as a summary or a clincher statement.

When you revise a paragraph that does not contain a directly-stated topic sentence, you have to make sure that your detail sentences actually support and strongly *imply* a central main idea. They should all work together to imply that main idea. If they do not, then you may have to delete some details that do not imply or support the main idea. You may even have to add other details. For example, consider these two paragraphs about Percival Lowell, an astronomer who studied Mars through his observatory telescope in the early 1900s.

Model A—Unrevised

Lowell's notebooks are filled with facts about the Mars he observed. He saw bright and dark areas, a hint of polar cap and canals. Lowell used a 24-inch refracting telescope and spent days observing and recording. He believed that the planet was inhabited. He noted many seasonal changes in the dark areas.

Model B—Revised

Percival Lowell's notebooks are full of what he thought he saw: bright and dark areas, a hint of polar cap, and canals, a planet festooned with canals. Lowell believed he was seeing a globe-girdling network of great irrigation ditches, carrying water from the melting polar caps to the thirsty inhabitants of the equatorial cities. He believed the planet to be inhabited by an older and wiser race, perhaps very different from us. He believed that the seasonal changes in the dark areas were due to the growth and decay of vegetation. . . .

—Carl Sagan, *Cosmos*

As you can see, Model A does not really focus on or imply a central or main idea. The details seem to strike out in various directions and suggest multiple ideas. Model B includes some of the details from Model A and excludes others, but it also adds information to those retained details. In addition, it contains other related details about Percival Lowell's conception of Mars. All the details in Model B work together strongly and clearly to imply a main idea. That main idea could be stated in a topic sentence like this one: *Lowell believed that Mars was in some ways like Earth.*

When you revise a paragraph that implies a main idea or topic sentence, look closely at your detail sentences. Make sure that each helps to suggest the paragraph's main idea.

CHECKLIST FOR REVISING THE TOPIC SENTENCE

1. If the topic sentence circles around the main idea without ever stating it directly, how can I revise it?
2. What noun or nouns would make the *subject* of the topic sentence more specific? What *verb* would express the action of the subject more accurately? What *adjective* or *adverb* would describe the main idea more precisely?
3. What is the scope of the topic sentence? Is it too large to be treated in one paragraph? Is it too specific to cover all that the paragraph needs to say?
4. Based on the topic sentence, what does the reader expect the rest of the paragraph to do?
5. What emphasis do I want to develop in the paragraph? How, if at all, would the topic sentence improve the paragraph if I moved it elsewhere in the paragraph?

6. If the main idea and topic sentence are not directly stated in my paragraph, do the supporting sentences strongly imply a main idea? Should some sentences be deleted? Should I add other sentences that further suggest or imply the main idea?

Objective

EXERCISE 2. Revising the Topic Sentence. Read the following paragraph and revise the underlined topic sentence. Move the topic sentence within the paragraph if necessary.

The Library of Congress in Washington, D.C., is a real library. The Library of Congress consists of several buildings and extensions. The total floor space of the buildings is almost 65 acres. A recent extension, the James Madison Memorial Extension, has 34.5 acres of floor space. More than 530 miles of shelves snake through this massive structure. Those shelves hold almost 20 million books and pamphlets. The Library of Congress also has an additional 60 million resource items.

Suggested Answer: The Library of Congress in Washington, D. C., is enormous.

REVISING THE PARAGRAPH					
Revising for Purpose and Audience	Revising the Topic Sentence	Revising Support, Development, and Organization	Revising for Coherence	Revising Word Choice and Sentence Structure	Editing, Proofreading, and Publishing

REVISING SUPPORT, DEVELOPMENT, AND ORGANIZATION

STRONG SUPPORT

The supporting sentences in a paragraph should be both strong and clear. During the revision process, you should review your prewriting notes to make sure that you have selected details, facts, examples, or reasons that best support your main idea. Also keep your audience and purpose in mind. Always select supporting statements that fulfill your purpose and that will have the greatest effect on your audience.

SUFFICIENT DEVELOPMENT

When you revise, make sure that your supporting statements actually contribute to the development of your main idea. Be wary of any supporting statements that merely restate the main idea or other points. In the following paragraph, the writer repeats the main idea using different words and phrases. This repetition does not provide sufficient development.

> Ice fishing can be a chilling experience, so dress warmly. Most importantly, wear thick work socks and waterproof boots. Layers of cotton or flannel shirts, a sweater, and a down parka are absolutely essential. Wind swirls across the ice, and the cold can be almost paralyzing. Heat escapes rapidly through your head and neck; prevent heat loss by wearing a heavy wool hat and a parka hood. Finally, keep your hands warm with thermal-lined gloves or mittens. It is cold out there on the ice; therefore warm clothing is absolutely necessary.

When you revise, you may have to delete sentences that are either repetitive or that do not relate directly to and support your main idea. Do not be afraid to cut sentences from your paragraph. Be selective about what supporting sentences you decide to include. Remember: A sentence that fails to provide sufficient support will not effectively convey your ideas.

When revising your supporting sentences, you should also consider the possibility of changing your method of development. As you reread your draft paragraph, you may see an opportunity either to add different kinds of supporting sentences or to change your entire method of development. For example, suppose that your paragraph on the difficulty of living on Mars consists primarily of facts and statistics. During revision, you suddenly realize that your paragraph is fairly dry and factual. At the same time, you see a way of conveying the information in those facts and statistics in a more interesting manner—by providing an imaginative example of a person living on Mars. Therefore, you decide to change your method of development, shifting from stating facts and statistics to telling about incidents and giving examples of "real" experiences. During revision, if you need to change your method of development, then change it. Revision involves changes, and such changes, more often than not, lead to better writing.

LOGICAL ORGANIZATION

During revision, look closely at the organization of your paragraph. Consider whether it is the best possible organization for your purpose. Think about other possibilities. For example, you may have used order of importance to tell about a series of related happenings during a recent hurricane. However, perhaps chronological order would be more effective, especially if you want to focus on how the events unfolded. Then again, perhaps a cause-and-effect order would be more effective, particularly if you want to emphasize the various effects of the hurricane. You may even consider combining methods of organization, for example, stating cause-and-effect *and* listing the effects of the hurricane in order of increasing or decreasing importance.

Changes in the organization of a paragraph often involve *rewriting* rather than simply rearranging sentences. It is usually easier to rewrite sentences than it is to rearrange them to fit a new organization. Do not hesitate to rewrite sentences when necessary. Rewriting is an important part of the revision process.

CHECKLIST FOR REVISING SUPPORT, DEVELOPMENT, AND ORGANIZATION

1. Which details, facts, examples, or reasons offer the strongest support for the main idea?
2. Which sentence or sentences, if any, merely repeat the main idea instead of developing it?
3. Which sentence or sentences, if any, do not provide sufficient, directly related support for the main idea?
4. Is my method of development the best possible one?
5. Is my method of organization the best possible one for fulfilling my writing purpose, or should I change it? Should I use a combination of organization methods?
6. Does my closing sentence do what I want it to do—restate the topic sentence or summarize main points or draw a logical conclusion or clinch the argument?

Objective

EXERCISE 3. Revising Support, Development, and Organization. Rewrite the following paragraph, revising for strong support, sufficient development, and logical organization. Rewrite, reword, rearrange, or replace any sentence to improve the paragraph.

The best-selling books of all time deal with very basic subjects—religion, philosophy and politics, spelling, and child care. The Bible ranks number one on the best-seller list. No one really knows how many Bibles have been sold, but a good estimate is three billion copies. Johann Gutenberg printed the first Bible in 1455. Number two on the list is *Quotations from the Works of Mao Tse-tung*, with eight hundred million copies in print. Millions of Chinese daily read Mao's philosophical and political thoughts. These best sellers focus on fairly common subjects. They are not your typical pot-boiler novels. Noah Webster's *American Spelling Book* and Dr. Benjamin Spock's *The Common Sense Book of Baby and Child Care* rank third and fourth, with one hundred million and twenty-four million, respectively, in print. About forty different authors every year produce books that sell a million copies each.

WRITER'S CHOICE #1

ASSIGNMENT: To write a paragraph on a subject of your own choice, or on one of the following topic sentences:
- The most important problem confronting our local area is [traffic, pollution, unemployment, or crime].
- In this technological age we [have become slaves to our machines or have been freed from the tyranny of mundane and boring tasks].

LENGTH: Eight to ten sentences
AUDIENCE: Your classmates
PURPOSE: To inform or to persuade
PREWRITING: Freewrite about your subject for five minutes.
WRITING: Consider your purpose and subject. Then organize your paragraph so that it is appropriate to your purpose and subject. For example, to inform you might choose order of importance; to persuade you might effectively use cause-and-effect order. Include details, facts, examples, or reasons in your support.
REVISING: Use the checklists on pages 58, 61, and 64.

WRITER'S CHOICE #2

ASSIGNMENT: To write a paragraph on a specific topic of your own choice. You may also narrow one of the following subjects into a specific topic that could be adequately developed in a single paragraph:
- solar system
- entertainment
- literature
- anger or happiness
- customs
- time

LENGTH: Your choice
AUDIENCE: Your choice
PURPOSE: Your choice
PREWRITING: Use the organization that seems appropriate to your topic and purpose—chronological order, spatial order, order of importance, or cause and effect, comparison and contrast.
REVISING: Revise your support and development according to the checklist on page 64.

WRITER'S CHOICE #3

ASSIGNMENT: To write a paragraph on any topic you choose, using your choice of development and organization. Determine and identify your own length, audience, and purpose. As you revise your support, development, and organization, use the checklist on page 64.

REVISING THE PARAGRAPH					
Revising for Purpose and Audience	Revising the Topic Sentence	Revising Support, Development, and Organization	Revising for Coherence	Revising Word Choice and Sentence Structure	Editing, Proofreading, and Publishing

REVISING FOR COHERENCE

A **coherent paragraph** is one in which the sentences are clearly and logically connected to one another. After you complete the larger-scale revision related to paragraph support, development, and organization, you should then revise for coherence.

REPEATED WORDS AND SYNONYMS

When you revise for coherence, see if you can effectively add repeated words and synonyms to improve the connections between ideas in different sentences. For example, in the following model the revised version includes both repeated words and synonyms that help give the impression of a single, continuous thought.

ORIGINAL: Many American political leaders in the eighteenth century had a diverse number of interests and talents. Ben Franklin worked in the fields of science, publishing, writing, and business.

REVISED: Many American political leaders in the eighteenth century had a diverse number of interests and talents. Ben Franklin, one of the eighteenth century's most renowned statesmen, exhibited a broad range of interests and talents in the fields of science, publishing, writing, and business.

PRONOUN REFERENCES

You can also use pronouns to connect ideas and sentences and thus achieve both coherence and conciseness. When you revise, make sure that your pronoun references will be clear to a reader.

ORIGINAL: The Baltimore Orioles, the Philadelphia Eagles, and the Chicago Black Hawks have one thing in common. The Orioles, the Eagles, and the Black Hawks are all named after birds.

REVISED: The Baltimore Orioles, the Philadelphia Eagles, and the Chicago Black Hawks have one thing in common. They are all named after birds.

TRANSITIONS

You can also use transitions to improve connections between sentences. In the following model the writer adds a transition to show a contrast between two statements and thus improves the coherence of the two sentences.

ORIGINAL: The Miami Dolphins sailed effortlessly through the regular football season, winning most of their games. They were soundly defeated by the San Francisco 49ers in the Super Bowl.

REVISED: The Miami Dolphins sailed effortlessly through the regular football season, winning most of their games. However, they were soundly defeated by the San Francisco 49ers in the Super Bowl.

CHECKLIST FOR REVISING FOR COHERENCE

1. Which words can I repeat and still give my sentences sufficient variety? What synonyms can I use?
2. Which pronouns can I use to achieve coherence and conciseness?
3. What kinds of transitions can I add to the paragraph: time or place transitions; transitions that show order of importance, cause and effect, or comparison and contrast; example transitions? (See the list of transitions in Chapter 3.)

Objective

EXERCISE 4. Revising for Coherence. Rewrite the following paragraph, revising for coherence by using repeated words and synonyms, pronoun references, and transitions. Use preceding checklist to help you revise.

Nuclear energy and solar energy are both potential energy sources. Nuclear energy and solar energy are not without their problems. Nuclear energy is generated through the process of fission, or the splitting of atoms. The process of fission must occur in safe nuclear reactors. Many of the present reactors have not maintained safety requirements over extended periods of time. Nuclear fission also involves nuclear waste. Nuclear waste requires safe disposal techniques or nuclear waste graveyards. Solar energy is a relatively safe energy source. Solar energy does not require supersophisticated reactors or waste disposal. Some solar energy systems involve the construction of light-sensitive collectors and solar-heat storage facilities. The collection and storage can be very expensive. Banks of silicon cells, which covert the sun's light into electricity, can cost thousands and thousands of dollars. That is an expensive proposition for the home owner.

REVISING THE PARAGRAPH					
Revising for Purpose and Audience	Revising the Topic Sentence	Revising Support, Devel-opment, and Organi-zation	Revising for Coherence	**Revising Word Choice and Sentence Structure**	Editing, Proof-reading, and Publishing

REVISING WORD CHOICE AND SENTENCE STRUCTURE

APPROPRIATENESS

Your choice of words should be appropriate to your *audience,* to the *subject,* and to the *occasion* for which you are writing. Inappropriate words may confuse your reader and make the purpose of your paragraph unclear.

When you think about appropriateness in terms of audience and occasion, consider such points as these: Are the terms you have used too unfamiliar or too elementary for particular readers? Are the words too formal or too informal for the age, interest level, and experience of your readers? (You will study more about word choice, or diction, in Chapter 5.)

CONSISTENCY

After you decide what level of word choice you want to use—formal or informal—then be consistent throughout your writing. If you begin on a formal level, then your reader will expect a continuation of that formal level throughout the writing. Try to avoid mixing formal and informal language, unless you purposely mean to create a humorous or shocking effect. Notice the mixed levels of diction in this example:

> A star in the Veil Nebula appears to be a teeny weeny microscopic fleck of flickering dust.

CHECKLIST FOR REVISING WORD CHOICE

1. Which words, if any, are not appropriate to the audience, to the occasion, to the subject? How should they be changed?
2. Which words or expressions, if any, are too formal or informal? How should they be changed?

Objective

EXERCISE 5. Revising Word Choice. Rewrite the following paragraph, paying particular attention to word choice. Use the preceding checklist to help you revise the word choice. Assume that your audience is your school basketball team. Your purpose is to convince them to develop a team attitude.

While ruminating yesterday about the lack of success our team has thus far had in subduing opponents throughout this fair season, several insightful perceptions struck me. Of primary import, we distinctly lack an *esprit de corps*, a merging of wills, a singular dedication of individual beings and talents. When we perform on the wooden arena, we function as individual egos. These individual efforts rarely fuse into a unit effort. We must first adopt a sharing attitude, then dedicate ourselves to our mutual interest—domination of the enemy. Let us enter into a pact and begin to function like a perfectly coordinated whole.

REVISING SENTENCE STRUCTURE

The typical English sentence begins with a subject followed by a verb. Other sentence elements tend to follow the verb. The great majority of sentences that you write will follow this subject-verb sequence. This sequence, however, can often become monotonous, especially when a number of sentences begin with the same subject. To avoid this kind of monotony, experienced writers deliberately vary the sentence structure by shifting to the beginning of sentences elements that normally come toward the end. In the first paragraph below, the sentence structure is tiresomely similar. In the second paragraph, the sentence structure is varied.

ORIGINAL: The first mate reversed the direction of the lifeboat. He stopped rowing after a few seconds. He made the boat drift slowly toward the rocky shore. He grabbed an overhanging tree branch when he was within a yard of the shore. He pulled on the branch, and the boat moved closer still. He leaped ashore with a shout of triumph. He tied a piece of rope around a tree trunk in a series of quick motions, securing the boat to the shore.

REVISED: The first mate reversed the direction of the lifeboat. After a few seconds he stopped rowing. Slowly he made the boat drift toward the rocky shore. Within a yard of the shore, he grabbed an overhanging tree branch. He pulled on the branch, and the boat moved closer still. With a shout of triumph, he leaped ashore. In a series of quick motions, he tied a piece of rope around a tree trunk, securing the boat to the shore.

CHECKLIST FOR REVISING SENTENCE STRUCTURE

1. Do too many sentences in the paragraph begin the same way?

2. Do some sentences contain modifiers that can be moved to the beginning to avoid sentence monotony?

Objective

EXERCISE 6. Revising Sentence Structure. The sentences in the following paragraphs all begin with subjects. Rewrite the paragraph, moving modifying phrases to the beginnings of some sentences.

One day a fox saw a beautiful bunch of grapes. The grapes hung from a vine high above his head. The grapes had ripened in the warm sun and looked absolutely delicious. The grapes beckoned to him in the light of midday. The fox wanted to eat the luscious fruit after a full day without food. He jumped high into the air and tried to bite them, but he could not reach the glistening prize. He jumped again, summoning all of his strength. He still could not reach the grapes. He jumped several more times in great desperation, but he fell short each time. He rested finally, worn out and exhausted. He then said to himself, "What a fool I am to want sour grapes. They are not worth the effort."

REVISING THE PARAGRAPH					
Revising for Purpose and Audience	Revising the Topic Sentence	Revising Support, Development, and Organization	Revising for Coherence	Revising Word Choice and Sentence Structure	Editing, Proofreading, and Publishing

EDITING, PROOFREADING, AND PUBLISHING

EDITING

The final stage of revision is editing. When you edit, you refine or polish your writing by correcting grammar, usage, capitalization, punctuation, spelling, and the physical appearance of your written manuscript. These refinements give your writing a final, clean, and correct appearance. That appearance is a very important part of your publication or presentation to a reader.

In general, **editing** means making changes in sentence structure and wording.

As you edit, use the following checklist to identify and correct errors in your writing drafts. The standard editing marks at the right of the page are a shorthand method of revising or commenting on any piece of writing. (Chapter 6 will provide practice in writing sentences in various structures. Part Two offers detailed instruction in grammar, usage, capitalization, and punctuation.)

Checklist for Editing

QUESTION	TYPICAL ERROR	STANDARD MARK
Does every verb agree with its subject?	Vincent van Gogh's paintings ~~has~~ ^have the quality of genius.	*agree*
Is every pronoun in the correct case?	~~Her and me~~ ^She and I will attend the concert.	*case*
Is every pronoun reference clear and correct?	Susan scheduled a meeting with Louise, but ~~she~~ ^Susan could not attend.	*ref*
Do my pronouns unnecessarily shift from third to second person?	A good writer respects readers, gives them ideas, and helps ~~you~~ ^them grow.	*p. shift*
Are all double negatives avoided?	Faulkner didn't write ~~no~~ ^any short sentences.	*neg*
Is each verb tense correct and consistent?	Although I ordered a complete set of books, the set ~~arrives~~ ^arrived incomplete.	*tense*
Shall I use an active rather than a passive verb?	~~The poem was written by~~ May Swenson~~.~~ ^wrote the poem.	*act. v.*
Are all comparisons properly expressed?	The ~~most~~ smallest of all birds is the bee hummingbird.	*adj.*
Are all clauses complete and properly joined?	~~A~~ ^Oates is woman who has won numerous literary prizes.	*frag*
	Thoreau saw little value in the hectic pace of civilized life, ^and he explored that theme in *Walden*.	*run-on*

QUESTION	TYPICAL ERROR	STANDARD MARK
Have all dangling or misplaced words been avoided?	~~Observing~~ As I observed the wild loon, it stared cautiously at me.	*dangling*
	The President spoke about challenges facing the nation at the beginning of the meeting.	*misplaced*
Has all redundancy (unnecessary repetition) and wordiness been avoided?	Others ~~people~~ never ~~ever~~ accept my ~~own personal~~ opinions.	*redundancy*
	The restaurant frequently offers ~~a daily menu of~~ fish ~~that are~~ fresh ~~and~~ vegetables ~~that are~~ frozen.	*wordy*

PROOFREADING

In general, **proofreading** means checking for errors in spelling, capitalization, and punctuation.

Use the following proofreading marks as you revise your own writing or comment on someone else's paper.

Checklist for Proofreading

MEANING	EXAMPLE	MARK
punctuation	Where does the boundary end?	*punct*
delete	A ~~seriously~~ concerned look	ℯ
insert	Twain wrote a number of bitingly sarcastic letters	∧
space	a few of the patterns	#
close up	the movie I wanted to see	⁀
capital	Mayor williams announced a new tax plan.	≡

MEANING	EXAMPLE	MARK
lower case	Most of the Mayors attended the conference.	/
spelling	what is so special about that occason?	sp
transpose	the sereis of indicated numbers	∽
new paragraph	. . . ended at noon. ¶ In the evening. . .	¶
stet (let stand something marked for change)	The trip across the desert was ~~interminable~~ and uneventful.	. . . . .

The following model paragraph demonstrates how editing and proofreading can apply the finishing touches to a piece of writing.

Paragraph with Editing and Proofreading Marks

One ~~word~~ seem to characteraze Modern life—*speed.* Everything and every one today are dedicated to a single ~~one~~ purpose, doing something ~~more~~ faster than ever. mail, which ~~use~~ to be delivered at a leisurely pace, is now zapped ~~with great rapidity~~ instantaneously ~~across the country~~ from San Francisco to washington, D.C. High-speed computers symbolize this fast-paced life ~~it~~ give you instance access to all the information you never needed. Then there is the fast meal instant burgers, instant gourmet food, and instant relief from indigestion instantaneously. Exhausted by all this speed, ~~jets~~ can ~~will~~ supersonically zoom you to a quick vacations on a slow-paced Caribbean island.

Final Revised Paragraph

One word seems to characterize modern life—*speed.* Everything and everyone today are dedicated to a single purpose, doing something faster than ever. Mail, which used to be delivered at a leisurely pace, is now zapped instantaneously from San Francisco to Washington, D.C.

High-speed computers symbolize this fast-paced life. They give you instant access to all the information you never needed. Then there is the fast meal—instant burgers or instant gourmet food, and instant relief from instantaneous indigestion. Exhausted by all this speed, you can supersonically zoom to a quick vacation on a slow-paced Caribbean island.

MANUSCRIPT PREPARATION

When you have completed your revisions and are ready to make a final copy, follow these rules of standard manuscript form. (Be sure to ask your teacher about any additional or different rules for your class.)

1. Use standard-size paper (8 1/2 by 11 inches) and blue or black ink or a black typewriter or word processor ribbon or cartridge.
2. If you are writing by hand use only one side of each page. If you are typing, double space.
3. Maintain an even margin of 1 1/2 inches on the left margin and about 1 inch on the right.
4. Indent the first line of each paragraph five spaces.
5. Be sure that every word is legible—readable—so that your audience does not have to strain.

Objective

EXERCISE 7. Editing and Proofreading. Revise the following paragraph, editing and proofreading to correct all errors.

A number of famous writers and artists was unknown, unacknowledged during there life times. For example, Henry David Thoreau had published only two books at the time of his death in the year 1862 few people had ever heard of him or it. Emily Dickinson who is today regarded as a great American poet. Her first collection of poems weren't published until four years after death. Paul gauguin and Vincent Van Gogh, two masterfull french painters, lived impoverished and obscure lifes Van Gogh exhibites today drew thousands upon thousands of admirors. However, during his lifetime only one painting was ever sold. Can it be that artistic genius is recognized only after death. For them artists and writers, obscurity—not fame—characterized their lives.

GENERAL CHECKLIST FOR REVISING

Purpose and Audience

1. Which sentence or sentences, if any, do not directly fulfill the purpose of the paragraph?
2. What changes should be made to make every sentence understandable or interesting to a reader?

Topic Sentence

3. If the topic sentence circles around the main idea without ever stating it directly, how can I revise the topic sentence?
4. What emphasis do I want to develop in the paragraph? Would moving the topic sentence improve the paragraph?
5. If the topic sentence is implied, is the main idea clearly implied? If not, how can I change the supporting sentences to imply the main idea clearly?

Support, Development, and Organization

6. Which details, facts, examples, or reasons form the strongest support for my main idea? Which sentence or sentences, if any, merely repeat the main idea? If necessary, should I change my method of development?
7. Is the method of organization used in the paragraph the best possible one, or should it be changed? Is it appropriate to my purpose?
8. Is my closing sentence effective? How can I make it more effective?

Coherence

9. Which words can I repeat and still give my sentences sufficient variety? What synonyms can I use?
10. Which pronouns can I use for coherence and conciseness?
11. What kinds of transitions can I use?

Word Choice and Sentence Structure

12. Which words, if any, are not appropriate to the audience, to the occasion, to the subject?
13. Which words or expressions, if any, mix levels of diction?
14. Which sentences can I change in length or structure to give my writing a sense of vitality and variety?

Editing and Proofreading

15. Does every verb agree with its subject?
16. Is every pronoun in the correct case? Is every pronoun reference correct and clear? Have I avoided unnecessary shifts from third-person pronouns to second-person pronouns?
17. Are all double negatives avoided?
18. Is each verb tense correct and consistent?
19. Should I use active- rather than passive-voice verbs?
20. Are all comparisons properly expressed?
21. Are all clauses complete and properly joined?
22. Have all dangling or misplaced words been avoided?
23. Has all redundancy and wordiness been avoided?
24. Has all proofreading been done carefully?
25. Have the rules of manuscript preparation been followed?

WRITER'S CHOICE #1

ASSIGNMENT: To write a paragraph on a topic of your own choice or on one of the following topics:
- the need to develop an alternate to the car as the primary means of transportation
- how people have become more (or less) self-centered than they were twenty years ago
- why modern rock music communicates (or does not communicate) to adolescents

LENGTH: Eight to ten sentences

AUDIENCE: Readers of a local newspaper's editorial page

PURPOSE: To inform or persuade

PREWRITING: Brainstorm or freewrite about your topic. Then identify your main idea, and list supporting ideas.

WRITING: Write a topic sentence that clearly expresses your main idea. Then write supporting sentences using facts, statistics, examples, details, or reasons. End with a sentence that summarizes your opinion.

REVISING: Refer to the general checklist on pages 74–75 and make all necessary revision and editing changes.

WRITER'S CHOICE #2

ASSIGNMENT: To write a paragraph on a topic of your own choice or to narrow one of the following general subjects:
- style
- communication
- work
- leisure

LENGTH: Eight to ten sentences

AUDIENCE: Young adult readers of a magazine distributed abroad

PURPOSE: To inform your readers of your attitude about the topic

OPTIONS: Freewrite or brainstorm about your topic for five minutes. Use examples, details, facts, and reasons for development. To revise, use pages 74–75.

WRITER'S CHOICE #3

ASSIGNMENT: To write a paragraph of your own choice, or use one of the following topics, narrowing it as necessary:
- important conservation issues
- four major poets or novelists
- the three most important events in history

You may also use the Writer's Sourcebook (pages 346–347) to generate a writing idea.

OPTIONS: Determine your own length, audience, and purpose. As you revise, refer to the checklist on pages 74–75.

THE WRITER

Susan Lynch, a student at Lacey Township High School, Lacey, New Jersey, has been the secretary of her class and a basketball cheerleader. She plans to attend college and major in business. Here she presents her first draft of a paragraph and then explains how she revised it for unity and coherence.

THE FIRST DRAFT

The tension in the American colonies had a large impact on whether or not the Revolutionary War would become a reality. The colonists reacted too radically to many incidents. They continued to threaten the king. The colonists did not try to settle anything rationally with the ruler of Britain. The colonists demanded too much without giving anything in return. They did not conduct themselves sensibly. The colonists were almost looking for revenge. They were setting up the beginning of a war. Better communication with England could have solved these problems.

THE WRITER AT WORK

One common writing problem is not giving enough detail to support the main idea. In some cases, however, the opposite is the major problem. I tend to look through my compositions and find that details need to be omitted.

My first draft of the paragraph on the colonists contained too many unrelated and unconnected details. Removing a few sentences and combining a few others helped solve the problem. This approach works well as long as I don't take out too much detail; certain sentences are needed to keep the paragraph flowing. The final paragraph still states my ideas, but it is more unified.

THE FINISHED PRODUCT

The tension in the American colonies had a large impact on whether or not the Revolutionary War would become a reality. The colonists reacted too radically to many incidents, sometimes making demands without giving anything in return. The colonists were almost looking for revenge, flirting with the launching of a war. Better communication with England could have solved these problems.

YOUR TURN **Revising a Paragraph**

Write a paragraph on any topic you choose, or choose a first draft you have already written. Revise the paragraph using the skills you practiced in this chapter.

CHAPTERS 2–4 THE WRITING PROCESS

CHAPTER 2 PREWRITING

Generating and Exploring Ideas (pages 11–16) Read these brainstorming notes, and answer the questions based on them.

- editorial cartoons
- famous news photographs
- favorite sections of the newspaper
- commercial art as a career
- famous comic strip characters
- history of comic strips

1. Which of the following ideas could be generated from these notes?
   (a) the importance of table manners
   (b) the role of science in everyday life
   (c) the most famous comic strip heroes and heroines
2. Which questions could be used to explore this idea?
   (a) Who are they? **(b)** How do they differ? **(c)** Why were they popular? **(d)** All of these

Topic, Purpose, and Audience (pages 16–23 and 23–24) Write the letter of the item that correctly answers the question.

3. Which of the following topics is the most focused?
   (a) the solar system **(b)** the sun **(c)** why solar eclipses occur
4. Which purpose would be most suited to this topic?
   (a) to persuade **(b)** to entertain **(c)** to explain a process
5. Which audience would probably be more interested in this topic?
   (a) students in a science class **(b)** students in an art class

Answers: **1.** c; **2.** d; **3.** c; **4.** c; **5.** a

Writing for Review Plan a paragraph about a topic that interests you. Generate writing ideas through brainstorming, and then explore one writing idea with questions. List your purpose and audience; state your main idea in a sentence. Hand in all your prewriting notes.

CHAPTER 3 WRITING THE PARAGRAPH

Answer the questions based on the following paragraph.

[1]The sun is the Earth's primary source of heat and light. [2]The sun's interior, which is the source of our sunlight, reaches a temperature of 40 million degrees. [3]That heat is generated by continuous thermonuclear reactions and explosions. [4]Other stars undergo similar nuclear explosions and thus emit starlight. [5]Scientists estimate that during the continuous solar explosions 400 million tons of hydrogen are converted into helium *each second.* [6]As a result of this conversion process, tremendous quantities of energy are released in the form of heat and light.

Topic Sentence (pages 34–36)

1. Which sentence is the topic sentence of the paragraph?
   (a) sentence 1 **(b)** sentence 2 **(c)** sentence 4 **(d)** sentence 5

Developing a Topic Sentence (pages 38–42)

2. The topic sentence in this paragraph is developed with
   (a) details **(b)** facts **(c)** examples **(d)** reasons

Unity (pages 44–46)

3. Which sentence is not directly related to the topic sentence?
   (a) sentence 2 **(b)** sentence 3 **(c)** sentence 4 **(d)** sentence 5

Coherence (pages 46–48)

4. Sentence 6 contains a transitional expression that shows
   (a) order of importance **(b)** cause and effect **(c)** time

Organization (pages 48–54)

5. The order used to organize the paragraph is
   (a) cause-and-effect **(b)** order of importance **(c)** chronological

Answers: **1.** a; **2.** b; **3.** c; **4.** b; **5.** b

Writing for Review Write a paragraph based on the prewriting notes you wrote in the Writing for Review for Chapter 2. (You may have saved these notes, or your teacher may have returned them to you.) If you wish, write a paragraph about a completely new topic.

CHAPTER 4 REVISING THE PARAGRAPH

Read the following paragraph and answer the questions based on it.

[1]The Chinese invented metal money. [2]Many centuries ago they introduced coins. [3]They introduced paper money as the primary currency. [4]The more valuable it was, the largest the piece of paper. [5]A bill measuring 9 by 13 inches was worth big bucks—1,000 copper coins.

Revising the Topic Sentence (pages 59–62)

1. Which of the following sentences is the better revision of sentence 1?
   (a) The Chinese invented metal money and coins.
   (b) The Chinese invented both metal and paper money.

Revising Support and Development (pages 62–64)

2. Which of the following revisions of sentence 2 provides the best support and development of the topic sentence?
   (a) Many years ago they introduced gold as coins.
   (b) About 4,000 years ago they introduced coins.
   (c) Coins were also invented by the ancient Egyptians.

Revising for Coherence (pages 66–67)

3. Which sentence needs the transition *almost 3,000 years later?*
   (a) sentence 1 **(b)** sentence 2 **(c)** sentence 3

Revising for Sentence Structure; Editing and Proofreading (pages 68–70, 70–75)

4. Which of the following sentences is the correct revision of sentence 4?
   (a) The more valuable it was, the largest the piece of paper.
   (b) The more valuable it was, the larger the piece of paper.

Revising Word Choice (pages 70–75)

5. Which sentence uses informal language inappropriately?
   (a) sentence 2 **(b)** sentence 4 **(c)** sentence 5

Answers: **1.** b; **2.** c; **3.** c; **4.** b; **5.** c

Writing for Review Revise the paragraph that you wrote in the Writing for Review for Chapter 3. (You may have saved this paragraph, or your teacher may have returned it.) If you wish, develop a new paragraph.

UNIT II
Words, Sentences, and Style

Style, according to essayist E. B. White, is that which is both "distinguished and distinguishing" about the way a writer expresses ideas. Because you are a writer, you already possess a writing style of your own, a style that distinguishes your work from the work of other writers. The purpose of this unit is to help you develop that style so that it is truly distinguished—a worthy expression of your creative best.

Style in writing is not like style in clothing, hair, or automobiles. Style in the latter is something added on, like chrome to a car or something that changes with every passing fad. Style in writing is much more basic: It is the *clarity, grace,* and *precision* with which you express your ideas in writing. The most effective style is one that comes naturally, though not without hard work, a style that lets *you* emerge from behind your words.

To achieve clarity in your writing, you will learn to pay attention to word choice and to sentence structure. The vocabulary of English is so vast that for every thought you want to express, an apt and exact word exists to help you express it. Search for that word. Similarly, the sentence structure of English gives you the practical means of expressing every subtle nuance of your thought—from thundering, majestic proclamations to the quietest of whispers—in a way that lets you control how your readers react to your words.

To achieve grace, you will learn to pay attention to the rhythm of your words. Why is grace important? You may already know the answer to this question if you have ever wanted to read a writer's words aloud just to feel the sound of them on your tongue or to share with others a particularly well phrased remark. A graceful style puts your reader immediately at ease and lets your reader focus on the meaning of your words without the interruption of awkward, labored language.

To achieve precision, your third goal, you will spend time learning to express your ideas clearly and vividly. The real trick to effective writing is to have your reader experience a scene exactly as you recall it or imagine it to be. The vitality of your images and language will compel your audience to read on.

This unit will give you practice in choosing exact and appropriate words, in writing and combining sentences for different effects and purposes, and in developing a writing style distinguished for its clarity, grace, and precision of expression. The work that you do here will have a far-reaching effect on the quality of all your writing.

CHAPTER 5
Choosing Words

The difference between the right word and the wrong word is the difference between lightning and a lightning bug.

—Mark Twain

Writers know the power of suggestion and the precision that words can have. Most writers love words. With words they form, shape, mold, and carve visions from their imaginations. Writers spend a lifetime exploring the innumerable shades of meaning that words suggest. Choosing the exact and precise word to convey the writer's meaning is the ultimate test of a good writer. As Twain implies in the preceding quotation, when you want to suggest lightning you do not choose a lightning bug.

In this chapter you will study the process of choosing words. Often referred to as **diction,** word choice means finding and using the word that fits exactly your meaning, tone, and purpose. In addition, you will also consider the appropriate level of diction—formal, middle, or informal—to communicate effectively with different audiences. You will practice the skills necessary for making informed choices about words:

- writing precisely
- writing concisely
- writing with figurative language

As you work through this chapter, you will recognize that word choice is a deliberate act. You control that act during prewriting, writing, and revising.

WRITING PRECISELY

CONNOTATION AND DENOTATION

Connotation is the unspoken or unwritten meaning associated with a word beyond its exact, dictionary meaning, or **denotation**.

Good writers choose exact words to communicate ideas clearly and precisely. Such writers are aware of both the denotations and connotations of words. A word's denotation is its obvious, or explicit, meaning. The dictionary lists denotative meanings for words. However, the dictionary rarely lists connotations for words. Connotations give words the power of suggestion. A writer takes advantage of that power by choosing words that will suggest or imply the writer's attitude toward something. Thus a writer's choice of words often reflects the writer's purpose. For example, consider the words *ineffective* and *incompetent.* They both have a similar denotative meaning, which is, "being incapable of doing or accomplishing something." However, each word implies or connotes a very different meaning or attitude. Use *ineffective* and then *incompetent* to complete the following sentence:

Giles is an ____________ guitar player.

When you state the Giles is an *ineffective* guitar player, you are not severely criticizing Giles. *Ineffective* is a wishy-washy word and suggests that Giles is not the best guitar player around. You could be suggesting that Giles is not a powerful player or does not know all his chords, or strums when he should be picking. Choosing the word *ineffective* to describe Giles as a guitar player reveals your attitude as well: You are critical but not harsh. On the other hand, if you state that Giles is an *incompetent* guitar player, then you are emphatically implying that Giles does not know a guitar string from a hamstring. If your purpose is to criticize Giles severely, then using the word *incompetent* will accomplish that purpose as well as reveal your negative attitude and assessment. The word *incompetent* connotes "total incapability, uselessness, and the absence of any redeeming talent." The contrasting connotations of these two words point to a simple lesson: Choose your words carefully so that they suggest exactly what you want to suggest.

Objective

EXERCISE 1. Determining Denotations and Connotations. Using the dictionary, write the denotation of each of the following words. Then list at least three connotations that you associate with each word.

SAMPLE: New York
DENOTATION: City located in lower New York state; includes five boroughs—Manhattan, Bronx, Brooklyn, Queens, and Staten Island; over 9 million inhabitants
CONNOTATIONS: Gargantuan; reverberating with energy; a symbol of contrasts—poverty and wealth, failure and success, the pragmatic and the creative, age and youth, the dying and the restored.

1. Olympics **3.** Texas **5.** jungle
2. literature **4.** mansion **6.** Mississippi River

Suggested Answer for 1: The word *constituted* connotes a high level of integration.

GENERAL AND SPECIFIC WORDS

A **general** word is all-embracing, indefinite, and broad in scope, while a **specific** word is explicit, definite, and narrower in scope.

GENERAL	SPECIFIC	MORE SPECIFIC
storm	snowstorm	blizzard
creature	bird	osprey
move	walk	saunter

Use as many specific words in your writing as possible. Specific words are narrow in scope and more informative than general words. Specific words convey exact meanings to your readers. When you use specific words, you eliminate vagueness from your writing. Try especially to avoid such vague words as *good, nice, interesting, lots of,* and *quite.*

Compare, for example, the level of detail in each of the following sentences. Notice how the model using general words conveys only a vague impression. The model containing specific words conveys an exact picture to the reader.

GENERAL: New York City is an interesting place.
SPECIFIC: New York City startles the first-time visitor—massive steel bridges stretching like fingers from its Manhattan palm, where skyscrapers stand poised like rockets.

Objective

EXERCISE 2. Rewriting Vague Sentences. Rewrite five of the following sentences. Replace any general or vague words with specific details.

impressive
1. The Rockies are beautiful mountains.
crept
2. The cat moved through the grass.
army ... marched
3. A bunch of interesting clouds went across the sky.
jazz band
4. The entertainment at the dance was very good.
books, old newspapers, and gym clothes
5. My locker is filled with things.

Suggested Answers are provided above the items.

CONCRETE AND ABSTRACT WORDS

Concrete words refer to a thing, or a quality that you can see, touch, taste, smell, or hear. Words are **abstract** when they refer to ideas, qualities, and feelings.

CONCRETE: bridge, hammer, dusty, sour, silent
ABSTRACT: despair, love, intelligent, complex, liberty

Concrete words convey precise meanings to readers. Even when you do write about such abstract ideas as love or liberty, use concrete words to make your ideas explicit. For example, this sentence offers the reader no specific description of a holiday dinner:

> Our Thanksgiving dinner was delicious.

The abstract word *delicious* could be made more exact by adding specific concrete details:

> The delicious Thanksgiving dinner consisted of succulent slabs of roast turkey, sweet yams, fresh green peas, buttered mashed potatoes, and hot crescent rolls.

This use of sensory details related to sight, taste, and touch tell explicitly *how* or *why* the dinner was delicious.

Sentences that contain concrete words usually can answer one or more of the following questions exactly and precisely: *Who? What? When? Where? Why?* and *How?* The answers to the questions are often concrete words or words that relate to the senses.

Objective

EXERCISE 3. Recognizing Concrete and Abstract Words. Read the following paragraph, and decide which of the underlined words are abstract and which are concrete. On a separate sheet of paper list the underlined words under the headings *abstract* and *concrete,* and indicate to which of the five senses each item on the concrete list refers. Some of the words may be put into more than one sense category.

> No, I do not think the <u>autumn</u> sad. It arouses in me a <u>nostalgia</u> for other days, but that is a sweet <u>sadness</u>, and one that I can bear. In a few more weeks, when the leaves come down, the harsh cry of the <u>blue jay</u> will be heard, and the <u>enameled</u> lapis of his <u>wings</u> seen through the open branches of the trees. The dark green of the spruces will stand out sharply against the blue waters of the <u>bay</u> and, if you keep out of the <u>wind</u>, the sun will be <u>warm</u> on your back as you kneel to your task in the <u>garden</u>.
>
> —Roy Barrette, *A Countryman's Journal*

LEVELS OF DICTION

The three levels of diction are informal, middle, and formal. Being aware of these levels will help you choose the right words for your writing—words that are appropriate to your purpose and audience. Some purposes and audiences require one treatment—for example, serious or conventional—and other purposes and audiences call for another treatment—for example, casual or offbeat. The words in the following lists present examples of the three levels of diction.

INFORMAL	MIDDLE	FORMAL
hassle	problem	complication
cops	police	law officers
grown-ups	adults	elders

Informal diction includes words used in everyday conversations with friends.

Informal diction is too casual for most school writing but is often perfect for narrative dialogue. For example, a character in one of your stories may say, "My friends are always hassling me." However, you probably would not use the preceding sentence as the topic sentence of a formal paragraph written for English class. If you are uncertain whether or not a word is informal, check the dictionary. There you may find the label *informal* or the labels for two other kinds of informal words—*colloquial* and *slang.*

Colloquial is a term that refers to everyday language used in conversation and in writing that is intended to have the same sound and rhythm as actual speech. Words such as *snappy, cinch* (meaning "simple"), and *jazzy* are typical colloquialisms. **Slang** is a label given to extremely informal or extremely colloquial words or meanings. Slang is composed mostly of new words or unusual uses of existing words. In both writing and speech slang creates a noticeable effect, such as humor or exaggeration. *Neat, dig, rip off,* and *goof off* are familiar slang words.

Neither slang nor colloquialisms are considered "incorrect" or "bad" English. What was slang twenty years ago may have become quite respectable today. The words *hippie* and *gobbler,* for example, began as slang and now belong to the category of middle diction.

Middle diction falls between informal and formal diction.

Middle diction comprises the words most often used in newspaper and magazine writing and in television newscasts. Middle diction is the best choice for your writing, whether for school, business, or the general public. Using middle diction enables you to present your ideas straightforwardly and unpretentiously. For example, if you are writing a letter to the editor of a local newspaper, you may begin with this sentence: "Conflict between individuals is often the result of a lack of communication; the same may be true of international conflict."

Formal diction is the language most often found in scholarly journals and books.

You are much more likely to read formal words than hear them or speak them. If you use formal words without knowing their connotations and denotations, your writing will sound unnatural and forced. Avoiding formal diction unless it is appropriate to your subject and audience eliminates the danger of **mixed diction,** a condition that can confuse your readers. For example, if you are writing a serious article on international conflict but mix formal, middle, and informal diction, your readers may find your explanations humorous: "Hassles between individuals are often the result of bad vibes due to an absence of interactive communication; the same may be true of international hassles."

Objective

EXERCISE 4. Determining Level of Diction. Categorize each of the following words according to its level of diction—*informal, middle,* or *formal.* Make a chart with the three levels, and write each word under the correct category. Use a dictionary, if necessary. Write a middle-level synonym for each word in your formal and informal categories.

1. gal informal; girl
2. eschew formal; shun
3. jerk informal; fool
4. mendacity formal; lying
5. surplus middle
6. reproach formal; blame
7. spiffy informal; well dressed
8. ostracize formal; exclude
9. uptight informal; nervous
10. elevator middle

Suggested middle level synonyms are provided for each formal or informal word.

Objective

EXERCISE 5. Revising for Mixed Diction. Revise and rewrite the following paragraph. Change the mixed level of diction so that it is consistently a middle-level diction. You will have to change words and phrases and restructure some sentences. Use a dictionary, if necessary.

Many high-class restaurants are rip-offs. First off, these joints serve diminutive portions of game and fish. Often the entrees are junked up with pungent spiceries and zesty saucified embellishments. The salads are consistently banal—a solitary lettuce leaf sporting a cheap slice of tomato. The supercilious waiters are stuffy and uptight. Then the grand finale occurs: the itemization for condiments, nutrients, and services rendered. We never take our leave from one of these clip joints without being destitute and broke.

IDIOMS

An **idiom** is an expression that is unique to a particular language.

Because idioms are unique expressions in a given language, they cannot be translated word for word from one language into another. The literal meaning of the individual words in an idiomatic expression is quite different from the expression's overall meaning. For example, the sentence "Melinda had time on her hands" means that Melinda had some free time or time for other tasks, not that her hands had time attached to them.

Idioms may be classified according to level of diction. "To reach a decision," "to take a peek," and "to plant an idea" are all examples of middle-diction idioms. "To bite the dust" and "to rip off someone" are among the idioms considered informal. If you are uncertain of the level of diction of an idiom, consult your dictionary. Most idioms are listed under the main entry of their key word, after the basic list of meanings (see the sample dictionary entry on page 665). For instance, the idiom "to stand in good stead" may be found under the main entry of its key word, *stead.* According to the dictionary, it is a formal idiom that means "to be in a position of acceptance or advantage." Informal idioms are labeled *informal, colloquial,* or *slang.*

Objective

EXERCISE 6. Finding Idioms. Using a dictionary, find an idiom based on each of the key words listed below. Then write a sentence using the idiom. Identify whether the idiom is informal, middle, or formal diction.

SAMPLE: take
take a shot
He took a shot at the new job. (informal)

1. bite
2. cross
3. discharge
4. drop
5. mind
6. cool
7. run
8. fall
9. capture
10. mountain

WRITING CONCISELY

INFLATED DICTION

Inflated diction is unnatural, pretentious, imprecise, overly formal language.

Writers who lack confidence in their ability to write simply and concisely will often use inflated diction to impress their readers. However, the readers will probably be too busy to be impressed, as they must struggle to translate the weighty verbiage into plain English. As a writer you can control inflated diction by asking yourself two questions: 1) How would I orally express the same idea? 2) Are my words specific and concrete enough to convey my meaning? For example, consider the following sentence. How might it be more simply stated?

> Wordsmiths should strive to eschew obfuscation in their verbal meanderings by paring and excising any verbiage that diminishes clarity.

An alternative to this sentence might be "Writers should aim toward clear, concise writing." One way to achieve clear, concise writing is to avoid use of inflated diction.

Objective

EXERCISE 7. Deflating Inflated Diction. Rewrite the following sentences by using middle-level diction. Asking yourself these questions will help eliminate inflated diction: How would I express the same idea in speech? Are the words concrete enough to convey the meaning?

1. All staff members of this corporation should ensure the cleanliness of their respective environments by disposing of any unneeded paper waste before departing for the evening.
2. Please establish verbal contact with your teacher before the close of day.
3. I receive a weekly disbursement of funds from my family.
4. My attitude toward the book is somewhat less than enthusiastic and borders on total rejection.
5. Lapidary objects littered the landscape.

Suggested Answers: **1.** Clean your office. **2.** Speak with your teacher before 3:20 P.M. **3.** My family gives me an allowance. **4.** I dislike the book. **5.** Stones covered the ground.

REDUNDANCY

Redundancy is the unnecessary repetition of words or phrases.

At times, the repetition of a word or phrase can be an effective connecting device between ideas and sentences. However, there are other times when repetition serves no useful purpose. For example, consider the repetition in the following sentence: "At 5:00 P.M. in the late afternoon, we met for a meeting to discuss the fate of the school newspaper." This sentence contains two redundant expressions. In each case the repetition adds no new information to the sentence. The elimination of redundant expressions leads to concise writing: "At 5:00 P.M., we met to discuss the fate of the school newspaper."

Objective

EXERCISE 8. Eliminating Redundant Expressions. Rewrite each of the following sentences. Make each sentence more concise by eliminating any redundant expressions.

1. We arrived at the school before 8:00 A.M. in the morning.
2. Twenty people in number were arrested for driving too fast in speed.
3. In the year of 1984 the federal deficit grew to two billion dollars in amount.
4. Chicago differs in different ways from the city of Dallas.
5. Now at the present time we can determine the future needs of our city for the year 2000.

Answers: Redundant expressions are underlined.

CLICHÉS

A **cliché** is an expression that has become trite through excessive use.

Clichés were once unusual, interesting, and effective expressions, but excessive use has made them trite, dull, and ineffective. Writing that contains clichés is unimaginative. When you write, try to avoid clichés by either inventing your own imaginative expressions or using straightforward language. Consider, for example, the following sentences:

CLICHÉ: Sandra is as cool as a cucumber during a tense basketball game.
REVISED: Sandra is calm and controlled during a tense basketball game.

CLICHÉ: He runs slow as molasses.
REVISED: He runs slowly, like sap trickling from a maple tree.

To decide whether or not an expression is a cliché, read the first few words of the expression and see if the last part automatically comes to mind. Try that approach with the following examples: "Hit the nail on . . . "; "honest as the day . . . "; and "smart as a. . . ."

Objective

EXERCISE 9. Replacing a Cliché with a Specific Word. Write one specific, carefully chosen word that would be an effective replacement for each of the following clichés.

1. in this day and age
2. nip in the bud
3. powers that be
4. fast as a bullet
5. pretty as a picture
6. sharp as a tack
7. busy as a bee
8. follow in the footsteps of
9. clear as crystal
10. tried and true

Suggested Answers: **1.** today; **2.** prevent; **3.** officials; **4.** swift; **5.** gorgeous; **6.** intelligent; **7.** industrious; **8.** imitate; **9.** obvious; **10.** reliable

Objective

EXERCISE 10. Eliminating Clichés. Rewrite the following sentences, substituting either original expressions or straightforward language for each cliché. Some sentences contain more than one cliché.

1. Even at the ripe old age of 70, Benjamin Franklin racked his brain for new inventions.
2. It stands to reason that taxation will send you to the poorhouse.
3. Carol is as smart as a whip in the chemistry lab.
4. We were caught like rats in a trap as our boat drifted helplessly across the bay.
5. At the crack of dawn, we waited with bated breath for the better-late-than-never school bus.

JARGON

Jargon is the specialized vocabulary of a group or a profession.

Computer sales people, lawyers, teachers, economists, auto mechanics, and many other groups or professions have their own jargon, or terminology. Jargon is appropriate and acceptable when used by a specialist writing or speaking to other specialists in the same profession. Jargon is inappropriate in school writing or in writing for a general audience. In such situations, jargon obscures the clarity of the writing. Jargon, like inflated language, often has to be translated into simple, straightforward English to be understood. Study the following examples.

JARGON: We must interface in either oral or written modes on a continual and daily basis in order to function effectively as an organization.

REVISED: Working as a team requires constant communication.

Objective

EXERCISE 11. Replacing Jargon. Write a specific, clearer word or phrase for each jargon expression listed below. Use the dictionary if necessary to determine the exact meaning of these words.

1. bottom line outcome
2. user-friendly uncomplicated
3. input information
4. detention center jail
5. shortfall shortage

Answers: Suggested specific words are provided next to the items.

WRITING WITH FIGURATIVE LANGUAGE

A **figure of speech,** or **figurative language,** is a word or phrase used in an imaginative, rather than a literal, sense. **Literal language** is language that means exactly what it says, word for word.

Prose writers as well as poets use figurative language to make their writing vivid and lively. Three figures of speech that you can use when you write are simile, metaphor, and personification.

SIMILES

A **simile** is a figure of speech that directly compares two seemingly unlike things using a comparing word such as *like* or *as.*

The two items being compared in a simile are basically different; however, they do share some characteristics. For example, when you write, "On the abandoned and lifeless rocky island, a single lighthouse guarded the coastline like a loyal, solitary sentry," you are comparing two different items—a lighthouse and a soldier or sentry—in relation to a shared characteristic, their aloneness. However, statements that compare alike items are *not* similes. "That building looks like a lighthouse" is not a simile.

METAPHORS

A **metaphor** is a figure of speech that makes an implied comparison between two seemingly unlike things.

Unlike a simile, a metaphor does not use a comparing word:

SIMILE: The airport is like a congested beehive.
METAPHOR: The airport is a congested beehive.

Both similes and metaphors make writing lively by revealing surprising similarities in things not normally considered alike. Unusual and imaginative metaphors can infuse a piece of writing with dramatic power and insight, as in the following examples from a poem and an essay:

> Morning is
> a new sheet of paper
> for you to write on.
>
> —Eve Merriam, "Metaphor"

> The Model T was full of tumors, but they were benign.
>
> —E. B. White, "Farewell My Lovely"

Merriam's poem uses a metaphor to make a *direct* comparison between "morning" and "a new sheet of paper." However, White's metaphor *implies* a comparison between the Model T car and a human body filled with benign tumors. In making this comparison, White suggests that the Model T had its mechanical problems, but none were terminal.

Both Merriam's and White's metaphors are effective; they are simple, and their images are coherent. Each comparison works. Sometimes, however, the comparison a metaphor makes is too complex, too diverse to function as an effective image. Such metaphors are commonly called **mixed metaphors,** as in this example:

MIXED METAPHOR: Life is a race in which you hitch your wagon to a star and step on the gas pedal.

The writer's comparison would have been more effective had it simply stated, "Life is a race." The introduction of additional comparative characteristics—"hitching your wagon to a star" and "stepping on the gas pedal"—only confuses the image and the reader. Avoid mixed metaphors by making your comparisons simple, clear, and visual. If a metaphor does not show an exact and consistent relationship between the two items being compared, then it will not effectively communicate a visual image.

PERSONIFICATION

Personification is a figure of speech in which an animal, object, or idea is given human qualities.

Personification implies that a nonhuman thing has personality, intelligence, or emotion. For example, consider the model simile from page 90:

> On the abandoned and lifeless rocky island, a single lighthouse guarded the coastline like a loyal, solitary sentry.

In this simile, the writer implies that the lighthouse has the human characteristics of a sentry—it is "loyal" and "guards." Personification can be a part of the comparison in a simile or a metaphor, or it can be used to directly describe something, as in this example:

> The moon slowly crept across the black sky, pausing to stare coldly with its single vibrant eye.

Objective

EXERCISE 12. Identifying Figurative Language. Identify in writing the figurative language in each of the following sentences, and note whether each is an example of simile, metaphor, or personification. Then write a sentence explaining why the figure is effective. Some of the sentences have more than one figure of speech.

personification metaphor simile

1. An apprehensive night crawled slowly by like a wounded snake, and personification sleep did not visit Rainsford. . . .

   —Richard Connell, "The Most Dangerous Game"

personification

2. January deals harshly with Newfoundland

   —Farley Mowat, *A Whale for the Killing*

simile

3. Arenas sprang up all over the [Roman] empire like shopping-center bowling alleys.

   —Tom Wolfe, "Clean Fun at Riverhead"

4. The artist is distinguished from all other responsible actors in society —the politicians, educators, and scientists—by the fact that he is his (metaphor) own test tube, his own laboratory, working according to very rigorous rules, however unstated these may be. . . .

   —James Baldwin, "The Creative Process"

Suggested Answers are provided above the items.

Objective

EXERCISE 13. Writing Figurative Language. Select five items from the following list. For each one, write a sentence that expresses an idea through figurative language. Write at least one example each of simile, metaphor, and personification.

1. sunset
2. the surf at the beach
3. silence
4. the way a person moves
5. an abandoned, rusted car
6. light
7. a plant or tree
8. a voice
9. a cloud
10. a bird

Suggested Answer to 1: The glowing embers of the sunset faded to ash.

CHECKLIST FOR CHOOSING WORDS

1. What are the denotations of my words? What are the connotations? Do the connotations fit my purpose? Would other words be more precise?
2. Which of my general words can I replace with specific words?
3. Which of my abstract words can I replace with concrete words?
4. What level of diction have I used—informal, middle, or formal? Does the level of diction fit my purpose? Is it appropriate for my audience? Which, if any, of my words should be changed to make my word choice more consistent?
5. Which, if any, idioms, clichés, or instances of inflated diction, redundancies, or jargon should be replaced?
6. What similes, metaphors, and personifications would improve my writing?
7. Have I avoided mixed metaphors and inconsistent comparisons?
8. Have I avoided far-fetched, elaborate figures of speech?
9. In sum, how appropriate is my word choice for my purpose and audience?

WRITER'S CHOICE #1

ASSIGNMENT: To write a paragraph about a place in which there is much activity, such as a city street scene, an amusement park, or a county fair

LENGTH: Eight to ten sentences

AUDIENCE: A friend who has never been there

PURPOSE: To describe the scene, its looks, noise, colors, smells, and so forth

PREWRITING: Use freewriting for five minutes. Try to create a flow of sensory images that describe the place.

WRITING: Begin by stating what you are describing and where it is located. Then use precise, vivid words—including similes, metaphors, and personification—to describe the sights, sounds, and other sensory impressions related to the scene.

REVISING: Make sure that you have used exact words to convey your impression of the scene. Ask yourself the questions on the checklist on page 93. Then edit and proofread your paragraph.

WRITER'S CHOICE #2

ASSIGNMENT: To write a paragraph about the names of professional teams associated with a sport

LENGTH: Eight to ten sentences

AUDIENCE: The editor of the sports section of your local newspaper

PURPOSE: To show how the connotations of sports teams' names imply certain team characteristics

WRITING: In your topic sentence, state your purpose. Then write six to eight sentences that explain the various connotations you associate with each team name. End with a clincher sentence about what kind of image the names of the teams and the respective connotations convey of the sport in general.

REVISING: Ask yourself the questions on the checklist on page 93. Then edit, proofread, and share your paragraph.

WRITER'S CHOICE #3

ASSIGNMENT: To write a paragraph on any topic

LENGTH: Your choice

AUDIENCE: Your choice

PURPOSE: To describe exactly what you see

OPTIONS:
- You may base your description on a photograph in the Writer's Sourcebook, pages 346–347.

THE WRITER

Robert Seal spent his early childhood in Milan, Italy. Besides playing in a concert group and in rock, jazz, and marching bands, he is involved in sports and the school paper. He also saves a little time to "lie back and think." As a student at Indian Hill High School in Cincinnati, Ohio, Robert wrote the following passage and commentary.

THE FINISHED PRODUCT

The tone of George Orwell's *1984* is one of bleak foreboding. This tone evokes the feeling of hopeless surrender among the people of Oceania. Orwell establishes this tone in the first paragraph of the novel:

> It was a bright cold day in April, and the clocks were striking thirteen. Winston Smith, his chin nuzzled into his breast in an effort to escape the vile wind, slipped quickly through the glass doors of Victory Mansions, though not quickly enough to prevent a swirl of gritty dust from entering along with him.

The fact that clocks are striking thirteen is enough to alert the reader that something is quite wrong with the picture. Winston Smith tries to escape the weather; symbolically, he can be seen as trying to escape the "vile wind" that pervades everything in Oceania. Winston turns inward to avoid the cold, a symbolic gesture that is elucidated later in the novel when he turns inward and questions the reality around him. With his creative use of language, Orwell paints the first few strokes on his canvas, depicting a bleak world from which there is no refuge.

THE WRITER AT WORK

I saw *1984* as a graphic warning to the world, a warning expressed in words that paint vivid pictures. As I wrote I deliberately chose words from painting—such as *canvas* and *strokes*—to show how the novel's tone comes from Orwell's visual images. In addition, I tried to "sculpt" my own words to create a form—a flow or rhythm—like the one I felt in Orwell's passage. For example, I used words such as *pervade* and *elucidate* because of their sound and rhythm. Words are symbols of reality, and I tried to use words to show the reader the reality I saw in Orwell's novel.

YOUR TURN **Using Vivid Language**

Paint a picture in words. Using visual details and vivid language, describe a subject of your choice—for example, a seascape, a busy street, a room.

6 CHAPTER
Writing and Combining Sentences

Good writers are those who keep the language efficient.
—Ezra Pound

Writing at its most basic level is a variety of sentences composed of words. The writer arranges and rearranges words in different patterns. During this process the writer constantly experiments with various sentence structures and often alters those structures to convey exact meanings in lively and interesting ways.

To help you write more lively, fluent, and engaging sentences, this chapter will give you practice in the following skills:

- expanding sentences with words and phrases
- combining sentences through coordination
- combining sentences through subordination
- combining sentences through coordination and subordination
- combining sentences by using other structures
- writing concise sentences and paragraphs
- creating variety in sentences

EXPANDING SENTENCES WITH WORDS AND PHRASES

A series of short, choppy sentences can sound halting and awkward. If you expand such sentences by adding concrete details, your writing will become smoother, clearer, and more specific.

You can expand choppy sentences by adding words and phrases that tell more about the nouns and verbs.

The APT is a train.
The **British** APT is a **powerful, fast passenger** train **with an electrical traction engine**. [expanded with adjectives and with a prepositional phrase that modifies the noun *train*]
The British APT can lean.
The British APT can **quickly** lean **inwards around curves to reduce air resistance**. [expanded with adverbs and prepositional and infinitive phrases that modify the verb *can lean*]

You can find and generate additional details about a sentence by asking questions like *how many? what kind? when? how? where?* and *why?*

As you add information to a sentence, you must decide where to place those additional words and phrases. You will often have choices about placement. Always try to position words and phrases near the terms they describe.

Objective

EXERCISE 1. Expanding Sentences by Adding Details. Rewrite the following sentences by adding words or phrases to each. The questions after each sentence will help you generate additional details.

SAMPLE: The wind blew.
(a) What kind of a wind was it?
(b) Where did the wind blow?

ANSWER: **A gusty, chilly** wind blew **across the frozen pond**.

1. Carla pedaled her bike.
(a) What kind of bike? **(b)** Where did Carla pedal her bike?
2. Runners struggled the last mile of the race.
(a) How many and what kind of runners? **(b)** Why did they struggle the last mile?
3. The boat sailed.
(a) Where did the boat sail? **(b)** When did the boat sail?
4. The dog barked.
(a) Which dog barked? **(b)** How did the dog bark?
5. Clouds drifted.
(a) What kinds of clouds? **(b)** How and in what direction did they drift?

Suggested Answer for 1: Carla pedaled her ten-speed bike through the park.

COMBINING SENTENCES THROUGH COORDINATION

When you coordinate sentences, you tie them together with coordinating conjunctions, such as *and, or, nor, but,* and *for.* You can use coordination in your writing to combine two closely related sentences into a single sentence. For example, these two distinct sentences are closely related:

> Lobsters are often featured in restaurant menus. Limited quantities of this seafood have led to high prices.

The ideas in these two sentences are almost equal in importance and so closely related that they can be combined by using *but* to show contrast:

> Lobsters are often featured in restaurant menus, *but* limited quantities of this seafood have led to high prices.

In the preceding example, two sentences were combined to make a single compound sentence. You can also combine short sentences to create compound subjects, predicates, and modifiers.

SEPARATE: Disk drives are an important part of a computer system. Software programs are also important.

COMBINED: Disk drives **and** software programs are important parts of a computer system. [compound subject]

SEPARATE: A hurricane severely battered several Florida coastal cities. It also severely damaged them.

COMBINED: A hurricane severely battered **and** damaged several Florida coastal cities. [compound predicate]

SEPARATE: Cross-country skiing is an exhilarating activity. Cross-country skiing is exhausting, though.

COMBINED: Cross-country skiing is an exhilarating **but** exhausting activity. [compound modifiers]

A paired coordinator, such as *both . . . and,* helps to strengthen the connection between two words, phrases, or sentences. You can combine elements that are almost equal in importance by using such paired coordinators as *both . . . and, either . . . or, neither . . . nor, whether . . . or, not only . . . but (also).*

SEPARATE: Sinclair Lewis received the Nobel Prize in Literature. William Faulkner also received the award.

COMBINED: **Both** Sinclair Lewis **and** William Faulkner received the Nobel Prize in Literature.

When some sentences are combined, words that refer to the same person or thing are sometimes unnecessarily repeated, as in this sentence:

Solar cells are expensive, and **they** are inefficient.

You can reduce such sentences by eliminating the repetition; for example:

Solar cells are expensive and inefficient.

If two sentences are closely related and almost equal in importance, stress their relatedness and equality by combining them through coordination.

When you use coordination to combine sentences, *be selective:* Do not overuse coordination. You do not want your writing to become an endless string of combined sentences. When you do use coordination, choose the coordinator that best expresses your meaning. The following chart groups the most common coordinating words and phrases and demonstrates the punctuation used with each kind of sentence structure. For rules about punctuating coordinated sentences, see Chapter 28.

Coordination Chart

PURPOSE	WORD OR PHRASE	EXAMPLE
To show an alternative	or nor otherwise either . . . or neither . . . nor whether . . . or	Wake up, **or** you will miss the train. **Either** the Red Sox **or** the Yankees will win the World Series this year.
To signal an addition	and also furthermore in addition similarly both . . . and not only . . . but (also)	The eclipse began at noon, **and** within minutes the sky turned dark. An abalone is a type of marine snail; **furthermore,** it is called the sirloin of the sea.
To show a reason	for	We worked quickly, **for** we needed to leave on time
To signal contrast	but yet instead nevertheless still however	An anemone has attractive **yet** poisonous tentacles. An anemone looks harmless; **however,** its tentacles contain a deadly poison.
To signal an example	for example for instance	Catfish are unusual fish; **for example,** one species of catfish actually walks on land.
To show a result	as a result thus so therefore	Harsh conditions characterize the lower depths of the ocean; **therefore,** fish at these depths rarely grow large.
To show balance	semicolon	Penguins have thick, protective coats; their features are dense and waterproof.

Objective

EXERCISE 2. Combining Sentences Through Coordination. Rewrite each pair of sentences as one sentence. When combining sentences, use a word or words or a phrase that expresses the relationship indicated in parentheses. Refer to the words and phrases on the preceding coordination chart.

SAMPLE: Tom was ready to leave. He was unsure of the directions. (contrast)

ANSWER: Tom was ready to leave but was unsure of the directions.

Jet engines burn kerosene as fuel, and hot gases. . . .

1. Jet engines burn kerosene as fuel. Hot gases from the burning fuel are expelled at high speed. (addition)

The gases shoot out through a rear nozzle; as a result, the. . . .

2. The gases shoot out through a rear nozzle. The jet develops a forward force called thrust. (result)

Fission is the process . . . , but fusion. . . .

3. Fission is the process of splitting an atom's nucleus. Fusion is the process of combining nuclei from atoms. (contrast)

Not only fission but also fusion can release. . . .

4. Fission can release tremendous amounts of energy during a nuclear reaction. Fusion can also release tremendous amounts of energy. (addition, paired coordinators)

Controlling . . . is difficult; however, it can. . . .

5. Controlling the process of fission is difficult. It can be accomplished in a nuclear reactor. (contrast)

Suggested Answers appear above each item.

Objective

REVIEW EXERCISE. Combining Sentences in a Paragraph. Rewrite the following paragraph, combining sentences through coordination. You may combine some sentences and leave others as they are presently written.

Animals have a wide range of normal skills. Some have developed extraordinary skills. Bats can detect objects ultrasonically. They can identify objects ultrasonically. They send out short wavelengths of sounds. The returning echoes indicate an object's size and position. The phrase "blind as a bat" has no basis in reality. It is totally incorrect. Another animal that has an unusual skill is the archer fish. It hunts insects. Its method of hunting is unique. The archer fish is an aquatic marksman. It shoots its victims with a pellet of water. The archer fish stuns insects with its fast, accurate shot. It shoots them down with successive, rapid-fire, follow-up shots. The *Mastophora* spider also has an unusual hunting technique. This spider hides behind cover. It waits for an unsuspecting fly or insect. The talented spider then lassoes a passing victim.

COMBINING SENTENCES THROUGH SUBORDINATION

Coordination, if used excessively, can lead to monotonous and unsophisticated writing.

The following passage uses some coordination, but it also varies sentence structure through subordination. To subordinate means "to place below another in rank or importance."

After it sprang from the gate, the horse galloped into the first turn. The track, which was a sea of wet, heavy mud, presented no obstacle for the horse. The animal surged into the lead and slowly pulled away from the field. When it was forty lengths ahead, it began to tire. The horse, which had first slowed to a walk, actually stopped. As the other horses caught and easily passed it, the animal dozed.

Subordinate a less important idea to a more important one.

Throughout the following pages you will practice using different kinds of subordination to combine sentences.

SUBORDINATING INFORMATION ABOUT NOUNS

How would you combine these two sentences?

1. George Lucas is a film genius.
2. George Lucas created *Star Wars.*

You can coordinate the two sentences, giving equal weight to each:

3. George Lucas is a film genius, and he created *Star Wars.*

Instead of giving equal importance to each statement, you can stress one statement and de-emphasize the other by using one of the following subordination techniques:

VERSION A: George Lucas, **who is a film genius,** created *Star Wars.* [Sentence 1 has been subordinated to an adjective clause that modifies the noun *George Lucas.*]

VERSION B: George Lucas, **who created *Star Wars,*** is a film genius. [Sentence 2 has been subordinated to an adjective clause that modifies the noun *George Lucas.*]

VERSION C: George Lucas is a film genius **who created *Star Wars.*** [Sentence 2 has been subordinated to an adjective clause that modifies the noun *genius.*]

Version A subordinates the statement about Lucas's film intelligence. Versions B and C subordinate information about one of Lucas's films. In all three versions the subordinated statement is introduced by the word *who.* In each case *who* replaces *George Lucas,* a noun in the original sentence.

Subordinate information in one sentence to modify a noun or a pronoun in another sentence by using the words *who, whom, whose, that, which, when,* and *where.*

The subordinated sentence that tells more about a noun is called a **relative clause,** or an **adjective clause.** The word that introduces the relative clause is called a **relative pronoun.**

Review the relative clauses above. Note that the relative clause in version A and the one in version B are separated from the rest of the sentence by commas. Neither is essential to the meaning of the rest of the sentence. These relative clauses merely give extra information. In version C, however, the relative clause is essential to the meaning of the sentence; that is, it limits or restricts the meaning of "film genius." Do not use commas to set off a clause that is essential to your meaning.

For additional information about essential and nonessential relative clauses see Chapter 21. For more information about punctuating relative clauses, see Chapter 28.

Here is a chart that illustrates the use of relative pronouns for subordinating information about nouns.

Subordinating Information About Nouns

ORIGINAL SENTENCES	COMBINED THROUGH SUBORDINATION
Phyllis Wheatly was a slave during the Revolutionary War period. She published her first poem at the age of sixteen.	Phyllis Wheatly, **who** was a slave during the Revolutionary War period, published her first poem at the age of sixteen.
She became a well-known poet. George Washington admired her.	She became a well-known poet **whom** George Washington admired.
We know very little about Phyllis Wheatly. She met Washington in 1776.	Phyllis Wheatly, about **whom** we know very little, met Washington in 1776.
Wheatly is a classical poet. I have read her poems.	Wheatly is a classical poet **whose** poems I have read.
She published a book. The book is called *Poems on Various Subjects, Religious and Moral.*	She published a book **that** is called *Poems on Various Subjects, Religious and Moral.*
Her poem about George Washington is an example of her classical style. Thomas Paine published it in 1775.	Her poem about George Washington, **which** Thomas Paine published in 1775, is an example of her classical style.
At the age of nineteen, she went to London. She became a celebrity there.	At the age of nineteen, she went to London **where** she became a celebrity.

Objective

EXERCISE 3. Subordinating Information About Nouns. Rewrite each of the following pairs of short sentences as a single sentence with subordinated information about a noun. In some cases you will have to choose which idea to subordinate. Refer to the preceding chart when choosing a method of subordination.

SAMPLE: I cannot find the place. I parked the car there.
ANSWER: I cannot find the place where I parked the car.

I know of a place where you can read. . . .
1. I know of a place. You can read about Texas there.

. . . tells about events that are taking place. . . .
2. The magazine called *D* tells about events. The events are taking place in Dallas.

. . . told about a graduate student who collects. . . .
3. A recent column told about a graduate student. The graduate student collects team nicknames.

In the 1,127 Texas high schools that he carefully studied, he found. . . .
4. In the 1,127 Texas high schools he found 178 team nicknames. He carefully studied those Texas high schools.

The writer, whose name I do not know, spent. . . .
5. The writer spent weeks gathering information. I do not know the writer's name.

. . . nicknames, which symbolize . . . of Texas, are. . . .
6. Some of the nicknames are expected: Ranchers, Cowboys, Pioneers. Those nicknames symbolize the spirit of Texas.

Bulldogs is the name that is the most popular of all.
7. Bulldogs is the name. That name is the most popular of all.

The writer found . . . schools in which the name . . . is used.
8. The writer lists ninety high schools. The name Bulldogs is used in those high schools.

Names that symbolize . . . , such as . . . , are also popular names.
9. Names such as Eagles, Tigers, and Panthers are also popular names. These names symbolize strength, agility, and courage.

The writer who did . . . also found. . . .
10. The writer also found fifty-three Wildcats and many Lions. That writer did the fascinating study.

Suggested Answers are provided above each item.

SUBORDINATING INFORMATION ABOUT VERBS

Information in one sentence can be subordinated to modify a verb in another sentence. One sentence can be subordinated to tell *when, where, how, why, to what extent,* or *under what conditions* the action of the verb is performed.

How many different statements can you make by combining these sentences through subordination?

I relax myself. I speak at the school assembly.

Here are some combinations:

I feel tense **while I speak in public.**
I feel tense **before I speak in public.**
I feel tense **if I speak in public.**

The important information in each sentence is *I feel tense.* The less important information in each sentence concerns *when, why,* and *under what conditions* the speaker feels tense. The subordinated information is in adverb clauses that modify the verb *feel.*

Subordinate one sentence to another to tell *when, where, how, why, to what extent,* or *under what conditions* the action of the other sentence was performed.

You have several options when using this kind of subordination. First you can choose *which idea to subordinate*:

> Jerome is a professional singer. He has trained for years.
> Jerome is a professional singer **because he has trained for years.**
> Jerome has trained for years **because he is a professional singer.**

You can also try placing the subordinated information in *different positions.* Note how the emphasis changes in each version:

> **Because he has trained for many years,** Jerome is a professional singer.
> Jerome, **because he has trained for many years,** is a professional singer.
> Jerome is a professional singer **because he has trained for many years.**

You also have the option of determining the *exact relationship* you want to emphasize between two ideas. The word you use to introduce a subordinated idea will clarify that relationship:

> Writers write **because** they have a need to communicate.
> Writers write **when** they have a need to communicate.
> Writers write **as long as** they have a need to communicate.

You will find more information about adverb clauses in Chapter 21. For information about punctuating adverb clauses, see Chapter 28. Here is a list of words that can introduce subordinated ideas about verbs:

1. To introduce subordinate ideas that tell *when:*

after	as soon as	since	when	while
as	before	until	whenever	

2. To introduce subordinate ideas that tell *where:*

where wherever

3. To introduce subordinate ideas that tell *how:*

as as if as though

4. To introduce subordinate ideas that tell *why:*

as because in order that since so that

5. To introduce subordinate ideas that tell *to what extent:*

as far as as fast as as long as than

6. To introduce subordinate ideas that state *conditions:*

although	(even) if	so long as	whether (or not)
considering (that)	inasmuch as	unless	while

Objective

EXERCISE 4. Subordinating Information About Verbs. Rewrite each of the following pairs of sentences as a single sentence with a subordinate idea that tells more about its verb.

SAMPLE: The sun was shining. The day was still quite cold.
ANSWER: Although the sun was shining, the day was still quite cold.

. . . made her film debut when she. . . .

1. Shirley Temple made her film debut. She was only three years old.

. . . cautiously form snowplow turns whenever the slopes. . . .

2. Beginning skiers cautiously form snowplow turns. The slopes drop off at a steep angle.

Because problems seem . . . , everyone looks forward. . . .

3. Problems seem to disappear under the glow of the sun. Everyone looks forward to a day at the beach.

. . . stretch before us as far as the human eye can see.

4. The Rockies stretch before us. The human eye can see them far into the distance.

After . . . use their electronic calculators, they double-check. . . .

5. Hong Kong bank tellers use their electronic calculators. They then double-check each calculation on an abacus.

Suggested Answers are provided above each item.

SUBORDINATING TO CREATE A NOUN SUBSTITUTE

The following two sentences can be combined by subordinating the underlined sentence:

<u>You are directing the play</u>. We will see the play.

Following are some possible combinations:

VERSION A: We will see the play **that you are directing**.
VERSION B: We will see the play **if you are directing it**.
VERSION C: We will see **whatever play you are directing**.

In version A, one sentence is inserted into another as an adjective clause to present more information about a noun. In version B, one sentence is subordinated to another as an adverb clause to tell more about a verb. Version C gives another method of subordination: One sentence is subordinated as a noun clause to take the place of a word—usually a noun or a pronoun—in another sentence.

The subordinated sentence that replaces a noun or a pronoun is called a **noun clause**. You can use a noun clause whenever you want to state a fact or include a question within another question, as in the following examples:

> The Earth was the center of the universe. At one time many people believed this statement.
> At one time many people believed **that the Earth was the center of the universe.**
> Should acid rain be a major environmental concern? This question has become an important issue.
> **Whether or not acid rain should be a major environmental concern** has become an important sentence.

When you want to state a fact or question within a sentence, subordinate the material, and use it in place of a noun or a pronoun.

You can use the following words to subordinate a sentence that you are adding to another sentence in place of a noun or a pronoun. Note that some sentences need to be reworded when they become noun clauses.

Creating Noun Substitutes

WORD TO INTRODUCE NOUN SUBSTITUTE	ORIGINAL SENTENCES	COMBINED WITH SUBORDINATION
who, whoever, whom, whom-ever, whose	Who directed the play? The director is very talented.	**Whoever directed the play** is very talented.
what, whatever	What is the central issue of the campaign? The committee discussed that topic.	The committee discussed **what the central issue of the campaign is.**
which, which-ever	Which script is better for television? The director argued about that fact.	The director argued about **which script is better for television.**
how, that, when, where, why, if, whether (or not)	Our baseball team lost the game by twenty runs. I heard this news.	I heard **that our baseball team lost the game by twenty runs.**

Objective

EXERCISE 5. Creating Noun Substitutes at the End of Sentences. Rewrite the following pairs of sentences so that one sentence is added to the *end* of the other in place of a noun.

SAMPLE: The coach decided something. Jason would be the new captain.

ANSWER: The coach decided that Jason would be the new captain.

. . . did not cite who discovered. . . .

1. Who discovered the planet Pluto? The textbook did not cite that fact.

We argued about which . . . is an original.

2. Which of the paintings is an original? We argued that question.

. . . Aristarchus proposed that the sun . . . lies. . . .

3. The sun rather than the Earth lies at the center of the planetary system. Around 280 B.C. Aristarchus proposed this fact.

. . . astronomers could not determine whose theories. . . .

4. Whose theories were correct? At the time astronomers could not determine the answer.

I wanted to learn how the . . . was formed.

5. How was the asteroid belt formed? I wanted to learn this fact.

Suggested Answers are provided above each item.

Objective

EXERCISE 6. Creating Noun Substitutes at the Beginning of a Sentence. Rewrite the following pairs of sentences so that one sentence is added to the *beginning* of the other in place of a noun.

SAMPLE: When will the train arrive? This fact is unclear.

ANSWER: When the train will arrive is unclear.

Whether we set up . . . is not an important issue.

1. Should we set up camp here or on that ridge? This is not an important issue.

Whoever solved . . . must have worked for hours. . . .

2. Who solved that physics problem? He or she must have worked for hours on it.

That the mayor refused . . . shocked. . . .

3. The mayor refused to talk with the city council. That fact shocked his advisors.

Where the airplane finally landed was unknown.

4. Where did the airplane finally land? That information was unknown.

What caused . . . could not be determined.

5. What caused the avalanche? This information could not be determined.

Suggested Answers are provided above each item.

SUBORDINATING WITH OTHER NOUN SUBSTITUTES

Another method of combining sentences involves changing the verb in one sentence to a gerund or a gerund phrase. A **gerund** is the *-ing* form of a verb used as a noun. In the following example, the verb *hiked* is changed to the gerund *hiking* and is inserted with its modifiers into the other related sentence:

We hiked across the Rockies. That hike was an adventure.
Hiking across the Rockies was an adventure.

In the preceding example, the gerund and its modifiers became the subject of the new sentence. You can also use gerunds as direct objects or as predicate nouns, as in these examples:

People **skate on that pond.** The owner forbids it.
The owner forbids **skating on that pond.**
Linda runs in marathons. **That is Linda's favorite activity.**
Linda's favorite activity is **running in marathons.**

Use a gerund or a gerund phrase to combine two sentences when you want to stress the action within the sentence that you subordinate.

Objective

EXERCISE 7. Using Gerunds to Combine Sentences. Combine each of the following pairs of sentences by changing the verb in one of the sentences into a gerund. Then insert the gerund and its modifiers into the other sentence.

SAMPLE: I weave rugs. That is my hobby.
ANSWER: Weaving rugs is my hobby.

Studying coral formations is the purpose. . . .
1. We study coral formations. That is the purpose of our Caribbean trip.

The harbormaster has outlawed swimming in. . . .
2. People swim in inner harbor. The harbormaster has outlawed this practice.

Solving quadratic equations is Alan's special talent.
3. Alan solves quadratic equations. That is Alan's special talent.

Researching . . . was an adventurous process.
4. I researched a topic about interstellar travel. It was an adventurous process.

Scraping barnacles . . . was a tedious job.
5. We scraped barnacles from the hull of our boat. That was a tedious job.

Suggested Answers are provided above each item.

COMBINING SENTENCES THROUGH COORDINATION AND SUBORDINATION

Another effective combining technique is the use of *both* subordination *and* coordination to combine short, related sentences. Read the following list of related sentences:

1. Few visitors reach the house.
2. The house is only a small cabin in the hills of Vermont.
3. A visitor may accidently discover the cabin.

4. The visitor will be escorted back to the main road by a snarling dog.

These sentences can be combined into a single sentence:

> Few visitors reach the house, which is only a small cabin in the hills of Vermont, and a visitor who accidently discovers the cabin will be escorted back to the main road by a snarling dog.

By mixing coordination and subordination, the new sentence clarifies the relationships among the various ideas. Statements 1 and 3 become the major ideas in the new sentence and are coordinated by using the word *and.* The word *which* subordinates statement 2 to tell more about the noun *house.* Then the word *who* subordinates statement 4 to tell more about the noun *visitor.*

You can use both **coordination** and **subordination** to join two or more equally important ideas with ideas that are less important.

Remember, however, that excessive use of lengthy sentences can weigh down your writing. Lengthy sentences are best used sparingly and are most effective when interspersed with short, simple sentences.

Objective

EXERCISE 8. Using Coordination and Subordination to Combine Sentences. Each of the following items contains several short sentences. Using both coordination and subordination, rewrite the short sentences in each item as a single sentence.

SAMPLE: He left the house. The sun was shining. No clouds filled the sky. Later in the day, heavy rains fell.

ANSWER: When he left the house, the sun was shining, and no clouds filled the sky; however, later in the day, heavy rains fell.

1. The town has no electricity. The tornado had knocked down power lines. Some homeowners had gas-driven generators. Supplies of gas were low.
2. Shopkeepers had frozen-food freezer units. These units could, in an emergency, be powered by gas-driven generators. None of the storekeepers owned generators. They wanted to borrow generators from homeowners.
3. The townspeople needed to decide something. Is it more important to have electricity in their homes? Is it more important to have a large supply of edible food available? Townspeople attended a meeting. Storekeepers attended a meeting.
4. They heard rescue teams arriving. This event ended all discussion. Everyone hurried to the center of town. In the center of town, they were given fresh food. They were given medical supplies.

Objective

REVIEW EXERCISE. Revising a Paragraph. Rewrite the following paragraph. Combine many of the sentences by using the methods you have practiced: (1) coordination, (2) subordination, and (3) coordination and subordination within one sentence.

During the bleak winter of 1777–1778, George Washington was camped in Valley Forge. His men were camped with him. Valley Forge is located about twenty miles from Philadelphia. He had picked the site for sound reasons. The nearby hills were tall. His army could easily survey the main routes. The routes led to supplies, gunneries, and powder mills. At first the location appeared ideal. It soon turned into a disaster area. The winter became severe. Food supplies were scarce. Medical supplies were scarce, too. Congress could not send supplies. Congress advised Washington to raid the nearby farms. Washington refused to do that. In the end Washington had a ragged army. It was starving, too. They held their position until spring. At that time the French entered the war. The French provided relief and supplies.

COMBINING SENTENCES BY USING OTHER STRUCTURES

Coordination and subordination are not the only structures used for combining ideas in single sentences. Next you will examine more concise structures for combining sentences.

COMBINING SENTENCES WITH APPOSITIVES

When you identify or describe a noun in a sentence, you can add either an entire statement or a shorter phrase or single word that does the same job more concisely. This word or phrase is called an **appositive**. For example, look at the different ways these two sentences can be combined:

Indian dance forms involve *mudras. Mudras* are hand gestures with recognized meanings.

VERSION A: Indian dance forms involve *mudras*, **which are hand gestures with recognized meanings.**

VERSION B: Indian dance forms involve *mudras*, **hand gestures with recognized meanings.**

When you form some appositives, you may have to add a word or repeat a word for clarity, as in these examples:

I enjoyed camping in the wilderness for a week. I had never done it before.

I enjoyed camping in the wilderness for a week, **something** I had never done before.

Sara sings songs from various cultures. They are simple yet moving.

Sara sings songs from various cultures, **songs** that are simple yet moving.

Appositives usually follow the nouns they identify or describe. In some instances, you might place one at the beginning of a sentence for emphasis, as in version B:

VERSION A: Hamlet, **a questionable tragic figure,** was the victim of his own sensitivity and intelligence.

VERSION B: **A questionable tragic figure,** Hamlet was the victim of his own sensitivity and intelligence.

Appositives are particularly useful in expository writing when you want to give your readers a brief definition of an unfamiliar term. For example, these appositives briefly define unfamiliar terms:

The microprocessor, **a thin wafer or chip of silicon,** contains many complex electrical circuits.

Dolphins and bats locate objects through a process of echolocation, **a process of sending, reflecting, and receiving echoed sound waves.**

For more information about appositives, see Chapter 20.

Objective

EXERCISE 9. Combining Sentences by Using Appositives. Rewrite each pair of sentences by using an appositive. Some may require that you add or repeat a word to form the appositive. In some cases you will have to decide which sentence to make into an appositive and where to place it.

SAMPLE: Venus is the closest planet to Earth. Venus is rocky and metallic.

ANSWER: Venus, the closest planet to Earth, is rocky and metallic.

London, a fascinating city to visit, is filled. . . .

1. London is filled with exciting shops, museums, and places of historic interest. London is a fascinating city to visit.

The Tower of London, a fortress that dates back . . . , is. . . .

2. The Tower of London is an imposing sight. It is a fortress that dates back to Norman times.

. . . brings the visitor to Greenwich, once the site of. . . .

3. A short boat ride on the Thames brings the visitor to Greenwich. Greenwich was once the site of The Royal Observatory.

The prime meridian, an imaginary line . . . , passes through Greenwich.

4. The prime meridian passes through Greenwich. The prime meridian is an imaginary line that divides east from west.

. . . attracts visitors from many countries, visitors who want a glimpse. . . .

5. Greenwich attracts visitors from many countries. These are visitors who want a glimpse into England's history.

Suggested Answers are provided above the items.

COMBINING SENTENCES WITH PARTICIPLES AND PARTICIPIAL PHRASES

How would you combine the following sentences to emphasize the sense of action?

> The salmon slowly climbed the dam's fish ladder. The salmon was wounded by jagged rocks.

Here is one possible combination:

> The salmon, **which was wounded by jagged rocks,** slowly climbed the dam's fish ladder.

The sentence is somewhat of an improvement over the two separate but repetitive sentences. However, there is another way to convey the action more concisely, as in this example:

> The salmon, **wounded by the jagged rocks,** slowly climbed the dam's fish ladder.

These concise statements capture the action more vividly. They condense the statement about the salmon's appearance into a participial phrase: *wounded by the jagged rocks.*

You can use **participles** and **participial phrases** to signal simultaneous action or to show how one action happens before another action. You can also use them to clarify cause-and-effect relationships.

The following three sentences refer to actions that take place simultaneously, or at the same time:

SIMULTANEOUS ACTION 1: The coach barked orders
SIMULTANEOUS ACTION 2: He stomped angrily
SIMULTANEOUS ACTION 3: He waved furiously.

Here the sentences are combined to show that the actions occur simultaneously. Whichever action remains in its original form will stand out as the main action in the new sentence.

VERSION A: **Stomping angrily and waving furiously,** the coach barked orders.
VERSION B: The coach waved furiously, **barking orders and stomping angrily.**
VERSION C: **Barking orders and waving furiously,** the coach stomped angrily.

The following two sentences express actions that happen at different times, one preceding the other.

> I played chess for three hours. Then I watched the news for an hour.

Using a participle that begins with *having* lets you combine the two sentences in a way that makes the time relationship obvious.

> **Having played chess for three hours**, I watched the news for an hour.

The following two events show another kind of sequence, one that expresses a cause and its effect:

> CAUSE: The voters were confused about the issues.
> EFFECT: The voters carefully questioned the candidates.

Here the events are combined to show the cause-and-effect relationship clearly:

> VERSION 1: **Confused about the issues**, the voters carefully questioned the candidates.
> VERSION 2: The voters, **confused about the issues**, carefully questioned the candidates.

In both versions the participial phrase *confused about the issues* is placed logically, near the noun or words it relates to, *the voters*. If they are misplaced, they can confuse a reader, as here:

> The voters carefully questioned the candidates, confused by the issues.

This sentence states that the candidates were confused by the issues. In fact, the voters were confused. For additional information about participles and participial phrases, see Chapter 20.

Objective

EXERCISE 10. Combining Sentences by Using Participles and Participial Phrases. Rewrite each of the following groups of sentences, combining them by forming one or more participles or participial phrases. You will need to choose which sentence to use as the main action. You will also need to keep in mind the time relationship in order to decide which participle to use.

SAMPLE: She went over Niagara Falls in a barrel. Annie Edison Taylor survived.
ANSWER: Having gone over Niagara Falls in a barrel, Annie Edison Taylor survived.

Needing money and deciding to take a chance, . . . Taylor planned. . . .

1. She needed money. She decided to take a chance. Annie Edison Taylor planned an adventure.

. . . a pamphlet giving an account. . . .

2. In 1902 she wrote a pamphlet. The pamphlet gave an account of her adventure.

. . . in a barrel measuring . . . and weighing. . . .

3. She went over the falls in a barrel. The barrel measured 4½ feet high and weighed 160 pounds.

Thrown about violently . . . , the barrel went out of control. . . .

4. The barrel went out of control upon landing. It was thrown about violently by the churning waters.

Having survived her ordeal, she made plans. . . .

5. She survived her ordeal. She made plans for a second attempt.

Suggested Answers are provided above each item.

COMBINING SENTENCES WITH ABSOLUTE PHRASES

When you write a narrative or a description, you often build an image by constructing a series of related details, as in these sentences:

> The sun edged toward the dark-pined horizon. The light spun across the lake like a spider's unfolding web. Shadows danced on the glimmering waves.

You can also combine these sentences by changing two of them into absolute phrases. An absolute phrase has no grammatical connection with the rest of the sentence but nevertheless adds to the meaning of the sentence. Here is how the preceding three sentences can be combined as a single sentence with two absolute phrases:

> The sun edged toward the dark-pined horizon, **light spinning across the lake like a spider's unfolding web, shadows dancing on the glimmering waves**.

Absolute phrases are usually most effective when placed in the middle or at the end of a sentence, where they construct a definite, absolute image for the reader to see. Here are two examples:

> The ancient, crippled car, **its engine groaning from years of misuse**, finally died in a seizure.
>
> The ancient, crippled car finally died in a seizure, **its engine groaning from years of misuse**.

Note that in both of these examples the effect of the absolute phrase is to shift from a description of the whole—the ancient car seizing—to a detailed description of a specific part—"its engine groaning with years of misuse." You can use absolute phrases to emphasize the specific parts of a scene or an action.

Objective

EXERCISE 11. Combining Sentences by Using Absolute Phrases. Combine each set of sentences by using an absolute phrase or phrases. Place them where they will be most effective and make sense.

SAMPLE: The stern eagle surveyed the mountain cliffs. Its eyes measured the familiar terrain.

ANSWER: Its eyes measuring the familiar terrain, the stern eagle surveyed the mountain cliffs.

Sharon turned . . . , her legs aching with pain, her mind spinning. . . .

1. Sharon turned toward the final one-hundred yards of the race. Her legs ached with pain. Her mind was spinning deliriously.

Its hull riddled . . . , its sails flapping helplessly, the old boat limped. .

2. The old boat limped across the bay. Its hull was riddled with scars of time. Its sails flapped helplessly.

. . . sat silently in . . . room, his eyes closed, his hands gently folded.

3. The elderly man sat silently in the empty room. His eyes were closed. His hands were gently folded.

Their faces twisted in anguish, the runners approached. . . .

4. The marathon runners approached Heartbreak Hill. Their faces were twisted in anguish.

Suggested Answers are provided above each item.

WRITING CONCISE SENTENCES AND PARAGRAPHS

When you revise your writing, you should eliminate any unnecessary words and work toward concise sentences that are uncluttered, compact, and direct.

You can make your writing **concise** by removing unnecessary or repetitious language and by simplifying long structures.

1. Eliminate unnecessary words and phrases, such as the following:
   - phrases such as "I think" or "I believe." Your reader knows that your writing is your opinion.
   - qualifying words such as "probably" or "somewhat." Say what you mean without hedging. Be direct.
   - redundant, or excess, words and phrases

Unnecessary words are shaded.

I believe that everybody in our town would probably benefit from the construction and building of bike paths, which in my opinion would eliminate the dangers of riding bikes on roads and reduce somewhat the high bike-auto accident rate.

Concise revision

Our town would benefit from the construction of bike paths, which would reduce the high bike-auto accident rate.

2. Combine related sentences, subordinating and coordinating ideas where possible..

CHOPPY: In the 1580s the Spanish had a large Armada. It consisted of 130 ships. It was the greatest naval fleet at that time. It sailed the Atlantic Ocean.

CONCISE: In the 1580s the 130-ship Spanish Armada was the greatest naval fleet sailing the Atlantic Ocean.

3. Reduce clauses to words or phrases.

WORDY: The Beatles were a singing group that was very talented.
CONCISE: The Beatles were a very talented singing group.

4. Break up rambling sentences into shorter sentences.

RAMBLING: Beatle fans were a dedicated group, and some would camp out for days in front of the box office, while others would offer all their worldly possessions for a single concert ticket, and it was obvious that Beatlemania had smitten these admirers.
CONCISE: Beatle fans were a dedicated group. Some camped out for days in front of the box office, while others offered all their worldly possessions for a single ticket. Beatlemania had smitten these admirers.

Objective
EXERCISE 12. Writing Concisely. Rewrite the following paragraph to make its sentences more concise. You will have to eliminate repetitious language and simplify long structures. You will have to combine short sentences and change some long sentences into two short sentences.

In my opinion, many civilizations throughout the world have probably been blindly upsetting nature's balance for years, decades, and generations. There are a number of causes for the threat to nature's balance. The causes are connected. Populations rapidly expanded. The need for living space has increased. This, in turn, led to increased development. That development sometimes threatens various species and types of animals with near extinction and destruction. One example of this vicious cycle comes to mind. It was the construction of the Welland Canal. The Canal was built in 1829. It was a passage to bypass Niagara Falls from Lake Ontario to Lake Erie. It opened the Great Lakes to the shipping industry. It also opened the lakes to the sea lamprey. The lamprey is an eel-like parasite. Its favorite food is the lake trout. By the 1950s sea lampreys had nearly destroyed the trout population from Lake Erie to Lake Superior, and so scientists had to quickly introduce a chemical that was toxic to lamprey larva and thus were able to control the lamprey population, and they thus prevented further loss of the trout population. In this case, a species of fish survived. Years were spent rectifying a situation. The situation was the result of blind development.

CREATING VARIETY IN SENTENCES

Thus far you have practiced a number of methods and techniques for combining sentences. In this section you will use those techniques in paragraphs to make your writing more interesting and effective.

VARYING SENTENCE LENGTHS AND STRUCTURES

If you vary the presentation of sentences in a paragraph by mixing short, simple structures with more complicated structures, your writing will sound lively and mature. More important, your readers will respond attentively.

Vary the length and structures of your sentences.

The following suggestions will help you create variety in the length and structure of your sentences:

1. Read a piece of your writing aloud, listening to the rhythm created by the sentence. Are all the sentences the same length, or do the lengths and structures vary. If all your sentences are short, combine some, making longer ones. If your sentences are mostly long and rambling, break up some of them.
2. To balance or contrast ideas and to create a series of items, use coordinated sentence structures.
3. For arranging and emphasizing ideas, use a variety of subordinated structures.
4. Use participles, appositives, gerunds, and absolutes to express information concisely or to create a feeling of dynamic action.
5. A single short sentence following a series of longer ones will indicate a change of thought, emphasize a point, or clinch a paragraph.

Objective

EXERCISE 13. Varying Sentence Lengths and Structures. Revise and rewrite the following paragraph by combining sentences and rearranging the information within them. Use a variety of sentence lengths and structures.

The ocean fascinates our family. The ocean surges with raw power. It soothes with a repetitive beat. Our son Joe wanted to see Sandy's beach. We decided to go with him. The family awoke at dawn. We picked up his friend. His friend's name is Marty. Almost all the traffic was going in the opposite direction. Many cars were heading into the city. Eventually we arrived at a place. At that place slate cliffs rose on our left. The sea fell on our right. The sea smashed against the cliffs. A small opening in the cliffs is Sandy's Beach. The cliffs there had been pulverized into sand. Sandy's beach is a stretch of fine grained, slate-colored sand. Sandy's beach is a stretch of fine grained, slate-colored sand. Joe and Marty put on their fins. They stood at the edge for a moment. They reached down. They touched the cold water. They did that before diving in. We watched. We were at a safe distance. They disappeared into foamy surf. The surf was swirling.

VARYING SENTENCE BEGINNINGS

An English sentence commonly begins with its subject. You can often give your writing greater impact by varying the ways you begin your sentences. The beginning of a sentence is a strong position; therefore, the words and details that you place there will receive greater emphasis.

Try to vary the beginnings of sentences.

1. You can begin a sentence with a single word set apart from the rest of the sentence:

   Angry, she marched up the steps and banged on the door.
   Sheepishly he cowered and quivered behind the door.

2. You can begin a sentence with a phrase:

   Chattering nervously, Robert paced back and forth.

3. You can begin a sentence with a subordinated idea:

   Even though the sun is dark during a solar eclipse, you should not look directly at it.

4. You can invert the order of a sentence from subject-verb-modifier to modifier-verb-subject:

   MODIFIER VERB SUBJECT
   Across the icy field stood frozen stalks of corn.

Objective

EXERCISE 14. Varying Sentence Beginnings. Rewrite the following paragraph by combining sentences and rearranging the structures within them to create a variety of sentence beginnings.

The year was 1766. That year Henry David Thoreau's grandfather staged a protest at Harvard College. Henry David Thoreau's grandfather was Asa Dunbar. Thoreau's grandfather disliked the quality of food at Harvard. He was agitated. He voiced his displeasure with a slogan. The slogan read, "Behold, our butter stinketh." The college faculty quickly reacted. They condemned Asa Dunbar for the "sin of insubordination." Their condemnation was a serious matter. That did not stop Dunbar and his followers. They held a student eat-out. They breakfasted off campus. This act may have been the first official student protest. It was eighty years after that incident. Dunbar's grandson protested a more serious issue. Dunbar's grandson was Henry David Thoreau. Thoreau refused to pay a tax. He protested government policies. The policies supported the Mexican-American War and slavery. Thoreau's aunt paid his fine. He did spend a night in jail. He wrote the essay *Civil Disobedience*. It resulted from that experience. The essay later influenced such people as Gandhi and Martin Luther King.

VARYING SENTENCE TYPES

Do you use declarative statements most of the time when you write? Try to vary those statements with an occasional question or command as in following paragraph:

Are you a top-notch, hard driving corporate executive? Could you survive five minutes in a wooded area other than your golf course? If not, a school in the rural hinterlands of New England has come to your rescue. Enroll in its two-week course and develop wilderness survival skills. The course teaches self-sufficiency but stresses *cooperative* effort. Then take a few of your acquired skills back to work. Your competitive business world would benefit from a transfusion of the cooperative spirit.

Objective

EXERCISE 15. Varying Sentence Types. Rewrite the following passage, combining choppy sentences to create sentences of varying lengths, structures, and beginnings. Use at least one question and one command.

Some people in our modern society have been captured by the television set. They watch television excessively. They spend four, six or twelve hours each day in front of the set. Critics of television call the medium a vast electronic wasteland. They argue that we have become its slave. Here is an example: A person spends six hours each day. He or she is glued to the tube. That same person watches programs for sixty years. That same person has wasted fifteen years of life. A four-hour-a-day viewer wastes time, too. That viewer wastes ten years of real living. That is over a sixty-year period. People could put such time to better use. They could read books. They could write. They could invent. They could help others less fortunate than themselves. Television has a control button. It should be used. People should control the television. It should not control people.

USING PARALLELISM FOR EFFECT

Using similar structure within a sentence or within a series of sentences helps to tie related ideas together. This technique is called parallelism. Parallelism means that ideas similar in content are expressed in similar sentence structures.

Use **parallelism** to emphasize the links between related ideas.

Parallelism, like any of the previously introduced techniques, should not be used to excess. When used to add variety to the sentence structures in your writing, parallelism can add grace and fluency to the rhythm of your sentences.

You can use parallelism to present a series of related ideas:

NOT PARALLEL: Dance marathons in the 1930s promised prizes and **that the winners would be recognized.**

PARALLEL: Dance marathons in the 1930s promised the winners **prizes** and **recognition.**

You can also use parallelism to balance or contrast ideas:

NOT PARALLEL: Dance in a natural rhythm, and **your manner should be relaxed as you move.**

PARALLEL: Dance in a natural rhythm, and **move in a relaxed manner.**

Objective

EXERCISE 16. Correcting Faulty Parallelism. Rewrite each of these sentences to express related ideas in similar or parallel structures.

. . . running, biking, hiking, and being outdoors.

1. Americans seem to like running, biking, hiking, and to be outdoors.

To try . . . to work . . . , and to excel. . . .

2. To try your best, to work your hardest, and excelling have long been American ideals in sports.

. . . not only in sports but in business.

3. These goals seem to hold not only in sports but also in doing business.

. . . winning or getting all the applause . . . as playing.

4. Remember, though, that winning or whether you get all the applause is not as important as playing.

Suggested Answers are provided above each item.

Objective

EXERCISE 17. Using Variety and Parallelism in a Paragraph. Rewrite the following paragraph, combining the short sentences to create a variety of sentence lengths, structures, and beginnings. Where appropriate, use parallelism and different types of sentences.

A movie critic's job is glorious. Many people think that. It is not an easy job. A critic spends years learning the job. The critic develops a writing style. The critic acquires a knowledge of film. The critic slowly understands the nature of film criticism. Critics often spend ten or more years in self-preparation. Those critics are dedicated to film. Most critics eventually can identify a good film. They can distinguish it from a bad one. They must, of course, view hundreds of films each year. That can be a rather long, boring experience. A few films produced each year are excellent. Most are inferior. Most lack originality. Most lack interest. The critic must make judgments about the quality of the acting. The critic also judges the quality of the direction and the editing. The script is also evaluated by the critic. The script is the film's storyline. Critics also interpret films. To interpret is to analyze a film's meaning. Then they must write their evaluation and interpretation in a review. The review often has a very rigid deadline.

WRITER'S CHOICE #1

ASSIGNMENT: To revise a passage from a lower grade-level textbook or a junior book

LENGTH: A passage of two or three paragraphs

AUDIENCE: General, adult population

PURPOSE: To revise a passage so that it is appropriate for an adult audience

PREWRITING: Choose a passage of two or three paragraphs from a fourth, fifth, or sixth grade elementary school textbook about science, history, or geography, or choose a passage from a junior book. Review the passage, carefully looking for sentences that you could subordinate, coordinate, or expand.

WRITING: Revise and rewrite the passage by using expansion, coordination, and subordination techniques.

REVISING: Make sure that you have used a variety of lengths and structures. Revise sentences that excessively repeat the same structural pattern.

WRITER'S CHOICE #2

ASSIGNMENT: To revise sentences in a piece of your own writing

LENGTH: Your choice

AUDIENCE: Your choice

PURPOSE: Your choice

OPTIONS:
- Choose a paragraph of your own of any length. Decide whether your sentences tend to be too short, too long, repetitious in their structures or in their beginnings.
- Rewrite the paragraph, directing your attention to its problems and using some of the techniques that you have practiced in this chapter to remedy those problems.

WRITER'S CHOICE #3

ASSIGNMENT: To write a campaign speech

LENGTH: Your choice

AUDIENCE: Your choice

PURPOSE: Your choice

OPTIONS:
- You may find an idea in the Writer's Sourcebook, pages 346–347.
- Follow the prewriting, writing, and revising steps you practiced in Chapters 1–4.
- As you revise, aim for variety in sentence lengths and structures.

7 CHAPTER
Developing a Writing Style

So, then, what is style? There are two chief aspects of any piece of writing: 1. what you say and 2. how you say it. The former is "content" and the latter is "style."

—Isaac Asimov

Writing, as Isaac Asimov, the American biochemist and well-known scientific and science-fiction writer, points out, involves both knowing what you want to say and saying it clearly and effectively. To Asimov, *how* a thing is said is as important as *what* is said. The "how," as Asimov states, is *style.*

You already have a writing style that is your own, one that you have been developing since you first began to write. It is increasingly important to continue developing that style so that it becomes both more effective and more truly representative of you.

Style is the characteristic way of writing that distinguishes one writer from another.

No matter what you expect your future involvement with writing to be, a pleasing and direct style will work for you. Whether you go on to produce short stories or articles as a professional writer or reports and letters as a member of business or industry, a clear, direct, and precise style will help you to get your message across. Clarity, grace, and precision are qualities that invite your readers to pay attention, to hear you out.

In this chapter you will learn how to add brightness and polish to your writing by sharpening the following skills:

- prewriting: choosing a suitable voice for subject and audience
- prewriting: finding your own voice as a writer
- writing: developing a personal style
- revising for style, voice, and tone

PREWRITING: CHOOSING AN APPROPRIATE VOICE FOR SUBJECT AND AUDIENCE

Your **voice** as a writer is the *you* behind your words. The **tone** of your voice reflects the attitude toward your subject that you want to communicate to your audience.

Each person has a voice that is distinctive and recognizable. When you answer a phone call from a friend, for example, the friend knows immediately by your voice that it is you. As a writer, however, you have several voices from which to choose. Which voice you decide to use depends on what you are writing about, your attitude toward your topic, and the nature of the audience for which you are writing. To attune your ear to the varied voices of a writer, read the following responses to a request for help with an unpleasant job:

VOICE 1: I seem to recall that I'm busy on Saturday morning. I'll have to check.

VOICE 2: Why should I help *you?*

VOICE 3: Of course, I'll help you. By the way, didn't you say I could borrow your car?

VOICE 4: I have better things to do with my Saturday mornings than to wash your car for you.

Each response speaks in a different tone and suggests a different attitude. Voice 1 is evasive; voice 2 is annoyed; voice 3 is self-serving; voice 4 is sarcastic. By adopting a different tone of voice, a writer can control an audience's response to the message behind the words.

A writer can and must adopt different voices for different audiences. Here are the several voices of one writer who is explaining volcanoes to two different audiences. What voice has the writer adopted in each case? Why would each voice be appropriate for the audience named at the start of the passage?

An Audience of Science Students

The most noticeable feature of a volcano's explosive eruption is the significant cloud of gases, vapor, and ash particles. The popular misconception that volcanoes are mountains on fire arises from the cloud's smoky and fiery appearance. This popular notion has always gained apparent support from the nature of the material that descends from the vapor cloud. This material, which closely resembles cinders and ash, is known to the geologist as *pyroclast.*

An Audience of Young Children

Have you ever wondered what makes a volcano form? The temperature under the surface of the earth becomes hotter the deeper you go. At about twenty miles below the surface, the temperature is hot enough to melt rock. When rock melts, the melted material moves upward through cracks in the earth. If these cracks lie close to the surface, the melted material can break through. Hot liquid and solid material are blown out. They pour out around the opening and form a cone-shaped mound or hill. This is the volcano.

The purpose of each paragraph—to teach the audience about volcanoes—is clear, but the tone of voice in each paragraph is very different. For the audience of science students, the writer adopts an analytical tone and freely uses technical and scientific vocabulary. Addressing younger readers, however, the writer chooses a simple and direct tone and avoids technical language completely. Because the tone of the writer's voice reinforces the writer's purpose, it is appropriate in each case.

Objective

EXERCISE 1. Identifying Voice in Writing. Indicate in writing whether the voice chosen by the author of each statement below is appropriate to the audience named in parentheses before the statement. Then in a sentence for each item, explain why you think the voice is appropriate or inappropriate.

1. (general audience) Have you ever wondered why grown men and women can become absolutely fascinated by colorful pieces of paper called postage stamps?
2. (fourth graders) Carbon-permeated fuels include lignite, bituminous and semibituminous coal, and anthracite.
3. (physicians) Myocardial oxygen requirements are generally increased by increases in heart rate, increases in contractility, and increases in total vascular resistance.
4. (financial experts) If many people want an item, its price will rise.
5. (senior citizens) The knowledge and experience of older Americans is extremely valuable and cannot be wasted.

Suggested Answers: **1**, **3**, and **5**—appropriate; **2** and **4**—inappropriate. In their evaluations students should consider the needs of each audience.

PREWRITING: FINDING YOUR OWN VOICE AS A WRITER

Effective writers express themselves with conviction and authority. You are already familiar with some of these authoritative voices: the magazine writer who exposes with forthrightness the existence of shoddy practices in a particular industry or the newspaper columnist who persuades readers to support a local bond issue. Their voices are so strong and clear that you are willing to be convinced by the power of their words. Good writers are always visible just behind their words, guiding and structuring your response to their message.

Writers achieve an authoritative voice by expressing themselves with such clarity and conviction that the reader is compelled to follow their presentation. One sentence draws you to the next. The tone of voice reveals the writer's beliefs, attitudes, and concerns.

Most of all, this tone makes you trust the writer's competence to handle the subject. In the passage that follows, H. L. Mencken, the American social critic and language expert, clearly establishes his credentials for discussing his chosen subject.

The American, probably more than any other man, is prone to be apologetic about the trade he follows. He seldom believes that it is quite worthy of his ventures and talents; almost always he thinks that he would have adorned something far gaudier. Unfortunately, it is not always possible for him to escape, or even for him to dream plausibly of escaping, so he soothes himself by assuring himself that he belongs to a superior section of his craft, and very often he invents a sonorous name to set himself off from the herd. Here we glimpse the origin of a multitude of characteristic American euphemisms, *e.g., mortician* for *undertaker, realtor* for *real estate agent, electrologist* for *electrical contractor, aisle manager* for *floor-walker, beautician* for *hairdresser, exterminating engineer* for *rat-catcher* and so on. . . .

—H. L. Mencken, *The American Language*

Mencken's style in this passage is forceful, direct, and mocking. As you read the passage, you are aware that the author is poking fun at the American penchant for fancy titles.

In contrast to the Mencken passage, how authoritative is the writer's voice in the following statement?

It is hoped that the economic climate might improve somewhat next year. Should that occur, the company could do a bit better.

Not only is the language in this statement indirect (Who is the *it* that is doing the hoping?), but the writer's voice clearly lacks conviction. Qualifying words—*might, somewhat, should, could, bit* —drain all vigor from the statement.

As you plan your writing, be aware of the authority that you want your voice to carry. Ask yourself the following questions to develop the power of your voice:

- How do I react to my topic? How do I want my readers to react? With sadness? With amusement? With anger? With fear?
- If I am writing to inform, how can I show that I understand my topic thoroughly?
- If I am writing to persuade, what argument most convinces me? How can I use the argument to convince others?
- If I am writing to explain, is any aspect of what I am explaining still hazy to me? What do I still need to explore or read more about in order to be convincing?

• If I am narrating a story, how can I guide and shape the audience's response to my characters and plot?

Objective

EXERCISE 2. Selecting an Appropriate Voice in Writing. Choose one of the following topics or a topic of your own. First identify the purpose and audience for which you are writing. Then describe the tone of voice you think is appropriate for that purpose and audience. Next, prewrite by brainstorming about your topic for five minutes.

1. budgeting personal expenses
2. the importance of exercise
3. a sensible diet
4. pets and responsibility
5. unkept promises
6. paying debts

Finally, reread your prewriting notes. Ask yourself the questions on pages 125–126 to help you write with authority and conviction in your voice. Save your prewriting notes for Exercise 6 on page 130.

WRITING: DEVELOPING A PERSONAL STYLE

All effective writing styles are graceful, clear, and precise. Writing is clear when it communicates directly, leaving no doubt in the reader's mind about what the writer means. Writing is graceful when it appeals to the reader's ear. Writing is precise when it contains nothing unnecessary, when every word and every phrase counts. Whether you are writing a paragraph or a longer work, you should always aim for a style distinguished by **clarity**, **grace**, and **precision**.

CONTROLLING THE RHYTHM OF YOUR PROSE

Like poetry, good prose has an obvious and unmistakable rhythmic quality. Rhythm in poetry is achieved through a regular pattern of stressed and unstressed syllables. In prose, however, rhythm comes from a pleasing variation in the rhythm and flow of words, phrases and clauses, and sentences.

Like poetic rhythm, prose rhythm appeals most directly to the ear. The best way to become fully aware of prose rhythm is to read a passage aloud. When you do, pay particular attention to the variety of sentence structures the writer uses and to the way punctuation helps to control the rhythm. For example, read aloud the following passage from Stephen Crane's short story "The Open Boat." Pay close attention to the rise and fall of the words.

It would be difficult to describe the subtle brotherhood of men that was here established upon the seas. No one said that it was so. No one mentioned it. But it dwelt in the boat, and each man felt it warm him. They were a captain, an oiler, a cook, and a correspondent, and they were friends—friends in a more curiously iron-bound degree than may be common. The hurt captain, lying against the water jar in the bow, spoke always in a low voice and calmly; but he could never command a more ready and swiftly obedient crew than the motley three of the dinghy. It was more than a mere recognition of what was best for the common safety. There was surely in it a quality that was personal and heartfelt. And after this devotion to the commander of the boat, there was this comradeship, that the correspondent, for instance, who had been taught to be cynical of men, knew even at the time, was the best experience of his life. But no one said that it was so. No one mentioned it.

—Stephen Crane

The rhythm of this passage should be obvious when it is read aloud. Notice, however, that this gracefulness is not due only to the sounds of the individual words. Rather, the graceful style arises from a number of factors. Varied sentence lengths, a wide variety of grammatical structures, different sentence types, and careful repetition all work together to give the passage its pleasing and effective rhythmic quality.

Keep the rhythm of your language in mind as you write. Experiment with varied sentence lengths, types, and structures. As you continue to develop as a writer, your efforts to achieve a graceful style will pay dividends, because what you write will be more pleasing and more memorable for your readers.

Objective

EXERCISE 3. Identifying Rhythmic Elements in Prose. Analyze the passage written by H. L. Mencken that appears on page 125. First, read the passage aloud. Then identify in writing the elements that make this passage rhythmic. Pay particular attention to Mencken's use of repetition and punctuation to create rhythm.

CONTROLLING SENTENCE STRUCTURE

Variations in the structure and length of sentences help you achieve a graceful prose rhythm. They are also important in achieving clarity, another key quality of effective writing. Sentence sameness has a monotonous effect that causes the reader's attention to wander away from the writer's message.

To make sure that your writing is clear, pay particular attention to eliminating short, choppy sentences, except when you are using them on purpose to achieve a staccato effect. In most cases, however, but a steady diet of short sentences fails to satisfy the reader and blocks communication. As you learned in Chapter 6, there are available to the writer a number of strategies to vary your sentences. Here are a few of them. Notice how each may be used most effectively to achieve clarity.

1. Expand sentences to vary the length and to add details that create a more precise image in the reader's mind.

   ORIGINAL: The clouds gathered.
   EXPANDED: The ominous black clouds gathered on the horizon.

2. Combine sentences to highlight certain ideas and place others in the background (see Chapter 6).

   ORIGINAL: Watercolor differs from other painting techniques. Its transparency makes it different. It is one of the most difficult mediums to master.
   COMBINED: One of the most difficult mediums to master, watercolor differs from other painting techniques because of its transparency.

3. Vary sentence structures and beginnings.

   ORIGINAL: Golden sunlight streamed through the open window.
   REVISED: Through the open window streamed golden sunlight.

4. Learn to use structures like participial phrases that let you add descriptive details in interesting ways (see Chapter 6).

   ORIGINAL: Lighter-colored, or "white," elephants were considered sacred in ancient times. They were even worshiped in certain parts of the world.
   REVISED: Considered sacred in ancient times, lighter-colored, or "white," elephants were even worshiped in certain parts of the world.

Objective

EXERCISE 4. Improving Clarity and Rhythm. Improve the clarity and rhythm of the following passage by varying the structure and length of the sentences. Make sure that your revision is clear and precise.

The nicknames of our states are interesting. They sometimes shed light on the history of the state and its people. Pennsylvania is called "The Keystone State." It occupied the middle area of the original thirteen colonies. It was the second state to approve the Constitution. Texas is called "The Lone Star State." A single star adorns its flag. "The Buckeye State" is Ohio. It is named for the large number of buckeye trees that once grew there. Delaware is often called "The Diamond State." It was small. It was of great value to the Union. It was the first state to join. Indiana has been given one of the more interesting names. It is known as "The Hoosier State." The river boatmen of Indiana were very tough in the early days. They were also rude. They could silence anyone in an argument. They were called "hushers." In time the word was pronounced "hoosiers." Wisconsin also has an unusual nickname. It is called "The Badger State." Very few badgers have ever set foot in Wisconsin. They live in more northerly areas. Early settlers came to work in Wisconsin's mines. They made homes for themselves in the earth. They built their homes somewhat like a badger does.

USING PRECISE NOUNS AND ACTION VERBS

Appropriate word choice makes what you say come alive by giving precision to your writing. Exact nouns and verbs allow readers to visualize what you are writing about. They give a crispness and freshness to your writing. The following principles will help you to choose effective nouns and verbs.

1. To give precision to your writing, always use specific nouns in place of general nouns.

GENERAL: A boat pulled a line of other boats.
SPECIFIC: A tug pulled a string of barges.

2. Always use specific nouns in place of the general pronouns *they* and *it*.

GENERAL: They say it will snow tomorrow.
SPECIFIC: Forecasters say it will snow tomorrow.

GENERAL: It says in the newspaper that winter will be mild.
SPECIFIC: The newspaper says that winter will be mild.

3. Use specific verbs that describe the action precisely. An exact verb makes a sentence come alive.

GENERAL: Clara hit the ball between first and second base.
EXACT: Clara slammed the ball between first and second base.

4. Whenever possible, use a single strong verb, not a weak verb and a noun, to convey the action you intend.

WEAK: The jet made a circle over the field.
STRONG: The jet circled the field.

5. Break the habit of beginning sentences with *there is* and other forms of this expression. To be more vivid and direct, use a noun and an action verb instead. Compare the two sentences that follow.

VERSION 1: There was confusion in the lobby.
VERSION 2: Confusion filled the lobby.

6. As often as possible, use the active voice of verbs to make your writing vigorous and direct. Active-voice verbs put the emphasis where it belongs—upon the doer of the action.

INDIRECT: The wall was designed and constructed by a skilled stonemason.
DIRECT: A skilled stonemason designed and constructed the wall.

Objective
EXERCISE 5. Using Precise Nouns and Action Verbs. Rewrite the following sentences by replacing general nouns with specific nouns and general verbs with action verbs, by concentrating the action in the verb, by replacing expressions that begin with *there,* and by using active-voice verbs.

An accident occurred . . .
1. There was an accident on South Main Street last night.
flickered
2. Candles burned in the dimly lighted room.
flock honked
3. A bunch of geese made noises throughout the night.
inched
4. We moved slowly along the narrow path.
The Romans originally engineered . . .
5. Some highways in Britain were originally engineered by the Romans.
An old inn stands...
6. There is an old inn on Mercer Street.
vanished into
7. The ship suddenly became invisible in the fog.
The student body has chosen . . .
8. Jennifer has been chosen to represent the school at the meeting.
trickled
9. A narrow stream ran through the center of town.
rounded
10. The train went around the sharp curve at high speed.

Suggested answers are given above each item.

Objective
EXERCISE 6. Writing with Grace, Clarity, and Precision. Reread your prewriting notes from Exercise 2 on page 126. Then write a paragraph on the topic you have chosen. As you write, pay attention to your writing style. Vary the rhythms and structure of your sentences. Be as precise, specific, and vivid as you can be in your wording of examples and details. Use active-voice verbs wherever possible. Save your paragraph for use in Exercise 9 on page 133.

REVISING FOR STYLE, VOICE, AND TONE

The revision stage is your opportunity to rework and polish your writing, to be sure that it represents your best effort. as you become a more practiced writer, you may find that your first draft already incorporates many elements that make it seem clear, precise, and graceful to you. In revising, however, you should try to "re-see" your writing from the viewpoint of someone who has not read it before. Will your writing be as clear to others as it is to you?

The following revision suggestions will help polish the style of your writing in preparation for the final draft.

AVOIDING AMBIGUITY

Ambiguity, or double meaning, is your enemy when you write because it prevents a reader from understanding your intended meaning. You know what your intended message is; but because of haste or inattention, you have expressed it in such a way that your reader receives more than one meaning. Learn to identify and eliminate the following sources of ambiguity.

Misplaced Modifiers

A misplaced modifier is a word, phrase, or clause that does not point clearly to the word it was meant to modify. In some cases the positioning of a single word in a sentence can change the meaning significantly. Notice, for example, the difference that the positioning of *almost* makes in the following pair of sentences.

> It *almost* rained on every day of our vacation. [It never really rained.]
>
> It rained on *almost* every day of our vacation. [It rained quite often.]

Far from the noun or pronoun they were intended to modify. To avoid ambiguity move the modifier nearer the word it modifies.

AMBIGUOUS: We admired the buildings driving down the street.
CLEAR: Driving down the street, we admired the buildings.

The second sentence in the pair makes clear who is driving.

In some cases a modifier is left dangling, with no noun or pronoun that it can logically modify. To avoid ambiguity, rephrase the sentence.

AMBIGUOUS: Sitting in the courtyard, the sun was warm.
CLEAR: Sitting in the courtyard, Cynthia enjoyed the warm sun.

Ambiguous Pronoun Reference

A pronoun must refer clearly to the word it replaces. If a pronoun can logically refer to more than one word in a sentence, the reader receives a double meaning. Eliminate the problem by rewriting the sentence to express the meaning you intend.

AMBIGUOUS: When Anne brought Nancy home from the play, we took photographs of her.
CLEAR: We took photographs of Anne after she brought Nancy home from the play.

CLEAR: We took photographs of Nancy after Anne brought her home from the play.

Faulty Punctuation

Ambiguity can also occur when punctuation is misplaced or omitted. The intended meaning can be made clear by eliminating or supplying punctuation as needed.

AMBIGUOUS: As I watched the hawk swooped down on its prey.
CLEAR: As I watched, the hawk swooped down on its prey.

AMBIGUOUS: At the kennel we inspected the cages, and the dog runs.
CLEAR: At the kennel we inspected the cages and the dog runs.

Objective
EXERCISE 7. Avoiding Ambiguity. Rewrite the following sentences to eliminate ambiguity. Look for problems of unclear punctuation, faulty pronoun reference, and misplaced modifiers.

As I lunged for the leash, the dog . . .
1. I lunged for the dog's leash, but it ran away.

After I had jogged for two hours, the water . . .
2. Having jogged for two hours, the water tasted wonderful.

When Shirley spoke, her words . . .
3. When Shirley spoke her words were audible in the back of the auditorium.

Gail first met Jenna when Jenna was . . . *or* . . . when Gail was . . .
4. Gail first met Jenna when she was seventeen.

We saw a herd of buffalo grazing...
5. Grazing quietly like cattle, we saw a herd of buffalo.

Suggested answers appear above each item.

AVOIDING EMPTY SUPERLATIVES

Avoid empty or meaningless superlatives—words like *outstanding, fantastic,* and *marvelous*—that have become stale from overuse. In their place, use vivid descriptive words and phrases that will allow your audience to visualize the experience you want to communicate.

Avoid as well the excessive use of exclamation marks. Your words, not the punctuation, should communicate the extent of your feeling.

WEAK: That was a fantastic sunset!
REVISED: The western horizon gradually turned crimson, then deep scarlet, and finally blood red. The sky was aflame with color.

Objective
EXERCISE 8. Avoiding Empty Superlatives. Rewrite the following sentences by changing empty superlatives into vivid words and phrases. To relate your exact meaning, you may change other words as needed.

1. My cousin prepared a fantastic meal!
2. What a terrific catch Judson made!
3. That is the greatest jacket I have ever seen.
4. The model ship had fabulous details.

Guidelines for Evaluation: Students should retain the main idea of each sentence but should provide a detailed description.

PARTICIPATING IN WRITING CONFERENCES

In almost every case, you write for an audience. It therefore makes sense to seek a reaction from the readers for whom you write. Writing conferences work best when they are structured. A set of questions such as the following can provide a structure:

1. What do you like best about this piece of writing?
2. What is the writer's purpose? Where in the piece of writing is the writer's purpose made clear?
3. Is the writing clear and precise? Is there one sentence or section of a paragraph in which the writing could be made clearer?
4. For what audience is this piece of writing intended? Where has the writer most effectively addressed the needs of this audience?
5. What has the writer done to maintain your interest?

Objective

EXERCISE 9. Revising Writing on the Basis of Readers' Reactions. Use the preceding list of questions or questions that your teacher provides as the basis for a writing conference. Share with one another the piece of writing for which you did prewriting in Exercise 2 and that you wrote in Exercise 6. Revise your writing, using the reactions you received during the writing conference and the items in the following checklist. Edit and proofread your work.

CHECKLIST FOR DEVELOPING A WRITING STYLE

1. Where are my own attitudes and convictions most strongly evident in my writing?
2. How can I express my ideas more simply and directly?
3. How can I improve the rhythm and grace of my writing?
4. Is my choice of voice and tone appropriate for my audience and my purpose? Is my voice consistent throughout?
5. How can I add variety to the sentence structures I use?
6. Where can I replace general nouns, pronouns, and verbs with specific nouns and verbs?
7. Is there any ambiguity in my writing? How can I add clarity?
8. Have I avoided using empty superlatives?
9. Have I used readers' reactions to improve my writing?

WRITER'S CHOICE #1

ASSIGNMENT: To revise a paragraph written earlier
LENGTH: Your choice
AUDIENCE: Same as for the initial writing
PURPOSE: Same as for the initial writing
PREWRITING: Already done
WRITING: Already done
REVISING: Would that audience recognize your purpose immediately? In what ways could you improve the style of the writing? Is the *you* visible behind your words? Is your writing straightforward? Does your writing have a pleasing rhythm? Do you use a variety of sentence structures? Are your sentences unambiguous? Have you used precise nouns and verbs?

WRITER'S CHOICE #2

ASSIGNMENT: To write a paragraph about something that means a great deal to you
LENGTH: Six to ten sentences
AUDIENCE: Your classmates
PURPOSE: To explain why you find the item attractive or the idea important
PREWRITING: Decide on several features or characteristics that make you value the object or the idea.
WRITING: Begin with a topic sentence. Be clear and direct and to write with authority and conviction. Vary the structure and the lengths of your sentences.
REVISING: Share your writing with others, if possible in a writing conference. Revise your paragraph on the basis of your readers' reaction.

WRITER'S CHOICE #3

ASSIGNMENT: To write a short paragraph on any subject
LENGTH: Your choice
PURPOSE: Your choice
AUDIENCE: Your choice
OPTIONS:
- You may revise a piece of writing from a previous assignment.
- You may base your writing on one or more of the items in the Writer's Sourcebook, pages 346–347.

REVISING: Be sure that your voice is clearly evident behind your words.

THE WRITER

Ken Sachar was born in Dhaka, Bangladesh, where his parents were stationed for two years. He now lives in Englewood Cliffs, New Jersey. His favorite activities and career interests are playing electric and acoustic guitar as well as writing music and lyrics. The following two paragraphs come from an essay that Ken wrote for a college application when he was a senior at the Rockland Country Day School in Congers, New York. He had been asked to choose an event in history and write an essay imagining an alternative outcome.

THE FINISHED PRODUCT

One day in 1861, a bearded man in his fifties was running through the woods of southern Italy. He stumbled into a local tavern and, breathing heavily, sat down at a wooden table. Exhausted, he bowed his head into his folded arms. Only minutes later, the tavern door swung open, and a patrol of Austrian soldiers swaggered in. Seeing nothing more than what they took to be a peasant slumbering at a corner table, they left. They had no idea that they had narrowly missed an opportunity to change history.

The bearded man was Giuseppi Garibaldi, a guerrilla hero with a price on his head. He was a flamboyant rebel fighting to unite Italy into one nation, independent of Austria. In the mid-nineteenth century, there was no single country of Italy; it was a collection of over a dozen small city-states, each with its own ruler, but all under the control of Austria. In the 1820s and 1830s, other local rebels had tried to overthrow their rulers, but none had succeeded. Garibaldi, though, was to be the spark who finally ignited the flame of Italian independence. . . .

THE WRITER AT WORK

Right at the outset, I wanted to seize the reader's attention. Setting the style of the first paragraph was like shooting a screenplay of vigorous, fast-paced action. Since I was describing a dramatic scene in the first paragraph, I needed to use strong visual images and action verbs. I replaced the bland verbs in my first draft with more vivid choices. For instance, Garibaldi didn't simply enter the tavern; he "stumbled" in. He didn't merely put his head down; we can sense his exhaustion as he "bowed his head into his folded arms." The soldiers didn't simply come into the tavern; we can almost hear their boots on the tavern floor as they "swaggered" in.

I also tried to keep a feeling of ongoing action in my sentence structure. Although the sentences vary in their length, none of them is very long and the action really stands out in all of them. In addition, I used participles and participial phrases such as "exhausted," "breathing heavily," and "Seeing nothing more..." to create a sense of simultaneous action.

Then, by the end of the first paragraph, it was time to shift gears from actions to ideas. I tried to keep the reader's curiosity piqued by the last sentence of the first paragraph. This final sentence serves as a transition to the next paragraph, which is written in a totally different style. In the second paragraph I was no longer painting an action picture. Instead, I was explaining the significance of the historical characters and events. The shorter, staccato sentences of the first paragraph give way to longer sentences presenting historical explanations. Each sentence presents several pieces of background information. Explanatory writing, though, must never be dull or confusing. I tried to maintain interest by introducing vivid adjectives and figures of speech as I edited this paragraph. The rebel became a "flamboyant" rebel. Finally, having set the stage and portrayed mid-nineteenth-century Italy as something of a tinder box, I made Garibaldi a "spark" who ignited a "flame."

In brief, then, I tried to make the style of each paragraph fit its particular purpose. The choice of each word or phrase and the construction of each sentence contributed to that style and helped create the mood I wanted.

YOUR TURN **Writing with Contrasting Styles**

Find a topic on which you can write two connected paragraphs with different purposes and styles. As Ken did, you may want to write one paragraph vividly, painting a scene or action, and a second paragraph expressing an idea or presenting background information about that scene or action. Be sure to choose words and build sentences that suit the purpose you have in mind for each paragraph.

CHAPTERS 5–7 WORDS, SENTENCES, AND STYLE

CHAPTER 5 CHOOSING WORDS

Writing Precisely and Writing Concisely (pages 81–87 and 87–90) Read the following passage, and indicate the letter of the item that correctly answers each question.

[1]Myron delivered a nice speech at yesterday's annual business meeting. [2]At first he seemed up-tight, but eventually he gained his composure and spoke with confidence. [3]After weeks of deliberation and much thought, he had reached a decision in his thinking. [4]Myron stated that he had tendered his resignation forthwith as manager of the Human Resources Department. [5]He indicated that he would be happy as a lark in his new role as interoffice mailman.

1. Which of the following words would be more specific and more richly connotative than *nice* in sentence 1?
   (a) good **(b)** interesting **(c)** striking
2. Sentence 2 mixes which levels of diction?
   (a) informal/formal **(b)** middle/informal **(c)** middle/formal
3. Indicate which of the following best describes the words "reached a decision" in sentence 3.
   (a) jargon **(b)** idiom **(c)** euphemism
4. How would you rewrite sentence 3 to eliminate the redundancy?
   (a) After weeks of deliberation and much thought, he had reached a decision.
   (b) After weeks of deliberation, he had reached a decision.
   (c) After deliberation, he had reached a decision in his thinking.
5. How would you improve the inflated diction in sentence 4?
   (a) . . . he had submitted his resignation. . . .
   (b) . . . he had committed himself to a course of resignation. . . .
   (c) . . . he had resigned. . . .
6. "Human Resources Department" in sentence 4 is an example of:
   (a) cliché **(b)** jargon **(c)** idiom
7. Which of the following is an example of a cliché?
   (a) happy as a lark **(b)** mailman **(c)** gained his composure
   (d) reached a decision
8. How would you change the sexist language to nonsexist language in sentence 5?
   (a) change *he* to *he or she* **(b)** change *lark* to *bird* **(c)** change *mailman* to *mail carrier*

Writing Figuratively (pages 91–94) Indicate the letter of the item that correctly answers each question.

9. Which of the following contains a simile?
   (a) The senator spoke for three straight hours, lost in the reverie of some long soliloquy.
   (b) Most of the audience, as silent as stone, slept through the three-hour speech.

10. Which of these contains both a metaphor and personification?
 (a) Spring is a single flower bud announcing its own rebirth.
 (b) Spring is like a single flower bud rising from the death of winter.

Answers: **1.** c; **2.** a; **3.** b; **4.** b; **5.** c; **6.** b; **7.** a; **8.** c; **9.** b; **10.** a

Writing for Review Write a paragraph about an event or a place that interests you. Be sure to use concrete, specific words and at least one figure of speech. Reread and revise your first draft.

CHAPTER 6 WRITING AND COMBINING SENTENCES

Combining Sentences with Coordination, Subordination, and Other Structures (pages 95–115) Read the following passage, and indicate the letter of the item that correctly answers each question.

[1]Ben Franklin is best known as a skilled political leader and inventor. [2]He was also an advertising copywriter. [3]Franklin wrote the first modern competitive ad. [4]It proclaimed the benefits of one of his inventions. [5]Franklin wrote the ad in the 1700s. [6]He published it in the *Pennsylvania Gazette.* [7]He had invented a new type of stove. [8]Franklin wanted to sell it to the public. [9]His ad argued that using his stove would reduce the problems of poor eyesight, dry skin, and rotting teeth.

1. Which of these pairs of sentences could you combine by using the word *although?*
 (a) sentences 2 and 3 **(b)** sentences 1 and 2 **(c)** sentences 6 and 7
2. Which of these pairs of sentences could you combine by changing one of the sentences into an adjective clause introduced by *which?*
 (a) sentences 6 and 7 **(b)** sentences 1 and 2 **(c)** sentences 3 and 4
3. Which of these sentences could you combine through coordination?
 (a) sentences 6 and 7 **(b)** sentences 4 and 5 **(c)** sentences 5 and 6
4. Which of these sentences should probably *not* be combined with another sentence?
 (a) sentence 1 **(b)** sentence 6 **(c)** sentence 7 **(d)** sentence 9
5. Which of these pairs of sentences could you combine by making one sentence into a participial phrase?
 (a) sentences 6 and 7 **(b)** sentences 2 and 3 **(c)** sentences 3 and 4

Writing Varied Sentences and Using Parallelism (pages 116–120) Read the following passage, and answer the questions based on it.

[1]The first subway was built in London. [2]The first subway was built in 1863. [3]A steam locomotive powered the subway cars. [4]The steam locomotive emitted a strong sulfurous smoke. [5]The subway cars, rattling with high-pitched noises and that smelled of sulfur, were without windows. [6]One might question how such a poorly designed method of transportation became popular. [7]I think its popularity was the result of its newness and also the curiosity of the public was aroused, and more than nine million people rode the underground subway in the first year of its initial operation.

6. Which pair of sentences could be combined by reducing one to a prepositional phrase?
 (a) sentences 1 and 2 **(b)** sentences 4 and 5 **(c)** sentences 6 and 7

7. Which pair of sentences could be combined by changing one to an adjective clause?
   (a) sentences 2 and 3 **(b)** sentences 3 and 4 **(c)** sentences 5 and 6
8. Which sentence could be written more concisely or perhaps even be divided into two or more separate sentences?
   (a) sentence 1 **(b)** sentence 3 **(c)** sentence 6 **(d)** sentence 7
9. To add variety, which sentence could you rewrite as a question?
   (a) sentence 1 **(b)** sentence 4 **(c)** sentence 6 **(d)** sentence 7
10. Which sentence contains structures that should be rewritten to make them parallel?
   (a) sentence 2 **(b)** sentence 5 **(c)** sentence 7 **(d)** sentence 4

Answers: **1.** b; **2.** c; **3.** b; **4.** d; **5.** a; **6.** a; **7.** b; **8.** d; **9.** c; **10.** b

Writing for Review Rewrite one of the paragraphs in the review for Chapter 6. Improve the sentences by writing concisely and by varying sentence lengths and structures.

CHAPTER 7 DEVELOPING A WRITING STYLE

Choosing an Appropriate Voice (pages 122–126) Indicate whether each statement is written in a voice that is **(a)** appropriate or **(b)** inappropriate for the audience named in parentheses.

1. (experienced mechanics) I would like to tell you how the internal combustion engine works.
2. (adults learning about computers) An interpreter is a special system program that translates a program written in a higher-level source code into an object code.

Developing a Personal Style (pages 126–130) Read each lettered pair of items. Indicate the letter of the item that is written with greater clarity or precision.

3. **(a)** In the newspaper it reported on this weekend's parade.
   (b) The newspaper reported on this weekend's parade.
4. **(a)** There was a very sudden thunderstorm yesterday afternoon.
   (b) A sudden thunderstorm struck the city yesterday afternoon.
5. **(a)** The police announced a crackdown on speeders.
   (b) The announcement said they will crack down on speeders.

Revising for Style (pages 130–133) Indicate whether the item is an example of **(a)** unclear pronoun reference, **(b)** unclear sentence structure, **(c)** misplaced modifier, or **(d)** empty superlative.

6. After the train chugged in the passengers boarded quickly.
7. Passing the test with a high score, my parents bought me a watch.
8. Karen made an ultra-fantastic play in the second quarter.
9. Tim told Caesar that he had to fill out an application.
10. I have always enjoyed walking, and hiking.

Answers: **1.** b; **2.** a; **3.** b; **4.** b; **5.** a; **6.** b; **7.** c; **8.** d; **9.** a; **10.** b

Writing for Review Following the steps of the writing process, write a paragraph describing a beautiful scene that you have witnessed. When you revise, pay special attention to your writing style.

UNIT III
The Modes of Writing

Each of the following paragraphs focuses on the same subject, a striped bass. Each paragraph, however, serves a fundamentally different purpose. As you read, try to see what that purpose is.

There in the quiet shallows, resting for just a moment, hovered a majestic striped bass, its bull-like body offset by the beauty of its markings—a dark olive-green-to-silvery-scaled body across which flashed a series of interrupted dark stripes. A wily fifty-pounder, how many hooks had it eluded in its passage to this spot?

Just as the sun slid behind the inland mountains, the huge fish struck. Bent in an arc, my pole strained against the raw power of the thrashing fish. After twenty minutes of battle, I guided the exhausted striped bass through the rocks to the sand. After removing the hook, I carefully placed him in the shallows near the ocean's edge. He stirred, breathed heavily several times, then slowly eased himself into the foamy surf—and disappeared.

The striped bass makes two distinct kinds of migration. In one, the fish travels inland to spawn; for example, schools of bass move from the salt water of the Atlantic to the upper, freshwater reaches of the Hudson River. The second type of migration is coastal, a northward passage from the Chesapeake area to the New England and Canadian coasts. This migration begins in the spring and ends with a return trip in the fall. During this spectacular trip, the fish gorge themselves; their voracious appetites make them easy prey for thousands of commercial and sport fishermen.

A federal law should be passed that will severely restrict or perhaps eliminate for several years both commercial and sport fishing for striped bass. In recent years this species of fish has drastically dwindled in numbers and is now in danger of becoming another extinct species. Pollution of spawning beds, toxic chemical intake, and excessive commercial and sport fishing have all contributed to the destruction of this glorious fish. It is time to halt the pursuit, before it becomes too late.

Each of these paragraphs explores a different approach to the subject of the striped bass. Each is in a different mode or type of writing—description, narration, exposition, and persuasion—with its own characteristics and techniques. During the next four chapters you will apply the writing process to each of these four modes of writing.

CHAPTER 8
Descriptive Writing

"Don't tell 'em—SHOW 'em!"

—George M. Cohan

George M. Cohan aimed his directive about "showing" and not "telling" at a young, inexperienced playwright. It is also good advice when applied to descriptive writing. To describe is to show. When you describe an object, a scene, or a person, you re-create your subject by showing your reader various sensory features of that subject.

Descriptive writing creates a clear and vivid impression of a person, place, or thing.

In this chapter you will practice the following steps and varieties of descriptive writing:

- prewriting: purpose and audience
- prewriting: sensory details
- prewriting: overall impression
- writing a description: organization and coherence
- writing a description: descriptive language
- writing a description: mood
- writing a character sketch
- revising, editing, and publishing descriptive writing

In the following pages you will write descriptions of various objects, places, and people. Your purpose will be to describe your subject so exactly that your reader will see it—and possibly hear, smell, taste, and touch it—through the suggestive power and vividness of your words.

PREWRITING: PURPOSE AND AUDIENCE

The main **purpose** in descriptive writing is to describe. You should, however, have a more specific purpose in mind when you begin to write a description. For example, you may want to describe a restored section of your home town in order to convince local government that urban redevelopment should be a major priority. On another occasion you may want to describe your pet boa constrictor to a friend so that your friend will appreciate its charms. Knowing specifically *why* you want to describe something or someone will help you to determine the best way of organizing and presenting your description.

You cannot write with a purpose unless you also have in mind a specific **audience,** the person or persons who will read your work. You must select your words, sentence structure, and organization to meet the needs of your audience.

To define your purpose and audience, ask yourself the following questions:

- Why do I want to write the description? To inform? To persuade? To gain sympathy? To entertain? Do I have another purpose or combination of purposes?
- Who is going to read the description? How much do my readers already know about my subject? Will they need special information to understand any part of my subject?

It may also be necessary to refine your purpose further after you have learned more about your subject and audience. For example, suppose you are writing a description of the Golden Gate Bridge for a high school magazine. During your research you discover some interesting facts and stories about the construction of the bridge. You decide that your readers would be interested in some of those historical facts. You have altered your purpose—after learning more about your subject and considering your audience. A change, or a refinement, of purpose often indicates that you are focusing on an aspect of your subject that truly interests you. That interest, in turn, should lead to interesting writing.

Objective

EXERCISE 1. Identifying Purposes for a Description. Study the following example. Then for each of the numbered subjects after the example, list at least two specific purposes that a writer could have in mind during the prewriting stage of descriptive writing.

SUBJECT OF DESCRIPTION	POSSIBLE PURPOSES OF DESCRIPTION
the insides of a microcomputer	• to inform readers about how the size of computers has been diminishing • to describe how deceptively simple a microcomputer appears • to convince readers that microcomputer circuits are extremely complex

1. a famous building
2. a sundial or some other instrument for measuring time
3. a food that you either enjoy or dislike

Suggested Answer for 1: Purposes might be to help readers visualize the structure and to explain its historical importance.

Objective

EXERCISE 2. Selecting an Audience for a Description. For each of the following subjects for a description, choose and list two intended audiences. One audience should be of experts in the general subject area; the other should be of nonexperts, people unfamiliar with the subject. Then select one of the subjects that follow. Write two or three sentences that tell how your purpose and description might differ for each of the two audiences.

1. a new but talented singing group or band
2. a new car model
3. a flower or a vegetable garden

PREWRITING: SENSORY DETAILS

Details are concrete, specific features of a person, object, place, or experience. **Sensory details** are details that appeal to the senses of sight, hearing, smell, taste, and touch.

People experience life through their senses. As a writer you can bring a subject to life by describing it through as many senses as possible. For example, when you describe a storm to your readers, try to make them see the frightening chaos—the brooding, dark sky, the massive coal-black clouds, the flashing lightning, and the steady downpour of rain. Better yet, try to make them *hear* the booming thunder rolls and *feel* the earth's trembling response.

RECOGNIZING SENSORY DETAILS

In the following passage Edwin Way Teale, author and naturalist, shares a sensory experience with his readers. To how many different senses do Teale's words appeal?

> Across the warm meadows, other crickets, crickets in uncounted numbers, are wide awake. The air pulsates with the shrill sound of their stridulating wings. The ringing, singing fields of late September!
>
> Rising and falling, the sound of this insect music is dominant in my ears as I stand, a little later, watching a butterfly migrant—a lone monarch, perhaps the last of the year. The journeying insect drifts by in the sunshine, coming from some place farther to the north, probably from Canada, perhaps from as far as the land below Hudson Bay. So late on its long journey, it moves without haste, with no indication of urgency. I follow its flight with my eyes. It crosses the pond and rises over the trees. It disappears and leaves me behind. I feel suddenly closer to the months of cold.
>
> —Edwin Way Teale, *A Walk Through the Year*

Teale refers to the senses of sight, hearing, and touch. Some descriptive details even combine senses. For example, the phrase *pulsates with the shrill sound* evokes sensations of motion and sound.

Teale's sensory details are absolutely necessary to the description. Without such details, the description would be barren, lifeless, like this:

> Many crickets were in the meadow. You could hear the noises. A monarch butterfly flew across the meadow, migrating from far away. It disappeared. Winter seemed nearby.

The preceding passage contains the same general information as Teale's description. This passage, however, evokes no response in a reader, shares no sensory experience, and does not reveal a writer's feelings or attitudes toward the subject. On the other hand, in Teale's original you can sense the writer's physical and emotional presence and his feelings of joy and sadness as he describes the meadow and the sensory signals of autumn and of impending winter.

Objective

EXERCISE 3. Thinking About Sensory Details. Read the following descriptive passage, and list the concrete sensory details that the author uses. On your list note which sense each detail evokes.

Early in the morning we set off again in the big deep canoe and wound our way through the man-made canals cut in the high grass that stretches for miles between the main river and Chambri Lake. It was very hot and still; the black water of the channels—black from its deposits of decaying vegetable matter—had a pungent odor that mixed strangely with the taste of the anchovies we had for lunch. The lake, smooth as glass, was as beautiful as it had been pictured, and the Tchambuli villages looked prosperous and full of promise for the work we wanted to do.

—Margaret Mead, *Blackberry Winter*

COLLECTING SENSORY DETAILS

In order to write effective description, you need to see and remember as many sensory details as you can. You have already used observation as a prewriting technique in Chapter 2. Now sharpen your powers of observation and your memory with questions like these:

1. What does my subject look like? What is its color, size, and shape?

2. What prominent or unusual features does it have? What do I notice first when I look at it?
3. What sounds can I associate with my subject?
4. What smells and tastes can I associate with it?
5. What does it feel like to the touch? Is it warm or cool, rough or smooth, hard or soft, sticky or wet?
6. How does my subject move?
7. How would I recognize my subject if I were blindfolded?

During prewriting you can record the answers to those questions on an observation table like the one that follows. In this chart details describing a baseball park during a game are listed sense by sense.

Observation Table

SUBJECT: *Baseball park during a game*			
SIGHTS	SOUNDS	SMELLS/ TASTES	TOUCH/ MOVEMENTS
• *lush green outfield* • *chalk-white lines from home plate to base of yellow foul pole at steel-gray fence* • *undulating rows and rows of fans* • *flags atop perimeter of stadium, rippling during wind shifts* • *balletlike movement and precision of second baseman during a double play*	• *groans, cries of fans* • *thunderous, rippling applause after a home run* • *sharp crack of bat meeting the ball* • *deep bellowing "out" call by umpire* • *still, dead silence during a pitcher-batter duel*	• *roasted peanuts, hot dogs* • *spicy mustard* • *cool, refreshing soft drinks* • *sweet smell of pines from nearby park* • *sharp smell of freshly painted seats* • *hot buttered corn*	• *blazing midafternoon sun* • *cool late-afternoon breezes and chilly shadows creeping across the field* • *explosion of spikes, dust, and players in a stolen-base play* • *blurred drift of the ball floating lazily toward center field* • *surging mass of people rushing toward exits*

You can use some of the sensory details in your observation chart later, when you write a description of your subject.

Objective

EXERCISE 4. Prewriting to Collect Sensory Details. Choose one of the places listed below, or choose any other place that you would like to describe. Think about your specific purpose and a possible audience. Ask yourself any appropriate questions from page 145, and list the answers in an observation table. Fill in columns for at least three different senses. Then save your observation table for use in Exercise 6.

1. a lake
2. a restaurant
3. a school laboratory
4. a shopping mall
5. your room
6. a sports arena

Suggested Answer: For example, for *a lake* students might note color of sky and vegetation and sounds of insects.

PREWRITING: OVERALL IMPRESSION

The details in a description should add up to a single **overall impression** of the subject.

A description is effective when all of its details relate to one another and create a single overall impression. When you are planning a description of something, you will often be struck by a single strong impression of your subject. At other times, you will discover several impressions among the details of your subject. In that case, you must decide which impression you want to convey to your readers. For example, look at the following list of details about a golf course:

- tiny, six-inch holes, called cups
- lush, green fairways
- undulating hills
- set in a wind-tunnel valley
- stretches of pines, maples, giant oaks
- small, dangerous ponds guarding the greens
- ribbons of clear streams, brooks
- massive, lurking sand traps
- narrow fairways
- firm, circular greens
- close-cropped carpets of rich green velvet
- snakes, alligators

Which of these details would support the following overall impression of the golf course?

> The golf course is a paradise, a striking example of manicured, natural beauty.

Some details do not support that overall impression—wind-tunnel valley; snakes, alligators; massive, lurking sand traps. Although these latter details are colorful and accurate, they do not support the impression of "manicured, natural beauty." Notice the details that the writer chose.

The golf course is a paradise, a striking example of manicured, natural beauty. Lush green fairways wind through the undulating hills. Stretches of pines, maples, and giant oaks line the fairways. Ribbons of crystal-clear streams and brooks ripple through the course. The circular-shaped, firm greens look like close-cropped carpets of rich green velvet.

Suppose, however, that you wanted to convey the following impression of the golf course:

> The golf course presents numerous obstacles to the average golfer.

Note the details used to support this overall impression.

The golf course presents numerous obstacles to the average golfer. The course itself is set in a wind-tunnel valley and winds rip across the fairways. Many of the fairways are very narrow, and treacherous. Massive, lurking sand traps and small, dangerous ponds guard the greens. Snakes and alligators frolic in those ponds. The golfer must conquer these obstacles and somehow manage to hit a tiny white ball into a six-inch cup.

Both descriptions focus on the same golf course, yet each description conveys a different overall or dominant impression of the golf course. Note that in each paragraph, the overall impression is clearly conveyed in the topic sentence.

Objective

EXERCISE 5. Prewriting to Create an Overall Impression. Look again at the observation table on page 145 about a baseball park during a game. On the basis of the details there, decide on two different impressions of the scene that you could present to a general audience. For each overall impression write a sentence that could serve as the topic sentence of a paragraph. Then list details that will develop each impression. You may add appropriate details of your own. Save your sentences and details for Exercise 8.

Objective

EXERCISE 6. Prewriting to Create an Overall Impression. Look back at the details that you listed in Exercise 4. Now write a sentence expressing one overall impression of the place you chose. List any additional details that can develop that impression. Save your notes for Writer's Choice #3 on page 152.

Objective

EXERCISE 7. Maintaining an Overall Impression. Read the following paragraph about an abandoned mansion, and identify in writing the overall impression the paragraph conveys. Then rewrite the paragraph to eliminate any details that do not contribute directly to the overall impression. You may replace those details with others that you think would be more appropriate.

The old abandoned mansion seemed ravaged by time. Shutters dangled loosely from the empty window frames. Bricks from the crumbling chimneys and pieces of slate from the caved-in roof were scattered in the weedy patches surrounding the house. A huge willow tree guarded the driveway. The solid oak front door seemed polished and restored by time and weather. Rotted gutters hung from the rafters like the broken limbs of a dying tree. The mansion had sixteen rooms.

Suggested Answer: Overall impression—deterioration; students should eliminate the details in sentences **4**, **5**, and **7**.

WRITING A DESCRIPTION: ORGANIZATION AND COHERENCE

An effective description should be **organized** so that the details build on each other naturally and logically.

A description may be organized in any one of several ways depending on its subject. Three methods of organization that work especially well for descriptive writing are spatial order, chronological order, and order of importance.

SPATIAL ORDER

Spatial order is a natural, effective way of linking together sensory details, particularly in a description of a place or an object. When you describe features or details as they appear in spatial order, you can clarify your description by using spatial transitions such as these to add coherence:

above	beneath	horizontally	opposite	there
ahead	down	inside	outside	under
around	far	near	over	vertically
below	here	next to	parallel	within

The following descriptive passage is organized spatially. Notice how the underlined transitions help clarify the spatial relationships between underwater features or details and add coherence to the flow of sentences.

She was surrounded by rushing streams of color. Above her, thousands of tiny silver minnows flowed past like an unfurling luminous ribbon. Below her was a school of heavy groupers and sea bass, their dark gray and brown forms slowly nosing along the sandy bottom. In front of and behind her, as if simultaneously leading and pushing her, schools of multicolored butterfly fish darted playfully in the sun-speckled green waters.

Objective

EXERCISE 8. Writing a Description by Using Spatial Order. Choose one of the two topic sentences you wrote about a baseball park during a game for Exercise 5, and write a descriptive paragraph that develops this topic sentence. As you write, use spatial order to arrange the details that support your topic sentence. After you have finished your first draft, be sure to revise and edit your paragraph. Then make a neat copy, and proofread the final version.

CHRONOLOGICAL ORDER

Chronological order is most often used to organize the events in a piece of narrative writing. Chronological order, however, can also be used effectively in a description when there is movement involved. If you are describing something from a moving vantage point—for example, from a train as it passes through a mountainous, wooded area—chronological order can help clarify the sequence of descriptive details. Transitions such as the following can give your chronologically organized description a sense of coherence:

after	before	meanwhile	soon
again	finally	next	then
already	first	now	when
at that time	formerly	occasionally	

The following description is organized chronologically. Note the underlined words, which help a reader follow the writer's movement through the scene, thus enabling the reader to see what the writer sees as the time sequence unfolds:

The mountain loomed straight ahead, about five miles down the stretch of tracks. <u>After</u> we passed through the vast flat plains, we <u>then</u> entered a valley surrounded by slopes of white birches and evergreens. Flashes of white bark and green pine branches rushed by the windows. <u>Soon</u> the valley moved away from us, and we <u>immediately</u> began a steep climb at the base of the mountain. <u>Now</u> cliffs, massive boulders, and scrubby timberline brush drifted lazily past. <u>At last</u> we reached the summit, some 3,000 feet above the valley floor and hidden in misty clouds.

Objective

EXERCISE 9. Writing a Description by Using Chronological Order. Think of a panoramic scene that you would like to describe—the desert, a ski slope, the coastline, or space. Then choose a vehicle that moves you through the scene. Freewrite for five minutes about the details that you see as you move through the scene. Use those details to write a description of the scene from a moving vantage point. Use chronological order to organize your description. Use transition words to give your sentences coherence. Revise and edit your first draft. Then make a neat copy, and proofread the final version.

ORDER OF IMPORTANCE

Another way of ordering details in a description is by arranging them in **order of importance**. You might, for example, begin with the most important or most interesting details and move on to the least important ones. You may also begin with the least important details and lead up to the most important ones. Whichever organizing method you choose, the following transitions will help you clarify relationships among details:

at first	last	most of all
first	latter	primarily
former	most important	second

The following description is organized by order of importance. Notice the underlined transition words: They give the description coherence and help a reader follow the sequence of details from less important to more important ones:

The first thing you notice about a shark is probably the least important feature—its huge torpedolike shape. This shape ripples with muscular power. Then you see its menacing facial features—the cold vacant eyes and tough-skinned snub nose. You cannot return the shark's stare, so your eyes drop to its most startling feature—its grinning mouth with rows of deadly, razor-sharp teeth.

Objective

EXERCISE 10. Writing a Description by Using Order of Importance. The following details refer to a movie set for a science-fiction film. Using at least four of the details, decide on an overall impression of the set. Then write a brief descriptive paragraph in which you arrange the details according to order of importance. Use transitions to connect your details. After you have written your first draft, revise and edit your paragraph. Then make a neat copy, and proofread the final version.

DETAILS

- monolithic, 300-foot spaceship
- boulders and rocks
- a lunar land rover
- metal robots
- mounds of sand and ash
- disk-shaped radio transmitter
- volcanolike craters
- dinosaurlike creatures
- buildings partially below ground
- plants with huge thorns

WRITING A DESCRIPTION: DESCRIPTIVE LANGUAGE

Effective descriptive writing uses exact and vivid **language**.

Remember the following points when you are choosing words for descriptive writing. For more information about any of these points, see Chapter 5.

1. Always pick the most specific word.

GENERAL: The bird soared over the grove of barren trees.
MORE SPECIFIC: The eagle soared over the grove of barren maples.

2. Never use a boring word with a modifier when a single, powerful word expresses the same meaning more vividly.

DULL: Lightning cut quickly across the night sky.
VIVID: Lightning scissored across the night sky.

3. Think about the connotations associated with a word.

GOOD: Rain beat on the canvas rain fly of our tent.
BETTER: Rain drummed on the canvas rain fly of our tent.

4. Use figures of speech to add an extra dimension to the subject of your description. When appropriate, try different kinds of figures of speech: simile, metaphor, or personification.

BLAND: Grapevines slipped through the crevices of the stone wall.
SPECIAL: Grapevines slithered like snakes through the crevices of the stone wall.

5. Avoid trite, overused expressions. Be inventive and *see* things with a fresh, vital vision.

CLICHÉ: The airplane shot across the sky as fast as a speeding bullet.
ORIGINAL: The airplane shot across the sky like a cosmic flare.

Objective

EXERCISE 11. Using Descriptive Language. Rewrite the following paragraph using more exact words and vivid language. Use a figure of speech in at least one sentence. Combine any sentences as you see fit.

Our rubber raft went quickly down the fast river. Cliffs of the surrounding gorge sped by like blinking lights. The current carried us rapidly. The raft moved up and down over the foamy waves and rocks. Then we entered a quiet piece of still water. The peace was nice. Finally we were as safe as a doorknob.

WRITER'S CHOICE

WRITER'S CHOICE #1

ASSIGNMENT: To describe an important local structure
LENGTH: A paragraph of six to eight sentences
PURPOSE: To describe the historical structure so that anyone could visualize it exactly
AUDIENCE: A friend or a relative who has never seen the structure
PREWRITING: Choose a historical structure; then on an observation table such as the one on page 145, collect details that will describe it exactly and vividly. Decide on an overall impression of your subject.
WRITING: Begin by identifying the historical structure and by stating its single most important detail. Use spatial order to organize the subject's other important features.
REVISING: Can you visualize the subject from your writing? Make sure to edit and proofread carefully.

WRITER'S CHOICE #2

ASSIGNMENT: To describe an abstract idea or feeling with concrete details
LENGTH: A paragraph of eight to ten sentences
PURPOSE: To convey how concrete, vivid details express an abstract idea or feeling
AUDIENCE: Your choice
PREWRITING: Select an abstract idea or feeling, such as freedom, solitude, joy, or affection. Brainstorm or freewrite for at least five minutes about the abstract idea or feeling. Generate a number of specific, concrete examples or details that precisely describe your abstract idea.
WRITING: Begin by stating what your abstract idea is and how you will make it real or concrete in your paragraph. Use the details you listed to write a description based on order of importance.
REVISING: Does your paragraph truly support the topic sentence? Do you need to change the topic sentence or add details to the paragraph?

WRITER'S CHOICE #3

ASSIGNMENT: To describe a subject of your choice
LENGTH: Your choice
PURPOSE: Your choice
AUDIENCE: Your choice
OPTIONS:
- You might describe the subject for which you did prewriting in Exercises 4 and 6.
- Be sure to revise and edit your first draft. Then copy and proofread the final draft.

WRITING A DESCRIPTION: MOOD

A **mood** is the emotional quality or atmosphere created by the details in a description.

When you write a description, you can create different moods by choosing details and language that call up different emotions in your readers. For example, if you are describing a rainstorm, do you want to create an oppressive mood by showing your readers heavy skies, muddy streets, and wet, clammy clothing? Or do you want to exhilarate them by showing raindrops bouncing on roofs and leaves shining wetly?

In the following passage, the writer creates a tense mood by describing the frenzied activity and feelings of confinement that he experienced on a subway at rush hour. What specific details contribute to the mood?

> Far down the track, in an eerie dark, the light of the express glared and winked, and then in a terrible roar and screech of brakes it was upon us. The crowds at the platform waited for the people to emerge from the car; then there would be one solid mass of flesh pushing forward through the doors. There was a loudspeaker in the station, and the voice would say, "Step lively, folks, step lively." And after a pause, "Get that arm out of the door, buddy!" or "Pull in that leg, sister!"
>
> —Willie Morris, "A Provincial in New York: Living in the Big Cave"

From the very beginning such details as the train's glaring light and screeching brakes set the tense, jarring mood of the passage. The crowd becomes a "mass of flesh" trying to squeeze through the subway doors, and the conductor barks orders at the passengers as they crowd in. All in all, the subway experience is made to seem like a kind of combat training.

Suppose, however, that the writer had decided to lighten the mood slightly. Say that he decided to convey a sense of camaraderie among the subway passengers. He might have written this:

> Far down the track the light of the express shone and winked, and then in a roar the train arrived at long last, much to the crowd's relief. Those on the platform waited for a few people to emerge from the car; then the crowd held its breath and pushed through the doors. The conductor's voice called out, "Step lively, folks, step lively." And after a pause, "Get that arm out of the door, buddy!" or "Pull in that leg, sister!" Eyeball to eyeball, a few of the passengers smiled and shook their heads ruefully.

In both of the preceding models, the descriptive details convey a distinct mood. That mood relates directly to the writer's overall or dominant impression of the subway scene. When you choose descriptive details to create a mood, make sure that those details and the mood fit your overall impression of the scene being described.

Objective

EXERCISE 12. Creating A Mood with Descriptive Details. Scenes change as seasons pass or as people move in and out of the scenes. Choose a place—for example, a lake shore, a beach, a city park, a wheat field, a school auditorium or gymnasium. Describe that place in two different paragraphs. In the first paragraph describe the scene during a summer or fall season or during a time when many people inhabit the scene. Make sure that your descriptive details convey a mood that fits your overall impression of the scene. In the second paragraph describe the same scene, but this time describe the scene during winter or during a time when the scene is abandoned. Choose details that convey a mood appropriate to your impression.

WRITING A CHARACTER SKETCH

A **character sketch** is a description that portrays an individual's psychological traits and physical appearance.

When you describe a human being, you want to tell your reader more about your subject than just physical appearance. You want to convey your subject's human qualities, his or her personality. You want to suggest a connection between the external person—how that person looks or acts—and the inner person.

In the following excerpt from Russell Baker's autobiography, notice how Baker reveals his mother's personality traits through a description of her physical appearance and actions. Notice also how the details he selects effectively shift the mood of the description from the sadness of a deathbed scene to the vibrancy of the headstrong, lively woman.

> At the age of eighty my mother had her last bad fall, and after that her mind wandered free through time. Some days she went to weddings and funerals that had taken place half a century earlier. On others she presided over family dinners cooked on Sunday afternoons for children who were now gray with age. Through all this she lay in bed but moved across time, traveling among the dead decades with a speed and ease beyond the gift of physical science. . . .

> She had always been a small woman—short, light-boned, delicately structured—but now, under the white hospital sheet, she was becoming tiny. I thought of a doll with huge, fierce eyes. There had always been a fierceness in her. It showed in that angry, challenging thrust of the chin when she issued an opinion, and a great one she had always been for issuing opinions. . . .
>
> "It's not always good policy to tell people exactly what's on your mind," I used to caution her.
>
> "If they don't like it, that's too bad," was her customary reply, "because that's the way I am."
>
> And so she was. A formidable woman. Determined to speak her mind, determined to have her way, determined to bend those who opposed her. In that time when I had known her best, my mother had hurled herself at life with chin thrust forward, eyes blazing, and an energy that made her seem always on the run.
>
> She ran after squawking chickens, an axe in her hand, determined on a beheading that would put dinner in the pot. She ran when she made the beds, ran when she set the table. One Thanksgiving she burned herself badly when, running up from the cellar oven with the ceremonial turkey, she tripped on the stairs and tumbled back down, ending at the bottom in the debris of giblets, hot gravy, and battered turkey. Life was combat, and victory was not to the lazy, the timid, the slugabed, the drugstore cowboy, the libertine, the mushmouth afraid to tell people exactly what was on his mind whether people liked it or not. She ran.
>
> —Russell Baker, *Growing Up*

As you prepare to write a character sketch, ask yourself the following prewriting questions:

1. What can I say about my subject's height, weight, hair color, complexion, face, and clothing?
2. What can I say about the way my subject speaks and moves? About my subject's facial expressions?
3. What can I say about the way my subject behaves toward other people? How do other people treat my subject?
4. What can I say about my subject's character traits, likes, dislikes, strengths, and problems?
5. What specific examples or anecdotes can I offer to show these character traits in action?
6. What overall impression of my subject's appearance and personality do I want to convey? Can I focus on one basic quality as a key to understanding this person?

7. What mood do I want to suggest in my description? Have I selected the exact and correct details to convey that mood?

Objective

EXERCISE 13. Writing a Character Sketch. Plan and write a character sketch about an interesting person you know. Prewrite by answering the questions on page 155, listing as many physical and psychological details as you can. Decide on an overall impression of that person, and write a sentence expressing that impression. You may organize the details in your description by beginning with physical features and moving to your subject's character traits. Be sure to revise and edit your first draft. When you are satisfied with what you have written, make a neat copy, and proofread it.

REVISING, EDITING, AND PUBLISHING DESCRIPTIVE WRITING

When you revise a piece of descriptive writing, you should ask yourself the general questions about paragraph revision (Chapter 4). In addition, descriptive writing requires you to ask special questions of the first draft—questions that will help you to revise it so that it will accomplish your purpose and be appropriate for your audience.

CHECKLIST FOR REVISING DESCRIPTIVE WRITING

1. What sensory details have I used? Which work best? Which could I do without? Which should I add?
2. What single, overall impression have I created? How should I change this impression to create a truer picture of my subject?
3. What kind of organization have I used to arrange my details? Would another kind of organization work better?
4. Which transitions add coherence to my description?
5. Which exact and vivid words help the reader picture my subject? What words or figures of speech could I add to make that description even more precise and vivid?
6. Do my descriptive details create and convey a mood? What details could I add that would help convey the mood more strongly?
7. In a character sketch, which details portray the subject's physical traits? Which ones communicate psychological traits? What overall impression have I created of this person? Does the mood fit the impression? What additional details does my reader need in order to see the subject as I do?

WRITER'S CHOICE #1

ASSIGNMENT: To write a character sketch about a famous historical figure

WRITING: Begin by identifying your subject and describing the feature you selected as a focus. End with an anecdote or brief anecdotes that illustrate your subject's personality.

REVISING: Will your reader be able to visualize your subject from the details you included? Do you connect those details to your subject's personality? Does the anecdote you used convey your subject's personality? Remember to edit and proofread your description.

LENGTH: A paragraph of eight to ten sentences

PURPOSE: To describe someone by focusing on an aspect of his or her appearance—clothing, hair, face, posture

AUDIENCE: A friend who is unfamiliar with your subject

PREWRITING: Decide on your subject, and then narrow the focus of your physical description. Pick a feature that is characteristic of your subject and that connects with your subject's personality. List a few brief anecdotes or a single, longer anecdote that illustrates your subject's personality.

WRITER'S CHOICE #2

ASSIGNMENT: To describe an inanimate object

LENGTH: Your choice

PURPOSE: To describe the physical characteristics of an inanimate object in such a way that you reveal the "personality" of the object

AUDIENCE: A group of young readers, ages eight and nine

OPTIONS:
- Use vivid, descriptive language to show the inanimate object's personality. Use metaphors, similes, personification, and allusion in your description.
- Try brainstorming to generate a list of connections between physical features and personality traits.
- Use spatial order or order of importance to organize your description.

WRITER'S CHOICE #3

ASSIGNMENT: To describe a subject of your choice

LENGTH: Your choice

PURPOSE: Your choice

AUDIENCE: Your choice

OPTION:
- You might use material in the Writer's Sourcebook (pages 348–349) as a springboard for your description.

THE WRITER

Susan Appel spends a great deal of her free time writing. She wrote the following descriptive passage and commentary as a student at Indian Hill High School in Cincinnati, Ohio.

THE FINISHED PRODUCT

Rain pounds down on the roof and the windows. I lie curled up tightly in my bed, my blanket drawn tightly to my chin, and I listen. The rain falls in great sheets, beating down loudly like an angry drummer. Each huge raindrop threatens to break through the glass of the window, or at least that's what I think. A flash of lightning cuts through the dark. I close my eyes, but I am too late; the light invades them anyway. The windows do little to shield out the light—they reach almost from ceiling to floor, and the gauzy white curtains are more decorative than practical. In that split-second flash of purply light, I can see everything in the room, even down to each individual slat in the closet doors. After the flash the television screen continues to glow for a few seconds. I burrow down deeper and count. One-Mississippi, two-Mississippi, three-Mississi.... Thunder shatters the silence. Suddenly it sounds as if something besides rain is striking the window. With my luck it's probably hail. I squeeze my eyes shut and bury my head under the pillow.

THE WRITER AT WORK

In writing this passage, my biggest problem was finding something to describe. I started out with the usual sitting-on-the-front-porch ideas, but there wasn't enough to say about them. So I began to think back to other times when I'd been drained of ideas and tried to remember what I'd done at those times. It dawned on me that I could write best about what came from my own experience. I thought back to places I'd been and things I'd seen. Eventually I drifted to thinking about rain—since it was raining out—and then to all the thunderstorms I'd been through. I remembered how much I dislike night thunderstorms because they keep me awake. When I listed all the things about them that annoyed me, it turned out that most of these concerned the light and the noises. I concentrated on these, and they became my paragraph.

YOUR TURN **Describing an Experience**

Find your own equivalent of Susan's thunderstorm—an experience that you have had often and that disturbs you. List the details you associate with that experience, and decide on your overall impression of it. Then write a paragraph describing it.

CHAPTER 8 DESCRIPTIVE WRITING

Sensory Details (pages 143–146) Indicate the sense to which each of these sentences appeals: **(a)** sight; **(b)** hearing; **(c)** smell; **(d)** taste; **(e)** touch or motion

1. The cold, wet drizzle completely soaked us.
2. The spicy chili with red-hot peppers burned my tongue.
3. Plumes of white smoke drifted lazily over the thick green pines.
4. The old bus clattered and groaned up the hills.

Organization (pages 148–150) Indicate whether each group of sentences uses **(a)** spatial order or **(b)** order of importance.

5. At the base of the mountain, clusters of white birches shone in the sunlight. The slate-gray cliffs loomed above the birches.
6. This computer has a well-designed keyboard and an easy-to-read monitor. Its best feature, however, is its portability.

Overall Impression, Descriptive Language, and Mood (pages 146–147, 151, and 153–154) Read the following paragraph, and indicate the letter of the item that correctly answers each question.

When we reached the landing, the last of the sun had bled into the river. . . . The waxed surface of the water had a glowing bloom to it. The force of the current made it bulge like a muscle. The color of it started as black under our feet, lightening to blue . . . then scarlet and yellow as it reached the horizon.

—Jonathan Raban

7. Which of the following states the overall impression created by the passage?
(a) The writer is totally indifferent to the sunset.
(b) The writer is confused by the sudden splash of color.
(c) The writer is dazzled by the various colors of the sunset.
8. The description of the water's surface as a "glowing bloom" suggests
(a) a dull sunset
(b) a sudden, vibrant sweep of colors
(c) darkness
9. Which of the following is a figure of speech?
(a) force of the current
(b) scarlet and yellow
(c) lightening to blue
(d) bulge like a muscle
10. What is the mood conveyed by this description of the sunset?
(a) gloom **(b)** bewilderment **(c)** peacefulness

Answers: **1.** e; **2.** d; **3.** a; **4.** b; **5.** a; **6.** b; **7.** c; **8.** b; **9.** d; **10.** c

Writing for Review Write a one-paragraph description of a place or a person. Use either spatial order or order of importance. After you write, underline at least four sensory details, three vivid words, and one figure of speech.

9 CHAPTER
Narrative Writing

> ***Of course a writer rearranges life, shortens time intervals, sharpens events, and devises beginnings, middles, and ends.***
>
> ***—John Steinbeck***

In the quotation you have just read, the American novelist John Steinbeck is talking about the process of compressing events and shaping details in fictional narratives. That same process of selection and compression occurs when a writer shapes a nonfiction narrative. The difference between the two types of narrative is, of course, that the nonfiction writer does not invent details, characters, and events.

Narration is the kind of writing that tells a story, real or imagined. A **nonfiction** is prose writing that tells a true story. A **fiction narrative** is prose writing that is made up or imagined.

In this chapter you will write a variety of nonfiction narratives, both single-paragraph and multiple-paragraph narratives. During the narrative writing process, you will practice the following skills:

- prewriting: recognizing the elements of a narrative
- prewriting: subject, purpose, and audience
- prewriting: preparing a narrative outline
- writing a narrative
- writing: using dialogue in a narrative
- writing: using vivid verbs in a narrative
- revising, editing, and publishing narrative writing

PREWRITING: RECOGNIZING THE ELEMENTS OF A NARRATIVE

Authors of nonfiction narratives often use the techniques and elements of a short story in presenting or narrating an incident. Such elements include a plot, a setting, and a point of view. Notice how John Updike uses those elements to maintain a reader's interest in the following narrative about Ted Williams's last batting performance for the Boston Red Sox.

. . . On the afternoon of Wednesday, September 28th, 1960, as I took a seat behind third base, a uniformed groundkeeper was treading the top of this wall, picking batting-practice home runs out of the screen, like a mushroom gatherer seen in Wordsworthian perspective on the verge of a cliff. The day was overcast, chill and uninspirational. . . .

Fisher, after his unsettling wait, was low with the first pitch. He put the second one over, and Williams swung mightily and missed. The crowd grunted, seeing that classic swing, so long and smooth and quick, exposed. Fisher threw the third time, Williams swung again, and there it was. The ball climbed on a diagonal line into the vast volume of air over center field. From my angle, behind third base, the ball seemed less an object in flight than the tip of a towering, motionless construct, like the Eiffel Tower or the Tappan Zee Bridge. It was in the books while it was still in the sky. Brandt ran back to the deepest corner of the outfield grass; the ball descended beyond his reach and struck in the crotch where the bullpen met the wall, bounced chunkily, and vanished.

Like a feather caught in a vortex, Williams ran around the square of bases at the center of our beseeching screaming. He ran as he always ran out home runs—hurriedly, unsmiling, head down, as if our praise were a storm of rain to get out of. He didn't tip his cap. Though we thumped, wept, and chanted "We want Ted" for minutes after he hid in the dugout, he did not come back. Our noise for some seconds passed beyond excitement into a kind of immense open anguish, a wailing, a cry to be saved. But immortality is non-transferable. The papers said that the other players, and even the umpires on the field, begged him to come out and acknowledge us in some way, but he refused. Gods do not answer letters.

—John Updike, "Hub Fans Bid Kid Adieu"

Updike might have simply told about Williams's last time at bat by stating only the basic facts: "In his last time at bat, Ted Williams hit a home run off pitcher Jack Fisher. Thousands of loyal fans cheered this amazing feat." The basic facts are there, but the statements lack the impact of Updike's narrative. His version stirs a reader's imagination and captures that reader's interest.

The **plot** is the sequence of events that occurs in a narrative. Often at the center of a plot is a problem, or **conflict.** As a person in a narrative tries to solve the conflict, the plot builds to the point of highest interest, or the **climax.** An effective **resolution** brings the narrative to a satisfying and likely conclusion.

Not all short narratives contain a conflict. For example, you can write a narrative about a raft trip down a wilderness river without introducing a conflict into the story line. You know from your own reading experiences, however, that a narrative with a conflict is usually more interesting to read. Conflicts in longer narratives set up tense situations and often introduce a problem that is resolved by the end of the story. One of these three general conflicts usually occurs in long narratives:

- conflict between people—for example, the batter-pitcher duel between Williams and Fisher in Updike's narrative
- conflict between a person and some outside force—for example, a person struggling to survive on a solo trans-Atlantic flight
- conflict within a person—for example, a person tormented by guilt, indecision, or an ethical dilemma.

The plot of an effective narrative—even that of a very short narrative—should have a meaningful and often dramatic or suspenseful sequence of action. For example, the plot in Updike's narrative centers on the duel between Williams—the batter—and Fisher—the pitcher. The climax and the resolution occur when Williams hits a home run.

The **setting** of a narrative is the time and place in which the narrative occurs.

A narrative's setting may include the geographical area, the landscape, the season, the weather, the historical period, or the culture in which the action takes place. The setting can be described in great detail, or it can be briefly described or suggested. The setting also establishes a **mood** or an **atmosphere** by means of details that evoke a particular response in the reader. Updike, for example, describes the day as "overcast, chill, and uninspirational." The gloomy day contrasts sharply with Williams's final inspirational performance.

Point of view represents the relationship of the narrator to the story.

Every narrative has a narrator who tells the story. A narrative told from the *first-person point of view* is related by the author, who participates in the story, speaks directly to the reader, and uses the first-person pronoun *I.* Updike's narrative, for example, is told from the first-person point of view. A narrative has a *third-person point of view* if the narrator is removed from the story and the story events are revealed from some distance. An author who adopts a third-person point of view uses third-person pronouns (*he, she, they*) to refer to characters.

Objective

EXERCISE 1. Recognizing the Elements of a Narrative. Read the following narrative about life with an unpredictable dog, and write answers to each of the numbered questions.

In his last year Muggs used to spend practically all of his time outdoors. He didn't like to stay in the house for some reason or other—perhaps it held too many unpleasant memories for him. Anyway, it was hard to get him to come in and as a result the garbage man, the iceman, and the laundryman wouldn't come near the house. We had to haul the garbage down to the corner, take the laundry out and bring it back, and meet the iceman a block from home. After this had gone on for some time we hit on an ingenious arrangement for getting the dog in the house so that we could lock him up while the gas meter was read, and so on. Muggs was afraid of only one thing, an electrical storm. Thunder and lightning frightened him out of his senses (I think he thought a storm had broken the day the mantelpiece fell). He would rush into the house and hide under a bed or in a clothes closet. So we fixed up a thunder machine out of a long narrow piece of sheet iron with a wooden handle on one end. Mother would shake this vigorously when she wanted to get Muggs into the house. It made an excellent imitation of thunder, but I suppose it was the most roundabout system for running a household that was ever devised. It took a lot out of Mother.

—James Thurber, "The Dog That Bit People"

1. Is this a nonfiction narrative? How do you know?
2. Briefly describe the plot of the narrative. What is the conflict, or problem? What is the resolution?
3. What are the setting and the mood of the narrative?
4. From what point of view is the story told?

PREWRITING: SUBJECT, PURPOSE, AND AUDIENCE

FINDING A SUBJECT

Narrative subjects can be found in everyday occurrences as well as in dramatic events. To find a subject for a narrative, think about people you know and experiences you have had. Use the prewriting techniques that you studied earlier—such as freewriting, brainstorming, observing, and charting—to generate and explore narrative ideas (see Chapter 2).

Throughout the remainder of this chapter you will follow one student in the preparation of a narrative. She chose to narrate a fairly dramatic experience that she had while on a camping trip in the Maine wilderness. You will follow the same steps to write a narrative of your own.

Objective
EXERCISE 2. Prewriting for a Narrative. Choose one of the subjects listed here or a subject of your own. Use one of the techniques of prewriting. Then ask the questions *who?, what?, when?, where?, why?,* and *how?*. Work for ten minutes to generate and explore ideas for your subject. Save your notes for a narrative that you will write later.

1. a trip
2. a sporting event
3. a work experience
4. a news event
5. surviving a hurricane
6. how you achieved or accomplished something

DEFINING PURPOSE AND AUDIENCE

A writer must be clear about the **purpose**, or goal of a narrative. Although the overall general purpose is, of course, "to narrate," a narrative may have an additional specific purpose. For example, a news narrative usually informs, a sports narrative or an adventure narrative often entertains, a historical narrative may make a point, and an autobiographical narrative may present a truth or an insight. Some narratives may serve several different purposes. A sports narrative, for example, might both entertain and inform.

In addition to defining a purpose for a narrative, a writer must consider his or her **audience.** As you plan and write your narrative, try to imagine your readers' reactions to it. Choose details and events that help them identify your purpose.

Objective
EXERCISE 3. Defining Purpose and Audience. Choose one of the subjects for which you generated ideas in Exercise 2, or choose a new subject, and answer in writing the questions on pages 22–24 in order to define purpose and audience for the narrative you will write later.

PREWRITING: PREPARING A NARRATIVE OUTLINE

CHOOSING EVENTS FOR A NARRATIVE

At this stage of prewriting, you may find it beneficial to ask and answer some questions about the events of your narrative. The following questions will force you to think about all the events of the experience and to focus on the critical incidents. The sample answers were written during this prewriting stage by the student preparing to write about her Allagash River experience.

QUESTIONS TO EXPLORE THE EVENTS OF A NARRATIVE	SAMPLE ANSWERS
1. In what way did the experience or incident begin?	*The experience began with three days of uneventful canoeing across lakes at the base of the Allagash River Wilderness Waterway in Maine.*
2. What problem, or conflict, did I or another character involved in the incident or experience face?	*We were totally unprepared for the surging Chase Rips--rapids--in the river and were caught in this dangerous stretch of water.*
3. What was my or another character's reaction to this problem?	*I was terrified. Karen looked anxious, but remained calm.*
4. In what way did I or another character solve the problem?	*We tried to ride out the rips, but the canoe tipped and we were thrown into the water. Our gear floated away. We tried to stay with the canoe.*
5. Did any obstacles prevent me or another character from solving the problem?	*The rips, the rocks, and the surging force of the river were all obstacles to getting up the river safely.*
6. What was the final outcome?	*Past the rips, the river changed. We and our gear floated safely to shore.*
7. What was my or another character's reaction to the final solution?	*We were exhausted but exhilarated. At first we laughed. Then we realized that we had not conquered the river. It had merely spared us. We were both relieved. We had also come to a deep respect for the power of the river.*

Objective

EXERCISE 4. Choosing Events for a Narrative. Use one of the narrative subjects you worked with in Exercises 2 and 3 or another of your own choosing. List the events of your narrative by writing an answer for each of the questions on page 165. Add any other important events not covered by the questions. Save your notes for use in Exercise 5.

ELIMINATING UNNECESSARY EVENTS

A well-developed narrative focuses only on important events. When considering whether each event is relevant, always keep your purpose in mind. For example, after prewriting additional events, the student found several that were not directly related to her purpose; she drew a line through them:

- *My sister and I were canoeing in the Maine wilderness.*
- *We had spent three uneventful days canoeing across several lakes at the base of the Allagash River Wilderness Waterway.*
- ~~*We saw a number of small streams and brooks entering into and flowing out of those lakes.*~~
- ~~*A huge moose crossed directly in front of our canoe at dusk of the third day.*~~
- *We entered the river itself and began our ninety-mile trek.*
- *We were caught helplessly in the Chase Rips, a dangerous stretch of water.*
- *The canoe tipped, we were thrown into the water, and our gear floated away.*
- ~~*Our canoe was an antique, a hand-crafted wooden model.*~~

Objective

EXERCISE 5. Eliminating Unnecessary Events. Look at the final list of events for your narrative that you made in Exercise 4. Delete any that are unnecessary or unrelated to the purpose and focus of your narrative.

COLLECTING NARRATIVE DETAILS

When you collect details for your narrative, think about how the characters looked, sounded, and acted. Think about their motivation for their actions. Consider the time and place of your setting, and then imagine sensory details associated with the setting. Think about the mood that you want to convey and about what sensory words and descriptive details will convey that mood. Making charts like those that follow may help you to focus on and organize the details of your narrative.

Characters in a Narrative

SUBJECT: *canoeing on the Allagash River*			
PEOPLE	CHARACTER TRAITS	BEHAVIOR/ REACTION	MOTIVATION
me	*stubborn, adventurous*	*terrified, dazed, relieved, and exhilarated*	*survival instinct, curiosity*
Karen (my sister)	*reserved, cautious, supportive*	*frightened but in control*	*need to command, to maintain self-control*

Setting for a Narrative

SUBJECT: *canoeing on the Allagash River*			
PLACE	TIME OF DAY/YEAR	WEATHER	DETAILS OF SETTING
chain of lakes at base of Allagash Wilderness Waterway	*late September*	*sunny, cool*	*wide, calm lakes, many small islands*
Chase Rips on Allagash River	*late September, early after-noon*	*sunny, cool*	*river: darkened channel in woods; surging current*

Mood for a Narrative

SUBJECT: *canoeing on the Allagash River*		
MOOD	SENSE WORDS	DESCRIPTIVE DETAILS
calm, serene	• *smooth, tranquil waters* • *water sparkled and shimmered, frosted blue*	• *expansive lakes, dotted with small islands* • *paddling lazily*
growing excite-ment	• *sweeping tunnel of color* • *kaleidoscope of filtered sunlight, autumn reds, browns, oranges*	• *exotic, jungly mesh of scrubby brush, gnarled trees, twisted vines*
fear, terror	• *thunderous hissing, popping, slapping* • *pulsating rapids* • *wall of deafening noise* • *slate-gray boulders* • *lurching, tipping* • *river pushed, pulled clawed at us*	• *surging power of current* • *turbulent river* • *choppy swirls of churning, foamy water* • *water hurls us past dangerous rocks strewn across river* • *Karen shouting* • *gear swirled away*
relief mixed with new respect	• *absence of noise*	• *river becomes gentle* • *we float to shore* • *gear bobs in water nearby* • *laughter, feeling of exhilaration* • *hulls of crushed canoes*

Objective

EXERCISE 6. Collecting Narrative Details. Using the narrative subject you have worked with in preceding exercises or another of your own choice, make three charts like those shown on pages 166 and 167. Use the same headings, modified if necessary, and fill in the information about the people, settings, and mood of your narrative. Save your notes for use in Exercise 7.

FILLING IN THE NARRATIVE OUTLINE

At this point in the prewriting stage, you are ready to make a narrative outline. Your outline should correspond to the model that follows. Notice that the outline begins by stating the purpose of the narrative and then lists the events in **chronological order.** This outline also contains descriptions of character and setting and includes sensory details that convey a mood. Thus the outline reflects all the prewriting work done up to this point.

Narrative Outline for Canoeing on the Allagash

I. Beginning

A. *State the purpose of your narrative in a sentence.*
I want to show readers how, on a recent camping trip in Maine's Allagash Wilderness Waterway, my sister Karen and I developed a deep respect for nature.

B. *Give important background information.*
This was our first canoeing and camping trip into a real wilderness area.

C. *Describe the setting.*
The base of the Allagash Waterway is a chain of expansive lakes dotted with small islands. The lakes lead to the Allagash River itself, which flows northward some ninety miles.

D. *Begin to tell what happened.*
We spent three uneventful days crossing the lakes. It was late September, sunny and cool, and the lakes sparkled and shimmered a frosted blue. At one point I complained to Karen about the lack of adventure. I felt that we were on a safe sightseeing cruise.

II. Middle

A. *Tell what happens next.*
We crossed the lakes and entered the Allagash River.

B. *Describe the new setting.*
The river was a channel that sliced into the heart of the wilderness, a jungly mesh of brush, trees, and vines. It was exotic. Karen, who is normally reserved and distant, remarked that she felt as if she were inside a sweeping tunnel of color, a kaleidoscope of autumn colors and sunlight.

C. *Introduce a conflict, or a problem.*

We were unprepared for the Chase Rips. We heard them first, an echoing avalanche of hissing, popping, and slapping. Suddenly we were caught in the rapids.

D. *Show your reaction and another character's reaction to the situation.*

I was terrified and screamed. Karen looked anxious, but remained calm, shouting orders about what to do.

E. *Build toward a climax, the point of highest interest.*

Helpless and powerless, we shot through the rips and their deafening noise. Choppy swirls of churning water hurled us past slate-gray boulders.

III. Ending

A. *Write a climax.*

The canoe tipped, and we were thrown into the foamy waters. Our gear floated away. Karen shouted to stay with the canoe. We struggled for several hundred yards as the river pushed, pulled, and clawed at us.

B. *Write a resolution.*

The river suddenly changed. The noise stopped, and the gentle current carried us toward the shore. Our lost gear bobbed in the water near a sandbank, as if patiently awaiting our late arrival. Wet, exhausted, and exhilarated, Karen and I began to laugh. We had not conquered the river; it had decided to spare us. Others had not been as lucky. The hulls of splintered, cracked, and crushed canoes were scattered along the banks.

Objective

EXERCISE 7. Preparing a Narrative Outline. Using the subject you developed in preceding exercises or another subject of your choice, write a narrative outline. Use the narrative outline on pages 168–169 as your model. Include as many of the categories in the outline as possible. Save your outline.

WRITING A NARRATIVE

CHRONOLOGICAL ORDER AND COHERENCE

At this point you should decide on the exact order in which you will present the events in your narrative. You can follow the order of your notes, progressing from the beginning to the middle to the end of your narrative. Another option is to begin at the end of your experience and then to go back to the beginning to show how you arrived there. Use transitions such as *after, finally, meanwhile, soon,* and *until* to give your writing coherence.

Objective

EXERCISE 8. Recognizing Transitions. Reread the narrative about Ted Williams on page 161. List at least one transition that indicates time order.

Suggested Answer: after

A MODEL NARRATIVE

The student whose progress you have been following throughout this chapter wrote the following five-paragraph narrative based on her prewriting notes. Not all narratives need to be five paragraphs long, however. In fact, had she narrowed the scope of her subject, she might have written a single-paragraph narrative that concentrated on the river experience itself.

The Chase Rips

On a recent camping trip in Maine's Allagash Wilderness Waterway, my sister Karen and I developed a deep respect for the power of nature. This was our first canoeing and camping trip into a real wilderness area. First we passed through the base of the Allagash Waterway, which is a chain of expansive lakes dotted with small islands. The lakes lead to the Allagash River itself, which flows northward some ninety miles. We spent three uneventful days paddling lazily across these smooth, tranquil waters. It was late September, sunny and cool, and the lakes sparkled and shimmered a frosted blue. At one point I remarked to Karen that the trip was not satisfying my thirst for adventure. I felt that we were simply drifting through the wilderness on a sightseeing cruise.

After crossing the lakes we entered the Allagash River, a channel that sliced into the heart of the wilderness. It passed through a jungly mesh of scrubby brush, gnarled trees, and twisted vines. It was exotic. Karen, who is normally reserved, remarked that she felt as if she were inside a sweeping tunnel of color, a kaleidoscope of autumn red, brown, green, orange, and crimson sprinkled with filtered sunlight. This change from the open, calm lakes to the enclosed river was both abrupt and symbolic.

We were totally unprepared for what happened next. We heard and felt the Chase Rips before we actually saw them. An echoing avalanche of thunderous hissing, popping, and slapping announced the surging power of the current. Suddenly, we were snared by this dangerous stretch of pulsating rapids. I was terrified and started to scream. Karen, too, stared anxiously at the turbulent river, but she remained calm and began to shout orders about riding with the current, paddling with the flow.

Surrounded by a wall of deafening noise, we shot through the rips. Choppy swirls of churning water bounced and hurled us past slate-gray boulders that were dangerously strewn across the river. Then the canoe lurched and tipped. We were thrown headfirst into the foamy waters. Our gear swirled away in the raging current. Karen shouted to stay with the canoe. For several hundred yards we struggled to stay afloat as the river pushed, pulled, and clawed at us.

Then as abruptly as we had entered the rips, we were past them. The river changed. The noise ceased, and a gentle current edged us toward the shore. Eventually it deposited us on a sandbank, where our lost gear bobbed in the water, as if patiently awaiting our late arrival. I looked at Karen and we began to laugh. We were wet, exhausted, and exhilarated. Then we grew serious. We had not conquered the river; it had simply decided to spare us, this time anyway. Others had not been as lucky. The hulls of splintered, cracked, and crushed canoes were scattered along the banks.

Objective

EXERCISE 9. Writing from a Narrative Outline. Write a narrative using the outline that you prepared in Exercise 7. Be sure to include all the elements of a narrative as well as specific significant details presented in vivid language. Present your narrative in chronological order, using transitions to help your reader follow the sequence of events. Your narrative can be one paragraph or several paragraphs long. Review your first draft to see what improvements you can make.

WRITING: USING DIALOGUE IN A NARRATIVE

Dialogue is the conversation between individuals in a narrative, quoted word-for-word and enclosed in quotation marks.

Dialogue adds realism to a narrative. People or characters in a narrative become real when they speak and exchange thoughts. Dialogue can also give a narrative a sense of immediacy, an I-was-there quality. For example, note how dialogue makes the following narrative both real and believable:

We watched the bear in silence for maybe five minutes. He was about fifty yards from us, but if he so desired he could be across the creek and in our midst within seconds. He was rooting slowly and quietly among the willows. Then he looked up and glanced across the creek, in our direction. He stopped feeding. He stood still, on his four legs, his head raised and pointed in our direction.

He had spotted us; or had sensed our presence somehow.

"If he starts across," Ray whispered, "bang the cooking pots together. I'll fire a shot in the air. That should stop him. If he keeps coming, climb the nearest tree you can find, and climb it as high as you can."

I looked around quickly. There was only one tree at the campsite which anyone could possibly climb. One tree, one bear, and five of us. "What about starting the fire?" I asked.

"Okay," Ray said. "Give it a try." What worried him, he added, was that we were so close to the road. This bear might be used to contact with people. Might be intrigued, rather than startled, by the presence of human beings along his creek. Otherwise, why hadn't he left when he'd seen us? Why was he still just standing there?

—Joe McGinniss, *Going to Extremes*

USING INDIRECT QUOTATIONS

Indirect quotations are paraphrases or restatements of the exact words a person used.

When writing a narrative, you can use indirect quotations in place of a person's exact words. In that case you do *not* use quotation marks. Indirect quotations are effective substitutes when you want to compress and summarize a speaker's exact words or when the dialogue itself is not memorable and adds little to the narrative. For example, in the final paragraph of the preceding model, all but the first two sentences is indirect quotation, a device which the writer uses to compress a series of statements by one of the characters.

PARAGRAPHING NARRATIVES

When writing a narrative, you should begin a new paragraph when:

- conversation is introduced
- the speaker changes
- the narrative resumes after dialogue
- the scene changes
- you, as the writer, move from one character to another for any length of time

Objective

EXERCISE 10. Paragraphing and Changing Indirect Quotations to Dialogue. Rewrite the following passage. Change the indirect quotations to direct quotations for a dialogue. Follow the guidelines for paragraphing, and begin a new paragraph when necessary. For punctuation rules with dialogue, see Chapter 28.

We were five miles offshore in a twenty-foot sailboat. The ocean was calm, and a steady but gentle wind guided us across the glassy surface. I told John that this was probably the best sailing day of the entire summer. He responded with a characteristic grunt and a short maybe. Then suddenly, as we turned the boat toward the shoreline, we saw a billowing, unfurling mass of dark clouds streaming toward us. The wind began to whip the waters into a choppy, frenzied turmoil. The sails flapped and rippled helplessly like broken wings, the halyards ripped free and clanked wildly, and a screeching wind tore through the boat. John began shouting and screaming about getting the sails down before the boat tipped. I told him to turn on the engine and take the wheel while I worked on the sails. I moved to the front of the boat, lashed myself to the deck, and began to pull feverishly at the sails. It took a half hour of hard work, but eventually the sails came down. When I returned to the rear of the boat, John was gripping the steering wheel tightly and smiling. He looked at me, laughed, and made some snide comment about what a great day for sailing it was.

REVISING, EDITING, AND PUBLISHING NARRATIVE WRITING

The general questions that you ask when revising paragraphs (see Chapter 4) apply also to narrative writing. In addition, you should consider the following checklist questions when revising your narrative first draft. These questions will help you revise with both your purpose and audience in mind.

When you have completed the final draft of your narrative, look for a forum in which to share your narrative with others. Perhaps you could enter it in a school-wide writing contest.

CHECKLIST FOR REVISING A NARRATIVE

1. What makes my narrative a nonfiction narrative as opposed to a fiction narrative?
2. What questions have I asked in order to define my purpose and audience?
3. What questions have helped me to choose events?
4. Which events are not really necessary to include?
5. What conflict, if any, does my narrative contain? How is the conflict resolved?
6. What narrative and sensory details have I included. Do those details convey the mood that I want to re-create?
7. Have I checked my first draft against my narrative outline to be sure that the first draft is complete?
8. What transitions give my narrative coherence?
9. Where can I add dialogue to my narrative?

WRITER'S CHOICE #1

ASSIGNMENT: To write a narrative paragraph
LENGTH: Eight to ten sentences
AUDIENCE: A friend
PURPOSE: To tell about an experience that led you to an understanding or an appreciation of something or someone
PREWRITING: List the events in chronological order.
WRITING: Begin by stating your subject and your purpose. Then tell what happened, listing the events in chronological order. End with a comment about what you learned or have come to appreciate because of the experience.
REVISING: Make sure that you have used transitions to clarify the order of events. Make sure that all of your details relate directly to your purpose. If necessary, add additional details. Edit your work, prepare a final version, and proofread it.

WRITER'S CHOICE #2

ASSIGNMENT: To write a historical narrative
LENGTH: Your choice
AUDIENCE: Your choice
PURPOSE: To recount an important historical event as if you had been a participant in the event
PREWRITING: List the events of the narrative in chronological order. Organize the details of setting, character, and mood in three charts.
WRITING: Use first-person point of view to narrate your account. Describe the setting first. Then introduce the events in chronological order. Introduce and describe the characters, their actions and motivations in vivid detail.
REVISING: Make sure that you have used vivid language to describe the events and characters. Make sure that you have consistently used first-person point of view throughout your narrative. Ask yourself: Do I appear as a participant in the event? Edit your work, prepare a final copy, and proofread it.

WRITER'S CHOICE #3

ASSIGNMENT: A narrative of any kind
OPTIONS:
- Write on any subject you choose.
- You may want to base your narrative on a photograph in the Writer's Sourcebook, pages 350–351.

THE WRITER

Michelle Siqueiros was born in Pasadena, California, and moved to Texas when she was eleven. She plans to earn a doctorate in history and hopes that one day she will be able to travel to Egypt and work as an Egyptologist. Michelle wrote the following personal narrative and commentary as a student at Eastwood High School in El Paso, Texas.

THE FINISHED PRODUCT

The noonday sun was shining brightly in the autumn air, but the crisp wind made the day colder than usual. The ranch looked homey in the sunlight; I felt tranquil. And the freshly cut hay and alfalfa burned my nostrils as it lay in the barnyard not far from the house.

There were nine of us in the jeep behind my aunt's ranch in the lower valley part of town. We decided to go riding around the ranch to see what mischief we could find.

Larry was driving, and Steve sitting next to him. Both of them were thirteen, and Steve had Laura, who was only a year old, on his lap. Angel, Marie, and I (all twelve), James (ten), Sylvia (four), and Ann-Marie (seven), were sitting in the back of the jeep. I sat in between the chrome roll bars on the back. These bars added a bit of style to the jeep, which was beige with at least three layers of dust on it.

We were about a mile from the house when we discovered a bumpy road that was really fun. We kept riding up and down that road, going faster each time.

"Hey, did you see that last hill we went over?"

"Yeah, let's do it again, faster!"

"Again, again!"

"Hold on—we're going to fall!"

"Hold on... hold—"

"Is everyone okay?"

We were thrown from the jeep. Luckily most of us had fallen into the bushes. Steve, who had thrown Laura out, and Larry were the only ones who got pinned inside the jeep.

"Ann-Marie! Where's Ann-Marie?"

"Angel, did you see what happened to Ann-Marie?"

"Help me, help me, please don't let her die—"

"She's too young, don't you understand, it could have been me!"

"It could have been me!"

On that last ride Ann-Marie and I had traded places, and she was sitting between the roll bars. We had gotten into a big fight, but I let her win because she began to cry.

We found Ann-Marie underneath the jeep, crushed from the waist down. She was pinned between the roll bars and couldn't jump out. She lay with her long golden-bronze hair in the dirt. Her clothes were torn, and she was bleeding. I stayed there and cried. Her eyes were empty and her smile had faded. And I knew her small, fragile body would never move again.

I still remember that day well, though it happened more than five years ago. And I know Ann-Marie will always be near me because I could have been the one to die. And it's sometimes when I feel really low and depressed that I pull out Ann-Marie's hair ribbon, the one she wore the day of the accident. I found it tangled up in a bush, flying in the air. I pull it out and gaze at it for a long time and cry for things I don't understand.

THE WRITER AT WORK

It took me two rough drafts before I finally wrote what I felt was right. I had to probe deeply to remember the details of the accident. It hurt to remember what happened, but it helped me to overcome the fear I had hidden for five years. I was supposed to relate an experience that had changed my life. And I still feel, even today, that this experience has really changed mine.

To remember more than the visual details of the accident, I went back to my aunt's ranch and walked around the place for a while. I found the scene of the accident, and I remembered the whole thing again. But instead of feeling sad, I felt better about coping with the whole thing, and wondered if I had finally grown up.

YOUR TURN **Writing a Personal Narrative**

Write about an event that you feel represents a turning point in your own life. The experience may be a sad one, like Michelle's, or a gratifying one. Relate the experience, and indicate how it changed you.

CHAPTER 9 NARRATIVE WRITING

Answer the questions based on the following paragraph.

[1]On December 17, 1903, at Kitty Hawk, North Carolina, Orville Wright lay stretched out on the lower wing of a strange-looking contraption. [2]It was a cold, windy day on the tree-barren sand dunes of Kitty Hawk. [3]At this point in history, people had only dreamed of flight; no one had actually flown. [4]After several minutes of warming the contraption's engine, Orville fearlessly released the wire that held the machine to its monorail track. [5]The huge machine lumbered down the track into a gusty twenty-seven mile-per-hour wind. [6]Orville's brother Wilbur ran alongside the swaying machine, holding onto it and balancing it on the track. [7]At the forty-foot mark, the machine lifted and erratically darted up, then down—a twelve-second, 120-foot flight. [8]Another aspect of nature had been conquered with this first flight. [9]The race to the stars had begun.

Narrative Elements (pages 160–162)

1. Which sentence identifies the setting?
(a) sentence 1 **(b)** sentence 3 **(c)** sentence 5

2. From which point of view is the narrative told?
(a) first-person **(b)** third-person omniscient

3. Which sentence identifies the conflict or central problem?
(a) sentence 1 **(b)** sentence 2 **(c)** sentence 3

4. Which sentence describes the climax of the narrative?
(a) sentence 3 **(b)** sentence 5 **(c)** sentence 6 **(d)** sentence 7

5. Which sentence states the resolution of the narrative?
(a) sentence 6 **(b)** sentence 7 **(c)** sentence 8

Narrative Details (pages 166–167)

6. Which sentence contains details about the setting?
(a) sentence 2 **(b)** sentence 3 **(c)** sentence 4

7. Which sentence contains details about the main character?
(a) sentence 3 **(b)** sentence 4 **(c)** sentence 5

Chronological Order and Coherence (pages 169–171)

8. Which of the following outlines the events in chronological order?
(a) Orville releases plane; Wilbur balances it; plane lifts.
(b) Orville releases plane; plane lifts; Wilbur balances it.

9. Which sentence contains a transition that indicates time?
(a) sentence 2 **(b)** sentence 4 **(c)** sentence 5 **(d)** sentence 6

10. Which sentence contains a verb that suggests the *slow* movement of the plane?
(a) sentence 5 **(b)** sentence 6 **(c)** sentence 7 **(d)** sentence 8

Answers: **1.** a; **2.** b; **3.** c; **4.** d; **5.** c; **6.** a; **7.** b; **8.** a; **9.** b; **10.** a

Writing for Review Write a narrative paragraph about a historical event. Make sure that your narrative contains a specific setting, characters, and a climax.

10 CHAPTER
Expository Writing

The only human value of anything, writing included, is intense vision of the facts.

—William Carlos Williams

Each of the following paragraphs exemplifies a type of expository writing you will learn more about in this chapter. What common element do these paragraphs share?

Humpbacks are baleen whales. That is, they have no teeth in their lower jaw, only closely spaced sheets of baleen—a material exactly like your fingernail—hanging from their upper jaw. They are filter feeders. A whale will just plow through a school of fish with an open mouth, and the water passes through the baleen while the fish are retained inside.

—Bill Lawton, "Tracking Leviathan"

Starting up a program on this particular computer is a simple process. You switch on the computer and place a floppy disk into drive A. The computer acknowledges it by making the letter *A* appear on the video display. You are now logged into Drive A, the computer is waiting for a command. The rest is up to you. You command it; it obeys.

In most parts of the world, pistachio nuts are still harvested and processed by hand. The red clusters are left to dry in the sun and then, at a later, more convenient time, soaked in water to facilitate hand hulling. The defect of this method, even in countries like Iran, where labor is cheap, is that it allows the pigment of the hull to stain and mottle the shells. Now if pistachios were sold as naked, shelled nutmeats, this would make no difference. But they are almost always roasted and salted in the shell because, ideally and usually, they emerge from the hull "smiling," with their shells split open at one end, easy for the eater to shell on his own.

—Raymond Sokolov, "A Delectable Drupe"

In ancient times, there were many fanciful theories about the origin of pearls. The real explanation is quite simple. Every mollusk that has a shell can produce a "pearl," and it will be inclined to do so whenever a foreign body enters its system. The mollusk's reaction is to cover the irritant with layers of the substance its shell is made of. However, only those mollusks that line their shells with nacre, or mother-of-pearl, produce what we know as pearls.

—Nigel Sitwell, "The Queen of Gems Comes Back"

Each of these paragraphs focuses on a different topic and presents that topic in a different form. One gives a definition and explanation of what a baleen whale is. The second tells how to do something—start a program on a computer. The third divides and classifies. The fourth explores a cause-and-effect relationship. Yet, as different in style and content as each passage is, they all have something in common: Each is an example of expository writing, or writing that *informs* a reader.

Expository writing is meant to inform the reader by presenting facts and explaining ideas.

In this chapter, you will learn various ways to shape and structure expository paragraphs. You will develop the following skills and methods of communicating information to a reader:

- determining purpose and audience for expository writing
- explaining a process
- explaining cause-and-effect relationships
- dividing and classifying
- defining
- comparing and contrasting
- analogy

DETERMINING PURPOSE AND AUDIENCE FOR EXPOSITORY WRITING

When you write an expository paragraph, you have a choice of many different approaches by which you may present information. Your choice of approach will depend upon your purpose and the interests of your intended audience.

Suppose, for example, that you want to inform your readers about a new high-speed computer with artificial intelligence. What specifically is your purpose? Do you want to point out the differences between this computer and earlier computers? If so, you probably should write a *comparison* or *contrast* of the two machines. To explore the meaning of artificial intelligence, you might want to draw an *analogy*, or extended comparison, between the computer's brain and a human brain. To emphasize the potential benefits or dangers of this artificial intelligence, then perhaps you should develop a *cause-and-effect* analysis. Each approach to the subject serves a different purpose, and the approach you select will dictate the nature of the information you will include.

In addition to your purpose for writing, you should keep your audience in mind when selecting a particular approach to your topic. For example, readers who know little about computers may be interested in a comparison or contrast of the new computer's features with those of earlier models. However, computer experts might find such a comparison uninteresting and uninformative.

To define your purpose and audience, ask yourself the following questions:

- Why do I want to write this expository piece? To explain a process? To explore causes and effects? To classify items into categories? To define something? To compare or contrast two items? To explain something complex by means of an analogy?
- Who is going to read my writing? How much do my readers already know about my subject? What approach is likely to interest them most?

After exploring your subject in greater depth, you may want to refine your purpose even further. For example, you may decide to inform *and* persuade your audience of the benefits of the high-speed, artificially intelligent computer. Even more specifically, you may decide to concentrate on benefits in two areas, education and medicine, and analyze the potential impact on these fields.

Objective

EXERCISE 1. Identifying Purposes for Expository Writing. For each of the following subjects, list two specific purposes that a writer could have in mind during the prewriting stage of expository writing.

1. television journalism
2. a recent book
3. acid rain pollution
4. a famous entertainer
5. migration patterns of birds
6. a recent invention

Suggested Answer for 1: Purposes might include to explain the power of TV journalism or to compare it with print journalism.

Objective

EXERCISE 2. Selecting an Audience for Expository Writing. Choose one of the following topics. Then write two or three sentences explaining whether you would prefer to write about this topic for an expert audience or a nonexpert audience.

1. playing a guitar
2. a professional basketball player

3. the birth and death of a star
4. the short-term and long-term effects of a recession

Suggested Answer for 1: Students might choose an expert audience in order to share a detailed knowledge of guitar technique.

EXPLAINING A PROCESS

Explaining a process means showing how something works or how a person accomplishes a particular task.

Do you want to explain how a color television set converts signals into color images? Do you want to explain how best to prepare for the SAT examinations? In each case you will be explaining a process. Your explanation must lead your readers step by step through each action or stage that makes up the total process. As you plan your explanation, you should keep in mind your intended audience and their familiarity or lack of familiarity with the process you are explaining.

PREWRITING

The first stage in writing about a process is to research the actual process and to take appropriate notes during your research. You can research a process in three ways:

1. by reading about it in a book; for example, a cookbook or a computer manual
2. by closely observing someone who is actually working through the process. This form of research is especially useful if you are explaining a technical process such as learning to drive a standard-shift car.
3. by working through the process yourself, whether it be something as simple as preparing an omelette or as complicated as constructing a bubble chamber to track atomic particles

The second stage in writing about a process is to list the steps in the process in **chronological**, or time, **order**. A chart like the following one, in which you answer the questions about the process, is a useful organizing tool. In this chart, the writer answers questions about the process of preparing to run in a twenty-six mile marathon.

Listing Steps in a Process

PROCESS: *Preparing for a marathon*	
QUESTIONS	SAMPLE ANSWERS
1. For what audience am I writing?	*Beginning runners who have never raced 26 miles in a marathon*

Listing Steps in a Process (continued)

QUESTIONS	SAMPLE ANSWERS
2. What are the steps in this process?	• *Set a plan or schedule, over a one-year period.* • *Make a serious commitment to preparing yourself physically and mentally.* • *Become a runner by working toward running 20 continuous minutes 3 times a week; may take 8–12 weeks.* • *Work toward a long-distance goal --20 miles a week.* • *Run the 20-mile weekly distance for at least 4–6 months.* • *Run in a marathon for experience.* • *Learn to pace yourself.* • *Race in a marathon.*
3. Should the order of the steps be changed?	*Reverse the first two; making a commitment comes first.*
4. Can any of the steps be combined?	*Combine learning to pace yourself with first-time running in a marathon.*
5. Does my audience need additional information to understand the process?	• *Stress purpose behind the gradual process of training: development of cardiovascular and muscle systems and mental confidence.*

Objective

EXERCISE 3. Prewriting: Ordering the Steps in a Process. The following steps, indicating the process by which paper is made, are out of order. On your paper list the steps in the order you think is correct. Group any steps that seem to belong together.

1. Debarked wood is reduced to pulp mechanically or with boiling chemicals.
2. Logs arrive at the paper mill.
3. The liquid wood pulp is partially dried.
4. Refining follows the Hydrapulper procedure.
5. At the paper mill, the bark is removed from the logs by machine.
6. After refining, pulp is mixed with chemicals and, sometimes, pigments.
7. A machine called the Hydrapulper breaks up the dried and pressed pulp.

8. The partially dried pulp is pressed.
9. Most of the water is extracted from the chemically treated pulp.
10. After extraction of the water, what remains is a kind of paper "cloth" that must be dried numerous times over mechanical drying cylinders.

Answer: The correct order is 2, 5, 1, 3, 8 (3 and 8 may be grouped), 7, 4, 6, 9, 10.

Objective

EXERCISE 4. Prewriting: Listing the Steps in a Process. Choose one of the processes listed here, or choose a different process that interests you. Then decide on an appropriate audience for an explanation of that process. Fill out a chart like the one on page 182. Save your notes for a paragraph that you will write later.

1. how a college basketball team reaches the NCAA final championship game
2. how to ski cross-country or downhill
3. how to prepare, plant, and grow a vegetable garden
4. the process of determining a presidential candidate—from primaries to national convention
5. how a sculptor creates

Suggested Answer for 1: Stages should include initial selection, preliminary rounds, semi-finals, and finals.

WRITING A FIRST DRAFT

Begin to write once you have a clear understanding of the process. Remember to choose language appropriate to your purpose and audience. If you are explaining how to perform a task, address your readers directly by using *you*. However, if your explanation focuses on the process itself rather than on how someone should perform it, use the third-person pronouns. In addition, always keep in mind your audience's level of expertise; define technical terms, if necessary.

Begin your explanation of the process with a topic sentence that tells the main idea of the paragraph. The topic sentence should identify the process and make a general statement about the purpose of your paragraph. Use chronological order to present the steps or stages of the process. Include transitions like the following to make your explanation coherent:

after	finally	immediately	meanwhile	so that
always	first	in order to	now	then
before	following	last	soon	until

Read the following explanation of how to prepare for a twenty-six mile marathon. Notice how the writer presents the steps chronologically and ties them together with transitions:

Preparing yourself to run in a twenty-six mile marathon involves a process of gradual but demanding training. First you must make a serious and total commitment to running. You will need to prepare yourself both physically and mentally by developing your cardiovascular system and building your mental confidence. A beginning runner needs to establish a one-year plan or training schedule. Before becoming a marathon runner, you need first to become a basic runner. Work toward a goal of running twenty minutes three times a week, a goal which may take you eight to twelve weeks to achieve. Then begin working toward a long-distance running goal of twenty miles each week, which may take you several months to achieve. Spend at least four to six months running the twenty-mile-per-week distance over various courses. Now you are ready to run in your first marathon—to gain experience and to learn to pace yourself. Soon, after several practice marathons, you can finally race in the New York or Boston Marathon with the goal of improving your time. If you run at your peak, you may even win the race.

REVISING, EDITING, AND PUBLISHING

When you finish your first draft, read it aloud. Listen for clarity and the logical progression of steps. Use the following checklist to help you revise, edit, and proofread your explanation. Then publish your final product by sharing it with your readers.

CHECKLIST FOR EXPLAINING A PROCESS

1. Which steps in the process should be added to my explanation? Which ones can be omitted or combined?
2. How can I present the steps in a more logical order?
3. What can I do to make the stages of this process clearer to a reader who does not know anything about it?
4. What transitions would add to the coherence of my writing?
5. Is each sentence a complete sentence? Have I avoided errors in verbs, pronouns, and modifiers?
6. Have I correctly capitalized and punctuated each sentence? Are all the words correctly spelled?
7. How can I effectively share my writing with others? By displaying it on a bulletin board? By sending it to the school or local newspaper?

Objective

EXERCISE 5. Writing and Revising an Explanation of a Process. Use the chart that you prepared for Exercise 4, and write a paragraph explaining the process you chose. Use appropriate transitions. Be sure to add any information that you think your audience needs. Then use the preceding checklist and revise, edit, proofread, and publish your writing.

EXPLAINING A CAUSE-AND-EFFECT RELATIONSHIP

PREWRITING

A **cause** is an event or condition that produces a result, which is known as an

When you explain the reasons behind or the results of a particular event, action, or condition, you are telling about a cause-and-effect relationship. Make sure that your events are cause-and-effect related and not simply linked by time. In a simple time relationship, one event merely follows another with no causal connection between them, as in this example:

> It began to snow at night.
> By sunrise a blizzard raged.

In a cause-and-effect relationship, the events are more closely linked in that one event actually *causes* the other to happen, as in this example:

> The blizzard dumped thirty inches of snow on the town.
> Schools were shut down for two days.

Because officials often cancel school in the aftermath of heavy snows, it is reasonable to think that the blizzard caused the closing of school.

Identifying Immediate and Long-Term Causes and Effects

Most cause-and-effect relationships are not as simple as the relationship between a blizzard and the closing of school. When you are examining cause-and-effect relationships during prewriting, you should also look for **immediate causes and effects**, or **underlying causes and effects**. An immediate cause, for example, of financial bankruptcy might be a person's inability to pay off a huge debt; while the underlying cause might be that person's mismanagement of funds or desire to acquire possessions regardless of cost. When writing about a cause-and-effect relationship, you want to present your reader with a complete understanding of the relationship.

Objective

EXERCISE 6. Identifying True Cause-and-Effect Relationships. Write whether each of the following pairs of sentences expresses a simple time relationship or a true cause-and-effect relationship.

1. Bill turned on the computer. He then inserted a disk in the drive system.
2. A truck jack-knifed on Route 302. Traffic was backed up for miles.

3. A high-velocity electron smashed into the atom's nucleus. The nucleus split into several atomic particles.
4. Folksinging was popular in the 1960s but faded in popularity in the 1970s. Today there is a renewed interest in folksinging.

Answers: **1.** and **4.**—simple time; **2.** and **3.**—cause-and-effect

Exploring a Cause-and-Effect Relationship

When doing prewriting for a cause-and-effect paragraph, narrow your topic and decide whether to stress causes or effects.

One useful method of exploring a cause-and-effect relationship is to brainstorm. First, list the event or condition that you want to focus on, and then generate ideas about either the *causes* or the *effects* related to that event or condition. In the following example, someone who is writing about the potential loss of East Coast marine life begins by charting or listing a series of related causes:

TOPIC: Potential loss of East Coast marine life

- People overfish and overconsume lobster population.
- Sea urchin population grows because fewer lobsters exist to prey on them.
- Urchins overgraze coastal kelp fields.
- Destruction of kelp fields, which are natural habitats for dozens of species of fish and other marine animals
- Loss of kelp habitat—shelter and food—results in loss of coastal marine life.

Objective

EXERCISE 7. Prewriting: Explaining Cause-and-Effect Relationships. Choose one of the subjects below or a subject of your own. Decide whether you want to focus on causes or effects, and make brainstorming notes like those in the preceding model. Save your notes for a paragraph that you will write later.

1. an inflationary period in the economy
2. a passing fad
3. a politician's defeat for re-election
4. the rebirth of a city or town
5. the popularity of the small, subcompact car
6. stress in modern life
7. an increasing number of career women in modern business
8. passivity
9. migration to the Sun Belt
10. laws mandating the wearing of automobile seat belts

WRITING A FIRST DRAFT

Before writing a first draft, review your prewriting notes. Then write a topic sentence stating your main idea. From your notes choose the points that seem to be the most important causes or effects. You will use those points as support; you might also use facts and quotations from your reading as additional support for your main idea.

As you write your cause-and-effect explanation, draw ideas from your notes, and connect those ideas with transitions. The following transitions can help add coherence to your explanation:

To Indicate Cause And Effects

as a result	consequently	is the effect of	therefore
because	if . . . then	leads to	the reason for
causes	is due to	since	

To Indicate Degrees Of Certainty

certainly	maybe	possibly	undoubtedly
likely	necessarily	probably	unquestionably

To Indicate Order Of Importance

finally	former	latter	second
first	last	primarily	

The following paragraph explains how a diminishing lobster population can potentially lead to a severe loss of other coastal marine life. Notice how the writer uses transitions to clarify cause-and-effect relationships.

A delicate chain of dependence exists among East Coast marine animals; the slightest alteration in that chain can lead to potential disaster. In recent years, consumer demand for lobsters has dramatically increased. As a result of that demand, lobstermen have increased their lobster catch. The increased fishing probably accounts for a diminishing lobster population. Because there are fewer lobsters, one of their favorite prey—the sea urchin—now exists in tremendous numbers. Urchins eat quantities of kelp, and their large numbers undoubtedly account for the overgrazing of marine kelp beds. Since these kelp fields are the natural habitat for dozens of species of fish and other marine animals, the destruction of the kelp means a loss of an important source of shelter and food. Finally, that loss can potentially lead to disaster for coastal marine life and to barren, lifeless coastal waters.

REVISING, EDITING, AND PUBLISHING

After writing your first draft, use the checklist to help you revise your cause-and-effect explanation. For additional guidelines on editing, proofreading, and publishing your work, see the checklist on page 184.

CHECKLIST FOR EXPLAINING A CAUSE-AND-EFFECT RELATIONSHIP

1. Where have I identified the causes or effects related to the event or condition on which I am focusing?
2. Which relationships are not true cause-and-effect relationships?
3. Which, if any, causes or effects should I add? Which should I delete?
4. What can I do to make clearer the connection between each cause and its effect? What transitions can I add?

Objective

EXERCISE 8. Writing and Revising a Paragraph About a Cause-and-Effect Relationship. Use the prewriting notes you made in Exercise 7 to write the first draft of a paragraph explaining a cause-and-effect relationship. Use transitions to clarify the cause-and-effect relationship. Refer to the preceding checklist and the checklist on page 184 to revise, edit, proofread, and publish your explanation.

DIVIDING AND CLASSIFYING

Division breaks an item into its main parts. **Classification** groups items together into categories.

Division is a good method for organizing information when you are explaining a complicated subject that has several distinct parts. For example, you could write about kinds of guitars and divide your subject into acoustic guitars and electric guitars or into modern guitars and early guitars.

Classification is another helpful method of organizing information. Use classification to explain how similar items can be sorted into categories. For example, if you were explaining your school's sports program, you might discuss tennis, golf, and swimming and show how these sports fall into the category of lifelong sports —sports that can be enjoyed well through one's adult years.

Division is the process of breaking a subject into smaller and smaller parts; classification is the process of grouping individual items into broader categories. Use the method that best suits your purpose and clarifies the point you want to make.

DIVISION: PREWRITING

The first step in dividing a subject is to determine a method of division that fits your purpose and allows you to say something meaningful about your subject. In the following example, a writer who wanted to explain how she learned to use a word processor found two ways in which she could divide her subject into meaningful parts. She then developed a chart to help organize her thinking.

Prewriting Chart for Division

SUBJECT FOR DIVISION: *Learning to use a word processor*	
METHOD OF DIVIDING	PARTS
METHOD 1: *stages of the learning experience*	*1. first dreadful day* *2. first week: confusion* *3. second week: experimentation* *4. third week: competence and understanding*
METHOD 2: *skills needed to learn it*	*1. dexterity* *2. patience* *3. problem-solving skills*

Objective

EXERCISE 9. Division: Prewriting. Choose one of the following subjects or a subject of your own. Think of two methods of dividing it. Then make a chart like the preceding one, listing each method and the distinct parts of division. Save your chart for a paragraph that you will write later.

1. the Olympics
2. fishing
3. celebrations
4. a shopping mall
5. a city
6. careers
7. music
8. the library

Suggested Answer to 1: Students might divide *the Olympics* into summer and winter Olympics or into categories of competition (swimming, etc.).

DIVISION: WRITING A FIRST DRAFT

Once you decide on a method of division to use, you should then choose an appropriate method of organization for your paragraph. For example, using spatial order would help you to explain the locations of the various rides in an amusement park. Chronological order would help you trace the stages of development in an artist's career. Order of importance would help you explain how your state government is divided into different branches. Remember to use transitions to connect ideas.

The following paragraph uses division to explore the various stages of learning to use a word processor. The writer uses chronological order to organize the paragraph.

Once you have purchased a home computer for word processing, you should anticipate three weeks of confusion until you discard your pencil for good. The first dreadful day begins with unpacking the computer. Unpacking is an easy enough task, but correctly connecting the printer, the monitor, and the main unit feels much like sorting cooked spaghetti into strands. With persistence, eventually everything is connected, but then begins the first week of mass confusion. Fear stalks your every press of the delete key. Will everything be erased? Unfamiliar nomenclature abets the confusion. *Files, floppies, backup disks*—who are these strange creatures? At the end of that initial week, however, you begin to understand it. You start experimenting with the dozens of commands for doing on a keyboard what you used to do with a lead pencil: writing words, erasing words, moving sentences around, and shaping paragraphs. At some point during the third week, though, you are competently writing with the word processor, your earlier frustrations forgotten. You may not know a modem from a widget, but you understand how to process words.

Objective

EXERCISE 10. Division: Writing and Revising. Review the chart you completed for Exercise 9. Choose one of the methods of division, decide on a method of organization, and write a paragraph using that method of division. Use transitions for coherence. Then revise your paragraph. For further guidance refer to the checklist on page 184, and look ahead to the checklist on page 192.

CLASSIFICATION: PREWRITING

When you classify, you group items by type or kind. For example, you might classify or group the selections in your literature textbook by literary genre—poems, plays, short stories, essays—or by theme. If you were grouping short stories by theme, you should be sure that each story you list truly embodies that theme.

Classifications should also be consistent and not overlap. For example, you could logically classify cars into the categories of *intermediate cars, compact cars,* and *subcompact cars.* If, however, you decided to group cars into *expensive cars, compact cars,* and *foreign cars,* you risk confusing your reader because your groupings are based on three different principles—cost, size, and source.

When you classify a subject, making a chart like the following one will help ensure that your categories are meaningful. The subject is magazines, classified two different ways.

Prewriting Chart for Classification

SUBJECT FOR CLASSIFICATION: *magazines*	
METHOD OF CLASSIFYING	CATEGORIES
METHOD 1: *subject matter*	*1. general-interest publications* *2. special-interest publications* *3. professional publications*
METHOD 2: *places where copies can be obtained*	*1. newsstands* *2. libraries* *3. magazine's subscription department*

Objective

EXERCISE 11. Classification: Prewriting. Choose one of the subjects listed here. Decide on two methods of classifying the subject. Then make a classification chart like the preceding one. List two or three meaningful categories into which you can classify parts of the subject. Save your notes for use in Exercise 12.

1. typewriters
2. foods
3. books
4. transportation
5. plants
6. musicians
7. politicians
8. planets
9. noises
10. triumphs

Suggested Answer to 1: Typewriters could be grouped into manual, electric, and electronic typewriters.

CLASSIFICATION: WRITING A FIRST DRAFT

When you group items into categories, you should arrange your categories in an order that makes sense to you and that will interest your readers. You may want to use chronological order, spatial order, or order of importance. Use the transition words and phrases listed on pages 47–48 to help you clarify the relationships among items. Read the following paragraph, which classifies magazines according to subject matter.

The magazine rack at the local library supplies magazines to meet every interest. The hobby magazines offer instruction and counsel about yachting, flying, amateur radio, photography, knitting, stamp collecting, and countless other fields of interest. As soon as more than two people show an interest in a subject, it seems, some market-conscious publisher decides to launch a new magazine to cover it. The recent spate of computer magazines serves as proof of this point. Computer magazines now form the most extensive subgroup of hobby magazines in the library's racks. News magazines are rarely found on the shelves. Dog-eared and well-thumbed, they lie in small piles on the tables where readers have left them. For the general reader sports and gossip magazines abound. Less thumbed but all the more interesting, however, are the literary magazines—*The New Yorker, Atlantic*, and many others that publish the short stories and poems that keep our literary heritage alive. The word *magazine* is derived from an Arabic word meaning "storehouse." Many treasures lie therein.

Objective

EXERCISE 12. Classification: Writing and Revising. Review your notes for Exercise 11. Write a paragraph that classifies the topic you selected. Be sure that your categories are meaningful and that you use appropriate transitions to link sentences. Then revise your first draft; refer to the following checklist and to the one on page 192.

REVISING, EDITING, AND PUBLISHING

After writing a first draft of a paragraph of division or classification, use the following checklist to help you revise your work. For additional guidance in editing, proofreading, and publishing your final version, see page 184.

CHECKLIST FOR DIVIDING AND CLASSIFYING

For division:

1. Into how many parts have I divided my subject? Are these enough? Too many? Are the divisions clear?

For classification:

Into how many categories have I grouped all the members of my subject? Are these categories meaningful and consistent, or do they overlap?

2. How can I clarify my reason for dividing or classifying my subject as I did?
3. How can I organize in a more logical way the divisions or classifications that I have set up for my subject?

DEFINING

A **definition** explains the meaning of a term.

When you want to explain to your readers what a *motif* is, what a *densitometer* measures, or what *holography* involves, you can write definitions of these generally unfamiliar terms. You can also write a personal definition of a more familiar term. For example, you might write your own definition of the term *riches* to indicate how for you it means something more than *having money.*

DEFINING AN UNFAMILIAR TERM: PREWRITING

When defining an unfamiliar term, you may first need to read about or research the meaning of the term. Then you should try to give your readers a wider, more familiar frame of reference in which to place the term. You can then explain how the term differs from the other terms in the same general category. To help your readers' understanding you should include examples or comparisons in your definition.

Begin defining an unfamiliar term by asking questions such as the ones in the following chart. Shown here are sample answers for a definition of a number with the intriguing name *googolplex.*

Prewriting Chart for Defining an Unfamiliar Term

TERM TO BE DEFINED: *googolplex*	
QUESTIONS	SAMPLE ANSWERS
1. Into what class or group of familiar items can I place the term?	*Numbers*
2. What distinguishes this item from the other items in its class or group?	*Its size--a googol is ten to the power one hundred, or a one followed by one hundred zeros; a googolplex is ten to the power of a googol.*
3. What examples or comparisons would help my readers?	*Comparisons to total number of atoms in a body = 10^{28}, or total number of protons, neutrons, and electrons in observable universe = 10^{80}. Example of piece of paper with a googolplex's zeros written out; the paper would not fit into the known universe.*

Objective

EXERCISE 13. Prewriting to Define an Unfamiliar Term. Choose a term that may be unfamiliar to many people. Your school courses, recent reading, or a special hobby may provide you with a generally unfamiliar term, such as *semiconductor* from a school computer course. Prepare a definition of the term by asking and answering questions like those in the preceding chart. If necessary, do research to discover comparisons or examples you might include. Save your notes.

DEFINING AN UNFAMILIAR TERM: WRITING A FIRST DRAFT

Use your prewriting notes as you write the first draft of your definition. Your topic sentence should identify the group or class of items to which the unfamiliar term belongs, as in the topic sentence. The next few sentences should detail the features that distinguish the item from the other items in the class or group. Complete your definition by providing concrete comparisons or examples of the defined term.

Like 1, 10, 100, or 1,000, a googolplex is quite simply a number. However, a googolplex is a very, very large number. It is a multiple of another number called the googol, which is ten to the power one hundred or a one followed by one hundred zeros. A googolplex, then, is ten to the power of a googol, or one followed by a googol zeros. 10^{100}, and a googolplex equals $10^{10^{100}}$. By comparison, the total number of atoms in the human body is only 10^{28}, and the total number of protons, neutrons, and electrons in the observable universe is a mere 10^{80}. If you were to write a googolplex with all of its zeros in a row on a piece of paper, that paper would not fit into the known universe.

Objective

EXERCISE 14. Writing and Revising a Definition of an Unfamiliar Term. Use your notes from Exercise 13 to write a definition of an unfamiliar term. After completing your first draft, revise your definition. For revision guidelines, use the checklist on page 184, and look ahead to the checklist on page 196.

DEFINING A FAMILIAR TERM: PREWRITING

When you define a familiar term, you have a more personal purpose in mind than a simple formal definition of the term. For example, you might want to define an abstract term like *joy* or *friendship* by explaining what it has come to mean to you.

You can prepare a definition of a familiar term by asking questions like the ones in this chart:

Prewriting Chart to Define a Familiar Term

TERM TO BE DEFINED: *Fiction*	
QUESTIONS	SAMPLE ANSWERS
1. What is the term's common meaning?	*Imaginative writing; entertainment*
2. In what ways does my definition differ from the common one?	*Fiction is more than simply imaginative writing or a source of entertainment--it is a way seeing the unseen and experiencing the unexperienced.*

QUESTIONS	SAMPLE ANSWERS
3. What incidents or examples might clarify my definition?	*Compare reading fiction to traveling through a new world. Point out the wide array of fiction.*

Objective

EXERCISE 15. Prewriting to Define a Familiar Term. Select a term from the following list, or choose a term of your own. Plan to write a personal definition of the term. Prewrite by answering questions like those on the preceding chart.

1. time
2. freedom
3. achievement
4. independence
5. perfection
6. silence
7. challenge
8. comfort

DEFINING A FAMILIAR TERM: WRITING A FIRST DRAFT

Because your term is a familiar one, your readers will at least have an understanding of its common meaning. You might, therefore, begin the definition by citing that common meaning and then giving your personal definition. You might also develop a topic sentence that captures your audience's attention. Remember to include examples, comparisons, or personal experiences that will help to clarify your definition.

In the following paragraph, the writer develops a personal definition of *fiction:*

Reading a piece of good fiction is like traveling through time and space into new, unexperienced worlds. Fiction is imaginative, entertaining writing, but it is more than that. Through fiction you see the previously unseen. You can travel back through history or leap forward into the future. You can inhabit the worlds of mystery, adventure, romance, and tragedy. You can share the successes, failures, and conflicts of kings and queens, astronauts and explorers, financial wizards and devious thieves. Fiction is a way of experiencing the misery and the glory of human existence.

Objective

EXERCISE 16. Writing and Revising a Definition of a Familiar Term. Use your notes from Exercise 15 to write a definition of a familiar term. Begin with a topic sentence that grabs your reader's attention. After completing your first draft, revise your definition. For revision guidelines, use the checklists on pages 184 and 196.

REVISING, EDITING, AND PUBLISHING

When you finish your first draft, use the following checklist to help you revise your work. For additional guidance in editing, proofreading, and publishing your final version, see page 184.

CHECKLIST FOR DEFINING

1. *For definitions of unfamiliar terms:* Have I indicated the wider category to which the term belongs? Have I explained what sets the term apart from the others in its same general category?
2. *For definitions of familiar terms:* How can I make even clearer my reasons for defining this term? What specific details and incidents can I add to clarify what the term means to me?

COMPARING AND CONTRASTING

When you **compare** items, you point out their similarities. When you **contrast** items, you point out their differences.

Depending on their complexity or your need for a detailed analysis, you can compare two items, contrast two items, or even compare *and* contrast two items by pointing out *both* their similarities and their differences. Regardless of whether you want to emphasize similarities, differences, or both, you must compare two items that have some common basis—for example, two types of canoes, two methods of communication, or two professional baseball teams. There is no reason to compare items, such as a canoe and a pencil sharpener; each has a very different function.

You should also have a *purpose* in mind when you compare and contrast items. For example, you might want to convince your reader that one item is more beneficial, more complicated, or more dependable than the other.

PREWRITING

Begin your examination of two items by listing *both* their similarities *and* their differences. Such a list will help you later to decide the most appropriate scope and focus for your writing. The list will also help you organize the points of comparison and contrast as you write.

One way of listing similarities and differences is to make a *comparison frame* as part of your prewriting. First identify and list the various points on which you will compare and contrast the items. Then, citing specific examples, indicate how the items are similar or different with regard to each of your points. The following comparison frame compares and contrasts two different types of solar energy, passive and active.

Comparison Frame

BASIS FOR COMPARISON	PASSIVE SOLAR ENERGY	ACTIVE SOLAR ENERGY
Construction	• *Uncomplicated, built into construction*	• *Can be complicated; depends on mechanical means (solar collectors or photovoltaic cells) to move, store heat*
Cost	• *Relatively inexpensive*	• *Can be very expensive; a photovoltaic roof can cost $60,000.*
Dependability	• *Dependable in southern climates* • *Undependable for 100% of heating needs in cooler climates*	• *Hot water system can provide 80%–100% of heating needs.* • *Electrical system can provide 40% of electrical needs.*
Future Outlook	• *Likely to be improved with new materials*	• *Likely to be improved with research--resulting in lower cost*

Objective

EXERCISE 17. Prewriting: Making a Comparison Frame. Choose one of the subjects from the following list, and identify the two specific items that you will compare and contrast. Write a purpose for comparing and contrasting the items. Then make a comparison frame: List at least four points on which you can compare and contrast the items, and for each point list specific similarities or differences. Save your notes.

1. two political parties
2. two states
3. two actors
4. two events in a track meet
5. two professional teams
6. two different sports
7. two methods of travel
8. two fads

WRITING A FIRST DRAFT

When you write a comparison or contrast, you can select one of the following methods of organization:

1. Order your information *item by item.* The type of organization is labeled AAABBB because you present all your information for item A and then all your information for item B.
2. Order your information *point by point.* Following this method, you present information about each main point for both items together. This type of organization is labeled ABABAB.

The following paragraph compares *and* contrasts passive and active solar energy by listing *both* similarities and differences in an ABABAB pattern of development. Note that the writer assumes a certain amount of knowledge on the audience's part but still uses transition words to maintain clarity and coherence.

Cost and dependability are the two factors that most stand in the way of a nationwide reliance on solar energy as a source of heat and electricity for the home. Passive solar energy is fairly inexpensive, but an active system such as a photovoltaic roof can cost $60,000. If you live in a southern climate, a passive system is dependable, but it will not supply one hundred percent of your heating needs in cooler climates. Likewise, active solar energy systems vary in dependability; for example, a water-based system can supply eighty to one hundred percent of a home's heating needs, while an electrical conversion system might supply only forty percent of the electrical energy needs of a home. Nevertheless, the future looks bright. Passive systems are likely to improve as new construction materials are developed. So too will active systems improve with additional research and lowered costs.

Objective

EXERCISE 18. Writing and Revising a Comparison and Contrast. Use the comparison frame you wrote for Exercise 17, and write a paragraph comparing and contrasting the two items you listed. Use either the AAABBB or ABABAB type of organization for your paragraph. Then revise your first draft, using the following checklist and the one on page 184.

REVISING, EDITING, AND PUBLISHING

After writing your first draft, read it aloud, and use the following checklist to help you revise. For additional guidelines in editing, proofreading, and publishing your final version, see page 184.

CHECKLIST FOR COMPARING AND CONTRASTING

1. How can I make my comparison-contrast clearer?
2. Have I used the AAABBB pattern of organization or the ABABAB pattern? Would the other have worked better?

ANALOGY

When you make an **analogy** between two events, situations, or actions, you use the more familiar of the two to help you explain the less familiar of the two.

When you use an analogy to explain something, you make an *extended comparison* between two *unlike* things. An analogy is a useful means of using a familiar item to help explain an unfamiliar item. For example, in the following analogy, the writer explains the function of an unfamiliar item, peptides, by comparing it to the function of a familiar item, a train:

> These tiny proteins, called peptides, consist of amino acids strung together in a row, like freight cars in a train. Just as a locomotive may haul many different kinds of rolling stock, peptides may contain any of the different amino acids that comprise the key molecules of life, all assembled in a straight line.

Similes, metaphors, and analogies have much in common. Both similes and metaphors are comparisons, either stated or implied (see Chapter 5). An analogy, however, is a comparison that is explored and developed throughout the paragraph, not just in a short phrase. When you develop an expository paragraph by means of an analogy, you must always keep in mind the purpose for using an analogy—to explain the unfamiliar by drawing parallels to more familiar events, situations, or actions. Used well, an analogy can help you bring great clarity to an explanation.

PREWRITING

The first step in creating an analogy is to identify the major aspects of the unfamiliar item that you want to explain. Then think of an item that is familiar to your audience and that shares many points of similarity with the unfamiliar item. During the prewriting stage, you may find it helpful to make an analogy frame like the one that follows to help you determine whether or not you have compiled enough similarities to make the analogy clear and forceful.

UNFAMILIAR ITEM: *Autofocus camera*	FAMILIAR ITEM: *The human eye*
• *Adjusts focus quickly and automatically* • *Motor moves the lens in or out.*	• *Adjusts focus quickly and automatically.* • *Muscles in the eye refocus the eye*

Analogy Frame (continued)

UNFAMILIAR ITEM: *autofocus camera*	FAMILIAR ITEM: *the human eye*
• *Electronic circuit controls focus.*	• *Human brain controls focus.*
• *Camera automatically readjusts itself to focus on moving objects.*	• *Eye automatically readjusts focus.*

Objective

EXERCISE 19. Prewriting: Making an Analogy Frame. Choose one of the following pairs of items, or choose two items of your own. Make an analogy frame to help you identify the points of similarity between the two items. Save your notes for Exercise 20.

1. termites and a wrecking company
2. a camera and the human eye
3. crime and disease
4. a spider and bridge builder
5. "All the world is a stage."
6. an athlete and an efficient machine

WRITING A FIRST DRAFT

The most effective method of presenting an analogy is the point-by-point, or ABABAB, method. Using this method, you focus on similarities between the two items, point by point throughout the explanation. Because your primary purpose is to explain the unfamiliar item with clarity, you should also select the method of development—chronological order, spatial order, order of importance, or some other method of development—that will best enable you to organize your information about the unfamiliar item. Remember to include a topic sentence that will let your audience see the point of the comparison immediately.

The following paragraph explains for a nonexpert audience how an autofocus camera works by drawing an analogy between the autofocus mechanism and the human eye and brain. The writer uses order of importance to organize the paragraph and presents the points of comparison in an ABABAB pattern.

Many of us prefer to be snapshooters rather than photographers and thus shy away from using a camera any more complicated than a simple disk camera. We just want to take pictures, not spend time fussing with camera adjustments. An autofocus camera may be just the camera for you: An autofocus camera adjusts its focus as quickly and as automatically as the human eye does. When you point an autofocus camera at an object, a small motor cranks the lens in or out until the object comes into sharp focus, just as the human eye automatically adjusts itself to focus on nearby or distant objects without conscious effort on your part. An electronic circuit inside the camera automatically makes the focus adjustment for you, just as your brain automatically adjusts the focus of your eyes. If you are photographing a moving object, the camera continues to adjust the focus of the lens, just as your eye maintains a constant focus on a moving object without your consciously telling it to do so. An autofocus camera can make picture taking as simple as seeing.

Objective

EXERCISE 20. Writing an Analogy. Using the analogy frame from Exercise 19, write a paragraph in which you develop an extended comparison between the two items you selected. Remember to include a topic sentence and to use transition words for coherence. Revise your first draft; refer to checklists on pages 184 and 201.

REVISING, EDITING, AND PUBLISHING

After writing your first draft, use the following checklist to help you revise your writing. For additional guidelines in editing, proofreading, and publishing your final version, see page 184.

CHECKLIST FOR DEVELOPING AN ANALOGY

1. How can I make the analogy more understandable to my audience? In what other ways do these two items resemble each other?
2. How have I organized the paragraph? Would some other method of development be more appropriate?
3. Have I developed the analogy clearly by using the ABABAB method of presenting the points of comparison?
4. Have I included a topic sentence? Have I used transitions to connect ideas and clarify relationships?

WRITER'S CHOICE #1

ASSIGNMENT: To explain a simple process or how to perform a simple task
LENGTH: One paragraph of six to eight sentences
AUDIENCE: Someone who is unfamiliar with the process
PURPOSE: To present the steps in the process clearly and exactly
PREWRITING: Choose one process or task, such as how water freezes or how to swim underwater, and list the steps involved in the process or task. Think about your audience and the specific information they will need to understand your explanation. If necessary, add or combine steps in your list.
WRITING: Begin with a clearly stated topic sentence that explains the purpose of your paragraph. Follow chronological or spatial order. Use language appropriate to your audience and explain any unfamiliar terms.
REVISING: As you revise your paragraph, use the checklist on page 184 to help you.

WRITER'S CHOICE #2

ASSIGNMENT: To explain a cause-and-effect relationship
LENGTH: Six to ten sentences
PURPOSE: To write an answer to one of these questions
- How does a jet engine work?
- Why do birds sing?
- How do rainbows form?
- What causes fog?
- Why do leaves change color in autumn?

AUDIENCE: Your choice
PREWRITING: Plan your paragraph carefully. Explore your topic by using the methods you learned in this chapter.
WRITING: Choose an appropriate method for developing your paragraph. Use transition words and phrases to make your paragraph more coherent.
REVISING: Is your purpose for writing clear? How could you organize your paragraph more clearly? For additional guidance, use the checklists on pages 184 and 188.

WRITER'S CHOICE #3

ASSIGNMENT: To define a term
LENGTH: Your choice
PURPOSE: To invent a term and write a logical definition of it
AUDIENCE: Your choice

PREWRITING: Decide on an *imaginary* term. You may make the term as far-fetched or as close to a real term as you wish. Determine the group of items to which the term belongs and the features that make it different from other items in the group.

WRITING: Follow the suggestions on page 195 for writing a definition of an unfamiliar term. Use examples.

REVISING: How well does your definition clarify the term for your audience

WRITER'S CHOICE #4

ASSIGNMENT: To compare and contrast two school subjects.

LENGTH: Your choice

PURPOSE: To show how each subject could be helpful to you in your possible future career.

AUDIENCE: Your choice

PREWRITING: Choose several points on which to base your comparison and contrast of your subject. Make a comparison frame that reflects their similarities and differences.

WRITING: Use either the AAABBB or the ABABAB type of organization. Use transitions for coherence.

REVISING: Are the subjects genuinely relevant to the career? How can you make their relevance clearer?

WRITER'S CHOICE #5

ASSIGNMENT: To explain an unfamiliar term by means of an analogy

LENGTH: Your choice

PURPOSE: Your choice

AUDIENCE: Your choice

PREWRITING: Make an analogy frame showing the similarities between the two items you have selected.

WRITING: Choose an appropriate method of development. Use transitions to make your writing more coherent.

REVISING: Be sure that your analogy is clear.

THE WRITER

Paul Monach was editor-in-chief of his school newspaper besides being active in band and track. He received the National Council of Teachers of English Award in Writing and plans a career in medical or scientific research. Paul wrote the following comparison of three dramatic heroines as a student at Indian Hill High School in Cincinnati, Ohio.

THE FINISHED PRODUCT

The plays *Medea, Hedda Gabler,* and *A Doll's House* all discuss the predicament of women tied to unfeeling or insensitive husbands. The three women in the plays respond with varying degrees of rebellion. Medea kills her own children as well as the woman that her husband wants to marry; Hedda kills herself; Nora in *A Doll's House* "merely" sets out for a new life on her own. All three women are victims of their husbands, but they are also plagued by isolation, both physical and spiritual.

Physically, Medea is isolated because Jason, her husband, has abandoned her for another woman. Hedda and Nora, on the other hand, are loved by their husbands but are still alone. Hedda, who married her husband for financial security, finds her husband terminally boring, and she feels that her marriage keeps her from a more interesting life. Nora is treated as a "doll": Her husband, though adoring, seems to regard her virtually as an attractive possession.

The gap between the women and their husbands goes deeper, however. Jason fails to see Medea's humanity and her dangerous emotions. Hedda's husband is completely absorbed in his work and believes, mistakenly, that she married him out of love. Nora's husband loves her but fails to see that she needs to be recognized as an intelligent individual, not merely admired as a pretty doll.

In essence, though, the three women are actually isolated from themselves. Medea has been blinded by her love of Jason and realizes too late that she has been used and discarded. Hedda betrays her own feelings when she marries for money, and she forfeits her happiness in the process. Nora is the only one who finally sees herself accurately, but this insight comes so late that she must leave behind all of her former life, including her husband and children.

Isolation in these three plays is tied closely to misunderstanding. In each of the husband-wife relationships, the wife overestimates her husband and fails to communicate with him. He then treats her poorly, whether through arrogance or ignorance. The roots of the conflicts, though, lie in the characters' inability to realize their own needs and desires.

THE WRITER AT WORK

For me, organization is the key to effective writing. A piece of writing must have a central idea and purpose; if I have my ideas in order, then I can easily develop a coherent, inclusive statement of my main idea.

I have found organization to be extremely valuable for two reasons. First, it makes a piece of writing more effective and easier to read; second, from the time-starved student's point of view, it helps save a tremendous amount of time. The more I have in my head before I start, the faster the words spill out, and in better order. I feel the same way about organizing as I do about using proper grammar and punctuation—it is so much easier to do it right the first time.

I would suggest to other writers that they do what they feel best to keep their writing coherent. Some like to outline on paper. I personally do not for the same reason that I would not flow-chart a computer program before writing it. To me the best writing is not only informative but also interesting, with an element of spontaneity to keep the words from just melting into the page.

YOUR TURN **Writing a Comparison**

Choose two or more subjects of your own to compare, and write several paragraphs developing the comparison. Begin by listing the points on which you will base your comparison, and indicate what you could say about each subject with respect to each point. Before you begin to write, be sure to state the main idea to be supported by your comparison.

REVIEW

CHAPTER 10 EXPOSITORY WRITING

Explaining a Process (pages 181–184) The following items list the steps in fly fishing for trout, *out of order.* Write each item on your paper, and next to it write **(a)** for the first step, **(b)** for the second step, and **(c)** for the third step.

1. When the trout strikes the lure, firmly counter by raising your fishing rod.
2. Try to determine the species of insect flying above the stream, and then tie a matching artificial fly to your line as a lure.
3. Cast your lure above the feeding trout, and let it drift to them.

Division and Classification (pages 188–192) Indicate the letter of the item that correctly answers each question.

4. Which item divides a novel in the most meaningful way?
   (a) characters/themes/plot **(b)** title/mood **(c)** author/setting/plot
5. Which item sorts sports into meaningful groups or classes?
   (a) winter sports/summer sports **(b)** spectator sports/football **(c)** televised sports/summer sports

Definition (pages 193–196) Read the following parts of a definition of the term *CPM.* Then indicate the letter of the item that correctly answers each question. **(a)** a computer operating system **(b)** operates only earlier 8-bit computers

6. Which phrase sets off the term from other members of its group?
7. Which phrase indicates the group to which the term belongs?

Comparing and Contrasting (pages 196–199) Read the following brief passage. Indicate the letter of the item that correctly answers each question.

Most dogs are voracious feeders and will eat whatever they are served. However, cats are generally delicate eaters and are also very particular about what they eat. Dogs are especially responsive pets and are easy to teach and train. On the other hand, cats are responsive only when *they* want to be.

8. Which type of organization does the passage follow?
   (a) ABABAB **(b)** AAABBB
9. Which would be a good topic sentence for this passage?
   (a) Dogs are very popular pets. **(b)** Cats are indifferent animals.
   (c) Cats and dogs are very different.

Analogy (pages 199–201) Indicate the item that correctly answers the question.

10. Which of the following pairs of items would be suitable for a paragraph developed by an analogy comparison?
    (a) a tree and a radio **(b)** gold and wealth **(c)** a healthy body and a strong government

Answers: **1.** c; **2.** a; **3.** b; **4.** a; **5.** b; **6.** b; **7.** a; **8.** a; **9.** c; **10.** c

Writing for Review Write a paragraph presenting either causes or effects for one of the following: (1) physical fitness, (2) loyalty, (3) lying.

CHAPTER 11
Critical Thinking and Persuasive Writing

Writing is thinking.

—Anne Morrow Lindbergh

Every type of writing is actually a way of thinking through a subject. One type of writing, however, involves a very rigorous form of thinking called critical thinking. That type of writing is persuasive writing.

Critical thinking refers to analyzing and evaluating information presented to you or information that you plan to present to others to support an opinion or a position.

You encounter persuasive writing every day. Every day you wade through a steady stream of advice, argument, and opinion, urging you to buy this or that product, agree with this or that opinion, or to follow a particular course of action. The purpose in each case is to *influence* your thinking or behavior.

Persuasive writing is writing that tries to influence a reader to accept an idea, adopt a certain position or point of view, or perform a certain action.

To be effective, persuasive writing demands both clarity of expression and clarity of thinking. Throughout this chapter, you will study the techniques of sound persuasive writing, and you will sharpen your thinking skills. You will concentrate particularly on the following areas of critical thinking and persuasive writing:

- prewriting: purpose and opinion
- prewriting: audience
- prewriting: support
- prewriting: inductive and deductive reasoning
- writing an argument
- revising, editing, and publishing: avoiding faulty methods of persuasion

PREWRITING: PURPOSE AND OPINION

In persuasive writing, purpose is very closely related to audience. Persuasive writing attempts to move someone to adopt a certain attitude or to follow a certain course of action. A writer who hopes to persuade an audience needs to keep both audience and purpose clearly in mind. Unlike some other types of writing, such as descriptive writing, persuasive writing requires that the writer adopt a serious and consistent stance. A persuasive writer cannot adopt a take-it-or-leave-it attitude toward a subject.

When you set out to write persuasion, you must be sure that your proposition, or opinion, is actually worth the effort of trying to persuade someone to accept it.

A **proposition** is the thought, idea, or point of view that you want others to accept.

Some propositions are simply not appropriate for persuasive writing. For example, it is hardly necessary to try to persuade someone of an accepted fact. Few people would argue a fact like "The sun is a major source of energy." A more suitable proposition for persuasion might be: "Every American home should employ solar heating." When determining a suitable proposition for persuasion, you should also avoid **truisms,** such as "Politicians should be honest" or "Journalists should report facts." Such statements are obviously true and would generate little or no discussion.

Your purpose and your proposition should also be suitable for the length of the writing task. For example, you could not adequately cover this proposition in a single paragraph: "American business should adopt Japanese management techniques to increase productivity." In fact, *books* have been written about this very subject. The same proposition, if narrowed, might be adequately covered in a multiple-paragraph essay: "American business should adopt the Japanese Theory Z management technique to increase worker productivity."

Objective

EXERCISE 1. Selecting Suitable Propositions for Persuasive Writing. Determine whether each of the following topics is suitable or unsuitable for persuasive writing. Write an explanation for each of your decisions.

1. It is important to be truthful.
2. The computer is the single most important invention of the twentieth century.
3. Computers can perform complex calculations.
4. Today's rock musicians are unimaginative and uninventive compared

with the musicians of the 1960s and 1970s.

5. National illiteracy is a serious problem.

Answers: **2** and **4** are appropriate; **1, 3,** and **5** are inappropriate.

Objective

EXERCISE 2. Selecting a Suitable Topic and Stating a Proposition. Choose one of the following general topics or a topic of your own. Then write a proposition that would be suitable for a persuasive essay.

1. television
2. school
3. business
4. advertising
5. international relations
6. cynicism
7. American life styles
8. diets
9. bureaucracy
10. leisure

Suggested Answer for **1**: Television news shows are too sensational.

PREWRITING: AUDIENCE

When a business is planning a new product, it often conducts extensive marketing research about the people for whom the product is being developed. Such research yields a profile of the intended customer. Likewise, when you are writing to persuade, you should have a good mental picture of your intended audience.

A **profile** is a brief sketch providing basic facts and relevant information.

Basically you will address two kinds of audience in your persuasive writing. First, you may address the universal audience, which you must assume consists of *all reasonable* people. Second, you may address a specific, specialized audience; for example, a well-defined group such as sports fans, city council members, or members of a management or union group.

To create a profile of your intended audience, make a list of questions that will yield useful information about your audience's needs and interests.

- Why are they likely to listen to me in the first place?
- What will catch and hold their attention?
- What attitudes are they most likely to have regarding my topic?
- What experiences have they had that relate to the topic?
- Would they prefer straight, plain language or more elegant or specialized language?

Answers to these questions will help you to adjust your argument so that it has a better chance of persuading. In some cases, you may not have to change an audience's mind. If your readers already agree with your opinion, it is not necessary to try to persuade them. For example, it would not be necessary to try to persuade an audience of professional baseball players to accept the opinion that the free agent rule is in their best interests. If, however, your audience is likely to be totally in disagreement with your opinion, you may have to reconsider and revise your proposition. For example, it may be futile to try to persuade a group of bankers to provide interest-free loans to all businesses; however, you may be able to persuade them to provide low-interest loans to small local businesses.

Objective

EXERCISE 3. Suiting Topic to Audience. Number your paper from 1 to 5. For each audience and opinion listed, write *a, b,* or *c* to tell which statement applies.

a. appropriate topic for this audience
b. inappropriate; unnecessary to persuade this audience
c. inappropriate; unlikely to persuade this audience

1. *Audience:* your classmates. *Opinion:* People should not be issued drivers' licenses until the age of twenty-one.
2. *Audience:* your classmates. *Opinion:* All drivers should be required to take a road test every ten years in order to renew their licenses.
3. *Audience:* your classmates. *Opinion:* Children six years of age should not be allowed to drive.
4. *Audience:* parent. *Opinion:* All first-time drivers should be issued temporary learners' permits that could be revoked on the spot for any major infraction of traffic laws.
5. *Audience:* parents and students. *Opinion:* Anyone involved in an accident while driving under the influence of alcohol or drugs should have his or her driver's license revoked permanently.

Answers: **1.** c; **2.** a; **3.** b; **4.** a; **5.** a

PREWRITING: SUPPORT

EVIDENCE: FACTS AND OPINIONS

If you want to persuade your audience to believe a certain opinion or to act in a certain way, you must present reliable evidence that supports your position. Such evidence must be precise, accurate, and relevant to the issue.

In persuasive writing **evidence** refers to the reasons that directly support your opinion. Usually the most effective reasons are facts.

A **fact** is something that is known to be true.

The following statements are examples of facts:

> An eight-cylinder car burns gas less efficiently than a four-cylinder car.
> Sacramento is the capital of California.

Facts are reliable evidence in support of a position because they cannot be argued; they can only be verified. They can be checked or verified either through direct personal experience or through a reliable source, such as an encyclopedia or an objective primary source.

An **opinion** is a personal judgment based on what one person believes or feels to be true.

People may disagree with an opinion, but they cannot do so with a fact once the fact has been verified. Compare the preceding facts with the following opinions:

> Eight-cylinder cars are more enjoyable to drive than are four-cylinder cars.
> Sacramento is a beautiful city.

Opinions are often expressed in words that have built-in judgments about the value or the worth of something. For example, in the preceding two opinions, the words *more enjoyable* and *beautiful* convey a personal judgment. Words like *bureaucrat, despicable,* and *failure* fall into the category of **loaded words,** words that have a strong emotional bias. Loaded words do *not* convert an opinion into reliable evidence; they simply tack emotion onto the opinion.

SOUND OPINIONS AND AUTHORITATIVE OPINIONS

Certain kinds of opinions, however, can be used as evidence to support an argument. You may use sound opinions and authoritative opinions to support a persuasive argument.

A **sound opinion** is one that is based on a sufficient number of precise and accurate facts. An **authoritative opinion** is one that comes from a reliable source, such as an eyewitness or a recognized expert.

When you quote a recognized authority's opinion, you should make sure that the person's opinion relates to his or her field of expertise. For example, a computer genius may be an expert in the field of computers, but that person's opinion on an international law issue may be no more informed than your own.

EVALUATING FACTS AND OPINIONS AS EVIDENCE

When gathering evidence for persuasion, you must make judgments about the reliability of your evidence. For example, imagine that you are supporting the following statement or proposition:

> Tanya is a better figure skater than Will.

Which of these statements present the strongest support?

1. Tanya is more graceful on the ice than is Will.
2. Tanya practices more often than Will.
3. The hockey coach stated that Tanya is a better figure skater than Will.
4. Tanya consistently receives higher scores in figure-skating competition than Will.
5. A group of figure-skating coaches recently voted Tanya the best figure skater in the state.

The first statement is an opinion. The second statement is factual but not relevant to the issue of which skater is the better figure skater. The third statement is an opinion by an authority, but the authority is an expert on hockey, *not* on figure skating. The fourth statement is a statement of fact. The fifth statement is an authoritative opinion—a statement by experts in the field. The fourth and fifth statements thus present the strongest support for the opinion.

When you gather and present evidence for persuasive writing, remember that your audience will most likely be persuaded by facts. Although sound opinions and authoritative opinions are acceptable evidence, they must also be judged according to the reliability and credibility of the source.

Objective

EXERCISE 4. Identifying Facts and Opinions. For each of the following items, write whether it is a fact, unsound opinion, sound opinion, a reliable authoritative opinion, or an unreliable authoritative opinion. Tell why each opinion is sound or unsound, reliable or unreliable.

1. Ernest Hemingway, an American novelist, wrote *The Sun Also Rises.*
2. *The Sun Also Rises* must be a very dull book; my best friend did not at all enjoy reading it.
3. My English teacher, who has never been fishing, stated that Hemingway was one of the most skillful fishermen of the twentieth century.
4. Based on the four Hemingway novels I have read, it is evident that he possessed a sharp, precise, and deceptively simple writing style.
5. According to his biographer and several literary historians, both Gertrude Stein and Ezra Pound had an important influence on Hemingway.

PREWRITING: INDUCTIVE AND DEDUCTIVE REASONING

In persuasive writing you present evidence to support an opinion that you want your audience to accept. Such writing requires clear and organized thinking.

Logic is the process of clear and organized thinking that leads to a reasonable conclusion.

This section will focus on two powerful tools for logical thinking: inductive reasoning and deductive reasoning.

INDUCTIVE REASONING

When you see a number of giraffes, each having a very long neck, and you conclude that all giraffes have long necks, in a very elementary way you have used the process of inductive reasoning to reach a conclusion.

In **inductive reasoning,** you move from specific facts to a general conclusion, or **generalization,** based on those facts.

When you are developing an argument by means of inductive reasoning, you want your audience to accept your conclusion as reasonable and true. To ensure the acceptance of a conclusion, you should present good evidence. The better the evidence, the higher the probability that the conclusion is reasonable. Here are some of the qualities that good evidence must possess.

1. Evidence must be **relevant** to the conclusion. For example, if you read the final draft of a piece of writing and note that it is scratchy with numerous crossouts, inkblots, and indecipherable words, you might reasonably conclude that the writer needs some advice on how to prepare a final manuscript. You have no grounds for concluding, however, that the writer is not a very imaginative thinker. The evidence is not relevant to such a conclusion.
2. Evidence must be **sufficient** to warrant the conclusion. For example, if you watch two new situation comedies on television, both of which have poorly developed characters and lack humor, you cannot yet conclude that *all* the new television shows are atrocious. Such a conclusion is *not* warranted by the evidence of *only* two bad shows.
3. The sample on which you base your conclusion should be **representative** of the group as a whole if it is to be offered as valid evidence in support of a conclusion. For example, if you interview several representatives of a local automobile union, all of whom argue that increasing benefits is their union's top priority, you have no grounds for concluding that *all* unions are primarily interested in additional benefits. Your sample (one union) is not representative enough to warrant a conclusion about *all* unions. Interviews with officials in unions other than the automobile union might yield different information and different priorities. For you to make a reasonable generalization

in this case, your sample should include a representative cross section of *various* unions.

Objective

EXERCISE 5. Analyzing Evidence and Conclusions. Determine whether each of the following arguments is reasonable. Ask yourself: Does the conclusion reasonably follow from the evidence? Is the evidence relevant, sufficient, and representative of the whole? Write an explanation for each of your decisions, citing specifics from the argument.

1. I bought a new foreign-made car last month. The steering column shakes. The engine will not start when the temperature rises above 60 degrees or falls below 50 degrees. When the engine does start, it burns three quarts of oil each day. No foreign manufacturer builds sturdy cars.
2. Advertising spots on television during the Super Bowl cost $1 million per minute. The cost of advertising today is outrageously high, and few companies can afford to advertise.
3. I know at least ten professional writers who are successful and use word processors. Word processors are perhaps the most important invention of the twentieth century.
4. Our class is composed of twenty boys and twenty girls. Of those twenty girls, fifteen voted in favor of creating a coed basketball team. Obviously, a majority of the girls in our school overwhelmingly want to establish a coed basketball team.

Sample Answer for 1: One defective car does not justify the conclusion that all foreign-made cars are poorly built.

LIMITING GENERALIZATIONS

The purpose of making generalizations about things we observe is to enable us to make judgments and predictions about things we have not observed. In order to make truthful, reasonable, and acceptable predictions, our generalizations must be based on evidence that is relevant, sufficient, and representative of the whole. Using irrelevant, insufficient evidence or unrepresentative samples leads to overgeneralizations, or hasty conclusions.

An **overgeneralization,** or **hasty conclusion,** is a statement that refers too broadly to people, places, animals, objects, or events.

You can test a conclusion or a generalization to find out if it is an overgeneralization or hasty conclusion. Asking questions like the following will help you determine whether or not a conclusion is reasonable:

Questions to Test Generalizations or Conclusions

1. Are the examples from which the conclusion is drawn really representative of the whole group?

2. Are there any important exceptions to the conclusions?
3. Would different or additional evidence strengthen the conclusion?
4. Is the conclusion too broad for the evidence given?

If you answer *yes* to each of these questions when testing a conclusion, then that conclusion is probably an overgeneralization and needs to be limited. Compare the following two statements:

OVERGENERALIZATION: The training manuals that accompany *all* computers are *always* poorly written.

LIMITED GENERALIZATION: The training manuals that accompany *some* computers are *frequently* poorly written.

The overgeneralized statement contains two absolute words: *all* and *always.* Note how the limited generalization tones down the sweeping, absolute nature of the original statement. This second statement contains **limiting,** or **qualifying, words,** which help provide for exceptions. Such words are an important part of persuasive writing. Following is a list of the most common limiting words and expressions:

almost never	in most cases	occasionally
a minority of	less than half	often
as a rule	many	rarely
certain	more than half	seldom
few	most	several
frequently	mostly	some
half	nearly all	sometimes
hardly ever	nearly always	the majority of
in general	not all	usually

Objective

EXERCISE 6. Limiting Opinions. Rewrite each of the following opinions so that they may be used as reasonable conclusions in persuasive writing. Use limiting words wherever necessary.

1. All major corporations pay little or no taxes.
2. Excessive government control and regulation always leads to a loss of all personal freedoms.
3. Good athletes are never good students.
4. Learning how to manage people is extremely difficult and can never be learned from a textbook.
5. All television shows are always dull and unimaginative.

Sample Answer for 1: Some major corporations often pay little or no taxes.

DEDUCTIVE REASONING

Deductive reasoning is sometines looked upon as the opposite of inductive reasoning. In inductive reasoning you work from the evidence to a generalization or conclusion. In deductive reasoning, however, you work from a generalization to reach a further conclusion that follows logically from that generalizaton.

In **deductive reasoning,** you start with a generalization, state a related fact or truth, and then arrive at a further conclusion about that truth.

A deductive argument often has three basic parts or statements. Together these statements form what is called a syllogism.

A formal statement of a deductive argument is called a **syllogism.**

Here is an example of a syllogism:

All the planets in our solar system rotate around the sun.
Pluto is a planet in our solar system.
Therefore, Pluto rotates around the sun.

Note that if the first two statements in a syllogism are true, then the conclusion drawn from them is called *valid.* For example, both statements in the model syllogism are true, so the conclusion (*Pluto rotates around the sun*) is valid.

Objective

EXERCISE 7. Completing Syllogisms. State in writing a conclusion that can be drawn from each of the following pairs of statements. Then indicate why your conclusion is valid.

1. All computers contain microchips. The Walnut P.C. is a computer.
2. All dictionaries contain definitions. This book is a dictionary.
3. All athletes must train hard. Marie Collins is an athlete.
4. All songs have rhythm. "All Night Long" is a song.

Answer for 1: Therefore, the Walnut P.C. contains a microchip.

USING DEDUCTIVE REASONING TO PERSUADE AN AUDIENCE

When you are trying to persuade an audience, you can use deductive reasoning to present your argument. Following is a brief argument in the form of a syllogism:

All good secretaries should receive promotions and pay raises.
Ms. Kearns is a good secretary.
Ms. Kearns should receive a promotion and a pay raise.

If you wanted to persuade your audience to accept the conclusion that "Ms. Kearns should receive a promotion and a pay raise," there are several things that you would have to show. First, you would need to clearly define what you mean by "good secretary," and you would have to persuade your audience to accept your definition of the qualities of a good secretary. You would also have to demonstrate that a promotion and a pay raise are justified ways of rewarding a good secretary's efforts. Most importantly, you would have to demonstrate that Ms. Kearns is indeed "a good secretary." That can only be accomplished by providing reliable evidence. Once you have accomplished all that, your audience will probably agree with your final conclusion that Ms. Kearns deserves a promotion and a pay raise.

Objective

EXERCISE 8. Turning a Syllogism into an Argument. Choose one of the three syllogisms that follow. Write an explanation of how you would use that syllogism as the basis for a deductive argument. Tell exactly what you would need to show in order to convince your audience. Also state the kind of audience that would be likely to be receptive to your argument.

1. All state colleges should be tuition-free. College X is a state college. College X should not charge tuition.
2. All good students should have to attend school only four days a week. I am a good student. I should have to attend school only four days a week.
3. All lazy students should receive extra homework. The students in our class are lazy. Our class should receive extra homework.

WRITING AN ARGUMENT

An **argument** is an ordered presentation of support for a position that you want others to accept.

An argument consists of your opening statement of position, any background information a reader may need in order to follow your argument, the evidence you will use to support your position statement, and a concluding statement. In addition, some arguments contain a rebuttal section in which opposing arguments are answered. The rebuttal section usually comes just before the concluding statement.

STATEMENT OF POSITION AND BACKGROUND INFORMATION

When you begin to write your argument, clearly and unemotionally indicate whether you are for or against what is being discussed. Your statement of position, or proposition, should be limited to a single opinion. In addition, a position statement should *not* contain any words that have built-in judgments, such as *shoddy* or *unfair.*

After making your position statement, give any background information a reader might need in order to follow your argument. For example, you may have to provide a source, name, or date, define a particular term, or give an example to ensure that a reader understands exactly what you mean.

ORGANIZATION OF SUPPORT

In the support section of your argument, you present evidence in support of your position statement. Present such evidence in a logical, clear order. For example, if you have four or five facts or authoritative opinions, present them one at a time, in order of importance. Always clearly inform your readers when you are stating a fact and when you are giving an authoritative opinion.

As you write, guide your readers from sentence to sentence by using the methods of achieving coherence described in Chapter 3: repeated words, pronoun references, and transitions. Transitions are particularly important in writing persuasively. They will help guide your reader through your argument to an understanding of your position. The following transitions are especially effective for persuasive writing:

To Present Evidence
first, second, third
most importantly
for example
for instance
the facts show that
according to

To State Your Opinion
in my opinion
I believe that
from my point of view
in my experience

To Deal with Conflicting Opinions
although
even though
conversely
in opposition to
in contrast to
still

Remember that the strongest support in an argument is reliable evidence; however, you may also convey personal comments to your readers. After all, you do want your readers to know that you feel strongly about your topic and that you are committed to a particular position. State any personal comments with a strong conviction, but avoid emotional outbursts.

ANSWERING OPPOSING ARGUMENTS

You may want to include a rebuttal section in your argument. In a rebuttal section you recognize and state an opposing view, and then you answer the opposing argument with your own counterpoints. A rebuttal has two important advantages: By recognizing the opposition's viewpoint, you demonstrate a sense of fairness to your audience and your confidence in your own views. Your fairness and confidence should make the audience more receptive to your argument. Note that although a rebuttal can be an effective part of an argument, not all arguments contain rebuttal sections.

CONCLUDING STATEMENT

In your concluding statement, you restate your opening position, summarize your evidence, and move your readers to action by urging them to think or act as you are recommending. The concluding statement can vary in length, depending on the length of your argument: A one-paragraph argument may include a one-sentence concluding statement; a multiple-paragraph argument may use an entire paragraph as a concluding statement.

The following annotated model demonstrates how each part of an argument works in a multiple-paragraph essay:

Proposition

The proposal that our city host the next Olympic Games should be defeated. The proposal itself is fiscally unwise, and the suggested long-term benefits to the city are not likely to materialize.

Background

This same proposal, in an only slightly different form, was defeated in a citywide vote last year by a two-to-one margin.

Statement of position

Proponents of the revised proposal, however, pay only minimal attention to the original objections to the plan, objections that can legitimately be raised anew.

First supporting argument

The estimated cost of hosting the Olympics is $350 million, a sum that is more than the city can afford and much less than the project will actually cost. This money is to be spent primarily on the construction of new sports facilities for track and field, swimming, soccer, and equestrian events. Voters must keep in mind, however, that the city is $50 million in debt this year and cannot possibly raise the taxes of an already overtaxed population. Furthermore, the estimated cost is not realistic. The experience of other cities that have hosted the Olympics indicates that $700 million would be a more accurate and realistic estimate of the cost of building these new sports facilities. As Regina Reese, president of the state's lagest construction company, recently indicated, "Reese Construction would not submit a bid of less than $700 million to complete all the proposed sites within the deadlines."

Second supporting argument

The second major objection to the proposal is that assuming such an enormous debt—$700 million minimally—could lead to economic disaster for the city. The mayor's economic adviser recently stated, "Such a debt would bankrupt the city and stifle any growth."

Answering opponents' arguments

Proponents of the plan argue that the facilities that the city builds for the Olympics will enhance the quality of life in our city. The potential uses for some of the facilities, however, are at best limited once the Olympics are over. For instance, the huge stadiums that would be constructed do not fit the dimensions for professional baseball and football; they would have to be rebuilt—at additional cost—to attract professional teams.

Conclusion

In conclusion, the immediate costs of the proposed Olympics construction as well as the negative long-term effects should be carefully weighed when our citizens go to the polls next month. I urge all voters to defeat this ill-considered proposal.

Objective

EXERCISE 9. Writing an Argument. Write a four- to six-paragraph argument about one of the following topics, or choose a topic of your own. State your position clearly; include any necessary background information. Develop your support with either reasons or facts. If possible, indicate the opposing arguments and answer them. Follow the stages of the writing process.

1. for or against increasing funding for the space program
2. for or against including computer instruction in the curriculum
3. for or against requiring all students to participate in programs of organized sports

REVISING, EDITING, AND PUBLISHING: AVOIDING FAULTY METHODS OF PERSUASION

Writing persuasion calls for sound reasoning. When you revise a written argument, be alert for any fallacies that may have found their way into your argument.

Fallacies are errors in reasoning.

For example, the hasty generalizations that you studied earlier in this chapter were fallacies. Following are descriptions of other kinds of fallacies that you should be aware of when you write and revise an argument or when you read and evaluate someone else's argument.

AVOIDING STEREOTYPES

A **stereotype** is an overgeneralization about someone or something that does not take exceptions into account. It usually refers to a belief held by many people who have not thoroughly examined the facts.

A stereotype is much like a hasty generalization and is the result of faulty thinking. For example, the generalization *College football players are not intelligent* is a stereotype that is absolutely false because it does not take into account all of the college football players who are top scholars, who graduate, and who are intelligent enough to *both* play football and perform well in the classroom. A more accurate and limited opinion might be: *Some college football players are intelligent and some are not intelligent.*

Objective

EXERCISE 10. Avoiding Stereotypes. Find the stereotypes in the following statements. Then explain in a few sentences why each is a stereotype. After your explanation, rewrite each of the stereotypes by using limited words to account for exceptions.

1. Writers are highly intelligent and sensitive people.
2. Journalists are extremely aggressive interviewers.
3. Large corporations are monolithic bureaucracies.
4. Large cities are dirty, unreliable, and dangerous.
5. All managers in businesses are strong-willed and tempermental.

Suggested Answer for 1: While it might be widely believed that writers are highly intelligent and sensitive, clearly *all* writers are not.

BANDWAGON

A **bandwagon** fallacy is an argument that attempts to persuade someone to do something because "everyone else is doing it."

The expression *to jump on the bandwagon* means "to join an enthusiastic crowd" in action or thought. The bandwagon argument states that something is correct or true because "everyone" does it or believes it. Bandwagon arguments are not logical; it is not necessarily true that one must like or believe something simply because of what others say, think, or believe. Often based on insecurity, bandwagon persuasion appeals to those who are unable or unwilling to think independently. Here is an example of the bandwagon fallacy:

> Buy a turbocharged Panther for your next car; thousands already have, and they love their Panthers.

Objective

EXERCISE 11. Identifying Bandwagon Fallacies. Identify the bandwagon fallacy in the following statements. Then write an explanation telling why the argument is not logical.

1. Millions of people use *Smile* toothpaste. You should use it, too.
2. Stop using sugar. Thousands of people have decided to kick the habit.
3. Hundreds of successful writers use word processors. Using one will make you a better writer, too.
4. *Spacedreams* is an absolutely fantastic movie; more than a million people saw it during the first week of its release.

Suggested Answer for 1: Millions of people could very well be wrong.

NAME-CALLING

Name-calling is a method of attacking the character of a person rather than addressing the person's views, position, and argument.

Name-calling is a false method of argument because an attack on a person's character is irrelevant to issues being argued. For example, the character of a person supporting the concept of government funding of medical care is unimportant; what matters are the arguments and evidence that person offers in support of such funding. Avoid name-calling in your own persuasive writing, and be alert for it in the arguments of others. A distractive method of argument, name-calling indicates a failure or an inability to focus on the real issues.

TESTIMONIAL

The **testimonial** is an attempt at persuasion based on the advice or testimony of a famous person.

This method of persuasion is both faulty and deceptive. It implies that a famous person is qualified to give good advice about any subject. In the following example, a famous football player gives this testimonial:

> "For years I have been on the receiving end of thousands of football passes. So I know how important it is to receive something quickly and on time. That's why I use Bullet Express to send all my mail and packages."

The football player may be an expert pass receiver, but that does not mean he is qualified to judge fast delivery services.

When confronted with a testimonial, apply your critical thinking. Ask yourself, *What is the logical connection between the person's knowledge and what he or she is trying to persuade me to do?*

Objective

EXERCISE 12. Identifying Name-Calling and Testimonials. Read each argument. Determine whether it is reasonable or contains a fallacy. If it contains a fallacy, write whether that fallacy is either name-calling or a testimonial. Then explain why the argument is not reasonable or logical.

1. In a television commercial, a famous writer states: "I have written over fifty novels, so I know quality when I see it. That's why I bought a Potato Computer, and you should buy one, too!"
2. You should vote for Ms. McCrimmon for the school board because she has had five years of experience working in the Education Department at City Hall. She has also taught for fifteen years in our school system. She has more experience with our educational system than any of the other candidates. She will be able to put that experience to good use while serving on the school board.
3. Senator X is an imbecile, incapable of sustaining a thought for more than ten seconds. There is no reason why we should consider his recommendations for trimming the state budget.

Sample Answer for 1: There is no connection between writing novels and knowing about quality in computers.

RED HERRING

When someone has a weak argument—or no argument—that person may attempt to pose a red herring to distract you.

A **red herring** is a second issue thrown in to distract attention from the first issue.

The term **red herring** comes from the practice of dragging a herring, strong-smelling fish, across a trail to make hunting dogs lose track of the original trail and follow the herring's scent. Here is an example of a red herring in an argument:

> The school budget does seem to be substantially larger this year than last year, and there are a number of excellent reasons for its increase. However, you should realize that some expenses are the same as or lower than last year. In addition, the preparation of this budget was a difficult process; much information was unavailable.

The person making this argument does everything *but* address the main issue of why the budget is larger this year. In fact the speaker throws in *two* red herrings to distract attention from the central issue. He introduces the irrelevant fact that some expenses are the same or lower, and he explains the difficulty in preparing the budget.

People introduce side issues when they feel that they cannot persuasively argue the central issue, or when they have no genuine, reliable evidence. You should not be taken in by red herrings, nor should you use them in your persuasive writing.

EITHER-OR THINKING

The **either-or** fallacy is an oversimplification that takes only two choices into account.

This kind of faulty reasoning limits a situation to a choice of one extreme or another without allowing for exceptions or possibilities in between the two extremes. Here is an example:

> Kim did not sign the petition to stop acid rain pollution. Since she did not sign the petition, she must be in favor of acid rain pollution.

The writer here is making the following illogical assumption: because Kim did not sign the petition, she favors acid rain pollution. This false reasoning stems from the writer's inability to see possibilities other than the *for* or *against* choices. In fact Kim may not have wanted to sign the petition for any number of personal reasons: Kim may have forgotten; she may not want to sign *any* petitions; she may not have had the time; she may want to sign a stronger statement or one not quite as forceful.

When you test a statement for an *either-or* fallacy, make sure that you *consider other alternatives.* Ask yourself, "Are there other answers or possibilities than the two that are being proposed?"

FAULTY CAUSE-AND-EFFECT THINKING

Faulty cause-and-effect thinking refers to establishing a false connection between a cause and an effect.

A faulty cause-and-effect argument is weak because the relationship between an effect and the proposed cause is nonexistent, unreasonable, or not clearly established, as in this example:

> The President should be re-elected to a second term. During his first term, the inflation rate fell almost 8 percent.

The writer of this argument is strongly implying that the inflation rate dropped eight percent *because* of the President's first-term actions. The writer has not specifically related which of the President's actions led to a lower inflation rate. The cause-effect relationship is not clearly established. In fact, the inflation rate could have fallen for any number of *other* economic reasons or actions that were totally unrelated to the President's action, such as consumers spending less and saving more, less consumer credit, no demands from unions for higher wages, or lower interest rates.

Review your writing for faulty cause-and-effect statements. Make sure that there is a truthful, reasonable, and clearly established relationship between your effect and its stated cause.

Objective

EXERCISE 13. Avoiding Red Herrings, Either-Or Thinking, and Faulty Cause-and-Effect. Identify the error in critical thinking in each of the following statements. Then explain in writing why the statement is a fallacy.

1. I dozed off while watching that concert on television. It must have been a very dull concert.
2. Before we decide whether to cut the funding for school athletics, let's first talk about how poorly our teams performed throughout the year and how a new coaching staff would raise the quality of performance.
3. Our government should supply arms and aid to all countries requesting them. If we do not, those governments will surely turn into communist states.
4. The ocean's fish population has significantly decreased in recent years. At the same time, the dumping of raw sewage into the ocean has increased drastically.

Sample Answer for 1: The possibility that the concert might have been dull is not proven by the viewer's dozing off.

CHECKLIST FOR REVISING PERSUASIVE WRITING

1. What is my purpose? What do I want the reader to do?
2. Is my position statement an overgeneralization?
3. What qualities in my audience do I want to keep in mind as I write? What kinds of support are most likely to persuade them?
4. Which pieces of evidence are facts, which are sound opinions, and which are authoritative statements? Which unsound opinions, if any, need to be eliminated?
5. What revisions are necessary to make sure that my opening statement is clear, specific, and directed toward my purpose?
6. Should I add any additional evidence to clarify my reasoning? Have I used transitions to help readers follow my reasoning?
7. How clearly is my conclusion stated? Have I restated my position and urged my readers to adopt that position?
8. Have I used any faulty methods of persuasion—bandwagon, testimonial, name-calling, red herring, stereotyping, either-or thinking, or faulty cause-and-effect thinking? What adjustments do I need to make to eliminate those faulty methods?

WRITER'S CHOICE #1

ASSIGNMENT: To write a persuasive essay for or against the following proposition:
PROPOSED: that the age for obtaining a driver's license be raised to twenty-one

LENGTH: Four to five paragraphs

AUDIENCE: Your choice, but develop an audience profile.

PURPOSE: To persuade

PREWRITING: Brainstorm to identify key points to support your position.

WRITING: Write your position statement in the first paragraph. Include any background information that a reader might need in order to follow your argument. In the next paragraph or two, give reliable evidence to support your position. If you wish, state an opposing view and then answer it. Your final paragraph should urge your readers to adopt your position.

REVISING: Apply all the questions in the checklist on page 225.

WRITER'S CHOICE #2

ASSIGNMENT: To develop a statement promoting something that you like or respect (a product, an event, a group, a person in a political campaign)

LENGTH: Four to five paragraphs

AUDIENCE: Someone who is unfamiliar with your subject.

PREWRITING: Use brainstorming or charting to generate a list of your subject's admirable qualities, and determine which qualities would appeal to your audience.

WRITING: Follow the procedures for organizing and presenting a convincing argument. Include a position statement and a main section that contains reliable evidence and that deductively or inductively supports your position statement. Avoid introducing fallacies in reasoning.

REVISING: Apply all the questions in the checklist on page 225.

WRITER'S CHOICE #3

ASSIGNMENT: To write a persuasive argument on a topic of your own choice

OPTIONS:
- You may find a writing idea in the Writer's Sourcebook, pages 354–355.

THE WRITER

Liza Steele is involved in such active pursuits as running, riding, and biking. She plans to study psychology in college. As a student at Midlothian High School in Midlothian, Virginia, Liza wrote the following persuasive piece and commentary.

THE FINISHED PRODUCT

Yesterday I looked inside the dusty cabinets and drawers about my house and found those gifts I received last Christmas from panicked last-minute shoppers. After cleaning away several cobwebs and clearing the shelves of old, unwanted items, I found my electric knife, my electric dust collector, and my electric toothbrush. Frankly, I have found these items to be three of the world's most useless gadgets.

In the last six months I have not once felt grateful for that supposedly indispensable electric knife. I think I used it last Christmas as friends and relatives watched the carving of the turkey, but I don't feel that using it once a year really justifies it. Besides, if a piece of meat needs to be cut with an electric utensil of any kind, I feel uncomfortable about eating it!

After excavating a bit further, I retrieved that wonderful cordless electric dust collector which I also received last Christmas. It sounds like a handy-dandy little gadget that makes cleaning up a simple, effortless task; however, it is quite the contrary. The charge on the battery is such that it runs out long before the completion of the task. In addition, it can hardly be called a vacuum cleaner because of its lack of any powerful suction. Admittedly, it is small and easy to use, but how many people have three days to vacuum out the car?

And as for that electric toothbrush... well, I think you get the picture.

Don't get caught in that last-minute shoppers' panic this year. Spend some time thinking about the gifts you are going to buy, and hope that your friends and relatives do the same! Finally, remember to be nice instead of naughty, or Santa Claus will bring you lots of nuts, bolts, and electric toothbrushes!

THE WRITER AT WORK

I found the introduction of this composition to be the hardest part to write because many of the introductions I tried did not give the effect that I had in mind. I found the conclusion to be fairly easy because I knew exactly how I wanted to tie up the paper before I actually got to the end.

In writing a paper I usually try to get my meaning down on paper and later go back to substitute better words and phrases. I find it rather difficult to get the right words down on paper on the first try. I usually reconsider as I write and make notes to myself as to what I will change. Personally, I prefer to write this way because I end up with several ways to say one thing rather than just one way.

When I finish a paper, I usually have numerous drafts to look at and compare, which I think is helpful. My first draft is usually very different from my final paper because I do so much revising and rewording. Sometimes I even feel the need to change my subject matter a bit to achieve my intended purpose or effect.

For this paper, I took my subject matter and tried to think of a catchy way to lead into what I planned to say about it. I did use a topic sentence because I feel it prepares the reader for the paper, and it gives an idea of what to expect. As for organizing, I usually keep in mind the three parts of a paper—the introduction, the body, and the conclusion. I feel that all three parts of this paper work together. The paper is fairly short and to the point, which I feel helps to hold it together also. Long, wordy papers often lose the reader's interest.

The purpose of the paper is to show the uselessness of certain household appliances which many people give as gifts. I tried to make the paper a bit humorous as well. I feel that any audience can appreciate a paper like that.

YOUR TURN **Writing Persuasively**

Write a persuasive paragraph on any subject you choose. You may want to do what Liza did and use a humorous approach to your subject. Write out a statement of your purpose and audience. State your opinion clearly, and present your evidence in a logical fashion. End with a strong concluding sentence, restating your main idea and, if you wish, moving the reader to action.

CHAPTER 11 CRITICAL THINKING AND PERSUASIVE WRITING

Selecting Suitable Topics (pages 208–210)

1. Indicate which of the following topics is a suitable topic for persuasive writing.
   (a) Smoking can be hazardous to your health.
   (b) Nonsmokers can be affected by smoke from nearby smokers.
   (c) Smoking should be prohibited on all airplane flights.

Identifying Facts and Opinions (pages 210–212) Indicate whether each of the following items is **(a)** a fact, **(b)** an unsound opinion, **(c)** a sound opinion, **(d)** a reliable authoritative opinion, or **(e)** an unreliable authoritative opinion.

2. According to a poll of sportswriters, the Tigers are the best team in professional baseball.
3. According to the record book, the Tigers had the best win/loss record in baseball last year.
4. The Tigers are a fantastic team because they are my favorite team in the league.
5. The Tigers, according to a poll of United States Senators, are the best team in professional baseball.

Faulty Methods of Persuasion (pages 220–225) Indicate whether each of the following statements demonstrates **(a)** a stereotype, **(b)** testimonial persuasion, **(c)** a red herring, **(d)** either-or thinking, or **(e)** faulty cause-and-effect thinking.

6. I failed to make the varsity basketball team because the coach dislikes me.
7. More than eighty percent of the professional basketball players wear and recommend ZOOM sneakers.
8. Ocean pollution is certainly a major problem that requires our attention. However, life is filled with complications and problems, all of which deserve our attention. For example, the Federal deficit is a major economic problem.
9. All government agencies are nothing but a huge, ineffective bureaucratic maze.
10. Unless you attend a prestigious college, you will not become successful in life.

Answers: **1.** c; **2.** d; **3.** a; **4.** b; **5.** e; **6.** e; **7.** b; **8.** c; **9.** a; **10.** d

Writing for Review Write a persuasive argument of at least three paragraphs on a topic of your own choice. Include a position statement, a main section that deductively or inductively supports your position with reliable evidence, and a concluding statement. If you wish, also include a rebuttal section in your argument. Then revise and edit your composition. Remember to proofread your final draft.

UNIT IV
The Essay and The Research Paper

In this unit you will apply what you have learned about the writing process, word choice and sentence structure, and the four modes of writing to the development of two longer pieces of writing: the essay and the research paper. Essays and research papers, like other written forms, are developed through prewriting, writing, and revising. They incorporate descriptive, narrative, expository, and persuasive elements, and rely on clarity, grace, and precision of expression for their effectiveness.

The essay and the research paper are similar in structure. Each contains a series of paragraphs that develops a single, focused idea or thesis. Each also begins with an introduction and ends with a conclusion.

These two types of writing differ, however, in several important ways. While a research paper is based on information from written sources or from interviews with experts on the topic, an essay is based on personal experiences, knowledge, and opinion. Thus, an essay is not nearly as formal as a research paper. As a matter of fact, essays have been written on almost every imaginable topic, from serious topics related to politics, science, religion, and culture, to less serious, even frivolous, topics such as sports, exercise, crabgrass, and the art of roasting a pig.

A research paper, on the other hand, draws its special usefulness from the fact that by doing research, the writer must look beyond personal experience to investigate what the ideas of other writers can contribute to the writer's understanding and analysis of a topic. Experts in all fields of study build on the data and findings of the thinkers, researchers, and experimenters who have preceded them. By writing a well-focused, well-executed research paper, you have the opportunity to become an expert about your topic. You will also have the opportunity to master those basic research skills that will be of much use to you at work and in school.

This unit will take you through the process of writing a formal essay and a research paper. Remember that all longer pieces of writing are but many shorter, easily written parts assembled into a unified and coherent whole by the insight and planning of a writer who values what he or she has to say.

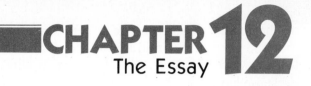

CHAPTER 12
The Essay

Do not lose your personality and your voice in the monotone of official prose. You should work like a scholar and a scientist, but you should write like a writer, one who cares about the economy and beauty of language.

—Sheridan Baker

Writing that expresses the writer's attitude toward a particular topic is called an essay.

An **essay** is a short composition that concentrates on one particular topic of strong interest to the writer.

The term *essay* can refer to a variety of writing forms. Editorials, many magazine articles, movie reviews, and biographies can be considered essays because each reveals what the writer thinks. The writer's views can be expressed with many degrees of formality. Depending on the tone and structure of the essay, the essay is either an informal essay or a formal essay.

An informal essay aims to entertain or please an audience while exploring a topic. The tone of an informal essay is generally light; its structure often has the looseness of a narrative. The informal essay allows for flexibility in the presentation of ideas, and its method of development depends more on the content than on any formal pattern of organization. In fact, the main point of an informal essay may be implied rather than directly stated. Informal essays often make use of descriptive and narrative elements to present the writer's viewpoint. The writer may relate personal anecdotes to develop the topic and enliven the narrative with entertaining descriptions of events or situations. Because the informal essay often makes personal references, it is sometimes called a **personal essay.** Here is an example of an introductory paragraph for an informal essay:

Some people are slow learners, and I suppose I fall into that category when it comes to babysitting. It is not that I need special training in the care and supervision of young children, but rather that I need practice in saying no to the Smiths the next time they ask me to sit for their darling little Jason. Few experiences in life can compare with an evening alone with three-year-old Jason.

The **formal essay**, on the other hand, is carefully structured so that the beginning, middle, and end are clearly defined and carefully developed. The ideas and arguments in a formal essay are presented in a logical order that is clearly apparent to the reader. Although the tone of a formal essay is most often serious, the writer's personal commitment to the topic is just as strong as in an informal essay. Read the following introductory paragraph for a formal essay about the same topic as the preceding informal essay:

> Successful babysitting requires sound judgment not only on the job but also in accepting jobs. Both the sitter and the parents should recognize that babysitting requires both the ability to care for a child and the desire to care for that particular child. A competent sitter has the good judgment to refuse to sit for a child who is uncontrollable and undisciplined.

In this chapter, within the context of the writing process, you will practice the various elements of the formal essay:

- prewriting: generating, exploring, and focusing ideas
- prewriting: organizing an essay
- writing a first draft
- revising, editing, and publishing the essay

PREWRITING: GENERATING, EXPLORING, AND FOCUSING IDEAS

If you are assigned an essay topic, you need to make the topic your own by finding some particular aspect of it that you find interesting. If you have to begin at the very beginning and generate a general topic of your own to write about, you must begin to focus and explore your topic. In either case, the prewriting skills that you practiced in Chapter 2 will help you get started. Here in Chapter 12 you will find examples of the prewriting notes produced by the student whose essay "Guiding Your Career Choices" appears at the end of the chapter.

GENERATING IDEAS

An essay is above all a personal statement. If you must generate an essay topic on your own, most experienced writers would suggest that you start with what you know best—yourself. What do you like? What do you dislike? The student who wrote the essay "Guiding Your Career Choices" was told to write an essay but was not assigned a topic. Here is how she began.

Freewriting

Freewriting is writing that is done continuously for a definite, brief period of time. Here is an example:

> *I have to write an essay. What can I write about? Lately I've been thinking about what I'm going to do after high school. We have had many speakers to talk about different careers, colleges, and job opportunities. Sometimes it seems as if everyone expects me to know what I'm going to do with my life. I need time to think about it. Maybe it's not so important to know just now. Maybe the point of all the questions and the speakers is to start me thinking. Well, I have been thinking, but it's not easy to answer the big question, "What are you going to be?"*

This writer has made a strong start: She has an idea for a topic.

Objective

EXERCISE 1. Freewriting for an Essay Topic. Freewrite for five minutes to find a topic for a brief essay. Do not worry if after five minutes you do not have a specific idea you want to write about. Save your notes for use in Exercise 2 and in later exercises.

Guidelines for Evaluation: Students should write continuously for five minutes. They should be evaluated for effort, not for results.

Brainstorming

Brainstorming can help you generate ideas by free association. Here is an example by the student.

- *Some jobs call for years of schooling or training.*
- *Who among family and friends has an interesting job? Aunt Karen always says how much she enjoys work. Maybe I could talk to her.*
- *Maybe I need to think about my goals.*
- *I know I'm good at math. What other talents do I have?*
- *Where can I find out what those people who work for big companies actually do all day?*

Through brainstorming, the student realizes that to answer questions about what she will be, she needs to ask more questions.

Objective

EXERCISE 2. Brainstorming for an Essay Topic. If the freewriting in Exercise 1 produced an idea that you want to develop, now is the time to brainstorm about it. If not, try brainstorming about one of the following suggestions. Save your notes for Exercise 3 and for later exercises.

1. television
2. maturity
3. part-time jobs
4. clothing fads
5. teen-agers and driving
6. table manners

Guidelines for Evaluation: Students should produce a number of details associated with the chosen topic.

Clustering

To explore her idea that choosing a career involves spending time asking questions, the writer used the clustering technique. She put the phrase *career choice* in the center of the paper and then grouped more specific ideas around those central words:

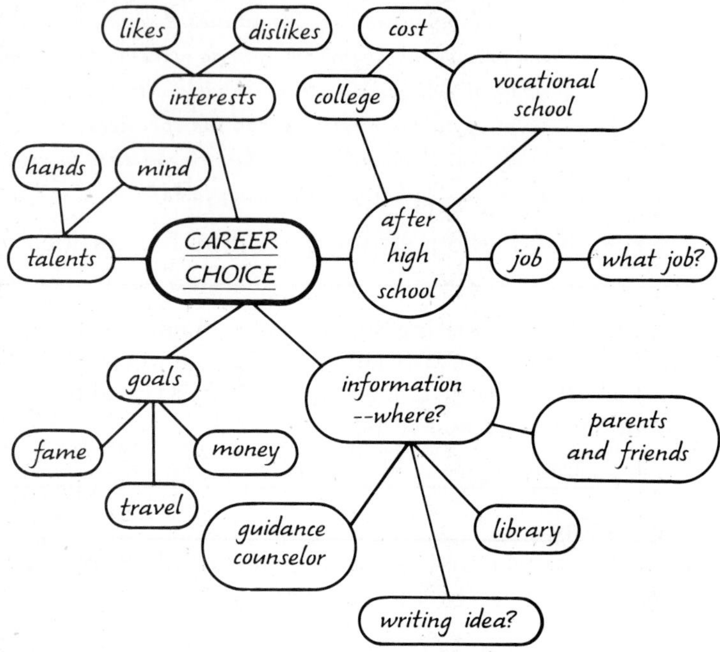

Clustering produced a few more ideas about special skills and training. Notice that she continues to focus on finding sources of information. The major theme of her essay is beginning to take form.

Objective

EXERCISE 3. Clustering to Find an Essay Topic. If a single word or phrase has emerged as a possible topic from Exercises 1 and 2, write the word or phrase in the center of a page. Draw a circle around it. Then write down other words that the central word calls to mind. You will be most successful with this exercise if you work quickly and write down very specific, concrete words associated with the central word. Draw a circle around each new word, and use lines to show how one word leads to another. If you do not have an idea to work with, put one of the following words in the center of a page, and begin clustering.

1. lunch **3.** blue
2. money **4.** age

EXPLORING SUBJECTS

Once you have a writing idea, you have to explore it further to be sure that you have enough material for an essay. As suggested in Chapter 2, you should ask yourself a series of informational, personal, creative, or analytical questions to add depth and detail to your thinking. The writer of the essay about career choice decided to ask a combination of informational and analytical questions.

INFORMATIONAL AND ANALYTICAL QUESTIONS TO EXPLORE A SUBJECT	ANSWERS
1. Who or what is my subject?	*Making choices about possible careers. I will focus on how you go about arriving at answers by asking other questions.*
2. Into what parts can I divide my subject?	*You start with yourself, your likes and dislikes, your dream about your future. You decide what is most important to you in terms of life goals. You list the skills you have.*
3. Can I relate a process to my subject?	*You talk to others. Interview people in different jobs. Read books and pamphlets on different careers. Talk to guidance counselors, parents, teachers, and others who know you. Also contact people who do not know you, but who have jobs that interest you. Find out about the practical details--necessary training, the kind of training (college, vocational school), salary, and so on.*

The questions and answers have helped this student recognize that to pick a career, you need to search within yourself as well as seek information from others.

Objective

EXERCISE 4. Exploring a Topic for an Essay. Prepare a chart with questions that will help you explore the topic that has emerged in Exercises 1–3. Your chart can contain informational, personal, creative, and analytical questions. Base your chart on the sample charts in Chapter 2, pages 17, 18, 19, and 20. If you still have not found an idea for an essay, use one of the following suggestions. Save your notes for use in Exercise 6 and in later exercises.

1. a sports figure you admire
2. what to do and what not to do when dieting
3. the problems facing our senior citizens
4. making the most out of summers

FOCUSING IDEAS

Now that you have explored your topic, you have produced many notes and ideas. You need to be sure, however, that your essay will be clearly *focused.* You will need to review your notes, and eliminate any ideas that would distract your reader from the main point of your essay. For example, the student who developed the essay about "Guiding Your Career Choices" realized that she wanted to explain the process of making a career choice and thus she should not focus on any one career in particular.

Objective

EXERCISE 5. Evaluating an Idea for an Essay. For each pair tell whether you would prefer to write about *a* or *b,* and why. Save your notes for use in Exercise 7.

1. **a.** pollution
   b. air pollution and health problems
2. **a.** this year's Grammy awards
   b. the recording business
3. **a.** outdoor activities
   b. backpacking
4. **a.** the two best films of the year
   b. movies produced this year
5. **a.** the joys of skiing
   b. winter sports

Answers: Students should recognize that the following are more focused: **1.** b; **2.** a; **3.** b; **4.** a; **5.** a

Objective

EXERCISE 6. Focusing an Idea for an Essay. If you have successfully completed Exercises 1–4, state a focused topic that has grown out of your prewriting activities. Save your response for Exercise 7.

Guidelines for Evaluation: Students should be able to start focusing on one topic, eliminating details that relate to other topics.

PURPOSE AND AUDIENCE

After focusing your topic, you need to decide on the *purpose* of your essay. A formal essay is usually written to *explain* something or to *persuade* the reader to adopt the writer's viewpoint. The student who wrote about "Guiding Your Career Choices" chose to explain how to go about answering career questions. Read the statement of purpose that she wrote.

I want to explain the steps involved in making a responsible career choice.

An important consideration in establishing the purpose of your essay is your audience. When writing for a general audience, assume that your readers are generally unfamiliar with your topic. Be sure to include important background information. Develop your topic carefully so that your essay is understandable to those with limited knowledge.

For example, the purpose of the essay "Guiding Your Career Choices" is to explain the steps involved in making these decisions. The writer cannot assume that a general audience will know what sources of information to use in researching careers. The author, therefore, needs to explain how to go about finding and contacting sources of information.

Objective

EXERCISE 7. Selecting a Purpose and an Audience. *If you were able to state a focused topic in Exercise 6,* now is the time to decide your purpose and audience. Decide whether your purpose is to explain or to persuade. Consider your audience. Most essays are written for a general audience. Now, state the purpose and the audience for the limited topic you stated in Exercise 6. *If you did not state a limited topic in Exercise 6,* review your answers to Exercise 5. For one of the topics you chose, write a possible purpose and a possible audience.

Guidelines for Evaluation: The purpose should be to persuade or to explain. The audience should be defined in detail or be noted as a general audience.

PREWRITING: ORGANIZING AN ESSAY

At this point some writers are ready to organize their prewriting notes informally and plunge into writing a first draft. Other writers prefer to prepare a formal outline as a way to structure their thinking.

An **outline** is a writing plan that shows main points, the sequence in which they will be discussed, and their relation to one another.

A **working outline** often provides sufficient organization for writing a first draft. The student who wrote the essay "Guiding Your Career Choices" organized her notes in a working outline, wrote a first draft, reviewed her first draft, and only then developed a formal outline to guide the writing of the final draft. The working outline helped her determine the order in which to present ideas and to distinguish between main ideas and supporting details. In the working outline that follows, note that each main idea was assigned a Roman numeral; each supporting detail was assigned a capital letter.

Working Outline

I. *Focus on self*
   A. *Define interests.*
   B. *Define talents.*
   C. *Think about goals.*
II. *Sources of information near at hand*
   A. *Guidance counselors*
   B. *People in careers*
   C. *Friends and relatives*
III. *Information about specialized careers*
   A. *College catalogs*
   B. *Visits*
   C. *"Career Day"*

Objective

EXERCISE 8. Writing a Working Outline. *If your work in Exercises 1–4 has produced many notes,* you can now organize and structure them into a working outline. First decide what your main headings will be. Then group supporting details under each main heading. Eliminate details that do not fit. *If you still do not have enough notes for an outline,* apply the prewriting techniques of freewriting, brainstorming, clustering, and asking questions to one of the limited topics in Exercise 5 or to another writing idea you may choose. Either way, you should develop a working outline with at least three main ideas. Save this outline; later in this chapter you will write an essay based on it.

WRITING A FIRST DRAFT

Follow your working outline as you write the first draft. Keep in mind that the first draft is not intended to be a finished piece of writing. Its purpose is to allow you to put your ideas onto paper in sentences and paragraphs.

THE THESIS STATEMENT

Just as a topic sentence helps to give direction to a paragraph, a thesis statement gives direction to an essay of several paragraphs. The thesis statement is usually the first or the last sentence in the opening paragraph.

The **thesis statement** performs three important functions: (1) It states the main point of your essay. (2) It indicates your attitude toward the topic. (3) It suggests the organization that the essay will follow.

As you write the thesis statement, review your working outline. Keeping your purpose and your audience in mind, compose a sentence that your reader can use as a guide in order to know what to expect in your essay.

The most effective thesis statement suggests some of the main topics on your outline. Try to make your thesis statement as precise as you can. Compare the two thesis statements that follow. Which statement provides the audience with an overview of the purpose, main points, and organization of the essay?

1. In thinking about careers, there are many different issues that need to be considered before making a decision.
2. Four simple guidelines can help you plan, not panic: Take a close look at your interest and abilities, think about your personal goals for the future, seek the assistance of people in your community, and, finally, explore carefully what opportunities lie beyond the world you know.

The first statement offers only a vague introduction to the topic. It fails to give the audience any sense of the writer's purpose or plan for the essay. The second statement is more precise. The audience knows that the essay will discuss the process of making career choices and will do so in a concrete and practical way aimed at reassuring an audience of those who may be upset or ill at ease with having to make the choice.

Many writers consider their thesis statements as working statements. That is, they often write a preliminary thesis statement that serves as a guide while they are writing the first draft. When they write the formal introduction after they complete the essay, they revise the thesis statement.

Objective

EXERCISE 9. Writing a Thesis Statement. Review your statement of purpose and audience from Exercise 7. Then review your working outline from Exercise 8. Write a thesis statement for your essay. Your sentence should provide your audience with a sense of your purpose, the main ideas of your essay, and how the essay will be organized. Save your thesis statement for Exercise 10.

Guidelines for Evaluation: The three criteria listed in the exercise should be met.

INTRODUCTORY PARAGRAPH

The introductory paragraph should create in the reader a set of expectations that will be fulfilled by the rest of the essay. This paragraph sets up the promise of what the rest of the essay will contain. A variety of openings can accomplish this goal and capture the reader's interest as well.

Consider using one of the following suggested openings when you write your introduction.

Asking a Question

The student writer in this chapter might have begun her first draft with this question: "Why do so many high school students feel a sense of panic when asked 'What are you going to do with your life?'"

Addressing the Reader Directly

The student writer might have begun with these words: "If you are like most people, you probably know little about choosing a career."

Stating an Interesting Fact or Statistic

The student writer could have stated, "The average American worker conducts a job hunt *every* 3.6 years. If you are thinking about what kind of job you want, you have plenty of company."

Telling an Anecdote

The student writer might have begun with an interesting or amusing incident from her life to introduce the topic: "When I was six I was *certain* I would grow up to be an astronaut; now that I'm seventeen I am not at all certain of what I want to be."

Taking a Strong Stand

The student writer could have provoked the reader's interest by making a strong opening statement: "When you consider that more than eleven thousand days of your life will be spent on the job, you would be foolish not to spend some time now planning your career."

Quoting from a Book, Poem, or Song

The student writer could have begun the essay by quoting novelist Joseph Conrad: "I don't like work—no man does—but I like what is in work—the chance to find yourself."

TONE AND DICTION

The **tone** of your essay reflects your attitude toward your topic and your audience. Your tone may be serious or humorous, persuasive or critical, emotional or reflective. Be sure to choose an appropriate tone. For example, you would probably use a serious tone to explain the need to provide adequate day-care facilities for working families but a humorous tone to describe your day as a helper at your sister's day-care center.

Pay attention as well to the level of **diction**, or word choice, that you use. A serious tone requires formal diction, whereas middle diction would be more appropriate for conveying a humorous tone. Remember to maintain a consistent tone and level of diction throughout the whole essay.

Objective

EXERCISE 10. Writing Introductory Paragraphs. Review the thesis statement you wrote in Exercise 9. Then write two different introductory paragraphs for your essay. Indicate in writing the version you prefer, and why. Save the preferred version for Exercise 11.

THE BODY PARAGRAPHS

The body paragraphs of an essay develop, or support, the thesis statement in the introduction. Your outline will be very useful when writing the body paragraphs. Follow the order established by your outline. Generally, each main head in the outline should become a separate paragraph.

As you write your paragraphs, keep in mind the different modes of writing you can use to develop a section of your outline. You may want to use expository writing to explain a process or a narrative style to relate supporting information. At this point, you may want to review Chapters 8–11 to recall these kinds of writing.

COHERENCE IN AN ESSAY

The reader should sense that each paragraph in your essay flows from the preceding paragraph and leads smoothly into the following paragraph. The transitional devices discussed in Chapter 3 and again in Chapters 8–11 will help make your writing coherent by connecting sentences within a paragraph and by providing bridges between paragraphs.

Repeated Words and Synonyms

You can make strong connections between paragraphs by using the same word or a synonym at the end of one paragraph and at the beginning of the next, as in this excerpt from the student essay:

> . . . will help you narrow your career choices.
>
> The third stage of your search for a career involves. . . .

Transitions

Transitional words and phrases help the reader follow your thoughts from one paragraph to the next. They signal the progression of ideas and thus make your writing easier to read. Here are some of the most common transitional expressions:

TIME:	after	first	later	soon
	always	following	meanwhile	then
	before	immediately	now	until
	finally	last	sometimes	

PLACE:	above	down	near	parallel
	ahead	far	next to	there
	around	here	opposite	under
	below	horizontally	outside	vertically
	beneath	inside	over	within

ORDER OF IMPORTANCE:	at first	former	latter	second
	first	last	primarily	secondarily

CAUSE AND EFFECT:	as a result	so
	consequently	then

COMPARISON AND CONTRAST:	but	just as	similarly
	however	like	unlike
	in contrast	on the contrary	
	in the same way	on the other hand	

EXAMPLES:	for example	namely
	for instance	that is

The sample that follows shows the effective use of transition words in the essay "Guiding Your Career Choices." Notice how the words *after* and *next* help you to understand the logical progression of ideas within the sentence.

> *After* thinking about your interests and abilities, the *next* step is to consider your personal goals.

THE CONCLUDING PARAGRAPH

A good concluding paragraph strengthens an essay in the same way that a strong closing sentence strengthens a paragraph. The list that follows includes some methods you may want to use in your concluding paragraph:

1. Summarize all the important points that you have presented in your essay.
2. Restate the central idea of your essay.
3. Describe your personal reaction to the topic.
4. Relate an anecdote that supports your thesis.
5. Suggest a solution to a problem that you have discussed.
6. Ask a question that leads the reader to think about the topic of your essay.

Objective

EXERCISE 11. Writing a First Draft. Using your working outline and the preferred introduction you wrote in Exercise 10, write the first draft of your essay. Use each main heading in your working outline as the main idea of a paragraph. Focus on putting your ideas on paper. You will have a chance to improve sentence structure, word choice, and organization when you revise your essay. Save your first draft. Your assignment in Writer's Choice #1 on page 249 will be to revise the draft by using the information discussed in the next few pages.

REVISING, EDITING, AND PUBLISHING THE ESSAY

The revision stage of writing gives you a chance to review and rethink your work. You may decide that some ideas require additional development. Other ideas may seem unnecessary or unrelated, and you will eliminate them. You may need to move a paragraph or revise your conclusion. The following checklist will help you revise your essay.

CHECKLIST FOR REVISING AN ESSAY

1. What is the purpose of my essay? Is my purpose clear to my audience?
2. Does my thesis statement present my main point clearly, indicate my attitude toward my topic, and suggest the organization that the essay will follow?
3. Does each point I discuss support the thesis?
4. Are my most important ideas developed carefully? Are they introduced in the right order?
5. Is each point related to the main topic? Should any points be eliminated?
6. Do my ideas flow smoothly? Are transitions between paragraphs clear to the reader?
7. Should the introduction or concluding paragraph be revised? Could they be made more forceful or interesting?
8. Are my sentences interesting? Do I avoid monotony in sentence structures and lengths?
9. What corrections need to be made in grammar, usage, word choice, spelling, capitalization, and punctuation?

Objective

EXERCISE 12. Revising a First Draft. Ask yourself the questions on the Checklist for Revising an Essay (page 243). Make notes on your first draft or on a separate page. These notes will guide you as you write your formal outline and a revised version of your essay in Writer's Choice #1 on page 249.

THE FORMAL OUTLINE

Earlier in this chapter you prepared a working outline and then used that outline to write the first draft of your essay. At this point you are ready to prepare a formal outline, which is somewhat more detailed than a working outline. Review the working outline written for the essay "Guiding Your Career Choices" on page 238. Compare it with the formal outline on page 244. The differences between the two reflect the changes made as the student revised her first draft.

Formal Outline

TOPIC: Guiding your career choices

I. Introduction
II. Looking at yourself
    A. Exploring your interests
        1. Listing what appeals the most
        2. Finding patterns within your interests
        3. Listing what appeals the least
    B. Assessing your abilities
        1. Academic abilities
        2. Nonacademic abilities
III. Looking toward your future
    A. Identifying goals
        1. Jobs vs. goals
        2. Qualities of a life style
    B. Investigating options
        1. Further training
        2. Immediate job
IV. Seeking the assistance of people in your community
    A. Seeking advice about your talents
        1. From parents, teachers, and friends
        2. From guidance counselor
        3. At school career center
    B. Seeking career information
        1. The people to question
            a. Relatives, neighbors, and family friends
            b. People you do not know
        2. The questions to ask
            a. About a typical workday
            b. About their likes and dislikes
V. Exploring career possibilities beyond your community
    A. Obtaining information
        1. From books and pamphlets
        2. From catalogs
    B. Contacting and visiting people in specific fields
    C. Attending "Career Day"
VI. Conclusion

Note that the outline shows the introduction and the conclusion of the essay. If you or your teacher prefers, you can omit these elements from your formal outline but not, of course, from your essay.

The formal outline follows a particular form. Study this summary of guidelines for writing a formal outline:

1. Place your topic at the top of the outline.
2. For each main idea, use a heading that begins with a Roman numeral. You must have a *II* if you have a *I*.
3. Under each main idea list supporting details or subordinate ideas. For each of these use capital letters. You must have a *B* if you have an *A*.
4. Under each subordinate idea, list any details that you want to remember to mention. For each of these use an Arabic numeral. You must have a *2* if you have a *1*.
5. Follow the indention scheme in the preceding model.
6. Begin each entry with a capital letter.
7. Entries for the same type of heading (Roman numeral, capital letter, or Arabic numeral) should be parallel in structure.

TOPIC OUTLINES AND SENTENCE OUTLINES

The formal outline you have just examined is called a **topic outline** because it uses phrases rather than sentences to indicate the topics of the essay. Note also the use of parallel structure. In *II*, for example, each supporting idea indicated by a capital letter begins with a gerund: *Exploring . . . Assessing.* Items B. 1 and B. 2 are both nouns: *abilities . . . abilities.*

A **sentence outline** uses complete sentences for the main topics, the subtopics, and the details listed under the subtopics. Be sure to end each sentence with a period. Here is a portion of the student's formal outline rewritten in sentence outline form.

Sentence Outline

II. The first step is to look at yourself objectively.
- **A.** You should begin by exploring your own interests.
  - **1.** You should list the jobs and tasks that appeal the most.
  - **2.** You should try to detect a pattern within your interests.
  - **3.** You should list the jobs and tasks that appeal the least.
- **B.** You should then assess your abilities.
  - **1.** Academic abilities are important to assess.
  - **2.** Nonacademic abilities should also be examined.

Objective

EXERCISE 13. Preparing a Formal Outline. Assume that you have written a first draft of an essay about your interests in volcanoes. After reading it, you are not satisfied with the first draft because your information is not well organized and the essay seems to wander from topic to topic. The weakness in your essay can be traced to a weakness in your working outline. Now is the time for you to prepare a better outline, a formal outline. You realize from reading your first draft that the body of your essay should be organized into three main topics: *the causes of volcanoes, kinds of volcanoes,* and *active volcanoes.* Your next step is to organize all the details from your first draft under those three headings. Prepare a formal outline with three levels: Roman numerals for the three main topics, capital letters for subtopics, and Arabic numerals for details within subtopics. Use all the notes on the following list in your formal outline.

Location of the volcanic zones
Lava
Shield volcanoes
Hot gases
Area surrounding the Pacific Ocean
Mt. St. Helens, Washington (May, 1980)
Ash
Active volcanoes
Kilauea, Hawaii (May, 1980)
The contents of a volcanic eruption
Cone volcanoes
The Mediterranean region eastward into Indonesia
Composite volcanoes

THE TITLE

The title for your essay should arouse the reader's interest and reflect some aspect of the essay's central idea. For example, for the sample essay in this chapter, the title "My Approach to Choosing a Career" is too dull. On the other hand, the title "Critical Choices" does not provide enough information about the central idea of the essay. "Guiding Your Career Choices," however, is livelier and more precise.

THE FINISHED ESSAY

The essay as finally written by the student interested in career choices appears on the following pages. The annotations written in the margin focus on some of the important points covered in this chapter and show how the parts of the essay correspond to the parts of the formal outline on page 244.

Guiding Your Career Choices

The introductory paragraph begins by posing a problem. Notice the underlined thesis statement.

When faced with the important question "What career are you going to choose?" many people panic because they cannot give an answer. If you are one of these people, a well-planned approach to choosing a career will help you make a responsible choice. Four simple guidelines can help you plan, not panic, when you face career choices: Take a close look at your interests and abilities, think about your personal goals for the future, seek the assistance of people in your community, and, finally, explore carefully what opportunities lie beyond the world you know.

This paragraph corresponds to I in the formal outline. Notice the writer develops the paragraph logically. The first two sentences provide the reader with an overview of the main points and indicate the three subpoints as well. Note the use of transition words.

First you should start with what you know best—yourself. A serious and systematic analysis of your interests, your abilities, and your goals in life is a strong, certain step toward deciding on a suitable career. Begin by listing your interests, including games, hobbies, extracurricular activities, subjects you enjoy reading about, and organizations in which you are active. Decide what aspects of these interests appeal to you, and then see if you can find a pattern of things you enjoy doing. It may be helpful during this process also to list what aspects you do not like, that you do not enjoy doing. This list, too, may form a pattern that might be helpful. After spending some time defining your interests, you should assess your particular abilities. Look closely at the areas of study in which you excel, because these can indicate where your talents lie. All talents are not academic, however, so be careful to consider such talents as working well with others or the skill of working neatly and paying close attention to detail.

This paragraph corresponds to II in the formal outline. The writer continues to develop the essay by using exposition.

After thinking about your interests and abilities, the next step is to consider your personal goals. Be careful not to confuse jobs with goals. Think of goals as the qualities of a life style that you value. Examples of life goals might include a strong family life, opportunities for travel, job security, or winning wealth, self-satisfaction, or even fame. Be sure to consider how much time and effort you are willing to spend after high school for further training for a profession. Then consider whether you would prefer less preparation and a more immediate entry into the job market. Try to compile a list of goals that seem important to you now. This list, as well as your lists of interests and skills, will help you narrow your career choices.

This paragraph corresponds to III in the formal outline.

The third stage of your search for a career involves seeking the assistance of people in your community. Start with the people who know you best—your parents, teach-

Notice the use of cause and effect to develop the idea that the more you learn, the greater the possible changes of your career goals.

ers, and friends. Ask them what they think your talents are. Your school guidance counselor can be an invaluable source of good advice and sound opinions. Work with your school career center if there is one. Compare the answers you receive from these sources with the skills you have already listed. Add new skills to your list. Continue to collect specific information about jobs and careers by interviewing a variety of people—relatives, neighbors, family friends—who have different kinds of jobs that interest you. Make appointments with people you do not know but whose professions are appealing. Ask these people what they do on a typical day; their descriptions can be very informative. Ask them what they like about their jobs—and what they dislike. Their answers may inspire you to amend your lists of interests and goals.

This paragraph corresponds to V in the formal outline.

The third stage of your search takes you beyond your immediate community to the consideration of more specialized careers. Here your school or public library can provide valuable material. Your librarian can furnish you with books and pamphlets that describe specific careers. In addition, catalogs from colleges, universities, and vocational schools, also available in libraries, can inform you about training requirements. Be creative in your investigation—here you may discover whole areas of possible careers you have not considered. It is possible for you to correspond with people in specific fields and even arrange to visit them at their jobs. If your school sponsors a "Career Day," the representatives from many schools, colleges, and industries can provide you with answers to many of your unanswered questions.

The conclusion states a personal reaction.

The process of making decisions about a career is not an easy one. Regardless, the benefits that result from the hard work can result ultimately in a happy and successful professional life.

Throughout this chapter you have followed the work of one writer while preparing to write an essay of your own. Now you will have the opportunity to put into practice what you have learned. The following Writer's Choice assignments give you practice in writing both formal and informal essays. Some of the assignments are structured with specific directions; others are open-ended, and you must determine how to proceed. Whichever assignments you choose, try to apply all of the writing skills you have learned in this chapter.

WRITER'S CHOICE #1

ASSIGNMENT: To write a formal outline and a final version of the essay you have been working on throughout this chapter
LENGTH: Five to seven paragraphs
AUDIENCE: As you stated in Exercise 7 and reconsidered in Exercise 12
PURPOSE: As you stated in Exercise 7 and reconsidered in Exercise 12
PREWRITING: You have already finished this stage by completing your first draft in Exercise 11.
WRITING: You have already finished this stage by completing your first draft in Exercise 11.
REVISING: Use the checklist on page 243 to review your first draft. Prepare a formal outline reflecting the changes you want to make in the organization of the essay. Follow the guidelines for a formal outline on page 245. Then use the formal outline and your first draft to write a final version of the essay. Be sure to edit and proofread the final draft of your essay and then share your essay with your readers.

WRITER'S CHOICE #2

ASSIGNMENT: To write a formal essay you will enter in a contest. Your essay must be about one of the following topics:

- the value of work
- a significant discovery
- the problems of combining part-time work with full-time school
- the value of travel
- the importance of the telephone in modern life
- the importance of education

LENGTH: Five to seven paragraphs
AUDIENCE: A general audience
PURPOSE: To explain or persuade
PREWRITING: Explore your subject with a series of informational, personal, or creative questions (see Chapter 2). Limit the topic, and organize the information you will present into a working outline.
WRITING: State your thesis clearly, and write a first draft.
REVISING: Refer to the Checklist for Revising on page 243, and then prepare a formal outline. Write your final version. Carefully edit and proofread the final draft of your essay, and then share your work with readers. If possible, enter your essay in an essay-writing contest sponsored by a community group.

WRITER'S CHOICE #3

ASSIGNMENT: To write a formal essay that you will enter in a national essay-writing contest. Choose one of the following topics, or choose a topic of your own.

- the greatest challenge facing today's teenagers
- popular music
- the effect of cable television on the nation's viewing habits

LENGTH: Five to seven paragraphs

AUDIENCE: A general audience

PURPOSE: To describe, inform, explain, or persuade

PREWRITING: Explore your subject by means of a series of informational, personal, creative, or analytical questions (see Chapter 2). Limit the topic, and organize your information into a working outline.

WRITING: State your thesis clearly, and write a first draft.

REVISING: Refer to the Checklist for Revising on page 243, and then prepare a formal outline. Write a final version of your essay. Carefully edit and proofread the final draft, and share your work with readers.

WRITER'S CHOICE #4

ASSIGNMENT: To write a formal essay on a topic of your choice

LENGTH: Your Choice

AUDIENCE: Your Choice

PURPOSE: Your Choice

OPTIONS: You may find a writing idea in the Writer's Sourcebook, pages 356–357.

- Follow these writing stages: working outline, first draft, formal outline, and final draft. Edit and proofread your work, and share your essay with an audience.

WRITER'S CHOICE #5

ASSIGNMENT: To write an informal essay on a topic of your choice

OPTIONS: Determine and state in writing the length, audience, and purpose of your essay. Use the prewriting technique that best fits the topic. The purpose of an informal essay is to entertain or please an audience while you explore a topic. The tone of your essay should be light, and you may rely heavily on descriptive or narrative elements to develop the essay. Follow these writing stages: prepare a working outline, a first draft, a formal outline, and a final version. Edit, proofread, and share your work.

CHAPTER 12 THE ESSAY

Topic (pages 232–237) Indicate the letter of the item that correctly answers the question.

1. Which of the following is the most focused essay topic?
   (a) jobs **(b)** photography **(c)** a hobby that can become a career

Outline, Introduction, and Thesis (pages 237–240) Read the following working outline, and then indicate the letter of the item that correctly answers each question.

I. Photography as a hobby
  A. Mastering the use of a camera
  B. Increasing knowledge of photographic techniques
II. Photography as a career
  A. Wedding photographs
  B. Yearbook photographs
  C. Advertising photographs
III. Difficulties of becoming a professional photographer
  A. Low pay at first
  B. Long hours
  C. Little recognition of your talents

2. Where in this outline would you place a point about the value of joining a camera club for amateur photographers?
   (a) in I under B **(b)** in II under C **(c)** in III under C
3. Which thesis statement best reflects this outline?
   (a) Photography can be an exciting career.
   (b) Why many amateur photographers want to become professionals.
   (c) Turning your hobby of photography into a career can have some drawbacks at first.

Body (pages 241–243) Indicate the letter of the item that correctly answers each question.

4. Which transition could you use to move smoothly from the final body paragraph to a concluding paragraph of an essay based on the preceding outline?
   (a) first **(b)** meanwhile **(c)** in summary **(d)** primarily
5. Which item would body paragraph 3 be most likely to discuss?
   (a) The beginning photographer must master how to produce a correctly exposed negative or slide.
   (b) An apprentice in a professional photo studio often just runs errands.
   (c) Photographing a company's products well requires a trained eye.

Answers: **1.** c; **2.** a; **3.** b; **4.** c; **5.** b

Writing for Review Write an essay about a topic that interests you. Begin with a paragraph that engages your reader's attention and leads up to your thesis statement. Make sure that the paragraphs in the body of the essay discuss all the points presented in your thesis. Write a concluding paragraph that summarizes your main points.

13 CHAPTER
The Research Paper

While you are studying (and) observing, . . . do not remain content with the surface of things. Do not become a mere recorder of facts, but try to penetrate the mystery of their origin.

—Ivan Pavlov

When you write a research paper, you do not merely record facts, ideas, and opinions. Yes, you gather information, but you also shape and adapt that information to provide support for your own insights into the topic. During the research process you begin to penetrate the mystery of the information you gather. You should try to do more than just catalogue the ideas of other writers. A good research report will include your own analysis of the information you uncover. Let your own insights into and judgments about the subject give focus to your research and writing.

A **research paper** deals with a limited topic and is based on information from written sources or from interviews with experts on the topic.

A research paper usually presents data gathered from five to eight sources of information and contains two to three thousand words, or eight to twelve typed pages. Your teacher may specify a different length, however.

As you write your research paper, you will use many of the prewriting, writing, and revising skills presented earlier in this book. You will also use one or more of the modes of writing: description, narration, exposition, and persuasion. This chapter focuses on the following skills:

- prewriting: selecting and limiting a topic
- prewriting: beginning your research
- prewriting: purpose, audience, and controlling idea
- prewriting: gathering material
- prewriting: taking notes
- prewriting: preparing a formal outline
- writing the first draft
- revising the first draft
- publishing the final draft

PREWRITING: SELECTING AND LIMITING A TOPIC

If your teacher does not assign a specific topic for your research paper, your first step will be to select a general topic that interests you, one that you can learn more about through additional reading and research. Then use prewriting techniques such as freewriting, brainstorming, charting, and asking informational and analytical questions to generate writing ideas for your topic (see Chapter 2).

Remember to choose a topic that is both interesting to you and manageable. Your topic should be one that can be researched in a reasonable amount of time and discussed in relatively few pages.

After selecting a general topic, you will have to limit its scope so that it can be covered thoroughly in an eight- to twelve-page paper. For example, suppose that you decide to write a research paper on the motion picture industry. Such a topic is too general to be examined adequately in two to three thousand words. You will have to focus on a more limited aspect of motion pictures. You may narrow the topic in the following way:

GENERAL: Motion picture industry
LESS GENERAL: Influence of famous directors
LIMITED: George Lucas's influence on the American film industry
TOO LIMITED: Set decoration in *Star Wars*

A topic that is overly limited may be unsuitable because too little information about it is available. Likewise, it may be difficult to find sufficient sources to research a topic that is too current, such as a film that was very recently released. Subjective topics, too, should be avoided because of limited sources. For example, it would be very difficult to find much research material suporting a subjective topic such as "Hemingway was a better writer than Faulkner."

In this chapter you will follow one student's progress as she moves through the various stages of writing a research paper. The student, Robin Spielberg, wrote about a literary topic. Note that her paper is based on research about that topic and is not a personal analysis of a literary work. Robin's assignment was to read three works by a playwright and to research and write about an idea or theme suggested by the works. Robin had become interested in Thornton Wilder when she played the part of Emily in a drama club production of *Our Town;* thus Robin decided to write about that play and two other works by Wilder. In order to give her paper a focus, she looked for similarities between the works.

CHECKLIST FOR SELECTING AND LIMITING A TOPIC

1. Why do I want to write about this topic?
2. Can I discuss the topic in the length specified, or is my topic too limited?
3. Can I cover all the important aspects of my topic in the length specified, or is my topic too general?
4. What books and articles about the topic are available? Do I have an adequate number of sources?

Objective

EXERCISE 1. Limiting a Topic. For five of the following general topics, suggest a limited topic for an eight- to twelve-page research paper. Then choose one of these topics (or another limited topic) for a research paper of your own.

1. life in Japan
2. Central America
3. the history of rock and roll
4. our solar system
5. rivers of North America
6. modern inventions

Suggested Answers: **1.** education in modern Japan; **2.** the Panama Canal; **3.** rock musicals; **4.** meteorites; **5.** the Ohio River; **6.** scuba gear

Objective

EXERCISE 2. Checking the Library for Sources. For the limited topic you chose in Exercise 1, consult the library card catalog, catalog book, or computerized catalog system and the *Readers' Guide to Periodical Literature.* Determine how much material about your topic is available. Find and list at least eight suitable sources. (For instructions on using the library, see Chapter 35.)

PREWRITING: BEGINNING YOUR RESEARCH

After choosing a limited topic for your paper, begin your research by reading one or more encyclopedia articles. Your purpose is to acquire an overview and to determine if you really want to write about the topic. Encyclopedia articles provide useful overviews of many subjects; in addition, such articles often contain lists of resource books on the subject.

The topic you selected may have its own entry in the encyclopedia, or you may have to use the index to find information about it in a more general article. For example, to find a discussion of the novel *The Bridge of San Luis Rey* you would probably look under the name of the author, Thornton Wilder, or in a general article like "American Novels" or "Pulitzer Prize Novels." Another source that you might consult to find background articles in magazines is the *Readers' Guide to Periodical Literature.*

Several biographical reference books, such as *Contemporary Authors,* also provide useful overview information. Robin read background articles about Thornton Wilder in both an encyclopedia and in *Contemporary Authors*. She also consulted a book called *Thornton Wilder: An Intimate Portrait*, which she found listed in an encyclopedia article. The articles and the book gave her a good overview of her topic. As she read this background information, she listed the important aspects of her topic.

Objective

EXERCISE 3. Finding General Information on a Topic. Read one or two encyclopedia articles for general information on the research paper topic that you chose in Exercise 1. If you cannot find general information about your topic in the encyclopedia, read one or two of the magazine articles that you identified in Exercise 2. List at least five important aspects of the topic discussed in the articles.

PREWRITING: PURPOSE, AUDIENCE, AND CONTROLLING IDEA

After selecting and limiting a topic and examining some background sources, you should define your purpose for writing the research paper. For example, if you were writing a paper about endangered species of animals, your purpose might be to inform your audience of the consequences of human intervention in the delicate ecosystem. State your purpose in a single sentence. A concise statement of your purpose can help you to identify the additional sources you may need.

Once you have defined your purpose, you should determine your audience. If your audience has expertise on your topic, you probably will not have to define basic terms or ideas. If your intended audience has a limited knowledge of the subject area, however, you will probably have to include explanations of many basic concepts.

The next prewriting step is to state your controlling idea. As you read through background sources on your topic, you jotted down ideas about it. You can use those ideas to develop a **controlling idea**, a main point that you want to develop and that you can support through your research. The controlling idea acts as a **working thesis statement** and performs three important tasks: (1) It clearly states the main point of the paper; (2) it conveys your attitude toward the topic; and (3) it suggests the direction your paper will take.

Keep notes as you read, preferably on three- by five-inch file cards or on a notepad. You will find that keeping notes helps you to focus on your controlling idea and to modify it as necessary when new information gives you new ideas.

Objective

EXERCISE 4. Determining Purpose, Audience, and Controlling Idea. For the research paper topic that you have chosen, state in writing your purpose, your audience, and your controlling idea.

PREWRITING: GATHERING MATERIAL

PREPARING A WORKING OUTLINE

A **working outline** will guide you in your reading and note-taking.

After you have developed an overview of your topic and a controlling idea for your research paper, you are ready to decide which aspects of the topic you want to cover and how to organize them. Your next step is to prepare a working outline to guide you as you read and take notes. You will probably revise your outline often by adding, changing, and dropping headings as you uncover new data.

To prepare a working outline, reread the list of important aspects of your topic, a list that you prepared in Exercise 3. Ask specific questions about these points; the questions you ask often become the major headings in your working outline. For example, here are some of the questions that Robin Spielberg asked herself about Thornton Wilder's works:

1. What themes consistently flow through Thornton Wilder's Pulitzer Prize plays and novel?
2. How and why does Wilder use audience participation in his plays?
3. What is the effect of Wilder's narrative style?
4. On what kinds of characters and events does Wilder primarily focus?
5. Why do Wilder's endings seem "endless," a part of a larger "continuous" pattern?

Robin then wrote a working outline based on her questions:

Thornton Wilder's Themes

I. Common themes
II. Wilder's use of audience participation
III. Narration
IV. Portrayal of everyday life
V. Wilder's endings

Answering the preceding questions helped Robin decide on the five principal ideas that she used as major headings to construct her working outline. Each topic became the heading for a list of research notes that Robin would make for her paper. Note how this working outline compares with Robin's final outline on page 262.

Now ask yourself these questions to start preparing your own working outline:

1. Where can I use description in my research paper?
2. Where can I use narrative prose?
3. What kind or kinds of explanatory prose should I use: process analysis, cause-and-effect analysis, division and classification, definition, or comparison and contrast?
4. Where can I use persuasive writing to develop arguments and to draw conclusions? What facts and opinions do I need to support my findings?

Objective

EXERCISE 5. Preparing a Working Outline. For the topic you chose in Exercise 1, list specific questions and answers about each important aspect that you identified in Exercise 3. Then prepare a working outline. Next to each point on the outline, write the kind of writing you might use to develop it.

FINDING INFORMATION

After developing a working outline, you are ready to review your research sources and, if necessary, find additional ones. First, locate the books and articles that you identified in Exercise 2. If you have problems finding a source in your library, use the card catalog and other reference books like the *Readers' Guide* or the *Humanities Index* to find additional sources. A two-thousand-word paper should be based on at least five sources, and a three-thousand-word paper should be based on at least eight sources.

FINDING RELIABLE SOURCES

When you identify sources for your research paper, make sure that they are reliable. A source is usually reliable if written by a highly regarded writer who has professional credentials in the subject area and who is respected by his or her peers. In addition, select only suitable books or articles; junior books, for example, are not appropriate sources for a research paper. If you are writing a historical research paper, do not rely on the blend of fact and fiction that you find in historical novels.

KEEPING A WORKING BIBLIOGRAPHY

A **working bibliography** is a list of books and other source materials that you will consult.

After locating a source, skim it to decide whether or not it will be useful, reliable, and suitable. If so, record the following information on a **bibliography card,** a three- by five-inch index card. Use a separate card for each source.

- the name of the author
- the complete title of the source
- the name and location of the publisher
- the copyright or date of publication
- the page numbers of magazine or newspaper articles, together with the name, date of issue, and the volume and number of the journals in which the articles appeared
- the library call number of the book (in case you need to find it later)

Number each of your bibliography cards in the upper left corner. When you take notes later, number each note card (see page 261) with the corresponding bibliography card number. You will also use the numbered bibliography cards when writing footnotes and preparing the bibliography for your final draft.

Bibliography Card for a Book

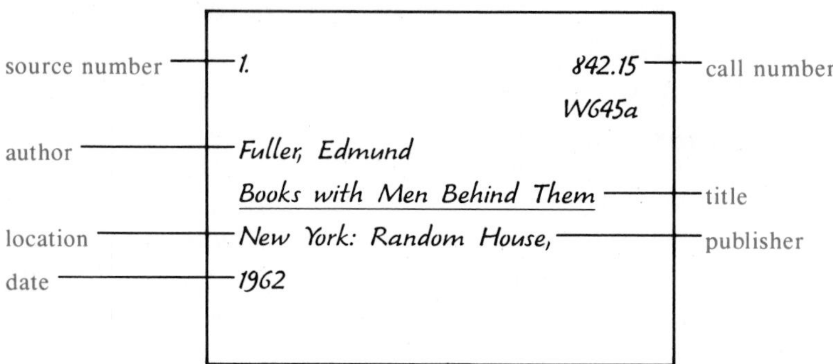

Bibliography Card for a Book with an Editor

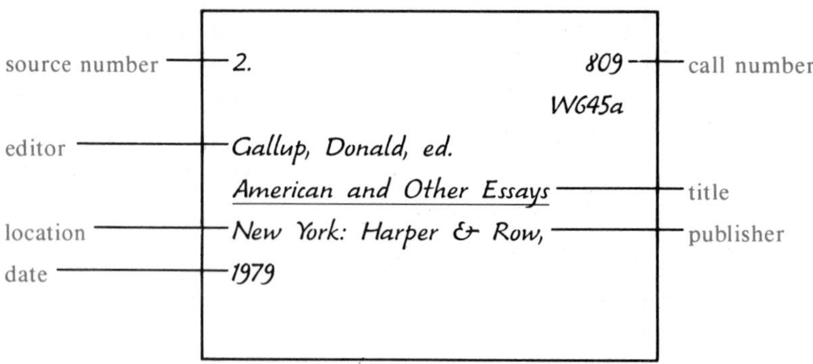

Bibliography Card for an Encyclopedia Article

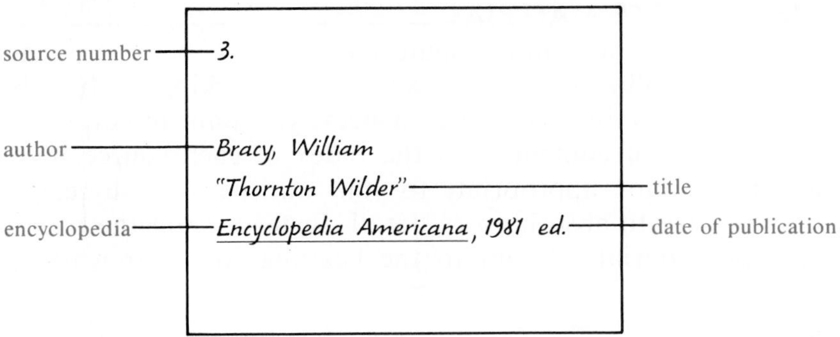

Bibliography Card for a Magazine Article

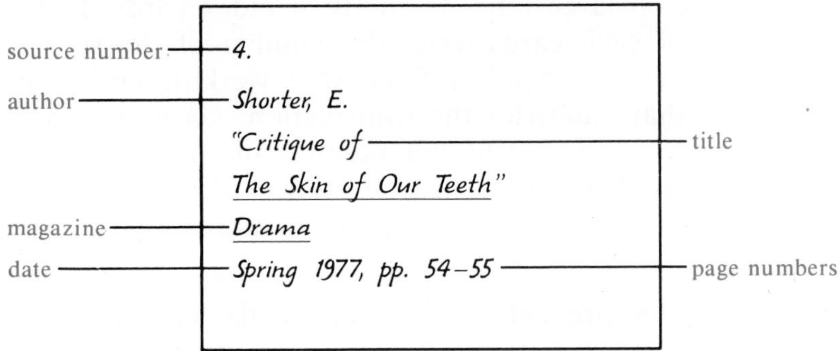

source number
4.
author
Shorter, E.
"Critique of
The Skin of Our Teeth"
title
magazine
Drama
date
Spring 1977, pp. 54–55
page numbers

Bibliography Card for a Newspaper Article

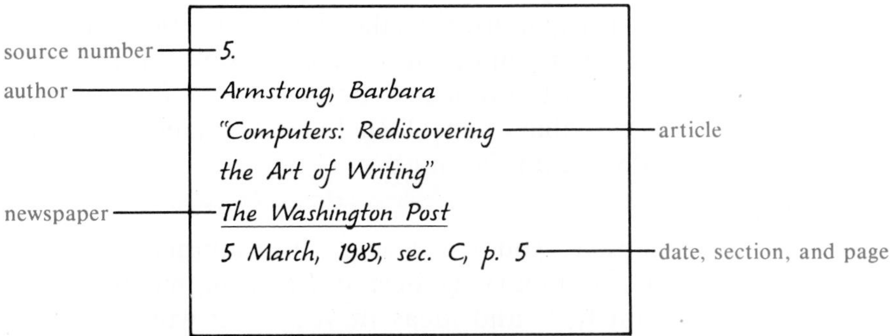

source number
5.
author
Armstrong, Barbara
"Computers: Rediscovering
the Art of Writing"
article
newspaper
The Washington Post
5 March, 1985, sec. C, p. 5
date, section, and page

Objective

EXERCISE 6. Finding Sources. You will need at least five sources for your paper. Review those that you found for Exercise 2. If you need more, use the book lists at the end of encyclopedia articles, bibliographies within your source books, the library's card catalog or computerized catalog system, and the *Readers' Guide to Periodical Literature.* Skim the sources; then write bibliography cards for those you plan to use. Follow the cards on pages 258–259 as models.

PREWRITING: TAKING NOTES

STUDYING SOURCE MATERIAL

After collecting your source material, you can begin to read and take notes. While doing so, keep your working outline in front of you as a reminder of which aspects you want to cover.

Study the table of contents and the index of each source book to locate information appropriate to your outline. As you read a source, do not try to absorb every detail. Instead, skim the pages, searching for material relevant to the headings on your working outline.

RECORDING INFORMATION

Write your notes on large four- by six-inch index cards. In the upper left corner of each card, write the number of the source. Below the number, write a heading from your working outline or a revised heading that identifies the information you will record. In the upper right corner, write the number of that particular note card. The notes that you record on each card will be direct quotations, paraphrases of information, or a combination of each.

Direct Quotations

A **direct quotation** presents the exact words used in your source. When you record a direct quotation on your note card, copy the exact words of the quotation carefully, and put quotation marks around them. Always recheck the copied quotation against the original source. If a quotation strikes you as particularly useful, you might include a comment at the bottom of the card indicating the quotation's relevance or potential use; for example, "good analogy" or "possible opener." Include the exact page number on which the information is found.

Paraphrasing

When you **paraphrase**, you write a concise summary of what you have read. This summary is best done from memory. You write down important facts and ideas in your own words, neither adding nor taking away from the author's original meaning. Include the exact page number on which the information is found.

AVOIDING PLAGIARISM

Remember that when you directly quote or paraphrase ideas, statements, or statistics from another source you must credit the source in your research paper. The direct quotes or paraphrased statements must be attributed in the footnotes and the bibliography of your paper.

Here is a note card on which Robin has recorded both a direct quotation and a paraphrase. Notice that quotation marks clearly set off the direct quotation.

Note Card Containing a Direct Quotation and a Paraphrase

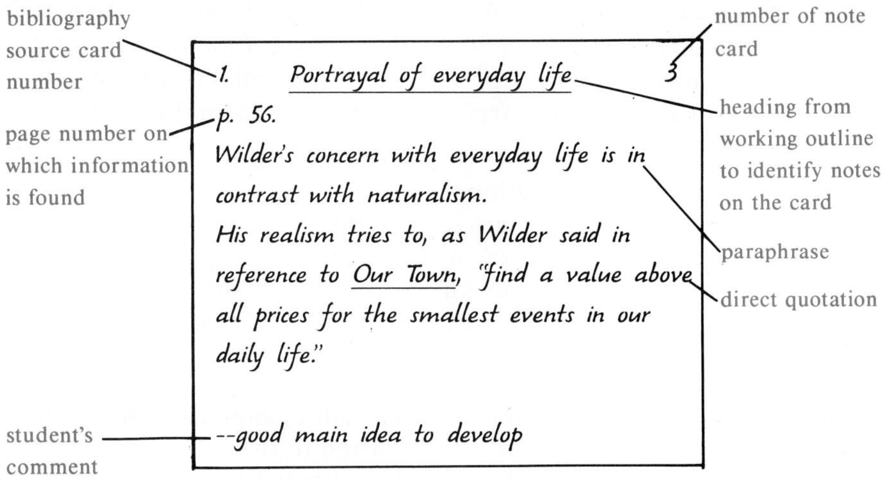

bibliography source card number
page number on which information is found
student's comment
number of note card
heading from working outline to identify notes on the card
paraphrase
direct quotation
1. Portrayal of everyday life 3
p. 56.
Wilder's concern with everyday life is in contrast with naturalism.
His realism tries to, as Wilder said in reference to Our Town, "find a value above all prices for the smallest events in our daily life."
--good main idea to develop

Objective

EXERCISE 7. Taking Notes. Take notes from the sources that you have assembled for your research report. Remember to identify each source by number and to write on each note card a heading from your working outline. Follow the directions for paraphrasing and quoting directly (see page 260).

PREWRITING: PREPARING A FORMAL OUTLINE

A **formal outline** will guide you in writing your first draft.

As you read and take notes, you will probably see the need to revise your working outline before making a final, formal outline. First, read over your notes carefully and group them into piles, one pile for each important aspect of your topic. If some cards are no longer appropriate to your topic, remove them. Compare your working outline with your piles of note cards, and ask yourself these questions:

1. How do the headings on the piles of note cards compare with the headings in my working outline? What other main headings should be added to the outline?
2. What other information do I need in order to support the main headings in my working outline? Where can I find the information?

3. What logical subdivisions can I introduce for the main headings?
4. What is the best order for presenting my ideas?

During her reading and note-taking, Robin Spielberg found additional information about common and related themes in three of Thornton Wilder's works, *The Bridge of San Luis Rey* (a novel) and *Our Town* and *The Skin of Our Teeth* (two plays). She revised her working outline and prepared the following formal outline:

The Themes of Thornton Wilder's Pulitzer Prize Winners

I. Similarities between the three works
  A. Common theme (note card 3)
  B. Common techniques (note card 4)
II. Routine life depicted against the vast dimension of time
  A. *The Bridge of San Luis Rey*
    1. Importance of the setting (note card 9)
    2. Relationship of setting to theme
    3. Parallels in Wilder's life (note card 7)
  B. *Our Town*
    1. The moral of the play (note card 14)
    2. Emily's embodiment of the moral
III. Wilder's use of narrative style
  A. First-person narration in *The Bridge of San Luis Rey*
  B. *Our Town*
    1. The role of the stage manager (note card 6)
    2. The playwright as stage manager (note card 5)
  C. *The Skin of Our Teeth*
    1. A play within a play
    2. The author's spokespersons (note card 12)
IV. Audience participation in Wilder's works
  A. *The Skin of Our Teeth* (note card 13)
  B. *Our Town* (note card 17)
  C. *The Bridge of San Luis Rey*
V. Wilder's "endless" endings (note card 2)
  A. The major themes
  B. Wilder's message

Objective

EXERCISE 8. Writing a Formal Outline. Using your note cards, your working outline, and the questions on pages 261–262, prepare a formal outline for your research paper. Follow the outline style shown above.

WRITING: THE FIRST DRAFT

You will need several hours of uninterrupted time for writing the first draft of your research paper. First, make sure that the sequence of your note cards corresponds to the sequence of headings in your formal outline. As you write, follow your outline, referring to the appropriate note cards for each section of your paper. Each time you use information from a note card, write the number of the note card in the sentence of your first draft; when you prepare your footnotes, you will know which idea you took from which card. Try to do more than merely expand your notes into sentences and paragraphs. Before writing, think of each section as a whole and decide what you want a particular section to tell your reader. Then use your notes to help fulfill that purpose. Remember to use transitional expressions to link the various sections together.

A research paper can be divided into three main sections, although these sections are not formally listed as such on your outline. These parts are the introduction, the body of the paper, and the conclusion.

INTRODUCTION

Every research paper needs an introduction in which you state the controlling idea of your paper. Some writers find that writing the introduction before beginning the body of the paper helps them develop a focus for their thinking. Other writers are more comfortable with composing the introduction after completing the main sections of the paper, when they know exactly what they have said. If you choose the latter option, keep your controlling idea in mind as you write the first draft of your paper.

THE BODY

As you write the body of your paper, concentrate on getting your ideas down in a clear sequence. Later, in a revision of your first draft, you can focus on fine-tuning those ideas and on polishing the wording of your sentences.

Strive to do more than simply expand your note cards into sentences and paragraphs, stringing bits of information together in a haphazard way. Be sure that each new item of information clearly adds to the development of your argument. Link your sentences and paragraphs together with transition words and phrases to show the logical progression of ideas.

Writing is also a thinking process, so do not be surprised when fresh ideas occur to you as you write. Evaluate those ideas, and include them in your paper if they are good. Always keep your purpose and your audience in mind.

THE CONCLUSION

The concluding paragraph should clearly convey the purpose and restate the main idea of the paper. A strong conclusion summarizes what you have accomplished and often echoes your opening statement.

After completing your first draft, do not begin revising it immediately. Put it aside for several hours or a day. When you return to it, you will be able to look at it with a clear mind.

Objective

EXERCISE 9. Evaluating Progress. In Writer's Choice #1 you will have a chance to write a research paper based on the work you have done so far. At this point, use the following questions to evaluate your progress in Exercises 1–8:

1. How satisfied are you with the limited topic that you chose for Exercise 1? In light of subsequent work, how might you change it?
2. How useful did the sources you identified in Exercise 2 turn out to be? Do you need additional sources?
3. Look at your responses to Exercise 4. What changes, if any, do you want to make in the purpose of your research report? In its audience? In its controlling idea?
4. How much did your working outline from Exercise 5 help your research?
5. How complete are your bibliography cards?
6. How clear and accurate are your note cards? Will you be able to understand them, or do you need more notes?
7. Based on changes in your notes, what changes, if any, should you make in your final outline?

REVISING THE FIRST DRAFT

The initial step in revising a first draft is to read the research paper carefully. As you read, try to answer the following questions objectively. You can then make the appropriate revisions as you rewrite.

1. How effectively have I introduced my paper? What ideas and opinions have I presented in the conclusion?
2. How closely does my paper follow the order of my outline? Are my ideas clearly and logically presented?
3. Do the various sections of the paper fulfill my purpose, and will my audience be able to understand my ideas? Have I included narration, description, and exposition that will effectively communicate my ideas to my intended audience?
4. How can I make my sentences easier to understand?

5. What details have I included? Are they effective? Should I add other examples?
6. What steps have I taken to make sure that my paper is free from errors in spelling, punctuation, capitalization, grammar, and usage?

USING FOOTNOTES

A **footnote** gives additional information, including source data, about a statement in your paper.

After rewriting your first draft, you should add footnotes to the paper. A footnote is necessary wherever you have directly quoted or borrowed an idea from someone else's writing. The footnote credits the author and allows your readers to consult and evaluate the original source.

A footnote has two parts. The first is a **superscript,** or raised number, placed in the text of your paper at the end of the quotation or borrowed idea. The superscript usually appears at the end of the sentence. In your draft you placed the number of the note card right into the sentence containing the borrowed idea. You can now replace those numbers with sequenced superscripts.

The second part of the footnote is the note itself. The information in the note consists of the data you recorded on the bibliography card for each source and the page number that you cited on the source card itself. Footnotes are placed at the bottom of the pages where the superscripts occur. Leave three lines of space between the text of your paper and the footnote or footnotes. You also have the option of placing all your footnotes at the end of the paper under the heading *Notes* (see page 272). Follow your teacher's instructions.

The first line of a footnote should be indented half an inch from the left margin of your paper, and the following lines should be even with the left margin. The information about the source should be given in a standard order with standard punctuation. Here is a sample footnote for a book. Use the Style Chart for Footnotes and Bibliography Entries on page 267 to help you punctuate footnotes correctly.

Footnote for a Book

[6]Edmund Fuller, *Books with Men Behind Them* (New York: Random House, 1962), p. 56.

Sources cited for a second time in a research paper, as in footnote ten that follows, need only the author's last name and the page number on which the information appears. If you have used more than one source by the same author, as in footnote fourteen that follows, include a shortened version of the title so that your readers can tell the two sources apart.

Footnote for a Repeated Reference to a Source

[10]Fuller, p. 57.

[14]Wilder, *Three Plays,* p. 9.

Objective

EXERCISE 10. Practicing Footnote Style. On a separate sheet of paper, practice writing footnotes based on the information in each of the following numbered items. Use the number of the item as the footnote number.

1. A book published in 1973 by Avon Books in New York entitled *The Secret Life of Plants* by Peter Tompkins and Christopher Bird. The information came from page 10.
2. A direct quotation from Winston Churchill found on page 23 of his book *Blood, Sweat and Tears.* The book was published by G. P. Putnam's Sons, New York, in 1941.
3. Information from page 375 of a book by Simone de Beauvoir entitled *The Coming of Age.* The book was published in New York by Warner Paperbacks in 1973.
4. The opening paragraph of an article in the *New York Times Magazine* entitled "How the West Was Won" written by Norman Podhoretz. It appeared on September 30, 1979, on page 17.
5. Several lines of a poem called "When the Year Grows Old" by Edna St. Vincent Millay in a collection of poems edited by Louis Untermeyer called *Yesterday and Today,* which was published in 1926 by Harcourt Brace Jovanovich in New York. The poem appears on page 197.

PREPARING THE FINAL BIBLIOGRAPHY

A **bibliography** lists all your sources.

The bibliography is an alphabetical list of all the sources you used in your research. It is the final page of your research paper. To prepare your final bibliography, alphabetize the cards of your working bibliography according to last name of the author. For sources in which the author's name is not given, use the first important word of the title.

Sample bibliography entries are listed with their equivalent footnote entries in the following chart. Note the differences in format, punctuation, and indention. Refer to this chart when you are preparing the footnotes and bibliography for your research paper.

Style Chart for Footnote and Bibliography Entries

	FOOTNOTE	BIBLIOGRAPHY ENTRY
Book	[1]Richard H. Goldstone, Thornton Wilder: An Intimate Portrait (New York: Saturday Review Press, 1975), p. 50.	Goldstone, Richard H. Thornton Wilder: An Intimate Portrait. New York: Saturday Review Press, 1975.
Periodical	[2]E. Shorter, "Critique of The Skin of Our Teeth," Drama, Spring, 1977, p. 54.	Shorter, E. "Critique of The Skin of Our Teeth." Drama, Spring, 1977, pp. 54–55.
Newspaper Article	[3]"U.S. Lets City Phase Out 9,100 CETA Jobs," New York Times, 29 Sept. 1979, p. 21.	"U.S. Lets City Phase Out 9,100 CETA Jobs." New York Times, 29 Sept. 1979, p. 21.
Encyclopedia Article	[4]William Bracy, "Thornton Wilder," Encyclopedia Americana, 1981 ed.	Bracy, William. "Thornton Wilder." Encyclopedia Americana. 1981 ed.
Book with an Editor	[5]P. E. Easterling, "Character in Sophocles," in Greek Tragedy: Modern Essays in Criticism, ed. Erich Segal (New York: Harper & Row, 1983), p. 138.	Easterling, P. E. "Character in Sophocles," in Greek Tragedy: Modern Essays in Criticism. Ed. Erich Segal. New York: Harper & Row, 1983.

Objective

EXERCISE 11. Practicing Bibliography Style. On a separate sheet of paper, practice writing a five-item bibliography based on the items listed in Exercise 10. Use alphabetical order for the entries in the bibliography. Check the bibliography form carefully.

PUBLISHING THE FINAL DRAFT

Your final draft may be typed, produced on a word processor, or written neatly in ink. Follow your teacher's instructions. A typed paper should be double-spaced, with a one-inch margin at the left, right, top, and bottom of each page.

If your teacher asks you to place your footnotes at the bottom of each page, be sure to leave enough room for them. If you put them at the end of your paper, place them on a separate page before the bibliography and write the title *Notes* at the top of the page.

As the final step, proofread your paper, and in ink neatly correct errors in typing, spelling, capitalization, and punctuation.

Now your paper is ready for publication. Normally a research paper is "published" by delivering it to your teacher within the stated deadline. Another option is to hold a symposium during which students who wrote about similar topics present their papers to one another.

THE FINISHED RESEARCH PAPER

You have followed Robin Spielberg's steps as she researched, planned, and organized her paper on themes in Thornton Wilder's Pulitzer prize winners. A partial version of her research paper is printed on the next several pages.

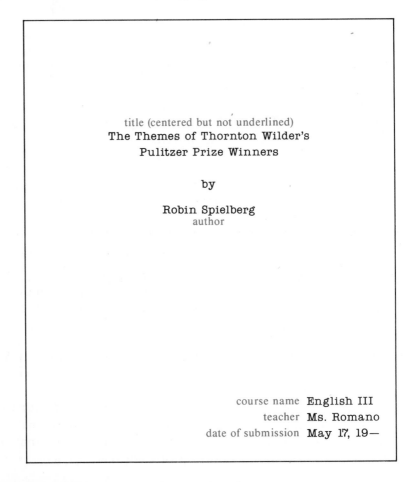

title (centered but not underlined)

The Themes of Thornton Wilder's
Pulitzer Prize Winners

by

Robin Spielberg
author

course name English III
teacher Ms. Romano
date of submission May 17, 19—

Notice the thesis statement about a common theme in Wilder's works.

2

Thornton Wilder, one of America's foremost novelists and playwrights, was concerned with the significance of human life in a vast universe. To him the fact that each individual life is but one of millions is not a cause for gloom but rather a reason for celebration. Wilder deals with this theme in his three Pulitzer prize–winning works: The Bridge of San Luis Rey, Our Town, and The Skin of Our Teeth. Even though two are plays and one is a novel, Wilder uses similar techniques to express this theme in all three works.

In this paragraph, the author uses comparison.

The three works all deal with time dimensions, and all concern "the smallest events in our daily life . . . against the largest dimensions of time. . . ."[1] Although each novel or play takes place over a long period of time, Wilder emphasizes the small and routine chores as well as the "unimportant" decisions of his characters.

3

In this paragraph, the author uses narrative to relate the novel's events.

The Bridge of San Luis Rey takes place in a small town in eighteenth-century Peru. No one knows why Wilder chose this setting: He does not seem to have shown any special interest in that time or place.[2] The tragic accident from which the novel unfolds is the collapse of the bridge on July 20, 1714. The facts of the victims' lives, however, are not revealed to the public until six years later. It is only after we learn about the victims' daily routine that we begin to appreciate their existence as individuals. Like Brother Juniper, the reader feels curious about these people, and realizes that common, typical lives can be important and meaningful. Wilder once stated, "Though I realize that my joy or grief is but 'one' in the ocean of human life, nevertheless it has its reality."[3] At the end of the novel, the authorities burn Brother Juniper along with his book about the lives of the five victims. Wilder writes, "But soon we shall die, and the memory of those five will have left the earth, and we ourselves shall be loved for a while and forgotten."[4]

Notice how the author uses quotations.

Notice the transition linking paragraphs.

4

In 1954 Thornton Wilder wrote something similar to that statement:

> After I'd graduated from college, I was sent to Europe to study archaeology. One day, our class in Rome was taken out into the country to dig a street. . . . Once thousands of persons had walked it . . . those who have uncovered such a spot are never the same again . . . the extent of this enlarged realization alters the whole view of life.[5]

This statement provides a clue to Wilder's purpose in choosing a remote setting for The Bridge of San Luis Rey.

Notice how the transition links the two paragraphs.

Our Town also deals with daily routine throughout a long time span. Wilder's "moral" in this play is "to find a value above all prices for the smallest events in our daily life."[6] We see the main characters in their childhood, married life, and death. The character of Emily, who after death desires to go back to the world of the living, finds that while alive she neglected to notice the "little" things in life, the "unimportant" things.

5

To present effectively the theme of the importance of human life in a vast universe, Wilder uses several techniques. One such technique is a personal narrative style that allows for direct communication between writer and reader (or audience). Although Wilder wrote The Bridge of San Luis Rey in the first person, the incidents involved are seen through the eyes of one character, Brother Juniper. In the first chapter, entitled "Perhaps an Accident," Wilder writes, "You and I can see that coming from anyone but Brother Juniper this plan would be the flower of a perfect skepticism."[7] Wilder uses the first person throughout his works as a means of direct communication with the reader or audience.

Notice that all direct quotations are footnoted.

Here, the technique is explored in a third work.

In Our Town, the Stage Manager communicates directly with the audience:

> Wilder found it necessary to place the Stage Manager in control of his imaginary world in order to guide the audience. He does not instruct the audience what to think . . . he guides the audience into understanding what the action presented on stage represents.[8]

Paraphrased statements of other sources are footnoted.

6

During Our Town's run on Broadway, Wilder himself replaced Frank Craven in the role of the Stage Manager. It is appropriate that the playwright should take on the role of the Stage Manager, since that character assumes the function of the playwright himself in setting the scene, creating characters, and offering commentary on the play's events.

In The Skin of Our Teeth, Wilder once again speaks through the characters in the play. The plot of this play concerns actors and actresses performing a play called The Skin of Our Teeth. The technique of having "characters in the play played by actors who are also characters in the play" again lets Wilder, as playwright, communicate on a more personal level with the audience.[9]

Parts IV and V of the paper are omitted here.

7

Notice how all the main points are summarized in the conclusion.

The Bridge of San Luis Rey, Our Town, and The Skin of Our Teeth are not only similarly presented, but all deal with "the events of our homely daily life . . . depicted against the vast dimensions of time and place."[16] By drawing the reader or audience into the action and by using a direct personal narrative style, Wilder reminds readers of their own importance as individuals and their involvement with the human race. To Wilder the human race includes all the people who have come before and all those who will follow. He tries to give the individual a sense of being part of this continuous history through his open-ended endings.

This paragraph restates the controlling idea.

"The development in Wilder's work had not been so much on what he wanted to say as on finding an adequate way to say it."[17] Once Wilder found the theme that concerned him most, his desire to communicate his ideas and feelings led him to use the techniques he needed.

Footnotes 10–15 are omitted here because the corresponding parts of the paper are not shown.

8

Notes

[1]Thornton Wilder, Three Plays (New York: Harper & Row, 1972), p. xi.

[2]Richard H. Goldstone, Thornton Wilder: An Intimate Portrait (New York: Saturday Review Press, 1975), p. 50.

[3]Donald Haberman, The Plays of Thornton Wilder: A Critical Study (Middletown, Conn.: Wesleyan University Press, 1967), p. 68.

[4]Thornton Wilder, The Bridge of San Luis Rey (New York: Grosset and Dunlap, 1927), p. 34.

[5]Haberman, pp. 54-55.

[6]Edmund Fuller, Books with Men Behind Them (New York: Random House, 1962), p. 56.

[7]Wilder, The Bridge of San Luis Rey, p. 20.

[8]Haberman, pp. 91-92.

[9]Haberman, p. 61.

[16]Wilder, Three Plays, p. xiii.

[17]Haberman, p. 11.

A line replaces the author's name in entries for additional works by the author.

9

Bibliography

Bracy, William. "Thornton Wilder." Encyclopedia Americana. 1981 ed.

Fuller, Edmund. Books with Men Behind Them. New York: Random House, 1962.

Goldstone, Richard H. Thornton Wilder: An Intimate Portrait. New York: Saturday Review Press, 1975.

Haberman, Donald. The Plays of Thornton Wilder: A Critical Study. Middletown, Conn.: Wesleyan University Press, 1967.

Shorter, E. "Critique of The Skin of Our Teeth." Drama. Spring 1977, pp. 54-55.

Wilder, Thornton. The Bridge of San Luis Rey. New York: Grosset and Dunlap, 1927.

———. Our Town. Acting Edition. New York: Coward-McCann, 1938.

———. Three Plays. New York: Harper & Row, 1972.

CHECKLIST FOR WRITING THE RESEARCH PAPER

1. What steps have I taken to limit my topic?
2. How many sources on my topic are available?
3. Where can I find general information on my topic?
4. For what purpose and audience am I writing?
5. What is my controlling idea (working thesis statement)?
6. What questions can I ask that will help me to write a working outline?
7. What modes of writing are appropriate to my topic?
8. What information belongs on the bibliography cards?
9. What are the best ways to take notes?
10. How should I use the formal outline to help me write the first draft?
11. When should I insert the footnotes, and should I place them on the same pages as the references or on a separate sheet at the end of the paper?
12. How should I revise the first draft?
13. What should I include in the final bibliography, and what forms should I follow?
14. What format should I use for the final paper?

WRITER'S CHOICE #1

ASSIGNMENT: A reseach paper based on the work you did in Exercises 1–8 and your practice with footnote and bibliography style in Exercises 10 and 11

LENGTH: Five to eight pages

AUDIENCE: As defined in Exercise 4 and revised in Exercise 9

PURPOSE: As you stated in Exercise 4 and revised in Exercise 9

PREWRITING: You have already finished this stage by completing Exercises 1–8.

WRITING: Prepare a formal outline and follow it carefully.

REVISING: Be sure that a thesis statement introduces the paper and that the conclusion summarizes properly. Share your finished paper.

WRITER'S CHOICE #2

ASSIGNMENT: A research paper on the use of computers in schools

LENGTH: Eight to fifteen pages

AUDIENCE: Your local school board and school administrators

PURPOSE: To gather information about the uses of computers in schools and the successes and failures of computers as instructional aids

PREWRITING: Check the *Readers' Guide to Periodical Literature* and the *New York Times Index* for articles. Skim a few of your sources, and develop a controlling idea. Make a working outline, and take notes. Write a formal outline.

WRITING: Write an introduction to your paper, highlighting your thesis statement. Write the body following your formal outline. End with a conclusion that sums up the main ideas of your paper.

REVISING: Make sure that your paper covers all points on your outline. Correct any errors in spelling, capitalization, punctuation, grammar, and usage. Share your finished paper with your intended audience.

WRITER'S CHOICE #3

ASSIGNMENT: A research paper on any topic

LENGTH: Your choice

AUDIENCE: Your choice

PURPOSE: Your choice

OPTIONS:
- Choose a subject area that interests you: art, science, literature, history, music, sports, or entertainment. Then choose a topic appropriate to that subject, and limit the topic so that you can adequately cover it in the length of your paper.

CHAPTER 13 THE RESEARCH REPORT

Limiting a Topic and Beginning Research (pages 253–255)

1. Which is probably the best topic for a research paper?
   (a) animals as architects **(b)** the animal kingdom **(c)** the largest beaver dam I have ever seen **(d)** animal behavior
2. Which controlling statement could best guide research on this topic?
   (a) Certain animals have developed complex architectural skills.
   (b) Many animals construct complex and unusual living quarters.
   (c) The beaver is a skilled dam builder.
3. Which of these information sources is most relevant to the topic?
   (a) a book about various classes of animals **(b)** an interview with a scientist who has studied how termites in Africa construct enormous mounds

Gathering Information (pages 256–262) Read the following note card, and then answer the questions based on it.

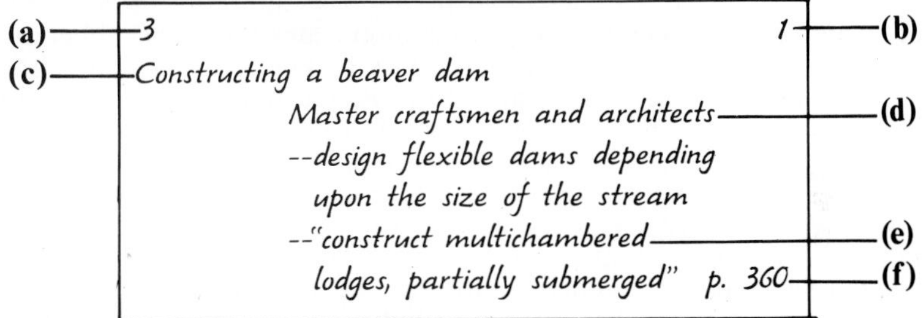

(a)
3
1
(b)
(c)
Constructing a beaver dam
Master craftsmen and architects
(d)
--design flexible dams depending
upon the size of the stream
--"construct multichambered
(e)
lodges, partially submerged" p. 360
(f)

4. Which item identifies where in the source the information is found?
5. Which item categorizes the information recorded on the card?
6. Which item identifies the source of the information?
7. Which item presents information from the source in the notetaker's own words?
8. Which item is a direct quotation from the original source?

Footnotes and Bibliography (pages 265–268)

9. Which item represents the correct footnote form for a *second* reference to a book?
   (a) [3]von Frisch, Karl, *Animal Architecture,* p. 82.
   (b) [3]von Frisch, p. 82.
   (c) [3]p. 82.
10. Which item represents the correct form for a bibliography citation?

(a) von Frisch, Karl. *Animal Architecture.* New York: Harcourt Brace Jovanovich, 1974.

(b) Karl von Frisch, *Animal Architecture,* New York: Harcourt Brace Jovanovich, 1974.

Answers: **1.** a; **2.** b; **3.** b; **4.** f; **5.** c; **6.** a; **7.** d; **8.** e; **9.** b; **10.** a

Writing for Review Choose a topic that interests you and that you can research. Limit and focus your topic, and find at least two sources about it. Then write a model note card for one source, and write footnote and bibliography entries for each source.

UNIT V
Writing Across the Curriculum

At this point in your education, you have probably written hundreds of paragraphs—and you did not write them all in English class. The variety of course work in school demands that you write well about many subjects—science, social studies, and literature, for example. In this unit you will apply your writing skills and the stages of the writing process to several specific subjects. This is what the phrase *Writing Across the Curriculum* means.

You probably find it easier to write for some subjects than for others. For example, you may be able to communicate easily the effect of a certain narrative technique in a short story by Poe or explain the underlying causes of the Revolutionary War. On the other hand, explaining the distinction between a proton, an electron, and a neutron might require more careful reading and research before you feel confident enough to write. Writing, however, is thinking on paper. In the very act of writing, while striving to express in clear, concrete language what you know or have learned about a topic, you may discover—as so many others have—that your understanding of the topic deepens. You know something truly well when you can explain it clearly and cogently to others. Conversely, nothing demonstrates more clearly your mastery of a subject, be it science, social studies, or literature, than a well-written report or essay.

Good writing should be your norm in all subject areas. Whenever you write, you should strive to achieve clarity, grace, and precision in order to make your writing an effective extension of yourself. In order to maintain a high quality of writing in all subject areas, you will find it beneficial to apply the stages of the writing process—prewriting, writing, and revising—as often as you can whenever you write, regardless of the subject area.

The four chapters in this unit will help you apply the writing process to writing about science and technology, writing about social studies and literature, and to creative writing. Although the content of each subject varies, the writing process remains the same, and the overall purpose of your writing remains the same: clear, coherent communication of your ideas to your audience.

CHAPTER 14
Writing About Social Studies

The first thing a foreigner has to try to take in about America—and it is not something automatically grasped even by all the natives—is the simple size of the place and the often warring variety of life that goes on inside it.

—Alistair Cooke, America

Social studies is the study of people living in groups and their ways of life. It includes history, geography, civics, economics, and sociology.

In this chapter you will apply the following writing skills to writing about social studies:

- prewriting: topic, audience, and purpose
- prewriting: evidence, sources, and documentation
- prewriting: making generalizations
- writing objectively
- writing chronologically
- writing about causes and effects
- writing with comparison and contrast
- revising, editing, and publishing a social studies report

PREWRITING: TOPIC, AUDIENCE, AND PURPOSE

When you write about a social studies topic, you should carefully focus your topic and clearly define your audience and purpose. You can usually focus a social studies topic by thinking specifically about the *who, what, when, where, how,* and *why* of the topic, as in this example:

industrial growth in America [*What*]
↓
industrial growth in America from 1860 to 1900 [*When*]
↓
steel industry in America from 1860 to 1900 [*What*]
↓
Andrew Carnegie's contribution to the steel industry [*Who*]
↓
Andrew Carnegie's creation of a steel monopoly [*How*]

To generate ideas, explore a subject, focus a topic, and form and develop a main idea, review the skills you learned in Chapter 2.

At this point in your life, your audience for social studies writing will most likely be your teacher. No matter who the audience is, however, always ask yourself two basic questions as part of your prewriting:

1. What does the audience need to know? (Include any terms you need to define.)
2. What kind of statements, what method of organization, and what level of diction will be most appropriate?

While prewriting you should also define your purpose clearly. Making your purpose clear will both allow your readers to follow your writing more attentively and make the writing task much easier for you. State your purpose in writing.

Objective
EXERCISE 1. Focusing a Topic in Social Studies. Choose a social studies topic from the following list, or choose a topic of your own. Ask yourself *Who?, What?, When?, Where?, How?,* and *Why?* questions to focus the topic into a manageable one for a three-paragraph paper.

- immigration in the United States
- Westward expansion in the United States
- the Civil War
- the growth of cities in the United States
- the Great Depression

Suggested Answer: immigration; *who?* immigration of eastern Europeans; *when?* immigration of eastern Europeans in the early 1900s

PREWRITING: EVIDENCE, SOURCES, AND DOCUMENTATION

Many facts are common knowledge and do not require supporting evidence. For example, you do not need to prove that Jamestown, the first successful English colony in America, was established in 1607. Yet some facts, although true, are generally unknown: For example, 144 settlers were involved in the establishment of Jamestown. Such facts as this require that a writer provide *sources* of information as **evidence.**

A **primary source** states the words of a person who was actually involved in the described event. A primary source may be a document, a personal journal, a letter, or an autobiography. A **secondary source** states the words of a person who, like a historian, has examined a primary source and then comments on it. For example, Abigail Adams, who was married to the second President of the United States, was a very vocal and strong supporter of women's rights. You can find this information in a primary source, her letters to John Adams, as in this March 31, 1776 letter:

> I long to hear that you have declared an independence—and by the way in the new Code of Laws which I suppose it will be necessary for you to make I desire you would Remember the Ladies, and be more generous and favorable to them than your ancestors. Do not put such unlimited power into the hands of the Husbands.

You can also find information about Abigail Adams's support of women's rights in a biography or a book about her—a secondary source. A primary source usually carries greater authority than a secondary source, because a primary source is closer to the event and is not secondhand information.

Documentation generally refers to providing specific source information, so that your reader can find that source. Documentation allows a reader to determine what degree of authority or importance to give your sources. If you use any sources during prewriting, keep complete and accurate records of them. Whether you use footnotes or endnotes when you write, follow the proper form described in Chapter 13, The Research Paper.

Whether you are stating your own opinion or someone else's opinion, always make clear that it is an opinion. Use an indicator like "In my opinion" or "I think that" to indicate clearly to a reader that what follows is your own opinion. When using the opinion of an expert, give the expert's authority or experience to help support the opinion, but make sure that both you and your reader are aware that it is still an opinion, not an established fact.

Objective

EXERCISE 2. Evaluating Evidence. Write whether each of the following items is a statement of fact, an opinion, a quotation from a primary source, or a statement from a secondary source.

1. a paragraph from a letter by Thomas Jefferson
2. a paragraph from *George III* by John Brooke
3. The stock market crashed in 1929.
4. The stock market crash caused the Great Depression

Answers: **1.** primary source; **2.** secondary source; **3.** fact; **4.** opinion

Objective

EXERCISE 3. Evaluating Resources for Research. Following is a list of resources on the general topic of the Great Depression of the 1930s. Explain in writing whether each resource would be useful or not useful for a social studies report on the topic.

1. a stockbroker's autobiography written during the 1930s
2. an encyclopedia article about the Depression
3. Herbert Hoover's presidential letters, from 1929 to 1932
4. an economist's article on the effects of the Great Depression.

PREWRITING: MAKING GENERALIZATIONS

Social studies writing often begins with facts and progresses toward **generalizations**—broad statements that are based on facts and may or may not be true. During prewriting you can form a *reasonable* generalization by closely examining the facts and by asking, What common elements do these facts share? For example, suppose that you gathered the following facts about events leading to war between the American colonies and Great Britain.

- The British Parliament levied a series of burdensome taxes on the colonists between 1764 and 1767, such as the Stamp Act and the Townshend Acts.
- Colonial opposition was strong, and the British, unable to enforce collection of these taxes, repealed the acts.
- George III had an inflexible, domineering attitude toward the colonies: "The Colonies must submit or triumph."
- In response to the Boston Tea Party, the British imposed a series of Intolerable Acts (as colonists termed them), which were designed to punish and restrain the people of Massachusetts.
- The colonists responded with the formation of the First Continental Congress (1774), which petitioned the king for relief from the Intolerable Acts and drew up a Declaration of Rights and Grievances.
- Massachusetts began to prepare for war. The British moved quickly to destroy the colonists' arms supplies in Lexington and Concord. The battles of Lexington and Concord (1775) were fought, and the war began.

You notice that three of the statements relate to England's attempt to control the colonists through oppressive mandates and to a ruler's inflexible attitude, and so you generalize: *England's attempt to exercise oppressive control over the American colonists was the cause of the Revolutionary War.* This generalization, however, does not account for all of the evidence in the other statements. It is a *hasty generalization* based on a first impression of the evidence. Try to avoid such broad, hasty generalizations. Instead, limit or qualify your generalizations, as in this example: *England's attempt to exercise oppressive control over the American colonists was one of the* major *causes of the Revolutionary War.*

When formulating a generalization make sure that your statement takes into account *all* of the evidence. Beware of absolute, or all-inclusive, statements, and do not hesitate to use qualifying words or phrases, such as *in most cases, one of, an important factor, some,* and *sometimes.*

Objective

EXERCISE 4. Making Generalizations. Choose a social studies topic of your own, or use one of the following topics. List at least five facts that you might collect during prewriting on that topic. Form a generalization that is supported by the facts. Refine it by using appropriate qualifying words and phrases.

1. results of inflation since World War II
2. accomplishments of labor unions in the twentieth century in the U.S.
3. the most important achievements of a famous American

WRITING OBJECTIVELY

When you write about social studies, it is important that you recognize the biases and prejudices of your sources and that your own writing be as detached, as objective, as possible. The following rules will help you to write objectively:

1. Give the facts in clear, straightforward language.
2. If you quote someone, quote *exactly* what he or she said.
3. If you are giving an opinion, label it as an opinion.
4. Watch out for judgment words. For example, use adverbs sparingly. One adverb can change a statement of fact into an opinion. For example, "The Minutemen fought at the battle of Lexington" is a fact. "The Minutemen fought valiantly" is a judgment that may or may not be justified by the evidence.
5. Avoid loaded words, words intended to evoke strong emotions in readers—for example, "*stubborn* and *inflexible* King George."

Objective

EXERCISE 5. Writing Objectively. The following paragraph is not an objective piece of writing. Revise and rewrite the paragraph, rewording any statements that are not objective.

After the Civil War a few people in American government intelligently and correctly observed the need for an expansionist policy. One of these noble champions for expansion was the Secretary of State, William M. Seward. When the Russians offered to sell Alaska to the United States for the paltry sum of $7.2 million, Seward anxiously and confidently jumped at the chance to own the huge territory. Seward probably saw the real value of the purchase and may have said to himself, "This is not only a good land value, but it is also a way to pressure the British out of Canada. Then Canada can become a part of the American empire!" Of course, a few despicable, irascible opponents called Seward's purchase a piece of worthless ice and ignorantly referred to it as "Seward's Folly."

WRITING CHRONOLOGICALLY

Social studies writing often requires that you describe events or processes in **chronological,** or time, **order.** Often it is important to tell whether one event takes place before or after another event, because the *order* of events makes a difference in determining the *significance* of each event. For example, in the following chronological description, we see a series of events related to the bonanza discovery of oil in 1859. As we learn from this account, however, oil had always been available, but it had no functional use. Only with the discovery of a distillation process, an event that preceded the 1859 major oil discovery, did oil become valuable.

> At the very start of this machine age there was something else, not an invention but a discovery, which helped transform this country from a farming republic into an industrial colossus. It began by a river in the Alleghenies, in western Pennsylvania. For a century or more Pennsylvania farmers had found their streams muddied by a kind of black glue. It turned up with good soil. First, the farmers cursed it, and then, on an old tip from the Indians, they bottled it and sold it as medicine. As early as 1849, the owner of a salt well put out the "black glue" in pocket-sized bottles with his own printed label: "Genuine petroleum. None genuine without the signature of Samuel Kier." Kier's petroleum was touted far and wide as a cure for asthma, rheumatism, gout, tuberculosis, cancer and fallen arches. . . . A man then discovered that it made a pretty good, though smelly, lighting fluid. After that came a distillation process that produced a purer liquid, almost odorless when burned—kerosene. And in 1859 came the bonanza.
>
> —Alistair Cooke, *America*

Review what you learned about chronological order in Chapter 3, Writing the Paragraph. As you write, use transitions that show the sequence of time, such as *first, after,* and *then.*

Objective

EXERCISE 6. Identifying Time Transitions. Reread the model paragraph about oil. Then identify the time transitions in the passage. Write each transition and explain how it is used to connect ideas.

Objective

EXERCISE 7. Writing Chronologically. Write a paragraph based on a series of social studies events. Describe the events in chronological order, using appropriate time transitions.

WRITING ABOUT CAUSES AND EFFECTS

Writing about causes and effects is perhaps the most common and most significant kind of social studies writing. The study of history is, after all, the study of related events. After a social studies writer identifies *what happened?* (the effect), he or she turns to the question *Why did it happen?* (the cause).

Human events usually have multiple causes and effects. For example, it would be inadequate to state, *Industrial growth accelerated during the 1860s because of favorable government policies, such as protective tariffs and cash subsidies.* Such a statement does not consider other causes related to that industrial growth, such as the invention of new technologies, the abundance of capital and labor, the construction of railroads, the immense wealth of undiscovered natural resources, and the formation of American corporations.

Also, remember that causes and effects can be short term or long term. A short-term, or immediate, cause or effect is usually a specific event that can be definitely identified. A long-term cause or effect is more difficult to identify but eventually is more important to a larger number of people. For example, one short-term effect of a recession is high unemployment, while a long-term effect is a weakened economy, which affects both the unemployed and the employed over a long period of time.

When you write about causes and effects, consider your topic from a variety of angles and ask yourself questions like these:

PERSONAL: Who was directly responsible? Who was directly affected? A single person? A group of persons? Was someone behind the scenes also responsible?

SOCIAL: What general beliefs or attitudes of the society made the event possible? In what way did the event change people's beliefs or attitudes? What system of government made the event possible? How did the event change the system of government?

ECONOMIC: What economic factors made the event possible? Who profited or lost because of the event?

Objective

EXERCISE 8. Writing About Causes and Effects. Write a paragraph about the causes or effects of a cultural or historical event. Choose an event of your own, or use one of the following. Consider the wide variety of possible causes or effects, and think carefully about the information your audience will need in order to understand completely the causes or effects of the event.

1. the invention of electricity
2. Roosevelt's New Deal policies

3. the development of nuclear arms
4. the improvement of relations between China and the United States during the 1970s and 1980s

WRITING WITH COMPARISON AND CONTRAST

Comparison is writing that describes similarities; **contrast** is writing that describes differences. Because historical and cultural events are often related, they are usually better understood when compared or contrasted with other events.

Writing a paragraph or an essay with comparison and contrast (Chapter 3, Writing the Paragraph) will be easier for you and clearer for your reader if you specifically detail the points of comparison and contrast during prewriting. Make a list, a chart, or a graph that identifies the similarities and differences between your subjects, as in this example:

Comparison/Contrast Chart

GREAT DEPRESSION OF 1784	GREAT DEPRESSION OF 1929
SIMILARITIES	
• *lasted several years* • *led to economic disaster and hardship* • *precipitated acts of open rebellion*	
DIFFERENCES	
• *caused primarily by excessive debt and overprinting of worthless paper money*	• *multiple causes--debt from World War I, agricultural slump, huge private debts, stock market speculation, and counterproductive government policies*
• *primarily hurt people in debt, particularly farmers*	• *hurt all sectors of society, rich and poor, employed and unemployed*
• *central Federal government not strong enough to control states and solve the conditions of the depression*	• *strong Federal government response during Roosevelt's first term--AAA and NRA relief programs, Federal jobs projects, 15 major recovery programs*

When you write, begin by identifying your subjects and telling your reader that you will compare and/or contrast them. Organize your paragraph or paper in one of two ways:

- in an *AAABBB* order—presenting all the points about one subject before introducing the next subject
- in an *ABABAB* order—comparing or contrasting each subject item by item

Whichever method you choose, make sure that your points of comparison are clear. You may conclude your paragraph with a general statement that summarizes your main idea and unites your points of comparison and contrast in a single, final observation. A chart like the preceding one for the two Great Depressions might evolve into the following social studies paragraph:

The Great Depression of 1784 and the Great Depression of 1929 were similar in several general ways. They both lasted several years and led to economic disaster and hardship for many Americans. During the course of each depression, the pain and suffering often translated into open acts of rebellion—Shays' Rebellion of 1787 and the Nebraska farmers with pitchforks (to drive off sheriffs with foreclosure notices) during the 1930s. Yet there were some significant differences between the two depressions. The depression of 1784 was caused primarily by excessive debt and overprinting of worthless paper money. While both public and private debt were also a cause of the 1929 depression, there were additional causes, such as the collapse of agriculture, stock market speculation, and counterproductive government policies in the tariff and tax areas. People in debt, particularly farmers, were the primary victims of the 1784 depression. In the 1930s, however, all sectors of society were hurt by the economic collapse—rich and poor, employed and unemployed, the farmer and the banker. In the 1780s the central government was weak and unable to either control the states' monetary policies or solve the depressed conditions. In the 1930s, however, a strong Federal government responded to the depression with fifteen major relief and recovery plans, such as the AAA, NRA, and the Federal jobs projects. While the depression of 1784 simply went away as the economy grew stronger, the depression of the 1930s had to be fought into submission during Roosevelt's first two terms in office.

Objective

EXERCISE 9. Writing With Comparison and Contrast. Write a paragraph comparing or contrasting two social studies subjects. You may choose one of the pairs of subjects provided or choose two subjects of your own. Research your subjects, making notes about similarities and differences between the two. Make a similarities and differences chart. Use the chart when you organize your comparison-and-contrast writing.

1. the central governments of the United States and of Canada
2. Abraham Lincoln and Franklin Roosevelt
3. inflation and recession
4. the nineteenth-century city and twentieth-century city
5. two periods in American history, such as the Civil War years and the World War II years

REVISING, EDITING, AND PUBLISHING A SOCIAL STUDIES REPORT

When you revise a paragraph, an essay, or a paper in social studies, use the basic revising skills you learned in Chapter 4, Revising the Paragraph. You should also revise with particular attention to the social studies skills you learned in this chapter. The following checklist will help you revise. Remember to edit and proofread the final version so that you can share your work with readers.

If you are writing an essay, review the special section on revising the essay in Chapter 12, The Essay. If you are writing a research report, review the section on revising in Chapter 13, The Research Report.

CHECKLIST FOR REVISING A SOCIAL STUDIES REPORT

1. What questions can I apply to the social studies topic to define and focus it—*Who?, What?, When?, Where?, How?,* or *Why?*
2. What basic social studies facts or definitions does the audience need? What statements or word choices, if any, are inappropriate to the audience? What is the purpose of this writing?
3. Is any source, primary or secondary, incorrectly or insufficiently identified? Is the proper format for documentation used in all cases?
4. What qualifying words and phrases should be used to revise any generalization?
5. Which statements are not as objective as possible? Which, if any, use unclear language, inexact quotations, unlabeled opinions, unnecessary adverbs, or loaded words?
6. Which transitions that show time can be used to make chronological statements absolutely clear?
7. Which causes and effects, if any, are not clearly identified? Which personal, social, or economic causes and effects need to be reconsidered and expanded?
8. Are any points of comparison or contrast unclear? Should any changes be made in the organization so that the point-by-point comparison or contrast will be easier for the reader to follow?

WRITER'S CHOICE #1

ASSIGNMENT: Write a comparative biographical sketch of any two of the following historical figures: Benjamin Franklin, Will Rodgers, Susan B. Anthony, Martin Luther King, Jr., Eleanor Roosevelt, Abigail Adams

LENGTH: One paragraph

AUDIENCE: Your teacher

PURPOSE: To inform and explain by comparison and contrast

PREWRITING: Make a chart of the similarities and differences between the two historical figures.

WRITING: Order your paragraph according to the *AAABBB* or the *ABABAB* structure. End with a general statement about the two figures. Use appropriate qualifying words.

REVISING: Refer to the checklist on page 286.

WRITER'S CHOICE #2

ASSIGNMENT: Choose one of the following historical events, or choose a different event that interests you. Write about the causes or the effects of the event.

- the stock market crash of 1929
- the transcontinental railroad
- the Cuban Missile Crisis

LENGTH: Your choice

AUDIENCE: Your choice

PURPOSE: To inform and explain

PREWRITING: Apply to your topic the personal, social, and economic questions listed on page 283.

WRITING: Clearly identify the short-term or long-term causes or effects you intend to discuss. Be sure to consider your topic from a variety of angles and to make your supporting details clear and relevant.

REVISING: Use the checklist on page 286. Edit your first draft, prepare a final copy, and proofread it.

WRITER'S CHOICE #3

ASSIGNMENT: A paragraph or brief essay about any social studies topic

OPTIONS: Determine your own length, audience, and purpose. You may want to refer to the Writer's Sourcebook (pages 358–361) for an idea. Use the checklist on page 286 to revise what you have written.

15 CHAPTER
Writing About Science and Technology

The most incomprehensible thing about the world is that it is comprehensible.

—Albert Einstein

From the solitary research scientist to the corporation employing thousands of technical writers, there is a continuous quest with pencil, typewriter, and word processor to make the findings of scientific and technological research comprehensible to experts and nonexperts.

Some writers address their reports to their scientific colleagues; others translate the results of their research into language that the average reader can understand. In both cases, however, the writer's purposes are the same—to further knowledge, to propose solutions to current problems, or to pose hypotheses that require additional research and investigation.

Scientific papers or technical reports follow a set format to present in clear, accurate, and concise language factual information based on research.

Writing about science and technology can be found in newspapers, in popular journals dedicated to science, and in journals and books written specifically for the scientific community. The style and organization of science writing in the popular journals resembles ordinary expository prose. In more formal research reports, however, scientific and technical writing employs a specific format and style of presentation that is different from the format and style of the research paper in literature, history, and other similar disciplines. The goal of both kinds of research report remains the same, however: the clear, coherent, and cogent presentation of information.

This chapter focuses on the various conventions for preparing scientific and technical reports and presents these conventions within the framework of the writing process:

- prewriting: finding a suitable scientific or technical topic
- prewriting: purpose and audience

- prewriting: gathering information
- writing a scientific or technical report
- revising, editing, and publishing a scientific or technical report

PREWRITING: FINDING A SUITABLE SCIENTIFIC OR TECHNICAL TOPIC

When you write a scientific or technical report, you may present information and findings from your own original research, or you may report the findings of others. In either case, the report itself must have a serious, objective **tone.** A reader looking for scientific or technical information is not interested in a writer's subjective feelings about a topic. In addition, the reader is probably looking for information and conclusions that are not readily available in other reports. You should keep the reader in mind as you generate and explore ideas for a suitable topic. Here are some examples of suitable and unsuitable topics for a scientific paper or technical report:

SUITABLE	UNSUITABLE
1. communication techniques among bees	why all students should learn about animal behavior
2. the effects of music on plant growth	the kinds of house plants I enjoy raising
3. nuclear waste disposal methods	my feelings about nuclear energy

Scientific and technical reports of course do convey the writer's beliefs and judgments, but these judgments and beliefs arise as a result of analyzing data about some feature or aspect of the natural world. The tone in analytical rather than subjective.

In this chapter you will see how a student planned and wrote a paper about nuclear waste disposal methods.

Objective

EXERCISE 1. Evaluating the Suitability of Topics. Read the following list of topics. On your paper write *suitable* if the topic is suitable for a scientific paper or technical report. Write *unsuitable* for each topic that is unsuitable, and explain why the topic is not appropriate.

1. why all students should learn to use computers
2. the mystery of animal migration patterns
3. the origins of asteroids
4. the computer as a weather-forecasting tool
5. my opinion of weather forecasters
6. the effect of ocean currents on weather
7. the joys of geology
8. how subatomic particles are detected
9. why chemistry is an interesting subject to study
10. how a violin produces musical notes

Answers: 1, 5, 7, 9, and 10—unsuitable (too subjective); 2, 3, 4, 6, and 8—suitable

Objective

EXERCISE 2. Selecting a Topic. Select one of the broad topics from the following list, or select another topic that interests you and that is suitable for a scientific or technical report. Begin to generate and explore writing ideas for your topic. Use one or more of the prewriting techniques that you learned about in Chapter 2. The purpose of this exercise is to find a topic that you will later develop into a scientific or technical report in Writer's Choice #1 on page 304.

1. the prospects of future space colonization
2. the effect of computers on education or on industry
3. acid rain: effects and solutions
4. insects as architects
5. ecological relationships
6. the use of lasers in medicine
7. the moons of Jupiter
8. how volcanos are formed
9. preservatives in food
10. the causes and effects of sunspots

PREWRITING: PURPOSE AND AUDIENCE

The main purpose of scientific or technical writing is to inform. The specific purpose of a scientific or technical report may be one of the following:

1. *to explain a process:* for example, to show how an invention works or how a scientific experiment was performed
2. *to analyze causes and effects:* for example, to explore or predict short-term or long-term consequences of a plan or project
3. *to divide and classify items:* for example, to divide a technical process into distinct parts and to study their interrelationships
4. *to define terms:* for example, to explain scientific or technical terms that are specific to a given field
5. *to compare and contrast items:* for example, to point out similarities and differences among scientific subjects or processes.

For more specific information about the types of expository writing, see Chapter 10.

In addition to determining your purpose, you must also focus on the nature and needs of your audience. Before you begin to write, ask yourself these questions:

1. Who is my audience?
2. How much do they know about my topic?
3. How interested are they in my topic?

If your audience is comprised of experts—members of a school science club, judges at a science fair, or fellow members of a research group, you can assume a more extensive level of knowledge about your topic than members of a nonexpert audience would generally possess. You can thus freely use the technical language of the field, correct in the belief that your audience will understand you. If you are writing for a nonexpert audience—people who are not trained in the field about which you are writing, be sure to explain basic concepts in language that is easy to understand. You may also find that you need to provide more of an overview rather than an in-depth analysis of a topic when you write for nonexperts. It is always wise to gauge the level of your audience's interest and knowledge as you plan your report. Telling readers more than they could ever care to know about your topic is a guaranteed way to lose their interest.

Objective

EXERCISE 3. Determining a Purpose. State a specific purpose for writing about the topic you selected in Exercise 2. Review the five kinds of purposes listed on page 290. Try to apply each of these purposes to your topic; then select one specific purpose that is appropriate for your topic. Write your purpose in a single sentence. Save your statement for Writer's Choice #1.

Objective

EXERCISE 4. Matching Audience and Writing. Read each of the following paragraphs. On your paper write *expert* if the paragraph is suitable for an audience of experts. Write *nonexpert* if the paragraph is better suited for an audience without specialized knowledge of the topic. Use specific examples from each paragraph to explain your answer.

1. This report describes some aspects of two methods of producing nuclear energy for fueling the space shuttle.
2. This report presents a study of the role of the orbiter in developing a functional space shuttle. Limited to an evaluation of potential fuels for the orbital maneuvering system, or OMS, the report will determine the efficiency of burning hypergolic monomethyl hydrazine and nitrogen tetroxide.

Objective

EXERCISE 5. Identifying Your Audience. Decide what type of audience you think would be interested in the report you have been planning in Exercises 2 and 3. Write a brief description of that audience, indicating who they are, the level of their knowldege—expert or nonexpert—about your topic, and the degree of their interest in it. Save your comments for Writer's Choice #1.

PREWRITING: GATHERING INFORMATION

The first step in gathering information about your topic is to discover what information you will need and to find the sources from which it will come. Questions such as the following will help you decide what information you will need in your report and how you will present it.

1. What problem or idea am I trying to solve or present?
2. What is the best way to solve or present it?
3. What does my audience need to know?
4. What questions do I need to answer in my report?
5. What sources will I use to find the answers?

You can begin your initial research by consulting a general reference book for an overview of your topic. Either of the following general reference works will provide topic overviews. Begin to take notes to record the data that you collect.

> *McGraw-Hill Encyclopedia of Science and Technology,* 5th ed. New York: McGraw-Hill, 1982. 15 volumes.
> *Van Nostrand's Scientific Encyclopedia,* 6th ed. New York: Van Nostrand Reinhold Co., 1983.

After consulting a general reference, try to find a major reference work for your specific topic. For example, the following reference books treat topics in specific scientific and technical fields:

> *Cambridge Encyclopedia of Astronomy.* New York: Crown Publishers, 1977. 1 volume.
> *Grzimek's Animal Life Encyclopedia.* New York: Van Nostrand Reinhold Co., 1974. 13 volumes.
> *How It Works: Illustrated Encyclopedia of Science and Technology.* London: Marshall Cavendish, Ltd., 1977. 20 volumes.
> *McGraw-Hill Encyclopedia of Environmental Sciences*, 2nd ed. New York: McGraw-Hill, 1980.

Once you have examined your sources, you should prepare a working outline to guide the rest of your research. Here is the working outline that the student prepared for his paper on nuclear waste disposal:

Nuclear Waste: Disposal Techniques and Problems

I. What nuclear waste is
II. The dangers of nuclear waste
III. Waste disposal techniques
IV. Waste disposal problems
V. Options and recommendations

Your next step is to locate specific, detailed information about your topic, especially information that relates to the items on your working outline. You may find lists of articles and books about your topic in the major reference books you read. You should also look through the library's card catalog for specific books. In addition, you should review recent volumes of periodical indexes, such as the *Readers' Guide to Periodical Literature,* to find current magazine articles. In addition to books and articles, you may be able to gather information from other sources, such as a company's product brochures, newsletters, bulletins, and research releases from manufacturers, businesses, and colleges. You might also gather firsthand knowledge of your topic by conducting interviews with appropriate professionals at local businesses and colleges.

For each promising source prepare a bibliography card and begin to take notes. For more information about these research techniques, see Chapter 13. When you have gathered enough information to begin writing, you are ready to prepare a formal outline.

Objective

EXERCISE 6. Gathering Information. Begin to research the scientific or technical topic that you selected for a report. Follow these steps during your research:

1. Ask general questions about the topic to guide your early research.
2. Check a general reference work to gather background information.
3. Prepare a working outline.
4. Locate specific sources, and begin reading and taking notes.
5. Decide whether your report would benefit from interviews and information that you would have to request by mail or telephone.
6. Prepare a formal outline.

PREWRITING: CHARTS, DIAGRAMS, AND ILLUSTRATIONS

As you research your topic, you should be aware of the value of including visual aids in your report. Scientific and technical reports often include sketches, tables, graphs, charts, and diagrams. Such aids may help you to clarify complex explanations or to simplify and summarize large amounts of data. As you gather information, try to think of ways to present it visually. When you create a visual aid, such as a graph, based on your own experiments or the work of others, remember to indicate the source of the data.

Among the kinds of visual aids you can decide to include are

- diagrams
- drawings
- photographs
- charts, graphs, and tables

Keep in mind that visual aids should be simple and clear. If you are representing a complex process, divide the process into its constituent parts and illustrate each part separately. Decide during prewriting which concepts are better presented by means of a visual aid. Later, when you are writing your report, remember to explain to your readers the meaning and implications of the information you present in this fashion.

WRITING A SCIENTIFIC OR TECHNICAL REPORT

STYLE AND TONE

A scientific or technical report should be accurate, logically developed, and unbiased. The report writer should use precise language and a serious, objective tone. First-person pronouns, such as *I* and *me,* should be avoided; third-person pronouns are more appropriate for scientific and technical writing even when you are reporting the results of your own work.

To become aware of the difference in tone between personal and impersonal styles, compare the following two examples:

THIRD PERSON: Nuclear waste is radioactive and is a dangerous by-product resulting from the splitting of atoms to produce energy.

FIRST PERSON: I am going to show that nuclear waste is radioactive and that I consider it a dangerous by-product of the splitting of atoms to produce energy.

Maintaining an objective tone and an impersonal style does not mean that you are any less committed to your ideas than is a writer who uses the first person. In fact, because a scientific or technical report is often the result of much intensive study, the writer is very eager to share those results with colleagues. As you learned in Chapter 7, Developing a Writing Style, good writers are always visible behind their words. In the example of an impersonal style that you have just read, for instance, notice the authority in the writer's voice. The writer sounds knowledgeable about the topic; the tone of the passage invites your trust. The writer presents facts—information that can be examined and verified by other members of the scientific community. The impersonal tone makes you believe that the writer's words carry weight. By comparison, the statement written in the first person sounds less confident and more open to dispute.

Objective

EXERCISE 7. Revising for Style and Tone. Rewrite the following paragraph, making corrections in word choice and tone. Make sure that your language is precise.

I believe that some insect communities have extraordinary construction and architectural talents. Some of the mound-building termites that I have studied design and construct complex living structures. Their moundlike homes contain multiple layers of chambers and interconnected passages. Some termite mounds even employ an unbelievable system of cross-ventilation, a kind of natural air-conditioning.

STRUCTURE

A scientific or technical report is usually divided into three sections. Here is a description of the three sections, which are usually labeled within the report:

Introduction

The introduction explains to the reader what general problem you intend to discuss in the paper or report and gives important background information, including the purpose of your report.

Discussion (or Body)

The discussion (or body) is the major section of the report and contains the results of your research. It focuses on facts, their relationships, and their importance.

The discussion portion of the report contains descriptions, comparisons and contrasts, analyses of causes and effects, and definitions of key concepts. For more information about writing descriptive and expository paragraphs, see Chapters 8 and 11.

Conclusions and Recommendations

This section summarizes your main ideas and states the implications of your findings. Because many scientific or technical reports analyze a specific problem, in the final section of the report, you can summarize the problem and make recommendations for solving the problem in the future.

In addition to these three major sections, a scientific paper or technical report has a number of other important features:

Title Page

The title page contains the title of the report, your name, your teacher's name, and the date.

Table of Contents

The table of contents lists in sequence all the sections of the report.

Abstract

An abstract is a one-paragraph summary of the contents of the report. The abstract provides the reader with an overview of the key points. You place the abstract on the title page below the title of the report or on a separate page just before the introduction.

Here is an example of an abstract. It is taken from the report about nuclear waste that you will read later in the chapter.

This report discusses the problem of nuclear waste. It specifically details and compares various techniques related to nuclear waste disposal. Problems relative to each technique are cited. This report does *not* recommend adoption of any single disposal technique; instead, it recommends a new commitment in time, effort, and money to analyze and refine multiple techniques for safeguarding the process of creating nuclear energy.

List of Illustrations

The list of illustrations tells your readers what visual aids your paper contains and their source.

Place the list of illustrations below the table of contents if there is room on the page. If, however, the abstract is on a separate page, the list of illustrations should be placed on a separate page following the table of contents.

Appendices

An appendix at the end may include supplementary materials that do not belong in the body of the report.

Graphs, tables, charts, and other more detailed explanations of topics that would distract from the overall coherence of your report or that would be of less interest to the nonexpert reader are often presented in the appendix. Not every scientific or technical report, however, has need of an appendix.

Bibliography

The bibliography, which lists all your sources, should be placed on a separate page with its own heading at the end of your paper. Use the formats suggested in Chapter 13.

MECHANICS

The term *mechanics* refers to the use of punctuation, capitalization, and abbreviations. The following rules or conventions should be followed in a scientific or technical report:

Abbreviations

Writers may use abbreviations in scientific or technical reports, especially to express units of measurement (for example, *mi, lb, cm*). Always spell out a unit of measure the first time it appears and also place its abbreviation in parentheses. Thereafter, the abbreviation itself is sufficient. Omit periods for units of measurement unless the abbreviation itself actually spells a word; for example, use *in.* for *inch*, not *in* without a period. Use the same abbreviation for both singular and plural references; for example, 21 *cm,* not 21 *cms.*

Numbers

In scientific or technical writing, the following rules apply to the use of numbers:

1. Write out numbers from one to ten (*eight feet*) except when using small numbers in a mathematical expression (*3 times 7*).
2. Use Arabic numerals for all numbers above ten (*27 feet*).
3. Write round numbers above one million as a combination of Arabic numerals and words (*8 billion*).
4. Use numerals to express fractions, percentages, decimals, page numbers, figures, monetary units, and exact measurements.
5. Never begin a sentence with numerals.

Documentation

Scientific papers or technical reports, unlike other research reports, do not include footnotes or endnotes. To provide information about the sources, an author–date–page number system is used. With this system you give in parentheses the author's last name, the year of publication, and the page reference when you cite the source, as in this example: (Masters, 1984, p. 162). If you use the same reference more than once, omit the date after the first citation. Remember to cite these sources in the bibliography.

Illustrations

Most scientific or technical reports use sketches, tables, and diagrams to help explain complex ideas. Number each sketch, table, or diagram, and refer to it by number in the body of the paper, as in this example: (*see Figure 2*). Place each sketch, table, and diagram on a separate page, and place its number, title, and source, if there is one, below it; for example, *Figure 2:* Core of a Nuclear Reactor.

Objective

EXERCISE 8. Analyzing a Scientific or Technical Report. In order to see how the preceding practices and conventions are observed in a report, examine the model report on pages 299–303. Write answers to the following questions.

1. How does the introduction differ from the discussion? How does the conclusions and recommendations section differ from the discussion?
2. How does the first acknowledgment of the Shapiro source differ from the other acknowledgments of that source?
3. Find one instance in which an idea rather than a direct quotation is attributed to a source.
4. What is the purpose of Figure 1?

REVISING, EDITING, AND PUBLISHING A SCIENTIFIC OR TECHNICAL REPORT

The general questions that you ask when revising a paragraph (see Chapter 4) apply also to scientific or technical writing. Such writing also requires that you ask other specific questions about your first draft of a scientific or technical report. The following questions will help you revise your work so that it fulfills your purpose and is appropriate for your audience:

CHECKLIST FOR REVISING A SCIENTIFIC OR TECHNICAL REPORT

1. What, if anything, distracts from the serious, impersonal tone of my report? Have I removed any references to personal experiences or opinions? Have I used third-person pronouns throughout?
2. What background information does the introduction provide? How well does the introduction state my general purpose and my specific purposes?
3. What, if anything, can I do to present my findings more concisely and objectively in the discussion?
4. What conclusions and recommendations have I stated? Are the conclusions and recommendations consistent with the facts presented in the introduction and the discussion?
5. What corrections, if any, do I need to make in the other elements of the report: on the title page, in the table of contents, and in the bibliography? Have all elements of mechanics been handled correctly?
6. What improvements can I make in the precision of my language?
7. What other editing should I do on a sentence-by-sentence basis?
8. How carefully have I proofread the final version?

After revising your report, you can share it with your audience. Whether your audience is your class, a teacher, a science club, or a community organization, you will be presenting a serious report that may lead to an understanding and a solution of a particular problem.

Nuclear Waste:

Disposal Techniques and Problems

David Doe*

Science 11
Ms. Williams
March 17, 19__

Table of Contents

List of Illustrations

3

Abstract

This report discusses the problem of nuclear waste. It specifically details and compares various techniques related to nuclear waste disposal. Problems relative to each technique are cited. This report does not recommend adoption of any single disposal technique; instead, it recommends a new commitment in time, effort, and money to analyze and refine multiple techniques for safeguarding the process of creating nuclear energy.

*This paper is based on research done by David Doe of Kentridge High School, Kent, Washington.

Introduction 4

Nuclear or radioactive waste is a dangerous by-product of the process of splitting atoms to produce energy. This separation of the nucleus of a heavy element, usually uranium, into two, small radioactive atoms is known as nuclear fission. (McGraw-Hill Encyclopedia of Science and Technology, 1982, ed., volume 9, p. 327.) Instead of splitting, some uranium atoms are changed into heavier atoms such as plutonium. This fissioning of uranium fuel creates heat, which in turn creates steam to drive generator turbines to produce energy. Although they do not release solid or chemical pollutants into the atmosphere, nuclear power plants do produce a radioactive waste.

The specific purposes of this paper are:

1. To clarify what nuclear waste is
2. To explain the dangers of nuclear waste
3. To analyze and compare various waste-disposal techniques and problems
4. To propose a commitment of time, effort, and money to analyze, refine, and develop methods of safeguarding the production of nuclear energy.

Discussion 5

Radioactive nuclear waste comes in various forms: liquids, solids, and gases. High-level wastes, such as cesium 137, strontium 90, and iodine 131, are formed when spent fuel containing valuable plutonium and uranium are reprocessed (Johansson, 1981, pp. 43–44). Low-level wastes include contaminated clothing, containers, filters, tools, machinery, and other items used in and around nuclear power plants. Trailings, the debris present after uranium ore is milled and mined, are also considered low-level nuclear wastes (Shapiro, 1981, pp. 8–12).

Nuclear waste contains radioisotopes that are highly toxic. Such waste poses a potential threat to living organisms and is particularly difficult to dispose of because of the very slow process of radioactive decay. The half-life, which is the time it takes a radioactive substance to dissipate to half its original strength, of iodine 131 is only eight days but is 30 years in strontium 90 and cesium 137. Some high-level wastes take centuries to dissipate to a safe level.

About one-third of the fuel assemblies, which are the rods where the rapid fissioning occurs, must be removed from the nuclear reactor core each year and replenished with fresh fuel. When it is first removed, spent fuel is

6

intensely radioactive and still generates large amounts of heat. This substance, which contains high-level wastes, is cooled by immersion in a holding tank, where it remains for several months to a year. The major controversy surrounding nuclear waste is how to dispose of it once it has cooled in the holding tanks. Several waste-disposal options have either been tried or proposed. Following is an analysis of various disposal techniques.

Partitioning and transmutation is a waste-disposal technique suggested by a number of nuclear physicists (Shapiro, pp. 226–227). Partitioning is the separation of high-level nuclear waste into shorter-lived components and far-longer-lived artificially produced elements, or transuranics. Waste disposal would be simplified because the two fractions could be stored in different facilities with varying time–storage requirements. Physicists have also suggested that transuranics could be further processed by transmitting them into stable, short-lived isotopes by bombarding them with neutrons. This technique, however, is not workable with current reactors.

7

A number of scientists have suggested sealed disposal because such sites are immune from earthquakes and remote from human habitation. High-level wastes have already been sealed in about 90,000 metal containers and dumped on the floor of the ocean; however, because of a combination of factors—corrosive marine environment, intense heat of the wastes, and underwater pressure—such containers are vulnerable and can crack and spill. Some spilled waste has already been discovered on the ocean floor and in marketable fish, which could eventually pose a threat to human life. An alternative to dumping containers is to embed them beneath selected oceanic sites, as proposed by some scientists (Hollister, 1984, p. 1325).

Deep underground disposal in salt beds is a method of disposing of nuclear waste that has already been used and is likely to be continued (Bethe, 1976, p. 28). There is, however, a danger of waste spillage because intense radioactive waste can eat through the thick concrete and steel containers and seep into the ground. In fact, recent measurements at the Maxey Flats, Kentucky, site where several million cubic feet of waste is buried in deep trenches, revealed that substantial amounts of radioactive plutonium had migrated thousands of yards through the soil (Shapiro, pp. 101–102). The government and many

8

scientists argue that underground disposal of waste can be a safe technique. Such waste could be encased in glass or ceramic canisters and buried thousands of feet below the surface in basalt, shale, granite, or salt foundations that are known to be free of earthquake, volcanic, or underground water activity. At present, however, a limited technology for utilizing this technique exists. Both scientists and environmentalists favor postponing a decision on it until there is more agreement on plans for isolating nuclear waste.

Another proposal is the reprocessing of spent fuel rods (Walker, 1983, pp. 191–192). In this plan, spent fuel could be recycled in the fission process (see Figure 1). Although reprocessing would reduce the need for developing numerous disposal techniques and sites, it would lead to the stockpiling of uranium and plutonium and to a greater risk of accidents due to the addition of a new, complicated step in the process of manufacturing nuclear fuel. In any event the risks of reprocessing spent fuel rods must be carefully analyzed in relation to the possible benefits.

9

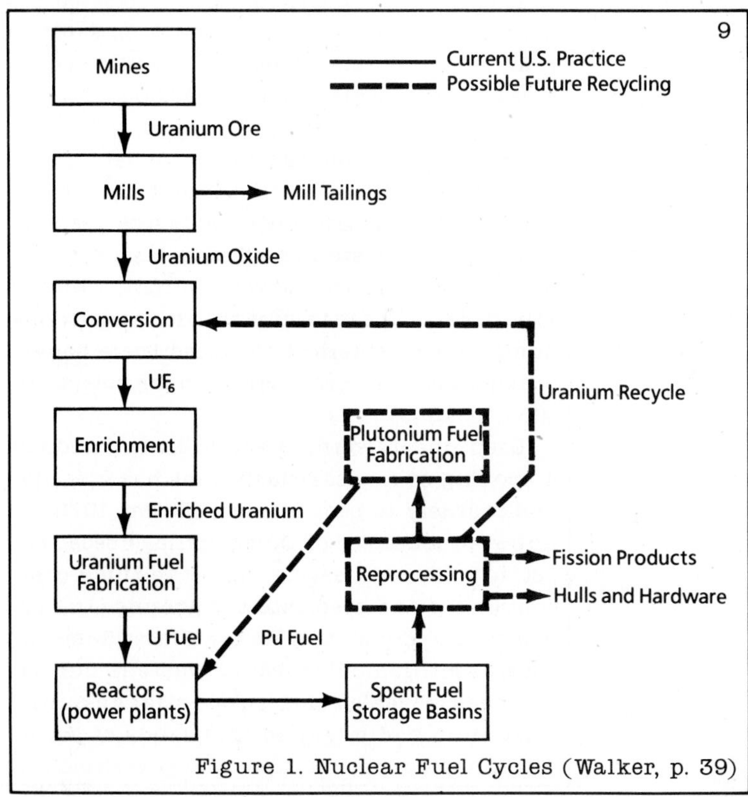

Figure 1. Nuclear Fuel Cycles (Walker, p. 39)

10

Conclusions and Recommendations

The disposal of radioactive waste, which is the deadly leftover material from the splitting of atoms to produce energy, is a complex, controversial issue. Numerous disposal techniques have been proposed: partitioning and transmutation, sealed disposal, deep underground disposal, and the reprocessing of spent fuel. It is not within the realm of this paper to recommend a specific disposal process as the ideal process. Unless it is decided that we abandon nuclear energy as an alternative energy source, then all techniques must continue to be analyzed, refined, and measured in terms of their potential risks and benefits. Much of the research and development effort and costs related to nuclear energy have been for the development of the product itself—energy. A continued utilization of that product demands that time, effort, and money be committed to safeguard the production of that product. Depending on the future energy needs of the world, a number of various nuclear waste disposal techniques may have to be carefully developed, tested, and adopted.

11

Bibliography

Bethe, H. A. "The Necessity of Fission Power." Scientific American, January 1976, pages 21–31.

Hollister, Charles D. (and others). "Seabed Disposal of Nuclear Waste." Science, January 1984, pages 1321–1326.

Johansson, Thomas B. and Steen, Peter. Radioactive Waste From Nuclear Power Plants. Berkeley, California: University of California Press, 1981.

McGraw-Hill Encyclopedia of Science and Technology. New York: McGraw-Hill, 1982 edition, volume 9, pages 309–338.

Shapiro, Fred C. Roadwaste. New York: Random House, 1981.

Walker, Charles A. (and others), editors. Too Hot to Handle? New Haven, Connecticut: Yale University Press, 1983.

WRITER'S CHOICE #1

ASSIGNMENT: A scientific or technical report based on your work in Exercises 2, 3, 5, and 6

LENGTH: 1,000 to 2,000 words

AUDIENCE: As you stated in Exercise 5

PURPOSE: As you stated in Exercise 3

PREWRITING: You have completed this stage in Exercises 2, 3, 5, and 6.

WRITING: Begin your first draft with the discussion, which should follow your formal outline. Then prepare an introduction and conclusions and recommendations. Add any illustrations you have planned. Prepare the other parts of the paper: the title page, the table of contents, the abstract, and the bibliography.

REVISING: Use the checklist on page 298 to review conventions of scientific and technical writing. Be sure to consider large issues, such as organization, as well as matters of editing and proofreading. Share your final draft.

WRITER'S CHOICE #2

ASSIGNMENT: To prepare a report comparing two or more similar technical products; for example, two televisions

LENGTH: At least four pages for the body of the report

AUDIENCE: A group unfamiliar with the products

PURPOSE: To compare and contrast the products

PREWRITING:
- Select two or more similar technical products and prepare a working outline that will help guide your research.
- Research the products by reviewing brochures, advertisements, and consumer evaluations. If possible, conduct interviews with manufacturers, sales people, or users. Prepare a bibliography card for each source.

WRITING: Prepare a first draft. Add any helpful illustrations, charts, or diagrams. Prepare the title page, table of contents, an abstract, any appendices you may need, and the bibliography.

REVISING: Use the checklist on page 298 as you revise your paper. Share the final draft with your audience.

WRITER'S CHOICE #3

ASSIGNMENT: To write a brief pamphlet describing the role of satellites in television transmission

LENGTH: Two or three pages for the discussion

AUDIENCE: Your classmates who are not familiar with how a TV signal is transmitted

PURPOSE: To illustrate and describe the transmission of a TV signal so that your readers will have no problem understanding how it is received into their homes

PREWRITING: Begin with a general reference work about satellites. You may wish to select a specific broadcast or cable TV network that uses satellites to transmit its signals. Prepare a working outline. For additional information, you can contact a local television station (broadcast or cable) and ask to speak with the public affairs office. You may also look for information in the *Readers' Guide to Periodical Literature.* Make sure to write a bibliography card for each source and take thorough notes as you read or talk to people.

WRITING: Prepare a first draft. Start with the body of the report. Then prepare the introduction and conclusions. Add illustrations and then prepare the other parts: title page, table of contents, abstract, list of illustrations, appendices, bibliography, and glossary.

REVISING: Use the checklist on page 298 to make sure that you have followed the rules for scientific and technical writing. Be sure to consider large issues such as organization as well as matters of editing and proofreading. It is in the revising that your paper becomes clear and as concise as it can be. When your final draft is ready, share it with your audience.

WRITER'S CHOICE #4

ASSIGNMENT: To prepare a report about the results of a scientific experiment that you have performed

LENGTH: Two to three pages for the discussion

OPTIONS:
- Choose an experiment that you have already performed in science class under the supervision of your teacher.
- Be sure to report results of your experiment in objective language.
- Include visual aids wherever they are needed to make your report clearer or more complete.
- Use the checklist on page 298 to make sure that you have followed the rules for scientific and technical writing.

WRITER'S CHOICE #5

ASSIGNMENT: To write a scientific paper or technical report on a topic of your choice

LENGTH: Your choice

OPTIONS:
- You may find a writing idea by looking in the Writer's Sourcebook, pages 362–365.
- You may want to discuss your choice of topic with your science teacher.

16 CHAPTER Writing About Literature

Literature, clearly, does not exist in a vacuum. It feeds on life and life feeds on it. . . . The keenest enjoyment of literature . . . derives from a sense of the continuing dialectic (interplay) between the formal aspects of art and the raw . . . reality that is the stuff of art.

—Cleanth Brooks, R. W. B. Lewis, and Robert Penn Warren

When you read literature, your first pleasure probably comes from your sense of how the work captures real life—recognizable people, places, events, feelings, images. Then you begin to think about what the work means—the insight into life communicated by the writer. When you write about literature, you focus on both the insight that the writer presents and the techniques that he or she has used to express that insight. In short, you explore the relationship between the "raw reality that is the stuff of art" and the "formal aspects of art" that allow the writer to shape this raw reality and give it meaning.

The following pages will give you practice in these skills:

- prewriting, writing, and revising a paper about a short story or novel
- prewriting, writing, and revising a paper about a dramatic scene
- prewriting, writing, and revising a paper about two poems

Your purpose will be to explain the meaning of each work and the techniques used to present that meaning. Sometimes your purpose will also be to evaluate the significance of the work in a book review.

WRITING ABOUT A SHORT STORY OR NOVEL

PREWRITING: FIRST RESPONSES TO A SHORT STORY OR NOVEL

If you are writing about a story, read it several times. During your first reading concentrate on the characters and the plot or events of the story. If you are writing about a novel, read it carefully the first time and then reread the most significant portions. Decide on your basic reaction to the work, and think about what the author's intention may have been in writing it.

Next, freewrite or brainstorm about your initial reaction to the work. Following is some freewriting based on a reading of Thomas Wolfe's short story "The Far and the Near." You will find Wolfe's story beginning on page 366 in the Writer's Sourcebook. Read the story before you look at the freewriting here.

> *Twenty years of building curiosity. Twenty years of building a comfortable image of those two women from far off. Then the engineer tried to get close. Why? Maybe to capture something beautiful forever? One thing for sure--the reality of the near destroyed the illusion of the far.*

PREWRITING: EXPLORING A STORY OR NOVEL

After stating your initial impression, you can begin to analyze why you reacted as you did and what the author's intention may have been. To help you analyze the parts of a short story or a novel, review the main elements of a work of fiction.

1. The **plot** is the sequence of events. The plot usually revolves around a **conflict**—a problem or struggle of some kind. The plot builds to a **climax,** or high point; after the climax, the conflict is resolved. Both stories and novels follow this pattern, but novels usually include several subplots related to the novel's main action.
2. We understand the **characters** in a work through their actions, words, the comments of other characters, and the comments of the narrator. Characters may be **flat** or **round**—that is, simple or highly developed. Characters who change are **dynamic;** those who remain the same are **static.**
3. The **setting** is the time and place of the action. The setting often creates an atmosphere, or mood, that colors the whole work.
4. The **point of view** of a short story or a novel is the relationship between the narrator, or storyteller, and the narrative. Some stories and novels are told from the **first-person** point of view—through the voice of a character. Others are told from a **limited third-person** point of view, in which the narrator relates the thoughts of only one character but speaks in the third person. Still others use an **omniscient,** or all-knowing, point of view, in which the narrator states the thoughts of all the characters.
5. The **tone** is the author's attitude toward the events and characters.
6. The **theme** is the underlying idea about life or impression of life conveyed by the work's events, characters, setting, point of view, and tone. A short story usually focuses on one theme. A novel, however, often communicates several themes.

You can explore short stories and novels by focusing on their elements with questions like the following ones. The sample answers here are based on "The Far and the Near."

QUESTIONS TO EXPLORE A SHORT STORY OR A NOVEL	SAMPLE ANSWERS FOR "THE FAR AND THE NEAR"
1. What is the main conflict?	*The engineer has constructed a fond, comforting image of two women from a distance. Close-up, he discovers that this image was an illusion.*
2. What is the climax?	*The engineer's awkward meeting with the unfriendly mother and daughter.*
3. How is the conflict resolved?	*The engineer realizes that the illusion he cherished is lost forever. He suddenly feels old.*
4. How would I describe the main characters? Are they sympathetic? Why, or why not?	*Engineer: sympathetic--old, wise, sensitive, seems lonely (his need for the image of the women)* *Two women: likable from afar, but restrained and suspicious up close--unsympathetic*
5. Describe the setting and atmosphere?	*The story takes place near a small American town. Seen from a train, everything seems pleasant; closer up, the setting becomes harsh and strange to the engineer.*
6. From what point of view is the story told?	*Limited third-person, through the eyes of the engineer.*
7. What tone does the author take toward characters and events?	*Shifts from a sense of romantic enrapture to a tone of despondent disillusionment.*
8. How would I state the theme, or underlying idea?	*What we idealize from a distance loses its wonder forever when we see it close.*

PREWRITING: MAIN IDEA AND SUPPORT

After exploring your ideas about the work, decide on the main idea you will present. State the work's theme and indicate the elements that most clearly convey that theme, as in this example:

In "The Far and the Near" the central character's changing relationship to the setting develops the theme of the passage from romantic vision to grim reality.

Objective

EXERCISE 1. Prewriting for an Essay About a Short Story or Novel. Plan to write an essay about a short story or novel of your own choosing. Begin by reading the work several times. Freewrite or brainstorm about your response to it. Then write your answers to exploring questions like those shown on page 308. Finally use your answers to these questions to help you state in writing your main idea.

WRITING ABOUT A SHORT STORY OR NOVEL: THE FIRST DRAFT

You should organize your response to a story or to a novel into several paragraphs. You might write those paragraphs in the following way:

Introduction and Thesis Statement

The introductory paragraph should contain your thesis statement, which expresses the main idea of your paper. Your thesis statement should indicate what you think the work's theme is and which literary elements you think contribute most to that theme.

Body

Write the body of your paper next. Here you should focus on the elements that you feel contribute most to the work's theme. Each paragraph should discuss a single element and should have its own topic sentence stating the paragraph's main idea.

Quotations

Back up your statements, using quotations from the short story or novel. Integrate quotations shorter than five lines into your text, enclosing them in quotation marks. Set quotations of five lines or more apart from the text by skipping a line, indenting, and single-spacing the quotation. You do not need to use quotation marks when you set a quotation apart in this way.

Conclusion

Conclude your paper with a paragraph that refers once more to your main idea. You might end with a clincher that expresses your overall response to the story or novel.

You can also apply these suggestions to responses that are only a paragraph long. If you are limited to a paragraph, begin with a strong topic sentence. Each of your following sentences should develop and support one aspect of the topic sentence.

The following paper analyzes "The Far and the Near." Note how the writer's prewriting feeds into this analysis.

"The Far and the Near"

Thesis statement expresses the theme and focuses on setting.

Thomas Wolfe's story "The Far and the Near" turns on a shift in perspective. In this story the main character's changing relationship to the setting conveys Wolfe's insight about life: that what we idealize from a distance may lose its wonder forever once we see it close.

Body paragraph 1 discusses the setting in the first part of the story.

The story falls into two parts. In the first section Wolfe introduces the central character, a railroad engineer. For twenty years this man has passed a "tidy little cottage" situated just outside a small town. As he passes every day the cottage in his train, he blows the whistle, and a mother and daughter wave back to him in a warm, friendly way. From the distance of the train, this man gradually constructs a tender, idealized image of the scene and the two figures. The cottage takes on "an air of tidiness, thrift, and modest comfort." The romantic setting dominates all, as the two women become "fixed" in the engineer's mind ". . . as something beautiful and enduring, something beyond all change and ruin and something that would always be the same. . . ."

Note the use of quotations to support ideas. Also note the format for short prose quotations.

Body paragraph 2 discusses the change in the setting, its effect on the main character, and its contribution to the theme.

The second part of the story shifts from the "far" to the "near" perspective. Upon retirement the engineer decides to visit the two women, perhaps to affirm his romantic vision. The visit is, however, a confrontation with a reality that turns out to be harsh. When seen close up, the quaint village and cottage suddenly strike the engineer as "unfamiliar," "strange," and "ugly." What had from a distance been a warm, familiar relationship between the engineer and the women becomes awkward and strange in their actual meeting. The engineer suddenly "knew that he was an old man," for he had lost his last illusion, the dream that somewhere in the world there existed a serene and shining place, "the imagined corner of that small good universe of hope's desire."

The concluding paragraph ends with a clincher.

Wolfe controls everything in this story through his selection of descriptive detail. As the details of the setting shift from "far" to "near," we and the story's main character pass from a romantic image to the grim truth. At the heart of the story, the near reality shatters the far illusion. The engineer learns that, in the real world, nothing remains "beautiful and enduring" and nothing is safe from "change and ruin"—including our most cherished dreams.

REVISING A PAPER ABOUT A SHORT STORY OR NOVEL

Before revising your first draft, set it aside for a while. Then revise it, edit it, and proofread it, answering these questions:

1. Which sentence is my thesis statement? How can it state the story's theme more clearly?
2. Are the ideas expressed in my thesis statement then taken up in the following paragraphs, with a topic sentence for each?
3. Each time I discuss one of the story's elements, what details from the story do I use? According to my paper, how does each element contribute to the theme?
4. What transitions and other techniques do I use to create effective, clear movement among sentences and between paragraphs?
5. How can I rewrite the ending to conclude in a more satisfactory, memorable way?

Objective

EXERCISE 2. Writing and Revising a Paper About a Short Story or Novel. Using the work you did for Exercise 1, write about the story or novel you have chosen. Include a thesis statement expressing your idea about the work's theme and identifying the elements that you think contribute most to that theme. Be sure to discuss each element mentioned in your thesis statement; make your writing coherent by using transitions and other devices. End by restating your main idea.

WRITING ABOUT A DRAMATIC SCENE

You can interpret a drama, or play, by focusing upon a single scene within it and telling how it advances the action, reveals the characters, and contributes to the themes developed throughout the play. Analyzed here will be a scene toward the end of William Gibson's *The Miracle Worker.* The play discloses how Annie Sullivan taught her pupil Helen Keller, who had been blind and deaf from the age of two, to communicate with the outside world. Read the scene, which begins on page 368 of the Writer's Sourcebook.

PREWRITING: FIRST RESPONSES TO A DRAMATIC SCENE

You should carefully read the entire play before writing about an individual scene. Then read your scene aloud, preferably with others taking different roles, to develop a feeling for the characters and the action. Then think about how the scene fits into the entire play. Next, freewrite or brainstorm about the scene.

PREWRITING: EXPLORING A DRAMATIC SCENE

Now begin to explore what is going on in the scene, and determine what it contributes to the play as whole. The following review of the basic elements of drama will help you explore the characters and action in your scene.

1. A play is made up of **dialogue**—the speeches of the characters—and **stage directions**—descriptions of the characters, setting, and action.
2. Like a story, a play presents a **plot,** a series of connected events. Each scene focuses on one event in the plot.
3. We understand the **characters** in a drama through their words and behavior and through others' treatment of them. Some characters are **flat,** developed around a single trait. Other characters are **round,** possessing a variety of traits.
4. Each scene in a play discloses some **conflict** between characters or within one character. The conflict arises when the characters pursue conflicting goals or when the goals of a particular character are contradictory.
5. The **setting** is the time and place in which the scene occurs. Setting influences a scene's characters and actions.
6. A play usually presents several **themes,** or ideas about life. One scene may develop one or more of these themes.

You can explore a particular scene by asking questions like the following. The sample answers for the scene from *The Miracle Worker* show how one reader analyzed the characters and action in the scene.

QUESTIONS TO EXPLORE A SCENE	SAMPLE ANSWERS FOR ACT 3 FROM *THE MIRACLE WORKER*
1. What happens in the scene?	*The Keller family and Annie are at a homecoming dinner celebrating Helen's return to the house. Helen repeatedly misbehaves to test Annie's will. Finally, Annie pulls Helen outside to the pump to refill the pitcher she had spilled. As the water flows, Annie spells w, a, t, e, r into the girl's palm, and suddenly Helen understands that words stand for real things. She discovers that she can communicate with other people.*
2. What is each character like? What is the goal of each?	*Helen: a willful, frustrated child, almost like a small animal, caged by her handicaps. Her goal is to rid herself of her teacher's demands. Annie: strong-willed and single-minded. Her goal is to force Helen out of her cage.*

QUESTIONS TO EXPLORE A SCENE	SAMPLE ANSWERS FOR ACT 3 FROM *THE MIRACLE WORKER*
3. What conflict occurs between characters? How is it resolved? Does conflict occur within a character?	*Conflict between Helen and Annie occurs when Helen tests her teacher. Annie will not allow Helen to slip back into the protective and undemanding hands of her family. The conflict is resolved when Helen finally discovers at the pump that words refer to real things. Helen finally understands and appreciates what Annie has been doing for her by trying to teach her language.*
4. What is the scene's setting? How might the setting affect the character?	*The setting of the scene is the Keller dining room and then the pump outside. The water at the pump triggers an old association for Helen, thus bringing about her breakthrough.*
5. Does the scene develop any of the themes of the whole play?	*Through dedication and love, Annie Sullivan teaches Helen that language can free her from her prison by allowing her to communicate as a human being.*

PREWRITING: MAIN IDEA AND SUPPORT

Once you have answered your exploring questions, decide on the main idea you want to communicate to readers. Then write a statement about how the scene contributes to the play as a whole:

> This scene from the final act of *The Miracle Worker* is important because it shows how the love and tenacious persistence of a dedicated teacher finally frees her pupil and allows her to become a full human being.

Objective

EXERCISE 3. Prewriting for a Paper About a Dramatic Scene. Plan to write a short paper about another scene from *The Miracle Worker* or from a play of your own choice. Begin by reading the whole work. Then read the scene aloud. Freewrite or brainstorm about your response to the scene. Then write your answers to exploring questions like those on pages 312–313. Finally, use your answers to help you state in writing your main idea about the scene.

WRITING ABOUT A DRAMATIC SCENE: THE FIRST DRAFT

In your introductory paragraph identify the scene and the play from which it comes. End your introductory paragraph with a thesis statement indicating why you think the scene is significant and what it contributes to the play as a whole.

Your first body paragraph should grow out of your thesis statement. Summarize the action of the scene, and briefly sketch the characters. You will then focus on the most important character or characters in the scene, noting any statements of actions that reveal personality traits, goals, and conflicts.

When you quote the words of a single character in a scene, integrate the quotation into your text. If the quotation is in prose, follow the format presented on page 310. If the quotation is in verse, follow the format illustrated on page 319. When you are quoting an exchange involving several characters, however, always set the quoted material apart as on page 315.

End with a paragraph that relates the scene to the whole play. You might state the scene's most important contribution to the play's central theme.

The following paper discusses a scene from the final act of *The Miracle Worker.* Notice how the writer used the exploring questions and main idea to write this paper.

The Final Scene in *The Miracle Worker*

The introduction identifies the play and in its final sentence, the thesis statement, explains how the scene fits into it.

William Gibson's *The Miracle Worker* is based on the early life of Helen Keller, a noted American author and lecturer, who was blind and deaf from the age of two. The play reveals how Annie Sullivan, her dedicated and persistent teacher, worked tirelessly to teach Helen language by spelling words into her hand. Helen, however, would not associate the touches with the real objects that they represented. She preferred to live undisturbed in her dark, silent prison. The final scene in the play is important because it shows how the love and persistence of a dedicated teacher finally free Helen from her prison.

Body paragraph 1 summarizes the first part of scene and describes the characters.

The scene opens in the dining room of the Keller house. The family has sat down to a homecoming dinner for Helen, who has returned from several weeks of seclusion with Annie. Up to this point in the play, Helen has resisted her teacher's efforts to teach her language. Helen is a violent, spoiled child, a kind of unruly pet to the Kellers. At dinner Helen repeatedly tests her teacher by disobeying her, as her parents try to excuse her behavior.

Body paragraph 2 summarizes the action,

As the scene progresses, the conflict between Annie and Helen builds. The teacher cannot bear to let Helen slip back into the protective custody of her parents, who

conflict, and resolution.

would allow the child to remain less than a human being. Kate, her mother, finally realizes that Helen deserves a human life. Reluctantly, she surrenders her child:

Note the format for quoting dialogue.

KATE. [*low*] Take her, Miss Annie.
ANNIE. Thank you.

The concluding paragraph restates the main idea and ends with a clincher sentence.

From this point on, Helen cannot rely upon her family's protection, and the teacher's persistence prevails. Annie pulls Helen into the yard to make her refill a water pitcher that had been spilled. As the water from the pump in the yard flows over Helen's hand, Annie spells the word *water* into the child's palm. And then "the miracle happens." For the first time Helen understands that the touches stand for a word and that the word represents the sensation that she feels. Led by her teacher's love and persistence, Helen finally breaks free from her dark, silent prison to become, for the first time, a fully human being.

REVISING, EDITING, AND PUBLISHING A PAPER ABOUT A DRAMATIC SCENE

The following questions focus on revising and editing a paper about a dramatic scene. For additional reminders about revising a paper about any literary work, see page 311.

1. Where do I identify the scene and the play from which it comes?
2. Where do I mention the scene's contribution to the play? How may I state this idea more clearly?
3. How might I summarize the action of the scene more clearly and succinctly?
4. When I discuss each character, what examples do I use of that character's speech and behavior?
5. Have I used the correct format for quoting dialogue? Have I remembered to identify each speaker?

Objective

EXERCISE 4. Writing and Revising a Paper About a Dramatic Scene. Using your work in Exercise 3, write a short paper about the scene you chose from *The Miracle Worker* or from another play. Be sure to include a thesis statement that expresses your idea about how the scene fits into the play. Summarize the action in the scene and discuss the characters, quoting their significant statements. End by restating your main idea in an interesting way.

WRITING ABOUT POETRY

A good way to understand a poem is to compare it with another poem that deals with a similar subject. Each poem may help you see something new about the other one. When you compare two poems, you consider the principal similarities and differences you see in the poems.

PREWRITING: COMPARING AND CONTRASTING TWO POEMS

Begin by reading both poems aloud several times, focusing on what happens in each. Then try freewriting or brainstorming about the similarities and differences of the poems. If you decide to brainstorm, you may find the technique of clustering particularly helpful (see Chapter 2). Following is an example of brainstorming with the clustering technique. The poems being analyzed are "The Secret Heart" by Robert P. Tristram Coffin and "Those Winter Sundays" by Robert Hayden. Before you read the example, look at the two poems, which appear on page 370 in the Writer's Sourcebook.

Brainstorming: Clustering Technique

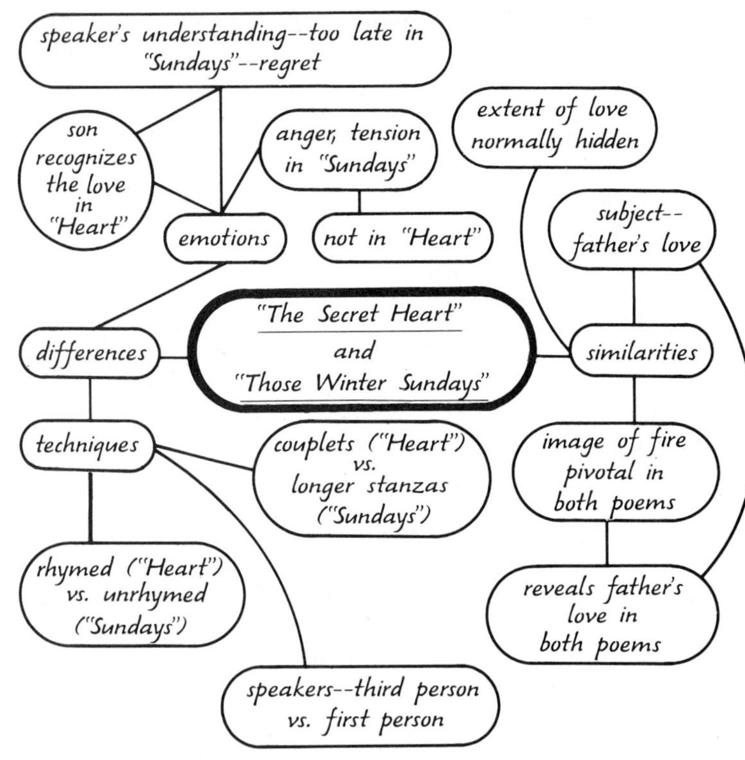

PREWRITING: EXPLORING POEMS

Once you have brainstormed, you can think more specifically about how the poets created their respective poems. Here is a brief review of the techniques that poets use to shape meaning:

1. The **speaker** of the poem is the voice we hear in the poem. Sometimes the speaker is the poet; sometimes the speaker is a character created by the poet.
2. The poet may use any number of sound effects, including the **repetition** of certain words or phrases; **rhyme**—the repetition of similar sounds; **rhythm**—the pattern of stressed and unstressed syllables; **onomatopoeia**—the imitation of a sound by a word or phrase; **alliteration**—the repetition of initial consonant sounds; **consonance**—the repetition of internal consonant sounds; and **assonance**—the repetition of vowel sounds.
3. A poem's **images** are its concrete sensory details.
4. **Figurative language** creates meaning by extending the literal facts. A **simile** compares two unlike items, using the word *like* or *as*. A **metaphor** compares two unlike items, without using these words. **Personification** describes an animal or object as if it had human traits.

You can explore two poems by asking questions that compare and contrast different aspects of the poems, as in this example.

QUESTIONS TO COMPARE AND CONTRAST TWO POEMS	SAMPLE ANSWERS FOR "THE SECRET HEART" AND "THOSE WINTER SUNDAYS"
1. Who is the speaker in each poem? What is each speaker doing?	*In "Those Winter Sundays" the speaker is a son who is reminiscing about his father's love.* *In "Secret Heart" the speaker is a third-person narrator who relates a son's memory of his father's love.*
2. What ideas and feelings are emphasized in each poem? How do they differ?	*In "The Secret Heart" the father's unspoken love is revealed by his appearance at the bedside of his sleeping son. The son glimpses and cherishes that sight.* *In "Those Winter Sundays" the father reveals his unspoken love for his family by making a fire for them. His son regrets that he did not recognize his father's love until years later.*

QUESTIONS TO COMPARE AND CONTRAST TWO POEMS	SAMPLE ANSWERS FOR "THE SECRET HEART" AND "THOSE WINTER SUNDAYS"
3. What images and figures of speech convey the main ideas in each poem?	*"Secret Heart": struck match, kindled spark, father's hands curved like a heart--a symbol of father's love for his son.* *"Winter Sundays": aching, "cracked" hands that bank a blazing fire--symbol of father's love, as he works to provide warmth for his family.*
4. What is the rhythm and rhyme of each poem? How do they contribute to the meaning of each?	*"Secret Heart": Rhymed couplets, fast-paced rhythm moves quickly through the poem, reinforcing the brief, fleeting glimpse the boy has of his father's hidden love.* *"Winter Sundays": no rhyme. First twelve lines use the rhythm of daily speech; last two lines include a repeated phrase and a formal question. Contrast highlights the importance of that final question.*

PREWRITING: MAIN IDEA AND SUPPORT

After answering exploring questions, decide on the main idea that you will present. Because you are comparing two poems, your main idea should focus on a major similarity or difference between them, as in this example:

> Although "The Secret Heart" and "Those Winter Sundays" express different emotions and have different speakers and poetic structures, both poems use the symbol of fire to express a father's hidden love for his child.

Objective

EXERCISE 5. Prewriting for a Paper About Two Poems. Plan to write about two poems of your own choice. Begin by reading the poems several times. Try brainstorming about the poems' similarities and differences. Then write answers to exploring questions like those on pages 317–318. Using your brainstorming and exploring notes, write your main idea about a major similarity (or difference) between the poems.

WRITING ABOUT TWO POEMS: THE FIRST DRAFT

The suggestions here apply specifically to writing a paper about two poems. For additional help in writing a paper about a literary work, see page 309.

When you write about two poems, you thesis statement should indicate the similarities and differences you see in the two poems. In the body paragraphs you can either analyze each poem separately or cover the similarities between the poems and then discuss their differences. In your concluding paragraph summarize your preceding discussion and end with a clincher sentence.

When quoting from a poem, be sure to quote exactly and to use the poet's original capitalization and line breaks. Integrate poetry quotations of three lines or less into your text, enclosing such short quotations in quotation marks, and marking ends of lines with a slash as in this example: "One instant, it lit all about, / And then the secret heart went out." Set quotations of four or more lines apart from text by skipping a line, and indenting and single-spacing the quotation. When setting a quotation apart in this way, you do not need to use quotation marks.

The following paper compares "The Secret Heart" and "Those Winter Sundays." Note how the writer used brainstorming, exploring questions, and main idea notes in writing this paper.

"The Secret Heart" and "Those Winter Sundays"

The thesis statement cites several contrasts between the two poems.

Robert P. Tristam Coffin's "The Secret Heart" and Robert Hayden's "Those Winter Sundays" are very different poems expressing different emotions through different speakers and poetic structures. Yet both poems focus on a father's unexpressed, hidden love, in both cases symbolized by the warmth of a flame.

Body paragraph 1 focuses on "The Secret Heart." Note the format for short quotations of poetry.

Coffin's "The Secret Heart" is a reminiscence of a simple incident in the life of a young boy: "Across the years he could recall/His father one way best of all." That "one way" is a bedside image he carries of his father, who late one night strikes ". . . a match to see/If his son slept peacefully." As the match glows in his father's cupped hands, the hands curve into ". . . the semblance of a heart." In this single action and image he glimpses his father's normally hidden love, "A bare heart on his hidden one. . . ." This single, strong image and symbol of a father's flaring yet unexpressed love for his son is further developed by Coffin's poetic structure. The rhymed couplet's and fast-paced rhythm move the poem along quickly, thus reinforcing the brevity of this boy's passing glimpse into his father's hidden heart and love.

Robert Hayden's "Those Winter Sundays" is also a reminiscence that focuses on a father's hidden love.

Body paragraph 2 focuses on theme, image or symbols, action, and poetic structure of the second poem.

Throughout the first twelve lines of the poem, Hayden builds an image of a tense home life (". . . chronic angers of that house"), an uncommunicative family ("Speaking indifferently to him"), and an unappreciated yet dutiful father ("No one ever thanked him"). The central symbol of the poem is the blazing fire that the father builds on cold mornings. He builds it with " . . . cracked hands that ached/from labor in the weekday weather. . . ." Hayden implies that the father's love for his family is unspoken; however, the father expresses his love by providing for their physical needs. The final two lines, with pounding repetition, force us to recognize the son's regret for his late recognition of his father's love: "What did I know, what did I know/of love's austere and lonely offices?"

The concluding paragraph ends with a clincher sentence.

Each of these poems has a different speaker and structure, and each expresses different emotions. Coffin's speaker is removed, and the poem passes quickly through a brief glimpse of a father's love. Hayden's speaker, the son himself, regrets his agonizingly late recognition of his father's love. Both poems, however, use the image and symbol of fire to illuminate a father's hidden heart.

REVISING, EDITING, AND PUBLISHING A PAPER ABOUT TWO POEMS

The following questions focus on revising a paper about a poem. For additional reminders about revising a paper on a literary work, see page 311.

1. Where do I state my idea about the meaning of each poem?
2. What specific poetic techniques do I discuss? How do the techniques contribute to each poem's meaning?
3. Which method of organization did I choose? Are the similarities and differences in the two poems presented clearly?
4. When I quote from a poem, do I write the words and lines exactly as the poet did?

Objective

EXERCISE 6. Writing and Revising a Paper About Two Poems. Using the work you did for Exercise 5, write a short paper about the two poems you chose. Be sure to include a thesis statement expressing the major similarities or differences between the poems. Decide whether to discuss each poem separately or whether to alternate, mentioning both poems for each point you raise. End by restating your main idea in an interesting way.

WRITER'S CHOICE #1

ASSIGNMENT: To write a review of a play
LENGTH: Your choice
AUDIENCE: General readership of a local newspaper
PURPOSE: To convince your readers that the play you are reviewing has a direct application to their lives
PREWRITING: Choose a play that interests you. Then choose a scene that reflects the major theme(s), action, and character conflict within the play. Freewrite or brainstorm about the scene, and ask exploring questions about it.
WRITING: Write your interpretation, relating it to modern life and presenting your favorable impression of the play. Conclude with a memorable clincher sentence.
REVISING: Be sure that your view of the play is clearly stated and that you have made no mistakes in grammar, usage, spelling, and punctuation.

WRITER'S CHOICE #2

ASSIGNMENT: To write a letter about a short story or a novel
LENGTH: Your choice
AUDIENCE: Your classmates and teacher
PURPOSE: To persuade them that your class should study the short story or novel
OPTIONS:
- You may want to write further about one of the works discussed in this chapter, or you may want to choose a short story or a novel that you recently read outside of class assignment.
- Be sure that your persuasive paper expresses your interpretation of the work and mentions why you think other students would benefit from reading it.

WRITER'S CHOICE #3

ASSIGNMENT: To compare two stories, scenes, or poems
LENGTH: Your choice
AUDIENCE: Your choice
PURPOSE: Your choice
OPTIONS:
- You may want to compare a work of your own choosing with one of the works you have read or written about in this chapter.
- Be sure to choose two works that have something in common. For example, you might compare "The Secret Heart" with another poem in which a child reminisces about a father or a mother.

17 CHAPTER
Creative Writing

The idea is to get the pencil moving quickly. . . . To write a scene, work up a feeling: ride in on it.

—Bernard Malamud

The process that leads to creative writing is different for every writer. In the opening quotation, Bernard Malamud suggests that the process begins with a feeling that the writer follows by riding on it as a surfer rides a wave. For some writers, a rigidly worked-out plan inhibits the creative imagination; these writers might not know how a scene will end before they start to write. Other writers begin by studying some place, person, or situation, which they then reinvent and re-create, eventually shaping a new reality.

is writing in which an author invents characters, situations, images, and emotions and puts these inventions into stories, novels, plays, and poems.

This chapter will provide you with several different ways of stimulating your creative imagination. You will focus on the following areas of creative writing:

- prewriting: purpose and audience
- writing a short story
- writing a dramatic scene
- writing a poem

PREWRITING: PURPOSE AND AUDIENCE

Although the general **purpose** of all creative writing is to entertain, you should also have a more specific purpose. You might want to make your audience laugh or cry, or you might want to share some event that has a special meaning for you.

Like all other kinds of writing, creative writing is done for a specific audience; the audience you choose will determine your style and presentation. A story for young children, for instance, will require a simpler treatment than will a story for your classmates. If you were writing for people your own age, you would write at the level of diction you use in speaking.

Objective

EXERCISE 1. Exploring Purpose and Audience. Think of a subject for a story and brainstorm for ten minutes about what aspects of it might interest each of three different audiences: second graders, teenagers, and adults. Generate ideas suitable for each audience. Then for each set of ideas write a specific purpose.

WRITING A SHORT STORY

Ideas for short stories are all around you. They may come from your own experiences, from fragments of overheard conversation, or from people you see on the street. All stories, however, will contain the same basic elements:

1. a **plot**—a sequence of events that builds to a **climax**, or high point. Your plot will develop a **conflict**, or problem. Conflict may occur between a person and an outside force such as nature or society, between two people, or within an individual. At the end of the story, the conflict is generally resolved.
2. one or more **characters**, who should have believable personalities and clear motives for their actions. In longer stories, major characters should be **round** as opposed to **flat** and **dynamic** as opposed to **static**.
3. a **setting**—a specific time and place in which the story occurs. Your description of the setting should help to convey to your readers an **atmosphere**, or **mood**, such as a feeling of tension or mystery or suspense.
4. a **tone**—an attitude that you, as the writer, express toward your subject. The tone can be casual, angry, sad, amusing, or reflect any other emotional attitude that is appropriate for your purpose. Once established, the tone should be maintained consistently throughout the story.
5. a **narrator** through whom you tell your story. A **first-person narrator** (referred to as *I*) is a character in the story; a **limited third-person narrator** relates the thoughts of only one character; an **omniscient narrator** relates the thoughts of several characters.
6. a **theme**—an idea or impression of life suggested by the specific situation, people, and environment of your story.

PREWRITING: GENERATING IDEAS FOR A STORY

To generate story ideas, consider your own experiences. Think about people, places, and situations. Look at books and magazines for interesting photos, and begin to invent stories about the people and places you see. Then create a chart like the following one:

Chart of Story Ideas

SITUATION/PROBLEM	CHARACTER(S)	SETTING
lost wallet and identification	*two tourists*	*a town miles from home*
Car breaks down.	*young driver*	*abandoned mission in southwestern desert*
time machine	*two teen-agers*	*2,000 B.C.*
wild boars	*two miners*	*Amazon jungle*
sudden snowstorm	*two backpackers*	*Rocky Mountains in late September*

Objective
EXERCISE 2. Prewriting: Generating Ideas for a Story. Generate ideas for a story by making a chart like the one above. If you wish, use the Writer's Sourcebook, pages 372–375, as one source of ideas.

PREWRITING: EXPLORING IDEAS FOR A STORY

Begin to explore a story idea by visualizing how your characters look and behave. You can use questions such as the ones on the following chart, which develops the fourth story idea.

STORY IDEA: *Two miners, searching for gold in the Amazon jungle, suddenly confront a herd of wild boars.*	
QUESTIONS TO EXPLORE A STORY IDEA	ANSWERS
1. Why would I like to explore the idea? Who is my audience?	*It is suspenseful and exciting.* *My audience: adventure-magazine readers*
2. What is the conflict?	*People vs. primitive jungle beasts*
3. Who are my main characters? How old are they?	*Two miners--Don and Dave--in their thirties*
4. What do they look like—height, weight, features, clothing?	*Don: medium height, thin, wiry; curly, brown hair, chiseled features; limps--result of old mining accident;* *Dave: tall, lean, strong; open, friendly features, blond hair*

QUESTIONS TO EXPLORE A STORY IDEA	ANSWERS
5. What are their personalities? How do they speak and act?	*Don: reserved and calm, soft-spoken, reasonable, logical; Dave: adventurous, energetic, excitable, self-confident*
6. How do they react to the situation?	*Initial panic; then Don reacts calmly; Dave, confidently*
7. What is the setting—locale, season, weather? What is the mood?	*Deep in Amazon jungle: late afternoon to morning of next day; humid summer tropics; mood: exotic, tense*
8. What point of view would work well?	*First-person narrator; told by the more excitable of the two characters*
9. What will be my tone?	*Excited; empathetic with characters*
10. What theme might this story express?	*Individuals vs. nature; survival; nature vs. nature*

PREWRITING: DEVELOPING A STORY OUTLINE

The writer planning the story about the miners' confrontation with wild boars made a working outline of story events. Notice that details about setting, conflict, climax, and resolution are part of the working outline in order to give the story a basic structure.

I. Beginning
- **A.** Describe the setting.
  Late afternoon; interior of Amazon jungle
- **B.** Introduce the main characters.
  Dave, the first-person narrator, tells about himself and his partner, Don.
- **C.** Establish basic situation.
  Dave and Don are traveling the Amazon jungle on foot. Their destination, two hundred miles inland, is an abandoned gold mine that they hope to restore.

II. Middle
- **A.** Introduce the conflict or problem.
  Suddenly they confront a herd of at least fifty wild boars.
- **B.** Show the characters reacting to the problem.
  Terrified, they instinctively try to flee.
- **C.** Lead up to the climax.
  They climb a giant tree and spend the night.

III. End

A. Present the climax.

They discover that the boars have been rooting under the tree all night and that the tree is ready to fall.

B. Wind down the action.

Don sees a way for them to escape. Grasping a vine overhead, they swing across a small river and drop to the other side.

C. Present the final action.

The boars jump into the stream, giving chase. Dave and Don watch as the boars are attacked by thousands of piranha. Dave comments that they have defeated the boars. Don responds that nature has defeated the boars.

Building Excitement or Suspense

To build excitement or suspense in your story, you have at least two sequencing options. You can tell the story in chronological order, building suspense with **foreshadowing**, or hints about future events. In the preceding story, for example, a character might mention how dangerous wild boars are. A second way to build excitement is to start in the middle of the story and use **flashbacks** to relate events that occurred before the main action. This technique allows you to begin at a moment of major excitement.

Objective

EXERCISE 3. Prewriting: Exploring and Outlining a Story Idea. Choose one story idea from the chart that you created in Exercise 2. Decide on your audience for a story. Explore your idea by asking questions like those shown on pages 325–326. Then outline the main events of your story.

WRITING THE FIRST DRAFT OF A STORY

Use the following suggestions to help you write your first draft.

Beginning

Introduce the characters and place them in the setting in an interesting way. Be sure to establish and maintain a consistent point of view. The writer of the story about the miners chose a character, Dave, as narrator; readers see the events through his eyes. Here is how the story begins:

My partner Don and I had been slogging for a week through the dense, trailless jungle. It was hot, humid, and dim, the sun barely penetrating the thick jungle canopy. The air vibrated with the beating wings of the insects, the cries of raucous-voiced birds, and the incessant chatter of monkeys.

Characterization and Motivation

When you describe your characters, use details that suggest their personalities and that reveal something about their nature and motives, as in the following passage:

After a short rest, I was ready to plunge on into the jungle. Yet I knew that Don was tired. He had begun to limp badly during the last two miles. Although he never complained, an old mining accident had permanently damaged his right leg, and he was often in pain. I saw relief flicker across his face as I pointed to a nearby spot and declared that we would camp for the night.

In the preceding paragraph, the writer uses descriptive details to reveal the personalities of both characters. Words like *plunge* and *declared* reveal the character of Dave. The description of Don reveals Don's character and Dave's compassion for him.

Dialogue

Instead of describing how a character acts or feels, use **dialogue** to let the characters speak for themselves. To create realistic dialogue, you must choose words for each character that are believable and written at an appropriate level of diction; consult Chapter 5 for a review of formal, middle, and informal diction. When you write dialogue, remember the following points.

- Start a direct quotation with a capital letter. If you interrupt the quotation in midsentence, begin the second part with a small letter. If the quotation contains more than one sentence, begin each new sentence with a capital letter.
- Begin a new paragraph each time you change speakers.
- Use commas to set off direct quotations.
- To help build mood, add descriptive explanatory details to speaker tags; for example, *he argued calmly.*

Here is an example of story dialogue:

"Why don't we set up the tent for tonight. That clearing over there looks like a good spot," I said.

Don nodded and muttered, "That sounds fine to me."

"Wait—what's that noise?" I whispered anxiously. "It's something moving toward us, squealing."

Don kept his voice low. "Dave," he said tensely, "look over near the rubber trees! It's a herd of wild boars."

Climax and Resolution

As your story nears its end, present the climax, the high point of the action. Then provide a resolution. One way of concluding the story is to show what the characters have learned.

We both got a firm grasp of the thick vine, and I swung us back and forth in an increasing arc over the angry, snorting boars. Gradually, we built up enough speed and force to swing out over the small river to the safety of the other bank.

The boars abandoned the uprooted tree and scrambled toward the river. "They're coming after us," Don stated matter-of-factly.

The boars leaped into the river and began swimming toward us, their snouts held high. At midstream the water suddenly turned into a broiling, thrashing frenzy, punctuated with the high-pitched squeals of the boars and the scissoring, snapping, slashing sounds of piranha teeth. Thousands of the tiny, deadly fish were attacking the boars. Snorting in panic and retreating to the safety of the shore, the survivors fled from the river.

I turned to Don and victoriously shouted, "We've beaten them! We've defeated the boars!"

"No, I don't think so. Nature got them. We only watched."

I gazed thankfully at the now-calm, shimmering river, its waters—giver of death, and life—coursing silently.

Title

Write a title that will attract a reader's interest. The writer of the story about Don, Dave, and the wild boars chose the title "The Survivors."

REVISING, EDITING, AND PUBLISHING A STORY

After you finish your first draft, you need to revise your story. Use the following checklist to help you.

CHECKLIST FOR REVISING, EDITING, AND PUBLISHING A STORY

1. Does my story fulfill my specific purpose? Will it interest my audience?
2. What details describe the setting? Do the details convey the mood of the story?
3. What physical details depict the characters? What personality traits do they display, and what words and actions convey these traits? What motives lie behind each character's actions? How clearly have I indicated these motives?
4. What point of view does the story use? Does the story stay within that point of view?
5. What conflict does the story present, develop, and resolve?
6. How is each event connected to what happens before and what happens after it?

7. Where do I use dialogue? How can I make it sound more true to life? Do I use the correct format for dialogue?
8. What moment is the climax of the story? How is the conflict resolved?
9. Is the language concrete and vivid?
10. Is each sentence a complete sentence? Have I avoided errors in verbs, pronouns, and modifiers?
11. Have I correctly capitalized and punctuated each sentence? Are all the words correctly spelled?
12. What might be a good forum for sharing my finished story—showing it to friends and teachers? Entering it in a contest?

Objective

EXERCISE 4. Writing, Revising, and Sharing a Story. Write a short story based on the notes and outline that you created for Exercise 3. Then use the preceding checklist to revise and edit your first draft. Make a finished copy, and present it to an audience.

WRITING A DRAMATIC SCENE

A **dramatic scene** consists entirely of dialogue and action. It is very much like a story scene without the narrator. The following passage dramatizes a part of "The Survivors."

> [*Sounds of the boars gnawing and slicing and snorting below the tree*]
> DAVE: [*Astonished*] They're trying to uproot this tree.
> DON: [*Calmly*] They're not trying; they're *doing* it. The tree! . . . it's swaying.
> DAVE: [*Fearfully*] What'll we do?

The elements of a dramatic scene include many of the same elements you used to write a story: **plot, conflict, climax,** at least two **characters,** a **setting, theme,** and **tone.** The form of a play, however, is different from that of a story. **Stage directions** in brackets provide descriptions of the characters' actions and motives and information about scenery, lighting, mood, and props—the items used by the characters in the scenes.

PREWRITING: GENERATING IDEAS FOR A SCENE

When you generate ideas for a dramatic scene, start by imagining at least two characters. To provide contrast, the characters should have different backgrounds, opinions, or attitudes. Next, try to imagine conflicts or problems that could surface between them. List possible scene ideas on a chart such as the one that follows.

Chart of Scene Ideas

FIRST CHARACTER	SECOND CHARACTER	CONFLICT
Businessman	*Artist*	*Who contributes more to society?*
Young man	*Young woman*	*Applying for the same job*
Beach lover	*Avid hiker*	*Where to go for vacation*
Famous fictional character from an earlier century	*Person from today*	*Manners, personalities*

Objective

EXERCISE 5. Prewriting: Generating Ideas for a Scene. Generate ideas for a scene by making a chart like the one above. Photographs in the Writer's Sourcebook, pages 372–375, might be a source of ideas.

PREWRITING: EXPLORING IDEAS FOR A SCENE

Next you can begin to develop one of your scene ideas. Imagine your characters in a situation that involves conflict. Then ask yourself questions such as the ones on the following chart. The writer of the chart decided to explore the humorous possibilities of **anachronism** by deliberately placing a character from the seventeenth century in a present-day setting.

SCENE IDEA: *A famous fictional character from the seventeenth century having lunch with a prospective employer in a modern restaurant*	
QUESTIONS TO EXPLORE A SCENE IDEA	ANSWERS
1. Who are the characters?	*Don Quixote: early seventeenth-century hero of a famous novel; Kimberly McGuire: rich, powerful ranch owner*
2. What do they look like? What are their distinctive features?	*Don Quixote: frail, short, long strands of straggly, thin, gray hair; shabby, torn court-attire from seventeenth century; Kimberly: perfectly groomed; stylish, expensive business attire*

QUESTIONS TO EXPLORE A SCENE IDEA	ANSWERS
3. What are their personalities like? How do they speak and act?	*Don Quixote: a romantic visionary; excitable, rambling, vague; Kimberly: businesslike, intelligent, assertive, direct*
4. What does each want in this scene?	*Don Quixote: a job on Kimberly's ranch; Kimberly: wants to get the interview over with*
5. Where does the scene take place? What props do the characters use?	*In a busy, elegant San Francisco restaurant at lunchtime; Don Quixote carries a bent, rusty sword; Kimberly carries a leather briefcase.*
6. What is my purpose? Who is my intended audience?	*To entertain by providing a humorous scene between characters from different centuries; audience: young adults and adults who have heard of Don Quixote*

PREWRITING: DEVELOPING A SCENE OUTLINE

You can organize your thoughts for a dramatic scene by outlining the main events. The writer planning the scene involving Don Quixote and Kimberly McGuire wrote the following outline:

I. Beginning
  A. Establish your characters' identities and their relationship to one another.
  Don Quixote and Kimberly meet and introduce themselves. He is a seventeenth-century Spanish courtier; she is a present-day businesswoman.
  B. Introduce the problem or conflict.
  Quixote has applied for a job on Kimberly's ranch. This scene is essentially Quixote's "interview."

II. Middle
  A. Present the characters' reactions to the conflict.
  Kimberly, who feels Quixote is wasting her time, wants to end the luncheon interview. Quixote, totally unaware of Kimberly's reaction to him, presses on, recounting his past experiences.
  B. Build toward the point of highest interest, or climax.
  Quixote, totally immersed in his past memories, begins ranting, swinging his sword; Kimberly unsuccessfully tries to calm him down.

III. Ending

A. Reach the point of highest interest.

Quixote swings his sword; Kimberly swats at him with her briefcase. He falls off the table.

B. Show the characters' reactions at the climax.

Kimberly shouts that Quixote, with his swinging sword, looks like a disjointed windmill. Stunned, he comes to his senses.

C. Present the final outcome.

Quixote calmly recounts a windmill experience he once had. Moved, Kimberly offers him a job as keeper of the windmills that supply her ranch with power. He graciously accepts.

Objective

EXERCISE 6. Prewriting: Exploring and Outlining a Scene Idea. Choose one of the scene ideas that you generated in Exercise 5, and think of an audience to whom that scene might appeal. Then explore your idea with questions such as those shown on pages 330–331. After exploring your idea, outline the action of the scene.

WRITING THE FIRST DRAFT OF A SCENE

Use the following suggestions to help you write a first draft of your scene.

Cast of Characters

List your characters in the order of their appearance and provide some identification of each, as in this example:

KIMBERLY McGUIRE: a wealthy rancher
DON QUIXOTE: seventeenth-century Spanish knight, hero of a famous novel

Setting the Stage

At the beginning of the scene, write stage directions describing the scenery, furniture, and lighting. Explain which characters are on stage, and describe them briefly. Enclose stage directions in brackets, as in the following example:

[*An elegant San Francisco restaurant. It is the lunch hour, and the restaurant is very busy. At the rear of the stage, people are seated at several tables and are eating or in the process of ordering. Kimberly McGuire enters and is shown a table in front center stage by a waiter. A strikingly attractive woman in her thirties, she is dressed in a stylish, expensive business suit and carries a leather briefcase.*]

Dialogue and Action

After setting the scene for your audience, you can begin the action and dialogue. Start by writing the name of the first character to speak and that character's first line of dialogue. Include stage directions that are clear enough for an actor to follow. Then begin the other character's first speech on a new line:

> QUIXOTE: Excuse me, but are you Ms. Kimberly McGuire? [*She nods, looking baffled by his appearance.*] My apologies for my lateness. It is very difficult to find a stable in this city. I have spent an entire morning riding up and down these magnificent hills. Finally, I simply tied my horse to a tree in Union Square. [*Looking exhausted, he drops down in the seat.*]
>
> KIMBERLY: [*Looking at him suspiciously.*] You, I take it, are the *same* "Don Quixote" [*Emphasizing his name*] who wrote me a letter requesting a job on my ranch?

Conflict and Climax

Follow your outline, using dialogue and stage directions to develop the problem or conflict. Build interest as your scene leads to its climax. Then present the climax.

> QUIXOTE: [*Jumping up from the table, he begins shouting and wildly swinging his sword. He leaps on top of the table and takes a vicious swing at the chandelier.*] Take that . . . you venomous beast . . . Knight of Deception . . . glittering beacon of malice. . . .
>
> KIMBERLY: [*Waving her briefcase at him.*] Mr. Quixote—Mr. Quixote! Sit down! This is a restaurant. We're not on some mystical battlefield. [*He continues jumping up and down on the table, thrusting at the chandelier with his sword.*]
>
> QUIXOTE: [*Screeching uncontrollably*] Truth . . . honor. . . . My fair lady . . . I will never. . . .
>
> KIMBERLY: [*Exasperated and angry, she swings her briefcase at him, causing him to fall off the table, and shouts.*] Stop it! You are acting like a windmill gone amok!
>
> QUIXOTE: [*On the floor, stunned, mumbles.*] Windmill . . . windmill. . . . Yes, I remember the windmills.

Resolution

Show the characters' reactions to the climax. Then present the resolution. Write final stage directions to end the scene.

> QUIXOTE: [*Continuing*] I thought the windmills were an attacking army. I fought them, but they defeated me. As a result of my defeat, I was placed in perpetual servitude to them. I spent decades servicing them, rebuilding them, and struggling to understand them. [*Laughs*] Do I

not know windmills! I know their every bearing, joint, and cogwheel; their evil, mechanical posturing and malevolence. . . .

KIMBERLY: [*Looking at some papers in her briefcase*] But Don, you never mentioned that in the resume you sent. [*She appears moved.*] I didn't know . . .

QUIXOTE: [*Confused*] Really . . . it must have slipped my mind. . . . I do . . . do . . . do . . . [*Straining to remember*] forget things. . . .

KIMBERLY: Perhaps. But I may have a position for you. You see, all of the power on our ranch comes from windmills, and. . . .

QUIXOTE: [*Smiling, interrupts*] I'll take it!

KIMBERLY: Of course, you'll be working hundreds of miles from civilization, and alone.

QUIXOTE: It sounds perfect. I cannot endure much more of this strange modern world. [*They smile at each other. Lights dim.*]

Title

Choose a title for your scene. It may refer to the situation, characters, setting, or a line of dialogue. The writer of the preceding scene chose the title "The Interview."

REVISING, EDITING, AND PUBLISHING A SCENE

Read your scene aloud. If possible, do a dramatic reading with friends. Then use the following checklist to revise and edit your writing:

CHECKLIST FOR REVISING, EDITING, AND PUBLISHING A SCENE

1. Does my scene fulfill my specific purpose? Will it interest my intended audience?
2. At the beginning of the scene, have I clearly identified each character? What more need I say about the setting?
3. Does each character speak and act consistently throughout? What personality traits does each character display in the scene? How can the dialogue and stage directions convey these traits more clearly?
4. What conflict does the scene present, develop, and resolve? How can I sharpen the presentation of this conflict?
5. What is the climax of the scene? What can I do to make the climax fit the scene better? How is the conflict resolved?
6. Is the format for dialogue and stage directions correct?
7. What might be the best way of presenting my scene to an audience—an informal reading? A full staging with costumes?

Objective

EXERCISE 7. Writing, Revising, and Publishing a Scene. Write a dramatic scene using the notes and outline that you created for Exercise 6. Then use the preceding checklist to revise and edit your first draft. Make a finished copy of your scene, and proofread that copy. Present the scene in a reading or in a performance.

WRITING A POEM

Poems come in all sizes, shapes, and forms. They may be profound or lighthearted, simple or complex. Anything may be the subject of a poem—a tree, a memory, a piece of machinery. Whatever their forms and subjects, however, all poems share several distinct qualities:

1. A poem communicates its meaning largely through **images**—specific, concrete details that appeal to the senses.
2. Poems often use **symbols.** A symbol is a person, object, or situation that, in addition to its literal meaning, represents something else.
3. Poetry often contains **figures of speech**. A **simile** compares two seemingly unlike items using the words *like* or *as*. A **metaphor** links two unlike things without using such words. **Personification** lends human qualities to inanimate animals, objects, or ideas.
4. Most poems use **sound effects**, which can include **repetition, rhyme,** and **rhythm.** Other sound effects are **onomatopoeia,** the imitation of a sound by a word; **alliteration,** the repetition of initial consonant sounds; **consonance,** the repetition of internal consonant sounds; and **assonance,** the repetition of vowel sounds.
5. Every poem has an overall pattern that gives it **form**. Some poems have set patterns of rhyme and rhythm and may be divided into **stanzas**, or groups of lines. Others, called **free verse**, have no set rhythm, rhyme, or stanza pattern.

PREWRITING: GENERATING IDEAS FOR A POEM

An idea for a poem may come from almost anywhere. In this section, you will learn about images, figurative language, sound effects, and form and how they can help you generate ideas for poetry.

Imagery

Images are concrete details as perceived by the five senses. You can practice creating concrete, vivid images by listing sensory details for an item in a chart like the one that follows.

ITEM:	
SENSE	IMAGES
Sight	*Dazzle of sun on water; dappled sunlight through leaves*
Sound	*Laughter of children on sunny day; hum of insects in summer*
Smell	*Moist-earth smell rising in response to warmth; newly mowed lawn; green smell of warm leaves*
Taste	*Sweet sun-ripened fruit--apricots, peaches*
Touch	*Warmth; grit of beach sand; sting of sunburn*

Figurative Language: Similes, Metaphors, Personification

You can use figurative language to highlight your subject. For example, note the dimension that each of the following figures of speech brings to its subject.

SIMILE: Autumn leaves fell from the trees like discarded memories.

METAPHOR: The fog was a heavy, wet blanket smothering the city.

PERSONIFICATION: The surf clawed at the beach with its long, white fingers.

Sound Effects

Poems can be written simply for the pleasure of the way words sound together, using the various sound effects that give poetry its special musical quality. One sound effect is **alliteration**, in which the first consonant sound is repeated:

*S*weet *s*pring *s*lipped *s*oftly. . . .

Onomatopoeia describes words that echo natural sounds:

The *hum* and the *buzz* of the bee . . .

Consonance and assonance often work together in a line of poetry to create subtle sound effects. **Consonance** repeats internal consonant sounds:

The ja*gg*ed ed*g*e of for*g*otten memories . . .

Assonance repeats internal vowel sounds:

The n*i*ght r*i*sing bl*i*nd . . .

Repetition, rhyme, and rhythm are the sound effects that give a poem its melody and help to make it memorable. Note, for example, the rhythmic pattern of the following line:

˘ ´ ˘ ´ ˘ ´ ˘ ´
I heard a thousand blended notes

The rhythmic pattern is based on an unstressed syllable followed by a stressed syllable. This grouping of syllables is called an **iamb,** and it is the most common pattern in English poetry. Here are three other common patterns of stress, with examples: the **trochee** (óut·lo͝ok); the **dactyl** (már·vĕl·oŭs) and the **anapest** (ĭn thĕ pínk).

Not all poems rhyme, but in the ones that do, there is usually a definite **rhyme scheme.** The **rhyme scheme** is the pattern of rhymes formed by the end rhymes in a poem. Rhyme scheme is indicated by assigning a different letter of the alphabet, starting with *a*, to each new rhyme.

Form

Sometimes the pattern and form of a poem will suggest content. For example, a two-stanza form lends itself to comparison and contrast. A form that is effective for brief descriptions is a single four- or five-line stanza, each line slightly longer than the next.

Charting to Generate Ideas for a Poem

A useful way to gather ideas for a poem is to make a chart like the one that follows. You can begin by listing general categories of subjects and then list specific subjects as they come to mind.

Chart of Ideas for a Poem

GENERAL CATEGORY	SPECIFIC SUBJECT FOR A POEM
A person (real or fictional)	*Jack--his birthday*
An animal (real or imaginary)	*My fat cat, Pudge*
An object or phenomenon (natural or artificial)	*The wind rattling my window*
An event (real or invented)	*The Labor Day parade*

Objective

EXERCISE 8. Charting to Generate Ideas for a Poem. Make a chart like the preceding one. For each general category fill in one specific item that you could write about in a poem. In addition, you might find ideas in the Writer's Sourcebook, pages 372–375. Save your notes.

PREWRITING: EXPLORING IDEAS FOR A POEM

After choosing a subject for a poem, you can explore that subject by asking and answering questions such as the ones on the following chart. They will help you to organize your ideas.

POEM IDEA: *The wind rattling my window*	
1. Why do I want to write about this subject?	*Strong sensory impression, evoking an emotional response I want to share*
2. What do I see, hear, smell, taste, and feel when I imagine the subject?	*Whispering, whistling, rattling; soft breezes in summer, biting cold in winter*
3. What emotions does the subject evoke in me?	*Feeling of solitude*
4. What figures of speech could I use?	*Personification--wind has a voice; sustained image of wind as person*
5. What sound effects could I use?	*Onomatopoeia: whispering, whistling, rattling; alliteration: cold, crying; assonance: cold, crying over snow;*
6. What words or phrases could I repeat?	*Perhaps "the wind has many voices"? probably none*
7. What kind of rhythm do I want to use? Do I want to use rhyme?	*Free verse, but mostly a stressed-unstressed pattern*
8. What form should my poem take?	*Two stanzas--one descriptive, one narrative*
9. Who is my audience? What is my purpose?	*General audience; to share a strong personal response*

Objective

EXERCISE 9. Exploring an Idea for a Poem. Review your chart of ideas for a poem. Using one of those ideas, plan a poem of any length, with or without rhyme. Consider the audience that you would like to have read your poem. Then explore your idea by using questions like those on the preceding chart.

WRITING THE FIRST DRAFT OF A POEM

Your first line should introduce your subject and establish in your reader's mind the tone of the whole poem. Then you can turn to other ideas, images, and figures of speech. Remember to use concrete language and sensory details.

The writer of the following poem began by personifying the wind and extended the image with sensory details. This writer did not use rhyme, but you may decide to include it in your poem.

The wind has many voices:
Soft sighing in tree branches,
Hushed whispering through the vines,
Shrill whistling down the chimney,
Cold crying over snow.

Try to save a striking and memorable image for the final lines.

Rattling my window
It clamors for admission,
Then—suddenly—is gone,
And silence, not the wind,
Is far too loud. I am alone.

After completing your poem, choose an appropriate title. The writer of the preceding poem called her poem "The Voice of the Wind."

REVISING, EDITING, AND PUBLISHING A POEM

Because every word in a poem is important, careful editing and revision are essential. Read your poem aloud, and ask yourself the following questions:

CHECKLIST FOR REVISING, EDITING, AND PUBLISHING A POEM

1. Will my audience understand my purpose?
2. To what senses do the images in my poem appeal? Which images can I sharpen or intensify?
3. What figures of speech have I used? Is each one clear?
4. Which of the following sound effects have I used—alliteration, onomatopoeia, assonance, and consonance? Is each sound effect appropriate?
5. How can I make my rhythm more effective?
6. Which words rhyme? Do I use rhyme consistently?
7. Which words or phrases do I repeat? Should I repeat any?
8. What form have I used? Have I followed it consistently?
9. Have I used correct spelling and punctuation?
10. What would be a good way of presenting my poem to my audience—in a dramatic reading? In a student anthology?

Objective

EXERCISE 10. Writing, Revising, and Publishing a Poem. Use the notes that you created in Exercise 9, and write a poem. Use any form for your poem, but use it consistently. Your poem may be rhymed or not. After writing a first draft, read your poem aloud, and revise it by asking the preceding questions. Complete a final draft; then proofread and present your poem to your intended audience.

WRITER'S CHOICE #1

ASSIGNMENT: To write a story or a dramatic scene
LENGTH: Your choice
PURPOSE: To re-create and fictionalize a historical event, altering the event as you wish
AUDIENCE: Your choice
PREWRITING: Choose a historical event, Decide whether you want to create a story or a dramatic scene. Then follow the prewriting suggestions presented in this chapter. When you write a plot outline, determine exactly how you will alter the historical event.
WRITING: Follow the suggestions for writing a story or a scene.
REVISING: Does your story or scene fulfill your purpose? For additional revision suggestions use the checklist on pages 328–329 or on page 334. Share your final version with your intended audience.

WRITER'S CHOICE #2

ASSIGNMENT: To write a poem of two to four stanzas
LENGTH: Your choice
PURPOSE: To reveal the unusual qualities that you see in a very common object
AUDIENCE: Your choice
PREWRITING: Brainstorm to find an interesting object. Then follow the prewriting procedures for exploring an idea for a poem on page 338.
WRITING: Follow the suggestions on pages 338–339.
REVISING: Read your poem aloud. Does it reveal unusual qualities of the common object you selected? For additional revision guidelines see page 339. Share your poem with your audience.

WRITER'S CHOICE #3

ASSIGNMENT: To write a story, scene, or poem
LENGTH: Your choice
PURPOSE: Your choice
AUDIENCE: Your choice
OPTIONS:
- You might use a story, scene, or poem idea that you generated but did not explore.
- You might also use the Writer's Sourcebook, pages 372–375, as a source of ideas.

THE WRITER

Brian Rowe has been writing poetry for several years. He was a student at Indian Hill High School in Cincinnati, Ohio, when he wrote the following poem and commentary.

THE FINISHED PRODUCT

My greatest performance—
To be seen by the President himself.
A career of studying
practicing
dedicated to one night.

The first act went well
My delivery impeccable,
The orchestra in perfect tune.

Then all went black
the crack of gunshot
that painful moan
"The President is dead."

My moment passed.
I was carried away
by a wave, then the
undertow pulled me back
—stung me
and pushed me off
the stage.

THE WRITER AT WORK

In my poem "Our American Cousin" I used a method known as adopting a *persona*, or speaker different from me. I've found this technique works best when I choose a participant in a major historical event, but not the figure who was the focus of the event. In the case of my poem, of course, the event is the assassination of Abraham Lincoln at Ford's Theater. By avoiding the obvious choices—Lincoln and John Wilkes Booth—I could present a decidedly different view of the assassination. I made my speaker an actor in the play *Our American Cousin.*

I divided my poem into four stanzas. The first stanza portrays the natural nervousness that every actor feels. The second tells how the play is going. The third presents the shock of the gunshot and the realization that the President is dead. Finally, the fourth stanza attempts to describe the almost unconscious feeling that the actor experiences as the perfect night turns into a nightmare.

YOUR TURN Writing a Poem with a Persona

As Brian did, choose a historical event, and write a poem about it using as a speaker a minor participant in the event.

THE WRITER

Steve Francis has spent most of his life in El Paso, Texas. A frequent flier, he has his own pilot's license. He wrote the following short short story and commentary when he was a student at Eastwood High School in El Paso.

THE FINISHED PRODUCT

> The sun was beating down on a small piece of flesh—me. The desert, relentless and indifferent, wore me down to near collapse as I struggled to see a sign of water. Then, just by chance, I kicked over a rock. A funny thing that rock. It was unlike any I had ever seen in the desert before. It seemed that this one rock, despite the destructiveness of this wasteland, had somehow kept its faint brilliance. Its jutting shape defied the erosive forces that I was battling. Its sparkle challenged the lifelessness that was overtaking me. I looked at that rock, a veteran of many wars with the elements, and saw in it a will to survive. And I went on.

THE WRITER AT WORK

I used a unique-looking rock as my springboard for this story. This rock was shaped with radial protrusions of glistening crystals extending from a body caked with dull, hardened sand. It immediately gave me the impression of opposing elements—the protruding crystals seemed to defy the sand.

Presenting a conflict between an individual and nature seemed the best way of expressing the opposing elements I saw in the rock. With this conflict in mind, I decided on my plot, character, and setting, all derived from my impression of the rock. The setting was easiest; the rock obviously came from a desert. The hostility of the desert—blistering sun, arid wind, waterless terrain—became my villain. I also got an impression for a main character and plot: It was to be a man struggling through a wasteland. The story seemed to need something more, so I placed the rock into the action as a kind of second "character." As I looked to my springboard for more ideas, I felt admiration for the rock, because it had survived many attacks on its brilliance. I decided to give the main character the same attitude toward the rock. This helped me work toward my ending, in which the man takes heart from the fact that the rock has endured.

YOUR TURN Writing a Story

Steve Francis looked at a rock and found a story. Find one concrete item and base a story of your own on it.

CHAPTERS 14–17 WRITING ACROSS THE CURRICULUM

CHAPTER 14 WRITING ABOUT SOCIAL STUDIES

Focusing on a Topic (pages 277–278)

1. Which of the following topics is the most narrowly focused?
   (a) westward expansion in the United States **(b)** the effect of the railroad on westward expansion **(c)** the American frontier

Evidence and Sources (pages 278–279) Indicate whether the item is **(a)** a primary source, **(b)** a secondary source, **(c)** a fact, or **(d)** an opinion.

2. A letter written by Teddy Roosevelt
3. Teddy Roosevelt was an extremely popular President.
4. A biography of Teddy Roosevelt
5. Before becoming President, Teddy Roosevelt was Police Commissioner in New York City and Governor of New York State.

Qualifying Words (page 280)

6. Which of the following statements is properly qualified?
   (a) Wage and price controls are the only effective means of halting inflation. **(b)** Wage and price controls can sometimes halt rising inflation. **(c)** Wage and price controls always lead to recessions.

Organization (pages 282–285) Indicate whether each statement demonstrates **(a)** chronological order, **(b)** cause and effect, **(c)** comparison, or **(d)** contrast.

7. The Russian's launching of *Sputnik* in 1957 ironically led to an improvement in science and math instruction in the United States.
8. Unlike the broader-based American curriculums, Russian education emphasized mathematics, science, and technology.
9. In 1957 Russia launched an orbiting satellite called *Sputnik*; the United States quickly followed with the *Explorer I* in 1958.
10. During the 1960s and 1970s, both the United States and Russia spent billions of dollars on their space programs.

Answers: **1.** b; **2.** a; **3.** d; **4.** b; **5.** c; **6.** b; **7.** b; **8.** d; **9.** a; **10.** c

Writing for Review Write a paragraph about a social studies topic of your own choice. Follow the complete writing process.

CHAPTER 15 WRITING ABOUT SCIENCE AND TECHNOLOGY

Topic and Purpose (pages 288–291) Indicate the letter of the item that correctly answers each question.

1. Which is a more suitable topic for a scientific or technical report?
   (a) how geologists locate oil **(b)** rock collecting as a hobby
2. Which purpose would probably best suit this topic?
   (a) to explain a process **(b)** to entertain **(c)** to contrast

Structure (pages 295–296) Match each part of a scientific or technical report in the left column with the phrase in the right column that is most likely to be found in that part.

3. Discussion
4. Abstract
5. Conclusion
6. Bibliography entry
7. Internal source citation

(a) This report recommends . . .
(b) (Knox, 1984, p. 207)
(c) This report will show . . .
(d) Igneous rocks, for example, . . .
(e) McBrearty, A. *Geology*. . . .

Style, Tone, and Mechanics (pages 294–297) Read the following passage and items 8, 9, and 10 that follow. For each numbered item, indicate whether **(a)** or **(b)** is correct for a paper about sciences.

The honeycomb in a beehive is **[8.]** __________ heavy. A comb measuring **[9.]** __________ can hold **[10.]** __________ of honey.

8. **(a)** unbelievably **(b)** extremely
9. **(a)** thirty-two by twenty-two centimeters **(b)** 32 by 22 cm
10. **(a)** 4 lbs **(b)** 4 lb

Answers: **1.** a; **2.** a; **3.** d; **4.** c; **5.** a; **6.** e; **7.** b; **8.** b; **9.** b; **10.** b

Writing for Review Write an abstract and an introductory paragraph for a paper about a scientific or technical subject of your own choosing. Follow the writing process.

CHAPTER 16 WRITING ABOUT LITERATURE

Writing About a Short Story or a Novel (pages 306–311) Indicate the letter of the item that correctly answers each question.

1. What would be the best limited topic for a paper about a novel?
   (a) the author's complete works **(b)** the major theme of the novel
2. What would be the best limited topic for a paper about a short story?
   (a) a comparison and contrast of the main characters' motives
   (b) an analysis of all themes, plots, and subplots

Writing About a Dramatic Scene (pages 311–315) Indicate the letter of the item that correctly answers each question.

3. Which statement is false?
   (a) A scene may develop one or more themes of the play. **(b)** A character's behavior is unimportant to the scene.
4. The setting for a scene is usually revealed
   (a) by the main character's actions **(b)** in the play's stage directions
5. Which would be the best limited topic for a paper about a scene?
   (a) the role of the setting **(b)** similar scenes in eight or ten plays

Answers: **1.** b; **2.** a; **3.** b; **4.** b; **5.** a

Writing for Review Write a short essay comparing two poems that treat a similar subject or theme. Follow the writing process.

CHAPTER 17 CREATIVE WRITING

Writing for Review Write a story, scene, or poem about something that you would like to happen. If you choose to write a story or a scene, decide on your characters and setting, and outline your plot. If you write a poem, select a subject and decide on the poetic techniques that you will use in the poem. Then write and revise your work.

RITER'S SOURCEBOOK

The Writer's Sourcebook is a collection of illustrations and assignments that correspond to many of the chapters in Part One: Composition. For example, as shown in the contents below, the Writer's Sourcebook opens with a section called "The Writing Process and Style," which presents paintings, photographs, and assignments coordinated with the first two units of the book.

Using the Writer's Sourcebook

You may work with the Writer's Sourcebook in a variety of ways:

- Just looking through the Writer's Sourcebook may help you generate ideas for writing.
- You may respond to specific material in the Writer's Sourcebook by completing the assignment suggested for each illustration.
- Illustrations from the Writer's Sourcebook will help you to complete certain Writer's Choice assignments, which appear throughout Part One: Composition.

For instance, in responding to Writer's Choice #5 in the chapter on narrative writing, you may choose the option that refers you to the photographs headed "Narrative Writing" in the Writer's Sourcebook. You may then write a narrative based on the action you see in the photographs.

Writer's Sourcebook Contents

HE WRITING PROCESS AND STYLE

1

ASSIGNMENTS

- **Generating and Exploring Ideas in Prewriting** *(pages 11–21).* Choose three illustrations on pages 346–347, and use various techniques of prewriting to generate and explore writing ideas for each.

- **Writing a Coherent Paragraph** *(pages 46–48).* Write a coherent paragraph based on a new topic or on one of the writing ideas that you developed in the assignment above. Be sure to vary your sentences, and use the best possible transitions.

- **Using Vivid and Precise Words to Evoke a Mood or Atmosphere** *(pages 81–84).* Write a descriptive paragraph that uses colorful and concise words to evoke the mood of an illustration on pages 346–347.

- **Revising for Style, Voice, and Tone** *(pages 131–133).* Imagine that you are an editor reading someone else's writing, and revise the paragraph you wrote for the assignment above.

3

4

2

5

The illustrations on these two pages complement the instruction in Chapters 1–7.

DESCRIPTIVE WRITING

ASSIGNMENTS

- **Using Descriptive Language** *(pages 151–152).* Use exact and vivid language to write a paragraph that describes the quilt shown in illustration 1. Be sure to include sensory details and to present an overall impression of the quilt. You may want to use figurative language in your description.
- **Writing a Character Sketch** *(pages 154–156).* Write a character sketch based on the photograph of Theodore Roosevelt in item 2. Begin with a topic sentence in which you express an overall impression. Include psychological traits as well as specific details in your portrait.
- **Creating a Mood** *(pages 153–154).* Describe painting 3 in a paragraph that creates a definite mood. Be sure to use colorful details from the painting and to include vivid, specific language in your description.
- **Using Spatial Order** *(pages 148–150).* Write a paragraph about illustration 4. Use spatial order to arrange the details that support your topic sentence. Be sure to use appropriate spatial transitions.

1

3

George Luks, *Armistice Night*, 1918. Oil on canvas. H. 37 in. W. 68¾ in.

The illustrations on these two pages complement the instruction in Chapter 8.

2

NARRATIVE WRITING

ASSIGNMENTS

- **Choosing Events for a Narrative** *(pages 164–166).* As preparation for writing a nonfiction narrative about item 1, 2, or 3 on pages 350–351, fill out a chart like the one on page 165.

- **Preparing a Narrative Outline** *(pages 168–169).* Make a narrative outline for one of the numbered items on pages 350–351. Give the purpose, setting, and background information, and then list the events in chronological order.

- **Writing a Narrative in Chronological Order** *(pages 169–172).* Using chronological order, write a narrative about one of the illustrations on pages 350–351. Include specific details. If you include dialogue, be sure to follow the format presented on pages 171–172.

- **Revising a Narrative** *(page 173).* Revise the narrative you wrote for the assignment above. Replace any weak verbs with vivid, precise verbs, and add narrative details that make your narrative richer and more informative.

1

2

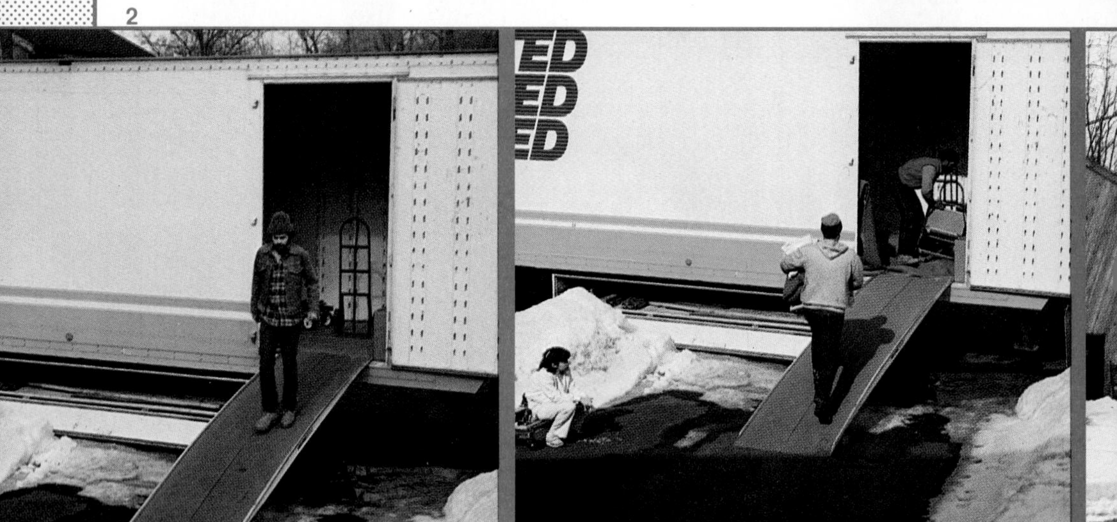

The illustrations on these two pages complement the instruction in Chapter 9.

3

XPOSITORY WRITING

ASSIGNMENTS

- **Defining an Unfamiliar Term** *(pages 193–194).* Illustration 1 shows a *daguerrotype.* Write a definition of this term. Prepare to write by consulting a reference work and creating a prewriting chart like that on page 193.
- **Comparing and Contrasting Items** *(pages 196–199).* Using a comparison frame, write a comparison-contrast based on the two subjects shown in illustration 2.
- **Explaining a Process** *(pages 181–184).* Write a paragraph explaining the process shown in illustration 3. As prewriting, fill out a chart listing the steps in the process (page 183).
- **Writing About Cause and Effect** *(pages 185–188).* As an alternative to the assignment above, write a paragraph about the *causes and effects* shown in illustration 3. Use transitional words to make your paragraph coherent.

1

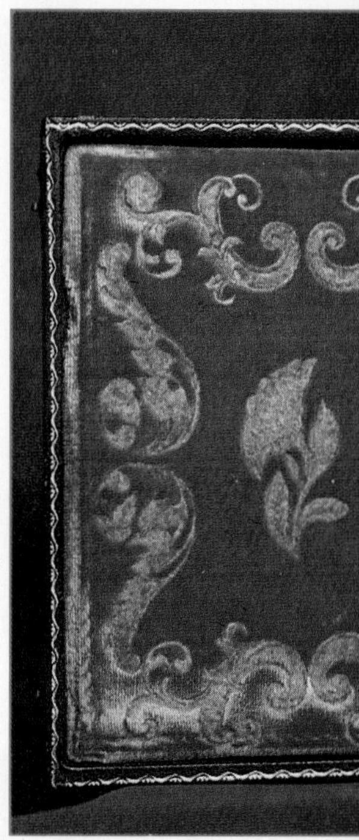

Litchfield Historical Society. Photo by James Miller.

3

2

Courtesy Shelburne Museum, Shelburne, Vermont.

The illustrations on these two pages complement the instruction in Chapter 10.

RITICAL THINKING AND PERSUASIVE WRITING

1

Courtesy New York Landmarks Conservancy.

ASSIGNMENTS

- **Selecting a Topic and Suiting Topic to Audience** *(pages 208–210).* The photographs on pages 354–355 focus on the subject of preserving historical structures. Study these photographs, and write a proposition to use as the basis for a persuasive paragraph. Be sure to express an opinion and to address an issue worthy of discussion. Then determine your audience by answering the questions on page 209.
- **Identifying Facts and Opinions** *(pages 210–212).* Using the photographs and any other sources of information that you can find readily, gather evidence in support of the topic identified in the preceding assignment. Then make a list of facts and a list of authoritative and sound opinions that directly support your proposition.
- **Writing an Argument** *(pages 217–220).* Based on the preceding assignment, first state your position clearly; include any necessary background information. Develop your support with either reasons or facts. If possible, indicate opposing arguments, and answer them. Use transitions to help your readers follow each step of your argument. End with a strong conclusion.

2

The illustrations on these two pages complement the instruction in Chapter 11.

HE ESSAY

ASSIGNMENTS

- **Generating, Exploring, and Focusing Ideas** *(pages 232–237).* Using the photographs on pages 356–357 as inspiration, prewrite for ten minutes to generate ideas for an essay. Then explore your ideas by filling out a chart like the one on page 235. Your chart may contain informational, personal, creative, or analytical questions. Focus your ideas by eliminating any insignificant details.

- **Making a Working Outline and Writing a First Draft** *(pages 237–243).* Use your notes from the preceding assignment to organize a working outline. Then write a first draft of your essay. Be sure to cover the main points and supporting details on your outline.

1

4

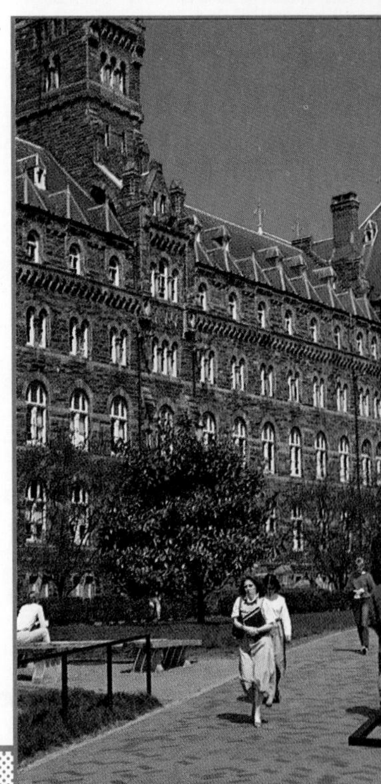

6

Writing a Final Version *(pages 243–246).* After reviewing your first draft from the preceding assignment, prepare a formal outline. Then, using your formal outline and first draft, write a final version.

The illustrations on these two pages complement the instruction in Chapter 12.

RITING ABOUT SOCIAL STUDIES

ASSIGNMENT

■ **Writing About Cause-and-Effect Relationships in History** *(page 283).* Item 1 on page 359 shows a nineteenth-century poster created by a railroad company in order to advertise the sale of land in Iowa and Nebraska. After the Civil War the railroads tried to encourage people to settle in the West. Items 2 and 3 show how railroad routes expanded between 1870 and 1890 and how the population of the western states changed during that time. Write a paragraph explaining the cause-and-effect relationship between the expansion of the railroads and the growth of the population in the West. You may want to begin by focusing on a few specific states, noting the change in population density and railroad service between 1870 and 1890. Once you note the general trend, you should check in your history textbook and other sources for specific information about the settlement of the West during this period. Write a topic sentence based on this information. Decide on your supporting information, and then write a paragraph explaining the cause-and-effect relationship between the growth of the railroads and the settlement of the West. You may want to use order of importance or generality to organize your writing.

2

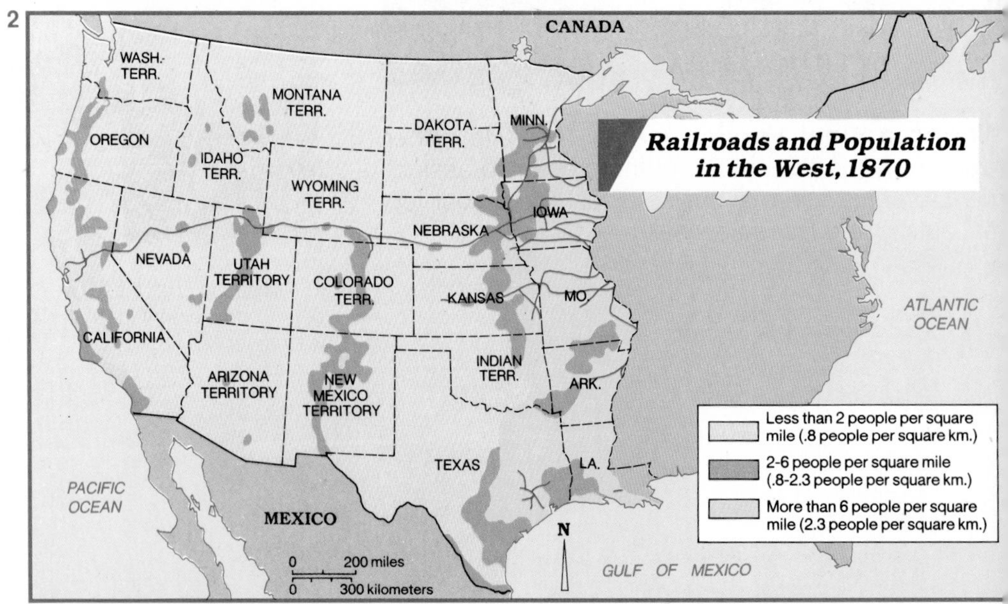

Railroads and Population in the West, 1870

The illustrations on these two pages complement the instruction in Chapter 14.

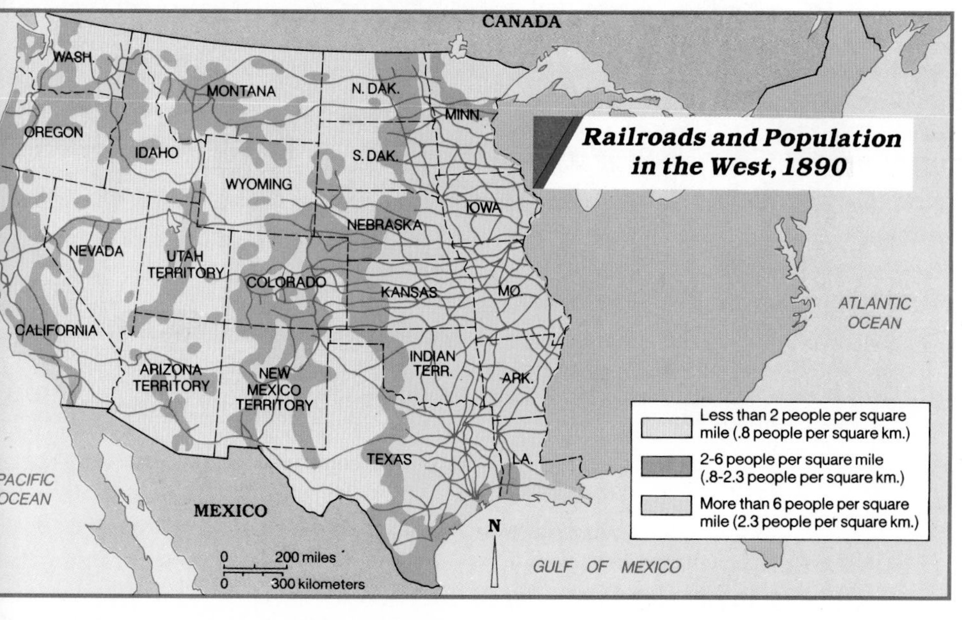

1

2

The illustrations on these two pages complement the instruction in Chapte

ASSIGNMENTS

Comparing and Contrasting *(page 284).* Illustration 1 on page 360 shows a twentieth-century artist's idealized conception of an American family dwelling in a sod house. Illustration 3 is a photograph of an actual Great Plains family living in a sod house in the 1880s. Write a paragraph comparing and contrasting the two illustrations. Decide on the overall impression that each creates. Then examine each closely, listing details about the setting and people portrayed in each. Decide on a main idea, and then write your comparison and contrast.

Making a Generalization *(page 280).* Examine items 1 and 3, which are photographs of American families living a century apart. Item 2 is a photograph of a contemporary American family living in a suburb. Item 3 is a photograph of a Great Plains family living in a sod house in the 1880s. Note the details in each photograph: the setting, the size of each family, and the appearance of each member. Then write a paragraph leading up to a generalization about how the American family has changed during the past century.

RITING ABOUT SCIENCE AND TECHNOLOGY

ASSIGNMENTS

■ **Writing About a Process in a Scientific Report** *(page 290).* Illustration 1 shows a solar heating system warming a house during the winter. Write a paragraph that explains how this warming process works. Begin prewriting by identifying your purpose and audience. Then list all the steps that are required for the process to take place. Arrange the steps in chronological order.

Once you have a clear understanding of the steps in the process, begin to write your paragraph. Choose precise language that is appropriate to your purpose and audience, and use third-person pronouns rather than first-person pronouns such as *I* or *me.* Present the steps of the process in chronological order, and use transitions to make sure that the order is clear and that the paragraph is coherent.

1

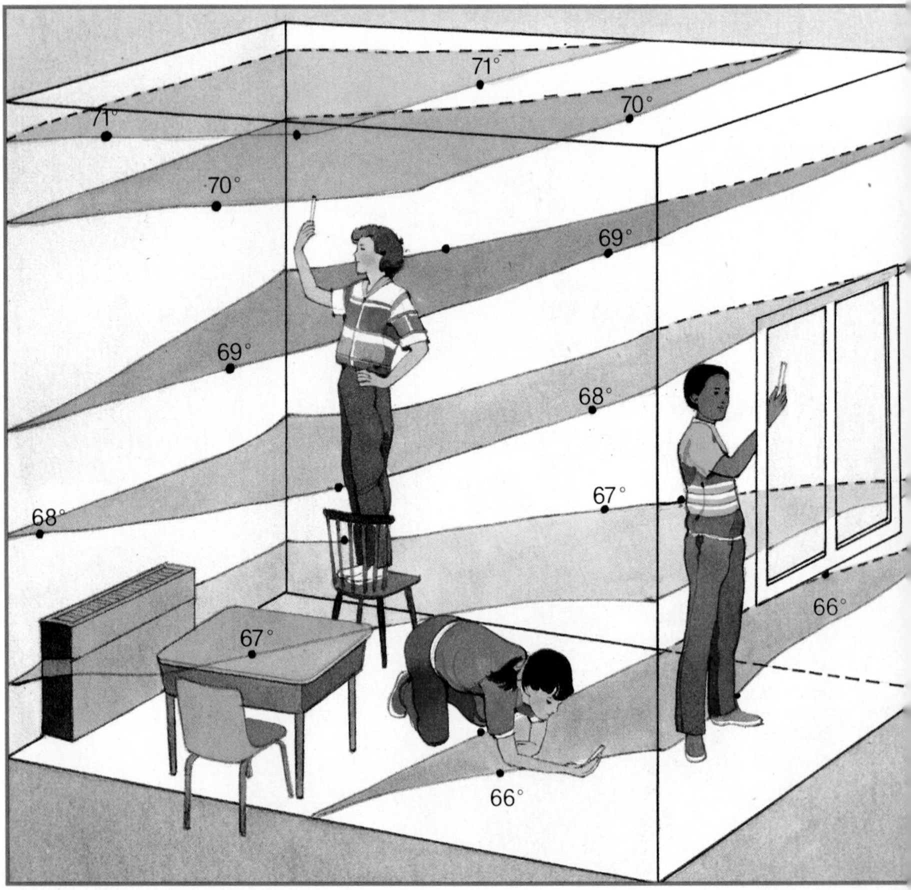

71°
71°
70°
70°
69°
69°
68°
68°
67°
67°
66°
66°

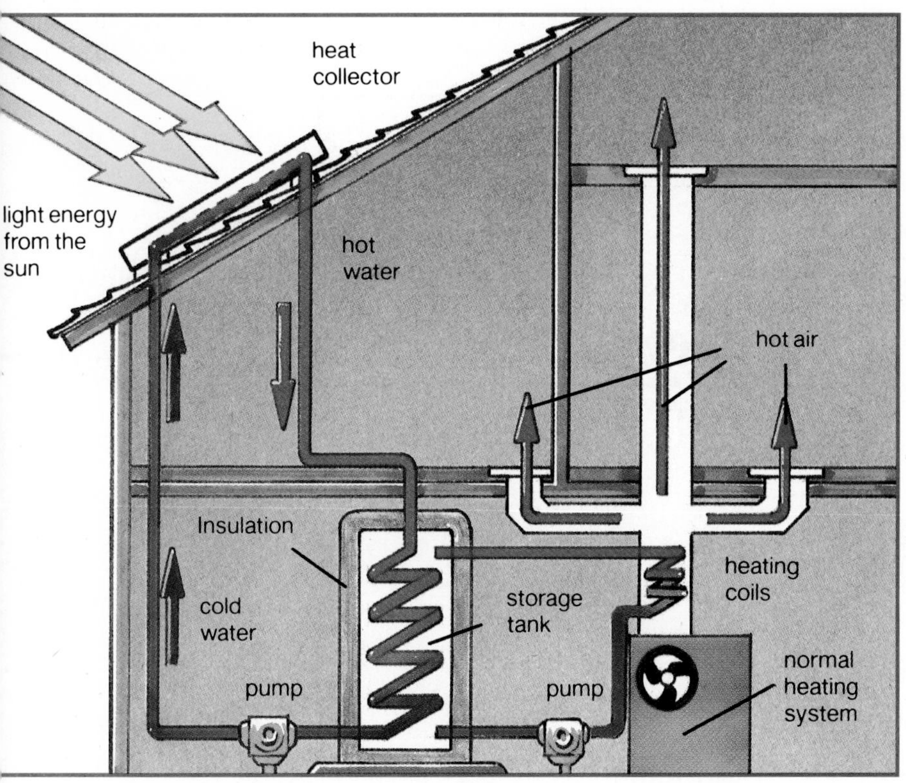

■ **Writing with Comparison and Contrast** *(page 290).* Write a paragraph that compares and contrasts the data in illustration 2 with findings of your own. Illustration 2 shows regions of equal temperature in different parts of a room. These regions are called *isotherms.*

As prewriting for your paragraph, measure the temperature of a room at the following heights: one foot above the floor, at the top of a table, halfway to the ceiling, and as close as possible to the ceiling. Make a list of the readings you obtain. Then draw a diagram indicating the position and measurement of each reading taken, using illustration 2 as your guide. Connect the points that show the same temperature with lines, and color the spaces between the lines with different colors. Finally, compare your data with the data in illustration 2, and write a paragraph about your findings.

The illustrations on these two pages complement the instruction in Chapter 15.

1

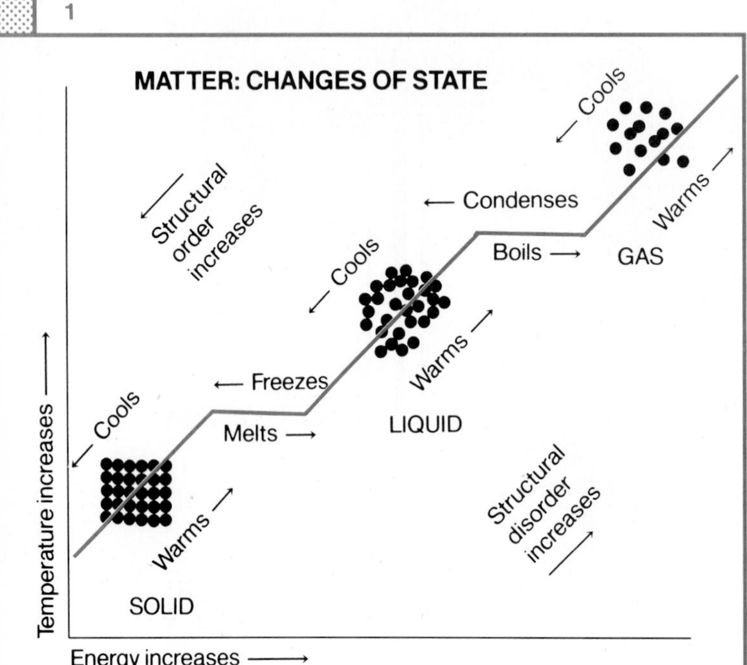

2

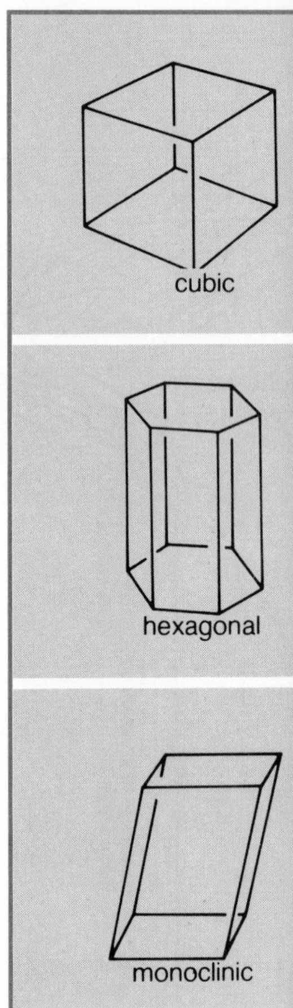

■ **Writing About Cause and Effect in a Scientific Report** *(page 290).* Write a paragraph about illustration 1, which shows the changes of state in matter. In your paragraph explain what causes matter to change from a solid to a liquid to a gas.

As prewriting, study the illustration, and make two lists of the different changes it shows. The first list should tell what happens when matter changes from solid to gas, and the second should explain what happens when matter changes from gas to solid. Be sure to consider all the information the illustration presents.

Begin your first draft with a topic sentence that expresses your main idea. Then follow a method of organization that presents your support in a logical way. Use transitions to help make the cause-effect relationships clear. Revise your first draft, making sure that you have included all causes and effects.

■ **Writing a Scientific Report** *(pages 263–266).* Use illustrations 2 and three as the basis for a short scientific report on crystals. Illustration 2 shows the basic shapes of crystals, and illustration 3 shows a variety of crystals that grow naturally in the earth's crust. Your report will define crystals, explain the process by which they are formed, and discuss the system by which they are classified.

As prewriting, ask general questions about your topic, and prepare a working outline. Then locate sources, and begin to take notes. You may want to prepare sketches and diagrams for your report. Once you have completed your preliminary work, prepare a final outline, and write a first draft. Use an author–date–page-number system (page 265) to cite your sources. Revise your draft using the checklist on page 266. Your final draft should have an introduction, a discussion section, and conclusion, and a title page, table of contents, and bibliography.

The illustrations on these two pages complement the instruction in Chapter 15.

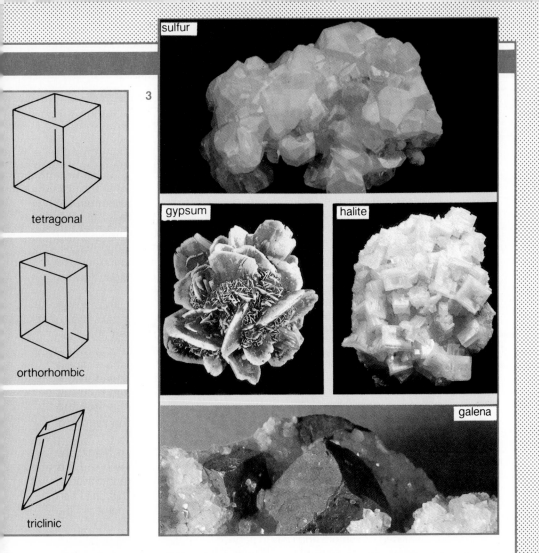

RITING ABOUT LITERATURE

Thomas Wolfe

The Far and the Near

On the outskirts of a little town upon a rise of land that swept back from the railway there was a tidy little cottage of white boards, trimmed vividly with green blinds. To one side of the house there was a garden neatly patterned with plots of growing vegetables, and an arbor[1] for the grapes which ripened late in August. Before the house there were three mighty oaks which sheltered it in their clean and massive shade in summer, and to the other side there was a border of gay flowers. The whole place had an air of tidiness, thrift, and modest comfort.

Every day, a few minutes after two o'clock in the afternoon, the limited express between the two cities passed this spot. At that moment the great train, having halted for a breathing space at the town nearby, was beginning to lengthen evenly into its stroke, but it had not yet reached the full drive of its terrific speed. It swung into view deliberately, swept past with a powerful swaying motion of the engine, a low smooth rumble of its heavy cars upon pressed steel, and then it vanished in the cut. For a moment the progress of the engine could be marked by heavy bellowing puffs of smoke that burst at spaced intervals above the edges of the meadow grass, and finally nothing could be heard but the solid clacking tempo of the wheels receding into the drowsy stillness of the afternoon.

Every day for more than twenty years, as the train approached this house, the engineer had blown on the whistle, and every day, as soon as she heard this signal, a woman had appeared on the back porch of the little house and waved to him. At first she had a small child clinging to her skirts, and now this child had grown to full womanhood, and every day she, too, came with her mother to the porch and waved.

The engineer had grown old and gray in service. He had driven his great train, loaded with its weight of lives, across the land ten thousand times. His own children had grown up and married, and four times he had seen before him on the tracks the ghastly dot of tragedy converging like a cannon ball to its eclipse of horror at the boiler head[2]—a light spring wagon filled with children, with its clustered row of small stunned faces; a cheap automobile stalled upon the tracks, set with the wooden figures of people paralyzed with fear; a battered hobo walking by the rail, too deaf and old to hear the whistle's warning; and a form flung past his window with a scream—all this the man had seen and known. He had known all the grief, the joy, the peril, and the labor such a man could know; he had grown seamed and weathered in his loyal service, and now, schooled by the qualities of faith and courage and humbleness that attended his labor, he had grown old, and had the grandeur and the wisdom these men have.

But no matter what peril or tragedy he had known, the vision of the little house and the women waving to him with a brave free motion of the arm had become

1. **arbor:** open-work lattice structure, usually shady and covered with vines.
2. **boiler head:** front section of a steam locomotive.

fixed in the mind of the engineer as something beautiful and enduring, something beyond all change and ruin, and something that would always be the same, no matter what mishap, grief, or error might break the iron schedule of his days.

The sight of the little house and of these two women gave him the most extraordinary happiness he had ever known. He had seen them in a thousand lights, a hundred weathers. He had seen them through the harsh bare light of wintry gray across the brown and frosted stubble of earth, and he had seen them again in the green luring sorcery of April.

He felt for them and for the little house in which they lived such tenderness as a man might feel for his own children, and at length the picture of their lives was carved so sharply in his heart that he felt that he knew their lives completely, to every hour and moment of the day, and he resolved that one day, when his years of service should be ended, he would go and find these people and speak at last with them whose lives had been so wrought[3] into his own.

That day came. At last the engineer stepped from a train onto the station platform of the town where these two women lived. His years upon the rail had ended. He was a pensioned servant of his company, with no more work to do. The engineer walked slowly through the station and out into the streets of the town. Everything was as strange to him as if he had never seen this town before. As he walked on, his sense of bewilderment and confusion grew. Could this be the town he had passed ten thousand times? Were these the same houses he had seen so often from the high windows of his cab? It was all as unfamiliar, as disquieting as a city in a dream, and the perplexity of his spirit increased as he went on.

Presently the houses thinned into the straggling outposts of the town, and the street faded into a country road—the one on which the women lived. And the man plodded on slowly in the heat and dust. At length he stood before the house he sought. He knew at once that he had found the proper place. He saw the lordly oaks before the house, the flower beds, the garden, and the arbor, and farther off, the glint of rails.

Yes, this was the house he sought, the place he had passed so many times, the destination he had longed for with such happiness. But now that he had found it, now that he was here, why did his hand falter on the gate; why had the town, the road, the earth, the very entrance to this place he loved turned unfamiliar as the landscape of some ugly dream? Why did he now feel this sense of confusion, doubt, and hopelessness?

At length he entered by the gate, walked slowly up the path and in a moment more had mounted three short steps that led up to the porch, and was knocking at the door. Presently he heard steps in the hall, the door was opened, and a woman stood facing him.

And instantly, with a sense of bitter loss and grief, he was sorry he had come. He knew at once that the woman who stood there looking at him with a mistrustful eye was the same woman who had waved to him so many thousand times. But her face was harsh and pinched and meager; the flesh sagged wearily in sallow[4]

---

3. **wrought:** formed; shaped
4. **sallow:** sickly, yellowish.

The literary works presented here complement the instruction in Chapter 16.

folds, and the small eyes peered at him with timid suspicion and uneasy doubt. All the brave freedom, the warmth, and the affection that he had read into her gesture vanished in the moment that he saw her and heard her unfriendly tongue.

And now his own voice sounded unreal and ghastly to him as he tried to explain his presence, to tell her who he was and the reason he had come. But he faltered on, fighting stubbornly against the horror of regret, confusion, disbelief that surged up in his spirit, drowning all his former joy and making his act of hope and tenderness seem shameful to him.

At length the woman invited him almost unwillingly into the house, and called her daughter in a harsh shrill voice. Then, for a brief agony of time, the man sat in an ugly little parlor, and he tried to talk while the two women stared at him with a dull, bewildered hostility, a sullen, timorous restraint.

And finally, stammering a crude farewell, he departed. He walked away down the path and then along the road toward town, and suddenly he knew that he was an old man. His heart, which had been brave and confident when he looked along the familiar vista of the rails, was now sick with doubt and horror as it saw the strange and unsuspected visage of an earth which had always been within a stone's throw of him, and which he had never seen or known. And he knew that all the magic of that bright lost way, the vista of that shining line, the imagined corner of that small good universe of hope's desire, was gone forever, could never be got back again.

William Gibson

from The Miracle Worker

from Act III, Scene iii. The KELLER *homestead in Tuscumbia, Alabama. The time is the 1880s.*

[HELEN KELLER *is a seven-year-old who has been blind and deaf since infancy. Her teacher is* ANNIE SULLIVAN, *who is twenty years old and specially trained to work with the blind and deaf.* ANNIE *persuaded* HELEN's *parents, who have always given in to their willful daughter, to allow her and* HELEN *to spend two weeks away from the family. During the time apart* ANNIE *taught* HELEN *to obey her and to spell a number of words in the finger alphabet of the deaf. The* KELLER *family is celebrating* HELEN's *homecoming with a special dinner. The group includes* HELEN *and* ANNIE, CAPTAIN KELLER *and his wife* KATE *(*HELEN's *parents),* AUNT EV *(*KELLER's *sister, and* JAMES *(*KELLER's *grown son by a previous marriage). The dinner seems to be going smoothly, and* HELEN *has been behaving herself.*]

KATE. Pickles, Aunt Ev?

AUNT EV. Oh, I should say so, you know my opinion of your pickles—

KATE. This is the end of them, I'm afraid. I didn't put up nearly enough last summer, this year I intend to—

[*She interrupts herself, seeing* HELEN *deliberately lift off her napkin and drop it to the floor. She bends to retrieve it, but* ANNIE *stops her arm....* ANNIE *puts the napkin on* HELEN. HELEN *yanks it off, and throws it down.* ANNIE *rises, lifts*

HELEN's *plate, and bears it away.* HELEN, *feeling it gone, slides down and commences to kick up under the table; the dishes jump.* ANNIE *takes* HELEN's *wrists firmly and swings her off the chair.* HELEN, *struggling, gets one hand free, and catches at her mother's skirt; when* KATE *takes her by the shoulders,* HELEN *hangs quietly.*]

KATE. Miss Annie.

ANNIE. No.

KATE. [*A pause.*] It's a very special day.

ANNIE. [*Grimly.*] It will be, when I give in to that....

AUNT EV. But what's the child done?

ANNIE. She's learned not to throw things on the floor and kick. It took us the better part of two weeks and—

AUNT EV. But only a napkin, it's not as if it were breakable!

ANNIE. And everything she's learned *is?*...

KATE. What do you wish to do?

ANNIE. Let me take her from the table....

KATE. [*Distressed.*] Will once hurt so much, Miss Annie? I've—made all Helen's favorite foods, tonight.

KELLER. [*Gently.*] It's a homecoming party, Miss Annie.

[ANNIE *after a moment releases* HELEN. *But she cannot accept it.*]

ANNIE. She's testing you. You realize?...

JAMES. [*To* ANNIE.] She's testing *you.*

KELLER. [*Testily.*] Jimmie....

ANNIE. Of course she's testing me. Let me keep her to what she's learned and she'll go on learning from me. Take her out of my hands and it all comes apart.

[KATE *closes her eyes, digesting it;* ANNIE *sits again, with a brief comment for her.*]

ANNIE. Be bountiful, it's at her expense. [*She turns to* JAMES, *flatly.*] Please pass me more of—her favorite foods.

[*Then* KATE *lifts* HELEN's *hand, and turning her toward* ANNIE, *surrenders her.*]...

KATE. [*Low.*] Take her, Miss Annie.

ANNIE. Thank you.

[*But the moment* ANNIE *rising reaches for her hand,* HELEN *begins to fight and kick, clutching to the tablecloth, and uttering laments.*]...

JAMES. [*Wearily.*] I think we've started all over....

[ANNIE *moves in to grasp* HELEN's *wrist, and* HELEN *flinging out a hand encounters the pitcher; she swings with it at* ANNIE: ANNIE *falling back blocks it with an elbow, but the water flies over her dress.* ANNIE *gets her breath, then snatches the pitcher away in one hand, hoists* HELEN *up bodily under the other arm and starts to carry her out, kicking.* KELLER *stands.*]

ANNIE. [*Savagely polite.*] Don't get up!

KELLER. Where are you going?

ANNIE. Don't smooth anything else out for me, don't interfere in any way! I treat her like a seeing child because I *ask* her to see. I *expect* her to see, don't undo what I do!

KELLER. Where are you taking her?

ANNIE. To make her fill this pitcher again!...

[ANNIE *pulls* HELEN *downstairs by one hand, the pitcher in her other hand, down the porch steps, and across the yard to the pump. She puts* HELEN's *hand on the pump handle, grimly.*]

ANNIE. All right. Pump.

[HELEN *touches her cheek,*[1] *waits uncertainly.*]

---

1. **Helen...cheek:** Touching her cheek is Helen's sign for her mother.

The literary works presented here complement the instruction in Chapter 16.

ANNIE. No, she's not here. Pump!

[*She forces* HELEN's *hand to work the handle, then lets go. And* HELEN *obeys. She pumps till the water comes, then* ANNIE *puts the pitcher in her other hand and guides it under the spout, and the water tumbling half into and half around the pitcher douses* HELEN's *hand.* ANNIE *takes over the handle to keep water coming, and does automatically what she has done so many times before, spells into* HELEN's *free palm:*]

ANNIE. Water. W, a, t, e, r. *Water.* It has a—name—

[*And now the miracle happens.* HELEN *drops the pitcher on the slab under the spout, it shatters. She stands transfixed.* ANNIE *freezes on the pump handle: There is a change in the sundown light, and with it a change in* HELEN's *face, some light coming into it we have never seen there, some struggle in the depths behind it; and her lips tremble, trying to remember something the muscles around them once knew, till at last it finds its way out, painfully, a baby sound buried under the debris of years of dumbness.*]

HELEN. Wah. Wah. [*And again, with great effort.*] Wah. Wah.

[HELEN *plunges her hand into the dwindling water, spells into her own palm. Then she gropes frantically,* ANNIE *reaches for her hand, and* HELEN *spells into* ANNIE's *hand.*]

ANNIE. [*Whispering.*] Yes.

[HELEN *spells into it again.*]

ANNIE. Yes!

[HELEN *grabs at the handle, pumps for more water, plunges her hand into its spurt and grabs* ANNIE's *to spell it again.*]

ANNIE. *Yes!* Oh, my dear—

[*She falls to her knees to clasp* HELEN's *hand, but* HELEN *pulls it free, stands almost bewildered, then drops to the ground, pats it swiftly, holds up her palm.* ANNIE *spells into it:*]

ANNIE. Ground.

[HELEN *spells it back.*]

ANNIE. Yes!

[HELEN *whirls to the pump, pats it, holds up her palm, and* ANNIE *spells into it.*]

ANNIE. Pump.

[HELEN *spells it back.*]

ANNIE. Yes! Yes!

[*Now* HELEN *is in such an excitement she is possessed, wild, trembling, cannot be still, turns, runs, falls onto the porch step, claps it, reaches out her palm, and* ANNIE *is at it instantly to spell:*]

ANNIE. Step.

[HELEN *has not time to spell back now, she whirls groping, to touch anything, encounters the trellis, shakes it, thrusts out her palm, and* ANNIE *while spelling to her cries wildly at the house.*]

ANNIE. Trellis. Mrs. Keller! *Mrs. Keller!*

[*Inside* KATE *starts to her feet.* HELEN *scrambles back onto the porch, groping, and finds the bell string, tugs it, the bell rings, the distant chimes begin tolling the hour, all the bells in town seem to break into speech while* HELEN *reaches out and* ANNIE *spells feverishly into her hand.* KATE *hurries out, with* KELLER *after her. . . .* HELEN, *ringing the bell, with her other hand encounters her mother's skirt; when she throws a hand out,* ANNIE *spells into it:*]

ANNIE. Mother.

[KELLER *now seizes* HELEN's *hand, she touches him, gestures a hand, and* ANNIE *again spells:*]

ANNIE. Papa—She *knows!*

Robert P. Tristram Coffin

The Secret Heart

Across the years he could recall
His father one way best of all.

In the stillest hour of night
The boy awakened to a light.

Half in dreams, he saw his sire[1]
With his great hands full of fire.

The man had struck a match to see
If his son slept peacefully.

He held his palms each side the spark
His love had kindled in the dark.

His two hands were curved apart
In the semblance of a heart.

He wore, it seemed to his small son,
A bare heart on his hidden one,

A heart that gave out such a glow
No son awake could bear to know.

It showed a look upon a face
Too tender for the day to trace.

One instant, it lit all about,
And then the secret heart went out.

But it shone long enough for one
To know that hands held up the sun.

1. **sire:** father.

Robert Hayden

Those Winter Sundays

Sundays too my father got up early
and put his clothes on in the blueblack cold,
then with cracked hands that ached
from labor in the weekday weather made
banked fires blaze. No one ever thanked him.

I'd wake and hear the cold splintering, breaking.
When the rooms were warm, he'd call,
and slowly I would rise and dress,
fearing the chronic angers of that house,

Speaking indifferently to him,
who had driven out the cold
and polished my good shoes as well.
What did I know, what did I know
of love's austere and lonely offices?

The literary works presented here complement the instruction in Chapter 16.

REATIVE WRITING

ASSIGNMENTS

1

- **Generating, Exploring, and Outlining a Story Idea** *(pages 323–326)*. Using one of the illustrations shown on pages 372–375, generate an idea for a short story. Answer the questions for exploring a story idea (page 324). Then write an outline of the events in the story's plot. Consider using techniques such as *flashback* and *foreshadowing* to create excitement and suspense in your story.
- **Writing a Story** *(pages 326–329)*. Write a story based on your work for the assignment above. Your story should include the following elements: beginning, setting, characterization and motivation, dialogue, climax and resolution, and a title.
- **Generating Ideas for a Scene** *(pages 329–330)*. Complete a chart of scene ideas (page 330) using three photographs from pages 372–375.

3

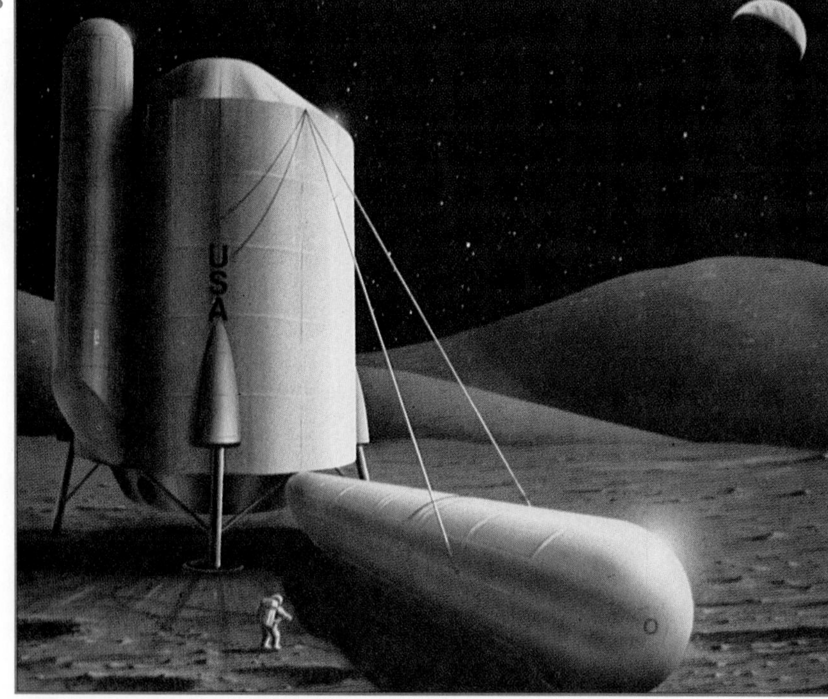

4

2

Edward Hopper (1882–1967), *Table for Ladies*. Oil on canvas. H. 48¼ in. W. 60¼ in.

5

Andrew Wyeth, *Christina's World*, 1948.

The illustrations on these two pages complement the instruction in Chapter 17.

1

Winslow Homer (1836–1910), *Eaglehead, Manchester, Massachusetts.*

2

4

© Joel Meyerowitz.

5

The illustrations on these two pages complement the instruction in Chapter 17.

3

ASSIGNMENTS

- **Exploring and Outlining a Scene Idea** *(pages 330–331).* Look over the chart you made for the previous assignment, and choose the idea that you like best. Explore your idea with questions like those on page 330–331. Then outline the scene's action.

- **Writing a Dramatic Scene** *(pages 332–334).* Write a dramatic scene based on your work for the assignment above. Your scene should include setting, dialogue, action, conflict, climax, a resolution, and a title.

- **Generating and Exploring Ideas for a Poem** *(pages 334–338).* Base an idea for a poem on an illustration on pages 341–344. Answer the questions for exploring ideas for a poem (pages 337–338).

- **Writing a Poem** *(pages 338–339).* Write a poem of any form and any length from the notes you created for the assignment above. Your poem need not rhyme.

UNIT VI
Grammar

Think of language as a wonderful machine and grammar as a kind of operator's manual for that machine: Grammar describes how a language *works*. Grammar explains how words interact to build structures that you can assemble in any number of ways into sentences that can express any number of ideas. Grammar sets forth the underlying "laws" that govern a language. For example, when your mind takes the isolated words *rain, field, the, to, wash, began,* and *gently,* and transforms them into *Gently, the rain began to wash the field,* you are applying the laws of English grammar to express a meaningful idea. You are making the machine of your language work.

Actually you became a grammarian at a very early age: You had mastered most of the laws of grammar by the time you were eight. If you knew your grammar so well then, why do you need to study it now? At eight you knew grammar *instinctively*; now you need to understand it *consciously.* Studying grammar will help you in a number of ways. First, becoming conscious of the grammatical laws that you instinctively obey will help you to think about these laws systematically, to recognize the orderly patterns that language follows. After all, it is always easier to obey a law when you understand why it exists. Second, knowing the terminology of grammar will sharpen your ability to pinpoint problems in your speaking and writing and to discuss these problems with your instructor. Third, understanding English grammar will aid you in studying a foreign language. In short, studying English grammar will increase your skill in communication, thus making you a better speaker and writer in any language.

This unit begins by setting forth the eight major categories of words, called *parts of speech*: nouns, pronouns, verbs, adjectives, adverbs, prepositions, conjunctions, and interjections. The next chapter analyzes the basic ingredients that make up sentences and explains the various roles that parts of speech play in forming sentences. The last two chapters of the unit focus on phrases and clauses, which are groups of words that function as single parts of speech within sentences. The final chapter describes the different sentence structures that you can create by combining clauses in different ways. In addition, this chapter presents guidelines for avoiding ungrammatical sentence structures. The four chapters in this unit will reinforce what you already know about your language and help you to expand that knowledge.

CHAPTER 18
Parts of Speech

NOUNS

A **noun** is a word that names a person, a place, a thing, or an idea.

A noun can name a person, place, or thing (living or nonliving) that occupies space.

PERSON: aunt, astronaut, son, daughter, child
PLACE: universe, village, park, bedroom
LIVING THING: shark, eagle, oak, foot
NONLIVING THING: table, sock, television, pencil

A noun can also name something that does not occupy space. Not only can we say, "We know about that *village,*" but we can also say, "We know about *honesty.*" In other words, some nouns allow us to take an aspect of experience—such as being honest—and talk about it as though it were a thing to which we could actually point. Here are some other examples of nouns that do not occupy space:

Their **anniversary** is in **February.**
We are studying **ethics** in this **course.**
The **inventiveness** of her **ideas** is the main **reason** for her **success.**

RECOGNIZING NOUNS

As you have just seen, you can classify a word as a noun if it names something. In addition, you can identify a word as a noun if it satisfies one of the following tests:

1. A word is a noun if it makes sense in one of the blanks in the following sentences:

She has a(n) ________.
I heard about (the) ________.
(The) ________ is (are) interesting.

2. The following noun-forming suffixes almost always signal that a word is a noun: *-acy, -age, -cy, -dom, -ee, -ence, -ency, -er, -ery, -ess, -et, -ette, -hood, -ian, -ics, -ion, -ism, -ite, -ity, -let, -ment, -ness, -or, -ship, -tion.*

freedom	adulthood
nominee	socialite
painter	insularity
hostess	actor
eaglet	courtship

CHARACTERISTICS OF NOUNS

Nouns also have the following characteristics:

1. Most nouns can be singular or plural, depending on whether they name *one* person, place, thing, or idea or *more than one.*

SINGULAR: mask, wrench, fly, knife, woman
PLURAL: masks, wrenches, flies, knives, women

Some nouns—such as *furniture, inventiveness,* and *honesty*—have no logical plural forms. (For rules on making the plural forms of nouns, see Chapter 30.)

2. Nouns have a form to show possession, ownership, or the relationship between two nouns.

SINGULAR	PLURAL
a **boy's** hat	the **boys'** hats
that **country's** laws	those **countries'** laws
a **woman's** smile	**women's** smiles

Objective
EXERCISE 1. Identifying Nouns. On your paper list the twenty nouns that appear in the following passage.

(1) Up until the twentieth century American drama made little impact on American literature as a whole. **(2)** The reasons for the lack of American drama are understandable. **(3)** Theaters such as the elitist European institutions of the eighteenth century did not flourish in our infant democracy. **(4)** Furthermore, the melodrama that became so popular in Victorian times never attracted serious American writers. **(5)** In the early twentieth century, however, American playwrights began to produce tragedies and psychological dramas that revolutionized American theater.

Objective
EXERCISE 2. Identifying Nouns with No Plural Forms. For each set of nouns, write the one that cannot logically be made plural.

1. hammer, equipment, tool

2. war, soldier, bravery
3. happiness, joy, smile
4. equality, similarity, equal
5. freedom, independence, liberty

PROPER AND COMMON NOUNS

A **proper noun** is the name of a particular person, place, thing, or idea.

A **common noun** is the general—not the particular—name of a person, place, thing, or idea.

The word *proper* comes from the Latin word *proprius,* which means "one's own." Therefore, a word that is "one's own"—such as a person's name—is considered *proper.* The important words in proper nouns are capitalized. (For rules on capitalizing proper nouns, see Chapter 27.)

PROPER NOUNS

PERSON: Richard Wright, Amelia Guitierrez, Dr. Salk, Eric the Red
PLACE: Pasadena, the Bering Sea, Nicaragua, the King Ranch
THING: King Kong, Volkswagen, Society of Friends, the *Titanic*
IDEA: the Augustan Age, Buddhism, the Indianapolis 500

Objective
EXERCISE 3. Matching Proper Nouns with Common Nouns. On your paper match the numbered proper nouns on the left with the lettered common nouns on the right.

1. London	**a.** month
2. Boston Marathon	**b.** car
3. Roxy Theater	**c.** race
4. Clara Barton	**d.** landmark
5. December	**e.** building
6. *New Orleans Picayune*	**f.** nurse
7. France	**g.** country
8. Wheatena	**h.** city
9. Toyota Celica	**i.** cereal
10. Statue of Liberty	**j.** newspaper

Answers: **1.** h; **2.** c; **3.** e; **4.** f; **5.** a; **6.** j; **7.** g; **8.** i; **9.** b; **10.** d

COLLECTIVE NOUNS

A **collective noun** names a group.

class	(the) military	congregation	(a) herd (of elk)
crew	(the) cast	chorus	(a) swarm (of bees)

A collective noun may be considered either singular or plural. You consider the collective noun singular when you talk about the group as a whole. You consider the collective noun plural when you talk about the individual members of the group. (For help with subject-verb agreement with collective nouns, see Chapter 23.)

SINGULAR: The **faculty** wants our cooperation.
PLURAL: The **faculty** have discussed the student proposal.

Objective
EXERCISE 4. Identifying Collective Nouns. Identify in writing the collective noun in each of the following sentences. Then indicate whether its meaning is singular or plural.

1. A herd of cattle fills the range in Sonoma County, Texas.
2. The pride of lions have different colored hides.
3. A gaggle is the name for a group of geese.
4. When startled, a school of fish dart in different directions.
5. A flock of domestic ducks follows a human being quite readily.

Answers: 1. sing.; 2. pl.; 3. sing.; 4. pl.; 5. sing.

COMPOUND NOUNS

A **compound noun** is a noun that is made up of more than one word.

brainpower	comic strip	master-at-arms
paintbrush	brake lining	foot-candle
payday	peace pipe	hurdy-gurdy

Sometimes two words are written as one to form a compound noun; sometimes they are written as two separate words; sometimes they are written with hyphens. Check a dictionary if you are not sure of the way a compound noun should be written.

Proper nouns may be compound: Margaret Thatcher, Yellowstone National Park, the Declaration of Independence.

Objective
EXERCISE 5. Forming Compound Nouns. Match the nouns in column 1 with the nouns in column 2 to form as many compound nouns as you can. (At least thirty-eight possibilities exist.)

	1		2	
air base	air	airfield	base	airline
air lock	ball	wheelhouse	field	air plant
airship	battle	air valve	house	ball field
ball valve	fire	battlefield	line	battleship
battle station	gas	wheelbase	lock	firehouse
firelock	ice	fireman/firewoman	man/woman	fire ship
fire station	space	waterline	plant	gas plant

gas station tree ice field ship icehouse
tree line water ice plant station spaceman/spacewoman
spaceship wheel space station valve tree house

Suggested Answers appear alongside the items.

CONCRETE AND ABSTRACT NOUNS

A **concrete noun** names an object that occupies space or can be recognized by any of the senses.

stone planet shout air sugar

An **abstract noun** names an idea, a quality, or a characteristic.

hardness roundness anger clarity dissonance

Objective

EXERCISE 6. Supplying Abstract and Concrete Nouns. For each concrete noun in item 1, write an abstract noun that names an idea with which the concrete noun can be associated. For each abstract noun in item 2, write a concrete noun that possesses the quality of the abstract noun.

SAMPLES: **1.** *astronaut*—fearlessness
2. *darkness*—cave

strength vibration scent sweetness pain
1. athlete, thunder, roses, honey, toothache
principal newspaper brook lemon murder
2. authority, truth, tranquility, sourness, guilt

Suggested Answers appear above the items.

NOUN PHRASES

A **noun phrase** is a group of words consisting of a noun and one or more other words that make the noun's meaning more specific.

The outrageous antics of my little sister delight me.

The noun at the heart of this noun phrase is *antics.* The other words in the phrase provide additional information about the noun.

Objective

EXERCISE 7. Identifying Noun Phrases. Reread the paragraph in Exercise 1 on page 378. Identify in writing at least five noun phrases contained in the paragraph.

Objective

APPLICATION EXERCISE. Creating Sentences with Nouns. Write five sentences about a close friend. Rely especially on concrete nouns to convey a vivid picture of the person.

Suggested Answer: Mark can spread his fingers as wide as a fan and hold a basketball in one hand.

REVIEW EXERCISE. Nouns. On your paper complete each sentence by filling the blanks with the kind of noun specified in italics. Be sure that your completed sentences make sense.

1. ___*proper*___ [Laura] saw a ___*compound*___ [bald eagle] near the ___*concrete*___ [river].
2. The ___*abstract*___ [versatility] of ___*common*___ [algebra] has always intrigued the ___*collective*___ [class].
3. The ___*collective*___ [choir] left their ___*concrete*___ [robes] at ___*proper, compound*___ [Grand Central Terminal].
4. Two ___*concrete*___ [lions] stalked a ___*collective*___ [herd] of ___*noun phrase*___ [timid, nervous gazelles].

REVISION EXERCISE. Nouns. In the following passage from *The Waves,* Virginia Woolf uses nouns effectively to describe sunlight flooding a room.

Sharp-edged wedges of light lay upon the window-sill and showed inside the room plates with blue rings, cups with curved handles, the bulge of a great bowl, the criss-cross pattern in the rug, and the formidable corners and lines of cabinets and bookcases. Behind their conglomeration hung a zone of shadow in which might be a further shape to be disencumbered of shadow or still denser depths of darkness.

Study the passage above closely, and try to apply some of Woolf's techniques when you write and revise your own work.

1. Whenever possible, use precise concrete nouns rather than general or abstract nouns. Notice that Woolf uses precise nouns to describe the objects that the sunlight illuminates in the room: plates, cups, a bowl, the rug, cabinets, bookcases. The list gives us a clearer picture of the room than it would if the author had merely said that the sunlight illuminated "the furnishings." Notice also, however, that in the last sentence Woolf does use general nouns to suggest the mysterious areas of darkness remaining in the room: zone of shadow, a further shape, depths of darkness.
2. Try to choose nouns for the effect of their sound as well as for their meaning. For example, notice how the *b* and *l* sounds in Woolf's phrase "the bulge of a great bowl" help accentuate the shape and size of the object.
3. Try to expand single nouns into noun phrases. Woolf expands the nouns *corners* and *lines* into "the formidable corners and lines of cabinets and bookcases." This expansion helps her make her point that light reveals the particular nature of general shapes.

Practice these techniques by revising the following passage on your paper. Pay particular attention to the italicized words.

When the *moon* slides above the horizon, everything slowly becomes bathed in *light.* The *field* shimmers, and the *trees* loom larger with their own *darkness. Anyone* out at *this time of night* is also washed in the *moonlight. Everything* is transformed into *something strange.*

PRONOUNS

A **pronoun** is a word that takes the place of a noun, a group of words acting as a noun, or another pronoun.

Pronouns allow you to avoid unnecessary repetitions when you speak or write. The word or group of words that a pronoun replaces is called its **antecedent**.

> Ezra Pound lived in Rapallo, Italy, where **he** wrote the *Cantos.* [The pronoun *he* takes the place of the noun *Ezra Pound.*]
>
> T. S. Eliot's *The Waste Land* and James Joyce's *Ulysses* appeared in 1922. **Each** had a profound effect on twentieth-century literature. [The pronoun *each* takes the place of the noun phrases *T. S. Eliot's The Waste Land* and *James Joyce's Ulysses.*]
>
> Gertrude Stein wanted to revolutionize writing. **This** is evident in her first major work, *Three Lives.* [The pronoun *this* takes the place of the phrase *to revolutionize writing.*]
>
> **Few** remembered to bring **their** notebooks to the lecture. [The pronoun *their* takes the place of the pronoun *few,* which stands for an unidentified group of people.]

The English language has about seventy-five pronouns, which fall into one or more of the following categories: personal pronouns, reflexive and intensive pronouns, demonstrative pronouns, interrogative pronouns, relative pronouns, and indefinite pronouns.

PERSONAL PRONOUNS

A **personal pronoun** refers to a specific person or thing by indicating the person speaking (the first person), the person being addressed (the second person), or any other person or thing being discussed (the third person). Personal pronouns also express **number**; they are singular or plural.

	SINGULAR	PLURAL
FIRST PERSON:	I, me	we, us
SECOND PERSON:	you	you
THIRD PERSON:	he, him she, her it	they, them

FIRST PERSON: **I** sent Angela a get-well card. [*I* refers to the person speaking.]
SECOND PERSON: Tell Mike to give **you** the key. [*You* refers to the person being addressed.]
THIRD PERSON: **She** told **them** the good news. [*She* and *them* refer to the people being discussed.]

Third-person pronouns express **gender**. *He* and *him* are masculine; *she* and *her* are feminine; *it* is neuter.

The personal pronouns include several forms that indicate possession or ownership. These **possessive pronouns** take the place of the possessive forms of nouns.

	SINGULAR	PLURAL
FIRST PERSON:	my, mine	our, ours
SECOND PERSON:	your, yours	your, yours
THIRD PERSON:	his her, hers its	their, theirs

Some possessive forms are used before nouns. Other forms can be used by themselves.

USED BEFORE NOUN: Where is **their** house?
USED ALONE: That house is **theirs.**

Objective

EXERCISE 8. Using Personal and Possessive Pronouns. Improve the following paragraph by replacing the underlined words or groups of words with personal or possessive pronouns. Write your answers on your paper.

(1) In November 1493 Christopher Columbus sighted an island that
he his
Christopher Columbus had not seen on Christopher Columbus' first
American voyage. **(2)** Columbus called the island Guadalupe, the name
it
that Guadalupe still bears. **(3)** When the explorer entered the island's
only village, the people there were Indian women and children who had
their
been kidnapped after a raid on the women and children's island.
he
(4) Using sign language, the women told Columbus how Columbus could
them their
return the women to the women's island, Borinquen. **(5)** When Borin-
him
quen was sighted, Columbus thought the island reminded Columbus of
you your
paradise. **(6)** How would the reader of this passage like to spend the
reader's next vacation on Borinquen?

REFLEXIVE AND INTENSIVE PRONOUNS*

Reflexive and intensive pronouns are formed by adding *-self* or *-selves* to certain of the personal pronouns, as shown below.

	SINGULAR	PLURAL
FIRST PERSON:	myself	ourselves
SECOND PERSON:	yourself	yourselves
THIRD PERSON:	himself herself itself	themselves

A **reflexive pronoun** refers to a noun or another pronoun and indicates that the same person or thing is involved.

We considered **ourselves** honored to be invited.

They think only of **themselves.**

An **intensive pronoun** adds emphasis to another noun or pronoun.

The Senator **herself** called.

They built that cabin **themselves.**

Objective

EXERCISE 9. Using Reflexive and Intensive Pronouns. Supply the appropriate reflexive or intensive pronoun for each blank. Write your answers on your paper.

1. Some of us athletes have trained ___ourselves___ as long-distance swimmers.
2. Swimming ___itself___ takes timing and coordination.
3. If you attempt long-distance swimming, you must be careful not to exhaust ___yourself___.
4. Some swimmers challenge ___themselves___ by attempting to cross bodies of water, such as the English Channel.
5. I ___myself___ have swum across Long Island Sound.

DEMONSTRATIVE PRONOUNS

A **demonstrative pronoun** points out specific persons, places, things, or ideas.

	NEAR	FAR
SINGULAR:	this	that
PLURAL:	these	those

Is **this** the jacket you like?
These are the only ones left.

Let me do **that.**
Bring **those** to me.

*Reflexive and intensive pronouns are also called *compound personal pronouns.*

Objective
EXERCISE 10. Identifying Demonstrative Pronouns. On your paper write the demonstrative pronoun in each sentence.

1. The rarest stamps in my collection are these.
2. This was the first postage stamp, a Penny Black.
3. That was issued without perforations.
4. I like those because they are triangular.

INTERROGATIVE PRONOUNS

An **interrogative pronoun** is used to form questions.

who? what? which?
whom?
whose?

Who were the winners? **Whom** did the comic impersonate?
Whose are these? **What** does this mean?
Which of these songs do you like?

The interrogative pronouns include the compound forms *whoever, whomever, whatever,* and *whichever.*

Whatever do you want?

RELATIVE PRONOUNS

A **relative pronoun** is used to begin a special subject-verb word group called a subordinate clause (see Chapter 21).

who which that
whom
whose

Whoever, whomever, whatever, and *whichever* can also function as relative pronouns.

The magazine praised the writer **who** won the prize. [The relative pronoun *who* begins the subordinate clause *who won the prize.*]
"Paul's Case," **which** was filmed for television, was written by Willa Cather. [The relative pronoun *which* begins the subordinate clause *which was filmed for television.*]
Our teacher praised the writer **whose** story was televised. [The relative pronoun *whose* begins the subordinate clause *whose story was televised.*]

Note that all the relative pronouns except *that* can also be used as interrogative pronouns to ask questions.

Objective
EXERCISE 11. Distinguishing Between Interrogative and Relative Pronouns. On your paper list the interrogative or relative pronoun in each

sentence. Next to each pronoun, indicate whether it is used as a relative or an interrogative pronoun.

1. Cleopatra, who (rel.) was of Macedonian descent, became queen of Egypt at the age of eighteen.
2. The coins that (rel.) were minted during her reign do not portray her as the beautiful woman of legend.
3. Julius Caesar first met Cleopatra in Alexandria, which (rel.) was Egypt's capital in the first century B.C.
4. Caesar fell in love with Cleopatra, whose (rel.) intelligence and charm he found captivating.

INDEFINITE PRONOUNS

An **indefinite pronoun** refers to persons, places, or things in a more general way than a noun does.

Some indefinite pronouns do not have clearly identifiable antecedents.

> Do you know **anyone** who can run that fast? [The indefinite pronoun *anyone* does not refer to a specific person.]
> **Many** prefer this style of jacket. [The indefinite pronoun *many* does not refer to specific people].

Other indefinite pronouns often have specific antecedents.

> When we opened the box of pears, **each** was already perfectly ripe. [The indefinite pronoun *each* has the specific antecedent *pears*.]

Some indefinite pronouns are listed in the following chart:

all	either	most	other
another	enough	much	others
any	everybody	neither	plenty
anybody	everyone	nobody	several
anyone	everything	none	some
anything	few	no one	somebody
both	many	nothing	someone
each	more	one	something

Objective

EXERCISE 12. Identifying Indefinite Pronouns and Their Antecedents. On your paper write the indefinite pronoun in each of the following sentences. If the indefinite pronoun refers to a specific person, place, or thing, identify its antecedent.

1. Everybody thinks that Alaskan Eskimos used to live in igloos.

2. No one seems to know that only Canadian Eskimos lived in igloos.

3. Anyone visiting Barrow, Alaska's biggest Eskimo town, finds homes heated by natural gas.

Eskimos
4. Few of the Barrow Eskimos have television sets.

Eskimos
5. In summer many of the Eskimos put wheels on their sleds.

teen-agers
6. Most of the teen-agers in Barrow prefer modern American dances to traditional Eskimo dances.

citizens
7. In winter some of the citizens of Barrow drive snowmobiles.

spirit
8. Some of the gold-rush spirit is still alive among aging prospectors.

wealth
9. Most of Alaska's mineral wealth now lies in oil, not gold.

salmon and crab
10. Some of the canned salmon and crab that you eat comes from Alaskan canneries.

Answers: Antecedents appear above the underlined pronouns.

Objective

APPLICATION EXERCISE. Following Models. Each of the following quotations has pronouns in it. Using each quotation as a model, write your own version with the same pronouns in the same positions. A sample response is provided for each item.

1. Heat not a furnace for your foe so hot
   That you do singe yourself.

—William Shakespeare, *Henry VIII*

SAMPLE ANSWER: Cook not a meal for your friends so meager
That you do starve yourself.

2. Hopes are but dreams of those who are awake.

—Pindar, *Fragment*

SAMPLE ANSWER: Dreams are but the reality of those who are asleep.

3. It is only when we forget all our learning that we begin to know.

—Henry David Thoreau, *Autumn*

SAMPLE ANSWER: It is only when we remember all our faults that we begin to grow.

4. Writers write for themselves and not for their readers. Art has nothing to do with communication.

—Rebecca West, "The Art of Skepticism"

SAMPLE ANSWER: Gardeners garden for themselves and not for their neighbors. Landscaping has nothing to do with neighborliness.

REVIEW EXERCISE. Pronouns. (a) On your paper list in order the ten pronouns contained in the following paragraph. **(b)** Identify each pronoun as personal, possessive, reflexive or intensive, demonstrative, interrogative, relative, or indefinite.

(1) Robin, in her (poss.) first draft, began the paper with this (demon.):

(2) Thornton Wilder, who (rel.) was one (indef.) of America's foremost novelists and playwrights and who (rel.) was born in Madison, Wisconsin, in 1897, has written over fourteen major novels and plays, including three that (rel.) won Pulitzer Prizes.

(3) When Robin read the first draft to herself (reflex.), she (pers.) realized the first sentence did not lead into the main idea well enough. **(4)** What (interrog.) would you (pers.) do to improve the opening?

VERBS

A **verb** is a word that expresses action or a state of being and is necessary to make a statement.

The verb is the part of speech that is essential to the formation of the sentence. The nouns and pronouns in sentences name people, places, or things, and the verbs tell what those people, places, or things *do* or *are.*

Penguins **swim.**
The gull **flew** west.
Penguins **are** underwater swimmers.
The gulls **became** noisy.

RECOGNIZING VERBS

1. You can test whether a word is a verb by seeing whether it makes sense in one of the blanks in the following sentences:

The group ________.
It ________ on the farm.
They ________ them there.
We ________ it to you.
The cold water ________ good.

2. Certain suffixes signal that a word is a verb. These verb-forming suffixes include *-ate, -en, -esce, -fy,* and *-ize.*

activate coalesce synchronize
sadden amplify

CHARACTERISTICS OF VERBS

The primary characteristic of a verb is its ability to express time—present, past, and future. Verbs express time by means of *tense* forms. (For rules on forming and using the tenses of verbs, see Chapter 22.)

PRESENT TENSE: We **see** the waves.
PAST TENSE: We **saw** the waves.
FUTURE TENSE: We **will see** the waves.

Objective

EXERCISE 13. Adding Verbs to Make Sentences. On your paper write five complete sentences by supplying a verb for each of the blanks in the items below.

1. The hot air balloons ___soared___ over the countryside.
2. They ___looked___ colorful against the white clouds.
3. Noticing the balloons, villagers ___raced___ out of their homes.
4. Moving with the summer wind, the balloons ___drifted___ noiselessly.
5. The gathering villagers ___appeared___ mesmerized.

Suggested Answers appear in the blanks.

ACTION VERBS

An **action verb** tells what someone or something does.

Some action verbs express physical action; others express mental action.

PHYSICAL ACTION: Skiers **swoop** down the mountainside.
MENTAL ACTION: Skiers **contemplate** each run.

Objective

EXERCISE 14. Identifying Action Verbs. On your paper write the action verb in each of the following sentences.

1. Backpackers often carry contour maps on a hike.
2. Contour lines on a map identify the elevation of each spot.
3. Numerals on a map's contour line tell the distance above sea level.
4. On steep slopes contour lines run close together.
5. Rivers, creeks, and rills always flow downward across the contour lines of a map.
6. Ups and downs of the countryside show vividly on a contour map.
7. The abbreviation *B.M.* (for bench mark) indicates the location of a tablet with the exact elevation of that spot.
8. Surveys by the United States place at least two bench mark tablets in each township.
9. Hikers use bench marks for reference.
10. With contour map, compass, and bench marks, backpackers find the right track.

Objective
APPLICATION EXERCISE. Creating Sentences with Action Verbs. Choose five of the action verbs that you identified in Exercise 14. For each verb, write one sentence.
Suggested Answer to 1: The movers carried the furniture into the house.

TRANSITIVE AND INTRANSITIVE VERBS

A **transitive verb** is an action verb that is followed by a word or words that answer the question *what?* or *whom?*

The word that answers the question *what?* or *whom?* after the action verb is called the *direct object,* or the *object of the verb.* (For more information about direct objects, see Chapter 19.)

> Athletes **win** medals. [The action verb *win* is followed by the direct object *medals,* which answers the question *win what?*]
> The athletes **obey** their coach. [The action verb *obey* is followed by the direct object *coach,* which answers the question *obey whom?*]

Many action verbs are not transitive. That is, they are not followed by words that answer the question *what?* or *whom?*

An **intransitive verb** is an action verb that does not have a direct object.

Intransitive verbs simply tell what someone or something does, or they are followed only by words that tell *when, where,* or *how* the action occurs.

> Our team **won.** [The action verb works alone.]
> The athletes **obey** immediately without protest. [The action verb is followed by words that tell *when* and *how.*]

Many action verbs can be transitive or intransitive, as you can see by comparing the two preceding sets of examples. Some action verbs, however, are either always transitive or always intransitive. That is, some action verbs make sense only with a direct object, and some make sense only without a direct object.

ALWAYS TRANSITIVE	ALWAYS INTRANSITIVE
Teams **capture** championships.	The ball **fell.**
Batters **avoid** the pitcher.	The sun **glowed** brightly.

Objective
EXERCISE 15. Recognizing Transitive and Intransitive Verbs. Look again at the verbs you identified in Exercise 14 on page 390. Indicate in writing whether each action verb is used as a transitive or as an intransitive verb.
Answers: **1.** vt.; **2.** vt.; **3.** vt.; **4.** vi.; **5.** vi.; **6.** vi.; **7.** vt.; **8.** vt.; **9.** vt.; **10.** vt.

Objective
APPLICATION EXERCISE. Creating Sentences with Transitive and Intransitive Verbs. For each of the following action verbs, write two sentences. First use the word as a transitive verb. Then use it as an intransitive verb.

1. ride
2. spin
3. plunge
4. fly
5. rush

Suggested Answer to 1: Children ride ponies. They ride around the track at the zoo.

LINKING VERBS

A **linking verb** links, or joins, a noun or pronoun (the subject of a sentence) with a word or expression that identifies or describes that noun or pronoun.

Be in all its forms—*am, is, are, was, were, will be, has been, was being*—is the most commonly used linking verb.

The hiker **is** an expert.
These animals **are** rare.
The noise **was** loud.
The bus **will be** late.

Sometimes rather than acting as a linking verb, the forms of *be* are used to state *where* something exists or *when* something happened. Such uses of the verb *be* are usually considered purely intransitive constructions.

Snow **is** on the roof.
Dinner **will be** soon.

Several other verbs besides the forms of *be* can act as linking verbs.

look	appear	taste
grow	seem	stay
feel	sound	smell
remain	become	

Objective
EXERCISE 16. Identifying Action and Linking Verbs. On your paper write the verb in each of the following sentences and identify it as either action or linking.

1. Yellow Springs, Ohio, was (linking) the childhood home of author Virginia Hamilton.
2. This southern Ohio area became (linking) part of the Underground Railroad system for runaway slaves.

3. Virginia Hamilton's ancestors lived [action] as slaves.

4. The setting of *The House of Dies Drear* by Virginia Hamilton is [linking] a southern Ohio community.

5. The large old houses of Hamilton's own community were [linking] hideouts for slaves during the Civil War.

6. *The House of Dies Drear* tells [action] a present-day mystery story with links to the Underground Railroad era.

7. From early childhood writing was [linking] Hamilton's strongest ambition.

8. Virginia Hamilton studied [action] at both Antioch College and Ohio State University.

9. Hamilton's husband is [linking] an author, too.

10. After many years in New York City, Hamilton resides [action] once again in Yellow Springs.

LINKING VERB OR ACTION VERB?

Except for the forms of *be* and *seem,* all the words listed as linking verbs on page 392 can also be action verbs. Each of the following sentence pairs shows a word first used as a linking verb and then as an action verb:

LINKING: The children **appear** ill.
ACTION: The children **appear** at the door.

LINKING: They **feel** faint.
ACTION: They **feel** their way along the hallway.

LINKING: They **look** pale.
ACTION: They **look** for their parents.

If you are unsure of whether a word is a linking verb, substitute the word *seem* in the sentence. If the sentence still makes sense, the word in question is probably a linking verb.

Houseplants **grow** [seem] more popular. [Here *grow* is a linking verb.]
Home gardeners **grow** crops for fun and profit. [Here *grow* is an action verb. *Seem* cannot be substituted for *grow.*]

Objective

EXERCISE 17. Distinguishing Between Action Verbs and Linking Verbs. For each of the following sentences, write the verb. Then indicate whether it is an action verb or a linking verb.

1. Nowadays fresh vegetables appear (action) in American supermarkets all year.

2. Around the world many people live (action) at or below subsistence level.

3. Food and health for everyone sounds (linking) like an impossible aim.

4. New agricultural methods and better food distribution become (linking) more and more important.

5. Plant breeders look (action) for strains of grain with short, stiff stems.

6. Most American farmers already grow (action) high-yield varieties of wheat with stiff stems.

7. Traditional thin-stemmed rice plants look (linking) top-heavy.

8. Roots of hybrid corn remain (action) in the ground through a storm.

9. Some modern varieties of fruits stay (linking) firm longer than old-time varieties.

10. Shoppers frequently feel (action) the ends of melons for ripeness.

11. Intelligent consumers smell (action) food for freshness.

12. New types of fertilizer also seem (linking) helpful for crop production.

13. Some agronomists feel (linking) uncertain about the long-range advantages of chemical fertilizers.

14. Many natural fertilizers smell (linking) worse than artificial fertilizers.

15. Some fertile land areas remain (linking) unproductive because of drought or flood.

16. Vegetables and grains stay (linking) expensive during years of drought or frost.

17. Farmland becomes (linking) efficient with contour plowing.

18. The highly mechanized systems of American agriculture appear (linking) inappropriate for some parts of the world.

19. Plans for energy conservation on farms grow (linking) important with current fuel shortages.

20. Average Americans taste (action) many kinds of different fruits and vegetables every year.

Objective

APPLICATION EXERCISE. Changing Linking Verbs to Action Verbs. Look again at the words in the preceding exercise that you identified as linking verbs. For each, write an original sentence using the word as an action verb.

Suggested Answer to 3: The guard sounds the alarm.

VERB PHRASES

The verb in a sentence may consist of more than one word. The words that accompany the main verb are called **auxiliary,** or helping, **verbs.**

A **verb phrase** consists of a main verb and all its or helping, verbs.

A main verb may have as many as three auxiliary verbs coming before it. The most common auxiliary verbs are the forms of *be* and *have.*

BE: am, is, are, was, were, be, being, been
HAVE: have, has, had

These auxiliary verbs help the main verb to express the various tenses. (For more information about using auxiliary verbs to form tenses, see Chapter 22.)

She **is talking.**
She **has talked.**
She **had been talking.**

Other auxiliary verbs are not used primarily to express time. Instead, they are used to help verbs indicate such states as ability, permission, possibility, certainty, obligation, request, invitation, negation, or interrogation. Because these auxiliary verbs express the attitude or mood of the speaker or writer, they are sometimes called *modal auxiliaries.*

do, does, did	would	will
may, might	should	shall
can, could	must	

He **did** talk.	He **would have talked.**	He **will talk.**
He **may talk.**	He **should be talking.**	**Shall** we **talk?**
He **can talk.**	He **must have been talking.**	

All of the auxiliary verbs on the preceding list, with the exception of the forms of *do,* can be used with the forms of *be* and *have* and the main verb.

Objective

EXERCISE 18. Identifying Verb Phrases. On your paper write the verb phrase in each of the following sentences. Put parentheses around the auxiliary verbs in each phrase. (Words that interrupt a verb phrase are not considered part of it.)

1. "We (must) think things, not words."
2. Justice Oliver Wendell Holmes, Jr., (had) spoken the above words in 1899, at the age of fifty-eight.
3. Justice Holmes (was) still expressing eloquent ideas thirty-two years later, at the age of ninety.
4. In 1864 Holmes (could) tackle Harvard Law School with enthusiasm.
5. After a year in George Shattuck's law office, Holmes (could) pass the Massachusetts bar exam.
6. Holmes (had) then expressed interest in the position of chief justice of Massachusetts.
7. Less than four years later, in 1902, Justice Holmes (would) move to Washington, D.C., as a member of the Supreme Court.
8. Future generations of law students (will) undoubtedly (be) reading Justice Holmes's Supreme Court opinions.
9. You (might) enjoy Francis Biddle's biography, *Mr. Justice Holmes.*
10. According to Justice Oliver Wendell Holmes, the law (must) be expedient for the community.

REVIEW EXERCISE. Verbs. On your paper write the verb that appears in each sentence in the following passage. Identify each as an action verb or a linking verb. Further identify any action verb as transitive or intransitive.

vt.
(1) Broccoli originally grew in Asia Minor. **(2)** In ancient times it
linking
was one of the favorite vegetables of the Romans. **(3)** Since then it has had a permanent place in Italian cuisine. **(4)** By the early eighth century,
vi. vt.
cultivation of broccoli extended to England. **(5)** Americans owe their familiarity with broccoli to nineteenth-century European immigrants. **(6)**
linking
A member of the cabbage family, this bright green vegetable is nutritious
vi.
and versatile. **(7)** It can serve as a side dish or as the principal ingredient
vt
of a main dish. **(8)** For example, you might serve broccoli with pasta and
vt.
oil and garlic. **(9)** At the grocery store choose only heads with unopened
linking
flowers. **(10)** This flavorful vegetable should be available year round.

Objective

APPLICATION EXERCISE. Creating Sentences with Vivid Verbs. Write five sentences that describe how a particular animal moves. Choose specific action verbs to convey a vivid sense of movement.

Suggested Answer: The python coils and slides along the branches.

REVISION EXERCISE. Verbs. Poets are particularly skillful at using verbs to crystalize images in their readers' minds. Here are some guidelines that poets—and prose writers, too—keep in mind as they write and revise their work.

1. Try to replace general verbs with more precise action verbs. For example, in a poem by Sylvia Plath about blackberries, instead of writing " . . . fat / With blue-red juices. They stain my fingers," the poet wrote " . . . fat / With blue-red juices. These they squander on my fingers." *Squander* is more precise and more vivid than *stains* and, in addition, suggests the abundance of the juices.
2. Try to reduce a group of words to one action verb. In describing a victorious athlete, A. E. Housman wrote, "We chaired you through the market-place." Notice how the single verb *chaired* vividly and succinctly captures the meaning "carried as if on a chair."
3. Whenever possible use action verbs rather than linking verbs. In "The Wild Swans at Coole" W. B. Yeats wrote, "Under the October twilight the water / Mirrors a still sky." The action verb *mirrors* gives the lines their power. Notice how a linking verb would have sapped their strength: "Under the October twilight the water / Is like a mirror for the still sky."
4. Think twice before beginning a sentence with "there is" or "there were." Instead, try to begin with a noun and follow up with an action verb. Denise Levertov began one of her poems "The house-snake dwells here still / under the threshold." Compare the economy of these lines with "There is a house-snake dwelling here still / under the threshold."

Practice these techniques by revising the following passage. Pay particular attention to the italicized words.

There are (1) on the island of Hawaii snowy peaks and sunny beaches that *are liked by* (2) tourists. The island's largest city, Hilo, *gives a surprise to* (3) many visitors. With its stone lanterns and bridges, Hilo *is like* (4) a Japanese city. Nearby, Akaka Falls *fall* (5) 442 feet into a beautiful rocky pool. In addition, *there are* (6) many colorful fields of orchids near Hilo. A short distance away *is* (7) Mauna Kea, Hawaii's highest volcano. At Kaimu the beach *consists of glistening* (8) black sand. At Kilauea scientists *are engaged in the study of* (9) the island's volcanic activity. Atop Mauna Loa *is* (10) an astronomical observatory.

ADJECTIVES

An **adjective** is a word that modifies a noun or pronoun by limiting its meaning.

Adjectives modify, or change, the meaning of a noun or pronoun by making it more specific. As the following examples show, adjectives can modify nouns and pronouns in any of four ways. The arrows point to the modified words.

1. Some adjectives *describe;* they answer the question *what is it like?*

   a **quiet** song   It tastes **sweet.**   a **blue** sky

2. Some adjectives *classify;* they answer the question *what kind is it?*

   adult frogs   **Italian** cuisine   **secret** documents

3. Some adjectives *identify;* they answer the question *which one?*

   that house   **these** shoes   **their** response   **her** vacation*

4. Some adjectives *quantify;* they answer the question *how much or how many?*

   an accident   **two** dollars   **many** guests   **no** time

Adjectives that identify or quantify nouns or pronouns are sometimes called *determiners.*

RECOGNIZING ADJECTIVES

1. The vast majority of adjectives can be used either before a noun or after a noun and a linking verb. That is, the vast majority of adjectives can logically fit in both blanks in the following sentences:

   The ________ desk is ________.
   The ________ speaker seems ________.
   The ________ idea is ________.

2. Certain suffixes signal that a word is an adjective. These adjective-forming suffixes include *-able* and *-ible, -al, -esque, -ful, -ic, -ish, -less,* and *-ous.*

usable	statuesque	selfish
spectral	pitiful	glamorous

CHARACTERISTICS OF ADJECTIVES

1. Many adjectives have different forms to indicate *degrees of comparison.* (For rules on forming and using the degrees of comparison, see pages 512–513.)

*Possessive pronouns, such as *their* and *her,* can be considered adjectives because they modify nouns in addition to serving their usual function as pronouns. Similarly, possessive nouns can be considered adjectives: *Fran's* vacation. For more information about pronouns that can be used as adjectives, see page 418.

POSITIVE	COMPARATIVE	SUPERLATIVE
fast	faster	fastest
happy	happier	happiest
beautiful	more beautiful	most beautiful

2. Adjectives may be used in various positions in relation to the words they modify.

> How **green** the leaves are!
> The **green** leaves shook in the breeze.
> The leaves are **green.**
> Sunlight makes the leaves **green.**
> The leaves, **green** as emeralds, shook in the breeze.

Objective

EXERCISE 19. Finding Adjectives and the Words They Modify. On your paper write the adjectives that appear in each sentence. Count pronouns that are used as adjectives, but do not count the words *a, an,* and *the.* After each adjective write the word it modifies.

trade century
1. Trade between Europe and America was heavy in the last century.
materials
2. Ships carried raw materials to Europe and then returned to America
products
with fine products.
materials materials
3. Materials like lumber were often difficult or cumbersome to transport.
space
4. On the trip back to America, vessels always had free space.
cargo ships
5. Captains preferred additional cargo so that the ship would be steady.
transportation
6. Shipowners began to offer inexpensive transportation to America.
immigrants country
7. Hopeful immigrants bought passage to the new country.
cargo weight
8. This cargo loaded and unloaded itself and shifted its weight during storms.
food food
9. Since passengers brought their native food with them, the ship-
profit
owners did not have to provide meals and so made a hefty profit.
fares it people
10. Low fares made it possible for even the poorest people to cross the ocean.

Answers: Modified words appear above the underlined adjectives.

Objective

APPLICATION EXERCISE. Creating Sentences with Adjectives. Select five of the adjectives from the sentences in Exercise 19. Write a sentence of your own for each one.

Suggested Answer to 1: Heavy rains flooded the roads.

ARTICLES

Articles are the adjectives *a, an,* and *the. A* and *an* are called indefinite articles. *The* is called the definite article.

INDEFINITE: I wrote **a** poem.
She wrote **an** essay.
DEFINITE: I wrote **the** poem.
She wrote **the** essay.

The definite and indefinite articles show how much you think the person that you are speaking or writing to knows about whatever you are discussing. If Richard says to Susan, "I wrote *the* poem," the definite article *the* shows that he thinks Susan can identify the particular poem he is talking about. If he does not think she can, he will use the indefinite article and say, "I wrote *a* poem."

Objective

EXERCISE 20. Identifying Articles. Find the articles in the following pairs of sentences. On your paper explain the differences in meaning between each pair.

1. Do you have the telephone book, Sandra? a particular telephone book
   Do you have a telephone book, Sandra? any telephone book
2. A shark surged through a school of fish. any shark and any school
   The shark surged through the school of fish. a particular shark and school

PROPER ADJECTIVES

A **proper adjective** is formed from a proper noun and begins with a capital letter.

Proper adjectives classify; they answer the question *what kind is it?*

The **Byzantine** Empire lasted a thousand years.
They believe in the **Jeffersonian** ideals of democracy.

The following suffixes are often used to create proper adjectives: *-an, -ian, -n, -ese,* and *-ish.*

PROPER NOUNS	PROPER ADJECTIVES
Caesar Augustus	Augustan
Canada	Canadian
China	Chinese
Finland	Finnish

Objective

EXERCISE 21. Forming Proper Adjectives. Write a proper adjective that may be formed from each of the following proper nouns. Consult a dictionary if you need help.

1. Austria
2. Andrew Jackson
3. Scotland
4. Norway
5. Panama
6. Venus
7. Turkey
8. John Milton
9. Rome
10. Japan

Answers: **1.** Austrian; **2.** Jacksonian; **3.** Scottish; **4.** Norwegian; **5.** Panamanian; **6.** Venusian; **7.** Turkish; **8.** Miltonian; **9.** Roman; **10.** Japanese

REVIEW EXERCISE. Adjectives. On your paper write the twenty adjectives including articles and possessives that appear in the following paragraph. Next to each adjective listed, write the word that it modifies.

critics poet poet
(1) Some critics consider Marianne Moore the most delightful
poet poems poems poems attention
American poet. **(2)** Her witty, sharp poems quickly grasp the attention
vision vision vision vision
of readers. **(3)** Her vision is original and precise but rather eccentric.
surfaces surfaces surfaces poems
(4) The brilliant and oblique surfaces of her poems are filled with observations of animals and nature. **(5)** Often she cryptically tosses in
quotations quotations reading reading
mysterious but appropriate quotations from her extensive reading.

Answers: Modified words appear above the underlined adjectives.

Objective

APPLICATION EXERCISE. Creating Sentences with Adjectives. Write five sentences about a place you have always wanted to visit. Describe the place as vividly as you can. Use a variety of adjectives, including those that describe, classify, identify, and qualify.

Suggested Answer: Many ancient temples stand alongside the narrow streets of the Roman Forum.

REVISION EXERCISE. Adjectives. Examine the following description of a wounded soldier from Stephen Crane's *Red Badge of Courage.* Note especially the effect of the italicized adjectives.

> The *spectral* soldier was at his side like a *stalking* reproach. The man's eyes were still *fixed* in a stare into the unknown. His *gray, appalling* face had attracted attention in the crowd, and men, slowing to his *dreary* pace, were walking with him. . . . As he went on, he seemed always looking for a place, like one who goes to choose a grave.

Here are some of Crane's techniques that you can apply when you write and revise your work.

1. Try to use adjectives that will make nouns more specific. Crane makes his nouns more specific by using vivid adjectives that describe color *(gray)*, shape or position *(spectral, fixed)*, and other visual characteristics *(stalking, appalling, dreary).*
2. Try to create an overall impression, or mood, through your choice of adjectives. Notice that all six of the italicized adjectives in the excerpt reinforce the overall impression that the wounded soldier is like a ghost or living corpse.
3. Try to use adjectives that suggest action. Notice Crane's use of the *-ing* words *stalking* and *appalling.* (For more on these verb forms used as

adjectives, see Chapter 20.) Within the context of the passage, these words emphasize the terrible effect that the soldier has on anyone who sees him. *Stalking* suggests a threatening action; *appalling* suggests a response of revulsion.

4. Do not feel that every noun you write needs an adjective. Try to determine where adjectives are helpful and where they are not needed. Notice how Crane uses his adjectives sparingly to focus our attention entirely on the wounded soldier. He does not add adjectives, for example, to the nouns *crowd* and *men* in the third sentence. To do so would divert our attention and weaken the strong picture we get of the spectral soldier.

Here is more of Crane's description but without his adjectives. Revise the passage, adding your own adjectives in the places indicated by the carets (^).

Something in the gesture of the man as he waved the ^ [bloody] and ^ [pitying] soldiers away made the youth start as if bitten. He yelled in horror. Tottering forward, he laid a ^ [quivering] hand upon the man's arm. As the latter turned his ^ [waxlike] features toward him, the youth screamed. . . . The ^ [tall] soldier held out his ^ [gory] hand. There was a ^ ^ [curious red] and ^ [black] combination of ^ [new] blood upon it.

Suggested Answers: Crane's adjectives appear above the carets.

ADVERBS

An **adverb** is a word that modifies a verb, an adjective, or another adverb by making its meaning more specific.

Like adjectives, adverbs are modifiers. Adjectives modify nouns and pronouns; adverbs modify verbs, adjectives, and other adverbs. Adverbs modify by answering the questions *when? where? how?* and *to what degree?* The following sentence illustrates the use of adverbs to modify an adjective *(intelligent)*, a verb *(leap)*, and another adverb *(high)*.

Surprisingly intelligent dolphins leap **very high.**

RECOGNIZING ADVERBS

1. You can determine that a word is an adverb by seeing whether it makes sense in one of the following sentences:

They did it ________.
I have ________ done it.
She is feeling ________ sleepy.
They did it ________ well.

2. Certain suffixes signal that a word is an adverb. By far the most widely used adverb-forming suffix is *-ly* when it is added to an adjective. Other adverb-forming suffixes include *-ward* and *-wise*.

absurdly	earthward	counterclockwise
regularly	downward	edgewise

CHARACTERISTICS OF ADVERBS

1. Like adjectives, some adverbs have different forms to indicate degrees of comparison. (For rules on forming and using the degrees of comparison, see Chapter 25.)

POSITIVE	COMPARATIVE	SUPERLATIVE
sat **near**	sat **nearer**	sat **nearest**
walks **slowly**	walks **more slowly**	walks **most slowly**
feels **ill**	feels **worse**	feels **worst**

2. When an adverb modifies a verb, it may be placed in various positions in relation to the verb. When an adverb modifies an adjective or another adverb, it immediately precedes the modified word.

MODIFYING A VERB: **Usually** we will dine there.
We **usually** will dine there.
We will **usually** dine there.
We will dine there **usually.**
MODIFYING AN ADJECTIVE: That restaurant is **very** fine.
MODIFYING AN ADVERB: **Only** seldom do we dine elsewhere.

Objective

EXERCISE 22. Identifying Adverbs. Write the adverb in each of the following sentences. Then write the word or words that each adverb modifies. (Remember that adverbs modify an entire verb phrase.)

1. The Honolulu Academy of Arts has a particularly [fine] fine collection of Early American furniture.
2. One handsome pine box is elaborately [is carved] carved in a style called Friesian.
3. An armchair on display in Honolulu was probably [was made] made in Connecticut.
4. Two mahogany side chairs in Honolulu once [belonged] belonged to William Smith of Hartford.
5. A drop-leaf table from Newport has claw-and-ball feet with rather [long] long claws.

Answers: Modified words appear above the underlined adverbs.

Objective
EXERCISE 23. Positioning Adverbs. (a) On your paper add an appropriate verb-modifying adverb to each of the following sentences. **(b)** Rewrite each sentence, placing the adverb in a different position.

SAMPLE: The marathon runner crossed the finish line.
ANSWER: **(a)** The marathon runner finally crossed the finish line.
(b) Finally, the marathon runner crossed the finish line.

1. The runners surged forward from the starting line.
2. Spectators cheered along the route.
3. The leaders established the pace for the others.
4. Many runners dropped out because of injury or fatigue.
5. Only the finalists will receive wreaths of victory.

Suggested Answer to 1: (a) The runners surged forward enthusiastically from the starting line. (b) Enthusiastically the runners surged forward from the starting line.

KINDS OF ADVERBS

An **adverb of time** tells *when.*

Some adverbs of time tell about a particular point in time *(yesterday).* Some tell about duration *(frequently).* Some tell about frequency *(always).*

I tried to telephone you **yesterday.**
My uncle calls me **frequently.**
He **always** calls me on Sunday.

An **adverb of place** tells *where.*

Some adverbs of place indicate position *(here).* Some indicate direction *(south).*

Sandy lives **here.**
Many birds fly **south** for the winter.

An **adverb of degree** tells *to what degree* or *to what extent.*

When adverbs of degree are used with adjectives or other adverbs, they are sometimes called *intensifiers* because they indicate the degree of intensity of the adjective or other adverb.

You have been **exceedingly** kind. [Adverb tells the degree of kindness.]
He **scarcely** spoke. [Adverb tells the degree of speaking.]
She was **rather** sleepy. [Adverb tells the degree of sleepiness.]

An **adverb of manner** tells how an action is done or the means by which it is done.

Adverbs of manner generally answer the question *how?* or *by which means?* Sometimes adverbs of manner modify adjectives.

HOW: **sloppily** arranged answered **excitedly**
acted **fairly** finished **quickly**

BY WHICH MEANS: **electronically** run   removed **surgically**
MODIFYING AN ADJECTIVE: **absurdly** happy   **hopelessly** sad

Most, but not all, adverbs of manner end in *-ly* (for example, *carefully, effectively*). The *-ly* is added to an adjective to form an adverb of manner. Be aware of other common words that do not end in *-ly* but are also adverbs of manner (for example, *together,* as in *ran together*).

Sometimes an adverb of manner may not modify a particular word in a sentence. Instead, it will provide a running commentary on the assertions that the speaker or writer is making. Such adverbs are sometimes called *sentence adverbs.*

> **Honestly,** only the strongest will succeed. [instead of "I'm being honest when I say that . . . "]
> The storm, **fortunately,** did little damage. [instead of "It is fortunate that the storm . . . "]

NEGATIVE WORDS AS ADVERBS

The word *not* and the contraction *n't* are considered adverbs. Certain adverbs of time, place, and degree have negative meanings.

The dolphin did **not** leap.   The dolphin **scarcely** leaped.
Dolphins are **nowhere** in sight.   That dolphin **never** leaps.
That is **hardly** a dolphin.   That fish can **barely** swim.

Objective

EXERCISE 24. Categorizing Adverbs. On your paper identify each of the italicized adverbs as (a) an adverb of time, (b) an adverb of place, (c) an adverb of degree, (d) an adverb of manner, or (e) a negative adverb.

1. travel *frequently*
2. pack *neatly*
3. depart *promptly*
4. *rarely* dangerous
5. *often* fly
6. hasten *away*
7. board *late*
8. *furiously* impatient
9. jump *down*
10. greet *excitedly*
11. drove *expertly*
12. accelerated *gradually*
13. *patiently* trudge
14. *barely* moving
15. *fully* open window
16. climb *aloft*
17. pedaling *uphill*
18. *homeward* bound
19. *utterly* reckless
20. *casually* wave

Answers: **1.** a; **2.** d; **3.** a *or* d; **4.** a; **5.** a; **6.** b; **7.** a; **8.** c; **9.** b; **10.** d; **11.** d; **12.** d; **13.** d; **14.** e *or* c; **15.** c; **16.** b; **17.** b; **18.** b; **19.** c; **20.** d

Objective

APPLICATION EXERCISE. Creating Sentences with Adverbs. Select five of the adverbs from Exercise 24. Write one original sentence for each adverb.

Suggested Answer to 1: My dogs frequently wait for me at the front door.

REVIEW EXERCISE. Adverbs. On your paper write the adverbs in each of the following sentences. Then write the word or words that each adverb modifies.

1. For athletes good health is vitally important. (important)
2. Each athlete needs a training program designed particularly for that person. (designed)
3. Athletes' bodies quickly respond to overuse. (respond)
4. Because athletes are alert to pain and lack of appetite, they undoubtedly save themselves from really bad performances. (save; bad)
5. It is hardly unusual for athletes to care for their feet constantly. (unusual; care)
6. A runner's shoes must fit well and never be worn down unevenly. (fit; be worn; be worn; be worn)
7. Shin splints, pains along the lower leg, usually result from a muscular problem. (result)
8. Sciatica pains in the lower back are often incorrectly diagnosed as calf "pulls." (are diagnosed)
9. Some back pains are relieved considerably by abdominal exercises. (are relieved)
10. Sore muscles are best treated immediately with cold water. (are treated; are treated)

Answers: Modified words appear above the underlined adverbs.

REVISION EXERCISE. Adverbs. Adverbs are often essential to the meaning of a sentence, as in "Geese fly *south* in autumn" or "Ostriches do *not* fly." Without *south* and *not* these sentences take on other meanings. Sometimes rather than being essential, adverbs "fine-tune" the sentence's meaning by adding either emphasis or subtlety. Keep in mind the following techniques when you write and revise your work.

1. Use adverbs to emphasize a point. In the following sentence from "The Cask of Amontillado," notice how Edgar Allan Poe uses adverbs to emphasize two actions:

   A succession of loud and shrill screams, bursting *suddenly* from the throat of the chained form, seemed to thrust me *violently* back.

   Poe could have omitted the two adverbs without altering the basic meaning of the sentence. Their inclusion, however, accentuates the suddenness of the screams and the violent effect they have on the narrator.

phrase. Sometimes, however, a preposition may follow its object, especially in informal conversations.

Which counselor should I meet **with?**

Objective

EXERCISE 25. Identifying Prepositions. On your paper list the prepositions in each of the following sentences. Remember that some prepositions are made up of more than one word. (The numeral in parentheses at the end of each item indicates the number of prepositions in that item.)

1. Jackson Hole Valley lies at the foot of the Teton Mountain range. (2)
2. Towering above Jackson Hole, the Tetons have ten peaks over ten thousand feet high. (2)
3. According to reports, the first white man within Jackson Hole was trapper John Coulter. (2)
4. With the exception of hardy mountain men hunting game, early pioneers stayed outside this valley. (3)
5. In the 1880s the first homesteaders became upset about the Jackson Hole elk. (2)
6. As a result, in 1912 National Elk Refuge was established within the valley. (3)
7. Above and beyond the elk was the problem of conservation. (3)
8. By 1929 Congress had established Grand Teton National Park along the eastern slopes of the Tetons. (3)
9. In the meantime, John D. Rockefeller, Jr., began to acquire acres of Jackson Hole land. (2)
10. Through the intervention of President Franklin D. Roosevelt, a 221,000-acre Jackson Hole National Monument was established. (2)
11. Many Jackson Hole residents were against all outsiders. (1)
12. All except a few Jackson Holers are now at peace concerning limited-growth regulations. (3)
13. In spite of protests, only 3 percent of Teton County's land is now in private hands. (3)
14. Aside from these small private holdings, the Jackson Hole area now forms a 310,000-acre Grand Teton National Park. (1)
15. Flying above Jackson Hole, you see vistas of breathtaking splendor. (2)
16. Beyond doubt, Jackson Hole's lakes and mountains are almost too spectacular for their own good. (2)
17. Because of the many clear streams, the fishing alone draws a host of visitors. (2)
18. Along the shore of Jackson Lake, a paved campground overlooks the marina of Coulter Bay. (3)
19. Amid the soaring peaks of Mount Moran, Grand Teton, and South Teton lies little Jenny Lake. (2)
20. Throughout Jackson Hole wildflowers carpet summer foothills with a riot of color. (3)

Objective
APPLICATION EXERCISE. Creating Sentences with Prepositions. Choose five prepositions from the lists on page 408. Use each one in a sentence. Add adjectives and adverbs wherever necessary.

Guidelines for Evaluation: Check to make sure that students did not use the words as conjunctions or adverbs.

CONJUNCTIONS

A **conjunction** is a word that joins single words or groups of words.

Conjunctions are very important because they clarify the relationship between parts of a sentence. English has four kinds of conjunctions: *coordinating conjunctions, correlative conjunctions, subordinating conjunctions,* and *conjunctive adverbs.*

Here we will study the first two in detail and cover the second two briefly. The last two will come up again when you study clauses in Chapter 21.

COORDINATING CONJUNCTIONS

A **coordinating conjunction** joins words or groups of words that have equal grammatical weight in a sentence.

The coordinating conjunctions are *and, but, or, nor, for,* and *yet.* All the coordinating conjunctions, except *for,* can join words, phrases, or clauses. *For* joins only clauses and nothing else.

> They stand **and** wait. [joins words]
> Put the boxes in the kitchen **or** in the garage. [joins phrases]
> We planted tulips, **but** they did not grow. [joins clauses]

Objective
EXERCISE 26. Completing Sentences with Coordinating Conjunctions. On your paper supply the coordinating conjunction that makes the most sense in each of the following sentences.

1. At the time of his birth in 1947, Ferdinand Lewis Alcindor, Jr., was 22½ inches long ___and___ weighed 12 pounds, 11 ounces.
2. By the sixth grade the six-foot Lew Alcindor already played basketball, ___but___ he was too clumsy to be good.
3. The school coach coaxed Lew to stay for practice at the gym until six ___or___ seven o'clock.
4. In the seventh grade Lew was tall enough (6 feet, 8 inches) to dunk the basketball, ___and___ other students grew proud of his ability.
5. Lew won a scholarship at Power Memorial Academy, ___for___ the coach there recognized his potential.
6. Lew became a member of the varsity basketball team as a freshman, ___but *or* yet___ he was still awkward.

7. With much practice Lew acquired considerable grace, ___and___ he was hailed as the most promising high school player in the country.
8. Lew's college basketball career at U.C.L.A. was lonely, ___but___ it brought many offers from professional recruiters.
9. At twenty-four Lew Alcindor was a renowned basketball star ___and___ was named Most Valuable Player of the NBA.
10. Now, of course, Alcindor is known as Kareem Abdul Jabbar, ___for___ he wanted to acknowledge his African heritage.

Answers appear in the blanks.

CORRELATIVE CONJUNCTIONS

Correlative conjunctions work in pairs to join words and groups of words of equal grammatical importance.

both . . . and	just . . . so	not only . . . but (also)
either . . . or	neither . . . nor	though . . . yet
		whether . . . or

You use the first part of the correlative conjunction before one word or group of words and the second part before the related word or group of words. Correlative conjunctions make the relationship between words or groups of words a little clearer than do coordinating conjunctions.

COORDINATING CONJUNCTIONS	CORRELATIVE CONJUNCTIONS
You **and** I should talk.	**Both** you **and** I should talk. [*You* and *I* are of equal value: They are related words. The correlative conjunction *both . . . and* makes the relationship clearer and stronger than does the coordinating conjunction *and*.]
You **or** I should talk.	**Either** you **or** I should talk. **Neither** you **nor** I should talk.
I speak French **and** Chinese.	I speak **not only** French **but also** Chinese.

Objective

EXERCISE 27. Identifying Correlative Conjunctions. On your paper write both parts of the correlative conjunctions in the following sentences.

1. Whether you are lost on a hike or stuck in a disabled car, your life may depend on finding shelter.
2. Both the severe cold of a snow-capped mountain and the burning heat of a desert require some kind of shelter.

3. In either hot or cold locations insects can be a serious problem.
4. Tarp shelters are not only quick and easy to put up but also light to carry if you are on the move.
5. A triangular tent can be formed either by leaning a pole into the crook of a tree branch or by lashing two poles together in an X.
6. Though the area may not have strong trees, yet there is hope.
7. A dense stand of either willows or sagebrush makes a fine shelter when the tops are tied together.
8. With neither tarp nor brush to help, you may be able to find a protected spot under a bank.
9. Though a dry wash may give shelter, yet flash floods can be dangerous in such spots.
10. In deep snow a simple trench roofed with evergreen branches provides both shelter and insulation from the cold.

Objective

APPLICATION EXERCISE. Creating Sentences with Coordinating and Correlative Conjunctions. Write four original sentences, using coordinating conjunctions. Then rewrite these sentences using correlative conjunctions.

Suggested Answer: Stuart is insensitive and rude.
Stuart is not only insensitive but also rude.

SUBORDINATING CONJUNCTIONS

A **subordinating conjunction** joins two clauses, or ideas, in such a way as to make one grammatically dependent upon the other.

The idea, or clause, that a subordinating conjunction introduces is said to be "subordinate," or dependent, because it cannot stand by itself as a complete sentence. You will learn more about these conjunctions when you study clauses in Chapter 21. Here are some examples of subordinating conjunctions in use:

> The orchestra applauded **when** maestro Ozawa appeared.
> **Wherever** the Boston Symphony played, critics praised it.
> Joan Sutherland took a curtain call **as** the audience cheered.

Here is a list of common subordinating conjunctions.

after	considering (that)	unless
although	if	until
as	inasmuch as	when
as far as	in order that	whenever
as if	provided (that)	where
as long as	since	whereas
as soon as	so long as	wherever
as though	so that	while
because	than	
before	though	

Objective

EXERCISE 28. Identifying Subordinating Conjunctions. Write the subordinating conjunction in each of the following sentences. Remember that some subordinating conjunctions are made up of more than one word.

1. Ed Parsons went to Alaska from Oregon because he had invented cable television too soon.
2. When he reached Circle Hot Springs, Alaska, Parsons took a job with Wien Airlines.
3. Since Wien had started, in 1924, its pilots had been flying with poor radio communication.
4. Where before there had been none, Ed Parsons established over one hundred radio stations.
5. In order that Scandinavian Airlines could fly the polar route, Parsons expanded the Barrow radio station.
6. Eskimos operated the Barrow station so that transpolar flights could maintain air-to-ground communications.
7. Bush pilots carry Ed Parsons' survival kit (another Parsons achievement) wherever they fly.
8. Whenever villages needed a landing strip, Ed Parsons flew in disassembled bulldozers.
9. As soon as bulldozer parts arrived, Wien mechanics helped villagers reassemble them.
10. Because twin-engine planes need only a short strip, an airstrip could be built quickly.

CONJUNCTIVE ADVERBS

A **conjunctive adverb** is used to clarify the relationship between clauses of equal weight in a sentence.

Conjunctive adverbs are usually stronger and more precise than coordinating conjunctions. Consider the difference in emphasis between the following two sentences:

COORDINATING CONJUNCTION:	The office was cold, the noise was intolerable, **and** he resigned.
CONJUNCTIVE ADVERB:	The office was cold, and the noise was intolerable; **consequently,** he resigned.

Note that a semicolon usually comes before a conjunctive adverb and that the adverb is usually followed by a comma.

There are many conjunctive adverbs, and they have several uses, as the following examples show:

TO REPLACE *AND*: also, besides, furthermore, moreover
TO REPLACE *BUT*: however, nevertheless, still, though
TO STATE A RESULT: consequently, therefore, so, thus
TO STATE EQUALITY: equally, likewise, similarly

Objective

EXERCISE 29. Identifying and Categorizing Conjunctive Adverbs. Each of the following sentences contains one conjunctive adverb. On your paper identify each conjunctive adverb, and indicate whether it is being used **(a)** to replace *and;* **(b)** to replace *but;* **(c)** to state a result; or **(d)** to state equality.

1. Every case that comes to police lab workers is different; however, all cases require two basic steps.
2. In criminal cases physical evidence should be identified; furthermore, it should be matched to an individual.
3. Scientists in police labs must be experts in one branch of science; moreover, they need common sense.
4. Each person's fingerprints are unique; similarly, each firearm fires bullets with unique groove marks.
5. Each chemical compound absorbs different wavelengths of light; therefore, police lab scientists can identify the contents of a pill or liquid.
6. Modern police labs use computers; thus, the matching of fingerprints or infrared curves takes only minutes.
7. Forged documents are frequent in fraud cases; consequently, police labs need document examiners.
8. Professional document examiners can usually match handwriting samples; moreover, they can often match typewriting to a specific typewriter.
9. With ultraviolet and infrared light, document examiners can bring out invisible writing; in addition, they can spot erasures and alterations.
10. Scientific analysis has helped convict many guilty people; likewise, it has helped free many innocent people.

Answers: **1.** b; **2.** a; **3.** a; **4.** d; **5.** c; **6.** c; **7.** c; **8.** a; **9.** a; **10.** d

REVIEW EXERCISE. Conjunctions. On your paper identify the conjunction in each of the following sentences and indicate whether it is **(a)** a coordinating conjunction, **(b)** a correlative conjunction, **(c)** a subordinating conjunction, or **(d)** a conjunctive adverb.

1. An Oklahoma farmer went looking for a sick calf; however, he found a meteor fragment.
2. When the Lost City Meteorite descended over Oklahoma, it was even seen in central Nebraska.
3. While the meteorite was descending, the sonic boom was heard from Tulsa to Tahlequah.
4. Not only was the Lost City Meteorite tracked photographically, but also its landing place was accurately predicted.

5. The first meteor fragment was found quickly and flown to the Smithsonian Institution.
6. Many airborne meteor particles were recovered because the photographic tracking was accurate.
7. Although the meteorite entered the earth's atmosphere at nine miles per second, it slowed to two miles per second at an altitude of eleven miles.
8. The fireball dropped a 9.85-kilogram meteorite out into the sky; nevertheless, it was found near Lost City.
9. Investigators found two more meteorites, so that the total mass recovered was 17.3 kilograms.
10. Before scientists tracked the Oklahoma fireball, they had tracked only one meteor by photography.

Answers: **1.** d; **2.** c; **3.** c; **4.** b; **5.** a; **6.** c; **7.** c; **8.** d; **9.** c; **10.** c

Objective

APPLICATION EXERCISE. Following Models. Each of the following quotations has conjunctions in it. Using each quotation as a model, write your own version with the same conjunctions in the same positions. A sample response is provided for each item.

1. I paint objects as I think them, not as I see them.

—Pablo Picasso

SAMPLE ANSWER: He does as he pleases, not as he should.

2. Dawn comes slowly, but dusk is rapid.

—Alice B. Toklas

SAMPLE ANSWER: War is easy, but peace is difficult.

3. Writers should be read—but neither seen nor heard.

—Daphne Du Maurier

SAMPLE ANSWER: Cars should be driven—but neither too fast nor too slow.

4. Singing is speech made musical, while dancing is the body made poetic.

—Ernest Bacon

SAMPLE ANSWER: Fiction is experience made permanent, while poetry is chaos made orderly.

REVISION EXERCISE. Conjunctions. Revise the paragraph below by replacing some of the coordinating conjunctions with more precise connectives. Use the following guidelines to help you:

1. Try to improve your writing by stressing the relationship between words with correlative conjunctions instead of relying on coordinating conjunctions.

EXAMPLE: She has written *not only* several short stories ~~and~~ *but also* a book of poems.

2. Try to replace coordinating conjunctions with conjunctive adverbs to state a result or to state equality.

EXAMPLE: The bus broke down; consequently, I arrived late for class.

3. Try to make the relationship between two ideas clearer by replacing coordinating conjunctions with subordinating conjunctions.

EXAMPLE: When the wrestlers entered the arena, the spectators cheered.

As you revise, pay particular attention to the italicized words and the places marked by carats (∧).

Ray spotted the great blue heron, *and* he stood as still as possible. The bird was ∧ the largest Ray had ever seen *and* one of the most beautiful. ∧ It stalked the shallows of the lake, *and* it peered intently beneath the surface. Suddenly the heron's long neck lunged downward; this time it did not catch a fish. Ray was delighted, *and* the bird flapped its great wings and soared directly overhead.

INTERJECTIONS

An **interjection** is a word or phrase that expresses emotion or exclamation. An interjection has no grammatical connection to any other words.

An interjection can be part of a sentence, or it can stand alone.

Well, such is life! **Ouch!** That hurts.
Ah, that's delicious! **Ssh!** Be quiet.

Interjections are used more frequently in informal speech than in writing.

Objective

EXERCISE 30. Using Interjections. On your paper fill the blank in the following sentences with an appropriate interjection from the list below.

yow oops help wow hi

1. Oops! I dropped an egg.
2. Hi, I'm your new neighbor.
3. Yow! The handle on this pot is hot.
4. Wow! Look at that sports car.
5. Help! The elevator's stuck.

WORDS AS MORE THAN ONE PART OF SPEECH

A word's part of speech is directly related to how the word is used in a sentence.

Many words can be used as more than one part of speech. Notice, for example, how the word *round* is a different part of speech in each of the following sentences.

NOUN: We played a **round** of golf.
VERB: **Round** the amount to the nearest dollar.
ADJECTIVE: The auditorium is in that **round** building.
ADVERB: The top spun **round.**
PREPOSITION: The campers gathered **round** the fire.

The following sections will explain how words normally considered one part of speech may often act as another.

NOUN OR ADJECTIVE?

Many words commonly listed as nouns in a dictionary may act as adjectives by modifying other nouns.

NOUNS: The news came as a total **surprise.**
The cool **water** was refreshing.

ADJECTIVES: My friends gave me a **surprise** party.
The **water** pitcher was almost empty.

Some combinations of nouns become so common that they are often thought of, to varying extents, as compound nouns.

question mark
sweat shirt
time zone

Objective

EXERCISE 31. Using Nouns as Adjectives. On your paper use each of the following nouns as an adjective by adding another noun that the given word may modify.

SAMPLE: pants
ANSWER: pants pocket

1. garden garden furniture
2. shirt shirt sleeves
3. country country house
4. shade shade tree
5. pine pine needles

6. radio radio program
7. furniture furniture polish
8. coal coal bin
9. wall wall divider
10. paper paper mill

Suggested Answers appear beside the items.

NOUN OR ADVERB?

Some words normally considered nouns may be used as adverbs of time or place.

NOUNS: My aunt has a **home** in San Francisco.
Today is my birthday.

ADVERBS: Flora stayed **home** from work **today.**

Objective

APPLICATION EXERCISE. Using Words as Nouns and Adverbs. your paper use each of the following words in an original sentence, first as a noun and then as an adverb.

1. year
2. tonight
3. mornings
4. tomorrow
5. home

Suggested Answer to 1: My sister switched colleges after a year.
My family visited Bavaria last year.

PRONOUN OR ADJECTIVE?

Many pronouns may be used as adjectives. Possessive pronouns, demonstrative pronouns, interrogative pronouns, and indefinite pronouns can all be used as adjectives when they modify a noun.

The following possessive pronouns, by their very nature, modify nouns by answering the question *which one?: my, your, his, her, its, our, their.*

POSSESSIVE PRONOUN: The car looks like **his.**

POSSESSIVE ADJECTIVE: **His** car is bright red.

This and *that* may modify singular nouns. *These* and *those* may modify plural nouns.

DEMONSTRATIVE PRONOUN: **These** taste sweet.

DEMONSTRATIVE ADJECTIVE: **These** strawberries taste sweet.

The interrogative pronouns *whose, what,* and *which* may be used as adjectives:

INTERROGATIVE PRONOUN: **What** are you reading?

INTERROGATIVE ADJECTIVE: **What** books have you been reading?

Many of the words listed on page 387 as indefinite pronouns often function as adjectives.

INDEFINITE PRONOUNS: **Many** were sold.
Give me a **few.**

INDEFINITE ADJECTIVES: **Many** tickets were sold.

Give me a **few** hints.

Objective

APPLICATION EXERCISE. Using Words as Pronouns and Adjectives. On your paper use each of the following words in an original sentence, first as a pronoun and then as an adjective.

1. those
2. his
3. which
4. each
5. some

Suggested Answer to 1: Hand me those, please. Hand me those books, please.

PREPOSITION OR ADVERB?

Many of the words listed as prepositions on page 408 can, in some sentences, be adverbs. If the word stands alone and answers a question such as *where?* or *when?* and if it does not connect a noun or pronoun to the rest of the sentence, consider the word an adverb. Otherwise consider it a preposition.

ADVERB: Please wait **outside.** [answers the question *where?*]
PREPOSITION: Wait **outside** the door. [connects the noun *door* to the verb *wait*]

Sometimes an adverb of place may be so closely linked in meaning to a verb that the adverb no longer seems to indicate where. Instead, the adverb helps form a two-word transitive verb.

The thunderstorm **put out** the brush fire.
Marsha **ran up** a large bill at the restaurant.

Notice the change in meaning when the adverb in a two-word verb is changed to a preposition.

Marsha ran **up** the steps. [The preposition *up* has as its object *steps. Ran* is an intransitive verb.]

Objective

APPLICATION EXERCISE. Using Words as Adverbs and Prepositions. On your paper use each of the following words in an original sentence, first as an adverb and then as a preposition.

1. across
2. in
3. inside
4. on
5. over

Suggested Answer to 1: We went across on foot. We went across the bridge on foot.

PREPOSITION OR CONJUNCTION?

The words *after, as, before, since,* and *until* can function in sentences as either prepositions or subordinating conjunctions. As prepositions these words connect a noun or a pronoun to the rest of the sentence. As subordinating conjunctions they will be followed by a word group that without the conjunction could stand alone as a sentence.

PREPOSITIONS:	We left **before** the end.
	The fireworks began **after** dark.
SUBORDINATING CONJUNCTIONS:	We left **before** the movie ended.
	The fireworks began **after** the spectators assembled on the lawn.

Objective

EXERCISE 32. Distinguishing Between Prepositions and Conjunctions. List on your paper the ten italicized words from the following sentences. Identify each word as a preposition or a conjunction.

Olympia served **(1)** *as* [prep.] the permanent site of the Olympic Games **(2)** *since* [conj.] the first recorded games occurred there in 776 B.C. For more than 1,100 years—**(3)** *until* [conj.] Emperor Theodosius banned the games in A.D. 394—the ceremonies attracted athletes to Olympia every four years. **(4)** *Before* [prep.] the Roman conquest of Greece, the games were religious festivals. **(5)** *As* [conj.] the religious significance declined, so did the quality of the games. **(6)** *After* [prep.] Theodosius' ban, Olympia survived **(7)** *until* [prep.] the sixth century, when an earthquake leveled the site. **(8)** *After* [prep.] a series of landslides and floods, Olympia lay buried under twenty feet of soil.

conj.
(9) *Before* the French and Germans excavated the site during the last century, Olympia had been largely forgotten. **(10)** *Since* the 1890s Olympia and the Olympic tradition have been recovered.
prep.

Objective

APPLICATION EXERCISE. Using Words as Various Parts of Speech. Write a sentence for each of the following words, using it as the part of speech indicated.

1. peace (noun)
2. peace (adjective)
3. whose (pronoun)
4. whose (adjective)
5. now (noun)
6. now (verb)
7. alongside (preposition)
8. alongside (adverb)
9. as (preposition)
10. as (conjunction)

Suggested Answers to 1 and 2: The diplomats discussed peace. The peace talks dragged on.

REVIEW

CHAPTER 18 PARTS OF SPEECH

Nouns (pages 377–383) Identify each of the ten underlined nouns as **(a)** proper, **(b)** common and concrete, **(c)** common and abstract, **(d)** collective, or **(e)** common and compound.

The noise of **(1)** firecrackers, orginally exploded to scare away evil spirits, heralds Chinese New Year. The date for this traditional **(2)** holiday varies because it begins the lunar **(3)** year, but it is always in **(4)** January or February. To celebrate this holiday, a **(5)** family share symbolic food, such as tangerines for good **(6)** luck and **(7)** fish for plenty. They decorate their houses with flowers and give **(8)** children money in red envelopes. (The color red symbolizes happiness.) In **(9)** China all **(10)** birthdays used to be celebrated on the New Year.

Answers: **1.** b or e; **2.** c; **3.** c; **4.** a; **5.** d; **6.** c; **7.** b; **8.** b; **9.** a; **10.** e

Pronouns (pages 383–389) Indicate whether the underlined pronoun is **(a)** personal or possessive, **(b)** reflexive or intensive, **(c)** demonstrative, **(d)** relative or interrogative, or **(e)** indefinite.

11. Nothing pleases her.
12. Everything pleases him.
13. He chose the lunch that I wanted.
14. I wanted the lunch that he chose.
15. You should be proud of yourself.
16. This is just too much.
17. Many have complained about that.
18. We help ourselves.
19. Who is that at the door?
20. I myself cannot answer for her.

Answers: **11.** a; **12.** e; **13.** a; **14.** d; **15.** b; **16.** c; **17.** e; **18.** b; **19.** d; **20.** b

Verbs (pages 389–398) Indicate whether each of the ten underlined verbs is **(a)** a transitive action verb, **(b)** an intransitive action verb, **(c)** a linking verb, **(d)** an auxiliary, or **(e)** a verb phrase.

The Federal Bureau of Land Management **(21)** has rounded up thousands of wild burros and **(22)** is offering them for adoption. The fee **(23)** is just seventy-five dollars for an animal who **(24)** will eat every weed it sees, and eventually be able to carry equipment or children on its back. The burros **(25)** are not native to the desert. Domesticated as beasts of burden for centuries, they **(26)** came to America with the Spanish. As the burros **(27)** found their way to freedom, they **(28)** increased alarmingly. Trampling tiny plants and animals, they **(29)** destroy the desert's ecosystem. To solve the problem that the herds cause in the Southwest, the government **(30)** must reduce the number of burros.

Answers: **21.** d; **22.** e; **23.** c; **24.** e; **25.** c; **26.** b; **27.** a; **28.** b; **29.** a; **30.** d

Adjectives (pages 398–402) Match the underlined adjective in the left column with the correct identification in the right column.

31. He had a guitar.	**(a)** comparative degree
32. She loved Spanish music.	**(b)** superlative degree
33. The best view was nearby.	**(c)** definite article
34. The night was moonlit.	**(d)** indefinite article
35. She wanted more romantic tunes.	**(e)** proper adjective

Answers: **31.** d; **32.** e; **33.** b; **34.** c; **35.** a

Adverbs (pages 403–407) Match the underlined adverb in the left column with the correct identification in the right column.

36. We wanted them to stay later.	**(a)** adverb of time
37. They had to go home.	**(b)** adverb of place
38. We could not convince them.	**(c)** adverb of degree
39. They became almost angry.	**(d)** adverb of manner
40. They left hurriedly.	**(e)** negative adverb

Answers: **36.** a; **37.** b; **38.** e; **39.** c; **40.** d

Prepositions, Conjunctions, and Interjections (pages 408–417) Indicate whether each of the ten underlined words as used here is **(a)** a preposition, **(b)** a coordinating conjunction, **(c)** a part of a correlative conjunction, **(d)** a subordinating conjunction, or **(e)** an interjection.

(41) Though city dwellers must often contend with pollution **(42)** and crime, the isolation of rural life can be quite stressful, too. Both medical care **(43)** and aid **(44)** for emergencies tend to be better in cities. **(45)** While population density causes stress, some psychologists believe that it also enhances social ties. Urbanites may be better able to cope with disrupted family relationships, **(46)** for they generally have varied friendships **(47)** outside the family **(48)** in addition to many cultural opportunities. **(49)** Yes, the differences between city and country life are enormous, **(50)** but the advantages are not all on one side.

Answers: **41.** d; **42.** b; **43.** c; **44.** a; **45.** d; **46.** b; **47.** a; **48.** a; **49.** e; **50.** b

Writing for Review Write one paragraph on any subject you choose. Underline and identify in your paragraph at least one example of each of the following parts of speech: noun, pronoun, verb, adjective, adverb, preposition, and conjunction.

19 CHAPTER
Parts of the Sentence

SIMPLE SUBJECTS AND SIMPLE PREDICATES

A **sentence** is a group of words that expresses a complete thought.

Every sentence has two basic parts, a *subject* and a *predicate.*

The **simple subject** is the principal noun or pronoun that tells what the sentence is about. The is the verb or verb phrase that tells something about the subject.

SIMPLE SUBJECT	SIMPLE PREDICATE
Sopranos	sang.
Senators	will attend.
Everything	has been discussed.

The simple subject is found by asking *who?* or *what?* about the verb. For example, in the first sentence above, the noun *sopranos* answers the question *who sang?*

COMPLETE SUBJECTS AND COMPLETE PREDICATES

In most sentences the simple subject and simple predicate are expanded or modified by the addition of other words and phrases.

The **complete subject** consists of the simple subject and all the words that modify it.

The **complete predicate** consists of the simple predicate and all the words that modify it or complete its meaning.

COMPLETE SUBJECT	COMPLETE PREDICATE
Sopranos from the opera company	sang at the inauguration.
The two senators from Ohio	will attend a local caucus.
Everything on the agenda	has been discussed by the committee.

Objective

EXERCISE 1. Identifying Subjects and Predicates. Copy each of the following sentences, and indicate with a vertical line the division between the complete subject and the complete predicate. Next underline the simple subject once and the simple predicate twice.

SAMPLE ANSWER: The care of our national parks|is a great responsibility.

1. During the 1800s visitors to the Montana Territory|returned with stories about geysers, hot springs, and bubbling mud.
2. These fascinating reports|prompted further exploration in a region known as Yellowstone.
3. As a result, in 1872 Congress|established the Yellowstone region as this country's first national park.
4. Since that time about fifty similar parks|have been established in this country.
5. These national parks|represent only one part of the entire National Park System.
6. The U.S. government|has declared nearly three hundred areas of historic importance, natural beauty, or recreational value as parks.
7. A staff of several thousand employees|is working to maintain the national parks throughout North America.
8. Every opening in the park service|will attract approximately forty applicants.
9. These park rangers|are working to preserve the parklands for future generations.
10. Each summer, temporary workers from across the country|join the full-time park employees.

COMPOUND SUBJECTS

A **compound subject** is made up of two or more simple subjects that are joined by a conjunction and that have the same verb.

Both **experience** and adequate **training** are necessary.
Neither the **bus** nor the **subway** goes there.
Crimson, cerise, and **vermilion** are shades of red.

Objective

EXERCISE 2. Identifying Compound Subjects. Write on your paper the compound subject in each of the following sentences.

SAMPLE: Both businesses and individuals rely on hotels.
ANSWER: businesses, individuals

1. Hotels, motels, and resorts constitute today's booming hotel industry.
2. Not only vacationers but also business travelers and conventioneers seek clean, comfortable facilities.

3. In many hotels, excellent service and sumptuous meals are available.
4. Attractive premises and spotless housekeeping are essential.
5. Prestige, glamour, and sophistication have long been associated with great hotels.
6. Both the Palace Hotel in San Francisco and the Waldorf-Astoria in New York were examples of luxurious hotels.
7. Neither the Planters Hotel in St. Louis nor the Paxton in Omaha could boast such luxuriousness.
8. At the turn of the century cities and towns everywhere acquired new hotels.
9. Today, over 22,000 hotels and 61,000 motels operate in the United States.
10. The restaurants, shops, and swimming pools of large resort complexes guarantee guests a pleasant stay.

COMPOUND PREDICATES

A **compound predicate** is made up of two or more verbs or verb phrases that are joined by a conjunction and that have the same subject.

Holograms **amaze** and **fascinate**.
The helicopter **hovered** briefly but **landed** almost at once.
Our guests **will eat** a light supper and **retire** before midnight.
The project coordinator **has been** and **may be** an officer of the company.

A sentence may have both a compound subject and a compound predicate.

S S P P
Crocuses and **daffodils** both **herald** and **symbolize** spring.

Objective
EXERCISE 3. Identifying Compound Predicates. Write on your paper the compound predicate in each of the following sentences.

1. The construction of a building requires many skills and provides good jobs.
2. Architects design the building and prepare the plans.
3. Construction supervisors both prepare budgets and hire workers.
4. They also contract for materials and coordinate the schedules.
5. Certain laborers will arrive first and prepare the site for the scheduled activities.
6. Carpenters not only construct the plywood forms for the concrete but also frame the walls.
7. Bricklayers and stonemasons either lay bricks or set the huge reinforced-concrete blocks of the outer walls.

8. Electricians and plumbers may run their respective lines and install the necessary fixtures.
9. In addition to these workers, thousands of others have manufactured and transported materials.
10. A slowdown in the construction industry may result from many things but usually leads to unemployment.

Objective
EXERCISE 4. Identifying Subjects and Predicates. On your paper copy the following sentences. Then underline the simple subjects once and the simple predicates twice. Some of the subjects and predicates are compound.

1. Earthquakes are some of nature's most destructive activities.
2. These deep, underground forces generally act without warning.
3. Few locations in the world are free from the risk of quakes.
4. Rare but devastating quakes have even struck the east coast of the United States.
5. More than four hundred instruments measure and record every unusual movement of the earth in California.
6. The San Andreas Fault, a seven-hundred-mile fracture in the earth's crust, is located there.
7. The place, time, and power of an earthquake are determined scientifically.
8. Scientists involved in the study of earthquakes are called seismologists.
9. They and the public are learning much about earthquakes.
10. Accurate prediction and control of these curious forces have not been determined.

Objective
APPLICATION EXERCISE. Expanding Subjects and Predicates. (a) Write five sentences, each with one subject and one predicate. **(b)** Expand each sentence by making both the subject and the predicate compound.

SAMPLE ANSWER: **(a)** Television provides entertainment.
(b) Television and radio both provide entertainment and disseminate information.

ORDER OF SUBJECT AND PREDICATE

In most sentences in English, the subject comes before the verb. There are exceptions, however, to this normal word order.

1. In commands or requests, the subject *you* is not expressed; it is "understood."

[You] **Listen!** [You] **Carry** it home. [You] **Please** see me.

2. At times a sentence is written in inverted order—that is, with the predicate before the subject. This reversal of the usual order is done to add emphasis. In the following examples the simple predicates and the simple subjects are in bold type.

PREDICATE	SUBJECT
Beneath the waves **lay**	an ancient **shipwreck**.
Over the years **had arisen**	many improbable **tales**.

3. The words *there, here,* and *it* are sometimes used as expletives. An *expletive* is a word used to introduce or to fill out a sentence. In sentences with expletives, the subject generally comes after the predicate. Very often the expletive is followed by a form of the verb *be*.

PREDICATE	SUBJECT
Here **is**	the **quilt** for my friend.
There **were**	**patterns** in a magazine.
It **is** certain	**that she will be pleased**.*

Objective

EXERCISE 5. Recognizing Word Order. Copy each of the following sentences, and draw a vertical line between the complete subject and the complete predicate. Next underline each simple subject once and each simple predicate twice. Some sentences are in normal subject-predicate order.

SAMPLE ANSWER: There are|many reasons for thinking of Washington, D.C., as one of this country's most beautiful cities.

1. Washington, D.C.,|has a distinctive atmosphere.
2. Of course, there is|the monumental quality of many of its public buildings.
3. The familiar Washington Monument|dominates the skyline.
4. Among the best of the contemporary buildings is|the stunning East Building of the National Gallery of Art.
5. Complementing the classical layout of the city are also|many broad, tree-lined avenues.
6. In addition, much of the land|is comprised of parks and gardens.
7. Below street level runs|Rock Creek Park, with miles of roadways and bicycle paths.
8. A complete lack of skyscrapers|reinforces the city's sense of openness.
9. A longstanding law|prohibits the construction of very tall buildings.
10. The city|has created a lasting impression on millions of visitors and residents.

*The subject here is a noun clause (see Chapter 21).

Objective
EXERCISE 6. Writing Inverted Sentences. Rewrite each of the following sentences as an inverted sentence with the predicate first.

Through the shutters filtered predawn light.
1. Predawn light filtered through the shutters.
On the cool morning air drifted the smell of moist earth.
2. The smell of moist earth drifted on the cool morning air.
Off the bare walls softly echoed the relentless drip of a faucet.
3. The relentless drip of a faucet softly echoed off the bare walls.
At the foot of the bed stretched two kittens.
4. Two kittens stretched at the foot of the bed.
From the radio on the desk suddenly erupted a deafening clamor.
5. Suddenly a deafening clamor erupted from the radio on the desk.

Suggested Answers appear above each sentence.

COMPLEMENTS

A **complement** is a word or group of words that completes the meaning of the verb.

A complement is anything that helps to make something else complete. A painting, for example, can be complemented by a frame. Similarly, a subject and a verb often need a *complement* in order for the meaning of a sentence to be complete. Note that the following sentences sound incomplete even though they include a subject and a verb.

Janice sold ______________.
This jacket looks ______________.

What complements would help complete the meaning of each of the preceding items?

The next four sections will discuss four kinds of complements that can be used to complete sentences: *direct objects, indirect objects, object complements,* and *subject complements.*

DIRECT OBJECTS

A **direct object** answers the question *what?* or *whom?* after an action verb.

The subject of a sentence usually performs the action indicated by the verb. That action may be directed toward or may be received by someone or something: the direct object. Nouns, pronouns, or words acting as nouns may serve as direct objects. Only transitive verbs have direct objects.

Janice sold her **typewriter**. [Janice sold *what?*]
Everyone watched the **diver**. [Everyone watched *whom?*]
They understood **what I said**. [They understood *what?*]

Like other sentence parts, direct objects may be *compound.*

Janice sold her **typewriter** and **radio**. [Janice sold *what?*]

Objective

EXERCISE 7. Identifying Direct Objects. On your paper write the action verb in each of the following sentences. Then list any direct objects. (One sentence has a compound object.)

1. Managers in industry coordinate various aspects of an enterprise. (DO: aspects)
2. They plan, in accordance with set objectives, the best way to achieve a goal. (DO: way)
3. These trained executives carefully organize their financial, physical, and human resources. (DO: resources)
4. As human relations specialists, they supervise each employee in their department. (DO: employee)
5. In addition, they diligently monitor all work in progress. (DO: work)
6. Conscientious managers constantly seek improvements in performance. (DO: improvements)
7. The best managers can elicit superior performance from all their personnel. (DO: performance)
8. High morale among employees and profitable operations reflect good managerial techniques. (DO: techniques)
9. Top-level managers must understand, among other things, industry trends, marketing development, and financial analysis. (DO: trends, development, analysis)
10. Every healthy business owes its success to its managers. (DO: success)

Answers: The action verb is underlined; the direct object is labeled.

Objective

EXERCISE 8. Adding Direct Objects. On your paper complete the following subjects and verbs by adding a direct object. You may also add any other words that you need for the sentence to make sense.

1. Most sports demand coordination.
2. Regular exercise builds muscles.
3. Athletes in training need a balanced diet.
4. A strong body affects one's mental outlook.
5. Determination may bring success.

Suggested Answers appear in the blanks.

Objective

APPLICATION EXERCISE. Creating Sentences with Direct Objects. Write five sentences describing how to make or do something. Use action verbs. Identify the subjects, verbs, and direct objects in these sentences.

Suggested Answer: A coat (S) of paint protects (AV) the surface (DO).

INDIRECT OBJECTS

An **indirect object** answers the question *to whom?* or *for whom?* or *to what?* or *for what?* after an action verb.

A sentence may have an indirect object only if it has a direct object. The indirect object will always come between the verb and the direct object, never after a preposition. Indirect objects are usually nouns or pronouns.

> Airlines give **passengers** bonuses. [Airlines give bonuses *to whom?*]
> The owner reserved **us** a table. [The owner reserved a table *for whom?*]
> The committee gave my **project** top priority. [The committee gave top priority *to what?*]

Indirect objects may be *compound.*

> Airlines give **passengers** and **employees** bonuses. [Airlines give bonuses *to whom?*]

Objective

EXERCISE 9. Identifying Indirect Objects. First write on your paper the direct objects in each of the following sentences. Then list any indirect objects. (Not all sentences will have indirect objects.)

IO DO
1. Collage offers the amateur artist an especially flexible technique.

DO
2. The collagist simply glues material to a chosen "ground."

IO DO
3. The use of diverse materials gives this genre an interesting effect.

DO
4. Some artists incorporate three-dimensional objects into their collages.

DO
5. Different types of paper provide the basic material for most work in this art form.

DO DO
6. Paint and ink can contribute variety and unusual effects.

IO DO
7. Photos of famous persons give the work a social or political edge.

DO
8. Abstract works, however, can also stir powerful feelings.

DO
9. An endless number of sophisticated techniques lend variety to this art form.

10. Multiple textures and layered effects provide extraordinary sensory DO detail.

OBJECT COMPLEMENTS

An **object complement** answers the question *what?* after a direct object. That is, it *completes* the meaning of the direct object by identifying or describing the direct object.

Object complements occur only in sentences with direct objects and only in sentences with action verbs such as the following:

appoint	find
call	make
choose	name
consider	render
elect	think

An object complement usually follows a direct object. An object complement may be an adjective, a noun, or a pronoun.

The accident rendered her car **useless**. [adjective]
I called the horse **Dusty**. [noun]
Aileen considers our house **hers**. [pronoun]
The board named Flo **president** and **treasurer**. [nouns]

Object complements may also be *compound*, as the last example demonstrates.

Objective

EXERCISE 10. Identifying Object Complements. Write the object complement (or complements) in each of the following sentences.

1. Many call Smith the perfect comptroller.
2. However, some critics consider him wasteful and stubborn.
3. Others consider him stingy but wise.
4. Still others make Smith the scapegoat for the city's fiscal problems.
5. The people elected him comptroller last year.
6. The mayor finds him miraculous.
7. In public she has called him a marvel.
8. Many journalists have dubbed his policies visionary.
9. Some opponents have thought him irresponsible.
10. Smith's policies render criticism moot.

SUBJECT COMPLEMENTS

A **subject complement** follows a subject and a linking verb and identifies or describes the subject.

A linking verb almost always needs one or more additional words in the predicate to complete its meaning. After all, a linking verb *links* a subject to something else. The "something else" is the subject complement. There are two kinds of subject complements: *predicate nominatives* and *predicate adjectives.*

A **predicate nominative** is a noun or pronoun that follows a linking verb and points back to the subject to identify it further.

Cellists are **musicians**.

The soloist for this concert is **someone** from Dallas.

Predicate nominatives are usually found in sentences that contain forms of the linking verb *be*. Often these are sentences that classify things. A few other linking verbs (for example, *become* and *remain*) can be followed by a predicate nominative.

Those two may be **thieves**.
Dolphins are **mammals**.
When did he become **treasurer**?
They will not remain **caterpillars**.

Like other parts of a sentence, predicate nominatives may be *compound*.

The divers remained **rivals** but **friends**.
The precipitation was neither **snow** nor **sleet**.

A **predicate adjective** follows a linking verb and points back to the subject and further describes it.

That cellist is **lovely**.

The soloist seemed **thoughtful**.

Predicate adjectives may follow any linking verb and may be *compound*.

Her tale sounded **preposterous**.
The runners looked **exhausted** but **happy**.
His manner was **coarse**.
We became quite **impatient**.

Objective

EXERCISE 11. Identifying Subject Complements. Write on your paper all the subject complements in the following sentences. Identify each as a predicate nominative or a predicate adjective. (Some sentences have more than one subject complement; others have none.)

(1) The Super Bowl has become an important event. **(2)** The original name of the Super Bowl was the World Championship Game. **(3)** "World Championship Game" sounded stuffy and prideful. **(4)** The nickname "Super Bowl" became the official title in 1969. **(5)** An important part of the entertainment is the pregame coverage. **(6)** Some football fans postpone all other activities on this Sunday. **(7)** Others give big parties that day. **(8)** This passion appears unwarranted and completely inexplicable to some people. **(9)** After all the fuss, the game itself is often disappointing. **(10)** Nevertheless, more than 100 million people watch the game on "Super Sunday." *Answers*: **1.** event—PN; **2.** World Championship Game—PN; **3.** stuffy, prideful—PA; **4.** title—PN; **5.** coverage—PN; **6.** NONE; **7.** NONE; **8.** unwarranted, inexplicable—PA; **9.** disappointing—PA; **10.** NONE

Objective
APPLICATION EXERCISE. Writing Sentences with Complements. Write four sentences about a natural phenomenon, such as an eclipse, a thunderstorm, or an earthquake. In each sentence use at least one of the four kinds of complements: direct object, indirect object, object complement, and subject complement. Label each of the complements in your sentences.

Suggested Answer: They considered the eclipse (DO) spectacular (OC).

REVIEW EXERCISE. Complements. On your paper write the complements that appear in the following sentences. Next to each complement, write what kind of complement it is: direct object, indirect object, object complement, predicate nominative, or predicate adjective. (One sentence has a compound complement.)

(1) American Sign Language (ASL) is the standard language of deaf children of deaf parents. **(2)** Like spoken languages, ASL has its own grammar and syntax. **(3)** With no real understanding of it, many linguistic "experts" call ASL primitive. **(4)** In reality, it is capable of great precision and subtle expression. **(5)** In comparison, Signed English is an uncomplicated system of conventional signs. **(6)** ASL affords deaf people an efficient means of communication. **(7)** A hearing learner can become expert only after years of practice. **(8)** Few ever become proficient.

Answers: **1.** language—PN; **2.** grammar, syntax—DO; **3.** ASL—DO, primitive—OC; **4.** capable—PA; **5.** system—PN; **6.** people—IO; means—DO; **7.** expert—PA; **8.** proficient—PA

BASIC SENTENCE PATTERNS

You regularly combine the parts of the sentence in ways that produce recurring patterns. You can express these patterns in a kind of shorthand using capital letters. Most sentences fall into one of the following patterns:

1. Subject + Action Verb (Intransitive)

S AV(I)
Accountants audit.

2. Subject + Action Verb (Transitive) + Direct Object

S AV(T) DO
Accountants balance accounts.

3. Subject + Action Verb (Transitive) + Indirect Object + Direct Object

S AV(T) IO DO
The ledgers are giving the accountants headaches.

4. Subject + Action Verb (Transitive) + Direct Object + Object Complement

S AV(T) DO OC
The owners found the accountants capable.

5. Subject + Linking Verb + Subject Complement (Predicate Nominative)

S LV SC(PN)
Accountants are advisers.

6. Subject + Linking Verb + Subject Complement (Predicate Adjective)

S LV SC(PA)
Accountants are indispensable.

You may expand each of these basic patterns by adding modifiers, such as adjectives and adverbs.

S AV(I)
The two new accountants work in our old office.

Another common method of expanding basic sentence patterns is by compounding. Sentences may have various combinations of compound subjects, verbs, and complements.

S S AV(T) DO
Both accountants and managers read financial statements
AV(T) DO
and ponder their implications.

Objective

EXERCISE 12. Identifying Sentence Patterns. On your paper write the basic sentence pattern of each sentence.

S LV SC(PN)
1. Sunsets become rainbows to the imagination.
S LV SC(PA)
2. Beautiful sunsets can be breathtaking.
S AV(T) DO OC
3. Clear days make the sky magnificent.
S AV(T) DO
4. Gradual shifts yield shades of brown, gray, and purple.
S AV(I)
5. These shades ultimately deepen into black night.

Objective

APPLICATION EXERCISE. Creating Sentences with Various Patterns. Write one sentence for each of the following sentence patterns. To make your sentence clear, you may need to add modifiers to your subjects, verbs, and complements.

1. S + S + AV(T) + DO Balloons and kites filled the sky.
2. S + AV(T) + DO + OC The doctor found the youngster delirious.
3. S + LV + SC(PA) Real celebrations are rare.
4. S + AV(I) + AV(I) The snow melted and disappeared.
5. S + AV(T) + IO + DO I gave the clerk my key.

Suggested Answers follow each pattern.

DIAGRAMING BASIC SENTENCE PATTERNS

Diagraming is a method of showing the relationship of various words and parts of a sentence to the sentence as a whole.

The following examples show the traditional method of diagraming the six basic sentence patterns summarized in the preceding section. The examples also show how to diagram modifiers, such as adjectives and adverbs, and how to represent compound sentence parts, such as compound subjects and predicates.

You begin to diagram a sentence by finding the simple subject, keeping in mind that a sentence may have a compound subject. After you have found the subject, find the action or linking verb that goes with it. Write the subject and the verb on a horizontal line. Separate them with a vertical line that bisects the horizontal line to indicate the division between the complete subject and the complete predicate of the sentence.

subject | verb

Additional sentence elements are added as indicated in the following examples:

1. Subject + Action Verb (Intransitive)

Trees grow.

subject | action verb

Trees | grow

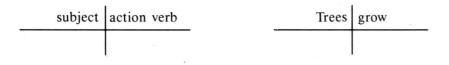

2. Subject + Action Verb (Intransitive), including adjectives and adverbs

Young pine trees grow especially fast.

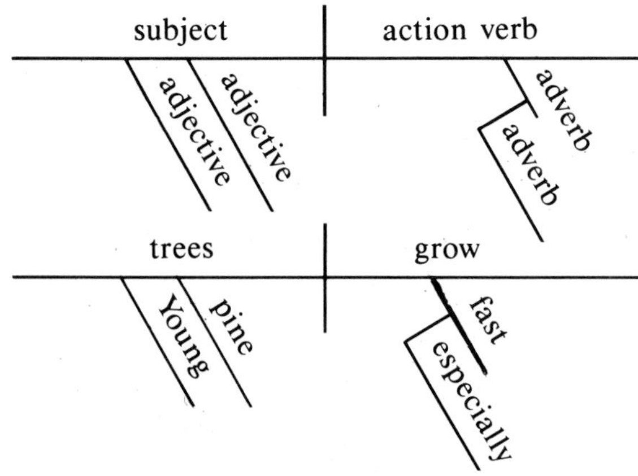

3. Understood Subject + Action Verb (Intransitive)

Observe carefully.

4. Subject + Action Verb (Transitive) + Indirect Object + Direct Object

Trees give us medicines.

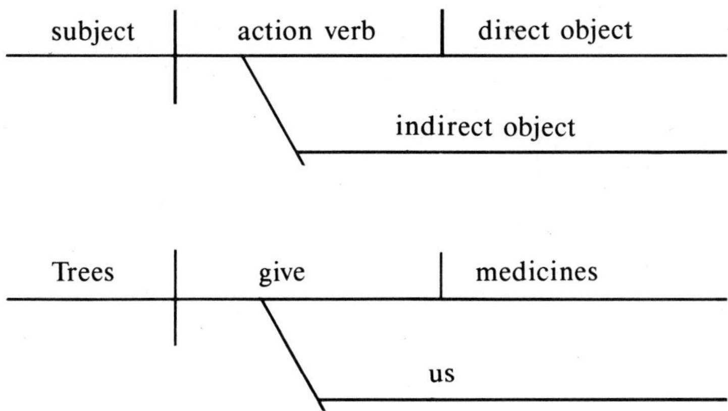

5. Compound Subject + Action Verb (Transitive) + Direct Object + Object Complement

Designers and carpenters consider hardwoods unsurpassed.

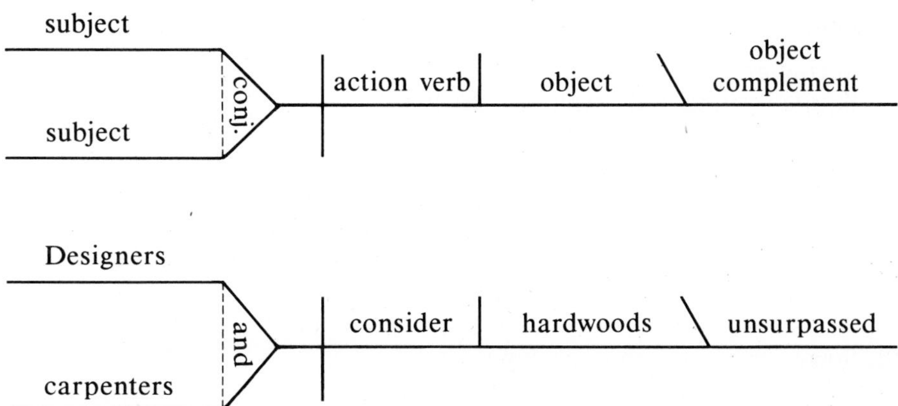

6. Expletive + Linking Verb + Subject

There is a Douglas fir.

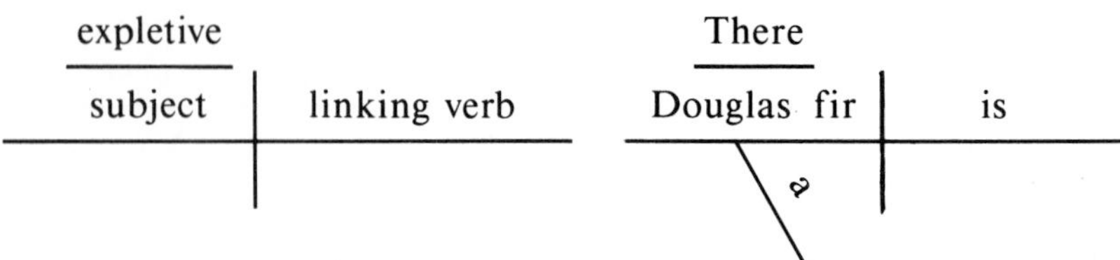

7. Subject + Linking Verb + Subject Complement (Predicate Nominative)

Trees become timber.

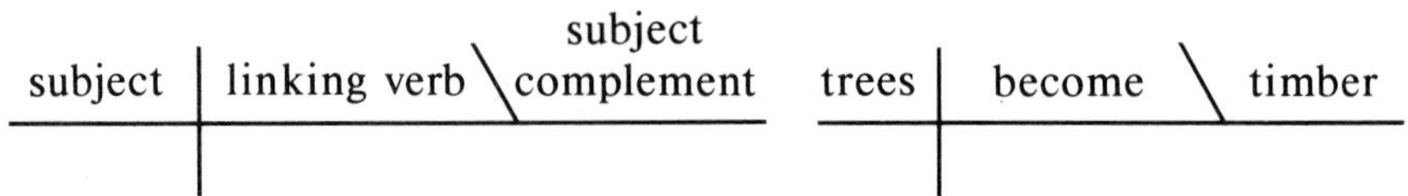

8. Subject + Compound Linking Verb + Compound Subject Complement (Predicate Adjective)

Conifers are numerous and will remain plentiful.

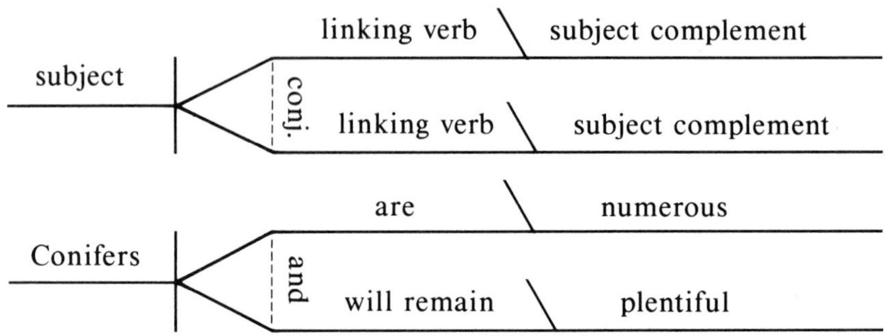

Objective

EXERCISE 13. Diagraming Basic Sentence Patterns. Use the preceding models as you diagram the following sentences.

1. Spring arrived.
2. Swollen young buds exploded thrillingly.
3. Their fragrance rendered everyone listless.
4. Joggers and cyclists considered the weather superb.
5. The season was a welcome visitor.
6. Winter seemed remote and long forgotten.
7. The long days gave her more light for her work.
8. Night rains released a familiar moldy scent.
9. The spring breezes were fresh but unpredictable.
10. Spring fever was an everyday malady.

CHAPTER 19 PARTS OF THE SENTENCE

Subjects and Predicates (pages 424–429) For each of the following sentences, identify the underlined word or words as **(a)** a complete subject, **(b)** a complete predicate, **(c)** a simple subject, **(d)** a simple predicate, or **(e)** a compound subject.

1. Several groups of Native Americans lived long ago in the Southwest.
2. One of these groups was the Anasazi.
3. The Navaho word *Anasazi* means "ancient ones."
4. The highly advanced civilization of the Anasazi vanished around A.D. 1300.
5. Drought or epidemic may have driven the people away.

Answers: **1.** c; **2.** b; **3.** a; **4.** d; **5.** e

Complements (pages 429–434) For each of the following sentences, identify the underlined word or words as **(a)** a direct object, **(b)** an indirect object, **(c)** an object complement, **(d)** a predicate nominative, or **(e)** a predicate adjective.

6. The Anasazi left their settlements behind.
7. Chaco in New Mexico is their largest settlement.
8. The Anasazi built their villages on high cliffs in steep-walled canyons.
9. Their extreme height made these villages secure.
10. Many of the Anasazi buildings are huge.
11. The Spaniards gave the Anasazi buildings a Spanish name.
12. They called these buildings *pueblos*, which is Spanish for "towns."
13. Anasazi pottery was highly distinctive.
14. Typical Anasazi crops were corn, beans, and squash.
15. The Spanish brought this area many new foods.

Answers: **6.** a; **7.** d; **8.** a; **9.** c; **10.** e; **11.** b; **12.** c; **13.** e; **14.** d; **15.** b

Basic Sentence Patterns (pages 434–435) Match the sentence in the left column with the sentence pattern in the right column. *Code*: S = subject, AV = action verb, LV = linking verb, IO = indirect object, DO = direct object, OC = object complement, SC = subject complement.

16. The Hopi are descendants of the Anasazi.	**(a)** S+AV+DO+DO
17. Both the Hopi and the Anasazi built on high plateaus.	**(b)** S+AV+IO+DO
18. The Hopi sell silver and turquoise jewelry.	**(c)** S+AV+DO+OC
19. The tourist trade brings the Hopi prosperity.	**(d)** S+LV+SC
20. Archeologists find the pueblos fascinating.	**(e)** S+S+AV

Answers: **16.** d; **17.** e; **18.** a; **19.** b; **20.** c

Diagraming Basic Sentence Patterns (pages 436–438) Indicate the letter of the position that each numbered word in the following sentence should occupy in the diagram below.

Stone and adobe (21) have given (22) the pueblos (23) centuries-old (24) permanence (25).

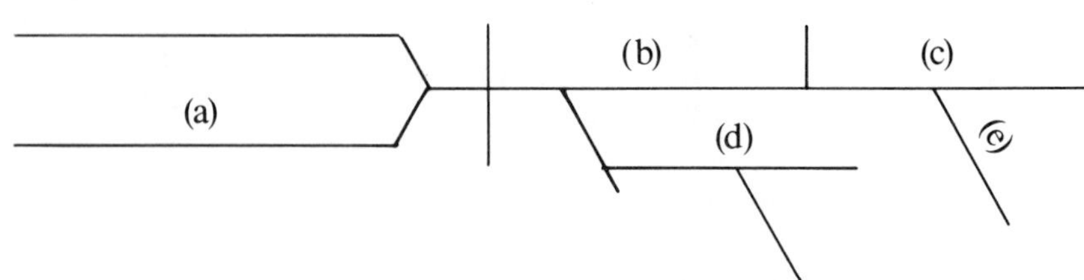

Answers: **21.** a; **22.** b; **23.** d; **24.** e; **25.** c

Writing for Review Write a paragraph on a topic of your choice. Demonstrate your knowledge of sentence parts by using a variety of sentence patterns. Underline and identify in your paragraph at least five of the following: simple subject, simple predicate, direct object, indirect object, object complement, predicate nominative, predicate adjective.

CHAPTER 20
Phrases

A **phrase** is a group of words that acts in a sentence as a single part of speech.

You have already learned about noun phrases and verb phrases (Chapter 18). In this chapter you will learn about four other kinds of phrases: *prepositional phrases, appositive phrases, verbal phrases,* and *absolute phrases.*

PREPOSITIONAL PHRASES

A **prepositional phrase** is a group of words that begins with a preposition and usually ends with a noun or pronoun, called the *object of the preposition.*

> This door leads **to the darkroom**. [*Darkroom* is the object of the preposition *to.*]
> That door is hazardous **for the waiters**. [*Waiters* is the object of the preposition *for.*]

(For lists of common prepositions, see page 408.)

Adjectives and other modifiers may be placed between the preposition and its object. In addition, a preposition may have more than one object.

> This door leads **to the expensive new darkroom**. [adjectives added]
> The door **to the basement and the garage** needs repair. [two objects]

Prepositional phrases also may occur in a series or sequence of two or more.

> The door **of the car with the skis on top** is scratched. [series of prepositional phrases]

A prepositional phrase normally acts in a sentence in the same way that an adjective or an adverb does. Used as an adjective, a prepositional phrase is called an *adjectival phrase;* it modifies a noun or a pronoun. Used as an adverb, a prepositional phrase is an *adverbial phrase;* it modifies a verb, an adjective, or an adverb.

Enter the door **in the rear**. [adjectival phrase modifying the noun *door*]

One **of these doors** is locked. [adjectival phrase modifying the pronoun *one*]

After work you could return this door **to the store**. [adverbial phrases modifying the verb phrase *could return*]

Automatic doors are fascinating **to children**. [adverbial phrase modifying the adjective *fascinating*]

The old door swings easily **for its age**. [adverbial phrase modifying the adverb *easily*]

Open the door **at the head of the stairs**. [adjectival phrase modifying the noun *door* followed by an adjectival phrase modifying the noun *head*]

Objective

EXERCISE 1. Identifying Prepositional Phrases. Write the following sentences on your paper, and underline each prepositional phrase.

1. Great environmental art is alive on the Great Plains.
2. From an airplane, the vast cultivated fields seem monumental abstract art.
3. The immensely varied designs result from modern farming methods.
4. The plowed fields are basically rectangular or square in shape.
5. Farmers plow along the natural contours of the land.
6. Red, brown, and black patterns with a variety of textures result from the plowing methods.
7. Modern irrigation equipment pivots around a central water source.
8. This technique produces huge circular areas that look like disks of bright green.
9. No one on the plains has consciously planned these designs.
10. They are the bonus of an unplanned collaboration between the farmer and nature.

Objective

EXERCISE 2. Identifying Adjectival and Adverbial Phrases. Look again at the prepositional phrases you underlined in Exercise 1. Write the word each phrase modifies. Then indicate whether each prepositional phrase is *adjectival* or *adverbial.*

Objective

APPLICATION EXERCISE. Expanding Sentences with Prepositional Phrases. Expand the following sentences by adding at least one adjectival phrase and one adverbial phrase to each.

1. The revelers set off fireworks.
2. Four nurses received awards.
3. Anyone could have seen it.
4. The spaceship transmitted messages.
5. The ruler was broken.

Suggested Answer to 1: The revelers on the riverfront set off fireworks after dark.

APPOSITIVES AND APPOSITIVE PHRASES

An **appositive** is a noun or pronoun that is placed next to another noun or pronoun to identify or to give additional information about it.

An **appositive phrase** is an appositive plus any words that modify the appositive.

> My sister **Kate** sells computer software. [The appositive *Kate* identifies the noun *sister*.]
> She works for Softwarehouse, **a new retail outlet.** [The appositive phrase, in bold type, identifies *Softwarehouse*.]

(For rules about using commas with appositives and appositive phrases, see Chapter 28.)

Objective

EXERCISE 3. Identifying Appositives and Appositive Phrases. On your paper write the appositive or the appositive phrase in each of the following sentences.

1. The music of American composer Virgil Thomson is known and enjoyed around the world.
2. Thomson's home during the 1920s and 1930s was Paris, the center of the musical world at that time.
3. Gertrude Stein, an expatriate American writer, collaborated with Thomson on an avant-garde opera.
4. The highly successful opera *Four Saints in Three Acts* featured cellophane sets and a celebrated all-black cast.
5. In 1949 the Pulitzer Prize Board awarded its musical prize to Virgil Thomson's film score *Louisiana Story*.

Objective

EXERCISE 4. Adding Appositive Phrases to Sentences. Each of the sentences below is followed by a group of words in parentheses. Rewrite each sentence, incorporating the group of words in parentheses into the sentence as an appositive phrase. Use a comma or commas to set off the appositive phrase from the rest of the sentence.

SAMPLE: The Washington Monument is located in Washington, D.C. (the nation's capital)

ANSWER: The Washington Monument is located in Washington, D.C., the nation's capital.

The most famous museum in Leningrad is the Hermitage, a magnificent former palace.

1. The most famous museum in Leningrad is the Hermitage. (a magnificent former palace)

The Sears Tower, the world's tallest building, can be found in Chicago.

2. The Sears Tower can be found in Chicago. (the world's tallest building)

The Great Wall, one of history's great engineering achievements, runs 3,500 miles across Chinese mountain ranges.

3. The Great Wall runs 3,500 miles across Chinese mountain ranges. (one of history's great engineering achievements)

Copenhagen is the home of Tivoli Gardens, a world-famous amusement park.

4. Copenhagen is the home of Tivoli Gardens. (a world-famous amusement park)

Suggested Answers appear above each item.

VERBALS AND VERBAL PHRASES

A **verbal** is a form of a verb that works in a sentence as a noun, an adjective, or an adverb.

While acting in sentences as nouns, adjectives, and adverbs, verbals retain some of the qualities of verbs. For example, verbals can show action and can have complements and modifiers.

A **verbal phrase** contains a verbal plus any complements and modifiers.

There are three kinds of verbals: *participles, gerunds,* and *infinitives.* All three can be expanded into phrases.

PARTICIPLES AND PARTICIPIAL PHRASES

A **participle** is a form of a verb that works in a sentence as an adjective.

Present participles end in *-ing. Past participles* often end in *-ed,* but they can also take other forms. Many of the adjectives that you commonly use in sentences are actually participles.

Rising prices are inevitable.

Julian Schnabel cleverly incorporates **broken** plates into his paintings.

The **opening** speech detailed many **needed** changes.

When a participle is part of a verb phrase in the predicate of a sentence, it is not acting as an adjective.

PARTICIPLE AS ADJECTIVE: The **lost** shipment has been recovered.

PARTICIPLE IN VERB PHRASE: The warehouse **had lost** a big shipment.

(For more information about forming present and past participles, see Chapter 22.)

A **participial phrase** contains a participle plus any complements and modifiers.

A participial phrase can have a present participle or a past participle. Participial phrases act as adjectives and can be placed in various positions in a sentence.

> **Preparing for the eclipse,** we set our alarms for the appropriate time.
>
> The full moon, **suspended in the sky,** was brilliant.
>
> **Delighted by the spectacle** but **badly needing sleep,** we maintained our vigil.

A past participle may be used with a form of the auxiliary verbs *have* and *be* to indicate the time of the action.

> **Having read about the eclipse,** we were steadfast.
>
> We watched the white light of the moon **being consumed by the dark shadow of our planet.**

(For practice in avoiding misplaced or dangling participles, see Chapter 25.)

Objective

EXERCISE 5. Identifying Participles and Participial Phrases. Write the participle or the participial phrase in each of the following sentences. Then identify the word each modifies.

effects

1. George Lucas has been responsible for the stunning special effects in many films.

he

2. Now known around the world, he is also the creator of the blockbuster *Star Wars* films.

Lucas

3. Having barely escaped death in a car crash, Lucas turned to films in the late 1960s.

effort

4. Lucas later sold *American Graffiti*, a full-length effort based on his own youth in California, to a major studio.

American Graffiti

5. Eventually becoming a huge success, *American Graffiti* was almost ruined by the editing of the studio.

Lucas

6. Having relinquished the rights to the film, Lucas had no legal

control over it—but learned a valuable lesson.

screenplay

7. The *Star Wars* screenplay, written by Lucas during the next two years, was destined for greatness.

Lucas

8. Suspecting a market for merchandise from *Star Wars*, a wiser Lucas sold the distribution rights but not the merchandising rights.

profits

9. The incredible profits derived from sales of such products as T-shirts, dolls, and bubble gum made him a wealthy man.

he

10. He became completely independent of the major studios, having been handsomely rewarded for his foresight.

GERUNDS AND GERUND PHRASES

A **gerund** is a form of a verb that ends in *-ing* and that is used in the same ways a noun is used.

> **Training** is essential. [gerund as subject]
> We considered **flying**. [gerund as direct object]
> We should give **speaking** more attention. [gerund as indirect object]
> Do I get credit for **trying**? [gerund as object of preposition]
> Their passion was **sculling**. [gerund as predicate nominative]
> Two skills, **planning** and **organizing**, are basic. [gerunds as appositives]

A **gerund phrase** contains a gerund plus any complements and modifiers.

A gerund phrase can vary in length, depending on how many complements and modifiers are added to the gerund.

> **Actively participating in sports** has many benefits.
> **Careful financial planning** is now a necessity.
> This suit shows **expert tailoring**.

The difference between a present participle and a gerund, both of which end in *-ing*, is that a present participle is used as an adjective and a gerund is used as a noun.

> **Waiting in line**, we grew impatient. [participial phrase]
> **Waiting in line** made us impatient. [gerund phrase]

Objective

EXERCISE 6. Identifying Gerunds and Gerund Phrases. List on your paper the gerunds and gerund phrases in the following sentences. The number of gerunds or gerund phrases is given in parentheses at the end of each sentence.

1. Decorative tinworking is an ancient craft still being practiced in New Mexico today. (1)
2. Only a few real experts, mostly retired Hispanic men and women, now give tinworking full attention. (1)
3. Often working with patterns from a century ago, these artisans begin by expertly cutting a new sheet of tin. (1)
4. Making indentations in the tin, or punching, is done with blunt tools of steel and iron. (2)
5. Piercing requires sharper implements and adds interest. (1)
6. The boxes, candleholders, mirrors, and religious objects have formal simplicity but fine detailing. (1)
7. The traditional tinworkers derive much satisfaction from creating beautiful but useful objects. (1)
8. Selling these masterful products is no problem. (1)
9. Many people enjoy decorating with these handmade pieces. (1)
10. Museums around the world have also been buying these objects for enriching their craft collections. (1)

Objective
EXERCISE 7. Identifying the Uses of Gerunds. Look again at your answers for sentences 2, 4, 6, and 7 in Exercise 6. On your paper identify the way in which each gerund or gerund phrase is used: as subject, direct object, indirect object, appositive, or object of preposition.

SAMPLE: Decorative tinworking
ANSWER: subject
Answers: **2.** indirect object; **4.** subject, appositive; **6.** direct object; **7.** object of preposition

Objective
APPLICATION EXERCISE. Writing Sentences with Gerunds. Select five of the gerunds that you identified in Exercise 7, and write one original sentence for each. Make sure that you use the *-ing* word as a gerund, not as a present participle or as part of a verb phrase.
Suggested Answer to 1: Tinworking requires patience and dedication.

INFINITIVES AND INFINITIVE PHRASES

An **infinitive** is a verb form that is usually preceded by the word *to* and is used as a noun, an adjective, or an adverb.

When you use the word *to* before a verb, the *to* is not a preposition but part of the infinitive form of the verb. Infinitives can be used in the same ways that nouns, adjectives, and adverbs are used:

To exercise is healthy. [infinitive as subject]
No one wishes **to volunteer**. [infinitive as direct object]
Their decision was **to merge**. [infinitive as predicate nominative]

I felt a need **to call**. [infinitive as adjective]

Everyone was prepared **to sacrifice**. [infinitive as adverb]

An **infinitive phrase** contains an infinitive plus any complements and modifiers.

The lawyers want **to continue the case.**
Would you prefer **to sleep until noon?**
To speak clearly and slowly was most important.

Occasionally, an infinitive may have its own subject. Such a construction is called an *infinitive clause.*

Circumstances forced **the gentlemen to duel**. [*Gentlemen* is the subject of the infinitive *to duel.* The entire infinitive clause *the gentlemen to duel* acts as the direct object of the sentence.]
The teacher asked **her to give a speech**. [*Her* is the subject of the infinitive *to give.* The entire infinitive clause *her to give a speech* acts as the direct object of the sentence.]*

Sometimes the word *to* is dropped before an infinitive.

Please [to] **call**.
We could have heard **a pin** [to] **drop**.
Shall we let **them** [to] **share our table?**

Objective

EXERCISE 8. Identifying Infinitives and Infinitive Phrases. Write the infinitive or the infinitive phrase that appears in each of the following sentences. (Note that one sentence has no infinitive.)

1. All the arts tend to thrive in Winston-Salem, North Carolina.
2. The nation's oldest brass band to operate continuously was formed in the little town of Salem in 1778.
3. It isn't surprising to discover that the first chamber music written in this country was composed in Winston-Salem.
4. In 1956, the Southeast Center for Contemporary Arts (SECCA) was founded to involve residents of the city with the arts.
5. To bring young artists to the public is a major aim of the SECCA.
6. One of the main concerns of this Winston-Salem gallery is to show the work of unrecognized artists.
7. The gallery does not plan to acquire a permanent art collection.
8. Each year, the SECCA awards fellowships to seven artists from the southeastern United States.
9. The works of the "Southeast Seven" artists are displayed for experts to judge.
10. Because most local business people are already involved with the arts, artists and executives find it easy to communicate.

*Note that the pronoun subject of the infinitive (*her*) is in the objective case.

Objective
EXERCISE 9. Identifying the Uses of Infinitives. Look again at your answers to the first five items in Exercise 8. Write whether each infinitive phrase is used as **(a)** a noun, **(b)** an adjective, or **(c)** an adverb.
Answers: **1.** c; **2.** b; **3.** a; **4.** c; **5.** a

Objective
APPLICATION EXERCISE. Writing Sentences with Infinitives. Jot down five action verbs. Use each in an infinitive phrase in an original sentence. Then underline the infinitive phrases.
Suggested Answer: It was wasteful *to discard the scraps.*

REVIEW EXERCISE. Verbal Phrases. On your paper write each of the verbal phrases in the following sentences. Tell whether each is a participial phrase, a gerund phrase, or an infinitive phrase.

1. Spelunkers are people who explore caves, searching for information.
2. Using equipment and techniques similar to those of mountain climbers, spelunkers probe the dark inner regions of caves for fun, profit, or research.
3. Tiny Rhode Island is the only state in which spelunkers have not been able to find any caves.
4. Most caverns are formed by the wearing away of rock by acid ground water.
5. The outpouring of molten rock from active volcanoes creates blister-like grottoes.
6. Sea caves, sandblasted by wave action against ocean cliffs, form along rocky coastlines.
7. Troglodytes, creatures that dwell in the innermost part of caves, are likely to be blind.
8. Eyeless cave fish live in dark underground lakes, detecting their prey with highly sensitive nerve ends.
9. Only plants that require no light are able to survive deep in caves.
10. The ceiling of some caves may be covered with tiny glowworms, gleaming like stars in a night sky.

Answers: **1.** participial; **2.** participial; **3.** infinitive; **4.** gerund; **5.** gerund; **6.** participial; **7.** infinitive; **8.** participial; **9.** infinitive; **10.** participial

ABSOLUTE PHRASES

An **absolute phrase** is a noun or pronoun that is modified by a participle or participial phrase and that has no grammatical relation to the rest of the sentence.*

An absolute phrase belongs neither to the complete subject nor to the complete predicate of a sentence. It stands "absolutely" by itself in relation to the rest of the sentence.

> **Its wings badly damaged in the storm,** the aircraft made an emergency landing.

*Absolute phrases are also known as *nominative absolutes.*

In some absolute phrases the participle *being* is understood rather than stated.

We took off on schedule, **the weather (being) perfect.**

Objective

EXERCISE 10. Identifying Absolute Phrases. Write on your paper the absolute phrase in each of the following sentences.

1. I spend many hours in the backyard, gardening being my favorite activity.
2. The soil rich in nutrients, everything grows quickly.
3. The radishes and beans having been planted a week ago, I now wait for the first signs of growth.
4. The plan of my vegetable garden is strictly geometric, everything laid out in neat rows.
5. The flower bed is more informal, the plants arranged mainly by color.

DIAGRAMING PHRASES

This section is a continuation of Diagraming Basic Sentence Patterns at the end of Chapter 19. Review the diagrams in that section before proceeding.

9. Prepositional Phrases

Place the preposition on a slanted line that comes down from the word modified by the prepositional phrase. Then draw a horizontal line from the slanted line. Place the object of the preposition on the horizontal line.

Lovers of old buildings spend millions of dollars for renovation.

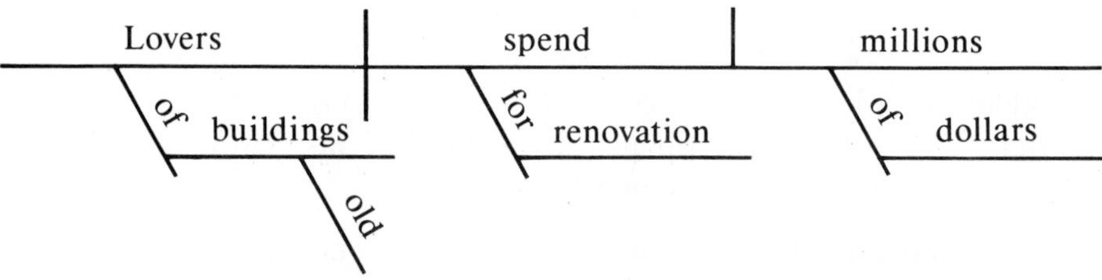

10. Appositives and Appositive Phrases

Place the appositive in parentheses after the noun or pronoun it identifies. Add any words that modify the appositive beneath it.

Monticello, the home of Thomas Jefferson, was restored by a private organization.

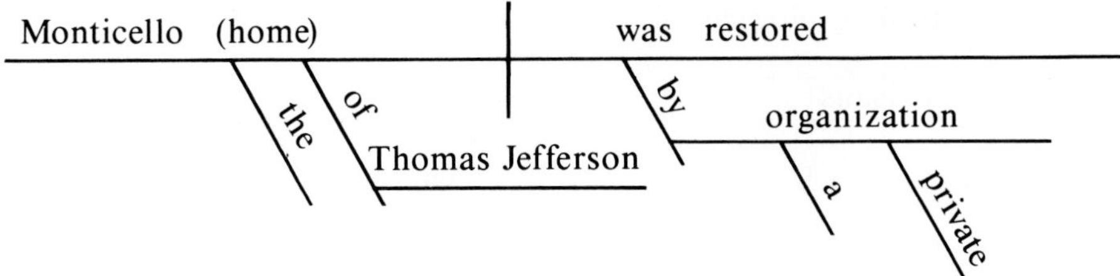

11. Participles and Participial Phrases

Curve the participle as shown below. Add modifiers and complements in the usual way.

Researching a building's history, one often encounters surprises.

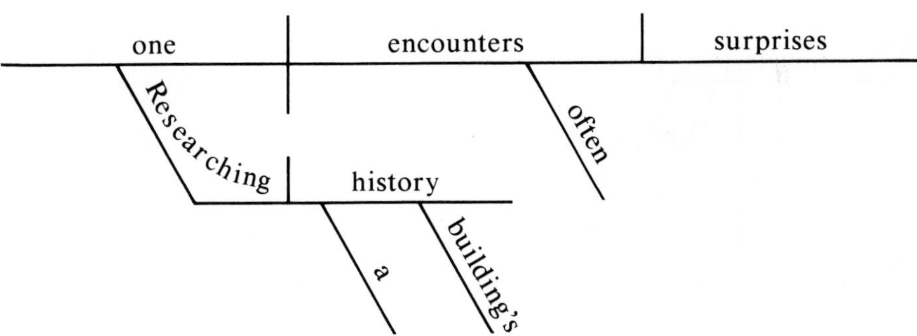

12. Gerunds and Gerund Phrases

Place the gerund on a step as shown below. The phrase in the subject position is placed on a "stilt" so that it will fit.

Finding original plans is a dream of every restorer.

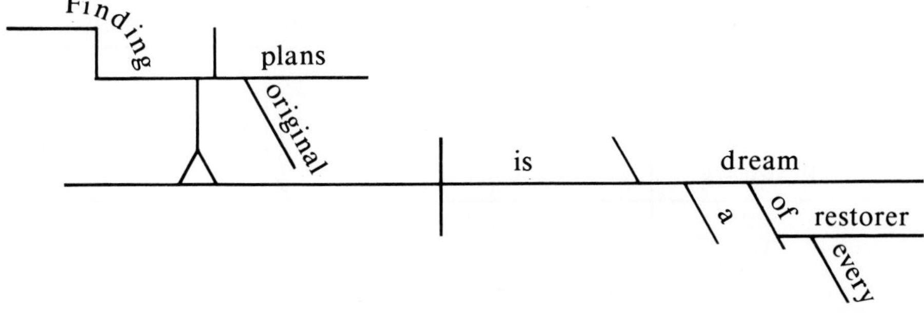

13. Infinitives and Infinitive Phrases Used as Adjectives or Adverbs

These infinitives are diagramed like prepositional phrases (see Diagram 9).

All artisans strive to re-create authentically.

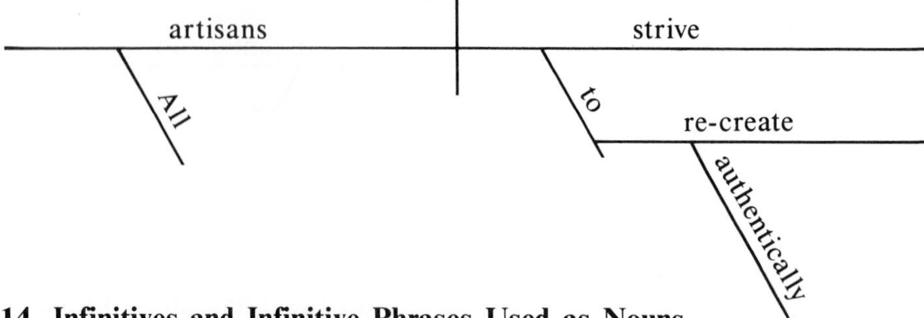

14. Infinitives and Infinitive Phrases Used as Nouns

Here you have to use stilts again.

To complete a restoration project is to feel a double accomplishment.

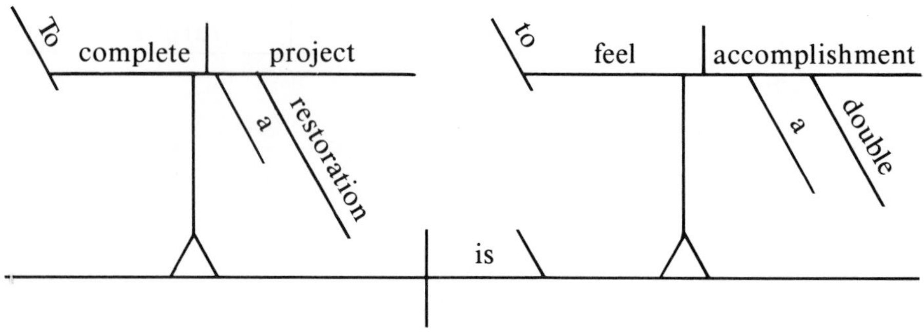

15. Subject of the Infinitive

The subject of the infinitive is added before the slanted line.

Restorers ask architects to provide plans.

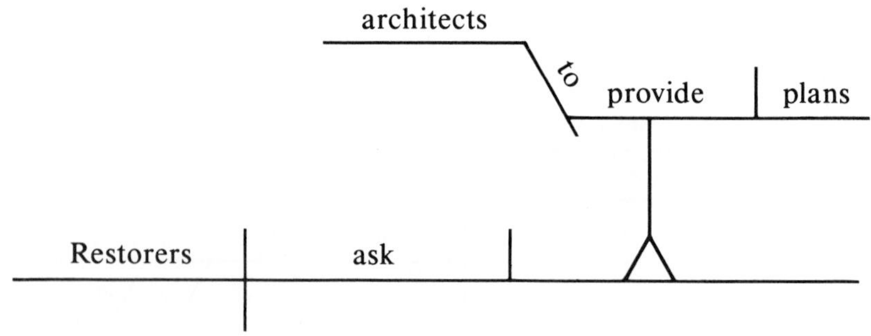

16. Absolute Phrases

An absolute phrase is placed above the rest of the sentence.

Its exterior freshly painted, the house looked almost new.

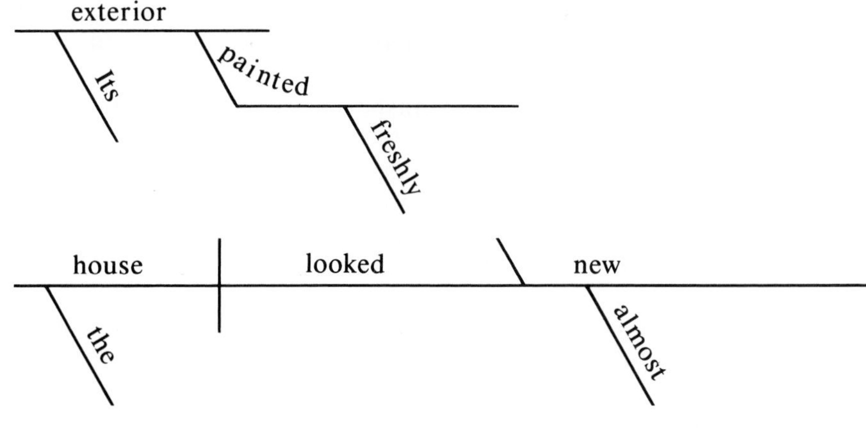

Objective

EXERCISE 11. Diagraming Prepositional Phrases. Using Diagram 9 as a model, diagram sentences 2, 4, 6, and 7 in Exercise 1 of this chapter.

Objective

EXERCISE 12. Diagraming Appositives and Appositive Phrases. Using Diagram 10 as a model, diagram the two example sentences preceding Exercise 3 of this chapter.

Objective

EXERCISE 13. Diagraming Participles and Participial Phrases. Using Diagram 11 as a model, diagram the five example sentences preceding Exercise 5 of this chapter.

Objective

EXERCISE 14. Diagraming Gerunds and Gerund Phrases. Using Diagram 12 as a model, diagram sentences 5, 8, 9, and 10 in Exercise 6 of this chapter.

Objective

EXERCISE 15. Diagraming Infinitives and Infinitive Phrases. Using Diagrams 13 and 14 as models, diagram sentences 2, 5, 6, and 7 in Exercise 8 of this chapter.

Objective

EXERCISE 16. Diagraming Absolute Phrases. Using Diagram 16 as a model, diagram sentences 1 and 3 in Exercise 10 of this chapter.

REVIEW

CHAPTER 20 PHRASES

Identifying Phrases (pages 441–450) In each of the following sentences, tell whether the underlined phrase is **(a)** a prepositional phrase, **(b)** an appositive phrase, **(c)** a participial or absolute phrase, **(d)** a gerund phrase, or **(e)** an infinitive phrase.

1. Known for her plays, Lorraine Hansberry was a highly committed person.
2. Writing about social injustice was important to her.
3. She began to write while still in high school.
4. *A Raisin in the Sun*, her first play, won several awards.
5. Her second play produced, Hansberry died at the age of thirty-four.

Answers: **1.** a; **2.** d; **3.** e; **4.** b; **5.** c

Prepositional Phrases (pages 441–443) In each of the following sentences, tell whether the prepositional phrase is (a) adjectival or (b) adverbial.

6. The phoenix legend probably began in Egypt.
7. The bird symbolized the sun with its power to "die" and rise again.
8. English kings used the phoenix symbol on their coats–of–arms.
9. Several oriental myths describe an immortal bird like the phoenix.
10. The phoenix inspired the *Firebird* ballet of Igor Stravinsky.

Answers: **6.** b; **7.** a; **8.** b; **9.** a; **10.** a

Gerund Phrases (pages 446–447) In each of the following sentences, tell whether the gerund phrase is used as **(a)** a subject, **(b)** a direct object, **(c)** an object of a preposition, **(d)** a predicate nominative, or **(e)** an appositive.

11. Have you ever considered owning your own business?
12. Coming up with a new idea is essential.
13. You will not succeed by copying someone else's ideas.
14. Management, creating good relationships, is often overlooked.
15. Your only goal must become making your business a success.

Answer: **11.** b; **12.** a; **13.** c; **14.** e; **15.** d

Infinitive Phrases (pages 447–449) In each of the following sentences, tell whether the infinitive phrase is used as **(a)** a noun, **(b)** an adjective, or **(c)** an adverb.

16. To save money, the mint now makes copper-coated zinc pennies.
17. Some people want to restore more copper to the penny.
18. Hoarding causes pennies to be in short supply.
19. To mint a penny costs much more than one cent.
20. The mint urges people to stop hoarding pennies.

Answers: **16.** c; **17.** a; **18.** a; **19.** a; **20.** a

Writing for Review Write a paragraph on any subject you choose. Include and underline at least one example of each kind of phrase—prepositional phrase, appositive phrase, participial phrase, gerund phrase, and infinitive phrase.

CHAPTER 21
Clauses and Sentence Structure

A **clause** is a group of words that has a subject and a predicate and that is used as a part of a sentence.

There are two kinds of clauses: *main clauses*, also called *independent clauses*, and *subordinate clauses*, also called *dependent clauses*.

MAIN CLAUSES

A **main clause** has a subject and a predicate and can stand alone as a sentence.

Every sentence must have at least one main clause. A sentence may have more than one main clause. Both of the clauses in the following example are main clauses because both can stand alone as a sentence.

MAIN CLAUSE 1: Manufacturers (S) produce (V), and MAIN CLAUSE 2: consumers (S) buy (V).

Manufacturers produce, and consumers buy.

SUBORDINATE CLAUSES

A **subordinate clause** has a subject and a predicate, but it cannot stand alone as a sentence.

A subordinate clause must be attached to a main clause in order for it to make sense. Subordinate clauses frequently begin with subordinating conjunctions (see page 413) or relative pronouns (see page 386).

MAIN CLAUSE: Consumers (S) buy (V) SUBORDINATE CLAUSE: whenever they (S) have (V) a need.

Consumers buy whenever they have a need.

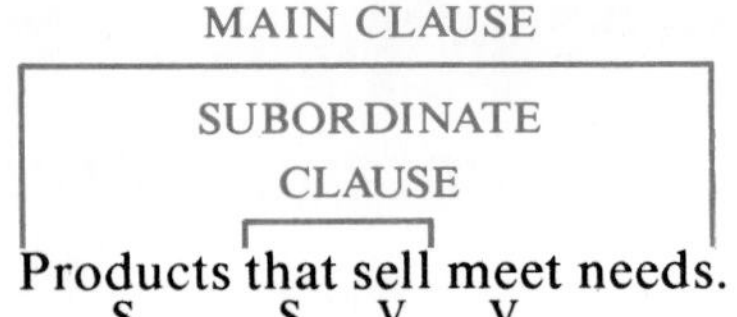

In the first example the subordinating conjunction *whenever* placed before *they have a need* creates a word group—*whenever they have a need*—that cannot stand alone as a main clause. In the second example the relative pronoun *that* begins a subordinate clause that comes between the subject and the verb of the main clause. *That* also serves as the subject of the subordinate clause.

In the following pages you will see how various combinations of main clauses and subordinate clauses form the four kinds of sentence structures: *simple sentences, compound sentences, complex sentences,* and *compound-complex sentences.* You will also see how subordinate clauses act in sentences as adverbs, adjectives, or nouns.

Objective

EXERCISE 1. Identifying Main and Subordinate Clauses. In each of the following sentences, the first clause appears in italics. On your paper write whether that clause is a *main* clause or a *subordinate* clause. (Remember that a subordinate clause cannot stand alone as a sentence.)

1. *Franchising is an idea* whose time has come.
2. *If the application is approved,* the franchisee is given the exclusive right to sell the product or service of a parent company.
3. *The franchisee usually pays the franchisor a flat fee plus a percentage of all the money* that the business makes.
4. *This is an advantage to the parent company* because it obtains a new sales outlet with almost no cash investment.
5. *When the franchisee signs the contract,* he or she does give up a certain freedom in operating the business.
6. *In return, the franchisee gets to sell a product* whose name and quality are well known.
7. *The franchisee also benefits from national advertising and operating procedures* that have proven successful in other outlets.
8. *Since customers know the name and quality of the product,* they are more likely to buy from a franchise outlet than from an untried independent.
9. *Unless franchisors maintain strict quality control,* the reputation of the entire chain will suffer.
10. *Because most franchisors are now very selective,* franchise failure rates are usually low.

Answers: **1.** main; **2.** subordinate; **3.** main; **4.** main; **5.** subordinate; **6.** main; **7.** main; **8.** subordinate; **9.** subordinate; **10.** subordinate

SIMPLE AND COMPOUND SENTENCES

Two kinds of sentences are made up of main clauses only: *simple sentences* and *compound sentences.*

A **simple sentence** has only one main clause and no subordinate clauses.

A simple sentence may have a compound subject or a compound predicate or both (see Chapter 19). The simple subject and the simple predicate may also be expanded in many other ways. Adjectives, adverbs, prepositional phrases, appositives, and verbal phrases may make some simple sentences seem anything but simple. Yet as long as the sentence has only one main clause, it remains a simple sentence.

> Consumers buy. [simple sentence]
> **Consumers** and **investors** buy. [simple sentence with compound subject]
> Consumers **compare** and **buy.** [simple sentence with compound predicate]
> S S V V
> **Consumers** and **investors compare** and **buy.** [simple sentence with compound subject and compound predicate]
> Most serious investors carefully consider alternative uses for their money. [simple sentence expanded]

A **compound sentence** has two or more main clauses.

As the following examples show, each main clause of a compound sentence has its own subject and predicate. Notice that the main clauses of a compound sentence are usually joined by a comma and a coordinating conjunction, such as *and, but, or, nor, yet,* or *for.*

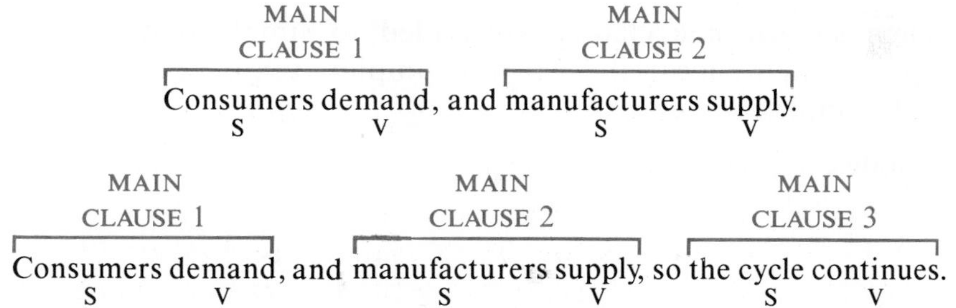

Two main clauses may also be joined to form a compound sentence by means of a semicolon (see Chapter 28).

MAIN CLAUSE 1 MAIN CLAUSE 2

Prices rise; demand falls.

Objective

EXERCISE 2. Identifying Simple and Compound Sentences. On your paper write whether each of the following is a simple or a compound sentence. (Remember that a single main clause can have a compound subject and a compound predicate.)

1. Crocodiles and dinosaurs are related, but crocodiles have survived extraordinary climate changes to the present day.
2. Crocodile brains are quite complex, and crocodile hearts are almost mammalian.
3. Full-grown crocodiles can range in length from three to twenty-five feet and can weigh more than a ton.
4. A crocodile is strong enough to kill a water buffalo but gentle enough to carry its newly hatched babies between its jaws.
5. A few species of crocodilians prefer to live alone; most, however, live in communities.
6. Crocodiles usually live in remote places, but hunters greedy for crocodile skins have no trouble in acquiring them.
7. In many places, crocodiles are protected by law but now face another problem.
8. People are moving into and radically changing the crocodile's natural habitat.
9. Engineers dam rivers, clear swamps, and build new towns to benefit people, but this "progress" does not help the crocodiles.
10. Have crocodiles survived 200 million years only to succumb to the unchecked desires of land developers?

Answers: **1.** compound; **2.** compound; **3.** simple; **4.** simple; **5.** compound; **6.** compound; **7.** simple; **8.** simple; **9.** compound; **10.** simple

COMPLEX AND COMPOUND-COMPLEX SENTENCES

When subordinate clauses are added to simple sentences and compound sentences, they form complex sentences and compound-complex sentences.

A **complex sentence** has one main clause and one or more subordinate clauses.

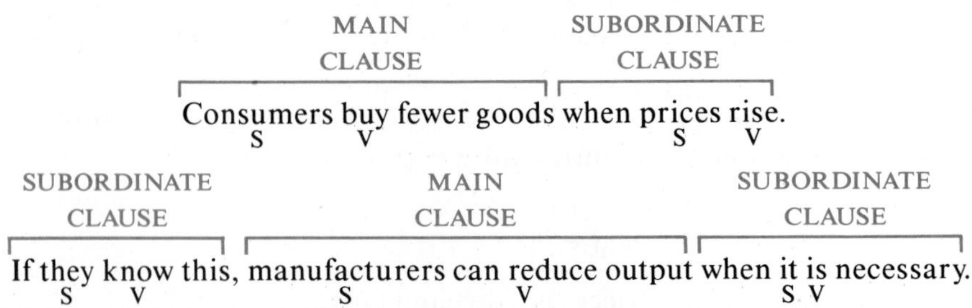

A **compound-complex sentence** has more than one main clause and at least one subordinate clause.

SUBORDINATE CLAUSE	MAIN CLAUSE		MAIN CLAUSE
If production increases,	prices may drop	and	consumers may buy more.
S V	S V		S V

Objective

EXERCISE 3. Identifying Complex and Compound-Complex Sentences. Write on your paper the subordinate clause in each of the following sentences. Indicate whether each sentence is a *complex* sentence or a *compound-complex* sentence.

1. Because most buildings last for many years, architecture plays an important role in creating a distinctive atmosphere in most cities.
2. Buildings have one kind of effect on the skyline, but they have a different effect on people who use them every day.
3. Municipal governments are concerned about both these aspects, and laws that control size and use of space are now common.
4. As soon as any major new design is announced, architectural critics review its features and predict its overall effects.
5. Many otherwise excellent buildings have failed because they were poorly integrated into their environments.
6. Unless a new building relates well to older structures near it, it will always seem awkward, and its merits may go unnoticed.
7. If buildings have inviting public spaces, people walk into them or through them, and this creates dynamic pedestrian traffic patterns.
8. However, even a building with a pleasing appearance will not be a total success if it is not designed for efficient use.
9. When the building is opened for use, its actual influence on human beings can be assessed.
10. Unless architects creatively integrate form and function, buildings will be less than successful, and we will be forced to live with the "mistakes." *Answers:* 1. complex; 2. compound-complex; 3. compound-complex; 4. complex; 5. complex; 6. compound-complex; 7. compound-complex; 8. complex; 9. complex; 10. compound-complex

Objective

APPLICATION EXERCISE. Writing Sentences with Various Structures. Write a simple sentence. Next rework it and make it a compound sentence. Rework it again, but now make it part of a complex sentence. Finally take your compound sentence and rework it into a compound-complex sentence.

SAMPLE ANSWER: I walked to school.
I ate breakfast, and I walked to school.
I ate breakfast before I walked to school.
I ate breakfast before I walked to school, yet I was soon hungry again.

ADJECTIVE CLAUSES

An **adjective clause** is a subordinate clause that modifies a noun or a pronoun.

An adjective clause normally follows the word it modifies.

Periodicals **that inform and entertain** make good reading.

Several writers **whom I admire** write regular columns.

I like a writer **whose style is distinctive.**

In addition to the relative pronouns (*who, whom, whose, that,* and *which*), the adverbs *where* and *when* may introduce adjective clauses.

I cannot remember a time **when I did not enjoy reading.**
Libraries are places **where many periodicals can be found.**

An adjective clause is sometimes essential to the sentence; that is, it is needed to make the meaning of the sentence clear. This kind of adjective clause is called an *essential clause*, or a *restrictive clause.* Without the essential adjective clause, the sentence would not make complete sense.

Magazines **that have no photographs** have little appeal for me. [essential clause]
Smithsonian is the magazine **that I like best**. [essential clause]

In the first example the meaning of the sentence would change without the essential clause *that have no photographs.* In the second example the adjective clause is needed because the sentence seems incomplete without it. The essential adjective clause *that I like best* limits or restricts the meaning of the noun *magazine* and helps the reader recognize *which* magazine is being discussed.

An adjective clause that is *not* needed to make the meaning of the sentence clear is called a *nonessential clause*, or a *nonrestrictive clause.* It may add information to the sentence, but the sentence would be perfectly logical without the clause.

Newspapers, **which I often read**, are always interesting. [nonessential clause]
Also informative are newsletters, **which are widely distributed by many organizations.** [nonessential clause]

You can use either *that* or *which* to introduce an essential clause, but you must always use *which* to begin a nonessential clause. Never use *that* before a nonessential clause.

Newsmagazines, **which are published weekly,** have excellent coverage of current events. [nonessential clause]
World events **that have major significance** are thoroughly covered. [essential clause]

(For rules about punctuating essential and nonessential clauses, see Chapter 28.)

Objective

EXERCISE 4. Identifying Adjective Clauses. On your paper write the adjective clause in each of the following sentences. Then write the word that the clause modifies.

1. The Pueblo Indians celebrate special occasions in the spring and summer with dances *dances* that have been performed for centuries.
2. These corn dances date from a time *time* when the Pueblo were the only humans in the arid Southwest.
3. Following a leader holding a tall symbolic pole, the chorus *chorus* who will accompany the dancers advance into the plaza.
4. The scores of males *males* who dance wear special jewelry and carry gourd rattles and sprigs of evergreen.
5. The women and girls carry bunches of evergreen branches and wear wooden headpieces *headpieces* that represent thunder and lightning.
6. The dancers circle the musicians, shaking rattles, gently waving evergreens, and treading the earth with steps *steps* that look deceptively simple.
7. The rhythms *rhythms* that fill the air are both subtle and complex.
8. About midday, the dancing stops and food is offered to all *all* who are present.
9. The dances, *dances* which in many pueblos are performed by two groups alternately, continue until sunset.
10. By performing this ceremony, the Pueblo Indians hoped to insure rain for the crops and blessings for those *those* who lived in the pueblo.

Objective

EXERCISE 5. Recognizing Essential and Nonessential Clauses. Here are five pairs of sentences. For each pair write the adjective clause, and then identify it as an essential clause or a nonessential clause.

1. a. People who are handicapped (essential) have impairments of sensory, physical, or mental faculties.
   b. Handicaps, which may be mild to severe (nonessential), can be classified as sensory, motor, or mental.
2. a. Most people, who tend to associate mental impairment with physical impairment (nonessential), react stereotypically to those with handicaps.
   b. People who deal with handicapped people (essential) must take care to see each individual as unique.
3. a. New technology in vans, wheelchairs, and electronic equipment is available to those who need it (essential).
   b. Application of new electronic technology to equipment for the handicapped, who make good use of it (nonessential), is growing steadily.
4. a. New laws have made transportation, which has long been a problem for physically handicapped people (nonessential), more readily available.
   b. Physically handicapped people have waited much too long for transportation that is reliable and relatively inexpensive (essential).
5. a. Menial jobs, which offer little mental challenge (nonessential), are not appropriate for blind or deaf persons of normal intelligence.
   b. The handicapped are gradually gaining access to jobs that are suitable to their full capabilities (essential).

ADVERB CLAUSES

An **adverb clause** is a subordinate clause that modifies a verb, an adjective, or an adverb. It tells *when, where, how, why, to what extent,* or *under what condition.*

> **Wherever I go**, I take a magazine. [The adverb clause modifies the verb *take.* It tells *where.*]
> I stay happy **as long as I can read**. [The adverb clause modifies the adjective *happy.* It tells *under what condition.*]
> I enjoy magazines more **than I usually enjoy a book**. [The adverb clause modifies the adverb *more.* It tells *to what extent.*]

Subordinating conjunctions such as those listed on page 413 introduce adverb clauses. Being familiar with those conjunctions will help you recognize adverb clauses. Remember also that an adverb clause may come either before or after the main clause. Notice that the first example on page 462 might have been written in this way.

I take a magazine **wherever I go**.

Occasionally words may be left out of an adverb clause. The omitted words can easily be supplied, however, because they are understood, or implied. Such adverb clauses are described as *elliptical.*

Few can read faster than I [can read].
Reading makes me happier than [it makes] him [happy].

Objective

EXERCISE 6. Identifying Adverb Clauses. On your paper write the adverb clauses in the following sentences. (Some sentences have more than one adverb clause.)

1. Until Annie Oakley came along, sharpshooting had been a rather tame affair.
2. Since Annie's widowed mother was very poor, Annie provided for the family by shooting birds that she sold to hotels and restaurants.
3. When Annie was visiting her sister in Cincinnati, she entered a contest against a champion sharpshooter, because it might bring in extra money.
4. After he lost a close match, the sharpshooter, Frank Butler, fell in love with Annie and married her.
5. Frank taught Annie tricks of the sharpshooting trade so that she could join his stage act.
6. Wherever they went, Frank's act was a big success as long as Annie was featured.
7. After Annie was established as a star, Frank retired from the act, though he continued as Annie's manager.
8. Annie attracted many fans because she was entertaining as well as skillful.
9. Annie befriended orphans and paid the bills of many poor families, as she remembered her own unhappy childhood.
10. Although Annie Oakley established sharpshooting records, her greatest feats were perhaps her kind deeds.

NOUN CLAUSES

A **noun clause** is a subordinate clause used as a noun.

You can use a noun clause in all of the ways that a noun can be used—as a subject, a direct object, an object of a preposition, or a predicate nominative.

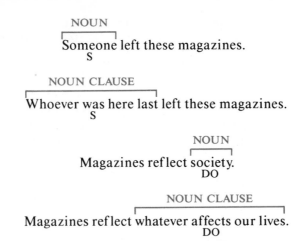

NOUN

Someone left these magazines.
S

NOUN CLAUSE

Whoever was here last left these magazines.
S

NOUN

Magazines reflect society.
DO

NOUN CLAUSE

Magazines reflect whatever affects our lives.
DO

In the preceding examples notice that each noun clause forms an inseparable part of the sentence's main clause. In the second sentence, for example, the noun clause is the subject of the main clause. In the last sentence the noun clause is the direct object of the main clause. Notice also that the examples with the nouns are simple sentences because each contains only one subject and one predicate. The examples with the noun clauses are complex sentences because each has a main clause (the entire sentence) and a subordinate clause (the noun clause).

Some of the words that can be used to introduce noun clauses follow.

how	when	who, whom
that	where	whoever
what	which	whose
whatever	whichever	why

Here are additional examples of noun clauses.

Do you know **which magazine is my favorite?** [as a direct object]
This article is about **how microchips work**. [as an object of a preposition]
This is **where I get most of my information**. [as a predicate nominative]

Objective
EXERCISE 7. Identifying Noun Clauses. On your paper write the noun clauses in each of the following sentences. (Two of the sentences have two noun clauses each.)

1. Whatever you achieve in life depends greatly on how clearly your basic goals have been visualized.

2. A primary consideration, of course, is how you expect to earn a living.
3. You should also understand what your other needs and priorities are.
4. Not seriously considering educational, health, and psychological aspects is where many people fall short in their planning.
5. You must decide how important each of these areas is to you and what you need to accomplish in each one.
6. Whoever wishes to be free to pursue other goals must maintain excellent health.
7. Beyond this, decisions are based on whatever interests, abilities, and personality traits the individual has developed over the years.
8. That everyone is free to pursue such personal goals is a basic tenet of a free society.
9. Goals and priorities, however, are affected by whatever influences are most powerful at any given moment.
10. We must, therefore, expect that our goals will change from time to time.

Objective

APPLICATION EXERCISE. Using Subordinate Clauses in Sentences. Write four original sentences. In the first use an adverb clause. In the second use an adjective clause. In the third use a noun clause as a subject. In the fourth use a noun clause as a direct object. *Suggested Answer:* Because the weather was bad, we arrived late. My companion, who was the guest of honor, apologized. That we were embarrassed was obvious. I considered what we might have done.

REVIEW EXERCISE. Clauses. On your paper write each subordinate clause in the following sentences. Then write whether the subordinate clause is **(a)** an adverb clause, **(b)** an adjective clause, or **(c)** a noun clause.

1. Tulsa, Oklahoma, is called the "Oil Capital of the World" because more than 850 petroleum companies have headquarters there.
2. The city, which is on the Arkansas River, is the second largest in the state.
3. Although many people do not realize it, Tulsa is also a thriving center of art and distinguished architecture.
4. Philbrook Art Center, which sponsors an annual competition for North and South American Indian artists, has an outstanding collection.
5. History buffs will find it difficult to decide how they can best spend their time at the Gilcrease Institute of History and Art.
6. Tulsa has many distinctive new buildings, although carefully selected older ones have been successfully preserved.
7. The civic center and a unique high-rise Art Deco church are only two of the structures that have received widespread acclaim.
8. The futuristic campus of nearby Oral Roberts University is remembered by all who visit it.

9. That the fountains and shade trees of the new pedestrian mall are special attractions in themselves is clear.
10. Many surprises await whoever visits this fascinating and progressive city.

Answers: **1.** a; **2.** b; **3.** a; **4.** b; **5.** c; **6.** a; **7.** b; **8.** b; **9.** c; **10.** c

FOUR KINDS OF SENTENCES

Sentences may be classified according to their purpose. The four types of sentences are *declarative, imperative, interrogative,* and *exclamatory.*

A **declarative sentence** makes a statement.

The sun will rise at 6:17 A.M. It is already light outside.

A declarative sentence normally ends with a period. It is the type of sentence used most frequently in speaking and writing.

An **imperative sentence** gives a command or makes a request.

Get up and take a walk with me.
Please close the door quietly.

An imperative sentence usually ends with a period. The subject "you" is understood (see Chapter 19).

An **interrogative** asks a question.

Is anyone else awake?
Do you think we should wait for the others?

An interrogative sentence ends with a question mark. It often begins with an interrogative pronoun (see Chapter 18) or with an auxiliary verb.

An **exclamatory sentence** expresses strong emotion.

The sunrise over the water was glorious!
What a great idea this was!

An exclamatory sentence is a declarative, imperative, or interrogative sentence expressed with strong emotion. The exclamation point at the end of the sentence conveys the strong emotion to the readers.

Objective

EXERCISE 8. Identifying Kinds of Sentences. On your paper write whether each of the following sentences is **(a)** declarative, **(b)** imperative, **(c)** interrogative, or **(d)** exclamatory.

1. How intriguing "common" crows can be!
2. Have you ever turned your full attention to one of these impressive birds?
3. Observe their shiny blackness and note their superbly confident bearing.
4. They seem to be harboring deep secrets.
5. Can you understand why Edgar Allan Poe featured ravens in several of his most mysterious works?
6. Watch carefully as a crow lifts itself into flight.
7. Can't you almost feel the great weight?
8. How big and black they are!
9. Their deep-throated, raucous caws are rivaled by few other birds.
10. A crow perched atop a snag creates a powerfully haunting image.

Answers: **1.** d; **2.** c; **3.** b; **4.** a; **5.** c; **6.** b; **7.** c; **8.** d: **9.** a: **10.** a

Objective

APPLICATION EXERCISE. Writing Four Kinds of Sentences. Write four sentences about a recent news story. Use one declarative, one imperative, one interrogative, and one exclamatory sentence.

Suggested Answer: The chemical plant has polluted the river again. Look at its past record. Do you think those people will ever learn? I surely hope so!

SENTENCE COMPLETENESS

Unless you are mimicking conversation in your writing, your sentences should be complete. They should have at least one subject and one predicate and express a complete thought (see Chapter 19). Incomplete sentences, or sentence fragments, are considered a serious error because they confuse readers. Another kind of sentence error occurs when two or more sentences run on in such a way that readers cannot tell where one ends and the next begins.

SENTENCE FRAGMENTS

In general, avoid sentence fragments in your writing. A **fragment** lacks a subject or a predicate or does not express a complete thought.

Sentence fragments are usually phrases or subordinate clauses that have mistakenly been capitalized and punctuated as if they were complete sentences. Often you can correct a sentence fragment by joining it to an idea that comes before or after the fragment. Sometimes, however, you may need to add missing words to form a complete sentence.

FRAGMENT: **The first radioactive element that was discovered.** It was polonium.

COMPLETE SENTENCE: Polonium was the first radioactive element that was discovered.

FRAGMENT: The discoverer of polonium was Marie Curie. **Who was born in Poland.**

COMPLETE SENTENCE: The discoverer of polonium was Marie Curie, who was born in Poland.

FRAGMENT: **A year later also discovered radium.** More than 20 elements are radioactive.

COMPLETE SENTENCE: A year later she also discovered radium. More than 20 elements are radioactive.

Objective

EXERCISE 9. Identifying Sentence Fragments. Indicate in writing whether each of the following numbered items is a complete sentence or a sentence fragment.

(1) A number of the chemical elements are named after figures from mythology. **(2)** Uranium, titanium, and the rare-earth element promethium, three examples. **(3)** Uranus was the father of the Titans. **(4)** Giants who were thought by the ancient Greeks to rule the world. **(5)** One of the Titans, Prometheus, the bringer of fire. **(6)** Mercury, neptunium, and plutonium are other elements named for gods. **(7)** Obviously, the names of planets in our solar system and of many constellations. **(8)** Drawn from the rich sources of ancient lore. **(9)** Fascinating connection between science and mythology. **(10)** Both are attempts to understand the world.

Answers: **1.** sentence; **2.** fragment; **3.** sentence; **4.** fragment; **5.** fragment; **6.** sentence; **7.** fragment; **8.** fragment; **9.** fragment; **10.** sentence

Objective

REVISION EXERCISE. Correcting Sentence Fragments. Revise the preceding paragraph by correcting each fragment that you identified in Exercise 9. Whenever possible, combine the fragments with other sentences in the paragraph.

RUN-ON SENTENCES

Avoid run-on sentences in your writing. A **run-on sentence** occurs when main clauses are run together without proper punctuation. Do not use a comma alone to separate two main clauses.

The errors that cause run-on sentences are called *comma splices* or *comma faults.*

RUN-ON: Prose can be precise, poetry often creates a sharper image.

You may correct run-on sentences like the preceding example in any of four ways:

1. with a comma *and* a coordinating conjunction

    Prose can be precise, **yet** poetry often creates a sharper image.

2. with a semicolon

Prose can be precise; poetry often creates a sharper image.

3. with a period and a capital letter

Prose can be precise. **P**oetry often creates a sharper image.

4. by turning one of the main clauses into a subordinate clause

Although prose can be precise, poetry often creates a sharper image.

Objective

EXERCISE 10. Correcting Run-on Sentences. Rewrite each of the following run-on sentences. Use each of the four methods for correcting run-on sentences at least once in this exercise.

1. Many ancient peoples conceived works of environmental art, and huge patterns in earth and stone resulted from their extraordinary efforts.
2. Some of these creations had religious significance. Indian mounds in North America, and the Nazca lines in South America are examples.
3. Some contemporary artists are returning to the concept of environmental art, because elements of nature stimulate their aesthetic sensibilities.
4. The scale of these artists' works is tremendous; no painting or museum gallery could provide such a powerful effect.
5. An observer is forced to sense space and shape in startling new ways. This is a primary goal of the environmental artist.

Suggested Answers appear above.

REVIEW EXERCISE. Sentence Completeness. Rewrite the following paragraph, correcting all sentence fragments and run-on sentences.

(1) Physics, the most intriguing of the natural sciences. **(2)** Although the mathematical calculations can be tedious. **(3)** The fundamental concepts are exciting indeed, applied physics has made our lives easier, theoretical physics stretches our imaginations. **(4)** No one yet explain gravity. **(5)** Whether light is a wave or a particle not resolved, add to this the results of experiments that lead only to the conclusion that atoms can think! **(6)** The question of the origin of the universe also physics. **(7)** Questions of physics all other sciences. **(8)** Dealing with mind-boggling questions of physics puts our individual lives in a different perspective.

DIAGRAMING CLAUSES

This section is a continuation of Diagraming Basic Sentence Patterns (Chapter 19) and Diagraming Phrases (Chapter 20). Review the diagrams in those sections before proceeding.

17. Compound Sentences

Place each main clause in a diagram of its own. If the main clauses are connected by a semicolon, use a vertical dotted line to connect the verbs of each main clause. If the main clauses are connected by a conjunction, place the conjunction on a solid horizontal line.

Trial lawyers argue their cases, and juries consider the evidence.

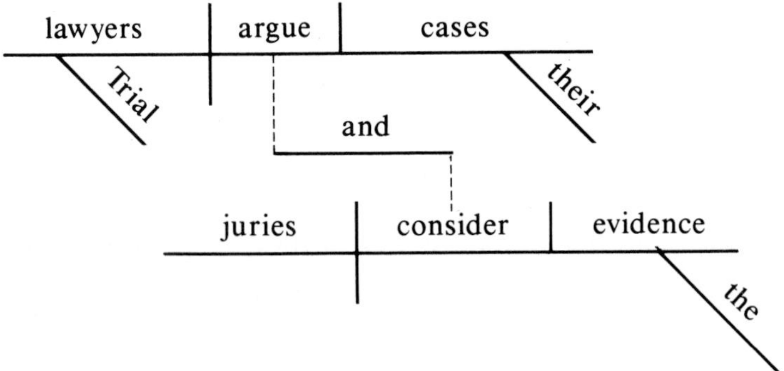

18. Complex Sentences: Adjective Clauses

Place the main clause in one diagram and the adjective clause beneath it in another diagram. Use a dotted line to connect the relative pronoun or other introductory word in the adjective clause to the modified noun or pronoun in the other clause.

A judge, who presides over the trial, rules in procedural matters that may arise.

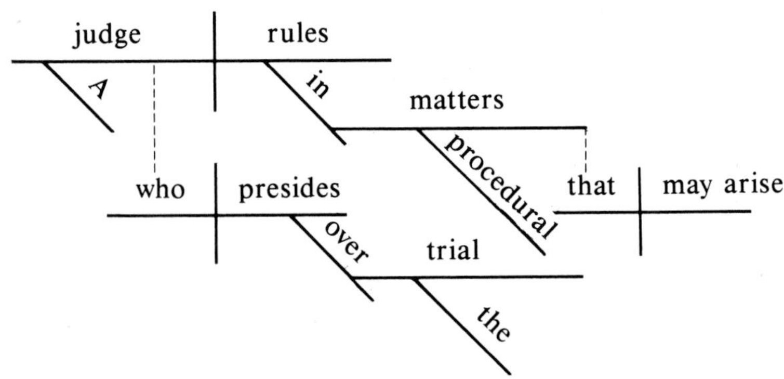

19. Complex Sentences: Adverb Clauses

Place the main clause in one diagram and the adverb clause beneath it in another diagram. Place the subordinating conjunction on a diagonal dotted line connecting the verb of the adverb clause to the modified verb, adjective, or adverb of the other clause.

Before witnesses testify, they must take an oath.

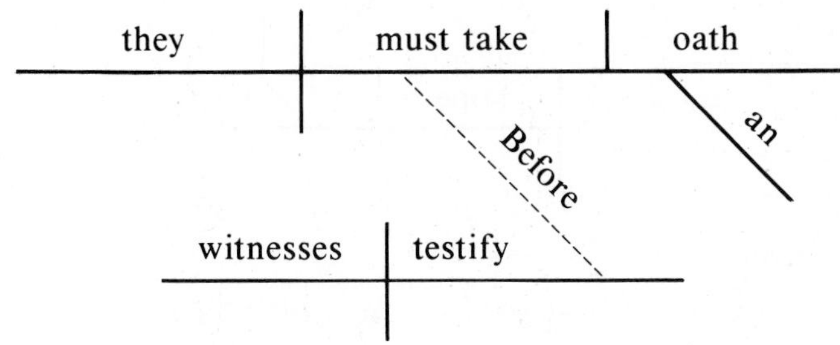

20. Complex Sentences: Noun Clauses

To diagram a sentence with a noun clause, first decide what role the noun clause plays within the main clause: subject, direct object, predicate nominative, or object of preposition. Then diagram the main clause with the noun clause on a stilt rising out of the appropriate position. Place the introductory word of the clause as the subject, object, or predicate nominative within the noun clause itself. If the introductory word merely begins the noun clause, simply place it on a line of its own.

AS SUBJECT

Whatever the witnesses say will influence the jury.

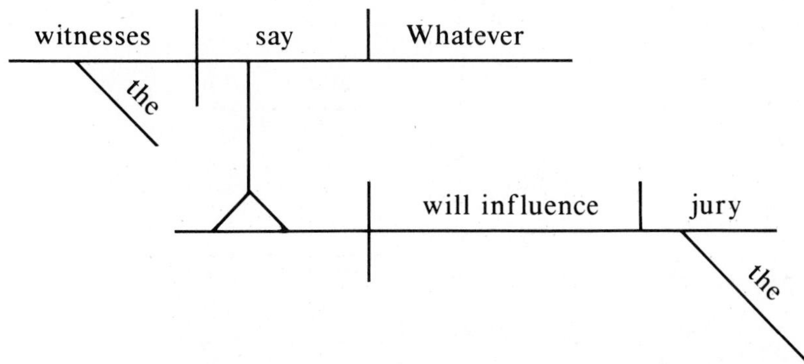

AS DIRECT OBJECT

Both the plaintiff and the defendant hope that the jury will believe them.

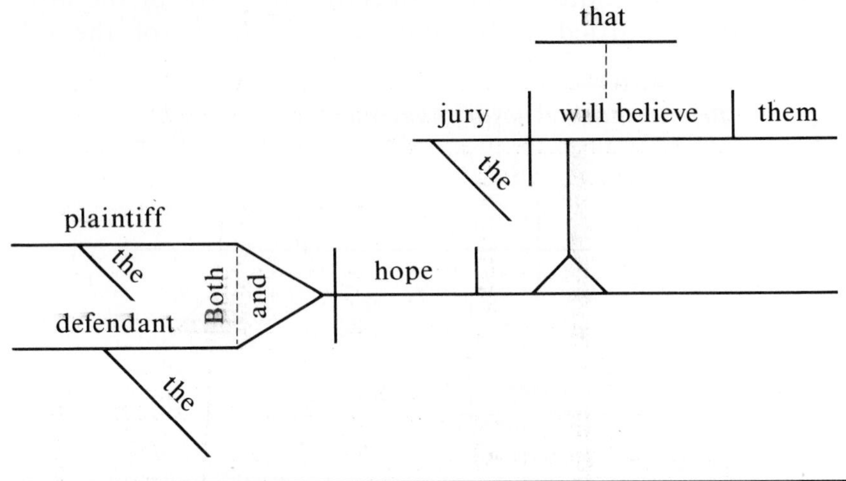

Objective

EXERCISE 11. Diagraming Compound Sentences. Using Diagram 17 as a model, diagram sentences 1, 2, 5, and 6 in Exercise 2 of this chapter.

Objective

EXERCISE 12. Diagraming Adjective Clauses. Using Diagram 18 as a model, diagram sentences 1a, 4a, 4b, and 5b in Exercise 5 of this chapter.

Objective

EXERCISE 13. Diagraming Adverb Clauses. Using Diagram 19 as a model, diagram sentences 1, 4, 5, and 10 in Exercise 6 of this chapter.

Objective

EXERCISE 14. Diagraming Noun Clauses. Using Diagram 20 as a model, diagram sentences 3 and 8 in Exercise 7 of this chapter.

CHAPTER 21 CLAUSES AND SENTENCE STRUCTURE

Clauses and the Sentences They Form (pages 455–459) Indicate whether each of the following sentences is **(a)** simple, **(b)** compound, **(c)** complex, or **(d)** compound–complex.

1. Colonial Williamsburg is a section of Williamsburg, Virginia.
2. This section, which was restored, is interesting to visit.
3. Craftspeople work in the shops, and they explain how the colonists did each of their jobs.
4. A master, who owned the shop, might not practice the trade at all, but he or she would hire others to do the work.
5. The colonists respected all the trades; each one of them was essential.

Answers: **1.** a; **2.** c; **3.** d; **4.** d; **5.** b

Kinds of Clauses (pages 455–465) Identify the underlined clauses in each of the following sentences as **(a)** a main clause, **(b)** an adjective clause, **(c)** an adverb clause, or **(d)** a noun clause.

6. Fairbanks, Alaska, is a far northern city that has severe winters.
7. Summers are quite pleasant since the days are very long.
8. Fairbanks was founded after gold was discovered there.
9. Gold, which was mined in the early 1900s, caused a boom.
10. That oil has replaced gold as the source of Alaska's prosperity cannot be denied.

Answers: **6.** b; **7.** a; **8.** c; **9.** b; **10.** d

Kinds of Sentences (pages 466–467) Indicate whether each of the following sentences is **(a)** declarative, **(b)** imperative, **(c)** interrogative, or **(d)** exclamatory.

11. Have you heard about "comfort foods"?
12. Psychologists say that some foods have comforting effects on the human brain and body.
13. Some foods may comfort because they bring back pleasant memories.
14. How unfortunate it is that comfort foods are often fattening!
15. To feel good, try drinking some warm milk with a little honey in it.

Answers: **11.** c; **12.** a; **13.** a; **14.** d; **15.** b

Sentence Completeness (pages 467–469) Identify each of the following items as **(a)** a fragment, **(b)** a run-on, or **(c)** a complete sentence.

16. Johann Sebastian Bach, one of the world's greatest composers.
17. During his lifetime he was best known as an organist.
18. He was born into a musical family, he took his first music lessons from an older brother.
19. Perfecting the art of polyphony in baroque music.
20. Of Bach's twenty children, four sons became famous composers.

Answers: **16.** a; **17.** c; **18.** b; **19.** a; **20.** c

Writing for Review Write a paragraph on a topic of your choice. Use sentences with a variety of clauses. Identify at least one of each of the sentence types: simple, compound, complex, and compound-complex.

UNIT VII
Usage

Your knowledge of English is something that you share with one-tenth of the entire population of this planet. Since the 1600s English has spread from Britain to such distant and disparate places as California, India, Zambia, and Australia. Because English is used in such widely different cultures, it is to be expected that people who speak English in different parts of the world will speak the language differently from one another. English, as you know, can vary greatly in pronunciation, word choice, and sentence structure even within the boundaries of the United States. Such variations are called *dialects*; everyone who speaks English uses one or more dialects.

This book is designed to help you understand the dialect known as standard American English. Standard American English is the most widely known and accepted dialect of English spoken and written in the United States. Three subcategories exist within this dialect: informal standard, middle standard, and formal standard. These subcategories are the different levels of standard English that are appropriate for different situations. Informal standard English is the level of English used in magazine and newspaper articles, news broadcasts, most contemporary novels, social correspondence, and general speeches to large audiences. Formal standard English, on the other hand, is the level of English used in serious research studies, works of criticism, and formal speeches. Middle standard English, as the name implies, falls somewhere between informal and formal English and can be used in many situations. It is difficult to define clearly the boundaries of each subcategory of standard English. However, in general, you fill find that formal English is characterized by longer, more complicated sentences consisting of longer, less common words.

Nonstandard English refers to dialects less widely accepted than standard English. Nonstandard dialects are, of course, completely understandable; they are, however, generally not spoken or written by as wide a population as is standard English.

Your ability to speak and write well—both now and later in life—depends on your ability to distinguish between standard and nonstandard usage and to recognize which level of usage is appropriate to a given situation. Whereas grammar *describes* how English works, usage *advises* how you can make English work to your best advantage. This unit, therefore, will help you apply your knowledge of grammar and recognize the preferred usage of standard American English. You will focus first on the various forms of verbs, and then you will practice making verbs agree with their subjects. Next you will study the correct and clear use of pronouns and modifiers. Finally you will learn to distinguish between items that are commonly confused or misused in standard American English.

CHAPTER 22
Verb Tenses, Voice, and Mood

PRINCIPAL PARTS OF VERBS

All verbs have four **principal parts**—a *basic form,* a *present participle,* a *simple past form,* and a *past participle.* All the verb tenses are formed from these principal parts.

BASIC FORM	PRESENT PARTICIPLE	PAST FORM	PAST PARTICIPLE
walk	walking	walked	walked
listen	listening	listened	listened
fall	falling	fell	fallen
try	trying	tried	tried
speak	speaking	spoke	spoken
be	being	was/were	been

The basic form is sometimes called the *present form* because it is the principal part used to form the present tense. The basic form is also called the *infinitive form* because it is the form that is used with *to.* The present participle is always formed by adding *-ing* to the basic form of the verb.

The basic form and the past form can be used by themselves as main verbs. To function as the simple predicate in a sentence, the present participle and the past participle must always be used with one or more auxiliary verbs.

Dolphins **splash**. [basic or present form]
Dolphins **splashed**. [past form]
Dolphins **are splashing**. [present participle with auxiliary verb *are*]
Dolphins **have splashed**. [past participle with auxiliary verb *have*]

REGULAR AND IRREGULAR VERBS

Verbs are regular or irregular depending on how their past form and their past participle are formed.

A **regular verb** forms its past and past participle by adding *-ed* to the basic form.

BASIC FORM	PAST FORM	PAST PARTICIPLE
employ	employed	employed
watch	watched	watched
laugh	laughed	laughed

Some regular verbs undergo spelling changes when a suffix beginning with a vowel is added.

advertise + **-ed** = advertis**ed**
study + **-ed** = stud**ied**
skim + **-ed** = skim**med**

An **irregular verb** forms its past and past participle in some way other than by adding *-ed* to the basic form.

Some of the oldest and most common verbs in English are irregular.

BASIC FORM	PAST FORM	PAST PARTICIPLE
be	was, were	been
bear	bore	borne
beat	beat	beaten *or* beat
become	became	become
begin	began	begun
bite	bit	bitten
blow	blew	blown
break	broke	broken
bring	brought	brought
burst	burst	burst
cast	cast	cast
catch	caught	caught
choose	chose	chosen
come	came	come
creep	crept	crept
dive	dived *or* dove	dived
do, does	did	done
draw	drew	drawn
drink	drank	drunk
drive	drove	driven
eat	ate	eaten
fall	fell	fallen
feel	felt	felt
find	found	found
fling	flung	flung
fly	flew	flown
freeze	froze	frozen
get	got	got *or* gotten

BASIC FORM	PAST FORM	PAST PARTICIPLE
give	gave	given
go	went	gone
grow	grew	grown
hang	hanged *or* hung	hanged *or* hung
have, has	had	had
know	knew	known
lay*	laid	laid
lead	led	led
lend	lent	lent
lie*	lay	lain
lose	lost	lost
put	put	put
ride	rode	ridden
ring	rang	rung
rise*	rose	risen
run	ran	run
say	said	said
see	saw	seen
set*	set	set
shake	shook	shaken
shine	shone *or* shined†	shone *or* shined
shrink	shrank *or* shrunk	shrunk *or* shrunken
sing	sang	sung
sink	sank *or* sunk	sunk
sit*	sat	sat
slay	slew	slain
speak	spoke	spoken
spring	sprang *or* sprung	sprung
steal	stole	stolen
sting	stung	stung
swear	swore	sworn
swim	swam	swum
swing	swung	swung
take	took	taken
tear	tore	torn
tell	told	told
think	thought	thought
throw	threw	thrown
wear	wore	worn
win	won	won
write	wrote	written

*For more detailed instruction on *lay* versus *lie, raise* versus *rise,* and *sit* versus *set,* see Chapter 26.

†*Shone* is intransitive. (The sun *shone.*) *Shined* is transitive. (I *shined* my shoes.)

Objective

EXERCISE 1. Supplying the Correct Principal Part. On your paper complete the following sentences by filling the blanks with the principal part indicated in parentheses.

1. Cities typically ___began___ as small villages. (past form of *begin*)
2. Over time, the villages spontaneously ___grew___ larger. (past form of *grow*)
3. Enterprising people have ___seen___ ways of accelerating this process. (past participle of *see*)
4. Alexander the Great (336-323 B.C.) ___planned___ seventy new cities in great detail. (past form of *plan*)
5. Today several nations are ___designing___ urban experiments, new types of cities to meet specific needs. (present participle of *design*)
6. Britain has ___taken___ the lead in planning new cities. (past participle of *take*)
7. The British have ___built___ new towns primarily to relieve housing shortages and traffic jams in cities. (past participle of *build*)
8. Some planned cities have ___become___ popular with their inhabitants only after many years. (past participle of *become*)
9. Israel has ___reclaimed___ more than sixty-five percent of its desert through irrigation. (past participle of *reclaim*)
10. Architects and city planners have ___given___ excellent designs for new towns to many nations. (past participle of *given*)

TENSE OF VERBS

The **tenses** of a verb are the forms that help to show time.

Depending on which principal part of a verb you use and which, if any, auxiliary verbs you put before the principal parts, you can show *when* the action or condition you are describing occurred.

There are six tenses in English: *present, past,* and *future* and *present perfect, past perfect,* and *future perfect.*

THE PRESENT TENSE

The present tense of any action verb and of every linking verb other than *be* is the same as the verb's basic form. The following is a *conjugation*, or list of forms, for the present tense of *help:*

	SINGULAR	PLURAL
FIRST PERSON:	I **help**.	We **help**.
SECOND PERSON:	You **help**.	You **help**.
THIRD PERSON:	She, he, or it **helps**.	They **help**.

Note that in the present-tense forms of the third-person singular, an *-s* is added to the basic form. In the following conjugation note that the present tense of *be* has three forms:

	SINGULAR	PLURAL
FIRST PERSON:	I **am** honest.	We **are** honest.
SECOND PERSON:	You **are** honest.	You **are** honest.
THIRD PERSON:	He, she, or it **is** honest.	They **are** honest.
	Joseph **is** honest.	Children **are** honest.

The **present tense** expresses a constant, repeated, or habitual action or condition. It can also express a general truth.

> Water **erodes** rock. [not just now but always—a constant action]
> Terry **drives** defensively. [now and always—a habitual action]
> Steel **is** an alloy. [a condition that is always true]

The **present tense** can also express an action or condition that exists only now.

> Jessica **seems** interested. [not always but just now]
> I **agree** with you. [at this very moment]

The **present tense** is sometimes used in historical writing to express past events and, more often, in poetry, fiction, and reporting—especially sports reporting—to convey to the reader a sense of "being there."

> The applause **continues** as the soloists **step** forward and bow.
> The ball **hovers** on the rim of the basket and finally **slips** through the net.

Objective

EXERCISE 2. Using the Present Tense. On your paper write your answer to each of the following questions in a complete sentence, beginning with *Yes.* (This exercise will help you practice using singular present-tense action verbs that end in *s, es,* and *ies.*)

SAMPLE: Does a college send brochures?
ANSWER: Yes, a college sends brochures.

Yes, a student applies to several colleges.
1. Does a student apply to several colleges?
Yes, community colleges offer a two-year degree.
2. Do community colleges offer a two-year degree?
Yes, a job placement office helps students find jobs.
3. Does a job placement office help students find jobs?
Yes, the faculty teaches classes in English as a Second Language.
4. Does the faculty teach classes in English as a Second Language?
Yes, an admissions office tries to locate prospective applicants.
5. Does an admissions office try to locate prospective applicants?
Yes, extracurricular activities impress interviewers.
6. Do extracurricular activities impress interviewers?

Yes, a college stresses equal access for disabled students.
7. Does a college stress equal access for disabled students?
Yes, work experience makes a good impression.
8. Does work experience make a good impression?
Yes, each college places different emphasis on test scores.
9. Does each college place different emphasis on test scores?
Yes, education changes a person's life.
10. Does education change a person's life?

Objective
APPLICATION EXERCISE. Expressing the Present Tense in Sentences. Write a sentence using each of the following verb forms. Make the content of your sentence express the kind of present time indicated in parentheses.

SAMPLE: speaks ("now and always")
ANSWER: She speaks Spanish fluently.

1. plays ("now and always") He plays tennis regularly.
2. tastes ("just now") This soup tastes salty.
3. are ("always true") Diamonds are crystals.
4. accepts ("at this moment") She accepts the job.
5. walk ("always") I walk my dog.

Suggested Answers appear beside the items.

THE PAST TENSE

Use the **past tense** to express an action or condition that was started and completed in the past.

Everyone on the team **swam** well. We **won** by a big margin.

All regular and irregular verbs—except *be*—have just one past-tense form, such as *talked* or *wrote.* When you use *be,* you must choose *was* or *were* depending on whether the person or thing you are talking about is first, second, or third person, singular or plural.

PAST TENSE OF *BE*

I **was** strong.	We **were** strong.
You **were** strong.	You **were** strong.
He, she, or it **was** strong.	They **were** strong.

Objective
EXERCISE 3. Using the Past Tense. Complete each of the following sentences by writing on your paper the correct past-tense form of the verb in parentheses.

1. In Ohio two different families __adopted__ identical twin boys shortly after birth. (adopt)
2. Thirty-nine years later the twins __spoke__ to each other for the the first time. (speak)

3. The twins discovered that each had married a woman named Linda. (discover)
4. Identical twin women, also separated at birth and unknown to each other, had daughters named Kirsten. (have)
5. Twin sisters in Staunton, Virginia, took standardized tests in opposite corners of a classroom. (take)
6. The results were remarkable. (be)
7. Both sisters wrote the same kind of story—on the same subject. (write)
8. Male twins became professional basketball players. (become)
9. They made surprisingly similar basketball records. (make)
10. After studying more than fifteen thousand pairs of twins, Professor Luigi Gedda of the Gregor Mendel Institute of Rome developed a theory about twins. (develop)

THE FUTURE TENSE

You form the **future tense** of any verb by using *shall* or *will* with the basic form: *I shall paint, you will clean* .

Use the **future tense** to express an action or condition that will occur in the future.

Jerry **will buy** a car.
I **shall finish** my homework.

The following are other ways to express future time besides using *shall* or *will:*

1. Use *going to* with the present tense of *be* and the basic form of a verb.

   Jerry **is going to** buy a car.
   I **am going to** finish my homework.

2. Use *about to* with the present tense of *be* and the basic form of a verb.

   Jerry **is about to** buy a car.
   I **am about to** finish my homework.

3. Use the present tense with an adverb or an adverbial phrase that shows future time.

   Rosemary **graduates tomorrow**.
   Rosemary **graduates on the fifteenth of June**.

Objective

EXERCISE 4. Identifying Expressions of Future Time. Write on your paper the words that express future time in the following sentences.

SAMPLE: Next week we plan to buy a computer.
ANSWER: Next week, plan

1. Two families are going to share the cost of a computer.
2. We are going to get a color monitor and a printer, too.
3. Our family will have the computer at our home every other week.
4. Each of us will take a class on computer operation.
5. My class in Basic begins next month.
6. Tomorrow we shall look at personal computers made by two different companies.
7. Computer classes at school are about to start.
8. I am going to use the computer to type my résumé.
9. I shall be able to correct my mistakes so easily with a computer!
10. The printer will give me as many copies as I need.

Answers: The words that express future time are underlined.

Objective

APPLICATION EXERCISE. Expressing Future Time in Sentences. Write five statements or predictions about the future. Your sentences can be as realistic or as imaginary as you wish. Try to use at least two other ways of expressing future time in addition to *shall* or *will.*

SAMPLE ANSWER: Every home in America is going to have a computer in every room.

THE PERFECT TENSES

In this section you will learn how to form and use the three perfect tenses—the *present perfect tense,* the *past perfect tense*, and the *future perfect tense.* The term *perfect* comes from the Latin word *perfectus,* meaning "completed," and all of these tenses refer to actions or conditions that are or will be completed.

To make the perfect tenses you must use a form of the auxiliary verb *have* with the past participle of the main verb.

PRESENT PERFECT TENSE

You form the present perfect tense by using *has* or *have* with the past participle of a verb: *has lived, have begun.**

Use the **present perfect tense** to express an action or condition that occurred at some *indefinite* time in the past.

She **has fished** in the Atlantic.
The birds **have migrated** south.

*Do not be confused by the term *present perfect;* this tense expresses *past* time. *Present* refers to the tense of the auxiliary verb *has* or *have.*

The present perfect can refer to completed action in past time only in an indefinite way. Adverbs such as *yesterday* cannot be added to make the time more specific.

The days **have grown** longer. [indefinite past]

To be specific about completed past time, you would normally use the simple past tense.

The days **grew** longer after December 21.

The present perfect can also be used to communicate the idea that an action or a condition *began* in the past and *continues* into the present. This use normally involves adverbs of time or adverbial phrases.

She **has waited for a long time**.
The talk show host **has answered** telephone calls **for two hours**.
They **have watched** for shooting stars **all night**.

PAST PERFECT TENSE

You form the **past perfect tense** by using *had* with the past participle of a verb: *had lost, had danced.*

Use the **past perfect tense** to indicate that one past action or condition began *and* ended before another past action started.

PAST PERFECT ... PAST
She **had earned** ten thousand dollars before she **resigned**.
[She earned; she stopped earning; she resigned.]

PAST ... PAST PERFECT
By the time Joel **arrived**, all of the other guests **had left**.
[The other guests left; they finished leaving; Joel arrived.]

FUTURE PERFECT TENSE

You form the future perfect tense by using *will have* or *shall have* with the past participle of a verb: *will have met, shall have met.*

Use the **future perfect tense** to express one future action or condition that will begin *and* end before another future event starts.

In two more laps, she **will have run** four hundred meters.
[The four hundred meters will be finished by the time another future event, the completion of two more laps, occurs.]
By the end of the month, each student **will have submitted** three essays to the contest.

Objective

EXERCISE 5. Identifying the Perfect Tenses. On your paper write the tense of the italicized verbs in each of the following sentences.

1. Seattle *has covered* eight miles of its old city with new streets and sidewalks. present perfect
2. With its maze of interesting passageways, the old city *has become* an underground tourist attraction. present perfect
3. By 1930 Seattle's builders *had washed* away Denny Hill to make room for city expansion. past perfect
4. Since it opened in 1906, colorful Pike's Place Market *has sold* produce, seafood, homemade delicacies, and all kinds of imported and handcrafted goods. present perfect
5. Once you have driven over Evergreen Point Bridge on Seattle's Lake Washington, you *will have crossed* the world's longest floating bridge. future perfect
6. The Seattle Space Needle's revolving restaurant *has served* breakfast for several years. present perfect
7. The Seattle Opera *will have performed* Wagner's *Ring* cycle by the end of the summer. future perfect
8. The monorail *has carried* visitors from downtown Seattle to Seattle Center for many years. present perfect
9. The Pacific Northwest Dance Ballet Company *will have opened* its spring season by the first of March. future perfect
10. By the end of last season, The Seattle Repertory Theatre *had staged* six plays. past perfect

Objective

APPLICATION EXERCISE. Expressing the Present Perfect Tense in Sentences. **(a)** Rewrite each of the following sentences, changing the tense of the verb from past to present perfect. **(b)** Add appropriate adverbs or adverbial phrases to each of your new sentences to communicate the idea that an action or condition began in the past and continues into the present.

SAMPLE: We wrote term papers.
ANSWER: **(a)** We have written term papers.
(b) We have written term papers every year.

He has talked two hours. He has talked continuously for two hours.
1. He talked two hours.
The drama club has presented skits. The drama club has presented skits each semester.
2. The drama club presented skits.
I have studied French. I have studied French since ninth grade.
3. I studied French.
Our senators have opposed this bill. Our senators have opposed this bill for two years.
4. Our senators opposed this bill.
We have visited Yosemite National Park. We have visited Yosemite National Park for the
5. We visited Yosemite National Park.
last three summers.

Suggested Answers appear above the items.

THE PROGRESSIVE AND EMPHATIC FORMS

Each of the six tenses has a **progressive** form that expresses a continuing action.

You make the progressive forms by using the appropriate tense of the auxiliary verb *be* with the present participle of the main verb.

PRESENT PROGRESSIVE: They ***are*** **thinking.**
PAST PROGRESSIVE: They ***were*** **thinking.**
FUTURE PROGRESSIVE: They ***will be*** **thinking.**
PRESENT PERFECT PROGRESSIVE: They ***have been*** **thinking.**
PAST PERFECT PROGRESSIVE: They ***had been*** **thinking.**
FUTURE PERFECT PROGRESSIVE: They ***will have been*** **thinking.**

The present and past tenses have additional forms, called **emphatic**, that add special force or emphasis to the verb.

You make the emphatic forms by using *do* or *did* with the basic form of the verb:

PRESENT EMPHATIC: I **do think.**
PAST EMPHATIC: I **did think.**

Objective

EXERCISE 6. Using the Present Progressive. For each of the following sentences, write the present progressive form of the verb that appears in parentheses.

are recording
1. Some photographers (record) nature in great detail.
are capturing
2. With today's fast shutters, photographers (capture) objects in motion.
are describing
3. Photographers (describe) on film objects frozen in time.
are providing
4. Satellites (provide) photographic evidence of ancient civilizations.
is making
5. Photography (make) invisible worlds visible.

Objective

EXERCISE 7. Using the Past Progressive. For each of the following sentences, write the past progressive form of the verb in parentheses.

was performing
1. Mozart (perform) his own compositions in European courts at the age of seven.
was earning
2. Haydn (earn) his living as a church singer at five.
was playing
3. Yehudi Menuhin (play) violin recitals at the age of ten.
were touring
4. In the 1930s musical child prodigies (tour) everywhere.
were vanishing
5. By their teens, many of these gifted youngsters (vanish) from the concert stages.

Objective

APPLICATION EXERCISE. Expressing Past Time in a Paragraph. Write a paragraph of at least five sentences about an important event in your past. Underline five verbs or verb phrases that you have used, and identify the tense of each underlined item. (Remember that the perfect tenses as well as the simple past tense can be used to express past actions.)

Objective

EXERCISE 8. Supplying the Appropriate Verb Form. On your paper complete the following sentences by filling the blank with the verb form indicated in parentheses.

1. A volunteer program established in 1961 to assist underdeveloped countries, the Peace Corps __is making__ a comeback.
2. In January 1985 Director Loret Ruppe __called__ for ten thousand volunteers with agricultural skills. (past tense of *call*)
3. By the end of two months, more than eighteen thousand Americans __had responded__ to the call. (past perfect tense of *respond*)
4. Many of the new volunteers __are__ older people with a great deal of technical knowledge and experience. (present tense of *be*)
5. Older people __were volunteering__ for government service after raising their families and retiring from careers. (past progressive of *volunteer*)
6. Most of the new Peace Corps volunteers __will work__ in Africa's drought-stricken countries. (future tense of *work*)
7. The Peace Corps __has learned__ from its past mistakes (present perfect tense of *learn*)
8. In its early years, the Peace Corps __did encourage__ primarily young volunteers. (past emphatic of *do*)
9. Mature volunteers, however, __do have__ a greater depth of knowledge on which to draw. (present emphatic of *have*)
10. In most of the twenty countries served by the Peace Corps, the people __have accepted__ older volunteers readily. (present perfect tense of *accept*)
11. If the current trend continues, by the year 1995 the average age of a Peace Corps volunteer __will have reached__ forty. (future perfect tense of *reach*)

COMPATIBILITY OF TENSES

The various verb tenses enable you to show whether two or more events occur at the same time and whether one event precedes or follows another.

Do not shift, or change, tenses needlessly when two or more events occur at the same time.

INCORRECT: He **dived** into the pool and **swims** to the other side. [The tense needlessly shifts from the past to the present.]

CORRECT: He **dived** into the pool and **swam** to the other side. [Now it is clear that both events happened at nearly the same time in the past.]

In general, shift tenses only to show that one event precedes or follows another.

INCORRECT: When we **hiked** three miles, we **stopped** for a rest. [The two past-tense verbs give the mistaken impression that both events happened at the same time.]

CORRECT: When we **had hiked** three miles, we **stopped** for a rest. [The shift from the past perfect tense *(had hiked)* to the past tense *(stopped)* clearly indicates that the hiking of three miles happened before the rest stop.]

INCORRECT: Since I **got** a part-time job, my grades **improved**. [It is not clear which event came first.]

CORRECT: Since I **got** a part-time job, my grades **have improved**. [The past tense *(got)* indicates a completed action. The present perfect *(have improved)* indicates another past action, one that has continued into the present.]

Objective

EXERCISE 9. Making Tenses Compatible. First find the verbs in each of the following sentences. Then rewrite each sentence making the tenses compatible.

1. The twin-engined Douglas DC-3 is a workhorse of an airplane that carries (has carried) passengers and freight for more than fifty years.
2. It hit (has hit) a mountain in Arizona and flown home with twelve feet missing from one wing. (*or,* hit...flew)
3. One DC-3 that has left (left) the factory in 1942 used (has used) up 700 tires, 35,000 spark plugs, and 100 engines, but it was (is) still in service with the French navy today.
4. In the many years that pilots have been flying the DC-3, they have (have had) relatively few problems.
5. The reliable DC-3 still has been used (is being used) today for short runs to small airports when delivery time is not especially important.

Answers: The verbs are underlined, and the correct tense appears above each incorrect form.

VOICE OF VERBS

An action verb is in the **active voice** when the subject of the sentence performs the action.

The coach **encouraged** the team.

An action verb is in the **passive voice** when its action is performed on the subject.

The team **was encouraged** by the coach.

Both of the preceding examples say the same thing, but in the first sentence the *coach* (the subject of the sentence) performs the action. In the second sentence the *team* (now the subject of the sentence) takes center stage, and the coach is reduced to something called an *agent.*

As a writer you often have a choice between using a verb in the active or passive voice. It is often a question of whom you want to place in center stage—the coach or the team, for example.

Generally the active voice is stronger, but there are times when the passive voice is preferred or, in fact, necessary. If you do not want to call attention to the performer or if you do not know the performer, use the passive voice, as in the following examples:

The book **was returned**. [You may not know by whom.]
The glass **was broken**. [You may not know who broke it.]

You form the passive voice by using a form of the auxiliary verb *be* with the past participle of the verb. The tense of a passive verb is determined by the tense of the auxiliary verb.

The team **is encouraged** by the coach. [present tense, passive voice]
The team **was being encouraged**. [past progressive tense, passive voice]
The team **will have been encouraged** by the coach. [future perfect tense, passive voice]

When a verb is in the passive voice, the performer of the action may be stated as the object of the preposition *by.*

Products are advertised **by television commercials**.

Objective

EXERCISE 10. Changing the Voice of Verbs. In each of the following sentences, change the active voice to the passive or the passive voice to the active.

Sometimes, whaling captains were accompanied by their wives on voyages.

1. Sometimes, their wives accompanied whaling captains on voyages.

Charlotte Jernegan and her husband, Captain Jernegan, had spent four years aboard his whaling ship.

2. Four years had been spent by Charlotte Jernegan and her husband, Captain Jernegan, aboard his whaling ship.

On board the *Niger*, Charlotte inhabited a large pantry.

3. On board the *Niger*, a large pantry was inhabited by Charlotte.

The ship's tables were kept horizontal by stone weights.

4. Stone weights kept the ship's tables horizontal.

Charlotte's husband temporarily left her in Chile to have their son.

5. Charlotte was left temporarily by her husband in Chile to have their son.

Charlotte's daughter Amy followed her sea-going.

6. Charlotte's sea-going was followed by her daughter Amy.

Amy practiced hobbies aboard her husband's ship.

7. Hobbies were practiced by Amy aboard her husband's ship.

Whaling captains took whaling ships to more remote regions every year.

8. Whaling ships were taken by whaling captains to more remote regions every year.

The sounds of whales off the African coast were heard by Lucy Smith aboard her husband's ship, the *Nautilus*.

9. Lucy Smith, aboard her husband's ship, the *Nautilus*, heard the sounds of whales off the African coast.

Charity Norton, the wife of Captain John O. Norton, crossed Cape Horn six times.

10. Cape Horn was crossed six times by Charity Norton, the wife of Captain John O. Norton.

MOOD OF VERBS

In addition to tense and voice, verbs also express mood.

A verb expresses one of three **moods**: the **indicative mood**, the **imperative mood**, or the **subjunctive mood**.

The indicative mood—the most frequently used—makes a statement or asks a question. The imperative mood expresses a command or makes a request.

INDICATIVE MOOD: She takes the bus home.
IMPERATIVE MOOD: Take the bus home.

The subjunctive mood, although often replaced by the indicative mood in informal English, has two important uses in contemporary formal English.

1. To express, indirectly, a demand, recommendation, suggestion, or statement of necessity:

   We demand (*or* recommend *or* suggest) that she **take** the bus home. [The subjunctive mood drops the *-s* from the third-person singular.]
   It is necessary that you **be** home before dark. [The subjunctive mood uses *be* instead of *am, is,* or *are*.]

2. To state a condition or a wish that is contrary to fact:

If she **were** late, she would take the bus home. [Use *were,* not *was.*]

They complained to me as if I **were** the one in charge. [Not *was.* Notice that this use of the subjunctive always requires the past tense.]

I wish that I **were** a genius.

Objective

EXERCISE 11. Using the Subjunctive Mood. On your paper rewrite the following sentences, correcting any errors in the use of the subjunctive.

1. To photograph someone with a pet, it is necessary that the photogra-
choose
pher chooses a time of day when the animal is neither too lively nor too sleepy.
2. were
If the owner was agreeable, he or she would hold the pet; a small pet such as a hamster or a parakeet could be set on the owner's shoulder or hand.
3. To get prize-winning impact, it is recommended that the photographer
get
gets both pet and owner to look at the camera at the same time.
4. Before the photograph is finally taken, the photographer will probably
were
wish that the pet's owner was an animal trainer.
5. keep
It is also suggested that the photographer keeps the background
take
uncluttered, and takes the picture at a distance of four or five feet.

CHAPTER 23
Subject-Verb Agreement

A verb must agree with its subject in person and number.

With most verbs the only change in form to indicate agreement occurs in the present tense. An *s* (or *es*) is added to the basic verb when its subject is third-person singular. The linking verb *be* changes in both the present and the past tense.

SINGULAR	PLURAL
She **advises.**	They **advise.**
He **is** there.	They **are** there.
It **was** mysterious.	They **were** mysterious.

In verb phrases the auxiliary verbs *be, have,* and *do* change in form to show agreement with third-person subjects.

SINGULAR	PLURAL
She **is advising.**	They **are advising.**
She **has left** work.	They **have left** work.
Does he **speak** there?	**Do** they **speak** there?

Making a verb agree with its subject involves not only recognizing subjects and verbs but also telling whether a subject is singular or plural. In some sentences it may be easy to mistake another word for the actual subject. In other sentences determining whether the subject is singular or plural may be difficult.

INTERVENING PREPOSITIONAL PHRASES

Do not mistake a word in a prepositional phrase for the subject of a verb.

The simple subject is never within a prepositional phrase. Make sure the verb agrees with the actual subject, not with the object of a preposition.

The giant ***tortoise*** of the Galapagos Islands **weighs** more than five hundred pounds. [The subject *tortoise* is singular;

of the Galapagos Islands is a prepositional phrase; therefore, the verb *weighs* is singular.]

Baby ***tortoises*** near an adult **have** to be careful. [The subject *tortoises* is plural; *near an adult* is a prepositional phrase; therefore, the verb *have* is plural.]

Objective

EXERCISE 1. Making Subjects and Verbs Agree When Prepositional Phrases Intervene. First find the simple subject in each of the following sentences. Then write on your paper the verb in parentheses that agrees with the subject of each sentence.

1. A long chain of volcanoes (stretch/stretches) across the Pacific Ocean for 3,300 miles.
2. Communities on the main island of Hawaii (lie/lies) near two active volcanoes, Mauna Loa and Kilauea.
3. Solidified flows of one kind of lava (is/are) rough, sharp-edged, and chunky.
4. Snowstorms near the summit of Mauna Loa sometimes (catch/catches) hikers by surprise.
5. Lava from Kilauea's eruptions often (push/pushes) into the sea, creating new land.

AGREEMENT WITH LINKING VERBS

Do not be confused by a predicate nominative that is different in number from the subject. Only the subject affects the number of the linking verb.

The ***footprints*** in the mud **were** the only clue. [The plural verb *were* agrees with the plural subject *footprints,* not with the predicate nominative *clue.*]

My favorite ***breakfast*** **is** eggs scrambled with onions. [The singular verb *is* agrees with the singular subject *breakfast,* not with the predicate nominative *eggs.*]

Objective

EXERCISE 2. Making Linking Verbs Agree with Their Subjects. First find the simple subject in each of the following sentences. Then write on your paper the verb in parentheses that agrees with the subject of each sentence.

1. Since the invention of the tape recorder, interviews (has become/have become) a new way of acquiring and recording information.
2. Television or radio interviews with a political figure (is/are) sometimes a battle of wits.
3. Tape-recorded conversations with an elderly relative (is/are) a priceless family keepsake.
4. Beginning as a high school English project, *Foxfire* (has become/have

become) remarkable collections of the stories, songs, history, and practical knowledge of the mountain people of Georgia.

5. The interviews in *Foxfire* (is/are) an internationally acclaimed treasury of folk wisdom.

AGREEMENT IN INVERTED SENTENCES

When a subject follows its verb, carefully locate the simple subject and make sure that the verb agrees with the subject.

Inverted sentences are those in which the subject follows the verb. Inverted sentences often begin with prepositional phrases. Do not mistake the object of the preposition for the subject.

SINGULAR: Beyond the Milky Way **lies** (V) the Andromeda ***galaxy*** (S).
PLURAL: Beyond the Milky Way **lie** (V) countless ***galaxies*** (S).

In inverted sentences beginning with the expletive *there* or *here*, look for the subject after the verb. An expletive is never the subject of a sentence.

SINGULAR: There **is** (V) one possible ***explanation*** (S).
Here **comes** (V) my best ***friend*** (S).
PLURAL: There **are** (V) two possible ***explanations*** (S).
Here **come** (V) my ***friends*** (S).

In questions an auxiliary verb may come before the subject. Look for the subject between the auxiliary verb and the main verb.

SINGULAR: **Does** (V) that ***man*** (S) **teach** (V) in this school?
PLURAL: **Do** (V) these ***schools*** (S) **teach** (V) Latin?

Objective

EXERCISE 3. Making Subjects and Verbs Agree in Inverted Sentences. First find the simple subject in each of the following sentences. Then write on your paper the verb in parentheses that agrees with the subject of each sentence.

1. There (has been/have been) many attempts to explain the gigantic explosion in a remote area of Siberia in 1906.
2. In the book *Black Holes* by Walter Sullivan (appear/appears) a discussion of the theory that the blast was caused by the crash of a minute —but superdense—black hole.
3. (Don't/Doesn't) Sullivan make this bizarre idea sound quite plausible?

4. According to Sullivan, in 1906, in a straight line through the earth—entering in Siberia and exiting in the North Atlantic—(plummet/plummets) a "mini black hole" with the size of an atom and the mass of an asteroid.
5. Here (is/are) the recorded effects of the earth's encounter with that mysterious object: widespread devastation, disturbance in the earth's magnetic field, and atmospheric shock waves traveling around the planet in both directions.

AGREEMENT WITH SPECIAL SUBJECTS

Some subjects require careful attention when you select a verb to agree with them.

COLLECTIVE NOUNS

A *collective noun* names a group. (See Chapter 18.) Consider a collective noun singular when it refers to a group as a whole. Consider a collective noun plural when it refers to each member of a group individually.

SINGULAR

THE ***jury*** **leaves** the courtroom.
The ***orchestra*** **rises.**
My ***family*** **loves** to travel.

PLURAL

The ***jury*** **argue** among themselves.
The ***orchestra*** **are voting** for their new conductor.
My ***family*** **take** turns choosing places to go.

SPECIAL NOUNS

Certain nouns that end in *s,* such as *mumps, measles,* and *mathematics,* take singular verbs.

SINGULAR: ***Mathematics*** **is** my best subject.

Certain other nouns that name one thing but that end in *s,* such as *eyeglasses, pants, scissors,* and *binoculars,* take plural verbs.

PLURAL: These ***binoculars*** **are** a bargain.
The ***scissors*** **were made** in France.

Many nouns that end in *ics* may be singular or plural depending on meaning.

SINGULAR: ***Ethics*** **is** the branch of philosophy that most interests me. [one subject of interest]
PLURAL: His ***ethics*** in this matter **are** questionable. [more than one ethical decision]

NOUNS OF AMOUNT

When the noun of amount refers to a total considered as one unit, it is singular. When the noun refers to a number of individual units, it is plural.

SINGULAR: Two ***dollars*** **is** the fee. [one amount]
PLURAL: Two ***dollars*** **are** in his pockets. [two individual bills or coins]

SINGULAR: Five ***days*** **seems** like a long time. [one unit of time]
PLURAL: Five ***days*** **are spent** at school.

TITLES

A title is always considered singular even if a noun within the title is plural.

SINGULAR: ***Millions of Cats*** by Wanda Gag **is** my three-year-old nephew's favorite book.

THE NUMBER, A NUMBER

The number is considered singular. *A number* (meaning "some") is considered plural.

SINGULAR: The ***number*** of high grades **is** gratifying.
PLURAL: A ***number*** of seniors **have contributed** time.

Objective
EXERCISE 4. Making Verbs Agree with Special Subjects. First find the subject in each of the following sentences. Then write on your paper the verb in parentheses that agrees with the subject of each sentence.

1. Party-goers (is/are) happy people.
2. *Parties and More Parties* (is/are) a book for all party planners.
3 Students in Jackson, Michigan, (has/have) a big party every year.
4. A number of planners (oversees/oversee) preparations for the parties.
5. Four weeks (is needed/are needed) for planning each party.
6. The number of tasks to be completed (is/are) overwhelming.
7. Nonetheless, the planners (motivates/motivate) the students.
8. Economics (is/are) an important aspect of the planning.
9. Two hundred dollars (is/are) the cost of each party.
10. The *Jackson High News and Views* (prints/print) photographs taken at the party.

AGREEMENT WITH COMPOUND SUBJECTS

When the subject of a sentence is compound (Chapter 19), you must pay attention to the conjunction that joins the compound parts and to the meaning of the entire subject. Only then can you know which verb form agrees with a particular compound subject.

1. Compound subjects joined by *and*

Usually compound subjects joined by *and* or by *both . . . and* are considered plural. However, when the parts of the compound subject are actually parts of one unit or when they refer to the same person or thing, the subject is considered singular.

PLURAL: The ***librarian*** *and* the ***student*** **are reading.**
Both ***duck*** *and* ***chicken*** **are** poultry.
SINGULAR: ***Fever*** *and* ***nausea*** **is** typical of influenza. [Compound subject is one unit.]
Macaroni *and* ***cheese*** **tastes** delicious. [Compound subject is one unit.]
Her ***teacher*** *and* ***counselor*** **meets** with her. [One person is both the teacher and the counselor.]

2. Compound subjects joined by *or* or *nor*

With compound subjects joined by *or* or *nor* (or by *either . . . or* or *neither . . . nor*), always make the verb agree with the subject nearer the verb.

PLURAL: *Neither* the ***librarian*** *nor* the ***students*** **are reading.**
SINGULAR: *Either* the ***librarian*** *or* the ***student*** **is reading.**
Neither the ***librarians*** *nor* the ***student*** **reads.**

3. *Many a, every,* and *each* with compound subjects

When *many a, every,* or *each* precedes a compound subject, the subject is considered singular.

SINGULAR: *Many a* ***cook*** and ***waiter*** **works** late.
Every ***student, teacher,*** and ***parent*** **wants** good grades.
Each ***librarian*** and ***student*** **is reading.**

INTERVENING EXPRESSIONS

Certain expressions, such as *accompanied by, as well as, in addition to, plus,* and *together with,* introduce phrases that modify the subject but do not change its number. Although their meaning is similar to that of *and,* they do not create compound subjects.

If a singular subject is linked to another noun by an intervening expression, such as "accompanied by," the subject is still considered singular.

SINGULAR: ***Loyalty,*** in addition to similar interests, **is** essential to a long-term friendship.
The ***cook*** as well as the ***waiter*** **works** hard.

Objective
EXERCISE 5. Making Verbs Agree with Their Subjects. On your paper write the appropriate form of the verb in parentheses in each of the following sentences.

1. Every chef and gourmet (knows/know) that the proper kitchen tool makes any job easier.
2. Preparing food as well as serving the meal often (depends/depend) on having the correct utensils.
3. Many an inexperienced cook and homemaker (is/are) surprised by how many utensils are needed.
4. A food processor accompanied by several different attachments (makes/make) everything from juices to garnishes.
5. For carving meat, a fork and a sharp knife (is/are) essential to produce smooth, even slices.
6. A kitchen scale together with measuring cups (helps/help) cooks to measure ingredients.
7. A slotted spoon and tongs (makes/make) hot or greasy food easy to handle.
8. A strainer plus colanders of various sizes (is used/are used) to sift flour or to shake water from foods.
9. Many a lover of fudge or boiled eggs (finds/find) a timer or a stop-watch useful.
10. A grater and a blender (is/are) very useful for making delicious soups and sauces quickly.

Objective

APPLICATION EXERCISE. Writing Sentences with Compound Subjects. Write a sentence, using each of the following compound subjects. Make the compound subject agree with a present-tense verb.

SAMPLE: strawberries and cream
ANSWER: Strawberries and cream is an easy dessert.

1. bread and water singular verb if used as a single unit
2. neither the table nor the chairs plural verb
3. both the *New York Times* and the *Boston Globe* plural verb
4. Uncle Alfred or my grandmother singular verb
5. many a bird and beast singular verb

The number of the verb required in each sentence appears beside each item.

INDEFINITE PRONOUNS AS SUBJECTS

A verb must agree in number with an indefinite pronoun subject.

Indefinite pronouns (see Chapter 18) can be divided into the following three groups: those that are always singular; those that are always plural; and those that can be either singular or plural, depending upon the nouns to which they refer.

Here are the indefinite pronouns that are always singular:

each	everyone	nobody	anything
either	everybody	nothing	someone
neither	everything	anyone	somebody
one	no one	anybody	something

These are the indefinite pronouns that are always plural:

several few both many

These indefinite pronouns may be singular or plural:

some all any most none

The verb that you use with an indefinite pronoun from the third group often shows whether you are assigning the pronoun a singular or a plural meaning.

SINGULAR: ***Some*** of his music **was** quite sophisticated. [*Some* is used here in the sense of "part," which is singular.]
PLURAL: ***Some*** of his songs **were** fun to sing. [*Some* is used here to refer to *songs,* which is plural.]

Objective

APPLICATION EXERCISE. Making Verbs Agree with Indefinite Pronoun Subjects. Write a sentence, using each of the following indefinite pronouns as the subject of a present-tense verb.

SAMPLE: several
ANSWER: Several of the students have interesting science projects.

1. everyone Everyone in the class has an exhibit.
2. many Many of the experiments use electricity.
3. one One of the students displays a solar oven.
4. everything Everything is ready on time.
5. each Each of the science teachers is a judge.

Suggested Answers are beside each item.

AGREEMENT IN ADJECTIVE CLAUSES

The verb in an adjective clause must agree with its subject. The subject of an adjective clause is often a relative pronoun. (See Chapter 21.) The number of the relative pronoun subject depends on the number of its antecedent in the main clause.

The Mexican grizzly is one of the ***bears*** **that were thought to be extinct.** [The antecedent of *that* is *bears,* a third-person plural noun.]
The baleen whale is the only ***one*** of the whales **that has two rows of baleen (whalebone) instead of teeth.** [The antecedent of *that* is *one,* a third-person singular pronoun.]

If the expression "one of" appears in the main clause, you must take care to determine if the antecedent is "one" as in the second example above or the noun that follows it, such as "bears" in the first example. (The word *the* before *one* indicates that *one* is the antecedent.)

The action or linking verb in an adjective clause with a relative pronoun subject must agree with the antecedent to which the relative pronoun refers.

She is ***someone*** who **wants** to succeed.

Objective

EXERCISE 6. Making Subjects and Verbs Agree in Adjective Clauses. On your paper complete the following sentences by choosing the correct form of the verb in parentheses.

SAMPLE: Johann Sebastian Bach was the only one of the great eighteenth century composers who (was/were) the father of several outstanding musicians.

ANSWER: was

1. The Asian tree shrew is one of the mammals that (is/are) difficult to classify.
2. The little spacecraft Pioneer 10 is the only one of humanity's artifacts that (has traveled/have traveled) beyond the solar system.
3. Celia Thaxter was one of the nineteenth-century American poets who (was writing/were writing) primarily for children.
4. The Rocky Mountain spotted fever tick is one of the insects that (causes/cause) disease.
5. Jesse Owens of the United States was the only one of the Olympic competitors who(has set/have set) six world records in one day.

REVIEW EXERCISE. Subject-Verb Agreement. The following ten sentences contain errors in subject-verb agreement. Rewrite the sentences with the correct verb forms that agree with their subjects. (Some of the sentences will have more than one subject-verb combination.)

(1) On a sunny Saturday in May both Charles and Anna tramps the neighborhood, stapling signs to posts. **(2)** Then they join the rest of their family which are working madly, hauling old toys, clothes, and furniture to the garage. **(3)** "Here come the crowd!" yells Anna, as three cars pull up to the curb and a number of people gets out. **(4)** Everyone swarm over the lawn. **(5)** "There is toys for sale here?" asks a small boy, the first to arrive. **(6)** On top of some boxes sit a huge teddy bear. **(7)** Neither worn-out clothes nor a broken toy sell well at a garage sale. **(8)** Everything that are clean and useful, however, manage to find a new home. **(9)** By sunset nothing except empty containers are left. **(10)** A garage sale is one of the activities that seems to please everyone.

24 CHAPTER
Using Pronouns Correctly

Several pronouns change their form depending on how they function in a sentence. Consider, for example, the following:

Tim greeted Mrs. Edwards. He greeted her.

Notice that the nouns in the first sentence can be reversed *(Mrs. Edwards greeted Tim)* but that the pronouns in the second sentence cannot. *Her greeted he* is simply not normal English. This chapter will explain why pronouns such as *he* and *her* can fill only certain functions in sentences and not others. The last part of this chapter will discuss the relationship between pronouns and their antecedents and give guidelines for making them agree.

CASE OF PERSONAL PRONOUNS

Personal pronouns have three **cases**, or forms. The case of a personal pronoun depends on the pronoun's function in a sentence (whether it be a subject, object, etc.). The three cases are called **nominative, objective,** and **possessive**.

The following chart lists the case forms of personal pronouns according to the pronouns' function in sentences:

	PRONOUNS		
	SINGULAR	PLURAL	FUNCTION
NOMINATIVE CASE:	I, you, she, he, it	we, you, they	subject or predicate nominative
OBJECTIVE CASE:	me, you, her, him, it	us, you, them	direct object or indirect object or object of preposition
POSSESSIVE CASE:	my, mine, your, yours, her, hers, his, its	our, ours, your, yours, their, theirs	replacement for possessive noun(s)

You and *it* rarely cause usage problems because they have the same form in both the nominative and the objective cases. Learn to recognize the forms and functions of the other pronouns according to their case.

You can avoid errors involving the case of personal pronouns if you keep the following rules in mind:

1. Be sure to use the nominative case for a personal pronoun in a compound subject.

> Alice and **I** repaired the fence. [*not* me repaired]
> **She** and Jeff fixed the gate. [*not* Her and Jeff fixed]
> **He** and **I** mowed the lawn. [*not* Him and me mowed]

2. Be sure to use the objective case for a personal pronoun in a compound object.

> Henry brought Jeff and **me** some lemonade. [*not* Jeff and I]
> He shared some sandwiches with Alice and **me.** [*not* with Alice and I]

When you have to choose the correct pronoun in a sentence with a compound subject or object, it is helpful to say the sentence to yourself without the conjunction and the other noun or pronoun subject.

3. In general, use the nominative case of a personal pronoun after a form of the linking verb *be.*

> The most skillful gardener was **he**. [*not* was him]
> Alice said that the best supervisor was **I**. [*not* was me]
> I said that the best workers were **they**. [*not* were them]

In speaking, people often use the objective case after a form of the linking verb *be:* they say "*It's me,*" and "*It was him.*" In writing, however, you should use the nominative case after the linking verb *be.*

4. Be careful not to spell possessive pronouns with apostrophes.*

> This lawnmower is **hers.** [*not* her's]
> The lawn is ours. [*not* our's]

It's is a contraction for *it is.* Do not confuse it with the possessive pronoun *its.*

5. Be sure to use possessive pronouns before gerunds (*-ing* forms used as nouns).

My, your, his, her, its, our,* and *their* are sometimes called possessive adjectives because they modify nouns: *This is* ***her* *garden*, for example.

Your working late will be helpful. [*not* You working late will be helpful]
She was grateful for **our** playing the piano. [*not* for us playing the piano]

Objective

EXERCISE 1. Choosing the Correct Case Form. In each of the following sentences, write the personal pronoun or pronouns that correctly complete the sentence.

1. My friend Tom and (I/me) are learning to play tennis.
2. Tom's cousin Ed gave him and (I/me) a few lessons.
3. The key to a good ground stroke is (you/your) gripping the racket correctly.
4. Ed demonstrated the proper grip for Tom and (I/me).
5. He said that (me/my) keeping my arm straight was important.
6. Tom and (I/me) practice three times a week at the local courts.
7. Sometimes (it's/its) difficult to find an empty court.
8. Tennis is not a hard sport to learn; (it's/its) rules are quite simple.
9. Several players came over last week to compare their rackets with (our's/ours).
10. Ed says that (us/our) playing regularly is the only way to improve.

PRONOUNS IN APPOSITIVE PHRASES

Pronouns often appear with nouns in appositive phrases that follow other nouns or pronouns. (See Chapter 20.)

The official scorers, **Grace and I**, listened closely to the debaters. [The pronoun *I* is part of a phrase that is in apposition to the noun *scorers*.]

Use the nominative case for a pronoun that is in apposition to a subject or predicate nominative.

The first team, **she and Sam**, debated brilliantly. [*Team* is the subject.]

They were the runners-up, **Sam and she**. [*Runners-up* is the predicate nominative.]

Use the objective case for a pronoun that is in apposition to a direct object, indirect object, or object of a preposition.

The principal congratulated the winners, **Helen and her**. [*Winners* is a direct object.]

The judge gave the funniest speakers, **Tom and her**, a special award. [*Speakers* is an indirect object.]

He had some good words for the scorers, **Grace and me**. [*Scorers* is the object of the preposition *for*.]

In appositive phrases with *we* and *us*, choose the case of the pronoun on the usual basis of its function in the sentence.

> **We sisters** love horseback riding. [*We* is the correct form because *we* is the subject of the sentence.]
> Uncle Paul gave **us brothers** a new pool table. [*Us* is the correct form because *us* is the indirect object.]

It is often helpful in choosing the correct pronoun to say the sentence without the noun.

Objective

EXERCISE 2. Choosing the Correct Pronoun in Appositive Phrases. Write the pronoun or pronouns that correctly complete each sentence.

1. Our coach told (us/we) seniors that it was our responsibility to lead.
2. The co-captains, Joan and (she/her), are two of the best players.
3. The win was due to two forwards, (Sally and she/Sally and her).
4. They are my best friends in class (Gene and she/Gene and her).
5. (We/Us) seniors are going to celebrate the team's victory.

PRONOUNS IN ELLIPTICAL ADVERB CLAUSES

In elliptical adverb clauses using *than* and *as* (see Chapter 21), choose the case of the pronoun that you would use if the missing words were fully expressed.

> They arrived at the party earlier than **she** [arrived].

The nominative pronoun *she* is the subject of the adverb clause *than she arrived.*

> The play amused our guests as much as [it amused] **us**.

The objective pronoun *us* is the direct object of the adverb clause *as much as it amused us.*

Objective

APPLICATION EXERCISE. Using Pronouns in Elliptical Adverb Clauses. Expand each of the following expressions into a complex sentence containing an elliptical adverb clause. End each sentence with a personal pronoun other than *you* and *it.*

SAMPLE: more astonished than
ANSWER: No one in class was more astonished than he.

1. more helpful than
2. as attractive as
3. less amiable than
4. as athletic as
5. sterner than

Suggested Answer for 1: In arranging the party Susan was more helpful than they.

CORRECT USE OF REFLEXIVE AND INTENSIVE PRONOUNS

A reflexive pronoun refers to a noun or another pronoun in the sentence and indicates that the same person or thing is involved. An intensive pronoun adds emphasis to another noun or pronoun. (See Chapter 18.) Take care to avoid the following errors in the use of these pronouns.

1. Do not use *hisself* or *theirselves;* they are incorrect forms. Always use *himself* and *themselves.*

> Paul corrected the error **himself.**
> My parents **themselves** put out the **fire.**

2. Be sure to use a reflexive pronoun when the pronoun refers to the same person as the subject of the sentence.

> INCORRECT: I bought me a book.
> CORRECT: I bought **myself** a book.
>
> INCORRECT: He found him a comfortable chair.
> CORRECT: He found **himself** a comfortable chair.

3. Do not use a reflexive pronoun unnecessarily. Remember that a reflexive pronoun must refer to the same person as the subject.

> INCORRECT: Lila and myself are going to the mall.
> CORRECT: Lila and **I** are going to the mall.

WHO AND *WHOM* IN QUESTIONS AND SUBORDINATE CLAUSES

The pronoun *who* can function as an interrogative or a relative pronoun. (See Chapter 18.) It has these case forms:

> NOMINATIVE: who
> OBJECTIVE: whom
> POSSESSIVE: whose

In questions, use *who* for subjects and *whom* for direct and indirect objects and for objects of prepositions.

> **Who** did you say called me? [*Who* is the subject of *called.*]
> **Whom** are you photographing? [*Whom* is the direct object of the verb *are photographing.*]

In questions with interrupting expressions, such as "did you say" or "do you think," it is often helpful to drop the interrupting expression in order to determine whether to use *who* or *whom.*

> **Who** [do you think] will arrive first?

When *who* and *whoever* or *whom* and *whomever* are used as relative pronouns to introduce subordinate clauses, the choice of case is determined by the function of the relative pronoun in the subordinate clause.

Use *who* and *whoever* for subjects and predicate nominatives in subordinate clauses.

> Tell me **who** is in charge here. [*Who* is the subject of the noun clause *who is in charge here.*]
> She knows **who** her supervisor is. [*Who* is the predicate nominative of the noun clause *who her supervisor is.*]
> The prize will be given to **whoever** deserves it. [*Whoever* is the subject of the noun clause *whoever deserves it.*]

Use *whom* and *whomever* for direct and indirect objects and objects of prepositions in subordinate clauses.

> They asked her **whom** she had seen at the party. [*Whom* is the direct object of the verb *had seen* in the noun clause *whom she had seen at the party.*]
> Warren G. Harding is a President about **whom** I know very little. [*Whom* is the object of the preposition *about* in the adjective clause *about whom I know very little.*]
> The winner will be **whomever** the people select. [*Whomever* is the direct object of the verb *select* in the noun clause *whomever the people select.*]

When choosing whether to use *who* and *whoever* or *whom* and *whomever* in subordinate clauses, remember to look at the subordinate clause only and to determine how the relative pronoun functions in that clause.

In informal speech, people generally use *who* in place of *whom* in sentences like this one: *Who did you ask?* In writing and in formal speaking situations, however, people are expected to make the distinctions between *who* and *whom.*

Objective

EXERCISE 3. Choosing *Who* or *Whom*. Write on your paper the appropriate form of the pronoun in parentheses in each of the following sentences.

1. (Who/Whom) did Shakespeare present as the leader of the plot to assassinate Julius Caesar?
2. The key conspirator was Marcus Brutus, (who/whom) Caesar regarded as one of his closest friends.
3. Caius Cassius, (who/whom) realized that Caesar's favorite would lend prestige to the conspirators' cause, appealed to Brutus's patriotism.
4. A soothsayer (who/whom) Caesar encountered warned him to beware the Ides of March.

5. The main characters of Shakespeare's tragedy, about (who/whom) he read in Plutarch's *Parallel Lives,* are Caesar, Brutus, and Antony.

Objective

EXERCISE 4. Choosing *Whoever* or *Whomever*. Write on your paper the appropriate form of the pronoun in parentheses in each of the following sentences.

1. (Whoever/Whomever) performs best at the auditions will be offered a summer internship with the orchestra.
2. The judges will schedule (whoever/whomever) applies by Friday for an audition.
3. A newspaper article will appear about (whoever/whomever) the judges select.
4. The auditions will be worth attending, (whoever/whomever) wins.
5. Helen says that she will interview (whoever/whomever) the audience applauds the most.

PRONOUN-ANTECEDENT AGREEMENT

An *antecedent* is the word or group of words to which a pronoun refers or which a pronoun replaces. All pronouns must agree with their antecedents in number, gender, and person.

AGREEMENT IN NUMBER AND GENDER

A pronoun must agree with its antecedent in number (singular or plural) and gender (masculine, feminine, or neuter).

A pronoun's antecedent may be a noun, another pronoun, or a phrase or clause acting as a noun. In the following examples the pronouns appear in bold type and their antecedents in bold italic type. Notice how they agree in both number and gender.

> ***George Eliot*** published **her** masterpiece, *Middlemarch*, in installments in 1871-72. [singular, feminine pronoun]
> Fred's ***sisters*** took **their** boat out on the bay. [plural pronoun]
> ***Frank Lloyd Wright*** constructed many of **his** innovative houses in the Midwest. [singular, masculine pronoun]
> Rita's ***brothers*** are highly respected in **their** business. [plural pronoun]
> We should consult this ***magazine*** for **its** comprehensive article on whales. [singular, neuter pronoun]
> ***Dogwoods*** and ***azaleas*** are admired in spring for the beauty of **their** blossoms. [plural pronoun]

Traditionally, a masculine pronoun is used when the gender of the antecedent is not known or may be masculine or feminine.

A good ***diver*** must practice **his** routine daily.

If you do not wish to use a masculine pronoun when the antecedent may be feminine, you can frequently reword the sentence so that the pronoun is plural or eliminated entirely.

Good ***divers*** must practice **their** routines daily. [plural pronoun]
Good divers must practice routines daily. [no pronoun]

AGREEMENT WITH COLLECTIVE NOUNS

When the antecedent of a pronoun is a collective noun (see Chapter 18), the number of the pronoun depends on whether the collective noun is meant to be singular or plural.

The ***group*** boarded **its** bus promptly at eight. [The collective noun *group* is being used in the singular sense of one unit of persons. Therefore, using the singular pronoun *its* is correct.]
The ***group*** bought **their** souvenirs before leaving. [The collective noun *group* is being used in the plural sense of several persons. Therefore, using the plural pronoun *their* is correct.]

Objective

EXERCISE 5. Making Pronouns and Antecedents Agree. On your paper complete the following sentences by filling the blank with an appropriate possessive pronoun. Also write the antecedent of each pronoun that you supply.

1. As we look at some animals in zoos, it never enters ___our___ minds how clever and resourceful they are in the wild.
2. Many mammals in cold climates survive during the winter by reducing ___their___ diet and avoiding unnecessary activity.
3. A badger, for example, spends much of the winter in ___its___ burrow.
4. The female black bear gives birth to ___her___ cubs in a den during the winter.
5. Smaller animals, like woodchucks and hedgehogs, prolong ___their___ winter sleep until the warmer spring weather awakens them.

Answers: Pronouns appear in blanks; antecedents are underlined.

Objective

EXERCISE 6. Making Pronouns Agree with Collective Noun Antecedents. On your paper complete the following sentences by filling the blank with an appropriate possessive pronoun. Also write the antecedent of each pronoun that you supply.

1. The majority expressed ___its___ will loudly and clearly.
2. The audience left ___their___ cars in the parking lot.
3. The group found ___its___ way to the theater with difficulty.
4. The committee agreed on ___its___ weekly agenda.
5. The band brought ___their___ own instruments to the concert.

Answers: Pronouns appear in blanks; antecedents are underlined.

AGREEMENT IN PERSON

Pronouns must agree with their antecedents in person. Pronouns are in the first person, second person, and third person. (See Chapter 18.)

Do not use the second-person pronoun *you* to refer to an antecedent in the third person. Either change *you* to an appropriate third-person pronoun, or replace it with a suitable noun.

POOR: John and Susan are going to Ravenna, where you can admire the remarkable Byzantine mosaics.

IMPROVED: John and Susan are going to Ravenna, where **they** can admire the remarkable Byzantine mosaics.

IMPROVED: John and Susan are going to Ravenna, where **tourists** can admire the remarkable Byzantine mosaics.

Objective

EXERCISE 7. Making Pronouns and Antecedents Agree in Person. On your paper rewrite each of the following items, eliminating the inappropriate use of *you* by substituting a third-person pronoun or a suitable noun.

1. The audiences of English medieval plays enjoyed the spectacle immensely. They You watched the plays outdoors.
2. The spectators gathered in churchyards. They You would often be celebrating a feast day or holiday.
3. In the towns of Wakefield, Chester, York, and Coventry, a person you might see many short dramas in the course of a single day.
4. Each guild provided actors for the plays. The actors You would circulate through the town in a pageant wagon, which served as a moveable stage.

Suggested Answers appear above the items.

AGREEMENT WITH INDEFINITE PRONOUN ANTECEDENTS

In general, use a singular personal pronoun when its antecedent is a singular indefinite pronoun, and use a plural personal pronoun when the antecedent is a plural indefinite pronoun. (See page 498 for the list of singular and plural indefinite pronouns.)

Each of the boys in class wrote **his** own sonnet.
Each of the girls wrote **her** own speech.
Several of my friends presented **their** work.

Notice that the plural nouns in the prepositional phrases—*of the boys, of the girls*—do not affect the number of the personal pronouns. *His* and *her* are singular because *each*, their antecedent, is singular. In speaking, however, people often use the plural pronoun *their* in such sentences.

INFORMAL: ***Neither*** of the boys wrote **their** own sonnets.

Writers traditionally make a masculine pronoun agree with an indefinite antecedent when no gender is specified.

Everyone should write **his** own research paper.

If you do not want to use a masculine pronoun when the indefinite pronoun may refer to a female, try rewording your sentence. You might substitute a plural indefinite pronoun for the singular one or eliminate the personal pronoun entirely. Although some people use two pronouns *(he or she, him or her, his or her),* many writers consider such wording awkward.

All should write **their** own research papers.
Everyone should write a research paper. [no pronoun]

Objective

EXERCISE 8. Making Pronouns Agree with Indefinite Pronoun Antecedents. On your paper supply the missing possessive personal pronoun in each of the following sentences. Then write the antecedent of each pronoun that you supply.

1. Each of the Native American tribes had ___its___ own way of life.
2. Most of this cultural variety had ___its___ roots in the climate and the terrain.
3. In the Southwest several of the tribes made ___their___ homes in pueblos, or villages.
4. Almost all of the Pueblo tribes built ___their___ stone homes on the mesas.
5. Among the Zuñi, houses were the property of women, and each could sell or trade ___her___ home without hindrance.
6. A few of the Southwestern tribes earned ___their___ livelihood as shepherds.
7. Most of the Pueblo tribes farmed the land, raising corn, beans, and squash as ___their___ principal crops.

8. Any of the tribes that relied on hunting and gathering for ___their___ food had to journey with the seasons.
9. If most of an area received little rain, ___its___ residents had to travel in search of food.
10. Many of the Plains Indians relied on the availability of buffalo for ___their___ survival.

Answers: Pronouns appear in blanks; antecedents are underlined.

CLEAR PRONOUN REFERENCE

Make sure that the antecedent of a pronoun is clear and that a pronoun cannot possibly refer to more than one antecedent.

To correct unclear pronoun reference, either reword the sentence to make the antecedent clear or eliminate the pronoun.

UNCLEAR ANTECEDENT: When the large dogs approached the small cats, **they** were intimidated. [Which word is the antecedent of *they*? Were the dogs or the cats intimidated?]

CLEAR ANTECEDENT: The large dogs were intimidated when **they** approached the small cats.

NO PRONOUN: When the large dogs approached the small cats, the dogs were intimidated.

NO PRONOUN: The large dogs were intimidated by the small cats.

Do not use the relative pronoun *which* without a clearly stated antecedent.

NO ANTECEDENT: In 1906 many buildings in San Francisco burned, **which** was caused by the great earthquake of April 18. [What was caused by the great earthquake? A fire was caused, but *fire* does not appear in the sentence.]

CLEAR ANTECEDENT: In 1906 a fire, **which** was caused by the great earthquake of April 18, burned many buildings in San Francisco.

Objective

EXERCISE 9. Making Pronoun Reference Clear. On your paper rewrite each of the following sentences, making sure that all pronoun references are clearly stated.

1. William Blake was apprenticed to an engraver, which he used when he

illustrated and published his own poems.

2. Blake told his father that he had little interest in being a tradesman.
3. Blake's first major poems appeared during the early years of the French Revolution, which were pivotally important.
4. Blake compares the effects of the Industrial Revolution to an individual's loss of innocence, which is a key Romantic idea.
5. When Blake's poems are read alongside his mystical prose works, they are often illuminated.

REVIEW EXERCISE. Pronoun Usage. Rewrite each of the following sentences, eliminating any mistakes in the use of pronouns. Each sentence has one error.

I

1. My brother and me have enjoyed classical music since we were very young.

I

2. I enjoy attending concerts because you can hear a wide variety of musical works.

he

3. Bob collects recordings, and it was him who first introduced me to the operas of Giuseppe Verdi.

It is Verdi's mastery of Italian opera which accounts . . . lifetime.

4. Verdi was the master of Italian opera, which accounts for his great popularity during his lifetime.
5. Verdi took the plots for several of his operas from Shakespeare,

who

whom, I understand, was his favorite playwright.

its

6. Each of Verdi's operas features a highly dramatic plot in it's libretto.

whoever

7. These operas can appeal to whomever enjoys a good play.

Theresa's (*or* my sister's)

8. My sister's friend Theresa says her record collection is more extensive than Bob's.

his

9. Each of our friends has their own favorite among the Verdi operas.

me

10. However, *Otello* has always seemed to Bob and I to be the composer's masterpiece.

Suggested Answers appear in red.

25 CHAPTER
Using Modifiers Correctly

This chapter will discuss how adjectives and adverbs are used to make comparisons. In addition, it will show you how to avoid certain errors in making comparisons and how to correct misplaced and dangling modifiers.

THE THREE DEGREES OF COMPARISON

Most adjectives and adverbs have three degrees: the positive, or base, form; the comparative form; and the superlative form. A modifier in the **positive** degree is the form used as the entry word in the dictionary; it does not make a comparison. A modifier that shows two things being compared is called **comparative**. A modifier that shows three or more things being compared is called **superlative**.

POSITIVE: The pianist's hands are **large.**
The nightingale sang **sweetly.**

COMPARATIVE: The pianist's hands are **larger** than mine.
The nightingale sang **more sweetly** than the cardinal.

SUPERLATIVE: Of the three women, her hands are the **largest.**
The nightingale sang the **most sweetly** of all.

The following are rules to guide you in forming the comparative and superlative degrees of adjectives and adverbs.

1. In general, add *-er* to form the comparative and *-est* to form the superlative of modifiers with one syllable.

slow, slow**er**, slow**est**
The local is **slower** than the express.
bright, bright**er**, bright**est**
That is the **brightest** tie I have ever seen.

In some cases, there will be spelling changes when you add *-er* and *-est*. (See Chapter 29.)

white, whit**er,** whit**est** merry, merr**ier,** merr**iest**
flat, flat**ter,** flat**test**

Sometimes it may sound more natural to use *more* and *most* with some one-syllable modifiers.

brusque, **more** brusque, **most** brusque
Mr. Wilson is **more brusque** than Mr. Stein.

2. Add *-er* to form the comparative and *-est* to form the superlative of most two-syllable adjectives.

little, littl**er,** littl**est**
That kitten is **littler** than this one.
friendly, friendl**ier,** friendl**iest.**
The Burmese kitten is the **friendliest** of the three.

If *-er* and *-est* sound awkward with a two-syllable adjective, use *more* and *most.*

prudent, **more** prudent, **most** prudent
No one was **more prudent** with money than John.

3. Always use *more* and *most* to form the comparative and superlative degrees of adverbs ending in *ly.*

loudly, **more** loudly, **most** loudly
Jeff sang **more loudly** than Henry.
slowly, **more** slowly, **most** slowly
Of all the trees, that dogwood grows the **most slowly.**

4. Always use *more* and *most* to form the comparative and superlative degrees of modifiers of three or more syllables.

talented, **more** talented, **most** talented
This actor is **more talented** than that one.
cordially, **more** cordially, **most** cordially
Of all the officials, the mayor greeted the guests the **most cordially.**

5. *Less* and *least,* the opposite of *more* and *most,* can also be used with most modifiers to show comparison.

Ed is **less reflective** than Harriet.
Mark is the **least reflective** person I know.

Some adjectives, such as *unique, perfect, empty, full, dead, square,* cannot be compared. They have no comparative or superlative forms because they describe an absolute condition. A person or thing cannot logically be "more dead" or "most unique." However, you can sometimes use "more nearly" or "most nearly" with these adjectives.

That painting is the **most nearly perfect** that I have seen.

IRREGULAR COMPARISON

A few modifiers form their comparative and superlative degrees irregularly. It is most helpful simply to memorize their forms.

POSITIVE	COMPARATIVE	SUPERLATIVE
good	better	(the) best
well	better	(the) best
bad	worse	(the) worst
badly	worse	(the) worst
ill	worse	(the) worst
far	farther	(the) farthest
far	further	(the) furthest
little (amount)	less	(the) least
many	more	(the) most
much	more	(the) most

Objective

EXERCISE 1. Identifying Degrees of Comparison. On your paper write the degree of comparison of the italicized modifier in each of the following sentences.

SAMPLE: This cereal is *more healthful* than that candy.
ANSWER: comparative

1. Swimming is one of the *best* sports for people of all ages who wish to keep fit and healthy.
2. Many people consider swimming *healthier* for the body than jogging or weightlifting.
3. Swimmers are *more likely* to exercise all of their body muscles than are runners or gymnasts.
4. Swimming is also *less expensive* than many other sports, such as riding and skiing.
5. A daily swim is a *good* way to stay in shape.

Answers: 1. superlative; 2. comparative; 3. comparative; 4. comparative; 5. positive

Objective

EXERCISE 2. Making Correct Comparisons. On your paper complete the following sentences by filling the blank with the correct form of the modifier in parentheses.

SAMPLE: Sue is the ________ singer in our group. (good)
ANSWER: best

1. Many people consider James Joyce the __most imaginative__ writer of English fiction in the twentieth century. (imaginative)
2. Joyce exploited __more__ new techniques in the novel than virtually any other writer of his generation. (many)
3. His short stories are generally __more accessible__ than his novels. (accessible)
4. One of his great stories, "The Dead," explores the conflicts in Irish

society between the younger generation and older, more traditional characters. (traditional)

5. In this story, Joyce skillfully presents a number of character types, based on real people the author knew in Dublin. (skillfully)
6. The novel *Ulysses* is considerably more complex in style and narrative technique than Joyce's short stories. (complex)
7. The main character of *Ulysses,* Leopold Bloom, feels that he is one of the most isolated men in Dublin. (isolated)
8. Although *Ulysses* is epic in scope, Bloom wanders no farther than the city limits of the capital. (far)
9. Bloom finally meets the young Stephen Dedalus, who becomes a surrogate son to him. (finally)
10. Joyce used Homer's epic, the *Odyssey,* as a prototype for his novel, although the end effect is far different from that of the earlier work. (early)

Objective

APPLICATION EXERCISE. Writing Sentences That Make Comparisons. Select five of the irregular modifiers from the list on page 514. Write a sentence for each, using the positive and comparative degrees of the modifier to make a comparison. Underline your modifiers.

SAMPLE: well
ANSWER: Susan speaks French well, but Marie speaks it better.

DOUBLE COMPARISONS

Do not make a double comparison by using *-er* or *-est* and *more* or *most.*

INCORRECT: Rhode Island is more smaller than Connecticut.
CORRECT: Rhode Island is smaller than Connecticut.

Objective

EXERCISE 3. Correcting Double Comparisons. Rewrite each of the following sentences, correcting the double comparison.

1. Mont Blanc is one of the most highest of the Swiss Alps, a favorite of tourists and mountain climbers.
2. Many tourists say that they have never seen more greater views than from the slopes of Mont Blanc.
3. The English poet Percy Bysshe Shelley memorialized Mont Blanc in one of his most memorablest poems.
4. The winter storms that occur in this area are among the most worst experienced in Europe.

5. The sight of the cable cars ascending the mountain is one of the most exciting excitingest views possible.

Suggested Answers appear above. Other answers are possible.

INCOMPLETE COMPARISONS

Do not make an incomplete or unclear comparison by omitting *other* or *else* when you compare one member of a group to the other members.

UNCLEAR: New York has more skyscrapers than any city in America.
CLEAR: New York has more skyscrapers than any **other** city in America.

UNCLEAR: Helen received more prizes than anyone.
CLEAR: Helen received more prizes than anyone **else.**

Be sure your comparisons are between like things.

UNCLEAR: The population of Morocco is less than Egypt. [One country's population is being compared illogically to a whole country.]
CLEAR: The population of Morocco is less than **Egypt's**. [The word *population* is understood after *Egypt's*.]
CLEAR: The population of Morocco is less than **that of Egypt.**

Objective

EXERCISE 4. Making Complete Comparisons. Rewrite each of the following sentences to correct the incomplete comparison.

1. The cheetah can run faster than any ^other mammal.
2. Its speed of over seventy miles per hour on short runs is greater than ^that of the lion or the jaguar.
3. Cheetahs have more distinctive tails than those of any ^other large cat.
4. On our safari to Africa, Henry spotted more cheetahs than anyone ^else.
5. Cheetahs are often difficult to spot, since they are more nocturnal than many ^other animals.

Suggested Answers appear above the items. Other answers are possible.

GOOD OR *WELL*; *BAD* OR *BADLY*

Always use *good* as an adjective. *Well* may be used as an adverb of manner telling how ably something was done or as an adjective meaning "in good health."

Paul is a **good** violinist. [adjective]
Paul looks **good** in that sweater. [adjective after linking verb]
Paul plays the violin **well.** [adverb of manner]
Paul is not **well** this week because of a cold. [adjective meaning "in good health"]

Always use *bad* as an adjective. Therefore, *bad* is used after linking verbs. Use *badly* as an adverb. *Badly* usually follows action verbs.

The player made a **bad** throw. [adjective]
The broccoli smelled **bad**. [adjective following linking verb]
I feel **bad** about losing that money. [adjective following linking verb]
Her nose is bleeding **badly**. [adverb following action verb]

Objective

EXERCISE 5. Choosing the Correct Modifier. On your paper complete the following sentences by correctly filling the blank with either *good, well, bad,* or *badly.*

1. A person who studies ___well___ can be confident of making good grades on examinations in college.
2. Doing poorly on an examination can make any student feel ___bad___.
3. ___Good___ organization is essential to studying effectively.
4. A ___badly___ organized study schedule can cause you to lose a great deal of precious time.
5. A ___good___ schedule allows enough time for the points and subjects that you find difficult to grasp.
6. Even a student who is doing ___well___ should give some thought to structuring study time.
7. If you start out ___badly___ in a course, there is all the more reason to budget more time for studying that subject.
8. Most people feel ___good___ when they go into an examination if they know that they have devoted sufficient time to studying.
9. You must know the material very ___well___ if you expect to receive top marks.
10. Some students perform ___badly___ on examinations if they are unduly nervous on the day of the test.

DOUBLE NEGATIVES

In general do not use a **double negative**, two negative words in the same clause. Use only one negative word to express a negative idea.

INCORRECT: I didn't hear ~~no~~ noise.
CORRECT: I didn't hear any noise.

INCORRECT: She hasn't had ~~no~~ visitors.
CORRECT: She hasn't had any visitors.
CORRECT: She has had no visitors.

INCORRECT: He never looks at ~~no~~ cartoons.
CORRECT: He never looks at any cartoons.
CORRECT: He looks at no cartoons.

Objective

EXERCISE 6. Avoiding Double Negatives. On your paper rewrite each of the following sentences, eliminating the double negative.

1. Serious dieters do not eat ~~no~~ any snacks during the day.
2. They lose weight by not eating ~~no~~ desserts.
3. Some people on a diet, when faced with the temptation of desserts, cann~~o~~t do nothing.
4. They say to themselves that they will diet tomorrow, and they ne~~v~~er deny themselves nothing.
5. To their dismay, these dieters discover that they never lose ~~no~~ any weight!

Suggested Answers appear above. Other answers are possible.

MISPLACED AND DANGLING MODIFIERS

Place modifiers as close as possible to the words they modify in order to make the meaning of the sentence clear.

Misplaced modifiers modify the wrong word or seem to modify more than one word in a sentence. To correct a sentence with a misplaced modifier, move the modifier as close as possible to the word it modifies.

MISPLACED: The beaches of Martinique impress many tourists **with their beautiful, calm surf.** [prepositional phrase]

CLEAR: The beaches of Martinique, **with their beautiful, calm surf,** impress many tourists.

MISPLACED: The lifeguard revived the swimmer **using first aid.** [participial phrase]

CLEAR: **Using first aid,** the lifeguard revived the swimmer.

Sometimes a misplaced modifier can be corrected by rephrasing the sentence.

MISPLACED: **Blowing from the north,** the pines were tossed by the wind.

CLEAR: The pines were tossed by the wind **which blew from the north.**

CLEAR: **Blowing from the north,** the wind tossed the pines.

Dangling modifiers seem to modify no word at all. To correct a sentence with a dangling modifier, you must supply a word the dangling phrase can sensibly modify.

DANGLING: **Excavating the site,** a new Roman temple was discovered.

CLEAR: **Excavating the site,** archaeologists discovered a new Roman temple.

Be sure to place the modifier *only* close to the word you wish it to modify, or the meaning of your sentence may be unclear.

UNCLEAR: Jean **only** has band practice on Tuesday. [Does she have nothing else to do on Tuesday or no band practice on any day but Tuesday? Or is Jean the only person (in a group) who has band practice on Tuesday?]

CLEAR: Jean has **only** band practice on Tuesday. [not French class or play rehearsals]

CLEAR: Jean has band practice **only** on Tuesday. [not on any other day of the week]

Objective

EXERCISE 7. Correcting Misplaced and Dangling Modifiers. On your paper rewrite the following sentences to correct the misplaced or dangling modifiers.

1. Blue jeans are now worn by people all over the world, created in California during the Gold Rush.
2. Guaranteed not to rip, gold prospectors liked jeans for their durability.
3. Designed originally for rough conditions, only prospectors and laborers at first wore denim pants.
4. Jeans first gained popularity in the West, worn by cowboys for work and for dress wear.
5. No longer associated with bucking broncos, men and women alike now consider jeans to be high fashion.

26 CHAPTER
Glossary of Specific Usage Items

The glossary that follows presents some particularly troublesome matters of preferred usage. The glossary will give you guidance, for example, in choosing between two words that are often confused. It will also make you aware of certain words and expressions that you should avoid completely when speaking or writing for school and business purposes.

a, an Use the article *a* when the word that follows begins with a consonant sound, including a sounded *h*: *a rocket, a helicopter.* Use *an* when the word that follows begins with a vowel sound or an unsounded *h*: *an endowment, an heir.* Use *a* before a word that begins with the "yew" sound: *a eucalyptus, a union.*

a lot, alot This expression is always written as two words and means "a large amount." Some authorities suggest avoiding it altogether in formal English.

> **A lot** of people attended the final game of the season.

a while, awhile *A while* is made up of an article and a noun. *In* and *for* often come before *a while,* forming a prepositional phrase. *Awhile* is an adverb.

> The musicians paused for **a while**.
> The musicians will pause **in a while**.
> The musicians paused **awhile**.

accept, except *Accept* is a verb that means "to receive" or "to agree to." *Except* may be a preposition or a verb. As a preposition it means "but." As a verb it means "to leave out."

> Please **accept** my apologies.
> Everyone **except** Paul can attend the meeting.
> If you **except** Brazil, South America is a Spanish-speaking continent.

adapt, adopt Adapt means "to change something so that it can be used for another purpose" or "to adjust." *Adopt* means "to take something for one's own."

> It was difficult to **adapt** the play for a young audience.
> Dinosaurs became extinct because they could not **adapt** to a changing environment.
> The general must **adopt** a new strategy to win this battle.

advice, advise *Advice* is a noun that means "helpful opinion." *Advise* is a verb that means "to give advice or offer counsel."

> Cheryl asked her guidance counselor for **advice** in choosing a college and hoped he would **advise** her well.

affect, effect Although *affect* and *effect* sound nearly the same, they should not be confused. *Affect* is a verb that means "to cause a change in, to influence." *Effect* may be a noun or a verb. As a noun it means "result." As a verb it means "to bring about or accomplish."

> This information will certainly **affect** our decision.
> What **effect** will this information have on your decision?
> What could **effect** such a change in her outlook?

ain't *Ain't* is unacceptable in speaking and writing unless you are quoting somebody's exact words. Instead use *I am not, she is not, he is not*, and so on.

all ready, already The two words *all ready* should not be confused with the adverb *already*. *All ready* means "completely ready." *Already* means "before or by this time."

> The boys were **all ready** to take the test, but by the time they arrived, the test had **already** begun.

Objective

EXERCISE 1. Making Usage Choices. For each of the following sentences, write the correct choice of the two expressions in parentheses.

1. Ragtime played (a/an) important role in the development of American music.
2. First popular in the early 1900s, it enjoyed a revival for (a while/awhile) in the 1970s.
3. Many musical phrases used in early jazz were (adapted/adopted) from ragtime.
4. Ragtime also (affected/effected) the music of classical composers such as Charles Ives, Igor Stravinsky, and Claude Debussy.
5. Scott Joplin had perhaps the greatest (affect/effect) on ragtime.
6. Joplin's "Maple Leaf Rag," (all ready/already) well-known by 1900, helped popularize ragtime throughout the United States.
7. The public quickly (accepted/excepted) Joplin's later piece, "The

Entertainer," which became one of ragtime's most famous numbers.

8. (A lot/Alot) of ragtime pieces have been reproduced on piano rolls for player pianos.
9. In his published piano music, Joplin offered excellent (advice/advise) on how to play ragtime.
10. Although ragtime compositions (ain't/aren't) easy to play, they remain highly popular with pianists today.

---

all right, alright Write this expression as two words. Although often seen in print as *alright,* most authorities prefer *all right.*

> Is it **all right** for the baby to have ice cream?

all together, altogether Use *all together* to mean "in a group." Use the adverb *altogether* to mean "completely" or "on the whole."

> They decided to leave **all together,** but it was **altogether** impossible for them to fit into one car.

allusion, illusion *Allusion* means "an indirect reference"; *illusion* is a false idea or appearance.

> The candidate made a disparaging **allusion** to his rival's plan for lowering taxes.
> It is an **illusion** that taxes can be lowered this year.

and etc. Use *etc.* without the *and. Etc.* is an abbreviation for the Latin expression *et cetera,* which means "and the rest." To put *and* before this would be repetitive.

> At the beginning of the school year, we buy paper, pens, pencils, **etc.**

anywheres, everywheres Write these words and others like them without an *s*: *anywhere, everywhere, somewhere.*

bad, badly See Chapter 25.

being as, being that Many people use these expressions informally to mean "because" or "since." In writing use *because* or *since.*

> **Since** the weather is bad, they have decided to stay at home.
> **Because** the weather is bad, we have decided not to go.

Objective

EXERCISE 2. Making Usage Choices. For each of the following sentences, write the correct choice of the two expressions in parentheses.

1. It is certainly an (allusion/illusion) to imagine that patchwork quilts are a thing of the past.

2. Today Americans (everywhere/everywheres) are rediscovering these beautiful and practical coverlets.
3. Patchwork quilts were made by early Americans who needed warm covers (bad/badly).
4. They discovered that the colorful quilts were not merely (all right/alright) but quite extraordinary as bed covers.
5. Most patchwork patterns have quaint names—Log Cabin, Sunburst, Nine Patch, Grandma's Flower Garden, (and etc./etc.)
6. Some quilt patterns contain symbols that make (allusions/illusions) to important events of life, such as birth and marriage.
7. (All together/Altogether), there are hundreds of different patchwork patterns.
8. (Being that/Because) it is difficult and time-consuming to quilt a coverlet, people often work together at quilting parties, called quilting bees.
9. When a number of people work (all together/altogether), a quilt can be completed quite quickly.
10. (Being that/Since) some quilts are quite elaborately and beautifully made, it is not uncommon to see them used as decorative wall hangings.

beside, besides These are two different words with different meanings. *Beside* means "at the side of" or "next to." *Besides* means "moreover" or "in addition to."

> Who is that little girl sitting **beside** Joanne?
> **Besides** Sergio, I am inviting James, Karl, and Luiz.
> Sonia is too busy to attend the play; **besides**, she is feeling ill.

between, among Use *between* in referring to two persons or things, or use it to compare one person or thing to other persons or things. *Between* may also be used when referring to more than two persons or things when they are considered when a close relationship.

> Lucinda sat **between** Tamara and Don.
> What is the difference **between** this novel and the author's previous books?
> ANZUS is a treaty **between** Australia, New Zealand, and the United States.

Use **among** when you are referring to three or more persons or things or when you are indicating a group rather than separate persons or things.

> The four women talked **among** themselves.
> This soprano is **among** the finest singers in the world.

borrow, lend, loan *Borrow* and *lend* have opposite meanings. *Borrow* is a verb meaning "to take something with the understanding that it must be returned." *Lend* is a verb meaning "to give something with the understanding that it will be returned." *Loan* is a noun. It may be used as a verb, but most authorities prefer *lend*.

May I **borrow** your car? [verb]
Will you **lend** me your bike? [verb]
Jessica will ask the bank for a **loan**. [noun]

bring, take Use *bring* to mean "to carry to" or "to cause to come with." Use *take* to mean "to carry away" or "to cause to go with." *Bring* is related to *come* as *take* is related to *go*.

Will you **bring** me a pineapple when you **come** back from Maui?
Don't forget to **take** your camera when you **go** to Hawaii.

can, may *Can* indicates the ability to do something. *May* expresses permission to do something.

You **may** keep my typewriter till Monday.
Laura is so strong that she **can** lift a typewriter with one hand.

can't hardly, can't scarcely These terms are considered double negatives because *hardly* and *scarcely* by themselves have a negative meaning. Therefore, avoid using *hardly* and *scarcely* with *not* or *n't*.

That story is so outlandish that I **can hardly** believe it.
It is so dark that I **can scarcely** see the path.

continual, continuous *Continual* describes action that occurs over and over, but with pauses between occurrences. *Continuous* describes something that goes on in space or time with no interruption.

The **continual** banging of the door and the **continuous** blare from the TV made it difficult to concentrate.

could of, might of, would of After *could, might, should*, and *would*, you need another verb form, not the preposition *of*. Use the helping verb *have* after *could, might, must, should*, or *would*.

I **would have** gone to the meeting if I had known it would be so important.

Objective

EXERCISE 3. Making Usage Choices. For each of the following sentences, write the correct choice of the two expressions in parentheses.

1. At a potluck supper people eat and chat for hours; the event is one of (continual/continuous) enjoyment.
2. Lively conversation takes place (among/between) the guests.
3. (Beside/Besides) enjoying good conversation, the guests can sample a great many foods.
4. The guests (can/may) bring a variety of dishes to the supper.
5. Often the table (can scarcely/can't scarcely) hold all the food.
6. The host may need to (borrow/lend) extra plates or cups.
7. (Between/Among) the main course and the dessert, people like to pause for conversation.
8. Years ago, the dessert (might have/might of) been homemade ice cream, hand-cranked by the guests.
9. Today's potluck suppers may not have homemade ice cream, but at least one guest usually (brings/takes) an apple pie.
10. When the supper is over, there is still so much food that guests often (bring/take) some dishes home.

---

credible, creditable, credulous *Credible* means "believable." *Creditable* means "praiseworthy." *Credulous* means "ready to believe or accept without proof; gullible."

> A realistic novel should have a **credible** plot.
> On her first day in the emergency room, the intern did a **creditable** job in treating the patients.
> Brad is so **credulous** that he believes everything he reads.

data *Data* is the plural form of the Latin *datum.* In informal English *data* is usually used with a singular verb. In formal English it should be followed by a plural verb.

> The available **data** seem to support the theory of black holes.

different from *Different from* should be used before nouns, pronouns, and gerunds.

> A canoe is **different from** a rowboat.
> Trout fishing is **different from** deep-sea fishing.

disinterested, uninterested The word *interested* can mean "involved or concerned for one's personal advantage"; *disinterested* is the opposite of this. *Disinterested* means "not influenced by selfish motives" or "impartial." *Interested* can also mean "curious" or "concerned." *Uninterested,* which is the opposite, means "not curious," "paying no attention," "not concerned."

> Umpires must be **disinterested** in the outcome of a game, but they cannot be **uninterested**.

doesn't, don't *Doesn't* is the contraction of *does not* and should be used with *he, she, it,* and singular nouns. *Don't* is the contraction of *do not* and should be used with *I, you, we, they,* and plural nouns.

> I **don't** like sweet apples.
> Margie **doesn't** like them either.

emigrate, immigrate *Emigrate* means "to go from one country to another to live." *Immigrate* means "to come to a country to settle there." Use *from* with *emigrate* and *to* or *into* with *immigrate.*

> Many people **emigrated** from Europe before the turn of the century.
> Thousands of Irish people **immigrated** to the United States during the potato famine of the 1840s.

enthuse This verb is derived from the noun *enthusiasm*, but it is not yet accepted in formal English. Use *be enthusiastic* or *become enthusiastic* instead. (A similar verb to avoid is *burgle*, which comes from the noun *burglar*; use *burglarize* instead.)

> The critics **were enthusiastic** about the film.

farther, further *Farther* should be used to refer to physical distance. *Further* should be used to refer to time or degree.

> My house is **farther** from school than yours.
> I cannot give you **further** information about the course.

Objective

EXERCISE 4. Making Usage Choices. For each of the following sentences, write the correct choice of the two expressions in parentheses.

1. Many people have (emigrated/immigrated) to the United States throughout the country's history.
2. In fact, data (show/shows) that more people have come here to settle than to any other country in the world.
3. Immigrants have made (credible/creditable/credulous) contributions to the life of the country.
4. Jacob Riis, humanitarian and journalist, (emigrated/immigrated) from Denmark in 1870.
5. American moviegoers have given (enthused/enthusiastic) responses to the suspense thrillers of British-born Alfred Hitchcock.
6. Hitchcock received (farther/further) recognition when he was knighted in 1980.
7. Many people (doesn't/don't) realize that the actresses Ingrid Bergman and Marlene Dietrich immigrated to the United States.
8. Russian-born George Balanchine came to the United States and developed a ballet style very different (from/than) that of classical ballet.

9. Most people were (disinterested/uninterested) in the fate of Yosemite Valley until John Muir brought it to national attention.
10. Muir's (disinterested/uninterested) efforts on behalf of forest conservation brought about the creation of Yosemite National Park.

fewer, less Use *fewer* when referring to nouns that can be counted. Use *less* when referring to nouns that cannot be counted. *Less* is also used to refer to figures used as a single amount or quantity.

> The store sells **fewer** ice-cream cones during the winter than during the summer months.
> People usually eat **less** ice cream during the winter than in summer.
> The flight to Paris took **less** than six hours. [Six hours is treated as a single period of time.]
> The dollar is worth **less** than ten French francs. [The money is treated as a single sum.]

good, well See Chapter 25.

had of Do not use *of* between *had* and a past participle.

> I wish I **had** seen him before he left for Europe.

hanged, hung *Hanged* and *hung* are the past-tense and past-participle forms of the verb *hang.* Use *hanged* when you mean "to put to death by hanging." Use *hung* in all other instances.

> Phil **hung** the picture above his desk.
> The soldier who had deserted was caught and **hanged**.

in, into, in to In formal English, use *in* to mean "inside" or "within" and *into* to indicate movement or direction from outside to a point within. *In to* is made up of an adverb (*in*) followed by a preposition (*to*) and should be carefully distinguished from the preposition *into.*

> The president was working **in** his office.
> A secretary walked **into** the office and greeted him.
> Every morning the secretary goes **in to** the president and discusses the day's agenda.

ingenious, ingenuous *Ingenious* means "clever," "inventive," or "skillful." *Ingenuous* means "frank and open," or "having a childlike innocence or simplicity."

> Karen came up with an **ingenious** solution to the chess problem.
> Her **ingenuous** manner immediately put me at my ease.

irregardless, regardless Use *regardless.* The prefix *ir-* and the suffix *-less* both have negative meanings. When used together, they produce a double negative, which is incorrect.

> Ron maintains an optimistic outlook, **regardless** of unfavorable circumstances.

this kind, these kinds *Kind* is singular. Therefore, the singular form, *this* or *that,* modifies it. *This* and *that* should also be used with *sort* and *type* (*this type, that type, this sort, that sort*). *Kinds* is plural. Therefore, the plural form, *these* or *those*, modifies it. Use *these* and *those* with the plural nouns *sorts* and *types.*

> **This kind** of dog is easy to train. [singular]
> **These kinds** of dogs are easy to train. [plural]

lay, lie These words are often confused. *Lay* means "to put," or "to place"; it takes a direct object. *Lie* means "to recline" or "to be positioned"; it never takes an object.

> Please **lay** the book on the table.
> The cat loves to **lie** in the sun.

Problems arise particularly in using the principal parts of these verbs. Notice, for example, that the past tense of *lie* is *lay.* Learn all the principal parts of these verbs.

BASIC FORM:	lay	lie
PRESENT PARTICIPLE:	laying	lying
PAST FORM:	laid	lay
PAST PARTICIPLE:	laid	lain

> Max **laid** the packages on the chair.
> The cat **lay** next to the fireplace.

Objective

EXERCISE 5. Making Usage Choices. For each of the following sentences, write the correct choice of the two expressions in parentheses.

1. It does not take an (ingenious/ingenuous) mechanic to follow home-repair manuals.
2. In fact, some meticulous people can do home-repair jobs just as (good/well) as a professional.
3. It is always wise to consider the cost before calling a plumber or a carpenter (in/into/in to) your home.
4. Many people are quick to call for a specialist (irregardless/regardless) of the problem.
5. Then they may incur expenses that they could have avoided if they (had/had of) considered the problem carefully.
6. Fixing a broken drawer or a clogged drain poses (fewer/less) difficulties than many people imagine.

7. Many homeowners also find that they can (lay/lie) new tiles or linoleum themselves.
8. If a new door needs to be (hanged/hung), however, it would be wise to call a carpenter.
9. Installing new fixtures (in/into/in to) the kitchen or bathroom can also become too complicated for the average homeowner.
10. (This kind/These kinds) of repair, which takes more time and expertise, requires professional assistance.

---

learn, teach These words have different meanings. *Learn* means "to receive knowledge," and *teach* means "to give knowledge."

Many young children easily **learn** a second language.
These instructors **teach** Spanish.

leave, let *Leave* means "to go away," and *let* means "to allow" or "to permit." Some people use the expressions *leave alone* and *let alone* to mean the same thing, but they have different meanings. *Leave alone* means "to go away from," and *let alone* means "to permit to be alone" or "to refrain from disturbing."

The plane to Phoenix **leaves** in two hours.
Please **let** us help with the dishes.
The baby will cry if we **leave** him alone.
If the children do not **let** the cat alone, she will scratch them.

like, as *Like* is a preposition and introduces a prepositional phrase. *As* and *as if* are subordinating conjunctions and introduce subordinate clauses.

He looks **like** a nervous person.
He felt nervous, **as** he does before every performance.
He looks **as if** he feels nervous.

loose, lose Use *loose* to mean "free," "not firmly attached," or "not fitting tightly." Use *lose* when you mean "to have no longer," "to misplace," or "to fail to win."

That button is **loose**, and you are sure to **lose** it.

passed, past *Passed* is the past tense and the past participle of the verb *to pass. Past* can be an adjective, a preposition, an adverb, or a noun.

The time **passed** quickly. [verb]
Denise has grown during the **past** months. [adjective]
The truck drove **past** our house this morning. [preposition]
The truck shifted gears as it went **past**. [adverb]
All of that happened in the **past**. [noun]

persecute, prosecute *Persecute* and *prosecute* should not be confused. *Persecute* means "annoy constantly" or "treat a person or group cruelly or unfairly." *Prosecute* means "to bring a case before a court of law for trial."

> Sir Thomas More was **persecuted** for his beliefs.
> He was **prosecuted** and convicted of high treason.

precede, proceed Use *precede* when you mean "to go or come before." Use *proceed* when you mean "to continue" or "to move along."

> An elegant dinner **preceded** the concert.
> The speaker **proceeded** to the dais and began her lecture.

raise, rise The verb *raise* means "to cause to move upward"; it always takes an object. The verb *rise* means "to go up"; it is an intransitive verb and does not take an object.

> Many people **raise** their voices when they become angry.
> Antonio **rises** every morning at six and runs two miles.

reason is because Do not use this expression. Since *because* means "for the reason that," it is repetitious. Use either the *reason is that* or *because.*

> The **reason** Jane cannot come to the party **is that** she will be away.
> Jane cannot come to the party **because** she will be away.

Objective

EXERCISE 6. Making Usage Choices. For each of the following sentences, write the correct choice of the two expressions in parentheses.

1. A family reunion is (like/as) a page from the past.
2. As family members recall their favorite memories, they are surprised at how much time has (passed/past).
3. Some relatives no longer look (as/like) they once did.
4. In the afternoon, parents (leave/let) their children play games such as tug-of-war and hide-and-seek.
5. There is hardly a child who has not at some time felt (persecuted/prosecuted) by his or her cousins during such games.
6. Later, everyone (precedes/proceeds) to the dining room for supper.
7. When the family finally (raises/rises) from the table, the hour is late.
8. After supper the cooks often (learn/teach) one another old recipes.
9. At the end of the reunion, the family promises not to (loose/lose) touch.
10. The reason family reunions are popular is (because/that) they bring the family together again.

respectfully, respectively Use these words carefully. *Respectfully* means "with respect." *Respectively* means "in the order named."

> The audience listened **respectfully** to the Nobel laureate.
> Peggy and Michael are, **respectively**, author and editor of the book.

says, said *Says* is the third-person singular of *say. Said* is the past tense of *say.* Be careful not to use *says* when you mean *said.*

> Yesterday he **said** that he would meet us outside the theater.
> He always **says** he will be on time, but he never is.

sit, set *Sit* means "to place oneself in a sitting position." *Sit* rarely takes an object. *Set* means "to place" or "to put" and usually takes an object. *Set* may also be an intransitive verb when it is used with *sun* to mean the sun is "going down" or "sinking out of sight." When *set* is used in this way, it does not take an object.

> Mother and Father **sit** at opposite ends of the table.
> Please **set** this casserole dish on the table.
> We watched the sun **set** into tumbling layers of orange and red.

slow, slowly *Slow* is an adjective that is occasionally used as an adverb in expressions such as *Drive slow* and *Go slow. Slowly* is an adverb and is preferred in formal writing.

> Ann's typing is very **slow**. [adjective]
> Ellen spoke **slowly** because she had forgotten her lines. [adverb]

than, then *Than* is a conjunction used to introduce the second element in a comparison; it also shows exception.

> Yesterday was busier **than** today.
> We have had no visitors other **than** Mrs. Peterson.

Then is an adverb that means "at that time," "soon afterward," "the time mentioned," "at another time," "for that reason," "in that case," and "besides."

> Pamela was in high school **then**.
> The musicians tuned their instruments and **then** played.
> By **then** they had already left town.
> Colleen has been to Europe twice; she visited England and Scotland, **then** she toured France and Italy.
> She found a pleasant hotel, and **then** felt contented.
> Salads are refreshing, and **then** they are healthful.

this here, that there Avoid using *here* and *there* after *this* and *that.* Use only *this* and *that.*

Debbie wants to buy **this** sweater.
Please give me **that** pencil on the desk.

who, whom See Chapter 24.

Objective

EXERCISE 7. Making Usage Choices. For each of the following sentences, write the correct choice of the two expressions in parentheses.

1. Quite often, more (than/then) one person has been instrumental in an invention or discovery.
2. For example, there were many people (who/whom) contributed significantly to the invention of the automobile.
3. As early as 1690, Denis Papin, inventor of the pressure cooker, proposed a steam-powered vehicle in which people could (sit/set) and ride.
4. (This/This here) idea of Papin's was not realized until 1769, when Nicolas Cugnot successfully drove his steam-powered creation down a street in Paris.
5. Cugnot reached a speed of 2.5 miles per hour in his odd-looking contraption, and (then/than) collided with a tree.
6. Historians (respectfully/respectively) recognize two men, Gottlieb Daimler and Karl Benz, as the true fathers of the modern automobile.
7. These two men, neither of (who/whom) met the other, were both working on a gas-powered vehicle in 1885.
8. Later, after making successful trial runs with their inventions, each (said/says) that he was the actual inventor of the automobile.
9. (This/This here) rivalry had a surprising ending when in 1926 the companies started by Daimler and Benz merged.
10. Daimler's and Benz' companies were, (respectfully/respectively), Daimler and Benz; they merged to form the Mercedes-Benz Company.

REVIEW EXERCISE. Usage (Part 1). For each of the following sentences, write the correct choice of the two expressions in parentheses.

1. Field lacrosse is a sport that has become popular (between/among) both men and women in America.
2. At the beginning of the game, the referee (sets/sits) the ball in the center of the field.
3. The attackers are supposed to get the ball (in/into/in to) the net of the opposing team.
4. Three midfielders (bring/take) the ball toward the attackers.
5. Dodging the defending players, the attackers make (continual/continuous) attempts to score.
6. Skill and speed are especially important at (this/this here) point in the game.
7. In their attempts to score, the attacking team must be careful not to

(loose/lose) the ball to the defenders.

8. An attacker who is (anywhere/anywheres) near the goal may attempt to score.
9. None of the players (accept/except) the goalies may touch the ball with their hands.
10. (Beside/Besides) needing speed and agility, lacrosse players must be able to judge distance.
11. (Disinterested/Uninterested) referees oversee every aspect of the game.
12. In lacrosse, it is (all right/alright) for players to block one another with their bodies.
13. Referees are careful not to (leave/let) all the players bunch up at one end of the field.
14. Lacrosse is (a/an) French name for a game that originated with Native Americans.
15. *La crosse* means "the cross"; the term (might have/might of) referred to the stick used by each player.
16. Today, lacrosse is (all together/altogether) different from the game played by the Iroquois and Hurons.
17. It is still fast-paced, however, and players (ain't/aren't) allowed to set the ball down on the ground.
18. (Being that/Since) a lacrosse games lasts sixty minutes, players must have endurance.
19. People who know ice hockey will see that it is not very different (from/than) lacrosse.
20. Football players (who/whom) play lacrosse find that it develops their speed and agility.

REVIEW EXERCISE. Usage (Part 2). For each of the following sentences, write the correct choice of the two expressions in parentheses.

1. Many people who are not particularly interested in history become more (enthused/enthusiastic) when they visit restored villages.
2. History books describe how people in the (past/passed) probably lived.
3. Restored villages show people actually living (like/as) they did many years ago.
4. Obviously, there are (fewer/less) restored villages than there are history books.
5. The restored villages that exist, however, create a strong (allusion/illusion) of stepping into the past.
6. Restored villages are (everywhere/everywheres) in the United States.
7. They can be found in New England, the South, the West, (and etc./etc.)
8. In these restored villages, many (ingenious/ingenuous) methods are used to recreate the past.
9. Often, historians (advice/advise) the people doing the restorations.
10. In Old Town San Diego and Historic St. Augustine one can sample,

(respectfully/respectively), traditional Mexican dishes and old Spanish recipes.

11. St. Augustine, Florida, is the oldest (continual/continuous) settlement in the United States.
12. (Beside/Besides) the James River in Virginia are restored buildings from the Jamestown settlement.
13. The restoration of Williamsburg, Virginia, is (all together/altogether) impressive.
14. Walking through the streets of Williamsburg, visitors (can hardly/can't hardly) believe they are in the twentieth century.
15. The Pennsylvania Farm Museum of Landis Valley is especially important (being that/because) the Pennsylvania Dutch way of life is slowly changing.
16. These settlers (immigrated/emigrated) to the Pennsylvania area during the 1600s and 1700s.
17. Artisans at the ancient Cherokee village of Tsa-La-Gi, Oklahoma, are concerned about the (affect/effect) of modern civilization on their heritage.
18. In an effort to preserve their language, (a lot/alot) of these artisans speak only Cherokee.
19. At Plimoth Plantation, Massachusetts, restorers (respectfully/respectively) use the original spelling of the town's name.
20. Having left England because they were being (persecuted/prosecuted) for their religious beliefs, colonists established the town in 1620.

REVIEW EXERCISE. Usage (Part 3). For each of the following sentences, write the correct choice of the two expressions in parentheses.

1. (Irregardless/Regardless) of the dangers involved, many people are interested in cave exploration.
2. People grow interested when they (learn/teach) of the treasures supposedly hidden in caves.
3. Legends say that some pirates (laid/lay) their booty in caves hundreds of years ago.
4. Some cave explorers are (credible/creditable/credulous) enough to take these stories seriously.
5. Spelunkers—cave explorers—(precede/proceed) cautiously through caves, using headlamps and flashlights.
6. Since little or no sunlight enters a cave, spelunkers (cannot/may not) see without a good source of light.
7. An experienced spelunker (doesn't/don't) go into a cave without a hard hat and heavy clothing.
8. An improperly equipped spelunker could be (bad/badly) hurt.
9. Caves are the homes of unusual animals (like/as) blindfish, bats, and transparent crayfish.
10. These animals have (adapted/adopted) to their sunless world by developing keen senses of touch and smell.

11. Green plants, such as mosses and ferns, grow (good/well) in the outer parts of caves, where some sunlight penetrates.

12. (Farther/Further) back in a cave, fungi, which need no sunlight, may grow.

13. Caves also hold clues about life (like/as) it was thousands of years ago.

14. Archaeologists explore caves, gathering data that (help/helps) them understand how prehistoric people lived.

15. Rather (than/then) build shelters in the open, some prehistoric people lived in caves.

16. Archaeologists think that the reason cave dwellers chose to live at a cave's entrance is (because/that) the interior was too dark, cold, and damp.

17. People (who/whom) visit the Carlsbad Caverns in New Mexico will see some spectacular mineral formations.

18. (This kind/These kinds) of formations are called stalagmites and stalactites.

19. Water seeping (slow/slowly) through a cave deposits the minerals, creating the formations.

20. Stalactites hang from the ceiling of the cave; stalagmites (raise/rise) from the floor.

CHAPTERS 22–26 USAGE

CHAPTER 22 VERB TENSES, VOICE, AND MOOD

Principal Parts of Regular and Irregular Verbs (pages 475–478) Select the verb part that correctly completes each sentence.

1. Public television has ____ fine television programs for years.
   (a) offer **(b)** offering **(c)** offered
2. PBS stations recently have ____ severe federal budget cuts.
   (a) beared **(b)** bore **(c)** bored **(d)** borne
3. When federal contributions ____, viewers were asked to increase their contributions.
   (a) shrinked **(b)** shrank **(c)** shrunken **(d)** shrinking

Tense of Verbs (pages 478–484) Complete each sentence by choosing the verb tense requested in capital letters.

4. *Masterpiece Theatre* (PRESENT PERFECT PROGRESSIVE) for over ten years.
   (a) has been airing **(c)** is airing
   (b) had been airing **(d)** will have been airing
5. The series (PRESENT PERFECT) to the television screen such classic novels as *Anna Karenina* and *Pride and Prejudice.*
   (a) has been bringing **(b)** brings **(c)** brought **(d)** has brought
6. *Upstairs, Downstairs* (PAST) the life of wealthy people and their servants in turn-of-the-century England.
   (a) depicted **(b)** had depicted **(c)** was depicting **(d)** depicts
7. Despite stiff competition, *Masterpiece Theatre* (PRESENT EMPHATIC) a loyal viewing audience.
   (a) has attracted **(b)** is attracting **(c)** does attract **(d)** did attract

Compatibility of Tenses (pages 487–488)

8. In which of the following sentences are the tenses compatible?
   (a) After it had succeeded in a half-hour format, *The MacNeil/Lehrer Report* expanded to one hour.
   (b) Young children watch *Sesame Street* and have enjoyed its Muppet characters.
   (c) Since they first appeared on *Sesame Street*, the Muppets become big stars.

Voice and Mood of Verbs (pages 488–490) Complete each sentence by choosing the appropriate verb.

9. The science program *Cosmos* ____ by Carl Sagan.
   (a) hosted **(b)** was hosted **(c)** were hosted **(d)** be hosted
10. If I ____ home, I would watch *Nova.*
   (a) am **(b)** was **(c)** were **(d)** be

Answers: **1.** c; **2.** d; **3.** b; **4.** a; **5.** d; **6.** a; **7.** c; **8.** a; **9.** b; **10.** c

Writing for Review Write a paragraph relating an incident that happened to you in the past. Check to be sure that you have used verbs correctly.

CHAPTER 23 SUBJECT–VERB AGREEMENT

Agreement in Number (pages 491–498) Indicate the verb that agrees with its subject in each of the following sentences.

1. Among the many recent urban redevelopment projects in America (a) is/(b) are the South Street Seaport Museum in New York City.
2. A group of Dutch colonial buildings along with wharves and other waterfront structures (a) stands/(b) stand in the South Street area.
3. Each of these buildings (a) has/(b) have been restored.
4. New and diverse restaurants are one of the many attractions that (a) draws/(b) draw tourists to South Street.
5. A rare shell or a ship's flag (a) is/(b) are on sale at one of the shops.

Answers: **1.** a; **2.** a; **3.** a; **4.** b; **5.** a

Writing for Review Write a short description on a topic of your choice. Demonstrate your mastery of subject-verb agreement by including in your description various compound subjects and intervening phrases.

CHAPTER 24 USING PRONOUNS CORRECTLY

Personal Pronouns Usage (pages 500–503) Indicate the correct case of the personal pronoun in each sentence.

1. Mike and (a) I/(b) me run a carpet-cleaning company.
2. The owners of the company are Mike and (a) I/(b) me.
3. The fees are split between the owners, Mike and (a) I/(b) me.
4. Aunt Jody gave Mike and (a) I/(b) me her industrial vacuum cleaner.
5. The vacuum cleaner is as heavy as (a) she/(b) her.

Who* and *Whom (pages 504–506) Indicate the correct case of the pronoun.

6. I wonder (a) who/(b) whom our next customer will be.

Pronoun–Antecedent Agreement pages (506–508) Indicate the correct pronoun.

7. The head of the bakers' union has (a) their/(b) her office downstairs.
8. Before a union declares a strike, (a) it/(b) they must poll members.

Agreement with Indefinite Pronoun Antecedents (pages 508–509)

9. Which of the following sentences has correct agreement between pronouns?
   (a) Both of the unions asked their members to meet on Thursday.
   (b) Each of the unions polled their members.
   (c) Only one of the two unions held their annual elections.

Clear Pronoun References (pages 510–511)

10. In which sentence does the pronoun clearly agree with its antecedent?
    (a) When the campers first met the counselors, they were friendly.
    (b) The new campers complained about the food, which made the counselors laugh.
    (c) The counselors organized a swimming race, which Lola won.

Answers: **1.** a; **2.** a; **3.** b; **4.** b; **5.** a; **6.** a; **7.** b; **8.** a; **9.** a; **10.** c

Writing for Review Write a paragraph describing your family's activities during a summer vacation. Demonstrate your mastery of pronoun usage by including a variety of personal and indefinite pronouns in your paragraph.

CHAPTER 25 USING MODIFIERS CORRECTLY

The Three Degrees of Comparison (pages 512–513) Select the correct comparative or superlative form in each sentence.

1. Of the three islands, Antigua has the ____ beaches.
   (a) more attractive (b) attractiver (c) most attractive (d) attractivest
2. Of the two outermost planets, Neptune is the ____.
   (a) larger (b) more large (c) largest (d) most large
3. Pluto is the planet ____ from the sun.
   (a) farrest (b) more far (c) farther (d) farthest

Double and Incomplete Comparisons (pages 515–516) Indicate the correct form of the modifier in each sentence.

4. The space shuttle landed (a) sooner/(b) more sooner than planned.
5. Astronauts travel farther than (a) anyone/(b) anyone else.
6. I like astronomy better than (a) any/(b) any other science.

Double Negatives (pages 517–518) Indicate the correct usage.

7. I have (a) read/(b) not read nothing about the recent space launch.

Misplaced and Dangling Modifiers (pages 518–519) For each pair indicate the sentence in which modifiers are placed correctly.

8. (a) Visiting Florida, Cape Canaveral is very interesting.
   (b) Visiting Florida, tourists find Cape Canaveral very interesting.
9. (a) Cape Canaveral attracts many visitors with the Kennedy Space Center.
   (b) Cape Canaveral with the Kennedy Space Center attracts many visitors.
10. (a) Only last month we stopped at Cape Canaveral.
    (b) We only stopped at Cape Canaveral last month.

Answers: **1.** c; **2.** a; **3.** d; **4.** a; **5.** b; **6.** b; **7.** a; **8.** b; **9.** b; **10.** a

Writing for Review Write a paragraph in which you compare one thing with another, such as the city with the country. In your paragraph use modifiers to make comparisons.

CHAPTER 26 GLOSSARY OF SPECIFIC USAGE ITEMS

Preferred Usage (pages 520–535) Indicate the preferred usage of the choices given in each sentence.

1. Celia could not find him (a) anywhere/(b) anywheres.
2. The writer (a) adapted/(b) adopted her book for the screen.
3. Poe's poems make many (a) allusions/(b) illusions to mythology.
4. The camera bag contained film, flashbulbs, (a) etc./(b) and etc.
5. Snails crawl (a) slow/(b) slowly along the ground.
6. Columnist Ann Landers gives (a) advice/(b) advise to readers.
7. The child was naive and (a) credible/(b) creditable/(c) credulous.
8. The data (a) shows/(b) show that many viruses are airborne.
9. Many Americans (a) enthused/(b) were enthusiastic about the tax cut.
10. Buffalo, New York, experienced (a) continual/(b) continuous blizzards last winter.
11. Many notorious outlaws of the West were (a) hanged/(b) hung for their crimes.

12. During the social unrest of the 1840s, many people (a) emigrated/(b) immigrated from Germany.
13. An arbitrator in a labor–management dispute must be a(n) (a) disinterested/(b) uninterested party.
14. New medical discoveries have (a) affected/(b) effected the average life expectancy of Americans.
15. Some people cannot (a) accept/(b) except the facts no matter how clearly those facts are presented.
16. (a) Can/(b) May I borrow the car?
17. The sign said that trespassers will be (a) persecuted/(b) prosecuted.
18. I (a) can hardly/ (b) can't hardly read the small print.
19. The basketball finals attracted (a) alot/(b) a lot of viewers.
20. After waiting in line, we went (a) into/(b) in to the movie theater.

Answers: **1.** a; **2.** a; **3.** a; **4.** a; **5.** b; **6.** a; **7.** c; **8.** b; **9.** b; **10.** a; **11.** a; **12.** a; **13.** a; **14.** a; **15.** a; **16.** b; **17.** b; **18.** a; **19.** b; **20.** a

Writing for Review Demonstrate your knowledge of the dinstinction between the terms in each of the following pairs by writing a sentence for each term.

all together, altogether   farther, further
between, among   lend, loan

UNIT VIII
Mechanics

Kiki and Ellen, we're looking for the map. Why? It's not here.
Kiki and Ellen were looking for the map. Why, it's not here!

How do you know that you should read these two lines differently? You know because of the punctuation and capitalization that each contains. When you speak, your voice rises, dips, speeds up, slows down, and thus helps your reader to follow your ideas. When you write, on the other hand, you must rely on the visual clues of capitalization and punctuation to tell your reader how you want your writing to be read. To make your writing meaningful and expressive, you add to it such signals as commas for "Brief Pause," periods for "Full Stop," parentheses for "Short Detour," and italics for "Extra Emphasis." Sometimes the clarity of your sentences will depend on your use of capitalization and punctuation. For example, "telephone bill" means something entirely different from "Telephone, Bill?" or "Telephone *Bill*!"

Many rules of capitalization and punctuation are matters of tradition. For example, tradition indicates when to capitalize the first letter of a word. Traditions, or conventions, vary from place to place and change over time. At one time people who wrote English capitalized all nouns. This practice continues today in German, which shares a common linguistic history with English. In English, however, we no longer capitalize common nouns. Here is another example of change over time: If you compare a contemporary novel to one written during the Victorian period, you will find that the modern novel uses much less punctuation.

The following two chapters outline the basic rules of mechanics—the technical aspects of writing—as they are practiced by writers in the United States today. You will find that you are already familiar with many of these rules. However, you may also find that you need to study others carefully in order to correctly capitalize and punctuate the various kinds of writing that you are doing now. Review these chapters, and refer to them in particular when you proofread your writing.

CHAPTER 27 Capitalization

CAPITALIZATION OF THE PRONOUN *I*

Capitalize the pronoun *I*.

> This week **I** am on vacation.

CAPITALIZATION OF SENTENCES

Capitalize the first word of every sentence, including the first word of a direct quotation that is a complete sentence.

> **D**id you know that Beethoven was completely deaf by the time he composed his Ninth Symphony?
>
> **T**he poet Edna St. Vincent Millay responded to a Beethoven symphony by writing, "**S**weet sounds, oh beautiful music, do not cease!"

Capitalize a sentence in parentheses that stands by itself.

> Scott Joplin composed ragtime piano music. (**R**agtime music was originally called rag music.)

Do not capitalize a sentence in parentheses that is contained within another sentence.

> Fiddles and banjos (**t**he piano was used later) were the original instruments in a ragtime band.

Do not capitalize quoted words that cannot stand as a complete sentence.

> The British writer Thomas Carlyle said that music is "**t**he speech of angels."

Do not capitalize an indirect quotation. (An *indirect quotation* conveys the meaning of an original statement without repeating it word for word. It is often introduced by the word *that*.)

> Beethoven said that **m**usic should bring tears to the eyes.

Objective

EXERCISE 1. Capitalizing Sentences and the Pronoun *I*. Rewrite correctly any of the following sentences that have errors in capitalization. Write *Correct* if a sentence has no errors.

1. What is the driving force in people's lives? my brother and i examined a book of quotations to learn how famous people of the past and present have addressed this question.
2. Many of the quotations suggested that a desire for freedom is of primary importance. the writer Ralph Waldo Emerson, for example, said that his angel was named freedom, and he told his readers to choose this angel for their king.
3. Dignity was another quality to which many of the quotations pointed. Booker T. Washington said that no race can prosper until it learns that there is as much dignity in tilling a field as in writing a poem. Correct
4. Neil Armstrong (He was the first human to walk on the moon) once said that The single thing that made people happiest was the feeling that they had worked up to the limit of their abilities.
5. Architect Frank Lloyd Wright wrote, "individuality is the most precious thing in life." (individuality is amply displayed in the many buildings that Wright designed.)
6. The singer Billie Holiday wrote about "The kind of fight it takes to record what you want to record the way you want to record it."
7. Opera star Beverly Sills (she presently directs the New York City Opera) wrote, "there is something in me—I just can't stand to admit defeat."
8. A famous anonymous quotation says that it is love that "Makes the world go round." (This quotation was used in a Gilbert and Sullivan operetta and, more recently, in a popular song.)
9. "Love is only chatter," wrote Gelett Burgess. "friends are all that matter."
10. According to philosopher George Santayana, "life is not a spectacle or a feast; it is a predicament."

CAPITALIZATION OF PROPER NOUNS

Capitalize a proper noun.

Do not capitalize a common noun unless it is the first word of a sentence.

Capitalize only the important words in proper nouns composed of several words. Do not capitalize articles (*a, an, the*), coordinating conjunctions (*and, but, for, or, nor, yet*), or prepositions of fewer than five letters.

Most proper nouns fall into the following fifteen categories:

1. Names and nicknames of individuals

Tracy Austin	Buffalo Bill
Ulysses S. Grant	Sugar Ray Leonard
Cleopatra	Catherine the Great

2. Titles of individuals

Capitalize titles used before a proper name and titles used in direct address (naming the person or persons to whom one is speaking).

President Truman	Prime Minister Benjamin Disraeli
Sir Arthur Conan Doyle	Pope John Paul II
Queen Victoria	Yes, Senator [direct address]
Lord Byron	

Capitalize titles used after a proper name and titles that replace a proper name when you wish to show respect or indicate a high official. (For example, when referring to the President of the United States, always capitalize the title.) Do not capitalize titles used as common nouns to refer to a general class or type.

the Senator from Arkansas	*but*	the work of a senator
Crazy Horse, Chief of the Sioux		the chiefs of various tribes

In general, capitalize a title showing a family relationship if it is used with or in place of a proper name. Do not capitalize the title if a possessive is used before it (unless the title is considered part of the name).

I wrote to Aunt Olga.	*but*	My aunt Olga lives abroad.
We spoke to Father.		Our father is a lawyer.

3. Names of national groups, ethnic groups, and languages

Americans	Iroquois
West Germans	Japanese
Mexican Americans	Swahili

4. Organizations, institutions, political parties and their members, and firms

Girl Scouts of America	the Republican party
Salvation Army	a Democrat
House of Representatives	American Express Company

Note that the word *party* is not capitalized. Do not capitalize common nouns such as *museum* or *university* unless they are part of a proper noun.

She applied to the state university.
She applied to the University of Indiana.
He visited the art museum on his lunch hour.

5. Monuments, bridges, buildings, and other structures

Grant's Tomb	John Hancock Center
Delaware Memorial Bridge	Graybar Building
Mayo Clinic	Hoover Dam

6. Trade names

a Chevrolet	Tide detergent
Kleenex tissues	Ivory soap

7. Documents, awards, and laws

the Bill of Rights	the Pulitzer Prize
the Treaty of Paris	the Heisman Trophy
the Declaration of Independence	the Civil Rights Act of 1968

8. Geographical terms

Capitalize the names of continents, countries, states, provinces, counties, cities, villages, specific bodies of water, topographical features, regions, streets, and roads.

North America	Richmond	Red River Valley
Greece	Atlantic Ocean	Painted Desert
Illinois	Lake Superior	Tropic of Capricorn
Alberta	Mackinac Island	Central America
Chester County	Pocono Mountains	Michigan Avenue

9. Planets and other heavenly bodies

Uranus	Little Dipper
Milky Way	Polaris

Do not capitalize the words *sun* and *moon*. *Earth* is capitalized only when it is used in conjunction with the names of the other planets. It is never capitalized when used with the definite article *the*.

The sun is setting, and the moon is visible.
The planets Mars and Earth are similar in many respects.
Different constellations are visible from different areas of the earth.

10. Compass points

Capitalize the words *north, east, south,* and *west* and compounds of these words when they refer to a specific area of the country or the world or when they are part of a proper name.

Do not capitalize *north, east, south,* and *west* and compounds of these words when they merely indicate direction.

the Far East	*but*	the east coast of Australia
South Carolina		south on Route 9
the Southwest		a southwest wind

11. Ships, planes, trains, and spacecraft

U.S.S. *Constitution*
Concorde
City of New Orleans
Apollo 12

12. Historical events, cultural movements, eras, and calendar items

World War II	Dadaism
Battle of the Bulge	Middle Ages
Great Depression	Memorial Day

Do not capitalize a historical period when it refers to a general span of time.

the fifth century
the thirties

Capitalize the days of the week and the months of the year, but do not capitalize the names of the seasons (*spring, summer, autumn, fall, winter*).

a hot Sunday afternoon in the summer month of July

13. Religious terms

Capitalize names of deities, religions, denominations, and their adherents; words referring to a supreme deity; and religious books and events.

Allah	Church of England
Judaism	the Lord
Good Friday	Koran
Passover	Old Testament

14. School courses

Capitalize only those school courses that are the name of a language or the title of a specific course rather than the general name of a subject.

French	*but*	foreign language
World History I		history
Calculus 303		mathematics

15. Titles of works

Uncle Tom's Cabin	the *Philadelphia Inquirer*
"To Helen"	"You Were Always on My Mind"

Capitalize articles (*a, an, the*) at the beginning of a title only when they are part of the title itself. It is preferred practice not to capitalize (or italicize) articles preceding the title of a newspaper or a periodical. In general, do not capitalize (or italicize) the word *magazine* following the title of a periodical.

A Passage to India	*but*	a *Time* magazine article
The Red Pony		the *Chicago Tribune*

Objective

EXERCISE 2. Capitalizing Proper Nouns. Rewrite the following sentences correctly, adding or eliminating capital letters as necessary.

1. In the Sixteenth Century the spaniard Coronado described the land in Western north America as an uninhabitable waste.
2. Following the Louisiana purchase and the Mexican war, however, americans discovered that coronado was wrong.
3. The west proved to be a source of great wealth to the new nation.
4. The mormons in utah mined precious metals and trapped beavers; the california gold rush of 1849 made many people's fortunes.
5. Unfortunately, rapid expansion in the west was at the expense of Native american tribes.
6. When in 1851 the United States demanded that reservations for indians be established, the sioux and the cheyenne resisted.
7. One of the most vocal supporters of the Native Americans was the writer helen hunt jackson, author of *a century of dishonor.*
8. On june 25, 1876, general george custer made his stand against crazy horse and sitting bull in a famous conflict known as the battle of little big horn.

9. The battle was recounted in the dustin hoffman film *little big man*, which was nominated for various academy awards.

10. In 1887 congress passed the dawes act, which governed policy toward Native Americans, and in 1924 the united states granted full citizenship to Native Americans.

CAPITALIZATION OF PROPER ADJECTIVES

Capitalize proper adjectives (adjectives formed from proper nouns).

Most proper adjectives fit into the following two categories:

1. Adjectives formed from names of people

Georgian architecture	Jeffersonian agrarianism
Mosaic teachings [the teachings of Moses]	Marxist rhetoric

2. Adjectives formed from place names and names of national, ethnic, and religious groups

Athenian democracy	Irish folk music
Virginian soil	Hispanic cooking
African pottery	Jewish holidays

Many proper nouns do not change form when they are used as adjectives.

Vermont maple syrup	United States foreign policy
Eskimo artifacts	Beethoven symphonies

Objective

EXERCISE 3. Capitalizing Proper Adjectives and Proper Nouns. Rewrite the following sentences correctly, adding or eliminating capital letters as necessary.

1. On the morning of october 12, 1492, a sailor on the spanish ship *pinta* sighted an island in what are now the bahamas.
2. The italian captain of the *pinta,* christopher columbus, went ashore with the flag of spain and named the island san salvador.
3. Columbus' voyage opened up the north american regions to the people of europe, although this achievement had not been his original goal.
4. Originally, columbus had been seeking china, japan, and the east

indies, and he thought that these Eastern lands could be reached by sailing West from europe.

5. The demand for indian, chinese, and japanese products in europe was great.
6. Such asian spices as pepper, cinnamon, ginger, and cloves were important products to European people, and the european nations also prized asian foods such as rice, figs, and oranges.
7. Columbus persuaded queen Isabella to give him political control over the lands he discovered.
8. The spanish queen also wanted to establish roman catholic missions in the New World.
9. Although he had discovered a new continent, Columbus still believed that he had reached the east indies.
10. For this reason, Columbus called the new world inhabitants indians.

Summary of Capitalization Rules

CAPITALIZE:	DO NOT CAPITALIZE:
Before making repairs, the mechanic ordered parts for our car. (**O**ur car is a foreign model.)	The mechanic ordered parts for our car (**o**ur car is a foreign model) before making repairs.
Anne Frank said, "**I**n spite of everything, I still believe that people are really good at heart."	Anne Frank said that **i**n spite of everything she still believed that people are really good at heart.
Aunt Carmen	my **a**unt Carmen
Lieutenant **G**overnor **O**'Neill	a **l**ieutenant **g**overnor
Vanderbilt **U**niversity	the **u**niversity
San **D**iego **Z**oo	the **z**oo
a **T**oyota	a compact **c**ar
the **V**olstead **A**ct	an **a**ct passed by Congress
Mississippi **R**iver	the **r**iver
Ventnor **A**venue	an **a**venue
Mercury, **P**luto	a **p**lanet, the **s**un, the **m**oon
May, **T**hanksgiving **D**ay	**s**pring, a **h**oliday
the **W**est **C**oast	**w**est of the Rocky Mountains
the **R**enaissance	a period of **r**enaissance
the **B**ible, **B**uddhism	a **h**oly **b**ook, a **r**eligion
Geography 101, **C**reative **W**riting I	**g**eography, a **c**reative **w**riting class

Objective

APPLICATION EXERCISE. Writing Sentences with Capitalized Words. (a) Write a sentence using a direct quotation from a literary work, a political speech, or another source. (b) Write another sentence using an indirect quotation from a different source. Do not forget to name the sources of your quotations.

REVIEW EXERCISE. Capitalization. Write the letter of the one item that is correctly capitalized in each of the following pairs.

1. (a) My course in Greek Philosophy teaches the socratic method.
(b) My course in Greek philosophy teaches the Socratic method.
2. (a) Do you know the song "You do something to me"?
(b) Do you know the song "You Do Something to Me"?
3. (a) My cousin Anita met Mom and Dad at the shopping mall.
(b) My Cousin Anita met mom and dad at the Shopping Mall.
4. (a) Meet us at the Southwest corner of Maple avenue and Walnut street.
(b) Meet us at the southwest corner of Maple Avenue and Walnut Street.
5. (a) The book *Profiles in Courage* was written by President Kennedy.
(b) The book *Profiles In Courage* was written by president Kennedy.
6. (a) A musical work by Aaron Copland celebrates Appalachia.
(b) A musical Work by Aaron Copland celebrates appalachia.
7. (a) The Island nation of malta is in the Mediterranean sea.
(b) The island nation of Malta is in the Mediterranean Sea.
8. (a) The 1984 summer olympics were held in Los Angeles.
(b) The 1984 Summer Olympics were held in Los Angeles.
9. (a) The Declaration of Independence was signed in the summer of 1776.
(b) The declaration of independence was signed in the Summer of 1776.
10. (a) William the conqueror was the first norman King of England.
(b) William the Conqueror was the first Norman king of England.

Answers: **1.** b; **2.** b; **3.** a; **4.** b; **5.** a; **6.** a; **7.** b; **8.** b; **9.** a; **10.** b

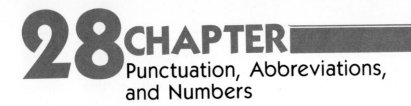

28 CHAPTER Punctuation, Abbreviations, and Numbers

PERIOD

Use a period at the end of a declarative sentence or at the end of a polite command.

DECLARATIVE SENTENCE: The banjo, a popular folk instrument, is native to America.
POLITE COMMAND: Think of some other instruments used by folk singers.

EXCLAMATION POINT

Use an exclamation point to show strong feeling and to indicate a forceful command.

You broke my guitar!
How I love Leonard Bernstein's music in *West Side Story!*
Help!
Don't you dare go without me!

QUESTION MARK

Use a question mark to indicate a direct question.

Is Aaron Copland an American composer?
Did Copland write *Appalachian Spring?*

Do not place a question mark after an indirect question (one that is reworded as part of a statement).

My friend asked whether Aaron Copland wrote *Appalachian Spring.*
She asked what Shaker folk tune is a central melody in *Appalachian Spring.*

In general, do not place a question mark after a polite request.

Will the chorus please be seated.

Objective

EXERCISE 1. Using End Punctuation. Rewrite the following sentences correctly, adding periods, exclamation points, and question marks where they are needed.

1. I was wondering whether you have read about Franklin Roosevelt.
2. What a great President he was!
3. Some people did not think that Roosevelt possessed the qualifications necessary for the presidency.
4. They wondered how Roosevelt could continue in politics after an attack of infantile paralysis.
5. When Roosevelt became President, the Great Depression had reached its peak.
6. What terrible times those years were!
7. What would you have done if you were President during the Depression?
8. Imagine yourself in Roosevelt's place.
9. Roosevelt's plan to end the Depression was called the New Deal.
10. Will you please read about the New Deal in your history textbook.

COLON

Colons to Introduce

1. Lists

Use a colon to introduce a list, especially after a statement that uses such words as *these, the following,* or *as follows.*

> Listen to a recording of one of the following black concert vocalists: Paul Robeson, Grace Bumbry, or Leontyne Price.
> A teacher often gives the following instructions: **(1)** Find books on your topic, **(2)** take notes, **(3)** write an outline, and **(4)** write a first draft.

Do not use a colon if the list immediately follows a verb or a preposition.

> Three important black composers are Ulysses Kay, Scott Joplin, and Arthur Cunningham.
> Scott Joplin wrote ragtime music such as "Maple Leaf Rag," "The Entertainer," and "Gladiolus Rag."

2. Illustrations or restatements

Use a colon to introduce material that illustrates, explains, or restates preceding material.

> Many African instruments are made of unusual materials: Pottery, shells, gourds, and beads are often used to make African percussion instruments.

Colons Before Quotations

Use a colon to introduce a long or formal quotation. A formal quotation is often preceded by such words as *these, the following,* or *as follows.*

> Patrick Henry's speech before the Virginia Provincial Convention closed with the following patriotic exclamation: "I know not what course others may take; but as for me, give me liberty or give me death!"

Poetry quotations of more than one line and prose quotations of more than several lines are generally written below the introductory statement (and indented on the page).

> Walt Whitman celebrated freedom in the following lines:
>
> The earth expanding right hand and left hand,
> The picture alive, every part in its best light,
> The music falling in where it is wanted, and stopping where it is not wanted,
> The cheerful voice of the public road, the gay fresh sentiment of the road.

Other Uses of Colons

Use a colon between the hour and the minute in writing the time, between chapter and verse in making biblical references, and after the salutation of a business letter.

5:40 A.M.	Ruth 3:4–18
8:30 P.M.	Dear Sir or Madam:
Matthew 2:5	Dear Ford Motor Company:

Objective

EXERCISE 2. Using the Colon. Rewrite the following sentences correctly, adding colons where they are needed. For the one sentence that needs no colon, write *Correct.*

1. The information that we need to remember can be classified into the following three categories:things we hear, things we see, and things we read.
2. In developing memory skills you might therefore focus on these three kinds of memory:aural memory, visual memory, and memory for written material.
3. Social situations often require you to use aural memory skills:At a party you will want to remember the names of the people you meet.
4. Your visual memory will be important if you witness a crime or an accident:A police officer may ask you about a person's clothes, height, and weight or a car's color, make, and license number.
5. Your memory for written material will help you improve your schoolwork, especially in subjects such as history, science, spelling, and foreign languages. Correct

6. The following steps will help you to remember information:(1) Concentrate on the information, (2) repeat the information in your mind, (3) write and rewrite the information, and (4) make up a jingle or another mnemonic device to help you remember the information.
7. A mnemonic device to remember the colors of the rainbow is the name *Roy G. Biv,* which stands for the following colors:red, orange, yellow, green, blue, indigo, and violet.
8. By using a series of mnemonic devices, Angela memorized portions of the Bible, including Genesis 1:1–31 and Psalms 23:1–6.
9. To remember the locker combination 53–07–15, you could use this mnemonic device:"We often have dinner from 5:30 to 7:15."
10. Rhymes and repetition make it easy to memorize the following stanza from "The Raven," a poem by Edgar Allan Poe:

    Once upon a midnight dreary, while I pondered, weak and weary,
    Over many a quaint and curious volume of forgotten lore—
    While I nodded, nearly napping, suddenly there came a tapping,
    As of someone gently rapping, rapping at my chamber door—
    "'Tis some visitor," I muttered, "tapping at my chamber door—
        Only this and nothing more."

SEMICOLON

Semicolons to Separate Main Clauses

Use a semicolon to separate main clauses that are not joined by the coordinating conjunctions *and, but, or, nor, yet,* and *for.*

George Gershwin wrote music during the Jazz Age; his compositions were influenced by jazz music.

Use a semicolon to separate main clauses joined by conjunctive adverbs (such as *however, therefore, nevertheless, moreover, furthermore,* and *consequently*) or adverbial expressions (such as *for example, that is,* and *in fact*).

In general, a conjunctive adverb or an adverbial expression is followed by a comma.

Much of jazz music is improvised; however, all the instruments are played in the same key.

Semicolons and Commas

Use a semicolon to separate the items in a series when these items contain commas.

Three important black musicians are Leontyne Price, an opera singer; Henry Lewis, a conductor; and André Watts, a pianist.

Use a semicolon to separate two main clauses joined by a coordinating conjunction when such clauses contain several commas.

> Arthur Mitchell, as a leading dancer with the New York City Ballet, danced in *A Midsummer Night's Dream, Agon,* and *Western Symphony;* but he is also famous as the founder of the Dance Theater of Harlem, an internationally acclaimed dance company.

Objective

EXERCISE 3. Using the Semicolon. Rewrite the following sentences correctly, adding semicolons where they are needed.

1. Puerto Rico is an island of 3,434 square miles;its population is approximately 3 million.
2. Puerto Rico was discovered by Columbus on November 19, 1493; conquered by Ponce de León, the Spanish explorer, in 1509;and ceded to the United States after the Spanish-American War of 1898.
3. Sugar cane was introduced to Puerto Rico in 1515;it remains an important crop to this day.
4. Operation Bootstrap, begun in the 1940s, used a series of tax exemptions, low-interest loans, and other incentives to develop Puerto Rico's economy;and the island, a paradise in the Caribbean, now has the highest per-capita income in Latin America.
5. Manufacturing is important to Puerto Rico's economy;in fact, petrochemicals are among the island's chief products.
6. San Juan is the capital of Puerto Rico;Ponce and Mayagüez are two of the island's other important cities.
7. In addition to a warm climate and fine beaches, Puerto Rico offers a number of man-made tourist attractions;for example, tourists may visit the Old Walled City of San Juan, San Juan Cathedral, and the Ponce Museum of Art.
8. Puerto Rico is part of the United States, and its residents are American citizens;however, it is a self-governing commonwealth.
9. Residents of Puerto Rico, though they vote in national primaries, do not vote in national elections;on the other hand, they do not pay federal income tax for income earned in Puerto Rico.
10. Famous Puerto Ricans include Pablo Casals, an internationally acclaimed cellist;Roberto Clemente, the great baseball player and philanthropist;actors José Ferrer and Rita Moreno;and José Feliciano, a talented popular musician.

COMMA

Commas and Compound Sentences

Use commas between the main clauses in a compound sentence.

Place a comma before a coordinating conjunction *(and, but, or, nor, yet,* or *for)* that joins two main clauses.

The Marx Brothers were a comedy team, but each of them did work on his own.

Groucho Marx made wisecracks, and his brother Harpo played music on a harp.

You may omit the comma between very short main clauses unless it is needed to avoid confusion.

I prepared the meal and I washed the dishes. [clear]

I prepared the meal and the dishes needed washing. [confusing]

I prepared the meal, and the dishes needed washing. [clear]

Commas in a Series

Use commas to separate three or more words, phrases, or clauses in a series.

Director D. W. Griffith's silent film *Intolerance* is insightful, expressive, and powerful.

Early movie directors filmed adaptations of plays, short stories, novels, and nonfiction works.

Charles Chaplin wrote, directed, and starred in many classic film comedies.

Charles Chaplin made audiences laugh, Lillian Gish made them cry, and Buster Keaton amazed them with acrobatic stunts.

No commas are necessary when all of the items are connected by conjunctions.

The film *Intolerance* is insightful and expressive and powerful.

Nouns used in pairs *(spaghetti and meatballs, bacon and eggs, pen and ink)* are considered single units and should not be divided by commas. The pairs themselves must be set off from other nouns or groups of nouns in a series.

I ate bread and butter, ham and eggs, and fresh fruit every morning.

Commas and Coordinate Adjectives

Place a comma between coordinate adjectives preceding a noun.

Adjectives are *coordinate* if it would sound right to reverse their order or to put the word *and* between them.

She wore a long, thick scarf.

She wore a long, soft, thick scarf.

Do not use a comma between adjectives preceding a noun if they sound unnatural with their order reversed or with *and* between them. Adjectives that do not need commas between them usually describe different aspects of the word to which they refer —for example, size, age, and material.

She wore a long wool scarf.

Objective

EXERCISE 4. Using the Comma (Part 1). Rewrite the following sentences correctly, adding commas where they are needed. For the two sentences that do not need commas, write *Correct.*

1. Silent-screen star Mary Pickford was vibrant and talented and beautiful. Correct
2. Pickford was born in Canada, worked on the New York City stage, and became a film actress in Hollywood.
3. Her delicate beauty and strong, versatile acting ability made her a Hollywood star overnight.
4. Pickford beguiled, charmed, and won the hearts of many Americans.
5. This popular screen actress was famous for portraying children, and she became known as America's Sweetheart.
6. Pickford once played a mistreated orphan on a farm run by a vengeful old man. Correct
7. She was praised for her roles in *Suds*, in *Little Lord Fauntleroy*, and in a stage play called *A Good Little Devil.*
8. Pickford was married to fellow actor Douglas Fairbanks, and the couple was among Hollywood's most popular celebrities.
9. Mary Pickford, Douglas Fairbanks, Charles Chaplin, and D. W. Griffith together established United Artists.
10. The company flourished, Pickford became a successful producer, and she retired a very wealthy woman.

Commas and Nonessential Elements

1. Adjective clauses

Use commas to set off a nonessential adjective clause.

A *nonessential (nonrestrictive) clause* can be considered an *extra* clause because it gives additional information about a noun. An *extra* clause does not change, but adds to, the basic meaning of a sentence. Therefore, it is set off by commas.

Hedda Hopper, who acted in a number of American films, was famous for her collection of fabulous hats. [nonessential clause: *who acted in a number of American films*]

Do not set off an essential adjective clause. An *essential (restrictive) clause* gives necessary information about a noun. It is needed to convey the exact meaning of a sentence.

The person who actually films a movie is called the camera operator. [essential clause: *who actually films a movie*]

2. Appositives

Use commas to set off an appositive if it is not essential to the meaning of the sentence.

A nonessential (nonrestrictive) appositive can be considered an *extra* appositive; it calls for commas.

> James Wong Howe, a famous American camera operator, was born in China.
> Howe first worked for Cecil B. De Mille, a director of many American films.

A nonessential appositive is sometimes placed before the word to which it refers.

> A camera operator for Cecil B. De Mille, James Wong Howe was an important talent in the film industry.

An essential (restrictive) appositive gives necessary information about a noun and is not set off.

> James Wong Howe operated the camera for Martin Ritt's film *The Molly Maguires.* [If commas were placed around the essential appositive *The Molly Maguires,* the sentence would imply that this was Martin Ritt's only film.]

3. Participles, infinitives, and their phrases

Use commas to set off participles, infinitives, and their phrases if the words are not essential to the meaning of the sentence.

> Barbara Loden, having acted, became a director. [participle]
> Robert Redford, earning fame as an actor, turned to directing. [participial phrase]
> Redford played a skier in *Downhill Racer* and an aging baseball star in *The Natural,* to name just two of his many acting credits. [infinitive phrase]

Do not set off participles, infinitives, and their phrases if they are essential to the meaning of the sentence.

> The most famous documentary directed by Robert J. Flaherty is *Nanook of the North.* [participial phrase tells *which* documentary among those that Flaherty directed]
> Flaherty made the film to show the realities of Eskimo life. [infinitive phrase tells *why*]
> To film *Nanook of the North* was a difficult undertaking. [infinitive phrase used as subject]

Commas with Interjections and Conjunctive Adverbs

Use commas to set off interjections (such as *yes, no,* and *well*), parenthetical words and expressions (such as *however, therefore, moreover, on the other hand,* and *for example*), and conjunctive adverbs and adverbial expressions (such as *however, therefore, moreover, on the other hand,* and *for example*).

> Yes, director Francis Ford Coppola is also a scriptwriter. [interjection]
> He did, for example, write the screenplay for *Patton*. [parenthetical expression]
> Coppola is highly regarded as a director; for example, he won an Academy Award for directing *The Godfather*. [conjunctive adverbial expression]
> Moreover, Coppola comes from an artistic family. [parenthetical word]
> Talia Shire is Francis Ford Coppola's sister; moreover, she is a talented actress. [conjunctive adverb]

Objective

EXERCISE 5. Using the Comma (Part 2). Rewrite the following sentences correctly, adding commas where they are needed. For the one sentence that does not need any commas, write *Correct*.

1. Orson Welles' film *Citizen Kane* won only one Academy Award; however,it is now considered one of the finest movies ever made.
2. In fact,few films in the American cinema have been as influential as *Citizen Kane*.
3. The film,directed by and starring Orson Welles,has a newsreel quality that makes it seem very realistic.
4. The movie,which traces the life of a rich and powerful man,has had a stormy history,to say the least.
5. Some of those criticizing the film thought that Welles had insulted the powerful newspaper publisher William Randolph Hearst. Correct
6. The character Kane,played by Orson Welles,had many things in common with Hearst.
7. For instance,Kane built a great mansion,Xanadu,just as Hearst built a great mansion,San Simeon.
8. Yes,Orson Welles was severely criticized by those people who felt that he had exposed private lives to make his film.
9. On the other hand,in 1970 Welles was publicly voted one of the great American filmmakers.
10. He also received a special Oscar,which was given to him for his outstanding achievements in the film industry.

Commas and Introductory Phrases

1. Prepositional phrases

Use a comma after a short introductory prepositional phrase if the sentence would be misread without the comma.

During winter, snowstorms are common in New England. [comma needed]
In the distance we saw Mount Washington. [comma not needed]

Use a comma after a long prepositional phrase or after the final phrase in a succession of phrases.

On the rug by the fireplace, a large dog slept.

Do not use a comma if the phrase is immediately followed by a verb.

On the dresser lay an ivory mirror.
On the rug by the fireplace slept a large dog.

2. Participles and participial phrases

Use a comma after an introductory participle or participial phrase.

Smiling, I watched Diane Keaton clown in the film *Sleeper.*
Beginning as a comic actress, Sally Field graduated to more serious roles.

Commas and Adverb Clauses

Use commas to set off all introductory adverb clauses. Use commas to set off internal adverb clauses that interrupt the flow of a sentence.

Although Stanley Kubrick is an American director, he lives and works in Great Britain.
Ruby Keeler, although she retired in 1941, returned to Broadway in 1970.

In general, do not set off an adverb clause at the end of a sentence unless the clause is parenthetical or the sentence would be misread without the comma.

Let's go to the movies tomorrow if we have time.
The new Meryl Streep film is supposed to be good, if we can believe the reviews. [comma before parenthetical clause]
I was enjoying the movie, when the film projector suddenly broke. [comma to avoid misreading]

Use a comma if an adverb clause at the end of a sentence begins with *although, though,* or *while* meaning "whereas." Also use a comma if the clause begins with *since* or *as* and tells *why.*

The acting was superb, although the plot made little sense.
Some Walt Disney films star animated cartoon characters, while others star human actors.

Talented scriptwriters are highly paid, since their talents are in such great demand.

Do not use a comma before *while, as*, or *since* if the clause tells *when*.

Animation techniques have improved since the first Walt Disney cartoon was shown.

Commas and Antithetical Phrases

Use commas to set off an antithetical phrase.

An *antithetical phrase* uses a word such as *not* or *unlike* to make a contrast.

Augusta, not Bangor, is the capital of Maine.
Unlike Kansas, Colorado is very mountainous.

Objective

EXERCISE 6. Using the Comma (Part 3). Rewrite the following sentences correctly, adding commas where they are needed. For the two sentences that do not need commas, write *Correct.*

1. Unlike most singers, Alberta Hunter turned to a career in music late in life.
2. Retiring from the nursing profession at eighty-two, Hunter decided to start her new career as a singer.
3. Hunter had not sung since she was young. Correct
4. With a voice rich in expression, Hunter soon became a popular singer.
5. Singing in New York City, Hunter was able to fulfill one of her dreams.
6. Hunter, because she knew many languages, could sing almost anything.
7. She sang French songs when her audience was French. Correct
8. Because she sang the blues so well, many audiences requested blues songs.
9. In each song, lyrics and tone blended for a powerful rendition.
10. Although Hunter knew many languages, she never learned to read music.

Commas and Specifying Words and Phrases

Use commas to set off specifying words and phrases.

1. Titles of people

Use commas to set off titles when they follow a person's name.

Henry VIII, King of England, was a prolific songwriter and an accomplished musician.

2. Addresses, geographical terms, and dates

Use commas to separate the various parts of an address, a geographical term, or a date.

> The company is located at 840 Pierce Street, Southfield, Michigan, and has another office in Lansing, Michigan.
> Paris, France, is the setting of some of Hemingway's works.
> On Friday, October 12, 1492, Christopher Columbus landed on the New World island now called San Salvador.

Do not use commas if only the month and the day or only the month and the year are given.

> In July 1776 the Declaration of Independence was signed.
> The signing of the Declaration of Independence on July 4 is celebrated every year.

3. References

Use commas to set off the parts of a reference that direct the reader to the exact source.

> The theme is expressed in *The Scarlet Letter*, pages 3–4.
> We performed Act I, scene i, of Shakespeare's *Julius Caesar*.

Commas and Direct Address

Use commas to set off words or names used in direct address.

> Mona, can you meet me this afternoon?
> You, my dear, are leaving at once.
> Thank you for the book, Mrs. Gomez.

Commas and Tag Questions

Use commas to set off a tag question.

A *tag question* (such as *shouldn't I?* or *have you?*) emphasizes an implied answer to the statement preceding it.

> *The Sound of Music* starred Julie Andrews, didn't it?
> Andrews was not in the film of *My Fair Lady*, was she?

Commas in Letter Writing

Place a comma after the salutation of an informal letter and after the closing of all letters.

Dear Mario,	Yours truly,
Dear Cousin Agnes,	Love,

Use the following style for the heading of a letter:

> 23 Silver Lake Road
> Sharon, Connecticut 06069
> February 15, 1985

Misuse of Commas

Do not use a comma before a conjunction that connects a compound verb having only two parts.

INCORRECT: Our school never wins the championship, but every year has a spectacular losers' party.
CORRECT: Our school never wins the championship but every year has a spectacular losers' party.
CORRECT: Our school never wins the championship, but every year **it** has a spectacular losers' party.

The same rule applies to other compound elements, such as subjects.

INCORRECT: A book by Margaret Mead, and a book by Ruth Benedict were assigned to the students.
CORRECT: A book by Margaret Mead and a book by Ruth Benedict were assigned to the students.

Do not use only a comma to join two main clauses that are not part of a series. A sentence with this error is called a *run-on sentence.* (The error is also called a *comma splice* or a *comma fault.*) Use a coordinating conjunction with the comma, or use a semicolon.

INCORRECT: The navigator Cabrillo sighted land in 1572, the history of modern California had begun.
CORRECT: The navigator Cabrillo sighted land in 1572, **and** the history of modern California had begun.
CORRECT: The navigator Cabrillo sighted land in 1572; the history of modern California had begun.

Do not use a comma between a subject and its verb or between a verb and its complement.

INCORRECT: What she considered an easy ballet step to master, was quite difficult for me.
CORRECT: What she considered an easy ballet step to master was quite difficult for me.

INCORRECT: Popular tourist attractions in Florida include, Disney World, Palm Beach, and the Everglades.
CORRECT: Popular tourist attractions in Florida include Disney World, Palm Beach, and the Everglades.

Objective

EXERCISE 7. Using the Comma (Part 4). Rewrite the following letter, adding commas where they are needed and dropping them where they are incorrect.

4615 Oak Street
Kansas City, Missouri 64110
January 2, 1985

Dear Kim,

Happy New Year, Kim! We haven't spoken on the phone for some time, have we? I am enclosing an article about American colleges that appeared in the Sunday, December 30, 1984, issue of the *Kansas City Star.* You still haven't decided on a college, have you?

I've been looking through the college manuals at the local library. I'm thinking of applying to Bard, a small college in Annandale, New York, and to Hood College in Frederick, Maryland. If I apply for early enrollment, I'll begin school in January 1986.

The enclosed article contains up-to-date information and so should prove useful to you. Wouldn't it be nice if we could go to the same college, Kim? It's been three years since you moved to Winchester, Virginia, and left Kansas City. It would be fun to see more of each other again.

I hope to hear from you soon, Kim. Please give my best wishes and regards to your family.

Your friend,

Maureen

DASH

Indicate the dash in typing by two hyphens (--). Do not place a comma, a semicolon, a colon, or a period before or after a dash.

Dashes to Emphasize

Use a dash to set off and emphasize supplemental information or parenthetical comments.

> Yellowstone Park's geyser Old Faithful erupted faithfully—every hour on the hour—for over eighty years.

Dashes to Signal Hesitation

Use a dash to indicate an abrupt change in thought within a sentence or to show a hesitation or faltering in dialogue.

> "I think the answer is—I've forgotten what I was going to say."
> "I—I never was so scared," she stammered.

PARENTHESES

Use parentheses to set off extra material.

Commas and dashes are also used for this purpose; the difference between the three marks is one of degree. Use commas for extra material that is fairly closely related to the rest of the sentence. Use parentheses for material that is not intended to be part of the main statement but is nevertheless important enough to include. Use dashes for material that more abruptly interrupts the sentence and that you wish to emphasize.

> Mary Jane Cannary ("Calamity Jane") was a good friend of Wild Bill Hickok.

A complete sentence within parentheses is not capitalized and needs no period if it is contained within another sentence. If a sentence in parentheses stands by itself, both a capital letter and a period are needed.

> Mary Jane Cannary (she was known as Calamity Jane) was a good friend of Wild Bill Hickok.
> Paul Bunyan is a famous figure in American folklore. (You can learn all about him if you visit the Paul Bunyan Center in Minnesota.)

Parentheses with Other Marks of Punctuation

1. With a comma, semicolon, or colon

Always place a comma, a semicolon, or a colon *after* the closing parenthesis.

> Writer Bret Harte is associated with the West (his stories include "The Outcasts of Poker Flat" and "The Luck of Roaring Camp"), but he was born in Albany, New York.

2. With a period, a question mark, or an exclamation point

Place a period, a question mark, or an exclamation point *inside* the closing parenthesis if it is part of the parenthetical expression.

> The most famous guide of the Lewis and Clark expedition was Sacajawea. (A novel based on her life was published a few years ago.)
> Owatonna is the name of a Native American princess (a member of the Santee tribe?) who lived hundreds of years ago.

Place a period, a question mark, or an exclamation point *outside* the closing parenthesis if it is part of the entire sentence.

> The code of laws that governed Iroquois society was the Great Binding Law (known as the Iroquois Constitution).
> How surprised I was to learn that the British still call corn *maize* (which comes from the West Indian word for corn)!

Objective

EXERCISE 8. Using the Dash and Parentheses. Rewrite the following sentences correctly, adding dashes and parentheses where necessary.

1. The author John Steinbeck—a Nobel Prize–winner is one of the most popular American writers of the twentieth century.
2. Many people do not know that F. Scott Fitzgerald 1896–1940 wrote Hollywood films. He never liked to publicize this fact!
3. Emily Dickinson wrote many poems on the subject of death. She was also fascinated with religion and immortality.
4. Did you ever hear of Kate Chopin 1851–1904? She wrote a novel called *The Awakening* 1899, a short story collection called *Bayou Folk* 1894, and other short stories set in Louisiana.
5. Stephen Crane—the author of *The Red Badge of Courage* was once shipwrecked while traveling to Cuba. He led an adventurous life!

BRACKETS

Use brackets to enclose information that you insert into a quotation from someone else's work.

> We cannot be free until they [all Americans] are.
>
> —James Baldwin

Use brackets to enclose a parenthetical expression within parentheses.

> The name *Oregon* comes from the Algonquian word *wauregan* (which means "beautiful water" [referring to the Columbia River]).

ELLIPSIS POINTS

Use a series of spaced points called ellipsis points to indicate the omission of material in a quotation.

Use three spaced points if the omission is at the beginning of a sentence. Use the correct punctuation (if any) *plus* three spaced points if the omission is in the middle or at the end of a sentence. In using a period plus three spaced points, always put the period first, and do not put a space before it.

COMPLETE QUOTATION:

> I went to the woods because I wished to live deliberately, to front only the essential facts of life, and see if I could not learn what it had to teach, and not, when I came to die, discover that I had not lived. I did not wish to live what was not life, living is so dear; nor did I wish to practice resigna-

tion, unless it was quite necessary. I wanted to live deep and suck out all the marrow of life, to live so sturdily and Spartan-like as to put to rout all that was not life, to cut a broad swath and shave close, to drive life into a corner, and reduce it to its lowest terms, and, if it proved to be mean, why then to get the whole and genuine meanness of it, and publish its meanness to the world; or if it were sublime, to know it by experience, and be able to give a true account of it in my next excursion.

—Henry David Thoreau

QUOTED WITH ELLIPSES:

In explaining his reasons for retiring to Walden, Henry David Thoreau said, " . . . I wished to live deliberately, to front only the essential facts of life, and see if I could not learn what it had to teach, and not, when I came to die, discover that I had not lived."

Thoreau said, "I went to the woods because I wished . . . to front only the essential facts of life, and see if I could not learn what it had to teach, and not, when I came to die, discover that I had not lived."

Thoreau said, "I did not wish to live what was not life . . .; nor did I wish to practice resignation, unless it was quite necessary."

Thoreau said, "I wanted to live deep and suck out all the marrow of life. . . . "

EXERCISE 9. Using Brackets and Ellipsis Points. Examine the original passage from Ralph Waldo Emerson's "Self-Reliance," and then rewrite the second passage, adding brackets and ellipsis points where they are needed.

ORIGINAL PASSAGE:

A foolish consistency is the hobgoblin of little minds, adored by little statesmen and philosophers and divines. With consistency a great soul has simply nothing to do. He may as well concern himself with his shadow on the wall. Speak what you think now in hard words, and tomorrow speak what tomorrow thinks in hard words again, though it contradict everything you said today. "Ah, so you shall be sure to be misunderstood." Is it so bad then to be misunderstood? Pythagoras was misunderstood, and Socrates, and Jesus, and Luther, and Copernicus, and Galileo, and Newton, and every pure and wise spirit that ever took flesh. To be great is to be misunderstood.

PASSAGE TO BE REWRITTEN:

Ralph Waldo Emerson once said, "A foolish consistency is the hobgoblin of little minds. With consistency a great soul has simply nothing to do. . . . Speak what you think now in hard words, and tomorrow speak what tomorrow thinks in hard words, . . . though it contradict everything you said today. . . . Pythagoras [the Greek mathematician] was misunderstood, and Socrates [the Greek philosopher], . . . and Jesus."

QUOTATION MARKS

Quotation Marks for Direct Quotations

Use quotation marks to enclose a direct quotation.

Place quotation marks *only* around quoted material, not around an introductory or an explanatory remark. Generally separate such a remark from the actual quotation with a comma.

> "Weave us a garment of brightness," states a Native American song.
>
> Phil Rizzuto optimistically said, "They still can't steal first base."

When a quotation is interrupted by explanatory words such as *he said* or *she wrote,* use two sets of quotation marks.

Separate each part of the quotation from the interrupting phrase with two marks of punctuation, such as two commas or a comma and a period. If the second part of the quotation is a complete sentence, begin it with a capital letter.

> "The secret of my success," claims baseball pitcher Lefty Gomez, "was clean living and a fast-moving outfield."
>
> "The Lord prefers common-looking people," Abraham Lincoln once said. "That is the reason he made so many of them."

Do not use quotation marks in an *indirect quotation* (a quotation that does not repeat a speaker's exact wording).

ORIGINAL QUOTATION: Carl Sandburg once said, "Poetry is the achievement of the synthesis of hyacinths and biscuits."

INDIRECT QUOTATION: Carl Sandburg once said that poetry was the achievement of the synthesis of hyacinths and biscuits.

Use single quotation marks to enclose a quotation within a quotation.

> In speaking to her students, the teacher said, "Benjamin Franklin once wrote, 'Lose no time; be always employed in something useful.'"

In writing dialogue, begin a new paragraph and use a new set of quotation marks every time the speaker changes.

> "How do you do, Mr. Martin. Are you paying New York a visit? Or do you live here?"
>
> My father quickly shook hands with Jerome, somewhat to Jerome's surprise. "I'm just up for the afternoon, thank you. I live in a hick town in Pennsylvania you never heard of."
>
> "I see, sir. A quick visit."
>
> "This is the first time in six years that I've had a chance to see my brother."
>
> "Yes, we've seen very little of him these past years. He's a man we can never see too much of, isn't that right?"
>
> Uncle Quin interrupted. "This is my nephew Jay."
>
> "How do you like the big city, Jay?"
>
> "Fine." I didn't duplicate my father's mistake of offering to shake hands.
>
> —John Updike

Quotation Marks for Titles of Short Works

Use quotation marks to enclose titles of short works, such as short stories, short poems, essays, newspaper and magazine articles, book chapters, songs, and single episodes of a television series.

"To Build a Fire" [short story]
"Fire and Ice" [poem]
"Self-Reliance" [essay]
"Ahab" [chapter]
"The Star-Spangled Banner" [song]

Quotation Marks for Unusual Expressions

Use quotation marks to enclose unfamiliar slang and other unusual or original expressions.

Karen told her younger brother to "beat it."

Quotation Marks for Definitions

Use quotation marks to enclose a definition that is stated directly.

Ukelele comes from the Hawaiian word meaning "flea."

Quotation Marks with Other Marks of Punctuation

1. With a comma or period

Place a comma or a period *inside* the closing quotation mark.

"Love your Neighbor," Benjamin Franklin advised, "yet don't pull down your Hedge."

2. With a semicolon or colon

Place a semicolon or a colon *outside* the closing quotation mark.

Chuck Berry wrote "Johnny B. Goode"; the song was one of the first examples of rock-and-roll music.

There is only one main character in Ernest Hemingway's short story "Big Two-Hearted River": Nick Adams.

3. With a question mark or an exclamation point

Place a question mark or an exclamation point *inside* the closing quotation mark when it is part of the quotation.

We read Leonard Bernstein's essay "What Makes Music American?"

Walt Whitman's poem "Beat! Beat! Drums!" is about the Civil War.

Place a question mark or an exclamation point *outside* the closing quotation mark when it is part of the entire sentence.

Have you read Gwendolyn Brooks's poem "We Real Cool"?

How I adore old Cole Porter songs like "Anything Goes"!

If both the sentence and the quotation at the end of the sentence need a question mark (or an exclamation point), use only *one* question mark (or exclamation point), and place it *inside* the closing quotation mark.

Which French poet asked, "Where are the snows of yesteryear?"

Objective

EXERCISE 10. Using Quotation Marks. Rewrite the following sentences correctly, adding quotation marks where they are needed. For the one sentence that needs no changes, write *Correct.*

1. Johnny Carson was mentioned in an article in *The New Yorker* entitled "Fifteen Years of the *Salto Mortale.*"
2. Billy Wilder said that Carson's job is to do the *salto mortale,* a circus term meaning "an aerial somersault performed on the tightrope."
3. "What's more," said Wilder, "he does it without a net."
4. When Johnny Carson interviewed the actor Robert Blake on *The Tonight Show,* Blake said that Carson was "the ace comedian top-dog talk artist of the universe."
5. Comedian George Burns remarked about Carson, "When it comes to saving a bad line, he is the master."
6. The agent Irving Lazar called Carson "a mixture of extreme ego and extreme cowardice."
7. On one occasion Carson amused the audience by remarking, "I now believe in reincarnation. Tonight's monologue is going to come back as a dog."
8. "What makes television different from theater or cinema?" Carson once asked.

9. Carson says that after the monologue he works at the desk with Ed McMahon. Correct

10. "If you're happy in what you're doing, you'll like yourself," Carson once said. "If you don't like it," he continued, "stop doing it."

ITALICS (UNDERLINING)

Italic type is the slanted type that is used in printing. *(This is printed in italics.)* Indicate italics in typing or in handwriting by underlining. (This is underlined).

Italics for Titles

Italicize (underline) titles of novels and other books, lengthy poems and plays, films, television series, paintings and sculptures, and long musical compositions. Italicize the names of newspapers and magazines, ships, trains, airplanes, spacecraft, and court cases.

The Sun Also Rises [novel]
Our Town [play]
Nature [television series]
Places in the Heart [film]
St. Louis Post-Dispatch [newspaper]
U.S.S. *Constitution* [ship]*
Apollo 9 [spacecraft]
Leaves of Grass [long poem]
Furman v. *Georgia* [court case]**
Mona Lisa [painting]
Billy the Kid [musical work]
Psychology Today [magazine]
the *City of New Orleans* [train]
Air Force One [airplane]
David [sculpture]

Italicize (underline) and capitalize articles *(a, an, the)* written at the beginning of a title only when they are part of the title itself.

The Scarlet Letter *but* the *Los Angeles Times*
A Night at the Opera a *Business Week* reporter
An American Tragedy an *Atlantic Monthly* article

Do not italicize the apostrophe and *s* in the possessive of italicized titles.

Time's editorial *Macbeth*'s plot

Italics for Foreign Words

Italicize (underline) foreign words and expressions that are not used frequently in English.

Do not italicize a foreign word or expression that is commonly used in English.

Bob always says *hasta la vista* when he departs.
The health spa now offers courses in judo and karate.

---

*Do not italicize *U.S.S.* in the name of a ship.
**Do not italicize the *v.* in court cases.

Italics for Words and Other Items Used to Represent Themselves

Italicize (underline) words, letters, numerals, and symbols used to represent themselves.

> To make your essays read more smoothly, connect ideas with conjunctive adverbs such as *therefore* and *however.*
> The *t* and the *v* sometimes stick on this typewriter.
> There is no *9* in my phone number.
> Should I use the dollar sign (*$*) or spell out the word?

Objective

EXERCISE 11. Using Italics. Rewrite the following sentences correctly, underlining the parts that should be italicized.

1. The sociologist Alice S. Rossi published a collection of feminist literature entitled The Feminist Papers.
2. Rossi described such important writers as Betty Friedan, who wrote the book The Feminine Mystique.
3. Friedan's book was reviewed in many magazines, including Time and Newsweek.
4. Mary Shelley, who is included in Rossi's book, wrote the novel Frankenstein.
5. The horror film entitled The Bride of Frankenstein was loosely based on Shelley's book.
6. Famous airplanes include The Spirit of St. Louis, which Charles Lindbergh, Jr., used in his historic flight across the Atlantic.
7. The first steamboat, the Clermont, was invented by Robert Fulton.
8. The Clermont was named for Robert R. Livingston's Hudson River estate, which in turn took its name from the French words clair ("clear") and mont ("mountain").
9. The first satellite to orbit earth was Sputnik I, which was launched by the Soviet Union.
10. The United States put the first humans on the moon with the successful landing of Apollo 11 in 1969.

APOSTROPHE

Apostrophes for Possessives

1. Pronouns

Use an apostrophe and *s* for the possessive of an indefinite pronoun that is singular.

Do not use an apostrophe with other possessive pronouns.

no one's business	*but*	its paws
each other's books		The car is theirs.

2. Nouns not ending in *s*

Use an apostrophe and *s* to form the possessive of a singular or plural noun not ending in *s,* whether common or proper.

Arthur Cunningham's music
Mexico's deserts
children's activities
people's habits

3. Plural nouns ending in *s*

Use an apostrophe alone to form the possessive of a plural noun ending in *s,* whether common or proper

the Girl Scouts' code
the teachers' cafeteria
the Katzes' home
the books' prices

4. Singular nouns ending in *s*

The possessive of a singular noun ending in *s* (or an *s* or *z* sound), whether common or proper, depends on the number of syllables in the noun.

If the noun has only one syllable, use an apostrophe and *s.* If the noun has more than one syllable, you can usually use an apostrophe alone.

the bus's muffler
Langston Hughes's poetry
the princess' wardrobe
Rodolfo Gonzales' speeches

5. Compound nouns

Put only the last word of a compound noun in the possessive form.

my great-grandfather's watch
her brother-in-law's family
the foster child's happiness
my fellow employees' offices

6. Joint possession and separate possession

If two or more persons (or partners in a company) possess an item (or items) jointly, use the possessive form for the last person named.

my father and mother's house
Lerner and Loewe's musicals
Lord and Taylor's department store

If two or more persons (or companies) possess an item (or items) individually, put each one's name in the possessive form.

Julio's and Betty's test scores
Blair's and Leslie's shoes
Penney's and K-Mart's prices

7. Expression of time and money

Use a possessive form to express amounts of money or time that modify a noun.

The modifier can also be expressed as a hyphenated adjective. In that case no possessive form is used.

two hours' drive	*but*	a two-hour drive
eighty cents' worth		an eighty-cent loaf

Apostrophes in Contractions

Use an apostrophe in place of letters omitted in contractions.

A *contraction* is a single word made up of two words that have been combined by omitting letters. Common contractions combine a subject and a verb or a verb and an adverb.

you're	*formed from*	you are
it's		it is, it has
they're		they are
who's		who is, who has
she'll		she will
don't		do not

Use an apostrophe in place of omitted numerals in such expressions as *the summer of '82* and *the '84 convention.*

Apostrophes for Special Plurals

Use an apostrophe and *s* to form the plural of letters, numerals, symbols, and words used to represent themselves.

Italicize (underline) the letter, numeral, symbol, or word but not the apostrophe and the *s*.

> Cross your *t*'s and dot your *i*'s.
> I typed *4*'s instead of *3*'s.
> Please be sure to write *and*'s instead of *&*'s.

Do not use an apostrophe (or italics) in the plurals of dates.

> F. Scott Fitzgerald set many of his novels in the 1920s.

Objective

EXERCISE 12. Using the Apostrophe. Rewrite the following sentences correctly, adding apostrophes where they are needed. For the one sentence that needs no changes, write *Correct.*

1. Ishi, the last living Stone Age man found in North America, was introduced to civilizations [civilization's] wonders by Professor Thomas T. Waterman.
2. Waterman first learned of the mans [man's] existence from one of San Franciscos [Francisco's] newspapers.

3. The story attracted Waterman because of its human drama. Correct

ancestors'

4. Ishi was a member of the Yanas, a tribe of Native Americans who for centuries had lived in California and practiced their ancestors way of life.

Yanas'

5. The Yanas tragedy began in the 1840s.

California's Yanas'

6. With Californias Gold Rush many people moved into the Yanas territory.

There's

7. Theres no need to exaggerate the impact of this migration.

foreigners'

8. Slowly the foreigners desire to take over the land drove away the Yanas.

weren't

9. They werent given a chance to defend themselves.

Yanas' year's

10. The Yanas culture was practically destroyed in one years time.

HYPHEN

Hyphens for Prefixes and Suffixes

A hyphen is not ordinarily used to join a prefix or a suffix to the beginning or end of a word. There are a few exceptions.

1. Prefixes

Use a hyphen after a prefix joined to a proper noun or a proper adjective.

pro-Western pre-Columbian

Generally, do not use a hyphen if the proper noun or adjective loses its capital letter when the prefix is added. (When in doubt, check a dictionary.)

transatlantic Precambrian

Use a hyphen after the prefix *anti-* when it joins a word beginning with *i*. Use a hyphen after the prefixes *all-*, *ex-* (meaning "former"), *self-*, and, in most cases, *vice-*. (When in doubt, check a dictionary.)

anti-inflation	ex-actress	vice-consul
all-star	self-restraint	

Use a hyphen to avoid confusion between words that look alike but are different in meaning and pronunciation.

re-cover the sofa	*but*	recover a lost ring
re-mark the test papers		remark about her illness

2. Suffixes

Use a hyphen to join the suffix *-like* to a proper noun or to a word ending in double *l*.

Alaska-like weather	*but*	clocklike precision
a drill-like sound		pearllike beads

Hyphens in Compound Adjectives

Use a hyphen in a compound adjective that precedes the noun it modifies.

A compound adjective that follows the noun is usually not hyphenated.

up-to-date magazine	*but*	The magazine is up to date.
plum-colored shirt		The shirt is plum colored.

Compound adjectives beginning with *well-*, *ill-*, or *little-* are usually not hyphenated when they are modified by an adverb.

an ill-tempered man	*but*	a rather ill tempered man
a well-educated person		a very well educated person

An expression made up of an adverb ending in *-ly* and an adjective is not hyphenated.

a badly torn blanket   a happily married couple

Hyphens in Numbers

1. Compound numbers

Hyphenate any spelled-out cardinal or ordinal compound numbers up to ninety-nine and ninety-ninth.

forty-nine   eighty-fifth

2. Fractions used as adjectives

Hyphenate a fraction used as an adjective or an adverb (but not one used as a noun).

a two-thirds majority   *but*   two thirds of the members

3. Connected numerals

Hyphenate two numerals to indicate a span.

pages 151-218
1899-1968

When you use the word *from* before a span, use the word *to* rather than a hyphen. When you use *between,* use *and.*

from 1899 **to** 1968
between 2:45 **and** 3:15

Hyphens to Divide Words at the End of Lines

Words are generally divided between syllables or pronounceable parts. Because it is frequently difficult to determine where a word should be divided, check your dictionary. (For information on syllabification in dictionary entries, see Chapter 34.)

In general, if a word contains two consonants that occur between two vowels or if it contains a double consonant, divide the word between the two consonants.

bar-rel	hal-ter	skir-mish
gig-gle	rot-ten	won-der

If a suffix such as *-ing, -er,* or *-est* has been added to a complete word that ends in two consonants, divide the word after the two consonants.

black-est   fill-ing   tall-er

Objective

EXERCISE 13. Using the Hyphen. Rewrite the following sentences correctly, adding hyphens where they are needed and dropping them where they are incorrect. Then make a list of the italicized words, showing where each word would be divided if it had to be broken at the end of the line.

ex-roommate   all-around   highly motivated   ten-nis

1. My exroommate is a good all around athlete and a highly-motivated *tennis* player.

transatlantic   cross-ing   thirty-three

2. Charles Lindbergh, Jr., made the first solo trans-Atlantic flight in an airplane, *crossing* the Atlantic in just over thirty three hours on May 20-21, 1927.

12:15 to 1:15   crowd-ed

3. Since three fifths of the students eat lunch in the cafeteria from 12:15-1:15, the tables are very *crowded.*

self-reliant   nineteenth-century   fic-tion

4. The self reliant American is a popular character in nineteenth century *fiction.*

re-laying   brightly-colored   car-pet

5. The workers are relaying the brightly-colored *carpet* in the vice-chancellor's office.

well-known   sing-er   bell-like

6. Julie Andrews is a well known *singer* whose belllike voice has charmed music-loving audiences everywhere.

California-like   crop-killing   win-ter

7. For some months we had been enjoying Californialike weather, but then a crop killing *winter* frost set in.

whim-pers   three fourths

8. The *whimpers* of the ill tempered child disturbed three-fourths of the kindergarten class.

anti-British well respected fel-low

9. The antiBritish speaker is not well-respected by most of her *fellow* politicians.

10. The anti-inflation bill passed the state assembly with a two-thirds majority and was soon put into *effect* in twenty one counties.

ef-fect twenty-one

ABBREVIATIONS

Abbreviations are shortened forms of words. Abbreviations save space and time and prevent unnecessary wordiness. For instance, *200 B.C.* is more concise and easier to write than is *200 years before the birth of Christ.* Most abbreviations require periods. If you are unsure of a particular abbreviation, check a dictionary.

Use only one period if an abbreviation occurs at the end of a sentence that would ordinarily take a period of its own. If an abbreviation occurs at the end of a sentence that ends with a question mark or an exclamation point, use both the period and the second mark of punctuation.

He awoke at 5 **A.M.**
Did he awake at 5 **A.M.**

I visited Washington, **D.C.**
I loved Washington, **D.C.!**

Capitalization of Abbreviations

Capitalize abbreviations of proper nouns.

St. Croix **U.S.S.R.**
P.O. Box 43 **U.S.** Army

Abbreviations of organizations and government agencies are often formed from the initial letters of the complete name. Such abbreviations generally omit periods.

HUD **NATO** **CBS**
NBA **CIA** **RCA**

When using a person's initials, leave a space after each initial.

Robert **E.** Lee **W. H.** Auden

State names used in addressing mail may be abbreviated as shown in the following list. The official ZIP-code form consists of two capital letters with no periods.

Alabama **Ala. AL**
Alaska **AK**
Arizona **Ariz. AZ**
Arkansas **Ark. AR**
California **Calif. CA**
Colorado **Colo. CO**
Connecticut **Conn. CT**
Delaware **Del. DE**
Florida **Fla. FL**
Georgia **Ga. GA**
Hawaii **HI**
Idaho **ID**
Illinois **Ill. IL**
Indiana **Ind. IN**

Iowa **IA**
Kansas **Kans. KS**
Kentucky **Ky. KY**
Louisiana **La. LA**
Maine **ME**
Maryland **Md. MD**
Massachusetts **Mass. MA**
Michigan **Mich. MI**
Minnesota **Minn. MN**
Mississippi **Miss. MS**
Missouri **Mo. MO**
Montana **Mont. MT**
Nebraska **Nebr. NB**
Nevada **Nev. NV**
New Hampshire **N.H. NH**
New Jersey **N.J. NJ**
New Mexico **N.Mex. NM**
New York **N.Y. NY**
North Carolina **N.C. NC**
North Dakota **N.Dak. ND**
Ohio **OH**
Oklahoma **Okla. OK**
Oregon **Oreg. OR**
Pennsylvania **Pa. PA**
Rhode Island **R.I. RI**
South Carolina **S.C. SC**
South Dakota **S.Dak. SD**
Tennessee **Tenn. TN**
Texas **Tex. TX**
Utah **UT**
Vermont **Vt. VT**
Virginia **Va. VA**
Washington **Wash. WA**
West Virginia **W.Va. WV**
Wisconsin **Wis. WI**
Wyoming **Wyo. WY**

Capitalize the following abbreviations related to dates and times.

A.D. *(anno Domini),* "in the year of the Lord" (since the birth of Christ); placed before the date: A.D. 66
B.C. (before Christ); placed after the date: 500 B.C.
B.C.E. (before the common era); placed after the date: 300 B.C.E.
C.E. (common era); placed after the date: 80 C.E.
A.M. *(ante meridiem),* "before noon"
P.M. *(post meridiem),* "after noon"

Abbreviations of Titles of People

Use abbreviations for some personal titles.

Titles such as *Mrs., Ms., Mr., Sr.,* and *Jr.* and those indicating professions and academic degrees (*Dr., M.D., D.D.S., B.A.,* and so on) are almost always abbreviated. Titles of government and military officials and members of the clergy are frequently abbreviated when used before a full name.

Mrs. Nancy Reagan
Mr. John McEnroe
Ms. Vera Slade, **M.A.**
Henry James, **Jr.**
Victoria Proudfoot, **M.D.**
Dr. Jonas Salk
Gov. Thomas E. Dewey
Sen. John Glenn
Col. Greta Gold
Adm. Oliver Hazard Perry

Abbreviations of Units of Measure

Abbreviate units of measure used with numerals in technical or scientific writing but not in ordinary prose.

The abbreviations and symbols that follow stand for plural as well as singular units:

ENGLISH SYSTEM		METRIC SYSTEM	
ft.	foot	**cg**	centigram
gal.	gallon	**cl**	centiliter
in.	inch	**cm**	centimeter
lb.	pound	**g**	gram
mi.	mile	**kg**	kilogram
mph	miles per hour	**km**	kilometer
oz.	ounce	**l**	liter
pt.	pint	**m**	meter
qt.	quart	**mg**	milligram
tbsp.	tablespoon	**ml**	milliliter
tsp.	teaspoon	**mm**	millimeter
yd.	yard	**°C**	degrees Celsius or centigrade
°F	degrees Fahrenheit		

Objective

EXERCISE 14. Using Abbreviations. Write the abbreviations or initials for the italicized words or phrases in the following sentences.

Gov.

1. New York's *Governor* Mario Cuomo spoke at the convention.

T. S.

2. We read a poem by *Thomas Stearns* Eliot.

Dr.

3. Did you know that *Doctor* Joyce Brothers is an expert on boxing?

B.C.

4. King David lived in the ninth century *before the birth of Christ.*

A.D.

5. Columbus landed in the New World in *anno Domini* 1492.

NUMBERS AND NUMERALS

In nontechnical writing some numbers are spelled out, and some are expressed in figures. Numbers expressed in figures are called *numerals.*

Numbers Spelled Out

In general, spell out cardinal and ordinal numbers that can be written in one or two words. Spell out any number that occurs at the beginning of a sentence.

Two hundred and twenty singers performed.

Numerals

In general, use numerals to express numbers that would be written in more than two words.

There were **220** singers at the performance.
The area of Canada is **3,851,809** square miles.

Very large numbers are often written as a numeral followed by the word *million* or *billion.*

The area of Canada is roughly **3.85 million** square miles.

1. Money, decimals, and percentages

Use numerals to express amounts of money, decimals, and percentages.

> The bottle holds **1.5** quarts of liquid.
> The bank was paying interest at a rate of **9** percent.

Amounts of money that can be expressed in one or two words, however, should be spelled out.

> The apartment rents for **three hundred** dollars a month.

2. Dates and times

Use numerals to express years and days in a date and for specific reference to A.M. or P.M. time.

> Newfoundland became Canada's tenth province on March **31, 1949.**
> The movie was scheduled to begin at **7:05** P.M.

Spell out references to time used without the abbreviations *A.M.* or *P.M.* Spell out centuries and decades.

> The movie was scheduled to start at about **seven** o'clock.
> James T. Farrell's works depict America in the **thirties**.

3. Addresses

Use numerals for streets and avenues numbered above ten and for all house, apartment, and room numbers. Spell out numbered streets and avenues with numbers of ten or under.

> The office is located at **4** West **34th** Street, Room **9**.
> The restaurant is on West **Fourth** Street.

Objective

EXERCISE 15. Using Numbers and Numerals. Rewrite the following sentences correctly by making any necessary changes in the use of numbers and numerals. If no change is necessary, write *Correct.*

1. The Metropolitan Museum of Art in New York City is located on
   Fifth 82nd
   5th Avenue and Eighty-second Street.
2. For the convenience of art lovers, the museum is open Sundays and
   11:00
   holidays from eleven A.M. to 4:45 P.M.
3. 111th
   The Beverly Art Center in Chicago is at 2153 West One Hundred and Eleventh Street.
4. thirteenth-century
   Works of 13th-century French artists can be found at the Cloisters.

CHAPTERS 27–28 MECHANICS

CHAPTER 27 CAPITALIZATION

For each numbered item indicate the correct capitalization.

Riding the **(1)** cumbres and toltec Scenic Railroad from Antonito, Colorado **(2)** (The railroad used to run from Denver), to **(3)** Chama, New Mexico, is an exciting experience. The train runs in the **(4)** summer months through october of every year. You can learn more about it from John Albright's article in **(5)** the *New York Times.*

1. **(a)** Cumbres And Toltec **(b)** Cumbres and Toltec **(c)** cumbres and toltec
2. **(a)** (The railroad **(b)** (the Railroad **(c)** (the railroad
3. **(a)** Chama, New Mexico **(b)** Chama, new Mexico **(c)** chama, new mexico
4. **(a)** Summer months through October
(b) Summer months through october
(c) summer months through October
(d) summer months through october
5. **(a)** the *New York Times* **(b)** the New York *times* **(c)** *The New York Times*

Answers: **1.** b; **2.** c; **3.** a; **4.** c; **5.** a

Writing for Review Demonstrate your knowledge of capitalization by writing a paragraph that includes several different kinds of proper nouns, proper adjectives, titles, and quotations.

CHAPTER 28 PUNCTUATION

For each numbered item indicate the correct punctuation or usage.

According to William H. **(1)** Frey only human beings cry. **(2)** Animals tears fall if their eyes are **(3)** irritated however only human beings shed **(4)** tears when their emotions are touched. **(5)** Frey a biochemist has made a study of tears. He showed the movie **(6)** Brians Song **(7)** 1971 to see **(8)** peoples responses the film is about **(9)** 2 well known football **(10)** players and the untimely death of one of them.

1. **(a)** Frey only **(b)** Frey—only **(c)** Frey: only **(d)** Frey, only
2. **(a)** Animals **(b)** Animal's **(c)** Animals'
3. **(a)** irritated; however, **(b)** irritated, however **(c)** irritated, however,
4. **(a)** tears when **(b)** tears, when **(c)** tears. When **(d)** tears; when
5. **(a)** Frey a biochemist **(b)** Frey, a biochemist, **(c)** Frey, a biochemist—
6. **(a)** Brians Song **(b)** "Brian's Song" **(c)** *Brian's Song*
7. **(a)** 1971 **(b)** (1971) **(c)** (nineteen hundred seventy-one)
8. **(a)** peoples' responses. The **(b)** people's responses. The **(c)** peoples' responses, the **(d)** people's responses, the
9. **(a)** two well-known **(b)** two well known **(c)** 2 well-known
10. **(a)** players, and **(b)** players and **(c)** players; and

Answers: **1.** d; **2.** c; **3.** a; **4.** a; **5.** b; **6.** c; **7.** b; **8.** b; **9.** a; **10.** b

Writing for Review Write a paragraph that includes a short dialogue.

PART THREE: SKILLS AND RESOURCES

UNIT IX
Skills

Both in and out of school, situations will arise when you may need to write and speak fluently. Perhaps you will be preparing a written report, writing an office memo, filling out a job application, or preparing for a written test. These circumstances occur again and again during our lifetimes. The purpose of this unit is to help you learn skills that you will use in school and also in later life as you pursue a career, run a household, or make various business transactions.

Whether you are writing a lab report for a science class or preparing an office memo to fellow employees, a good vocabulary will help you communicate your ideas effectively. The first chapter of this unit examines a number of methods for improving your vocabulary.

The effectiveness of your lab report or your office memo could easily be undermined by a glaring error in spelling. In the second chapter of this unit, you will learn a number of ways to improve your spelling.

The third chapter of the unit focuses on actual business communications that you are likely to make now and in years to come. It includes information about the format and content of business letters and offers guidelines for filling out college applications and writing college-application essays.

Both in school and on the job, you will find that skill in listening and speaking is extremely valuable. The fourth chapter of this unit offers guidelines for improving your listening and speaking skills.

The final chapter of the unit examines a skill that is very important to you as a student: how to take tests. The information about test questions should prove especially helpful when you take standardized tests for jobs and promotions or to gain admission to a college or another school.

As you study the chapters in this unit, keep in mind that the skills you are learning are not merely to be applied to your work in English class. They are *life skills*—skills that you are likely to require again and again and again.

CHAPTER 29
Vocabulary Skills

A strong vocabulary is an important tool of effective communication. The more words you know and the more you understand distinctions between similar words, the more clearly you will be able to express yourself. This chapter examines ways to build vocabulary. It focuses especially on helping you improve the vocabulary you use in your writing.

WORDS IN CONTEXT

Perhaps the most natural way of building your vocabulary is by reading. When you read, you are likely to come across many new words. Often you understand the meanings of these new words because the words occur in sentences and in paragraphs—that is, they occur in *context.*

The **context** is the setting or surroundings in which a word appears.

By examining the context of an unfamiliar word, you can often figure out its meaning. You can also get an idea of how to use the word in your own writing. For example, consider these famous lines by the American poet Edwin Arlington Robinson:

> Whenever Richard Cory went down town,
> We people on the pavement looked at him:
> He was a gentleman from sole to *crown.* . . .

Robinson's use of the word *crown* may be unfamiliar to you, but the context gives you a strong clue to the word's meaning. Since *crown* is mentioned along with *sole*, you can figure out that *crown* in this quotation must mean "head."

Objective

EXERCISE 1. Determining Meanings from Context. Here are five quotations from famous works in American literature. Each quotation contains an italicized word that may be unfamiliar to you. Following each quotation are four possible meanings for the italicized word. Determine the meaning by examining the word's context, or surroundings. Then write the italicized word and its meaning.

1. Are fleets and armies necessary to a work of love and reconciliation? . . . Let us not deceive ourselves, sir. These are the implements of war and subjugation . . . What means this *martial* array, if its purpose be not to force us to submission?

—Patrick Henry

(a) friendly **(c)** warlike
(b) heavenly **(d)** sheriff

2. The dominant spirit, however, that haunts this enchanted region . . . is . . . a figure on horseback without a head. . . . The *specter* is known, at all the country firesides, by the name of the Headless Horseman of Sleepy Hollow.

—Washington Irving

(a) soldier **(c)** sword
(b) detective **(d)** ghost

3. The smith, a mighty man is he,
With large and *sinewy* hands;
And the muscles of his brawny arms
Are strong as iron bands.

—Henry Wadsworth Longfellow

(a) skinny **(c)** muscular
(b) small **(d)** weak

4. One of the wild suggestings referred to . . . was . . . that Moby Dick was *ubiquitous*; that he had actually been encountered in opposite latitudes at one and the same instant of time.

—Herman Melville

(a) present everywhere **(c)** living in water
(b) sinful **(d)** invisible

5. When I was a boy, there was but one permanent ambition among my comrades. . . . That was, to be a steamboatman. We had *transient* ambitions of other sorts, but . . . these ambitions faded out, each in its turn; but the ambition to be a steamboatman always remained.

—Mark Twain

(a) wanderer **(c)** permanent
(b) important **(d)** passing

Answers: **1.** c; **2.** d; **3.** c; **4.** a; **5.** d

Objective

APPLICATION EXERCISE. Writing Sentences. Show that the italicized words in Exercise 1 have become part of your writing vocabulary by using each word in a sentence of your own.

Suggested Answer for 1: Happy citizens celebrated the ending of martial law.

WORD PARTS

A second important way of building your vocabulary is by learning the meanings of the parts, or elements, that many English words contain. For instance, when you look at the parts of the word *unreachable,* you find *un-* ("not") + *reach* ("attain") + *-able* ("capable of"). You can therefore figure out that *unreachable* means "not capable of being attained."

When you write, you can put word parts together to make useful longer words. For example, instead of writing "Heavy snowfall made the mountaintop not capable of being reached," you can write "Heavy snowfall made the mountaintop unreachable." Notice how much stronger and clearer the second sentence is.

PREFIXES

A **prefix** is a word part that is attached to the beginning of a word or another word part.

Many English words contain prefixes. For example, *unreachable* contains the prefix *un-,* meaning "not." Knowing the meanings of common prefixes can help you figure out the meanings of words in which the prefixes appear. A knowledge of prefixes can also help you build new words to use in your writing.

Study the following chart of common prefixes:

PREFIX	MEANING	EXAMPLE
a-	without, lacking, not	apolitical
ante-	before	antedate
anti-	against, opposite	antiaircraft
auto-	self	autobiography
bi-	two	bilateral
circum-	around	circumnavigate
co-	together with, joint	coworker
com-, con-	together, with	compatriot, congenial
counter-	going against, opposite	counterproductive
de-	to reverse an action, to remove, to deprive of	decontrol, derail, demilitarize
dis-	not, opposite of, to remove, to reverse an action	discontent, disloyal, dislodge, disregard
en-	to put into, to make	encase, enlarge
ex-	previous, former	ex-manager, ex-singer
extra-	outside, beyond, more than	extraordinary
in-, il-, im-, ir-	not, without, lacking	incompetent, illegal, imbalance, irreverent
in-, im-	in, into	inflame, import

PREFIX	MEANING	EXAMPLE
inter-	between, among	interwoven
intra-	within	intraschool
macro-	large	macroeconomics
mal-	bad, wrongful, ill	malformed, maltreat
micro-	small	microcomputer
mid-	in the middle of	midway, mid-June
mis-	wrongly, bad, astray	misplace, misfortune
mono-	one, single	monotone
multi-	many	multilingual
neo-	new, recent	neocolonialism
non-	not	nonprofitable
omni-	all	omnipotent
post-	after	postwar
pre-	before	prepackage
pro-	in favor of, for	pro-West, prolabor
re-	again, back	relive, reemerge
semi-	half	semiconscious
sub-	under, beneath, less than	subbasement, subzero
super-	above, beyond, greater than	superimpose, superman
syn-, sym-	together, at the same time	synthesis, symbiotic
trans-	across	transoceanic
tri-	three	tricycle
ultra-	extremely, beyond	ultraconservative
un-	not, opposite of, to reverse an action, to deprive of	unimaginative, uncork, uncover
uni-	one	unilateral

Objective

EXERCISE 2. Using Prefixes. Rewrite each of the following ten sentences by replacing the awkward underlined phrase or clause with a single word that contains a prefix. Make sure that the new word is placed so that your revision reads smoothly.

SAMPLE: Susan B. Anthony was a leader in the movement that was in favor of suffrage.

REVISED: Susan B. Anthony was a leader in the prosuffrage movement.

1. In very different ways both Emily Dickinson and Henry David Thoreau were not conformists. *nonconformists*

2. The Pilgrims' voyage across the Atlantic ended at Plymouth, Massachusetts. *transatlantic voyage*

3. Harriet Tubman was an important figure in the movement against slavery of the nineteenth century. *antislavery movement*

4. The federal government handles issues involving commerce that occurs between the states. (interstate commerce)

5. George Washington Carver made important scientific discoveries using methods that were not orthodox. (unorthodox methods)

6. Special devices can remove the fog from the air. (defog)

7. Despite differences that seemed not reconcilable, Israel and Egypt were able to agree to a peace plan at Camp David. (irreconcilable differences)

8. Many early American buildings were designed in the style that was a new form of the classical style. (neoclassical style)

9. The general ordered an attack going against the previous attack by the enemy. (a counterattack)

10. Flight attendants must make many preparations before the flight before the passengers come on board. (preflight preparations)

SUFFIXES

A **suffix** is a word part that is attached to the end of a word or another word part.

A suffix has a grammatical function as well as a specific meaning. For example, the suffix *-able* is an adjective-forming suffix. In the word *reachable* the suffix *-able* turns the verb *reach* into an adjective. In addition, the specific meaning of *-able* is "capable of." Thus, *reachable* is an adjective meaning "capable of being reached."

Knowing the meanings and grammatical functions of suffixes can help you build new words to use in your writing. Study the following chart of common suffixes. The chart has been divided into sections that show the grammatical function of each suffix. Notice that a spelling change sometimes accompanies the addition of a suffix, as in the first example, where the *t* in *truant* is dropped when the suffix *-cy* is added.

Suffixes That Form Nouns

SUFFIX	MEANING	ORIGINAL WORD	NEW NOUN
-acy, -cy	state, condition	truant	truancy
-age	result, process	break	breakage
-al	action	survive	survival
-ance, -ence	state, quality	attend, persist	attendance, persistence

SUFFIX	MEANING	ORIGINAL WORD	NEW NOUN
-ant, -ent	agent, doer	contest, reside	contestant, resident
-ation, -ition, -ion	action, state, result	colonize, impose, elect	colonization, imposition, election
-dom	condition, state, domain	free, duke	freedom, dukedom
-ee	one receiving action	employ	employee
-eer	doer, worker, agent	puppet	puppeteer
-er, -or	doer, maker, resident	collect, island	collector, islander
-ful	amount	cup	cupful
-hood	state, condition	mother	motherhood
-ism	system, practice	capital	capitalism
-ity	state, quality	mature	maturity
-ment	action, result	astonish	astonishment
-ness	quality, state	bright	brightness
-(e)ry	people or things as a whole	artist, pot	artistry, pottery
-ship	state, condition	friend	friendship
-tude	quality, state	sole	solitude
-ure	act, result, means	please	pleasure
-y	result, action	photograph	photography

Suffixes That Form Adjectives

SUFFIX	MEANING	ORIGINAL WORD	NEW ADJECTIVE
-able, -ible	able, capable of	believe, collect	believable, collectible
-al	characteristic of	occupation	occupational
-ant, -ent	doing, showing	comply, pertain	compliant, pertinent
-ary	tending to	second	secondary
-ate	full of, having	affection	affectionate
-en	made of, like	wood	wooden
-ful	full of, having	sorrow	sorrowful
-ic	relating to, characteristic of	Islam, romance	Islamic, romantic
-ive	given to	protect	protective
-less	lacking, without	sense	senseless
-like	similar, like	web, bull	weblike, bull-like
-ly	like, characteristic of	coward	cowardly
-ous	full of, marked by	murder	murderous
-some	apt to, tending to	loathe	loathsome
-ward	in the direction of	east	eastward
-ly	like, showing	rust	rusty

Suffixes That Form Nouns and Adjectives

SUFFIX	MEANING	ORIGINAL WORD	NEW NOUN OR ADJECTIVE
-an, -ian	(one) belonging to	Mexico	Mexican
-ese	(something or someone) of a place or a style	China	Chinese
-ish	(something) characteristic of	Swede	Swedish
-ist	doer, believer, related to	Calvin	Calvinist
-ite	(someone) characteristic of	Brooklyn	Brooklynite

Suffixes That Form Verbs

SUFFIX	MEANING	ORIGINAL WORD	NEW VERB
-ate	become, form, treat	fluoride	fluoridate
-en	make, cause to be	short	shorten
-fy, -ify	cause, make	false	falsify
-ize	make, cause to be	modern	modernize

Objective

EXERCISE 3. Using Suffixes. Rewrite each of the following ten sentences by replacing the awkward underlined phrase or clause with a word that contains a suffix. You may have to make other changes so that the new sentence reads smoothly. Remember that you sometimes have to make small spelling changes when you add suffixes.

SAMPLE: Pretests are designed to measure how proficient a student is in advance.

REVISED: Pretests are designed to measure a student's proficiency in advance.

adjournment

1. The chairperson usually raps the gavel to signal the adjourned state of a meeting.

narrator

2. In *Our Town* the Stage Manager serves as the play's person narrating.

connotations, / the words' connotations

3. In choosing words poets are especially careful about what the words connote.

colonized

4. The Dutch made a colony of New York, which they called New Amsterdam.

alleviation of

5. Some drugs are designed for the action of alleviating pain.

an impressionistic painter

6. The American-born artist Mary Cassatt became a painter in the style of impressionism when she studied in Paris.

seizure of

7. The Coast Guard is often involved in the act of seizing smuggled goods.

alienated

8. Many people are made to feel alien by modern architecture.

impulsive

9. Wise shoppers are not given to impulse.

poisonous venom

10. Some snakes secrete a venom that is full of poison.

ROOTS

A **root** is the central part, or core element, of a word, to which other word parts may be attached.

In the word *unreachable* the prefix *un-* and the suffix *-able* have been attached to the root *-reach-*. While prefixes and suffixes can give you hints to a word's meaning, the real clue to a word's meaning lies in its root. Some roots, like *-reach-*, are also English words; others are not. For instance, consider the word *inaudible* in this sentence: The actress's lines were inaudible. The word *inaudible* contains the prefix *in-* ("not") and the suffix *-ible* ("able"), but the key to its meaning is its root, *-audi-*, which is not an English word. Only if we know that *-audi-* is a Latin root meaning "hear" can we figure out that *inaudible* is an adjective meaning "not able to be heard."

Latin Roots

Like *-audi-*, many roots come to English from Latin. A knowledge of Latin roots can therefore help build your vocabulary. Study the following chart of Latin roots:

ROOT	MEANING	EXAMPLES
-am-	love, friend	amorous, amity
-aqu-	water	aqua, aquarium
-audi-	hear	auditorium, audience
-ben-	good, well	benefit, benediction
-brev-	short	brevity, abbreviate
-cent-	hundred	cent, century
-cogn-	know	recognize, cognizant
-cred-	believe	discredit, incredible
-duc-	lead	duct, educate
-equ-	equal	equation, unequal
-fac-, -fec-	do, make	manufacture, affect
-frag-, -frac-	break	fragment, fraction
-gen-	kind, sort, origin	general, generate
-leg-, -lect-	read	illegible, intellect
-loc-	a place	locate, local
-man-	hand	manual, manufacture

ROOT	MEANING	EXAMPLES
-milli-	thousand	milligram, millimeter
-mit-, -miss-	send	mission, emit
-mor-	die	mortal, mortician
-ped-	foot	pedestrian, pedal
-pend-	weigh, hang	pendulum, suspend
-port-	carry	import, export
-reg-, -rect-	rule, right	regular, rectangle
-sci-	know	science, conscience
-scrib-, -scrip-	write	scribble, script
-son-	sound	consonant, sonar
-spect-	sight	inspect, spectrum
-temp-	time, season	temporary, temporal
-tract-	draw, pull	extract, tractor
-uni-	one	unite, unique
-ven-, -vent-	come	venture, advent
-vid-, -vis-	see	evident, television
-vit-	life	vital, vitamin

Objective

EXERCISE 4. Using Latin Roots. Using your knowledge of prefixes, suffixes, and Latin roots, write the meaning of the following words:

1. rectify
2. immortal
3. biped
4. unison
5. dislocation
6. aquatic
7. centipede
8. aqueduct
9. conscious
10. equable
11. transmittal
12. benefactor
13. fragmentary
14. incredulous
15. amiable

Objective

APPLICATION EXERCISE. Writing Sentences. Write an original sentence for each word in Exercise 4.

Sample Answer for 1: We will not pay the bill until the workers rectify their mistakes.

Greek Roots

Like Latin roots, Greek roots occur again and again in English words. For example, the word *phonograph* combines two Greek roots, *-phon-* ("sound") and *-graph-* ("writing"). A knowledge of Greek roots can help build your vocabulary. Study the following chart of Greek roots:

ROOT	MEANING	EXAMPLES
-aero-	air	aerospace, aerosol
-astro-, -aster-	star	astronomy, aster
-bio-	life	biography, symbiotic
-chrom-	color	chromatic, chromosome
-chron-	time	chronology, chronic
-crypt-	secret, hidden	cryptic, cryptogram

ROOT	MEANING	EXAMPLES
-gen-	race, kind	gene, genesis
-geo-	earth	geology, geography
-graph-, -gram-	write, writing	telegram, graphic
-hom-	same	homonym, homologous
-hydr-	water	hydrant, hydrogen
-log-	word, study	logic, biology
-metr-, -meter-	measure, instrument	metrical, barometer
-morph-	form, shape	endomorph, morphology
-naut-	ship, sail, sailor	astronaut, nautilus
-nym-	name	synonym, antonym
-path-	suffering, feeling	pathos, sympathy
-phil-	love	philanthropy, Anglophile
-phob-	fear	phobia, xenophobia
-phon-	sound	symphony, phonetic
-phot-	light	photograph, photosynthesis
-psych-	soul, mind	psychology, psychiatry
-scop-	examine, instrument	telescope, microscope
-soph-	wise	sophisticated, philosophy
-tele-	far, distant	television, telephone
-therm-	heat	thermometer, thermos

Objective

EXERCISE 5. Using Greek Roots. Using your knowledge of prefixes, suffixes, and Greek roots, write the meaning of the following words.

1. autograph
2. philosopher
3. homophone
4. synchronize
5. astral
6. hydrophobia
7. cryptography
8. pathology
9. geothermal
10. aeronaut
11. psychopath
12. nautical
13. amorphous
14. homogenize
15. astrology

Objective

APPLICATION EXERCISE. Writing Sentences. Write an original sentence for each word in Exercise 5.

Sample Answer for 1: Autographs of famous people often become valuable.

AMERICAN ENGLISH

American English is the English language spoken and written in America. It contains many **Americanisms,** words and expressions originating in or peculiar to America.

Americanisms come from a variety of sources. Early English settlers borrowed many words from the Native American tribes who lived in America before them. We see the influence of Indian languages in our place names (*Manhattan, Miami, Mississippi*), in our words for plant and animal life native to the Americas (*chocolate, skunk, tomato, woodchuck*), and in words naming the clothes, food, homes, tools, and customs of Native American peoples (*moccasin, powwow, succotash, tepee, toboggan, tomahawk*). Other Americanisms and American place names come from the languages of various peoples who settled in America along with the English—from French (*St. Louis, butte*), from Dutch (*kill* for "stream," as in *Catskill*), from the languages of Africa (*okra*), and especially from Spanish (*Los Angeles, San Diego, bonanza, canyon, mesa*). As other immigrants came to America, they often brought to American English their own words for their foods and customs. Americans now speak of eating *bagels* (Yiddish), *chili* (Mexican Spanish), *chow mein* (Chinese), *kielbasa* (Polish), *salami* (Italian), *souvlaki* (Greek), and *tempura* (Japanese), and they might buy many of these foods at a *delicatessen* (German).

Most dictionaries give a word's origins in brackets or parentheses before or after the word's definitions (see Chapter 34).

Objective

EXERCISE 6. Using Americanisms. Americans borrowed each of the following fifteen words from a language other than English. Look up the words in a dictionary, and then write their meanings and origins.

1. bayou
2. boondocks
3. cruller
4. depot
5. filibuster
6. gumbo
7. hex
8. kayak
9. mustang
10. pastrami
11. rutabaga
12. spelunker
13. totem
14. ukulele
15. zucchini

Objective

APPLICATION EXERCISE. Writing Sentences. Write an original sentence for each word in Exercise 6.

Sample Answer for 1: We spent Saturday fishing in the bayou.

REGIONAL DIALECTS

A **dialect** is a variation of a language spoken in a particular region or by a particular group of people.

Dialects may show differences in grammar, pronunciation, spelling, and vocabulary. The regional dialects of America often display differences in pronunciation; for example, the word *aunt* is pronounced differently in the South and in the North. America's regional dialects also have vocabulary differences. In New York

City you might eat a long sandwich called a *hero;* in Philadelphia a similar sandwich is called a *hoagie;* elsewhere the same sort of sandwich is called a *grinder,* a *sub* (short for *submarine*), or a *torpedo.*

Objective

EXERCISE 7. Examining Regional Dialects. For each of the following fifteen regional words and expressions, write another word or expression that some Americans use to mean the same thing. Look up unfamiliar words and expressions in a dictionary.

1. buckeye	**6.** goober	**11.** skillet
2. brook (noun)	**7.** larrup	**12.** smearcase
3. flapjack	**8.** mouth harp	**13.** stoop (noun)
4. friedcake	**9.** night crawler	**14.** teeter-totter
5. glowworm	**10.** polliwog	**15.** whirligig

SYNONYMS

Synonyms are words that have the same or nearly the same meanings.

For example, *finish* and *conclude* are synonyms. A knowledge of synonyms can help you improve your writing vocabulary. Consider this sentence:

> Some unproductive factories have obsolete management systems and obsolete machinery.

The use of the word *obsolete* in both phrases makes the sentence sound repetitious. Replacing the second *obsolete* with a synonym like *antiquated* would improve the passage.

In choosing among synonyms, be sure to keep in mind the **connotations,** or suggested meanings, of the different synonyms. For instance, *chubby* and *obese* both mean "fat," but the words have different connotations. If you were talking about a newborn baby, you would probably call the baby *chubby,* not *obese.* For more about word connotations, see Chapter 5.

Objective

EXERCISE 8. Using Synonyms. Rewrite each of the following ten sentences by replacing the repetitious underlined word with its synonym. Choose the appropriate synonym from the list below. Use each word only once.

abated	amalgamated	chivalrous	nocturnal	salutary
agrarian	augmented	domain	pilfering	voracious

1. Thomas Jefferson was interested in agriculture and envisioned an America with an agricultural (agrarian) economy.
2. The intensity of the winds lessened as the storm lessened (abated).
3. Exercise is healthful, but the healthful (salutary) effects of a balanced diet should not be underestimated.
4. The average family income has been increased (augmented) by wage increases.
5. Gallant knights were known for gallant (chivalrous) behavior.
6. Staffs are often combined when two businesses are combined (amalgamated).
7. The theft of office equipment has become a more serious problem than the theft (pilfering) of supplies.
8. The sounds of owls and other nighttime (nocturnal) creatures fill the woods at night.
9. The king's kingdom (domain) was vast.
10. Ravens are noted for their ravenous (voracious) appetites.

ANTONYMS

Antonyms are words that have opposite or nearly opposite meanings.

For example, *begin* and *conclude* are antonyms. A knowledge of antonyms can help you improve your writing vocabulary. Often you can strengthen statements by using an antonym for a word expressed with a weak negative. Consider these sentences:

WEAK NEGATIVE: Some trailers are not mobile.
REVISED WITH AN ANTONYM: Some trailers are stationary.

Instead of using *not* + *mobile*, the revised sentence uses an antonym for *mobile, stationary.* Notice that the revision is more direct and precise.

EXERCISE 9. Using Antonyms. (*Objective*) Rewrite each of the following ten sentences by replacing the awkward underlined phrase or clause with an antonym for the italicized word. For example, in the first sentence, provide an antonym for *permanent.* Make sure to place the antonym so that your revision reads smoothly. Choose the appropriate antonym from the list below. Use each word only once.

abet	condoned	docility	infringed (on)	succumb (to)
abjure	cursory	dubious	oblique	transitory

1. Like all fads, hula hoops and Nehru jackets were not *permanent.* transitory
2. Some modern poets make references that are not *direct* to Greek and Roman mythology. oblique references
3. Accomplices do not *hinder* criminals in the commission of crimes. abet
4. Some American colonists were not *certain* about the wisdom of rebelling against Britain. dubious
5. Hermits do not *partake* in the society of others. abjure
6. Some teenagers cannot *resist* the pressure of their peers. succumb to
7. The early Puritans condemned novels but did not *condemn* the writing of poetry. condoned
8. Poll taxes were abolished because they did not *respect* the constitutional right of all citizens to vote. infringed on
9. Some parents punish children for lack of *politeness.* impertinence
10. Many textbook sections require in-depth reading, but others require only reading that is not *thorough.* cursory reading

---

WORD LIST FOR WRITERS

The following list contains words that you will find useful in your writing. Try using each word in a sentence. If you have trouble at first, look up the meanings of unfamiliar words in a dictionary.

VERBS

abase	discern	initiate	provoke
absolve	deliberate		
acquiesce	deter	orient	saturate
advocate		overshadow	speculate
agitate	elaborate	overstate	stigmatize
alienate	embody		surmise
allege	endow	penalize	
	exalt	perceive	taunt
bewilder	exhort	permeate	thwart
		perpetuate	transcend
collaborate	implicate	perplex	
contemplate	impose	personify	venerate
	induce	peruse	verbalize
defer	inhibit	proliferate	vex

NOUNS

allusion	essence	metamorphosis	ritual
anomaly	euphemism		
atrocity		obscurity	serenity
aversion	façade		stagnation
		pallor	stigma
banter	hyperbole	paradox	
bias		periphery	tedium
	ideology	ploy	tranquility
caricature	illusion	predisposition	transformation
cataclysm	inference	preponderance	transition
chaos	intricacy	prestige	
	irony	prototype	vengeance
demeanor			virtuoso
devastation	jeopardy	rite	

ADJECTIVES

abject	fluent	objective	suave
aesthetic	frugal	oblique	succinct
affluent	futile	ominous	
ambiguous		opaque	tangible
analytic	immaculate		tenacious
arbitrary	impartial	pathetic	topical
	impenetrable	pedantic	trivial
bland	imperative	perverse	tumultuous
blatant	imperturbable	pompous	
boisterous	impervious	precarious	ultimate
	inane	premature	uncanny
candid	incorrigible	proficient	
capricious	individualistic	profuse	valid
copious	inexplicable	prophetic	vapid
	inflexible		vehement
deft	inherent	reticent	veritable
despondent	innocuous		versatile
disdainful	inordinate	sardonic	vigilant
dolorous	inscrutable	simultaneous	vital
	insidious	sinister	volatile
elusive	intrusive	skeptical	vulgar
eminent	irrational	solemn	
episodic		solicitous	whimsical
erratic	lavish	stark	
		strenuous	zealous
facile	mundane	stringent	

30 CHAPTER Spelling Skills

Good spelling is expected of every writer. Spelling mistakes in essays or short stories are certain to jar your readers and may prejudice readers against what you have to say. In job or college applications bad spelling can have even more serious consequences. This chapter looks at some of the ways in which you can improve your spelling.

SPELLING RULES

The spellings of many English words can be mastered with the help of the following spelling rules. Learning these rules and their exceptions will help you improve your spelling.

ADDING PREFIXES

When adding a prefix to a word, retain the spelling of the original word.

ir- + regular = irregular
un- + necessary = unnecessary

When adding a prefix to a lowercase word, do not use a hyphen in most cases. When adding a prefix to a capitalized word, use a hyphen. Always use a hyphen with the prefix *ex-* meaning "previous" or "former."

non- + standard = nonstandard
co- + author = coauthor
mid- + April = mid-April
ex- + actor = ex-actor

Objective

EXERCISE 1. Adding Prefixes. Combine the following prefixes and words, and write the resulting words.

1. dis- + appointed
2. dis- + satisfaction

3. ex- + wife
4. ir- + resistible
5. mid- + afternoon
6. mis- + spell
7. non- + fiction
8. pro- + Confederate
9. re- + commendation
10. re- + enlist

Answers: **1.** disappointed; **2.** dissatisfaction; **3.** ex-wife; **4.** irresistible; **5.** midafternoon; **6.** misspell; **7.** nonfiction; **8.** pro-Confederate; **9.** recommendation; **10.** reenlist

ADDING SUFFIXES

When adding a suffix to a word, do not use a hyphen in most cases. Do use a hyphen when adding *-like* to a capitalized word or to a word that ends in a double l.

American + -ism = Americanism
cat + -like = catlike
Chicago + -like = Chicago-like
bull + -like = bull-like

When adding *-ness* to a word that ends in *n*, keep the *n*.

lean + -ness = leanness
thin + -ness = thinness

When adding *-ly* to a word that ends in a single *l*, keep the *l*. When the word ends in a double *l*, drop one *l*. When the word ends in a consonant + *le*, drop the *le*.

annual + -ly = annually
beautiful + -ly = beautifully
dull + -ly = dully
incredible + -ly = incredibly

Objective

EXERCISE 2. Adding Suffixes. Combine the following words and suffixes, and write the resulting words.

1. bell + -like
2. Chicago + -an
3. cool + -ly
4. dog + -like
5. essential + -ly
6. keen + -ness
7. probable + -ly
8. subtle + -ly
9. sudden + -ness
10. Tokyo + -like

Answers: **1.** bell-like; **2.** Chicagoan; **3.** coolly; **4.** doglike; **5.** essentially; **6.** keenness; **7.** probably; **8.** subtly; **9.** suddenness; **10.** Tokyo-like

Words That End in *y*

When adding a suffix to a word that ends in a consonant + *y*, generally change the *y* to *i*. Do not change the *y* to *i* when the suffix begins with *i* or when the suffix is *-like*.

marry + -ed = married
duty + -ful = dutiful
marry + -ing = marrying
lady + -like = ladylike

Exceptions include certain one-syllable words combined with certain suffixes: *shy* + *-ly* = *shyly*, for example. When in doubt, check a dictionary.

When adding a suffix to a word that ends in a vowel + *y*, generally keep the *y*.

portray + -ed = portrayed
enjoy + -ment = enjoyment

Exceptions include *day* + *-ly* = *daily*, *gay* + *-ly* = *gaily*.

Objective

EXERCISE 3. Adding Suffixes to Words that End in *y*. Combine the following words and suffixes, and write the resulting words.

1. ally + -ance
2. city + -like
3. empty + -ed
4. forty + -eth
5. harmony + -ous
6. likely + -hood
7. marry + -age
8. mystify + -ing
9. vary + -ous
10. way + -ward

Answers: **1.** alliance; **2.** citylike; **3.** emptied; **4.** fortieth; **5.** harmonious; **6.** likelihood; **7.** marriage; **8.** mystifying; **9.** various; **10.** wayward

Words That End in Silent *e*

When adding a suffix that begins with a consonant to a word that ends in silent *e*, generally keep the *e*.

safe + -ty = safety
immediate + -ly = immediately

Exceptions include a number of one-syllable words and words that end in *dge* or two vowels; for example, *acknowledge* + *-ment* = *acknowledgment*, *argue* + *-ment* = *argument*, *awe* + *-ful* = *awful*, *judge* + *-ment* = *judgment*. When in doubt, check a dictionary.

When adding a suffix that begins with a vowel (including *-y* pronounced *e*) to a word that ends in silent *e*, generally drop the *e*. When adding a suffix that begins with *a* or *o* to a word that ends in *ce* or *ge*, keep the *e* so that the word will retain the soft sound of the *c* or the *g*.

love + -able = lovable	peace + -able = peaceable
ice + -y = icy	courage + -ous = courageous

Exceptions include certain one-syllable words and words that end in two vowels; for instance, *cage + -y = cagey, canoe + -ing = canoeing, mile + -age = mileage, toe + -ing = toeing.* A few one-syllable words that end in *i* + silent *e* change the *ie* to *y* when adding *-ing: lie + -ing = lying,* for example. When in doubt, check a dictionary.

Objective

EXERCISE 4. Adding Suffixes to Words That End in Silent *e*. Combine the following words and suffixes, and write the resulting words. If you think that a word may be an exception, check its spelling in a dictionary.

1. advertise + -ment
2. care + -less
3. conceive + -able
4. die + -ing
5. lace + -y
6. marriage + -able
7. notice + -able
8. severe + -ly
9. sincere + -ly
10. use + -age

Answers: **1.** advertisement; **2.** careless; **3.** conceivable; **4.** dying; **5.** lacy; **6.** marriageable; **7.** noticeable; **8.** severely; **9.** sincerely; **10.** usage

Words That End in a Consonant

When adding a suffix that begins with a vowel to a word that ends in a single vowel + a single consonant, double the final consonant if **(a)** the original word is a one-syllable word, **(b)** the original word has its accent on the last syllable and the accent remains there after the suffix is added, or **(c)** the original word is a prefixed word based on a one-syllable word.

wrap + -er = wrapper
pre•fer′ + -ed = pre•ferred′
counterplot + -ed = counterplotted (prefixed word)

Do not double the final consonant if the accent is not on the last syllable or if the accent shifts when the suffix is added.

mur′mur + -ed = murmured
pre•fer′ + -ence = pref′er•ence

Do not double the final consonants *x* and *w*.

box + -ing = boxing
flaw + -ed = flawed

When adding a suffix that begins with a consonant to a word that ends in a consonant, do not double the final consonant.

allot + -ment = allotment
regret + -ful = regretful

Objective

EXERCISE 5. Adding Suffixes to Words That End in a Consonant. Combine the following words and suffixes, and write the resulting words.

1. admit + -ance
2. allot + -ed
3. benefit + -ed
4. control + -able
5. defer + -ed
6. defer + -ence
7. equip + -ing
8. equip + -ment
9. prefer + -able
10. repel + -ent

Answers: **1.** admittance; **2.** allotted; **3.** benefited; **4.** controllable; **5.** deferred; **6.** deference; **7.** equipping; **8.** equipment; **9.** preferable; **10.** repellent

SPELLING PLURALS

RULES	EXAMPLES
To form the plural of most nouns, including proper nouns, add *s*. If the noun ends in *ch*, *s*, *sh*, *x*, or *z*, add *es*.	cat, cats Johnson, Johnsons box, boxes Jones, Joneses
To form the plural of common nouns ending in a consonant + *y*, change the *y* to *i* and add *es*.	cry, cries folly, follies secretary, secretaries
To form the plural of common nouns ending in a vowel + *y* and all proper nouns ending in *y*, add *s*.	day, days Carey, Careys Abernathy, Abernathys

RULES	EXAMPLES
To form the plural of common nouns ending in a vowel + *o* and all proper nouns ending in *o*, add *s*.	zoo, zoos patio, patios Renaldo, Renaldos
To form the plural of common nouns ending in a consonant + *o*, generally add *es*. For nouns from Italian that are related to music, add only *s*.	echo, echoes hero, heroes cello, cellos soprano, sopranos
To form the plural of most nouns ending in *f*, including all nouns ending in *ff*, add *s*. For some nouns ending in *f*, especially those ending in *lf*, change the *f* to *v* and add *es*.	belief, beliefs roof, roofs muff, muffs leaf, leaves wolf, wolves
To form the plural of some nouns ending in *fe*, change the *f* to *v* and add *s*.	knife, knives life, lives wife, wives
To form the plural of hyphenated or multiple-word compounds that consist of a noun and one or more modifiers, generally make the noun plural. Exceptions include hyphenated compounds with *-year-old*, as in *two-year-olds*.	heir apparent, heirs apparent mother-in-law, mothers-in-law eleventh grader, eleventh graders runner-up, runners-up
To form the plural of hyphenated or multiple-word compounds of a verb and one or more modifiers, make the entire compound plural.	push-up, push-ups spin-off, spin-offs take-in, take-ins
To form the plural of most compound nouns written as one word, make the entire compound plural.	cupful, cupfuls gooseberry, gooseberries werewolf, werewolves
To form the plural of letters, numerals, symbols, and words used as words, add an apostrophe and *s*. Exceptions include dates, which do not require an apostrophe: *1920s*, for example.	*b*, *b*'s ABC, ABC's *3*, *3*'s *, *'s *but*, *but*'s

RULES	EXAMPLES
Some frequently used nouns have irregular plural forms that must be memorized.	child, children man, men tooth, teeth
Some nouns, especially those ending in *s* and those naming animals, have the same form in the singular and the plural.	corps, corps series, series fish, fish sheep, sheep
Some nouns from foreign languages, especially Latin, form their plurals according to the patterns of their original languages. Some nouns from foreign languages have two acceptable plurals.	crisis, crises datum, data beau, beaus, OR beaux index, indexes OR indices

Objective

EXERCISE 6. Spelling Plurals. Write the plural form of each of the following nouns. If you are uncertain of the plural form, check a dictionary. If a noun has no plural listed in the dictionary, its plural is formed in accordance with the first plural rule on page 602.

analyses
1. analysis

attorneys general
2. attorney general

cargoes (preferred spelling)
3. cargo

catastrophes
4. catastrophe

chateaux
5. chateau

Connallys
6. Connally

crack-ups
7. crack-up

ghettos (preferred spelling)
8. ghetto

guesses
9. guess

headquarters
10. headquarters

Mendezes
11. Mendez

mosquitoes (preferred spelling)
12. mosquito

oxen
13. ox

parentheses
14. parenthesis

phenomena OR phenomenons
15. phenomenon

queries
16. query

shelves
17. shelf

trios
18. trio

valleys
19. valley

wrenches
20. wrench

SPELLING *IE* OR *EI*

Write *i* before *e* except after *c*,
Or when sounded like *a* as in *neighbor* and *weigh.*

I BEFORE *E*: believe, chief, grieve
EXCEPT AFTER *C*: conceive, deceit, receive
SOUNDED LIKE *A*: eighth, neigh, reign

Exceptions to this famous rhyme include *caffeine, codeine, either, financier, leisure, neither, protein, seize, weird,* and a number of words that contain a sound other than long *a* or *e,* such as *conscience, counterfeit, efficiency, foreign, forfeit, height, science, sufficient,* and *sovereign.*

Objective

EXERCISE 7. Spelling *ie* or *ei*. For each of the following incomplete words, decide whether you should add *ie* or *ei*, and then write the complete word.

1. defic__nt
2. hyg__ne
3. l__surely
4. n__ghborhood
5. n__ce
6. perc__ved
7. sc__ntific
8. s__ge
9. s__zure
10. y__ld

Answers: **1.** deficient; **2.** hygiene; **3.** leisurely; **4.** neighborhood; **5.** niece; **6.** perceived; **7.** scientific; **8.** seige; **9.** seizure; **10.** yield

SPELLING *SEDE, CEED,* OR *CEDE*

Use *sede* in only one word: *supersede.* Use *ceed* in only three words: *exceed, proceed,* and *succeed.* Use *cede* in all other cases: *concede, recede,* and so on.

Objective

EXERCISE 8. Spelling *sede, ceed,* or *cede*. For the following ten items, rewrite the misspelled words. If a word is not misspelled, write *correct.*

1. acceeding
2. conceded
3. exceeding
4. intersede
5. preceed
6. precedent
7. proceded
8. secede
9. succeded
10. supercedes

Answers: **1.** acceding; **2.** correct; **3.** correct; **4.** intercede; **5.** precede; **6.** correct; **7.** proceeded; **8.** correct; **9.** succeeded; **10.** supersedes

SPELLING UNSTRESSED VOWELS

Many English words contain an unstressed vowel sound pronounced like the *a* in *ago,* the *e* in *taken,* and the *i* in *pencil.* Dictionary pronunciations represent this unstressed vowel sound with the symbol **schwa** (ə).

To spell the unstressed vowel sound symbolized by a schwa, think of another form of the word in which the syllable containing the vowel sound is stressed, and then use the same vowel.

For example, to spell the last vowel in *simil_r,* think of *similarity.* In *similarity* the *lar* syllable is stressed, and you can clearly hear the *a*. Therefore, *simil_r* also uses an *a:* The correct spelling is *similar.*

Objective

EXERCISE 9. Spelling Unstressed Vowels. For each of the following incomplete words, determine how to spell the missing unstressed vowel by thinking of another form of the word in which the vowel is stressed. Write the complete word and also the form of the word that you used to figure out the spelling.

1. auth__r — author (authority)
2. emph__sis — emphasis (emphatic)
3. gramm__r — grammar (grammatical, grammarian)
4. horiz__n — horizon (horizontal)
5. hypocr__sy — hypocrisy (hypocrite, hypocritical)
6. lux__ry — luxury (luxurious)
7. par__lyze — paralyze (paralysis)
8. parenth__sis — parenthesis (parenthetic)
9. rever__nd — reverend (reverential)
10. symph__ny — symphony (symphonic)

EASILY CONFUSED WORDS

WORDS WITH SIMILAR SOUNDS

Some words with similar sounds are often confused. Learning the meanings and pronunciations of these words can help you avoid spelling problems. Study the following groups of words.

advice [əd vīs′] an opinion offered as guidance
advise [əd vīz′] to give guidance; to recommend

affect to influence; to act upon
effect a result; to achieve a result

breath [breth] air that is inhaled and exhaled
breathe [brēth] to inhale and exhale

conscience the ability to distinguish right from wrong
conscious physically and mentally awake; aware

desert [dez′ərt] a dry, barren region
desert [di zurt′] to abandon
dessert [di zurt′] the last course of a meal

formally politely; officially; according to custom or rule
formerly previously

personal [pur′sən əl] individual; private
personnel [pur′sə nel′] employees; staff

predominant having superior power or influence; prevailing
predominate to exert power or influence; to prevail

prescribe to give a direction or a recommendation
proscribe to prohibit; to condemn; to banish

Objective

EXERCISE 10. Spelling Words with Similar Sounds. In each of the following sentences, a choice of words is given in parentheses. Write the word that correctly completes the sentence.

1. He keeps (loose/lose) change in his pocket.
2. Job applicants are interviewed in (personal/personnel) departments.
3. Many doctors (prescribe/proscribe) aspirin for back pain.
4. Overeating is the (predominant/predominate) cause of obesity.
5. An earthquake's (affects/effects) can be devastating.
6. Nomadic tribes travel in (desert/dessert) caravans.
7. Ann Landers writes an (advice/advise) column.
8. It is dangerous to (breath/breathe) in asbestos particles.
9. He was troubled by a guilty (conscience/conscious).
10. The law will be (formally/formerly) adopted tomorrow.

Answers: **1.** loose; **2.** personnel; **3.** prescribe; **4.** predominant; **5.** effects; **6.** desert; **7.** advice; **8.** breathe; **9.** conscience; **10.** formally

HOMOPHONES

Homophones are words that have the same pronunciations but different spellings and meanings.

For example, *dear* and *deer* are homophones. Learning the meanings of homophones can help you avoid spelling problems. Study the following groups of homophones:

altar a table or platform for religious ceremonies
alter to change

ascent the act of climbing; upward movement
assent to agree; agreement

aural relating to listening or the ear
oral spoken; relating to the mouth

born brought into life
borne supported; endured

cite to quote or mention
sight the act of seeing; something seen
site a place or location

council an elected or appointed advisory group
counsel advice; to give advice; a lawyer or lawyers

idle not working or operating
idol an image of a god or a goddess; an admired person

principal the head of a school; greatest; first; main
principle a basic truth; a rule of conduct

stationary fixed; unmoving
stationery writing paper and envelopes

waive to relinquish a right or a privilege; to defer
wave to sway back and forth; a back-and-forth movement

Objective

EXERCISE 11. Spelling Homophones. In each of the following sentences, a choice of words is given in parentheses. Write the word that correctly completes the sentence.

1. The Constitution set down many (principals/principles).
2. He (waived/waved) his right to an attorney.
3. She was elected to the town (council/counsel).
4. Hebrew law prohibits the worship of (idles/idols).
5. I wrote the letter on white (stationary/stationery).
6. We saw the (cite/sight/site) of the Pilgrim's landing.
7. The hero's problems could not be (born/borne).
8. The ear doctor gave an (aural/oral) examination.
9. The mountaineer made a difficult (ascent/assent).
10. The bride and groom stood before the (altar/alter).

Answers: 1. principles; 2. waived; 3. council; 4. idols; 5. stationery; 6. site; 7. borne; 8. aural; 9. ascent; 10. altar

FREQUENTLY MISSPELLED WORDS

The following list contains words that are often misspelled by students in your grade. Master the words by **(a)** applying spelling rules where possible, **(b)** writing and rewriting the words, and **(c)** making up memory devices for problem words. For instance, if you have trouble spelling *penicillin,* remember: "There is an *ill in* the word *penicillin.*"

abridgment	aerosol	arctic	behavior
absence	aggravate	argument	bereavement
academically	aisle	Arkansas	beret
accelerator	allergic	ascend	biscuit
acceptance	allotted	assassination	blasphemy
accessible	all right	attendance	bookkeeper
accidentally	almanac	auditorium	brochure
accommodate	a lot	autumn	bruise
accountant	amateur	awful	budget
accuracy	analysis		bulletin
ached	anesthetic	bachelor	buoyant
acknowledgment	anonymous	ballet	
acquaintance	answered	balloon	cafeteria
acquire	anxious	banana	caffeine
adjacent	apparently	basically	calculator
advertisement	appreciation	beggar	calendar
adviser	appropriate	beginner	camouflage

campaign
cantaloupe
careless
Caribbean
carriage
castanet
catastrophe
caterpillar
cemetery
changeable
chassis
chlorine
chocolate
cocoa
coconut
cocoon
columnist
commissioner
committee
comparative
compatible
competence
complexion
concede
conceivable
conscience
conscientious
conscious
consistent
contemptible
controlled
corduroy
corroborate
counterfeit
coupon
courteous
criticize
cyclone

dealt
deceive
defendant
defense
deficient
delicatessen
deodorant
descend
desperate
development

disastrous
discipline
dissatisfied
divine
dominant
doughnut
dynamite

ecstasy
eerie
effervescent
efficiency
eighth
eke
elementary
eligible
embarrass
emperor
emphasize
endeavor
environment
epitaph
equipped
essentially
etiquette
exaggerate
exceed
excellence
excessive
exercise
exhilarated
extraordinary
extravagant

facility
fascinated
fatigued
February
feminine
fictitious
fiery
fluorescent
fluoride
foreign
forty
fourteen
funeral

gaiety
geyser

ghetto
glamorous
glamour
gnome
government
grammar
guarantee
guardian
gymnasium

handkerchief
harass
height
hereditary
hippopotamus
horizontal
hygiene
hymn
hypocrisy
hypocrite
hypothesis

Illinois
immaculate
immediately
incidentally
inconvenience
incredibly
independence
initiative
insistent
interference
interruption
irresistible
itinerary

jealousy
jeopardy
jewelry
judgment

kayak
kidnapped
kindergarten
knowledgeable

laboratory
laminate
larynx
leisure
leotard

library
license
licorice
likable
likelihood
liquor
livelihood
loathsome
lovable
luxury
lynx

maintenance
manageable
maneuver
marriage
martyr
Massachusetts
mathematics
meadow
memento
metaphor
millionaire
miniature
Minnesota
miscellaneous
mischievous
missile
Mississippi
misspell
moccasin
molasses
mosquitoes
municipal
murmured
mustache

naive
neither
nickel
niece
ninety
ninth
no one
noticeable
notoriety
nuclear
nuisance

occasion

occur
occurrence
offered
omitted
opponent

pagan
pamphlet
parallel
parentheses
partridge
pasteurize
pastime
penicillin
perceive
permissible
perseverance
persistent
Pharaoh
pharmacist
phenomena
phonetic
phosphorous
picnicking
playwright
pneumonia
polyester
porous
possession
prairie
precede
preferable
preference
prejudice
prevalence
privilege
procedure
proceed
professor
pronunciation
propaganda
propeller
psychology
pursuit

query
questionnaire

racism
receipt
reciprocal
recognizable
recommend
reference
referred
refrigerator
regretful
regretted
rehearsal
reign
relevant
remembrance
reminisce
renown
restaurant
résumé
rhinoceros
rhyme
rhythm
righteous
roommate
route

sacrilege
safety
sauerkraut
savvy
scenic
schedule
scholastic
scientific
scissors
seize
separate
several
severely
shriveled
sincerely
soccer
solar
souvenir
spatula
splendor
sponsor
strategy
strength
stubbornness
subtly
successful
suddenness
suede
sugar
sundae
superintendent
supersede
syllable
symphony
synonymous

tambourine
teammate
technique
temperamental
temperature
tepee
territory
thesaurus
tragedy
transcend
trespass
trigonometry
truly
turquoise
twelfth
tycoon
typhoid
tyranny

ulcer
undoubtedly
unmistakable
unnecessary
usage

vacuum
variety
versatile
vertical
veteran
villain
vinegar
volcano

Wednesday
weird
wholly
wintry
withhold
writ
writhe

yacht
yield

CHAPTER 31
Business Communication Skills

This chapter examines business writing and related skills that you will need to know when you are searching for a job, applying to a college or another school, or making other business communications. The chapter opens with a section about the format and content of business letters. It then examines college applications and the personal essays that they often require you to write.

BUSINESS LETTERS

A **business letter** is a formal letter written to communicate information or to request action. A letter is often more effective than a telephone conversation because it gives you an opportunity to organize your thoughts and to state them in specific, unmistakable terms. A letter also provides a dated written record that you can use for further reference or, occasionally, for legal proof of your communication. For these reasons, keep a copy of each business letter you write, at least until the matter under consideration has been resolved.

APPEARANCE AND FORMAT OF BUSINESS LETTERS

All business letters follow certain conventions of format and style. Generally, a business letter should be neat, clear, courteous, brief, and easy to read. It is therefore advisable to *type* business letters whenever possible. Use single spacing, and leave an extra space between paragraphs and between the different parts of the letter. To make the letter visually pleasing, use wide margins and center the letter vertically on the page. In order to center the letter, you will probably have to type it once, examine its length, and then type a centered final draft. Be sure that your final draft is free of spelling, grammar, and punctuation errors as well as messy erasures or typeovers.

The standard business letter is composed of six basic parts:

the heading	the body
the inside address	the closing
the salutation	the signature

On the following model business letter, the six parts are labeled. The model business letter is typed in **modified block style:** The inside address and the salutation align with the left-hand margin, while the heading, the closing, and the signature appear to the right of the center of the page and align on the left with each other. In modified block style each paragraph of the body may either align with the left margin or be indented. (Another example of a letter using modified block style appears on page 618.) In **block style** all six parts align with the left-hand margin. (An example of a letter using block style appears on page 619.)

The following subsections discuss the six parts of a business letter in detail.

The Heading

The **heading** contains your mailing address and the date of the letter. The name of your city, town, or village should be followed by a comma, your state, and your ZIP code. Also put a comma between the day and the year in the date. Do not put a comma before the ZIP code. If you are using stationery with a letterhead that gives your address, your heading consists of the date only.

In writing addresses, you should generally avoid abbreviations. However, you may use official post office abbreviations for the names of states (see Chapter 28).

The Inside Address

The **inside address** contains the name and address of the party to whom you are writing. It appears two lines below the heading. If you know the name of an individual to whom you should address your letter, put that person's name on the first line of the inside address. If you know the name of a room, a division, or a department to which you should send your letter, include this information as well as the name and address of the company or organization.

When you include the name of an individual, use the person's full name preceded by a **title of respect** if you know this information. Four titles of respect—*Mr., Mrs., Ms.,* and *Dr.*—should be abbreviated and require periods. Most other titles, including *Professor* and *Reverend,* should be spelled out. This title *Miss* is not followed by a period.

If you know the **business title** of the individual, you should usually put it on the same line as his or her name and separate it

Model Business Letter (Modified Block Style)

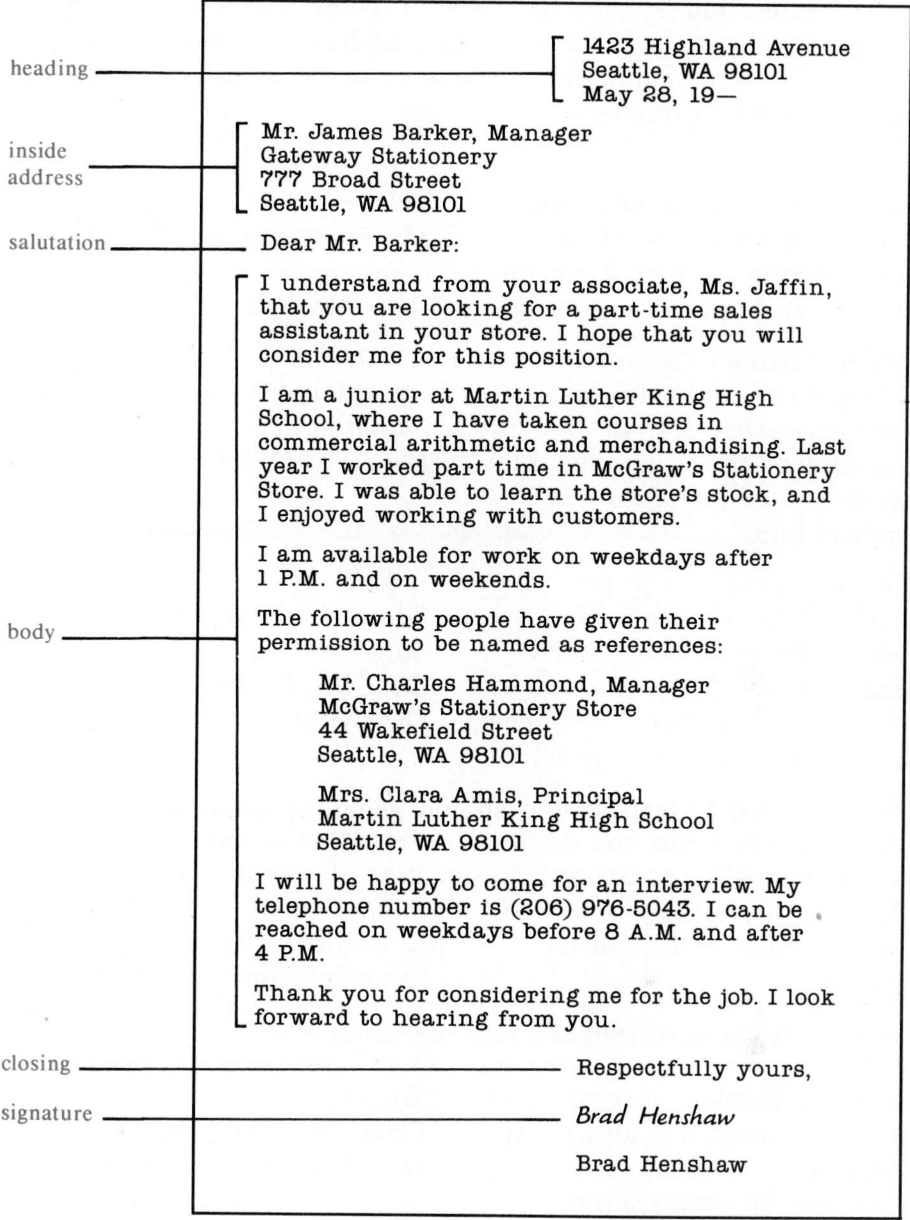

1423 Highland Avenue
Seattle, WA 98101
May 28, 19—

Mr. James Barker, Manager
Gateway Stationery
777 Broad Street
Seattle, WA 98101

Dear Mr. Barker:

I understand from your associate, Ms. Jaffin, that you are looking for a part-time sales assistant in your store. I hope that you will consider me for this position.

I am a junior at Martin Luther King High School, where I have taken courses in commercial arithmetic and merchandising. Last year I worked part time in McGraw's Stationery Store. I was able to learn the store's stock, and I enjoyed working with customers.

I am available for work on weekdays after 1 P.M. and on weekends.

The following people have given their permission to be named as references:

Mr. Charles Hammond, Manager
McGraw's Stationery Store
44 Wakefield Street
Seattle, WA 98101

Mrs. Clara Amis, Principal
Martin Luther King High School
Seattle, WA 98101

I will be happy to come for an interview. My telephone number is (206) 976-5043. I can be reached on weekdays before 8 A.M. and after 4 P.M.

Thank you for considering me for the job. I look forward to hearing from you.

Respectfully yours,

Brad Henshaw

Brad Henshaw

from the name with a comma. For example, in the model business letter, the business title *Manager* is included on the first line of the inside address. If adding the business title makes the first line look too long, you may put it on a second line and omit the comma.

Mr. Geraldo Martinez
Associate Editor

The Salutation

The **salutation** is a formal greeting to the reader of your letter. It appears two lines below the inside address and is followed by a colon. Different salutations are used in different situations, as the following chart explains.

SITUATION	EXAMPLE
When writing to a man whose name you know, use *Mr.* unless another title (such as *Reverend* or *Rabbi*) is appropriate.	*A letter to:* Mr. Francis Yeh *Salutation:* Dear Mr. Yeh:
When writing to a woman whose name and title you know, use *Ms., Miss,* or *Mrs.* as she prefers unless another title (such as *Dr.* or *Professor*) is appropriate.	*A letter to:* Miss Barbara Washington *Salutation:* Dear Miss Washington:
When writing to a woman whose name you know but whose title you do not know, generally use *Ms.* It is also possible to use her full name and omit the title of respect.	*A letter to:* Gloria Feldman, Director *Salutation:* Dear Ms. Feldman: OR Dear Gloria Feldman:
When writing to a specific person whose name you do not know, generally use *Sir or Madam.* It is also possible to use the business title of the person.	*A letter to:* Personnel Director Vasco Electronics Company *Salutation:* Dear Sir or Madam: OR Dear Personnel Director:
When writing to a company, an organization, a department, or a box number, generally use *Sir or Madam.* It is also possible to use the name of the company or organization.	*A letter to:* The Furness Corporation *Salutation:* Dear Sir or Madam: OR Dear Furness Corporation:

The Body

The **body** of a business letter begins two lines below the salutation and should be single-spaced, with double spaces between paragraphs. Although its contents will vary, the body should, in general, be brief, clear, and well organized. It should conclude with an expression of thanks or appreciation. If the letter follows up a previous letter or phone conversation, this fact should be mentioned in the opening paragraph.

The Closing

The **closing** appears two lines below the body and is followed by a comma. If the closing consists of more than one word, only the first word should begin with a capital letter. The tone of the closing may be very formal or a bit more personal, depending on your relationship with the reader or the tone you wish to achieve.

MORE FORMAL CLOSINGS	MORE PERSONAL CLOSINGS
Respectfully yours,	Sincerely yours,
Yours respectfully,	Sincerely,
Very truly yours,	Cordially yours,

The Signature

Your full name should be signed in ink just below the closing. Beneath your signature, type (or print) your name. If you have a business title, you may put it below your name, as Brooks Tillman does below. A woman writer may indicate how she wishes to be addressed by including a title of respect in parentheses before her name, as Amy Hern does below.

Respectfully,	Sincerely yours,
Brooks Tillman	*Amy Hern*
Brooks Tillman Class President	(Mrs.) Amy Hern

ADDRESSING ENVELOPES

On the envelope of a business letter, put your **return address**—your own name and mailing address—in the upper left-hand corner. Put the **recipient's address** just below and to the right of the center of the envelope. The envelope for the model business letter would look like this:

```
Brad Henshaw
1423 Highland Avenue
Seattle, WA 98101

                    Mr. James Barker, Manager
                    Gateway Stationery
                    777 Broad Street
                    Seattle, WA 98101
```

Be sure to include ZIP codes in all addresses. If you are unsure of a ZIP code, check a ZIP code directory at your post office or library.

KINDS OF BUSINESS LETTERS

Business letters are written for a number of different reasons. Among them are (1) to apply for a job or to a school, (2) to request information or services, (3) to place an order, (4) to make a complaint or ask for an adjustment, and (5) to make an inquiry.

The Letter of Application

Although most jobs and colleges require that you fill out a preprinted application form (see page 619), sometimes a letter of application may be all that is required. A **letter of application** asks that you be considered for a job, be allowed to enroll in a school or a course, or be permitted to join a club or another organization. An example of a letter of application is the model business letter in which Brad Henshaw applies for a part-time job at Gateway Stationery. You should follow these steps when you write a letter of application:

1. Identify the job, school, course, club, or organization to which you are applying.
2. Identify yourself.
3. Include relevant information concerning time, hours, and so on. For instance, if you are applying for a job, state the date you can begin and the hours that you will be available. If you are hoping to enroll in a special course, state the day, hours, and weeks or term during which the course is to be held.
4. Briefly explain your qualifications.
5. Include the names and addresses of people who may be contacted for references. If possible, give a **business reference**—a former employer or job supervisor—as well as at least one **personal reference**—a teacher, a neighbor, or another adult who knows you well. Always contact these people beforehand to make sure that they are willing to be named as references. Never list family members as references.
6. Include your telephone number and the best time at which you can be contacted.
7. Conclude courteously.

The Letter of Request

A **letter of request** asks for information or services from an organization or an individual. An example is the letter on page 618, in which Maria Ramirez writes to her state senator. Follow these steps when you write a letter of request:

1. Identify yourself.
2. Explain the reason that you need assistance.
3. State a specific request. If you are requesting the services of a

guest speaker or writing about another matter that involves a date, time, and place, be sure to specify the date, time, and place.
4. Conclude courteously.

The Order Letter

The **order letter** places an order for manufactured goods, magazines, or something else that requires payment. Follow these steps when you write an order letter:

1. Give the necessary information about the item or items that you are ordering. If you are ordering manufactured goods, for instance, specify the quantity, size, color, and price.
2. If you are enclosing payment, state the amount you are sending. Send a check or a money order; never send cash through the mail.
3. Keep a copy of the check or money order as well as the letter until the order has been filled to your satisfaction.

The Letter of Adjustment or Complaint

A **letter of adjustment or complaint** states a problem and asks that it be corrected. It is usually written to a company or an organization whose product or service has displeased you. Follow these steps when you write a letter of adjustment:

1. Give all the necessary details of the situation.
2. Be polite but firm. A courteous tone is more likely to get a positive response than a rude tone.
3. Ask for specific action, and indicate that you assume that this action will be taken.

The Letter of Inquiry

A **letter of inquiry** asks about job openings at a company or about the procedure for applying to a college or another school. An example of a letter of inquiry appears on page 619. You should follow these steps when you write a letter of inquiry:

1. Identify yourself.
2. Explain the reason or reasons that you are interested in a job at the company or in attending the school. If a specific job or subject area interests you, state it in your letter.
3. Ask for a copy of the company's job application or the school's application, and also request related printed material such as a school's course catalog or a company's list of current job openings.
4. Conclude courteously.

A Letter of Request (Modified Block Style)

13 Tremont Avenue
Orange, New Jersey 07050
November 3, 19—

The Honorable Cynthia MacPherson
The State Senate
Trenton, New Jersey 08625

Dear Senator MacPherson:

I am writing on behalf of the junior class at Thomas Jefferson High School. This year we are studying state government, and we would like to learn more about the work done by you and your colleagues in the State Senate.

I would like to invite you to speak to our class at any convenient time during the week of January 15. We are interested in learning about your role in preparing legislation that has helped the people of Orange. We would also like to hear about the many duties you perform as our representative in the State Senate.

Please let me know if you can speak to us. I can be reached at the above address or at (201) 737-8288 after 3 P.M. on weekdays.

Thank you for your interest and attention. I look forward to hearing from you.

Sincerely,

Maria Ramirez

Maria Ramirez
Secretary, Junior Class
Thomas Jefferson High School

Objective

EXERCISE 1. Writing Business Letters. For each item, write a letter *and* address an envelope. Use your name, address, and today's date.

1. Write a letter of application to Hiawatha Summer Camp, 82 Rosedale Street, Grand Rapids, Michigan 49506. You are applying for a summer job as an assistant counselor.
2. Write a letter of request in which you invite the President to speak at your school. Address your letter to The President, The White House, Washington, DC 20500. The correct salutation is *Dear Mr. President.*
3. Order a ream of 8-1/2″ x 11″ pink typing paper from Canon Office Supplies, Box 750, Hartford, Connecticut 06109. The price is $6.00.
4. Write a letter of adjustment to Canon Office Supplies (see item 3). The company sent you green typing paper by mistake.
5. Write a letter of inquiry to the admissions office of the college of your choice. Ask for an application and for related printed material.

Guidelines for Evaluation: Each letter should conform to the guidelines for that kind of business letter.

A Letter of Inquiry (Block Style)

32 Fountain Drive
Dallas, Texas 75224
September 18, 19—

Director of Undergraduate Admissions
University of New Mexico
Albuquerque, New Mexico 87131

Dear Sir or Madam:

I am a high school junior interested in anthropology and hoping to attend the University of New Mexico in September 19—. I would appreciate your sending me all available information on the procedure for applying to the university. Please include an undergraduate application, a copy of your undergraduate course catalog, and information on the possibilities of obtaining financial aid. I would also appreciate your sending me any additional printed material about courses offered by your anthropology department.

Thank you so much for your time and trouble. I look forward to receiving the requested materials.

Very truly yours,

Carol Pappas

Carol Pappas

COLLEGE APPLICATIONS

Most college applications are long forms with many sections. They require a good deal of advance planning and careful writing. Follow these steps when you fill out a college application:

1. Read the instructions carefully. Note the deadline for the application and the fee, if any, that must accompany it.
2. Read through the entire application, and make a list of the information that it requires. Arrange to take any required admissions tests, if you have not already done so. Also make arrangements with your parents or guardians, your teachers, your college adviser, and other people who may have to complete certain sections of the form. If the application requests written references from teachers and others, select people who will provide the best recommendations.
3. Familiarize yourself with related printed material supplied by the college admissions office—material like the course catalog or special guidelines for application.
4. Gather together the supplies and information that you will need to complete the application.

5. Make photocopies of the application, and work on these before you write anything on the actual application. Many applications require information about your interests, hobbies, achievements, and job experience; you will want to work carefully on your responses to these items. Be sure to include all your achievements and to state them in concrete, positive language.
6. Write, rewrite, and revise until you are satisfied with your responses. Show your responses to family members, teachers, or anyone else whose advice you feel will be helpful. Put your responses aside for a day or two and come back to them with a "fresh eye." Proofread carefully for spelling, grammar, and punctuation errors.
7. When you are completely satisfied with your responses, transfer them carefully to the actual application. Be sure not to introduce any new errors, and make sure everything is neat and legible.
8. Proofread your final copy carefully, and check to see that you have left nothing out.
9. Make photocopies of everything you submit in case your application is lost in the mail or misplaced at the college admissions office.

Objective

EXERCISE 2. Filling Out a College Application. The following portion of a college application is typical of actual applications that you are likely to encounter if you apply for admission to a college or another school. Main sections on the application have been given capital letters, and items have been numbered and sometimes further subdivided with small letters. Copy the appropriate letters and numerals for all items onto a separate sheet of paper. Next to each, write the information that you would provide if you were actually filling out the application.

APPLICATION FOR ADMISSION

Class of 19--

Please type or print in ink.

A. PERSONAL INFORMATION

1. Legal name ____________________
   Last First Middle (complete) Jr., III, etc.
2. Nickname or name you prefer to be called (if different) __________
3. Sex __________ 4. Birthdate ____________________
   Month Day Year
5. Mailing address ____________________
   No. Street City State ZIP code
6. Permanent address ____________________
   (if different) No. Street City State ZIP code
7. Telephone at mailing address ____________________
   Area Code Number

8. Permanent home telephone (if different) ________________
Area Code Number

9. Are you a citizen of the United States? ________________

10. If not, of what country are you a citizen? ________________

11. Have you applied to this university previously? ________________

12. If so, when? ________________

13. Do you plan to apply for financial aid? ________________

B. EDUCATIONAL INFORMATION

1. Area(s) of academic interest ________________

2. Probable career or professional plans ________________

3. School you attend now ________________

4. Address of your school ________________

5. Date of secondary school graduation ________________
Month Year

6. School telephone ________________
Area Code Number

C. PERSONAL INTERESTS, ACTIVITIES, AND HONORS

Please list, in order of importance to you, your hobbies and/or main school, community, and/or family activities.

	Name of Activity		Position Held or Special Achievements
1.	a. ________	b.	________
2.	a. ________	b.	________
3.	a. ________	b.	________
4.	a. ________	b.	________

5. Please note any scholastic distinctions or honors that you have earned during your years in high school. ________________

____

Please list any jobs you held during your years in high school.

	Employer	Position Held	Hours Worked Per Week	Dates
6.	a. ________	b. ________	c. ________	d. ________
7.	a. ________	b. ________	c. ________	d. ________
8.	a. ________	b. ________	c. ________	d. ________

9. Describe your summer activities, including jobs.

a. Last summer ________________

b. Two summers ago ________________

10. List the authors and titles of two books that most influenced you during the past year.

a. ___

b. ___

11. List two films, plays, musical events, or other cultural activities that most influenced you during the past year.

a. ___

b. ___

D. All information in my application is complete and correct.

1. ___ 2. ___
Signature Date

Guidelines for Evaluation: Students' answers should reflect careful adherence to the nine preceding guidelines.

THE PERSONAL STATEMENT OR ESSAY

Many college applications require you to write one or more **personal statements** or **essays.** Unlike most of the other responses on your college application, the essay does not provide objective information but instead gives you an opportunity to communicate subjectively with members of the college admissions board. The essay is your opportunity to make a personal impression in ways that test scores, school grades, and other factual data cannot.

One common request of college-application essays is that you write in general about yourself and the kind of person you are. Two examples follow:

> Initiative, creativity, organization, and perseverance are some of the qualities which contribute to success in college. . . . Acquaint us with examples of these qualities in your recent life.
>
> –The University of North Carolina at Chapel Hill

> Please provide information that you feel will give a more complete and accurate picture of yourself, e.g., unusual background, personal philosophy or traits, goals, etc.
>
> –Pomona College

Another common request is that you describe a single experience and explain how it has affected you. For example:

> Comment on an experience that helped you to discern or define a value that you hold.
>
> –Williams College

A third common request is that you describe a specific interest or idea that you have. For instance:

> Discuss some issue of personal, local, or national concern and its importance to you.
>
> —Hood College

A fourth type of essay asks you to explain the reasons that you wish to attend the particular school to which you are applying:

> Describe an intellectual interest or activity which you would like to explore in depth at Vassar.
>
> —Vassar College

A fifth type of essay asks you to display your imagination. For instance:

> Choose an event in history and imagine an alternative outcome. Describe the differences that one change would have made.
>
> —Pomona College

To see an excerpt from an actual answer to the last question, turn to Writers on Writing, Chapter 7.

Follow these steps when you write a college-application essay:

1. Read the directions carefully. Some directions specify the length of your essay; some require that you write more than one essay.
2. If there is a choice of topics, jot down your ideas on all topics before choosing one.
3. In choosing a topic, focus on an aspect of your life that you think will be interesting and memorable to the person or people reading your essay. Because members of college application boards will read many other essays along with yours, it is important that your essay be "special." Avoid topics that you think many other students will choose—like a summer job or vacation—unless you feel that your experience has special interest and relevance. Also avoid topics that show you in a negative light. Finally, while your essay can elaborate on a topic mentioned elsewhere in the application, do not simply repeat information that you have provided elsewhere.
4. Work from an outline, and write as many drafts as necessary.
5. Create an essay that is organized without being boring. Work on an introductory paragraph that not only states your topic but also captures the reader's attention. Create a closing paragraph that not only sums up your ideas but also makes the reader remember who you are. Organize the body of your essay into paragraphs, each of which focuses on a single main idea, and be sure to provide concrete details to support general

statements. Never be too general—specific details will make your essay more interesting. On the other hand, avoid a mere catalog of specific details that will read like a laundry list and bore your audience.

6. Consider the tone and style of your essay and the image of you that the essay presents. Does the essay sound too negative? Too self-critical? Too boastful? Too pretentious? Your essay should sound natural, honest, and positive. It should use good English but should avoid long-winded sentences and overly ornate language.
7. If possible, type the final draft of your essay; if not, print it neatly. Proofread your final draft to be sure that it contains no errors in spelling, grammar, or punctuation.

Objective

EXERCISE 3. Writing College-Application Essays. Write *two* college-application essays. Each should be from 200 to 500 words long. Respond to any of the sample essay questions provided in the preceding paragraphs or to any of the three additional essay questions provided below. (If you respond to Vassar College's question, you may change the name of the college to the school of your choice.)

1. "Between falsehood and useless truth there is little difference. As gold which he cannot spend makes no man rich, so knowledge which he cannot apply makes no man wise."—Samuel Johnson, *The Idler*, no. 84 Do you agree that there is such a thing as "useless" knowledge? Why or why not? (*The University of Chicago*)
2. Imagine the year is 1881. You may expect to live for another thirty-five years. What person would you most want to know well during that time? For what reasons? (*Swarthmore College*)
3. It is 12:35 P.M. on March 13, in the year 2002. Where are you, what are you doing, and what have you become? (*The University of Southern California*)

CHAPTER 32
Listening and Speaking Skills

Four score and seven years ago our fathers brought forth on this continent a new nation, conceived in Liberty, and dedicated to the proposition that all men are created equal.

—Abraham Lincoln

You may already be familiar with one of the most famous speeches in American history, Abraham Lincoln's Gettysburg Address. For decades, many American students have examined the power of Lincoln's language and attempted to deliver the speech themselves. These students discovered that language is not the only ingredient in making a speech effective. Voice, gestures, rapport with the audience—all these are important factors in effective speech-making.

The best speakers are often good listeners. They know that just as a good speaker makes listening easier, so a good listener makes speaking easier.

In this chapter you will study these two important aspects of oral communication—listening and speaking. To improve your listening skills, you will learn to practice responsive listening, to listen for main ideas and details, and to listen critically in order to evaluate the validity of what you hear. To improve your speaking skills, you will learn techniques for making your voice more effective and will examine how gestures and facial expressions can add to what you are saying. You will also study guidelines for reading aloud and reciting.

After studying listening and speaking skills, you will apply them to a number of situations that involve persuasion. These include formal persuasive speeches, formal debates, and informal group discussions. In applying listening and speaking skills to informal situations, you will also learn to make announcements.

IMPROVING LISTENING SKILLS

For five thousand years writing has been a transmitter of culture—but it was not the first one and certainly not the most important one for the majority of people. Throughout history, people *listened* to their teachers. They have concentrated on what was being said in order to extract meaning and to remember the important details. If they were unsure, they asked questions; if they wanted to show what they had learned, they made a speech.

RESPONSIVE LISTENING

To be a responsive listener, you must be an active listener. Listening involves more than just hearing what a speaker is saying. It also involves thinking along with the speaker. A responsive listener is engaged in an act of discovering the speaker's purpose, of uncovering the speaker's main ideas, and of determining the validity of the speaker's thoughts. The responsive listener must focus on what the speaker is saying, on keeping an open mind to avoid jumping to conclusions, and on demonstrating attentiveness through body language and facial expressions.

Objective

EXERCISE 1. Being a Responsive Listener. Working with a partner, take turns reading and listening. As the reader, choose an editorial from a newspaper or a magazine, and read it aloud at a faster-than-normal speed. As the listener, focus on what is being read, and when the reader is finished, try to repeat as much as you can of the editorial.

Guidelines for Evaluation: The speaker or another observer should determine the accuracy of the listener's statements.

LISTENING FOR MAIN IDEAS AND DETAILS

When you listen to a speaker, you are often listening for information that you want to understand and remember. You have to determine which information is most important and then focus on that information. Here are some techniques for determining and focusing on the speaker's main ideas and supporting details:

1. Be sure you understand the speaker's purpose. Is the speaker trying to inform, to entertain, or to persuade you to accept his or her beliefs? By understanding the speaker's purpose, you can focus on the information that supports the purpose.
2. Listen for words that tell you where the speaker is heading and how the ideas in the speech are connected. For example, some words indicate a time sequence *(first, then, last)*; some show spatial relationships *(near, far, in the middle)*; some indicate additional ideas *(besides, too, moreover)*; some indicate contrasting ideas *(however, nevertheless)*; and some signal results *(therefore, as a result, accordingly).*
3. As you listen, ask yourself questions to help identify the main ideas and supporting details. If, for instance, you have just heard three specific examples, you might ask yourself, "What do these examples support?" By asking yourself questions, you

will find that the speaker's ideas will become clearer to you and easier to remember.

4. Listen for words and phrases that signal new terms and definitions—words and phrases like *means, is called,* and *can be defined as.* Terms and their definitions are usually important details.
5. Pay attention to any visual aids that the speaker uses. For example, if a teacher writes a word or a list on the chalkboard as he or she is speaking, you can assume that the word or list is important.
6. As you listen, take notes on the important information. Taking notes will help you to organize the information and to remember it better. Do not try to write everything down; instead, focus on the information that you determine is important. Use abbreviations if you will understand them later, and use words and phrases rather than full sentences. Organize your notes, even if this means rewriting them later. Your notes should be organized to show the relationships between main ideas and supporting details. A good way to organize your notes is to use outline form.

Objective

EXERCISE 2. Listening for Main Ideas and Details. Listen while your teacher or a classmate reads the following passage. As you listen, take notes on the main ideas and important supporting details.

Most early societies had systems for transmitting messages. As civilization expanded, communication became an essential element in the ancient world. The earliest postal system originated about 2000 B.C. in Egypt as a means of prompt conveyance of orders from the pharaohs to their lieutenants in regions throughout the empire.

Although the Persians and the Greeks also developed communications systems, the Romans, with their well-unified empire and superb roads, conceived the most elaborate mail-delivery scheme, composed of numerous relay stations. Some historians contend that in a single day a Roman dispatch could cover 170 miles—a feat not equaled again in Europe until the 19th century.

The modern postal system dates back almost 150 years to a British treatise, *Post Office Reform: Its Importance and Practicability,* written by Rowland Hill, an educator and civil servant. The extensive study examined postal costs and concluded that the single fixed rate for all mail, regardless of weight or destination, did little to cover the costs of delivering a letter. From this idea sprang the practice of pricing a letter by weight and the distance it had to travel.

Hill also introduced the postage stamp, an adhesive label that served as a prepayment of postage for uniform rates and could be bought by the sender in advance at any post office. By 1840 stamps could be purchased in books of twenty. Questions have arisen over whether Hill or one of his assistants actually conceived the idea of a postage stamp, but in light of his vast renovations of an almost paralyzed system, the point becomes moot.

CRITICAL LISTENING

Good listeners hear not only what is said but also what is meant. They can test the validity of what they hear by spotting **fallacies,** erroneous statements that are the product of illogical or unreasonable thinking. Here are some common types of fallacies that you may encounter:

1. **Overgeneralization:** An **overgeneralization** is a statement that jumps to a broad conclusion based on too few facts. When listeners hear a speaker talk about "All teenagers" or "Students today," they have a right to be suspicious of the speaker's statements. Judicious use of *some* or *many* can cure this problem.
2. **Testimonial:** A **testimonial** aims to persuade people to do something because a famous person does it. The testimonial appeals to emotions, not reason, by implying that if you do what the celebrity does, you will be more like the celebrity.
3. **Either-or error:** An **either-or error** oversimplifies by stating that only two alternatives exist—either *X* or *Y.* An example is "Either we use calculators in math class, or we all fail." Either-or thinking is faulty because it fails to take into account that other options may be possible.
4. **Bandwagon:** The **bandwagon** approach attempts to make you think that you should behave in a certain way because everyone else does: "Everybody's doing it; why don't you?" The logic is faulty for two reasons: (a) not everyone is doing it, and (b) even if they were, popularity is not a valid reason.
5. **Personal attack:** A **personal attack** argues against a person instead of the ideas that the person believes or represents. Suppose, for example, that two students are debating an environmental issue and that one student says to her opponent: "What do you know about the environment? You got a *D* in biology last year." The remark attempts to invalidate the opponent's argument, but it actually has no logical connection to the issue of the debate.

Objective

EXERCISE 3. Recognizing Fallacies. Listen to commercials and speeches on TV or radio to find two examples of each of the preceding five fallacies. Share your findings with the class.

IMPROVING SPEAKING SKILLS

When you speak, deciding on a topic and finding the words to express your ideas are only half the battle. You also need to be able to speak in a way that will make others want to listen. If what you say is difficult to hear, if your manner and voice project boredom, if you fidget or seem ill at ease, your words will be less effective than if you look and sound convincing. People who depend on the way they speak to influence, persuade, entertain, or soothe others are often good models of effective speaking. Think, for example, of how doctors use their voices and gestures to calm patients, how lawyers sway juries, how salespeople convince customers, and how stand-up comics win over their audiences. They are all aware of the effect they have on others, and they adapt their manner to achieve specific goals.

USING YOUR VOICE EFFECTIVELY

Your lungs, voice box, tongue, and lips all help you to produce spoken words. To a great extent, effective speaking is a physical skill, and like all physical skills, it can be practiced and improved. Improving the quality of your voice will increase the effectiveness of your speaking and make you more confident. To analyze your voice production, keep these qualities in mind:

- **pronunciation**—the clarity and distinctness of your words
- **volume**—the loudness and strength of your voice
- **tempo**—the speed or rate of your speech
- **pitch**—the level or tone of your voice

Objective

EXERCISE 4. Analyzing Your Voice Production. Choose a favorite poem or a passage from a story, and read it aloud to a partner or into a tape recorder. Then use the following checklist to analyze your voice, or work with a partner and use the checklist to analyze each other's voices.

1. Do you pronounce words clearly and distinctly?
2. Do you speak at a suitable volume, neither too quietly nor too loudly?
3. Do you speak at a suitable tempo, neither too slowly nor too fast?
4. Is the pitch of your voice suitable, neither too high nor too low?

Guidelines for Evaluation: Use the preceding checklist to help students analyze their voices.

Improving Pronunciation

Learning to control pitch, volume, and tempo will make your voice more pleasing and increase the effectiveness of what you say. You also need to be comprehensible, or you will still have a hard time getting your message across. It is common to run words together in everyday speech, but slurring or swallowing your words can cause misunderstanding or block communication altogether. Separate your words just enough so that they can be heard, and pronounce them distinctly but naturally. Do not overemphasize the distinctions, or your speech will sound artificial.

Objective

EXERCISE 5. Improving Pronunciation. Read the following sentences aloud at a volume and tempo that will allow everyone in the class to hear you. Say the words as clearly as possible without overemphasizing the distinctions.

1. Did you learn anything?
2. I've got to stay here.
3. It's a story about a dog.
4. Whose idea is that?
5. Do you know where he is?
6. Can you avoid seeing her?
7. Joe is going to be a junior.
8. Lucy looked pale yesterday.
9. Alvin asked for a hundred dollars.
10. How did you lose your library card?

Guidelines for Evaluation: Refer to the analyses made in Exercise 4 to help students gauge the extent of their improvement.

Speaking Expressively

As you become more comfortable with your voice, you will be able to control it so that it helps express the content of your speech or your feelings about what you are saying. For example, you might speak softly (but distinctly) when you read a poem about a mouse, while you might speak loudly when you read a poem about a lion.

Objective

EXERCISE 6. Speaking Expressively. Choose one of the sentences below, and practice saying it in one of the ways suggested in parentheses. Ask the class to identify the emotion you tried to express.

1. I don't know what you mean. (angry, frightened, bored)
2. That's one of my favorite colors. (surprised, determined to have your way, explaining patiently)
3. He's been waiting a long time. (sadly, enthusiastically, tiredly)

Guidelines for Evaluation: Evaluate students on how convincingly they express the emotions and how well they can be understood.

USING BODY LANGUAGE

When you talk to someone, you communicate not only through your words but also through your **body language**—your posture, your gestures, and your facial expressions. Body language can add to what you are saying or distract your audience from your speech. Here are some guidelines for improving body language:

1. Stand up straight, and keep your posture relaxed and natural. Since the quality and tone of your voice are affected by your ability to breathe deeply and easily, standing straight makes you sound better as well as look better.
2. Keep in touch with your audience through eye contact. Move your gaze around the room, and look directly at as many people as possible. Eye contact makes people feel that you are talking *to* them and not *at* them.
3. Keep your face expressive—that is, show the emotions appropriate to your speech. A stony expression bores the listener.
4. Use gestures and shifts of posture to emphasize ideas or statements that you wish to emphasize. When you are not using your hands to gesture, let them rest quietly.

Objective

EXERCISE 7. Using Body Language. Take turns delivering the following passages in front of the class. Use posture, eye contact, facial expressions, and gestures to enhance and emphasize what you are saying.

1. In the past we have had a light which flickered, in the present we have a light which flames, and in the future there will be a light which shines over all the land and sea.

   —Winston Churchill

2. You gain strength, courage, and confidence by every experience in which you really stop to look fear in the face. You are able to say to yourself, "I lived through this horror. I can take the next thing that comes along." . . . You must do the thing you think you cannot do.

   —Eleanor Roosevelt

READING ALOUD AND RECITING

There are many occasions when you may want or need to recite a poem or read aloud a passage from a book. Reading and reciting call on all the speaking skills you have just been practicing. In addition, you should keep the following guidelines in mind:

1. Select material that you understand and like. Unless you fully understand and are emotionally involved with the material, you will not be able to convey its meaning to an audience. If the material has been selected for you, make sure that you at least understand it before you read or recite it.

2. Consider your audience and purpose. Is your material appropriate for your audience? What do you want them to think, feel, or do after they have heard your recitation?
3. Rehearse your presentation several times. Short poems or selections can be recited—that is, repeated from memory. Longer selections can be read, but you should be familiar enough with the material so that you need only to glance at the words as you read. In either case, rehearse, paying special attention to your facial expressions, gestures, and the way you use your voice. Remember that you should appear and sound as natural as possible and maintain maximum eye contact with the audience.
4. Concentrate on your breathing. Breathe at the natural pauses within the sentence—at places marked by commas, for example, or between clauses. Pause between sentences to catch your breath and to give your audience time to think about what you are saying.

Objective

EXERCISE 8. Reciting a Poem. Select a short poem that you enjoy and practice reading it out loud. Then recite it for the rest of the class.

APPLYING LISTENING AND SPEAKING SKILLS IN FORMAL SITUATIONS

The free exchange of ideas is one of the greatest benefits of living in a democracy. Issues are confronted and problems are solved by people coming together in peace to discuss things. Since words are the instruments of change, those who use words wisely and forcefully are often able to win others over to their way of thinking. Learning the techniques of persuasive speaking and debating will help you present your ideas in the best possible way.

PREPARING AND DELIVERING A PERSUASIVE SPEECH

Like a persuasive essay, the purpose of a persuasive speech is to influence others. Sometimes the speaker will want the listeners to change their ideas about a certain topic or event. Sometimes the speaker will encourage the listeners to change their behavior. Whatever the aim, the subject is bound to be controversial because it represents the speaker's opinion. This opinion can be based on fact—for example, acid rain destroys forests and fish—but the speech itself presents the speaker's thoughts about that fact. A persuasive speech can also try to convince people that something they believe is bad is really good or vice versa. For example, a speaker at a career-day assembly might suggest that students who use calculators in math classes are more attuned to technology than those who rely on memory. The purpose of a persuasive speech can also be to dispute a fact. For example, a defense lawyer will argue that the defendant is not guilty, and the prosecutor will argue that the defendant is guilty.

Opinion and attitude alone do not make a good speech. Here are some successful strategies that can be used in preparing a persuasive speech.

1. Research your topic. Find out everything you can about the topic. Ask yourself questions you think your listeners will want to know. Try to answer the questions of someone who might disagree with you.
2. Offer solutions to the questions you raise. Anticipating what the opposition might say helps win your listeners to your point of view. You should also tell your listeners what could happen if your plan were put into effect.
3. List all the arguments. Before you make your final preparations for the speech, list all the arguments for and against the position you have taken. Look at each one closely. Then ask yourself: Has all the research I have done served to strengthen my original opinion, or do I want to change my mind? If you feel uncomfortable with your original position, now is the time to change it. The more convinced you are of the rightness of your statements, the more you will convince your audience.
4. State your purpose at the beginning. Make sure the purpose of your speech—to persuade—is clear to the audience and that the way you organize and present the material fits the purpose.
5. Capture the attention of your audience. Enrich your speech with definitions, examples, quotations, comparisons, and anecdotes. For example, if you are trying to persuade your school to allow calculators to be used in math classes, you might tell how one class succeeded in solving more complex math problems in less time because they were free to spend their mental energy on problem-solving rather than on adding and multiplying. Visual aids, charts, and graphs can also be helpful.
6. Focus your topic to suit your audience. A school principal will want to know how well the students who used calculators did on their SAT's. A math teacher will want to know what kinds of mathematical operations can be done on the calculators and what kinds cannot be done. Math students would probably want to know how quickly they can do their work.

7. Explain your position. Let your audience know how *you* arrived at this position. Then present your arguments and describe your solutions.
8. End with a request. Summarize your arguments and restate your position. Then direct your audience to do something about what you have just proposed. The **call to action** can be a request for support or for a vote or for a change of behavior—but it should always be strong.
9. Remember the differences between speech-writing and essay-writing. In essay-writing you turn your notes into sentences. In speech-writing, with the exception of the opening and closing of the speech, most of your notes remain notes. You will write a few key words and phrases or the main points of your outline on note cards and refer to them as you speak. Practice delivering your speech, and pay attention to the point where your audience might question your position.

Objective

EXERCISE 9. Preparing and Presenting a Persuasive Speech. Select a topic that you and your audience have strong feelings about. Prepare a speech to persuade your audience to your point of view. Use visual aids if they are appropriate. The speech should take about eight minutes. Rehearse your speech; then present it to the class. End with a call to action.

Objective

EXERCISE 10. Evaluating a Persuasive Speech. Use the following checklist to evaluate your classmates' speeches:

1. Did the speaker make the purpose clear?
2. Was the background of the topic given?
3. Did the speaker do sufficient research?
4. Were both sides of the argument presented?
5. Did the speaker capture your interest?
6. Was there enough information given to support the speaker's position?
7. Was there a strong call to action?
8. Were you convinced?
9. Was the speaker's voice clear and pleasing? Were the gestures and facial expressions appropriate?
10. Was the speaker relaxed and responsive to the audience?

DEBATING

A **debate** is an extremely formal discussion. Its purpose is to demonstrate, for judges and for an audience, the two sides of a question. The speakers on each side try to persuade the listeners that their point of view makes sense and that the opposing point of view cannot be defended.

Debating Procedure

A debate is conducted according to established rules and procedures. The following features usually characterize a debate:

1. The topic of a debate is usually worded as a **proposition,** or formal proposal. It begins with the word *resolved* and goes on to advocate, or support, a change in some existing policy: Resolved: *The President of the United States should be elected for one six-year term,* or Resolved: *Bicycle riders over the age of twelve should be licensed.*
2. Participants in the debate argue either for the proposition (**affirmative**) or against the proposition (**negative**).
3. There is an equal number of speakers (usually two) on each side of the question.
4. The debaters present a logical, carefully worked out series of arguments called a **case.** Each side prepares a **brief**—a detailed outline listing all the arguments on both sides of the issue.
5. The debate is divided into two parts. The first part is devoted to the presentation of each side's case, or to the **constructive speeches.** During the second part, or **rebuttal,** each side challenges the other's case.
6. At the end of the debate, the judges select the winning team. It is always the responsibility of the affirmative side to prove that the change in policy should be made. The negative side must demonstrate that the change is unnecessary or undesirable by responding to the affirmative side's attack.

Selecting and Wording a Debate Topic

The first step in a debate is selecting a topic and wording it correctly so that you have a debatable proposition. Keep the following points in mind:

1. The topic should be an issue that has two sides—for and against. It should, however, contain only one main idea. For instance, "Resolved: Our Community Could Benefit From Conservation Measures" doesn't state an issue clearly. "Resolved: Our Community Should Enact a Bottle Deposit Law and Open a Recycling Center" is better, but it complicates the proposition by making two recommendations. "Resolved: Our Community Should Enact a Bottle Deposit Law" is a proposition that debaters could readily take a stand for or against.
2. The topic should be worded so that debaters speaking for the proposition (affirmative) are in favor of the proposed change in

policy. Debaters on the negative side argue against the change; they do not recommend an alternative change.

3. The topic should be worded positively rather than negatively—"Resolved: Cigarette Advertising Should Be Banned from Magazines," rather than "Resolved: Cigarette Advertising Should Not Appear in Magazines."
4. The topic should avoid loaded, or biased, language. "Resolved: Our School Should Adopt a Dress Code" is preferable to "Resolved: Our School Should Penalize Students Who Dress Sloppily."

Objective

EXERCISE 11. Wording a Debate Topic. Write suitable propositions for debate by rewording each idea below.

1. Reduction in speed limits.
2. Nonsmoking sections in public buildings.
3. Change in the voting age.
4. Change in the driving age.
5. Use of animals in laboratory research.

Preparing for a Debate

Follow these steps when you prepare for a debate:

1. Examine both sides of the issue thoroughly. You will be better able to defend your position and to rebut the opposition if you have anticipated the points your opponents are likely to make.
2. Assemble factual evidence—statistics, examples, expert testimony, etc.—to back up your assertions or opinions. Remember that

   - Primary, or direct, sources are better than secondary, or indirect, sources. Find the views of a scientist in an article by the scientist rather than in an article about the scientist.
   - Expert testimony should be relevant and appropriate—given by people who know the subject well, not just by people who are famous.
   - Statistics and other numerical data should be up-to-date, valid, and reliable. Try to anticipate statistics your opponent might use that would cast doubt on your figures.
   - Make sure your evidence is not based on an incorrect underlying assumption—for example, arriving at the conclusion that the man sitting at the receptionist's desk is not a receptionist because you assume that men never work as receptionists.

3. Working with the other members of your team, prepare an outline of both your case and the attack you expect to make on

your opponents' case. Transfer the key points to note cards to use during the debate. Place each major argument on a separate card, with a code keying the rebuttal arguments to the assertions.

Conducting a Debate

In a debate with two speakers on each side, the procedure outlined below is common. The amount of time each speaker is given depends on the total time allotted for the debate.

1. In the first set of presentations—the **constructive speeches**—the speakers present evidence to support their views. Each one speaks for the same amount of time (for instance, six minutes) in the following order: Speaker A—Affirmative; Speaker B—Negative; Speaker C—Affirmative; Speaker D—Negative. In addition to presenting their case, speakers B, C, and D might also begin to challenge what their opponents have said and to defend themselves against the attacks of their opponents.
2. In the second set of presentations, or the **rebuttal,** the speakers concentrate on attacking their opponents' arguments. The time allotted for rebuttal speeches is shorter than that for the constructive speeches (for example, three minutes instead of six). The debaters would speak in this order: Speaker B—Negative; Speaker A—Affirmative; Speaker D—Negative; Speaker C—Affirmative.

Objective

EXERCISE 12. Taking Part in a Debate. Work in groups of four to six students to plan and present a debate. As you listen to the other groups debate, ask yourself the following questions:

1. How convincing is their evidence?
2. How well is it presented?
3. How sound are their arguments?
4. How well does each side answer the other's arguments?
5. How well does each team member speak?

Vote on which side—the affirmative or the negative—should win each debate.

Guidelines for Evaluation: Use the preceding guidelines and questions to evaluate each group's debate.

APPLYING LISTENING AND SPEAKING SKILLS IN INFORMAL SITUATIONS

Not all listening-speaking situations are structured as formally as a speech or a debate. You are often called upon to tell a group something on the spur of the moment or to discuss something with a group—for example, to plan an activity. There are no set procedures to follow for situations like these, but there are techniques you can keep in mind for more effective communication.

MAKING EFFECTIVE ANNOUNCEMENTS

From time to time, you may be asked to make announcements in class, at a meeting, or over the school's public address system. To ensure that your audience hears and understands what you have to say, follow the steps below.

1. Make sure you have the audience's attention before you begin. Often, an emphatic "Listen here" or "I have an announcement to make" may be all that is needed. If there is a great deal of noise, however, you might clap your hands or whistle sharply or stand where everyone will notice you right away.
2. Speak clearly and at a volume that everyone can hear. Be careful not to swallow or slur your words, and make sure your voice is loud enough to be heard even at the back of the room.
3. Speak with authority. Your audience will be more likely to listen carefully if you sound informed and confident.
4. Make sure the message is complete. For example, if you are announcing that the buses for the field trip will be leaving in five minutes, be sure to tell your listeners where the buses will be. An incomplete message can cause confusion and even serious trouble.

Objective

EXERCISE 13. Making Effective Announcements. Use the following data to prepare a brief announcement; then deliver your announcement to the class.

TOPIC: school play—*Romeo and Juliet*
PROBLEM: play canceled because student playing Romeo is sick
SOLUTION: Tonight's performance postponed until Friday, April 7, 8:30 P.M. Those wishing to return tonight's tickets may get refund.
PLACE: Room 212. Time: After school today only.
Tickets for tonight's performance will be honored on Friday.
Additional tickets for next Friday's performance will be sold.
TIME: Monday, April 3. Place: In the main office.

GROUP DISCUSSIONS

When you and your classmates discuss the meaning of a short story or a poem, or when you break up into small groups to edit each other's writing, you have a clear purpose in mind. The purpose is usually so clear that everyone in the group recognizes when it has been accomplished—the group agrees on the theme of the story or the changes that should be made in each other's writing. What most participants are unaware of, however, is how the decisions were made. In other words, how does group discussion work?

Objective

EXERCISE 14. Observing Group Behavior. During the next group discussion, observe and chart answers to the following checklist. Report your findings in a class discussion. Work with classmates to prepare a statement on how group discussions work in your classroom.

1. How many participants were there?
2. How many participants spoke more than once?
3. Did any of the participants react to what someone else said?
4. Did any of the participants disagree strongly with what someone said? If so, was the disagreement voiced courteously?
5. Did any student assume the role of leading or guiding the discussion?

Guidelines for Evaluation: Students' statements should incorporate answers to all of the preceding questions.

Improving Group Discussions

When you observed group discussion in your own classroom, you probably noted that some people seemed more involved than others in keeping the discussion going but that not all the best ideas came from those who talked the most. You also may have noted that disagreements often gave rise to new insights if they were handled courteously. If the discussion was a particularly fruitful one, you became aware of how effective it was when one speaker reacted to what someone else had said. A discussion in which all the participants feel free to say what they think to any other member of the group is called an **open-channel network.** Discussion groups that are open are usually more productive because nothing blocks the flow of ideas. When everyone feels that all ideas will be heard, more ideas—and more solutions—seem almost magically to spring forth.

If you want to improve the quality and effectiveness of group discussions, try to apply the following techniques:

1. Make everything group-centered. Each participant should not only participate fully but should also actively encourage the quieter members to share their ideas. Asking directly, "What do you think?" keeps the discussion moving.
2. Find a good leader when you need one. When a group is small, a leader may not be necessary. Larger groups benefit from a leader whose responsibility it is to keep the discussion focused, to encourage all members to contribute, to resolve conflicts,

and to sum up. Watch out for the type of leader who wants to turn the group discussion into a speech for one. A do-nothing leader who refuses to exercise any control is equally bad.

3. Choose a decision-making process. When the discussion period is over, how will your group come to a decision? You can decide to vote on the issue—in which case a simple majority will determine the decision. This is quick and sure, but it tends to leave a minority who feel that they lost. Decision-making by consensus takes longer because it is based on the group's arriving at a position that everyone can agree on. Compromises have to be worked out, and participants must be willing to give up something in order for group unity to be achieved. The advantage of consensus is that no one feels left out, and the group decision has a better chance of being acted on.
4. Learn to play productive roles in discussion. Participants should be aware of the kinds of behavior that encourage productive discussion:

   - **initiating**—starting the discussion and bringing up new questions
   - **supporting**—encouraging others by nodding and saying *yes*
   - **refining**—asking for supporting data or restating ideas so that everyone can understand them
   - **welcoming**—making sure that everyone speaks
   - **pacifying**—acting as mediator when difficulties arise
   - **focusing**—keeping the group on the target
   - **summarizing**—letting the group know what it has already decided so that the same ground need not always be covered

Objective

EXERCISE 15. Participating in a Group Discussion. With your classmates plan a group discussion around some issue that you all feel is important. You may choose an academic issue, or a nonacademic issue. In either case, the purpose of the discussion should be clear, and the outcome should be able to be stated so that everyone will understand the position of the class. Make sure that you (a) select a leader; (b) choose a decision-making process; and (c) play at least one of the productive roles you have studied. When the discussion is over, schedule a second discussion to analyze your group's behavior and its ability to interact.

Guidelines for Evaluation: Students should follow the preceding four guidelines in conducting their discussion and in analyzing the behavior of the group.

CHAPTER 33
Study and Test-Taking Skills

This chapter examines standardized tests and focuses on three important college-entrance examinations: the Scholastic Aptitude Test (SAT), the Preliminary Scholastic Aptitude Test (PSAT), and the English Composition Test (ECT). All examples and questions in the chapter are taken from the actual tests and will give you an idea of what to expect when you take these exams. Because the basic principles of test taking are the same for all standardized tests, the general advice in this chapter will also be helpful for licensing, certifying, and other career-oriented tests that you may take in the future.

STANDARDIZED TESTS

GENERAL INFORMATION AND STRATEGIES

A **standardized test** is a test designed to be given to a large number of participants. The participants start at a signal, are given a specified task to complete, and are all judged by the same criteria, or standards. Most of the standardized tests that you will take are either aptitude tests or achievement tests. An **aptitude test** is designed to measure general abilities and to predict future performance. An **achievement test** is designed to measure knowledge gained in a specific subject area.

No matter what standardized test you are taking, keep these general strategies in mind:

1. Read the directions carefully. Often, each section of the test has a separate set of directions.
2. Before beginning a section of the test, glance over it so that you can see the number of questions and the range of difficulty.

---

3. In multiple-choice questions, be sure to read *all* the answer choices before selecting the best answer.
4. Pay attention to key words in questions and in answer choices. Often, qualifying words such as *mainly, only, most important, least*, and *not* can guide you to the right answer.
5. For multiple-choice tests, find out if there is a penalty for a wrong answer. If there is *no* penalty, answer every question, even if you must make a wild guess. If there *is* a penalty for a wrong answer, do not guess unless you have eliminated some of the choices and are down to only two or three possible answers out of four or five choices. Cross out the answer choices that you have eliminated so that you can concentrate on the remaining possible answers.
6. Do not spend too much time on a single multiple-choice question. Put a mark next to the questions you do not answer. Then if you have time later, you can return quickly to questions that you skipped.
7. Be sure to mark your answer sheet correctly. Use the right type of pencil, and if you skip an item, be careful to skip the same numbered space on the answer sheet.
8. Try not to get nervous or flustered when you take the test. Relax. Since most tests begin in the morning, it helps to get a good night's sleep and to eat a good breakfast before taking the test.

SCHOLASTIC APTITUDE TEST (SAT) AND PRELIMINARY SCHOLASTIC APTITUDE TEST (PSAT)

The **Scholastic Aptitude Test (SAT)** is a multiple-choice test that many students take for college admission. The test is designed to predict future performance in college by measuring a student's ability to handle two systems of symbols—words (in the verbal section) and numbers (in the math section). On the SAT you lose points for a wrong answer that you would not lose if you left the item blank. Since there *is* a penalty for a wrong answer, you should guess an answer only if you have narrowed the choices to two or three possibilities out of the four or five choices given.

The **verbal portion** of the SAT contains four different kinds of multiple-choice questions, each of which is examined in the upcoming sections of this chapter: **antonym questions, analogy questions, sentence-completion questions**, and **reading-comprehension questions**. In addition, the SAT contains a thirty-minute **Test of Standard Written English (TSWE)** with questions similar to the **grammar-and-usage questions** and **sentence-correction questions** of the English Composition Test (see page 650).

The **Preliminary Scholastic Aptitude Test (PSAT)** is essentially a shorter version of the Scholastic Aptitude Test. Most students take the PSAT in October of their junior year in order to practice for the SAT test. In addition, the PSAT is the qualifying test for the National Merit Scholarship competition and is sometimes called the PSAT/NMSQT. On the PSAT, as on the SAT, there *is* a penalty for a wrong answer.

Antonym Questions

Antonyms are words that have opposite or nearly opposite meanings. For example, *good* and *bad* are antonyms. **Antonynm questions** on the SAT and PSAT ask you to choose the word or phrase that is most nearly opposite in meaning to a given word. Here is a sample antonym question:

SUBSEQUENT: **(A)** primary **(B)** recent **(C)** contemporary **(D)** prior **(E)** simultaneous

The correct answer is **(D)**, *prior.*

Follow these strategies when you answer an antonym question:

1. Read *all* the choices before selecting the answer.
2. Remember that few words are exact antonyms; you must decide which word is *most nearly the opposite* of the given word.
3. Remember that many words have more than one meaning or can be used as more than one part of speech.

The preceding sample question illustrates the importance of reading all the choices given. Choice (B), *recent,* seems as if it might be the opposite of *subsequent* because *recent* refers to a past action and *subsequent* refers to a future action. However, if you had chosen (B) without reading the rest of the choices, you would have chosen the wrong answer. Choice (D), *prior,* is most nearly the opposite of the given word.

Objective

EXERCISE 1. Answering Antonym Questions. Write the letter of the word or phrase that is *most nearly the opposite* of the word in capital letters.

1. DOUBTFUL: **(A)** practical **(B)** consistent **(C)** nonexistent **(D)** impervious **(E)** unquestionable
2. VENTURESOME: **(A)** lacking agility **(B)** lethal **(C)** fragile **(D)** timid **(E)** without significance
3. RELAPSE: **(A)** carelessness **(B)** improvement **(C)** obstruction **(D)** composure **(E)** kinship
4. ALTRUISTIC: **(A)** groveling **(B)** stubborn **(C)** selfish **(D)** forthright **(E)** sagacious
5. DEPRESS: **(A)** force **(B)** allow **(C)** clarify **(D)** elate **(E)** loosen

Answers: **1.** E; **2.** D; **3.** B; **4.** C; **5.** D

Analogy Questions

An **analogy** makes a comparison between things that are alike in certain respects but are otherwise unlike. **Analogy questions** on the SAT and PSAT require you to understand the relationships between pairs of words. Here is a sample analogy question:

REQUEST : ENTREAT : : **(A)** control : explode
(B) admire : idolize
(C) borrow : steal
(D) repeat : plead
(E) cancel : invalidate

You should read an analogy question in the following way: *Request* **is to** *entreat* **as** *control* **is to** *explode;* **as** *admire* **is to** *idolize*; and so on. Your first step is to figure out the relationship between the given pair of words. Your next step is to choose the pair with the relationship most like the relationship of the given words. In this sample question, the correct answer is choice (B): *Request* is to *entreat* as *admire* is to *idolize.*

Follow these strategies when you answer an analogy question:

1. Think about the kind or quality of relationship that exists between the given pair of words. Is the relationship one of large to small? Weaker to stronger? Cause to effect? Part to whole? Are the two words synonyms or antonyms?
2. Pay careful attention to the order of the words in each pair. A pair of words with the relationship of small to large, for example, is not analogous to a pair of words with the relationship of large to small.
3. Make up a sentence expressing the relationship between the given pair of words. Then substitute each of the other pairs of words in your sentence to see which makes the best sense. Be sure to consider *all* the choices before selecting your answer.

In the sample analogy question, the relationship between the given pair of words is one of weaker to stronger: Although both words have similar meanings, to *entreat* expresses a stronger degree of feeling than to *request.* You could make up this sentence expressing the relationship: "To *request* with strong feeling is to *entreat.*" If you then plug in the choices, you will find that choice (B) makes the best sense: "To *admire* with strong feeling is to *idolize.*"

Objective

EXERCISE 2. Answering Analogy Questions. Write the letter of the pair of words that expresses a relationship *most like* the relationship expressed by the pair of words in capital letters.

1. AMPLIFIER : HEAR : :
   (A) turntable : listen
   (B) typewriter : spell
   (C) platter : eat
   (D) camera : feel
   (E) microscope : see
2. HOMESTRETCH : RACE : :
   (A) finale : opera
   (B) goal : contest
   (C) boundary : journey
   (D) terminal : station
   (E) platform : campaign
3. TREPIDATION : TREMBLING : :
   (A) luminescence : perceiving
   (B) recollection : remembering
   (C) intoxication : drinking
   (D) lamentation : wailing
   (E) sonority : hearing
4. SWILL : SWINE : :
   (A) roe : fish
   (B) coop : poultry
   (C) mutton : sheep
   (D) pesticide : vermin
   (E) fodder : cattle
5. AESTHETE : BEAUTY : :
   (A) enthusiast : cause
   (B) hunter : nature
   (C) administrator : government
   (D) advocate : legality
   (E) philanthropist : money

Answers: **1.** E; **2.** A; **3.** D; **4.** E; **5.** A

Sentence-Completion Questions

A **sentence-completion question** consists of a sentence that is missing one or two words. You are to select the word or words that best complete the sentence. Your understanding of the incomplete sentence helps you fill in the blanks. Key words within the sentence control the possible word or words that can be substituted for the blanks.

Here is a sample sentence-completion question with two words missing:

> One thing that makes *Othello* a great play is the way it takes jealousy, a characteristic flaw__________ to most of us, and __________ it into tragedy.
> **(A)** known . . . denigrates
> **(B)** horrifying . . . projects
> **(C)** common . . . magnifies
> **(D)** realistic . . . modifies
> **(E)** unnoticeable . . . elevates

The key part of this sentence is: *it takes jealousy . . . and* __________ *it into tragedy.* This implies that jealousy is changed in some way. Jealousy is described as *characteristic of most people.* This description matches *common* in choice **(C)**. To change jealousy, a common trait, into tragedy is to make it larger than life, or to *magnify* it. Since *magnify* is also given in choice **(C)**, choice **(C)** is the correct answer.

Notice that choice **(A)** begins with a word that itself would make sense in the first blank: Jealousy is, indeed, *known* to most of us. However, the second word in choice **(A)** does not make sense in the sentence: To *denigrate*, or criticize, jealousy would not be to turn jealousy into tragedy. Since the second word in choice **(A)** does not make sense in the sentence, choice **(A)** is not the correct answer. In a sentence-completion item that is missing two words, *both* words in an answer choice must fit the sentence.

Follow these strategies when you answer a sentence-completion question:

1. Be alert to the clues contained in the sentence. The given parts of the sentence will always provide clues to the correct answer.
2. If the sentence has two blanks, try to understand how the missing words are related to each other. For example, are they similar in meaning? Are they opposite? Does the second word reduce or increase the quality identified by the first word?
3. Be sure to consider *all* the choices before selecting the answer.

Objective

EXERCISE 3. Answering Sentence-Completion Questions. Write the letter of the word or words that *best* completes the meaning of each of the following sentences.

1. Many predatory animals are remarkably ________, crouching motionlessly for hours until they detect potential prey.
   (A) energetic
   (B) vicious
   (C) fleet
   (D) patient
   (E) massive
2. Even if they have no inclination toward doing what is ________, most people feel an urge to resist a prohibition for the sake of resistance.
   (A) absurd
   (B) arduous
   (C) prosaic
   (D) essential
   (E) forbidden
3. The valley would be ________ were it not for the flocks of ________ crows looking for a roost in the trees.
   (A) undisturbed . . . silent
   (B) agitated . . . tranquil
   (C) beautiful . . . majestic
   (D) secluded . . . tumultuous
   (E) quiet . . . raucous
4. Unfortunately, to speak and to ________, with some people, are but one and the same thing.

(A) infer
(B) relate
(C) illustrate
(D) offend
(E) enjoy

5. The contemporary student of ancient Greek science is struck by the ______ between that science and our own, no less than by the differences between them.
(A) affinities
(B) ruptures
(C) animosities
(D) distinctions
(E) inconsistencies

Answers: **1.** D; **2.** E; **3.** E; **4.** D; **5.** A

Reading-Comprehension Questions

The SAT and PSAT include questions based on reading passages of varying length and difficulty. These **reading-comprehension questions** are usually designed to test your understanding of a passage in several specific ways. Each question will usually ask you to do one of the following:

1. Understand the main idea of the passage.
2. Recall or identify facts and ideas in the passage.
3. Make inferences, or conclusions, from the facts and ideas given.
4. Evaluate the author's purpose, tone, or attitude.

Here is a sample passage followed by four reading-comprehension questions:

With our eyes we can distinguish objects whose sizes are as small as three thousandths of an inch. A microscope is used to see detail on a much finer scale, but the wave nature of light limits the detail that can be observed. Theory predicts and experiment confirms that with even the most perfect optical instrument, we cannot see anything smaller than the wavelength of the light used; for visible light, this is about a thousand times the diameter of an atom and a hundred million times the diameter of an atomic nucleus. Thus, in the conventional sense, we cannot see an atom, nor can we ever hope to do so.

One way to try to "see" to atomic distances and beyond is to use X-rays, light of a wavelength much shorter than normal visible light. Such forms of light are high energy waves, and the higher the energy, the shorter the wavelength. The sources of short-wavelength radiation are based on the fact that when an electron hits a target, radiation is emitted; the greater the energy of the electron, the shorter the wavelength of the radiation. Beams of electrons cause the radiations from X-ray tubes, betatrons, and electron synchrotrons.

However, short-wavelength light is not the only tool used to explore down to atomic dimensions and below, nor is it even the main one. A beam of particles can be used like a beam of light to probe the atom. "Wave-particle dualism" means that particles of matter—electrons, protons, and all the rest—behave like light waves in many phenomena. When a particle moves, it has a wavelength which decreases as the energy of motion increases. An electron microscope, which utilizes an electron beam instead of visible light, resolves finer details because the electrons used have wavelengths that are smaller than those of visible light. Of course, a "look" with a beam of electrons gives a picture different from that obtained with visible light. Beams of energy protons furnish still another view of our submicroscopic universe. Thus, these various tools provide descriptions which differ in the information they give. It is as if we were to photograph our landscape with different cameras, one of which films only the houses, another the trees, and a third the streets.

1. Which of the following statements about the observations of atoms is supported by the passage?
- **(A)** We may not be able to see atoms, but we can get a "look" at them.
- **(B)** The inner structure of an atom can never be examined.
- **(C)** Particles that cannot be seen cannot enable people to see atoms.
- **(D)** Theoretically, the most effective equipment for "seeing" atoms is the electron microscope.
- **(E)** The ultimate achievement in seeing would be to see an atom.

Question 1 requires you to recall facts from the passage. Choices **(B)** and **(C)** are direct contradictions of the information in the passage. Choice **(D)** is inaccurate because two other ways of "seeing" atoms are described in the passage. Choice **(E)** is irrelevant to the sense of the passage, which tells how, in fact, atoms *are* seen. Choice **(A)** is supported by the facts in the passage and is the correct answer.

2. Which of the following titles best describes the content of the passage?
- **(A)** Submicroscopic Particles of Matter
- **(B)** Electron Microscopes and Their Use

(C) Optical Instruments for Measuring Atomic Particles
(D) Wave-Particle Dualism
(E) Tools for the Investigation of Submicroscopic Particles

Question 2 requires you to understand the main idea of the passage, which the author indicates in the last two sentences. Choices **(A)**, **(B)**, and **(D)** are subtopics covered in the passage, but none is the *main* idea. Choice **(C)** is incorrect because the instruments are *not* optical: We do not "see" the particles in a conventional way, as the passage states. Once choice **(E)** offers a comprehensive title that adequately covers the main idea of the passage. Choice **(E)** is therefore the correct answer.

3. If you were told that X rays from an electron synchrotron can be used to take pictures of smaller particles than can X rays from an X-ray tube, you could conclude that
(A) the X-ray tube is inappropriate for the observation of large atomic particles
(B) electrons in the synchrotron have higher energies than those in the X-ray tube
(C) more electrons per second pass through the synchrotron than through the X-ray tube
(D) the synchrotron is more useful than the X-ray tube in the study of atoms
(E) laboratories will replace their X-ray equipment with electron synchrotrons

4. It can be inferred from the passage that one of the characteristics of X rays is that they
(A) are not directly visible
(B) do not behave like light waves
(C) have longer wavelengths than most other forms of light
(D) have an energy identical for all X-ray beams
(E) are used primarily by physicists in the study of atoms

Questions 3 and 4 each require you to make an inference.

The passage states that the shorter the wavelength, the higher the energy of motion of the wavelength. Logically, therefore, choice **(B)** is the correct answer to question 3. In **(A)**, the opposite would be the correct deduction to make; the X-ray tube would be *appropriate* to use to "see" large atomic particles. Choices **(C)**, **(D)**, and **(E)** do not offer logical conclusions to the question as stated.

In question 4 choice **(B)** is wrong because the passage does suggest that X rays behave like light waves. Choice **(C)** is unwarranted because the passage says that X rays have shorter wavelengths than visible light; the passage does not mention that X rays have longer wavelengths than most other forms of light. Choice **(D)** is wrong because it contradicts information about the energy of motion in wavelengths given in the second and third paragraphs of the passage. Choice **(E)** is incorrect because the passage tells of methods other than X rays that physicists use in the study of atoms. Only choice **(A)** can be inferred from the information provided in the passage.

Follow these strategies when you answer reading-comprehension questions:

1. Before you read the passage, glance at the questions at the end to get an idea of what you should be looking for when you read.
2. As you read the passage, concentrate on *what* is being said and on *how* it is being said. Underline the main idea and key details so that you can find answers quickly.
3. In answering the questions, be sure to consider *all* the choices and to choose the *best* answer from the choices given.

ENGLISH COMPOSITION TEST (ECT)

The **English Composition Test (ECT)** is one of the College Board Achievement Tests. These tests are designed to measure knowledge gained in specific subjects; the ECT, as its name implies, measures knowledge of English composition. In the ECT there *is* a penalty for a wrong answer. You should therefore not guess the answer to a multiple-choice question unless you have narrowed the choices to two or three possibilities out of the four or five choices given.

The ECT contains three different kinds of multiple-choice questions: **grammar-and-usage questions, sentence-correction questions**, and **construction-shift questions**. These three types of questions are discussed in the following sections. Once a year the ECT is administered with a twenty-minute **essay question** designed to predict a student's writing potential. For information about answering these essay questions, see the last section of this chapter.

Grammar-and-Usage Questions

A **grammar-and-usage question** tests your ability to recognize an error in grammar or usage. The grammar-and-usage questions that appear on the ECT each consist of a sentence with four underlined parts labeled **(A)** through **(D)**. An error may exist in any *one* of these parts, *or* the sentence may have no error. Here is a sample grammar-and-usage question:

> Rather than discussing the issues on which (A) this campaign should be decided (B), Mr. Richards resorts to (C) insult, exaggeration, and he lies (D). No error (E).

On your answer sheet you would mark the letter—**(A)**, **(B)**, **(C)**, *or* **(D)**—of the sentence part that contains an error, *or* you would mark **(E)** if the sentence contains no error. In this sample sentence, the error is in part **(D)**. Parallel structure (see Chapter 6) demands that the third item in a series of nouns should also be a noun. In the sample sentence, however, the series beginning with the nouns *insult* and *exaggeration* has as its third item not a noun but a brief clause, *he lies.* The series should read as follows: . . . *Mr. Richards resorts to insult, exaggeration, and lies.*

Objective

EXERCISE 4. Answering Grammar-and-Usage Questions. For each of the following sentences, write the letter—**(A)**, **(B)**, **(C)**, or **(D)**—of the part that contains an error in grammar or usage. If the sentence contains no error, write **(E)**.

1. Dylan's turned (A) thirty, as well as (B) the Beatles' breaking up, signified (C) the end of a distinctive period in (D) rock music. No error (E).
2. While modernizing (A) the factory, the company ran out (B) of money and must (C) secure a loan so that it could finish buying (D) the new equipment. No error (E).
3. Freud suggests that there is no such thing (A) as (B) a slip of the tongue, for they are (C) actually what the subconscious mind intends us (D) to say. No error (E).
4. A good many modern musicians have begun (A) composing (B) pieces that call for (C) using electronic devices as (D) musical instruments. No error (E).

Answers: **1.** A; **2.** C; **3.** C; **4.** E

Sentence-Correction Questions

Sentence-correction questions are designed to test your skill in using the most concise and logical structures in a given sentence.

A typical sentence-correction question on the ECT contains an underlined element that may be wordy, awkwardly phrased, or illogical. You are to select from listed choices a replacement that corrects the sentence. If there is no error in the original sentence, select choice **(A)**, which always repeats the underlined element.

Here is a sample sentence-correction question:

> A thorough study of a foreign language helps people learn about other cultures and <u>attitudes different from theirs are better understood.</u>
> **(A)** attitudes different from theirs are better understood
> **(B)** different attitudes from their own are better understood
> **(C)** understand attitudes that are different from their own
> **(D)** their understanding of different attitudes is better because of it
> **(E)** a better understanding of different attitudes is possible

The problem with this sentence is that the verb in the first clause, *helps*, is in the active voice, but the verb in the second clause, *are understood*, is in the passive voice. The idea of the sentence is that study helps people learn something and understand something. Since study helps people to do two things, those verbs must be expressed in the same voice. The only choice that properly corrects the problem of the mismatched verb voices is choice **(C)**, which provides the active-voice verb *understand*. (For more information on the active voice and the passive voice, see Chapter 22).

Objective

EXERCISE 5. Answering Sentence-Correction Questions. For each of the following sentences, write the letter of the choice that *best* corrects the underlined element in the sentence. If there is no problem in the underlined element, select choice **(A)**, which repeats the underlined element. Do not make a choice that changes the meaning of the sentence.

1. <u>Early in her career Gwendolyn Brooks writing poetry</u> about a variety of subjects, but in recent years her writing has focused on the human concerns of black Americans.
   (A) Early in her career Gwendolyn Brooks writing poetry
   (B) Early in her career Gwendolyn Brooks wrote poetry
   (C) Gwendolyn Brooks wrote poetry early in her career and it was
   (D) Gwendolyn Brooks having written poetry early in her career
   (E) Although the early poetry of Gwendolyn Brooks's career was
2. Modern governments try <u>not only understanding but also to control</u> economic forces.
   (A) not only understanding but also to control
   (B) to not only understand but at controlling

(C) not only to understand but also to control
(D) not only to understand but also controlling of
(E) for not an understanding, only, but the control, as well, of

3. Napoleon has been and probably always will be fascinating to students of history.
   (A) has been and probably always will be
   (B) always has and probably will always be
   (C) was and always probably will be
   (D) has always and probably always will be
   (E) has been and probably will have been always
4. Prepared for the violent opposition he met with, Perez's attempt to organize the boycott succeeded.
   (A) Perez's attempt to organize the boycott succeeded
   (B) Perez succeeded in his attempt to organize the boycott
   (C) the attempt by Perez at organizing the boycott succeeded
   (D) there was success for Perez's attempted organization of the boycott
   (E) success was the result of the attempt by Perez to organize the boycott

Answers: **1.** B; **2.** C; **3.** A; **4.** B

Construction-Shift Questions

In a **construction-shift question** you must mentally rewrite a sentence according to instructions. You are told to substitute one expression for another in the sentence and to make any other additional changes that the substitution would require. Here is a sample construction-shift question from the ECT:

> In order to perform, the brain needs information about what is going on in time and space.
> Begin with Without information.
> Your revised sentence will include which of the following?
> (A) in performing
> (B) needs
> (C) cannot
> (D) not going
> (E) performed

By including the negative qualifier *without* in the sentence, you now need a negative verb in order to retain the meaning of the original sentence. Choice **(C)**, *cannot*, is correct. The revised sentence reads: *Without information about what is going on in time and space, the brain **cannot** perform.*

Objective

EXERCISE 6. Answering Construction-Shift Questions. Mentally revise each of the following sentences according to the directions that follow it. Do not change the meaning of the original sentence. Then write the letter of the choice that is included in your revised sentence. If you think of a sentence that contains none of the five choices, rephrase the sentence to include a word or phrase that *is* listed.

1. Owing to her political skill, Ms. French had many supporters.
Begin with Many people supported.
(A) so **(D)** because
(B) while **(E)** and
(C) although

2. Coming to the city as a young man, he found a job as a newspaper reporter. Change Coming to He came.
(A) and so he found **(D)** and then finding
(B) and found **(E)** and had found
(C) and there he had found

3. In the midnineteenth century, Prussia's population consisted entirely of Germans and a small number of Poles.
Begin with Germans and a small number of Poles.
(A) in its entirely **(D)** their entire
(B) were entirely **(E)** an entire
(C) the entire

4. Tchaikovsky was the composer of eleven operas, but he is better known for his symphonies.
Begin with Tchaikovsky is not as well-known.
(A) as his symphonies **(D)** as for his eleven operas
(B) as the composer **(E)** as he is for his symphonies
(C) as he composed

Answers: **1.** D; **2.** B; **3.** C; **4.** E

ESSAY QUESTIONS

Essay questions require you to write answers of several paragraphs or longer. The essay questions on the English Composition Test (ECT) are used to evaluate students' writing ability. Here is a sample essay question from the ECT:

> In the United States, competition has long been accepted as a proper stimulus to success. Recently, however, students of high school and college age have begun to show some resentment against the pressure of competition.
>
> *Assignment*: What are your opinions about competition? Illustrate your views with specific references to your reading, study, or observation.

The following are guidelines for answering an essay question:

1. Read the question carefully. Look for key words that tell you what you are expected to do—words like *compare, contrast, analyze, explain, define, prove, illustrate, describe*, or *summarize*. Be sure to respond to all parts of the question.

2. Prewrite your answer by listing the information that you plan to cover. Use an extra sheet of paper or the inside cover of your exam booklet. You may find that the best way to organize your list is to use outline form.
3. In your opening paragraph write a thesis statement that clearly expresses the general idea of your essay. Often your thesis statement will repeat portions of the essay question.
4. Organize the body of your essay into paragraphs, each of which has a single main idea related to the thesis statement in your opening paragraph. For example, if you were answering the sample essay question and using the thesis statement suggested in item 3, the main idea of the first paragraph of the body of your essay might be that competition in business stimulates successful business enterprises; the main idea of the second paragraph of the body might be that competition in sports stimulates successful athletic performances. State the main idea of each paragraph of the body in a topic sentence (see Chapter 3). Then go on to support the main idea with specific facts, details, and examples.
5. Use transitions like *therefore, thus, however, in addition, next,* and *last* so that sentences and paragraphs run together smoothly.
6. Conclude with a statement or a paragraph that summarizes the main ideas of your essay.
7. Reread your essay to see if it needs revision. Look especially for important points or examples that you may have omitted.
8. Proofread your essay to make sure that grammar, usage, spelling, punctuation, and capitalization are all correct.

Objective

EXERCISE 7. Answering an ECT Essay Question. Follow the eight guidelines for answering an essay question in writing your own response to the sample essay question *or* to the following essay question, which also comes from the ECT.

Each of us assumes a personality to satisfy each group into which we enter. That is, we do not act at home precisely as we act with the gang, in the classroom, or before an employer.

Assignment: What accounts for our changing behavior? Is there something false in these changes, or is there justification for them, or is there something of both falseness and justification? Make clear your view of this matter and, in doing so, support your view with examples from your reading, study, or observation.

Guidelines for Evaluation: Essays should reflect students' adherence to the eight preceding guidelines.

REVIEW

CHAPTERS 29–33 SKILLS

CHAPTER 29 VOCABULARY SKILLS

Using Context Clues (pages 583–584) and Greek and Latin Roots (pages 590–592). Determine the meaning of the underlined word in each sentence

1. The mathematician decoded the cryptogram.
   (a) secret location **(b)** secret message **(c)** skywriting **(d)** tomb
2. Do not draw conclusions until you are cognizant of the facts.
   (a) aware **(b)** intrigued **(c)** puzzled **(d)** relieved
3. A caterpillar undergoes a metamorphosis and becomes a butterfly.
   (a) change in shape **(b)** change of heart **(c)** disease **(d)** trauma

Using Prefixes and Suffixes (pages 585–589). Identify the word that could replace the awkward underlined portion of each sentence without changing the meaning of the sentence.

4. Many people feel that war is lacking in sense.
   (a) sensation **(b)** senseless **(c)** sensible **(d)** sensitive
5. Our businesses may suffer if we ship into port foreign products.
   (a) deport **(b)** export **(c)** import **(d)** transport
6. After physical therapy the injured runner qualified again for the race.
   (a) disqualified **(b)** prequalified **(c)** requalified **(d)** unqualified

Using Synonyms (pages 593–594) and Americanisms (pages 593–594). Identify the synonym for each word in capital letters.

7. DEPOT: **(a)** pledge **(b)** slope **(c)** station **(d)** valley
8. HEX: **(a)** anger **(b)** despise **(c)** hinder **(d)** jinx

Using Antonyms (pages 595–596) and Americanisms (pages 593–594). Identify the antonym for each word in capital letters.

9. BOONDOCKS: **(a)** catastrophe **(b)** countryside **(c)** mecca **(d)** shore
10. FILIBUSTER: **(a)** delay **(b)** facilitate **(c)** fracture **(d)** tame

Answers: **1.** b; **2.** a; **3.** a; **4.** b; **5.** c; **6.** c; **7.** c; **8.** d; **9.** c; **10.** b

CHAPTER 30 SPELLING SKILLS

Using Spelling Rules (pages 598–606). For each item, identify the one word that is spelled correctly.

1. **(a)** dissappointed **(b)** incredibly **(c)** niether **(d)** non-fiction
2. **(a)** courageous **(b)** intersede **(c)** preferrable **(d)** turkies
3. **(a)** defered **(b)** hypocrasy **(c)** sopranoes **(d)** supersede

Distinguishing Between Easily Confused Words (pages 606–608). Identify the underlined word that is spelled correctly in each sentence.

4. Although we are not **(a)** conscience of each **(b)** breathe we take, we would soon recognize the **(c)** affect of **(d)** altered breathing.
5. Because our **(a)** principal was **(b)** formally employed in a large company's **(c)** personal department, she can now **(d)** advice us on career planning.

Answers: **1.** b; **2.** a; **3.** d; **4.** d; **5.** a

CHAPTER 31 BUSINESS COMMUNICATION SKILLS

Examining Business Letters (pages 611–619) **and College Applications** (pages 619–624). Select the answer that best completes each of the following items.

1. The correct salutation for a letter addressed to A & M Records is
 (a) Dear Sir or Madam: **(c)** Both *a* and *b* are correct.
 (b) Dear A & M Records: **(d)** neither *a* nor *b* is correct.

2. In a letter using full block style, you should indent
 (a) the heading **(b)** the signature **(c)** each paragraph **(d)** nothing

3. A letter of request should always
 (a) include a check or a money order **(c)** conclude courteously
 (b) specify a date, time, and place **(d)** Choices *a–c* are all correct.

4. When you write a college-application essay, you should
 (a) work from an outline **(c)** choose an interesting topic
 (b) avoid overly ornate language **(d)** Choices *a–c* are all correct.

Answers: **1.** c; **2.** d; **3.** c; **4.** d

CHAPTER 32 LISTENING AND SPEAKING SKILLS

Examining Listening Skills (pages 625–628) **and Speaking Skills** (pages 629–632). Select the answer that best completes each of the following items.

1. Of what type of fallacy is the following statement an example? "Students today do not study enough."
 (a) overgeneralization **(b)** testimonial **(c)** bandwagon **(d)** personal attack

2. The level or tone of your voice is called the
 (a) pronunciation **(b)** volume **(c)** tempo **(d)** pitch

Answers: **1.** a; **2.** d

CHAPTER 33 TEST-TAKING SKILLS

Answering an Antonym Question (page 643). Identify the word that is *most nearly the opposite* of the word in capital letters.

1. PERMANENT: **(a)** facile **(b)** oblique **(c)** stationary **(d)** transitory

Answering an Analogy Question (pages 644–645). Identify the pair of words that expresses a relationship *most like* the relationship expressed by the pair of words in capital letters.

2. CARICATURE : EXAGGERATED :: **(a)** allusion : elusive **(b)** paradox : ironic **(c)** euphemism : sardonic **(d)** hyperbole : understated

Answering a Sentence-Completion Question (pages 645–647). Identify the word that *best* completes the following sentence.

3. To reach a fair verdict, a jury must be ____.
 (a) ambiguous **(b)** arbitrary **(c)** impartial **(d)** mundane

Answering a Grammar-and-Usage Question (page 651). Identify the letter of the underlined sentence part that contains an error in grammar or usage. If there is no error, choose *d.*

4. When (**a**) making bread, dry ingredients should be mixed (**b**) separately. (**c**) No error. (**d**)

Answers **1.** d; **2.** b; **3.** c; **4.** b

UNIT X
Resources

The dictionary, the thesaurus, the library—these are three of the most valuable resources available to you as a writer. Learning how to use these resources will not only help you improve your writing for school but will also assist you in all research and writing that you may need to do in years to come.

As you research, compose, revise, and proofread your writing, you will often have many questions that need answering. What does *indigent* mean? Where should you hyphenate the word *English*? Is *wildflower* one word or two? Can *misprint* be used as a noun? These are some of the kinds of questions that a dictionary can help you answer. In the next chapter you will study the dictionary and the valuable information it provides.

Have you ever had a word on the tip of your tongue but been unable to think of it? For instance, a word that means something like *selfish* but is much stronger, or a word that means something like *hammer* but is more specific? A thesaurus can assist you in solving this common writer's problem. In the next chapter you will also learn about that helpful writer's aid, the thesaurus.

How do you locate books in a library? Which books will be most useful in providing information for a particular research paper? In which newspapers or magazines can you find articles on the topic of your paper? What other library resources can best help you in your research? These are some of the questions that will be answered as you learn about libraries in the second chapter of this unit.

CHAPTER 34
The Dictionary and the Thesaurus

When you are writing, the two reference books that you will probably consult most often are a dictionary and a thesaurus. This chapter examines dictionaries, thesauruses, and the important information that they contain.

THE DICTIONARY

A **dictionary** of the English language is an alphabetical list of words, their meanings, and other useful information about the words.

An **unabridged dictionary** is the largest and most complete kind of dictionary. It lists over 400,000 words and gives detailed information about their histories and usage. The unabridged *Oxford English Dictionary*, or *OED*, is thirteen volumes long. *Webster's Third New International Dictionary, Unabridged*, lists 450,000 words and weighs fifteen pounds. Because unabridged dictionaries are costly and unwieldy, people most often use them at a library.

A **college dictionary**, also called a **collegiate dictionary** or a **desk dictionary**, is an abridgment, or shortened form, of an unabridged dictionary. It contains from 150,000 to 200,000 words and provides less detailed histories and examples of usage than an unabridged dictionary provides. College dictionaries are convenient for everyday use and are adequate for most students' needs. Four of the most popular college dictionaries in America are *Webster's New World Dictionary of the American Language, Second College Edition; Webster's New Collegiate Dictionary*; the *American Heritage Dictionary*; and the *Random House College Dictionary.*

A **concise, or condensed, dictionary** is an abridgment of a college dictionary. Because it contains fewer words than a college dictionary and often omits examples and word histories, a concise dictionary alone cannot meet the needs of most high school and college students.

While all college dictionaries contain similar information, no two dictionaries are exactly alike. For example, some dictionaries list people's names and place names in their main sections; others put them in special **biographical** and **geographical sections** near the back of the book. Some dictionaries use a star to indicate Americanisms; others use a different symbol or an abbreviation. To save time and get the most benefit from your dictionary, it is important to examine its general contents and its explanation of abbreviations and symbols used in the work. The **table of contents** and a **list of abbreviations and symbols** are usually found near the front of the dictionary.

The main part of a dictionary is composed of alphabetically arranged word **entries**. Although the style of these entries varies slightly from dictionary to dictionary, most entries contain the same important information. In the model dictionary entries that follow, the different kinds of information have been labeled. The following sections explain the labels in detail.

ENTRY WORD

The **entry word** is the word being examined. Entry words are listed alphabetically in the main section of a dictionary and appear in bold (dark) print. To make specific entries easier to find, some dictionaries have **thumb indexes** that show you where the entries for each new letter of the alphabet begin. Dictionaries also print two guide words at the top of each page. The **guide words** identify the first and last entry word on the page; all other entry words fall alphabetically between the two guide words.

Homographs, or words that have the same spelling but different origins and meanings, are listed separately with superscript numbers after each entry word. In the model the entry words *crawl*[1] and *crawl*[2] are homographs.

The entry word shows you two important things about the word you are looking up—its **spelling** and its **syllabification**. It may also give you information about **capitalization**.

Spelling

Dictionaries provide correct spellings for all entry words. You can therefore use a dictionary to check the spellings of words and to find out if compound words are solid, hyphenated, or two-word compounds. For example, entry words in the current edition of *Webster's New World Dictionary* indicate that *offshoot* is a solid compound, *off-season* is a hyphenated compound, and *off year* is a two-word compound. (In the case of hyphenated compound adjectives like *off-key*, style rules dictate that the hyphens are used only when the adjective appears unmodified before the noun.)

Dictionaries also tell you if a word has **variant spellings,** or more than one correct spelling, and indicate which variant, if any, is preferred. Methods for indicating preferred spellings vary from dictionary to dictionary. Sometimes a dictionary indicates the preferred spelling by putting it first: **sheik, sheikh**. Sometimes *also* indicates a less-accepted spelling: **sheik** *also*, **sheikh**. Sometimes the preferred spelling is a main entry and the less-accepted spelling has a separate entry with a cross-reference: **sheikh** *same as* SHEIK.

If a variant spelling—like *odour* or *spectre*—is accepted only or mainly in Britain, an American dictionary will label it a British or chiefly British spelling.

Model Dictionary Entries

entry word

cra·ven (krā′vən) ***adj.*** [ME. *cravant* < OFr. < *cravanté*, pp. of *cravanter*, to break < VL. ****crepantare***, to cause to burst < L. ***crepare***, to rattle, creak < IE. ****krep-*** (whence RAVEN) < base ****ker-*** (see CRACK)] very cowardly; abjectly afraid **—*n.*** a thorough coward **—*SYN.*** see COWARDLY —

additional forms

cra′ven·ly *adv.* —cra′ven·ness *n.*

crav·ing (krā′viŋ) ***n.*** an intense and prolonged desire; yearning or appetite, as for food, drink, etc.

idiom

craw (krô) ***n.*** [ME. *craue* < OE. ****craga***, akin to MLowG. ***krage***, MDu. ***kraghe***, G. ***kragen***, collar, orig., neck < ? IE. base ****gwer-***, to swallow, whence L. *vorare*, to devour] **1.** the crop of a bird or insect **2.** the stomach of any animal **—to stick in the** (or **one's**) **craw** to be unacceptable or displeasing to one

pronunciation

inflected forms

☆**craw·dad** (krô′dad′) ***n.*** [fanciful alteration of CRAWFISH] [Dial.] *same as* CRAYFISH

usage label

craw·fish (-fish′) ***n.***, ***pl.*** **-fish′, -fish′es:** see FISH[2] *same as* CRAYFISH **—☆*vi.*** [Colloq.] to withdraw from a position; back down

part of speech

definitions

crawl[1] (krôl) ***vi.*** [ME. *craulen* < ON. ***krafla*** < Gmc. base ****krab-***, ****kreb-***, to scratch (whence G. ***krabbeln***): for IE. base see CRAB[1]] **1.** to move slowly by dragging the body along the ground, as a worm **2.** to go on hands and knees; creep **3.** to move or go slowly or feebly **4.** to move or act in an abjectly servile manner **5.** to swarm or teem (*with* crawling things) **6.** to feel as if insects were crawling on the skin **—*n.*** **1.** the act of crawling; slow movement **2.** a swimming stroke in which one lies prone, with the face in the water except when turned briefly sideward for breathing, and uses alternate overarm strokes and a continuous flutter kick **3.** [Brit. Slang] *same as* PUB-CRAWL **—crawl′er *n.***

synonyms

examples

***SYN.*—crawl,** in its strict usage, suggests movement by dragging the prone body along the ground [a snake *crawls*], and, figuratively, connotes abjectness or servility; **creep** suggests movement, often furtive, on all fours [a baby *creeps*], and, figuratively, connotes slow, stealthy, or insinuating progress

etymology

crawl[2] (krôl) ***n.*** [WIndDu. ***kraal*** < Sp. *corral:* see CORRAL] an enclosure made in shallow water for confining fish, turtles, etc.

—from *Webster's New World Dictionary, Second College Edition*

Syllabification

Most dictionaries break multisyllabic entry words into syllables by using spaces or midline dots. For example, in the model, the two-syllable word *craven* is broken into syllables indicated by a midline dot. Thus, if you have to type *craven* on two lines, the entry word tells you to hyphenate it after the *a*.

Capitalization

Dictionaries capitalize entry words that are always capitalized, like *America* or *Mexican*. For words that are sometimes but not always capitalized, a dictionary clarifies the instances in which capital letters may or should be used. For instance, while the word *continental* is not capitalized in *Webster's New World Dictionary*, the entry says [**C-**], indicating a capital *C*, before the definition "a soldier of the American army during the Revolution."

PRONUNCIATION

Dictionaries tell you the correct **pronunciation** of each entry word. If a word has more than one acceptable pronunciation, its different pronunciations will be given. Usually the pronunciation is given in parentheses, brackets, or slanted lines right after the entry word. In the model, pronunciations are given in parentheses.

Because there are only twenty-six letters in the alphabet but over forty sounds in spoken English, dictionaries use a special set of symbols, called **phonetic symbols**, to represent these spoken sounds. Different dictionaries use different phonetic symbols; for example, one dictionary shows the pronunciation of *fume* as [fyo͞om], while another shows it as [fyūm]. To understand the sounds represented by a dictionary's phonetic symbols, consult its **pronunciation key**. The full pronunciation key appears near the front of the dictionary, while a short form usually appears at the bottom of each right-hand page.

The pronunciation of a multisyllabic word indicates which syllable or syllables are **stressed**, or emphasized. To indicate stressed syllables, dictionaries use **accent marks** (**′**) either before or after the stressed syllables. If a word has more than one stressed syllable, the pronunciation indicates the **primary** (stronger) and **secondary** (lighter) **stresses**. Sometimes—as in the pronunciation for *crawdad* in the model—a bold accent mark indicates primary stress and a lighter accent mark indicates secondary stress. Sometimes an accent mark above the line indicates primary stress and an accent mark below the line indicates secondary stress.

PART OF SPEECH

Dictionaries tell you the **part of speech** of each entry word. Usually the part of speech is abbreviated and italicized. The abbreviation is placed before the definition or definitions to which it applies. For example, in the entry for *crawl*[1] in the model, the *vi.* before the first six definitions indicates that these definitions are for *crawl* as an intransitive verb; an *n.* then indicates that the last four definitions are for *crawl* as a noun. Some dictionaries have separate entries for each part of speech.

INFLECTED FORMS

Inflected forms include plurals of nouns and the past tense, past participles, and present participles of verbs. When these forms are irregular or confusing, a dictionary lists them in bold print near the entry word. For example, since the two acceptable plurals of *crawfish* may cause confusion, they are indicated after the entry word in the model.

When comparative and superlative forms of two-syllable adjectives are not made by adding *more* or *most*, a dictionary lists them in bold print near the entry word. For example, in the entry for *lovely*, a dictionary will list *lovelier* and *loveliest*.

ETYMOLOGY

The **etymology** is the origin and history of a word. Most dictionaries include a word's etymology in brackets or parentheses before or after its definitions. The etymologies in the model are given in brackets before the definitions. The etymology for *crawl*[2] indicates that the word comes from the West Indian Dutch word *kraal*, which in turn comes from the Spanish word *corral*.

SUBJECT AND USAGE LABELS

If a word or a definition is restricted in its use, many dictionaries include a subject or usage label explaining the restriction. **Subject labels** like *Music* or *Baseball* indicate that a word or a definition is restricted to a particular field or study. **Usage labels** indicate other restrictions; for example, a word may be rare, archaic, obsolete, colloquial, slang, or restricted to a particular region or dialect. Subject and usage labels appear right before the definition or definitions to which the restriction applies. They are often abbreviated and may be italicized or put in brackets or parentheses. In the entry for *crawfish*, the usage label [Colloq.] before the definition of the intransitive verb indicates that the intransitive verb *crawfish* should be used only in **colloquial**, or conversational, English.

DEFINITIONS AND EXAMPLES

An important function of a dictionary is to provide the **definitions**, or meanings, of words. If a word has more than one definition, each definition is numbered. Definitions for each part of speech are numbered separately. For example, in the entry for *crawl*[1], the six definitions for the intransitive verb *crawl* are numbered 1 to 6; new numbers are given to the four definitions of the noun *crawl.*

In order to illustrate a particular definition or shade of meaning, dictionaries sometimes include examples showing the word in context. To illustrate the distinction between the synonyms *crawl* and *creep* in the entry for *crawl*[1], the examples "a snake *crawls*" and "a baby *creeps*" are given.

IDIOMS

Toward the end of an entry for a particular word, dictionaries may list and define common **idioms**, or expressions, in which the word is a key element. For instance, in the entry for *craw,* the dictionary lists and defines the idiom *to stick in the* (or *one's*) *craw.* Note that the idiom appears in bold print.

SYNONYMS AND ANTONYMS

Dictionaries sometimes list **synonyms** or **antonyms** for an entry word. Usually they are labeled *Syn.* or *Ant.* and are listed near the end of an entry. At the end of the entry for *crawl*[1] in the model, a brief section clarifies the distinction between *crawl* and its synonym *creep.* In the entry for *craven,* a cross-reference to the entry for *cowardly* indicates that synonyms for *craven* are given in the entry for *cowardly.*

ADDITIONAL FORMS

At the end of an entry, dictionaries sometimes list **additional forms** of the entry word. These forms usually appear syllabified in bold print but without definitions. For example, at the end of the entry for *craven,* the adverb form *cravenly* and the noun form *cravenness* are listed. From your knowledge of suffixes (see Chapter 29), you can figure out that *cravenly* means "in a very cowardly manner" and that *cravenness* means "the state of being very cowardly."

Objective

EXERCISE 1. Using a Dictionary. Consult a college dictionary before writing your answers to each question.

1. Which of these words are spelled incorrectly? What are the correct spellings?

(a) affadavit
(b) Philippines
(c) rain storm
(d) X-ray

2. Is *traveler* or *traveller* the preferred American spelling? Where would you hyphenate the word?
3. For what meaning is the word *revolutionary* capitalized?
4. Does the *g* in *hegemony* sound like the *g* in *good* or the *g* in *gesture*? What does *hegemony* mean? What is its etymology?
5. Which syllable in *obligatory* gets the primary stress?
6. What are the comparative and superlative forms of the adjective *ill*?
7. In what dialect is the word *brae* used? What does it mean?
8. What does the idiom *(to) talk turkey* mean?
9. Does your dictionary list synonyms for *summit*? If so, what are they?
10. Does your dictionary list an adverb form of *belligerent* in the entry for *belligerent*? If so, identify and define the adverb form.

THE THESAURUS

A **thesaurus** is a list of words, their synonyms, and sometimes their antonyms.

When you use a thesaurus, you start with a meaning and find a word. For example, suppose you want to say that a person is snobbish but wish to use a stronger word than *snobbish*. A thesaurus will help you find that word.

Many thesauruses arrange entries alphabetically. In these thesauruses you would simply look up *snobbish* to find a stronger synonym. (If *snobbish* were not listed, you would look up the basic form of the word, *snob*.) Entries are subdivided according to part of speech and are followed by a list of synonyms. Antonyms may be listed as part of an entry, or a cross-reference may direct you to them.

Some thesauruses arrange entries in numbered categories based on the ideas they represent. Finding a word in this type of thesaurus is a two-step process. To find a synonym for *snobbish*, first look up *snobbish* in the alphabetical index at the back of the thesaurus. In the index to the *Original Roget's Thesaurus*, you would find:

snobbish *biased* 481adj. *fashionable* 848adj. *prideful* 871adj.
ill-bred 847adj. *affected* 850adj. *despising* 922adj.

Choosing *affected* as the word closest to the sense you are trying to convey, turn to item 850 and look at the adjective section. There you will find a list of synonyms including *artificial, pretentious, conceited,* and *posturing.* You can then choose the synonym that you find most appropriate. Before making your choice, you may need to look up the precise meanings of the synonyms in a dictionary.

Objective

EXERCISE 2. Using a Thesaurus. Look up the following words in a thesaurus, and write two synonyms for each word.

awkward, cumbersome
1. bulky

abrasive, caustic
2. corrosive

intensify, augment
3. enhance

destiny, fortune
4. fate

ceremonial, sententious
5. formal

crow, exult
6. gloat

apathetic, nonchalant
7. indifferent

ridicule, deride
8. mock

weary, haggard
9. tired

debilitate, delude
10. weaken

Answers will vary. Possible synonyms appear above each item.

Objective

APPLICATION EXERCISE. Writing Sentences. Write an original sentence that illustrates the meaning of each synonym in Exercise 2. Before writing your sentences, you may wish to consult a dictionary to find the precise meaning of each synonym.

Suggested Answer for 1: A scouring pad is abrasive.

CHAPTER 35
The Library

In the United States there are over 35,000 libraries. They range in size from the Library of Congress in Washington, D.C., with more than 18 million volumes, to traveling bookmobiles, with only a few hundred volumes. Most **public libraries** and **school libraries** (sometimes called **learning resource centers** or **media centers**) contain a wide variety of materials that can help you with your research and writing. This chapter examines the different types of materials available at libraries and explains how to find and use the materials that libraries contain.

FICTION AND NONFICTION BOOKS

Libraries have a wide selection of **nonfiction** (fact-based) books as well as **fiction** (novels and stories). Most nonfiction books provide detailed information on particular topics and can be valuable tools in your research. To determine whether or not a library has the book you need, you have to consult the card catalog.

THE CARD CATALOG

The **card catalog** is an alphabetical arrangement of individual file cards listing each of the books owned by a library.

Most fiction books in a library have two cards each, an **author card** and a **title card**. Most nonfiction books have three cards each, an **author card**, a **title card**, and a **subject card**. Usually the cards are kept in the drawers of special filing cabinets. Subject cards are usually filed in separate drawers and form the **Subject Index** of the card catalog. Author cards and title cards are usually filed together and form the **Author/Title Index**. Some large libraries do not use file cards but instead maintain **on-line,** or computerized, **catalogs** or print their catalogs in paperback volumes.

The main entry on an **author card** is the author of the book, with the last name first. Author cards are filed alphabetically by the author's last name. Thus, if you wanted to find author cards for books by Nathaniel Hawthorne, you would look in the Author/Title Index under *H.* If a book has two or three authors, there is usually a separate author card for each person. If a book has no credited author or is an anthology of many authors' works, the main entry on the author card is usually the editor (abbreviated *ed.*) or the publisher of the book.

The main entry on a **title card** is the title of the book. Title cards are filed alphabetically by the first word of the title, excluding *a, an,* and *the.* Thus, if you wanted to find the title card for *The Source,* you would look in the Author/Title Index under *S.*

The main entry on a **subject card** is the general topic of the book. Subject cards are filed alphabetically by these general topics. Thus, if you were looking for subject cards for books about New England, you would look in the Subject Index under *N.* If a book deals with more than one general topic, it will usually have more than one subject card.

In the following examples of catalog cards, the author card, title card, and subject card are all for the same book. Note that the three types of cards provide basically the same information. The important information on the subject card has been numbered 1 to 6. This information is

1. **Call number:** The **call number** is used to locate the book in the library. The number on the card corresponds to the number on the spine of the book. Library books are arranged by call number.
2. **Main entry:** The **main entry** is the primary heading on a catalog card. On this subject card, the subject *National characteristics, American,* is the main entry; the author and title come below it. Notice that the author's birth and death dates are given after her name.
3. **Publishing information:** The **publishing information** includes the location and name of the publisher and the date of publication.
4. **Collation:** The **collation** gives the number of pages or the number of volumes. Sometimes it gives the physical dimensions of the book; for example, on the sample subject card, the "21 cm." indicates that the book is 21 centimeters high. Sometimes the collation indicates whether or not there are illustrations (abbreviated *ill.* or *illus.*).
5. **Notes entry:** The **notes entry** tells whether a book has any special features, such as an introduction or a bibliography.
6. **Cross references to the card catalog:** The **cross references** indicate the book's other subject cards and can help give you a better idea of the topics covered in the book.

Sometimes you will find a fourth type of card in the card catalog—a cross-reference card. **Cross-reference cards** tell you to *see* or *see also* other cards in the catalog. For example, if you look up *Twain, Mark*, in the Author/Title Index, a card may tell you to "See *Clemens, Samuel L.*" This means that author cards for all books by Mark Twain are filed under the author's real name, Samuel L. Clemens. On the other hand, if you look up *Mississippi River* in the Subject Index, a cross-reference card may tell you to "See also *Steamboats, American*." This means that while subject cards for books about the Mississippi River are filed under the subject *Mississippi River*, subject cards for related books are filed under the subject *Steamboats, American.*

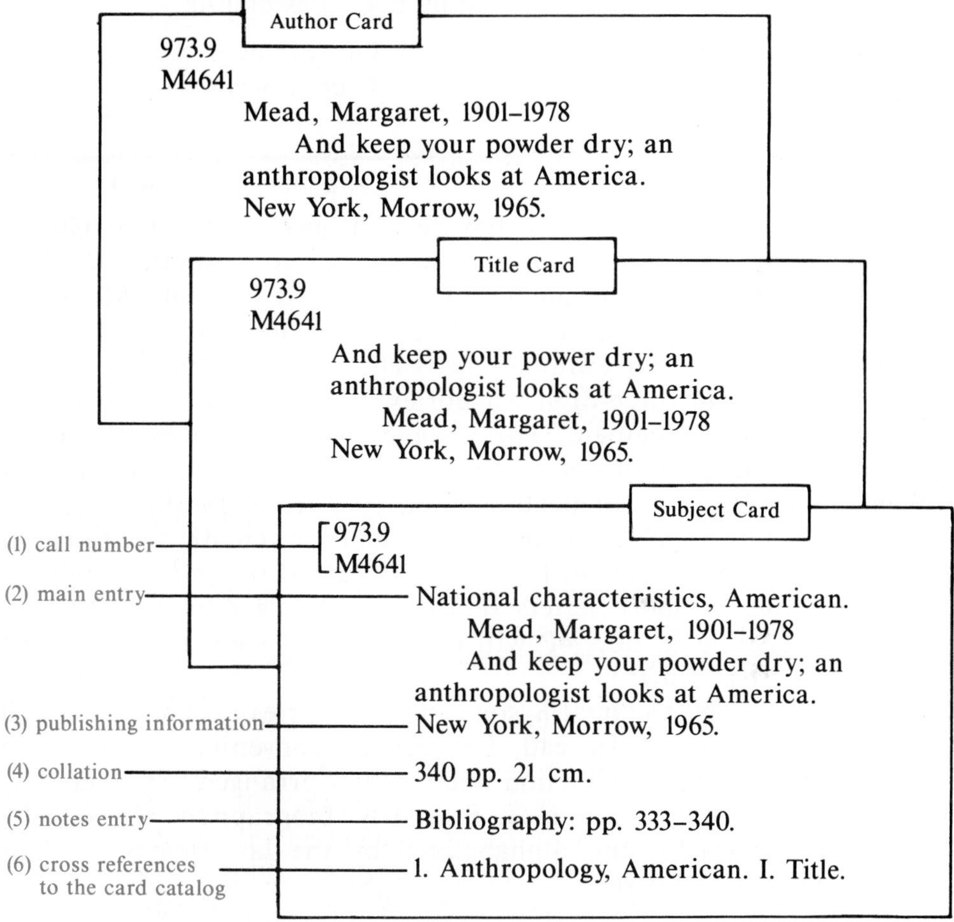

Author Card
973.9
M4641
Mead, Margaret, 1901–1978
And keep your powder dry; an
anthropologist looks at America.
New York, Morrow, 1965.
Title Card
973.9
M4641
And keep your power dry; an
anthropologist looks at America.
Mead, Margaret, 1901–1978
New York, Morrow, 1965.
Subject Card
(1) call number
973.9
M4641
(2) main entry
National characteristics, American.
Mead, Margaret, 1901–1978
And keep your powder dry; an
anthropologist looks at America.
(3) publishing information
New York, Morrow, 1965.
(4) collation
340 pp. 21 cm.
(5) notes entry
Bibliography: pp. 333–340.
(6) cross references to the card catalog
1. Anthropology, American. I. Title.

CLASSIFICATION AND ARRANGEMENT OF LIBRARY BOOKS

The **call number**, found in the upper left corner of a book's catalog card and on the spine of the book, is based on the Dewey Decimal System, the Library of Congress System, or the library's own classification system. Library books are arranged by call number in accordance with the classification system that the library uses.

Most American libraries classify and arrange books according to either the Dewey Decimal System or the Library of Congress System.

The Dewey Decimal System

In the **Dewey Decimal System**, the basic arrangement of library books is numerical.

The Dewey Decimal System organizes books by subject into ten very broad categories designated by multiples of 100:

000 General Works
100 Philosophy
200 Religion
300 Social Sciences
400 Language
500 Pure Sciences
600 Applied Sciences
700 The Arts
800 Literature
900 Geography and History

Each category is then further divided into another ten subdivisions designated by multiples of ten. For example, Applied Sciences, the 600s section, is further divided into 610—Medicine, 620—Engineering, and so on. Multiples of one further subdivide these categories. For example, 611 is Human Anatomy.

Within these three-digit categories, the use of decimals allows even greater refinement. For instance, a library may classify a book on the anatomy of the hands and arms as 611.974. The numerals after the decimal point often vary from library to library, but the numerals before the decimal point remain the same. If two books have identical topics, the library differentiates them by adding one or more letters of the authors' last names. Thus, a book classified as 611.974P will be written by someone whose last name begins with *P*.

In the Dewey Decimal System, most libraries do not assign call numbers to novels. Instead, for readers' convenience, novels are shelved in a separate Fiction Section and arranged alphabetically by the authors' last names. Similarly, biographies are usually shelved separately and alphabetized by the last names of their subjects (not authors).

The Library of Congress System

In the **Library of Congress System,** the basic arrangement of library books is alphabetical.

The Library of Congress System classifies books by subject into twenty broad categories designated by letters of the alphabet:

A General, Miscellaneous	**M** Music
B Philosophy, Religion	**N** Fine Arts
C History—Auxiliary Sciences	**P** Language, Literature
D History, Topography	**Q** Science
E–F America (including History)	**R** Medicine
G Geography, Anthropology	**S** Agriculture
H Social Sciences	**T** Technology
J Political Science	**U** Military Science
K Law	**V** Naval Science
L Education	**Z** Bibliography, Library Science

Subdivisions of these categories are designated by using two letters; for example, *PS* indicates American literature. Greater refinement is achieved by adding numerals and more letters.

LOCATING LIBRARY BOOKS

Use the **call number** to locate a book in the library.

The shelf area in which most books are kept is called the **stacks. Open stacks** are those that readers are allowed to enter in order to find books for themselves. Once you have obtained a list of books and their call numbers from the card catalog, you can go to open stacks to see if the books you want are available. **Closed stacks** are restricted to library personnel. If a library uses closed stacks, you will probably have to fill out a book-request slip and present it to a member of the library staff. The slip asks for information (such as the call number, title, and author of the book) that you can copy from a book's catalog card. If a book you want is not presently available, you can often **reserve** the book by filling out a special card or form.

Most libraries have **circulating books** that you can borrow and take home for a given period of time as well as **reference books** that you must use in the library. Reference books have *Ref* or *R* above their call numbers and are usually kept in a separate section of the library.

PARTS OF A BOOK

Once you have found a copy of a book for which you were looking, you may want to examine it to see if it is suitable for your purposes.

IF YOU WANT TO FIND:	LOOK FOR THE:
1. complete title, name of author or editor, edition number, name of publisher, place and date of publication, dates of previous editions	title page, copyright page

2. material explaining the nature, purpose, or scope of the book	preface, foreword, or introduction
3. a list of the general contents of the book and the page numbers on which the contents are found	table of contents
4. a list of the book's illustrations, charts, diagrams, maps, or tables	list of illustrations, maps, or tables
5. additional explanations not essential to the text itself	appendix
6. an alphabetical list of technical or unfamiliar terms used in the text	glossary
7. a list of the sources used by the author or additional readings suggested by the author	bibliography, references, or suggested readings
8. an alphabetical list of the topics used in the text, given with all of the page numbers on which they are found	index

Objective

EXERCISE 1. Using Catalog Cards. Refer to the sample catalog cards on page 669 in writing your answers to the following questions.

1. What is the book's call number? Into which of the ten basic Dewey Decimal categories has the book been classified?
2. What is the book's (a) title, (b) author, (c) publisher, and (d) date of publication?
3. How long is the book? Does it contain a bibliography? If so, how long is the bibliography?
4. Under what letter in the Author/Title Index would the title card for the book be filed?
5. Under what other subject in the Subject Index is a card for the book filed? *Answers:* **1.** 973.9/M4641, Geography and History; **2.** **(a)** *And Keep Your Powder Dry,* **(b)** Margaret Mead; **(c)** Morrow, **(d)** 1965; **3.** 340 pages, yes, 8 pages; **4.** *A;* **5.** Anthropology, American

Objective

EXERCISE 2. Finding Books in Your Library. Listed below are ten books, only five of which could be of possible value for a research paper on any aspect of colonial America before 1700. Visit a library, use the card catalog, and find and examine any of the ten books that are available at the library. For each of the books you find, write whether the book is *suitable* or *unsuitable* for the research paper. In identifying suitable books, also list their **(a)** call numbers, **(b)** publishers, **(c)** dates of publication, and **(d)** lengths. If you cannot find at least three suitable books from the list, you should substitute other books that are available at the library.

1. *The American Adam* by R. W. B. Lewis
2. *Anne Bradstreet* by Ann Stanford
3. *Apostles of the Self-Made Man* by John G. Cawelti
4. *The Birth of the Republic* by Edmund S. Morgan
5. *Builders of the Bay Colony* by Samuel Eliot Morison
6. *The Coming Fury* by Bruce Catton
7. *The First Gentlemen of Virginia* by Lewis B. Wright
8. *One Small Candle* by Thomas J. Fleming
9. *The Virgin Land* by Henry Nash Smith
10. *Winthrop's Boston* by Darrett Rutman

NEWSPAPERS AND PERIODICALS

Newspapers and **periodicals** (magazines and scholarly journals) contain short articles on specific topics and provide information that is usually up to date at the time of publication. Most libraries keep current newspapers and periodicals on shelves or racks in a reading room or area. Newspapers are usually alphabetized by the name of their city of origin. Periodicals are usually arranged by title.

Back issues of newspapers are normally kept on microforms (see page 679). Back issues of periodicals are sometimes kept on microforms and are sometimes bound together into hardcover volumes containing six months' or a year's issues. Bound periodicals are usually shelved in a separate section of the library and arranged alphabetically by title or according to call numbers.

Most libraries require that you use current or bound periodicals on the premises. If you need a copy of an article, you will probably be able to copy it on a photocopying machine in the library.

To find newspaper or periodical articles on a specific topic, you need to consult one or more indexes to newspapers or periodicals. These indexes are usually found in the reference section.

INDEXES TO NEWSPAPERS AND PERIODICALS

An **index to a newspaper or to periodicals** lists, in alphabetical order by subject, all articles published in the issues under consideration. It may also list the same articles by author, with the last name first.

The following list describes some of the most useful indexes to newspapers or periodicals. Most of the indexes are published a few times a year and are consolidated into bound volumes at a year's end. In the indexes you will find a list of articles along with their sources, dates, volume numbers, page numbers, and author information (if available).

General Science Index

The ***General Science Index*** is an index to articles on astronomy, biology, botany, chemistry, geology, physics, and zoology.

Humanities Index

The ***Humanities Index*** is an index to articles on archaeology, art, folklore, history, literature, music, performing arts, philosophy, and religion.

Social Sciences Index

The ***Social Sciences Index*** is an index to articles on anthropology, economics, law, political science, psychology, and sociology.

New York Times Index

The ***New York Times Index*** is an index to all articles published in the *New York Times.* It is a useful source for tracking down articles on either current events or history.

Readers' Guide to Periodical Literature

The ***Readers' Guide to Periodical Literature*** is an index to articles published in 180 periodicals throughout the United States and Canada. It is a useful source for tracking down articles in newsmagazines like *Newsweek* and *Time* and other general-interest magazines, such as *Sports Illustrated* and *Business Week.*

The following sample column from the *Readers' Guide to Periodical Literature* includes labels explaining entry elements. Notice that most names of periodicals are abbreviated. For explanations of abbreviations, look in the front of the *Readers' Guide.*

Objective

EXERCISE 3. Using the *Readers' Guide.* Refer to the *Readers' Guide* excerpt on page 675 in writing your answers to the following questions.

1. Who wrote the article "Spreading Starvation Stalks Africa"?
2. In what magazine did Andrea Fooner's article appear?
3. On what pages of the May 1979 issue of *World Tennis* did Gordon Forbes's article "Handful of Summers" appear?
4. What are the dates and volume numbers of the *Football* articles about ethical aspects of college football?

Answers: **1.** J. Kapstein; **2.** *Redbook;* **3.** 24–5+; **4.** June 1979; volume 68; May 21, 1979, volume 50

Readers' Guide to Periodical Literature

subject heading — **FOOD industry**
See also
Campbell Soup Company
Food additives
Food service
Lever Brothers Company

Advertising

Misleading cultural messages in TV ads. F. Small. USA Today 107:10-11 Je '79

FOOD laws and legislation

author of article — Case against poisoning our food. A. Johnson. bibl il Environment 21:6-13 Ap '79

Dangerous to your health: saccharin, cancer, and the Delaney clause. W. A. Thomasson. Atlantic 243:25-6 Je '79

Illusion of safety; the Federal government and the cancer epidemic; Delaney clause. E. M. Whelan. il USA Today 107:26-30 My '79

cross reference — *See also*
United States—Food and Drug Administration

FOOD stores

source of article (name of periodical, volume number, pages, date) — Aunt Tilly's way; Los Angeles health food store. J. Land. il Sat Eve Post 251:46-8 My '79

FOOD supply
See also
Grain supply
Production, Agricultural

Africa

Spreading starvation stalks Africa. J. Kapstein. Bus W p76 My 28 '79

author heading — **FOONER, Andrea**
Run, swim, jump and feel great! il Redbook 153:29+ Je '79

FOOTBALL
See also
Rugby
Soccer

FOOTBALL, College
See also
Football players

subhead — **Ethical aspects**

I feel betrayed; contract-breaking coaches. P. Good. il Sport 68:62-4+ Je '79

Some offers they coudn't refuse; sports agent M. Trope's tampering with college football players. W. O. Johnson and R. Reid. il por Sports Illus 50:28-30+ My 21 '79

FOOTBALL coaches
I feel betrayed; contract-breaking coaches. P. Good. il Sport 68:62-4+ Je '79

FOOTBALL players
Some offers they coudn't refuse; sports agent M. Trope's tampering with college football players. W. O. Johnson and R. Reid. il por Sports Illus 50:28-30+ My 21 '79
See also
Bradshaw, T.
Cousineau, T.
Namath, J. W.

Recruiting

name of article — How will your team do in the NFL draft? G. Usher. il Sport 68:35-7+ My '79

FORBES, Gordon
Handful of summers. il pors World Tennis 26:24-5+ My '79

FORBES, Timothy C.
Forbes goes Hollywood. il por Forbes 123:6 My 28 '79 *

FORCHÉ, Carolyn
Visitor; poem. Atlantic 243:67 Je '79

Objective

EXERCISE 4. Using Indexes to Newspapers and Periodicals. Use indexes to newspapers and periodicals to find three recent articles on each of the four topics listed below. Write the title of the article, the author (if known), the name of the newspaper or periodical, and the volume, date, and page or pages.

1. Ethiopia
2. America's trade deficit
3. actress Meryl Streep
4. videocassette recorders (VCRs)

One Suggested Answer for **1**: "Roots of Africa's Famine Run Deep"; K. R. Sheets; *U.S.News & World Report*; volume 97; December 3, 1984; page 32

GENERAL REFERENCE WORKS

The reference section of a library contains a number of **general reference works** that can help you to obtain information useful for your research. Among the most frequently consulted general reference works are encyclopedias, almanacs, atlases, dictionaries, and biographical reference works.

ENCYCLOPEDIAS

Encyclopedias are collections of articles on thousands of general topics. Articles are arranged alphabetically by subject.

Most encyclopedia articles are relatively brief; however, they are often good starting points for research projects. Some of the most frequently used encyclopedias are the *Encyclopaedia Britannica*, the *Encyclopedia Americana, Collier's Encyclopedia*, and the *World Book Encyclopedia.* Most of these encyclopedias contain from twenty to thirty volumes each, as well as a subject index to help you locate material and annually published supplements that contain up-to-date information on science, current events, and other changing fields. One- or two-volume **desk encyclopedias**, which contain shorter and fewer articles, include the *Lincoln Library of Essential Information*, the *New Columbia Encyclopedia*, and the *Random House Encyclopedia.*

Objective

EXERCISE 5. Using Encyclopedias. Use one or more encyclopedias to find answers to the following questions. Write down your answers along with the sources of your information.

1. What American President founded the University of Virginia?
2. Who invented the lightning rod?
3. In what city did America's first public theater open?
4. What was the capital of ancient Phrygia? Where was Phrygia located?
5. For what field was Lillian Gish famous?

Answers: **1.** Thomas Jefferson; **2.** Benjamin Franklin; **3.** New York City; **4.** Gordian, Asia Minor (present-day central Turkey); **5.** acting

ALMANACS

Almanacs (also called **yearbooks**) are annual collections of facts and statistics on geography, history, current events, science, sports, entertainment, and the arts.

An almanac is a relatively up-to-date source of information. It covers material through the year preceding the year on its cover. Popular almanacs are the *Official Associated Press Almanac*, the *World Almanac & Book of Facts*, and the *Information Please Almanac*. To locate information in an almanac, consult its index.

Objective

EXERCISE 6. Using Almanacs. Use one or more almanacs to find answers to the following questions. Write down your answers along with the sources of your information.

1. What is the state bird of South Dakota?
2. In what city were the 1984 Olympics held?
3. What was the population of Arizona in 1980?
4. Who won the 1983 Academy Award for Best Supporting Actress?
5. Who won the 1962 Nobel Prize for Literature?

Answers: **1.** the ring-necked pheasant; **2.** Los Angeles, California; **3.** 2,718,215; **4.** Linda Hunt; **5.** John Steinbeck

ATLASES

Atlases are collections of maps that may provide information on topography, population, climate, rainfall, or other geographical data.

Some of the best-known atlases are the *National Geographic World Atlas*, the *Hammond Contemporary World Atlas*, the *Rand McNally Cosmopolitan World Atlas*, and the *Historical Atlas of the United States.*

Objective

EXERCISE 7. Using Atlases. Use one or more atlases to answer the following questions. Write down your answers along with the sources of your information.

1. Into what body of water does the Colorado River flow?
2. Which is farther north, Missouri or North Carolina?
3. On which of the Great Lakes is Toronto, Canada?
4. What is the state capital of Alaska?
5. Of what European country is the island of Sardinia a part?

Answers: **1.** the Gulf of California; **2.** Missouri; **3.** Lake Ontario; **4.** Juneau; **5.** Italy

OTHER USEFUL REFERENCE WORKS

The following sections describe other types of library reference works that you may find useful in your research.

Language Reference Works

Language reference works provide information about words and usage. They include English-language dictionaries and thesauruses, foreign-language dictionaries, style manuals like the University of Chicago's *A Manual of Style*, and books on usage like the *Dictionary of American-English Usage* by Margaret Nicholson.

Biographical Reference Works

Biographical reference works give short life stories of noteworthy people, with entries arranged alphabetically by last name. These works include *Current Biography* and *Who's Who* books, which contain biographical information on *living* personalities; *Dictionary of American Biography, Dictionary of National Biography,* and *Who Was Who* books, which contain capsule biographies of noteworthy *deceased* persons; and *Webster's Biographical Dictionary,* which gives basic biographical information about contemporary and historical personalities from all over the world. To find the specific biographical reference work in which a particular person is listed, look under the person's last name in the library's *Biography Index.*

Books in Print

Books in Print is an annual index of books currently available from publishers. Books are listed in separate alphabetical volumes by author, title, and subject.

Books of Quotations

Books of quotations contain memorable quotations arranged by author, subject, or key word. Two well-known examples are *Bartlett's Familiar Quotations* and the *Oxford Dictionary of Quotations.*

Literature Handbooks

Literature handbooks include information about literary works and their authors. Examples are the *Oxford Companion to American Literature*, the *Oxford Companion to English Literature*, and the *Columbia Dictionary of Modern European Literature.* Literary terms are listed and defined in the *Reader's Guide to Literary Terms* by Karl Beckson and Arthur Glanz.

Reference Books in History and Geography

Reference books in history and geography include the *Oxford Companion to American History,* the *Oxford Companion to World History,* and *Webster's Geographical Dictionary.*

Reference Books in Science

Reference books in science include *A History of Technology, Van Nostrand's Scientific Encyclopedia*, and *The McGraw-Hill Encyclopedia of Science.*

Reference Books in Music and Art

Reference books in music and art include *The Encyclopedia of the Arts, Grove's Dictionary of Music and Musicians*, and *The McGraw-Hill Encyclopedia of World Art.*

Objective

EXERCISE 8. Using Other Reference Works. Use one or more of the books mentioned in this section to answer each of the following questions. Write down your answers along with your sources.

1. Who was Sojourner Truth? For what speech is she most famous?
2. Where and when did Stephen Crane die? What novels did he write?
3. What does the literary term *metonymy* mean?
4. In what poem did Ralph Waldo Emerson describe the first shot of the American Revolution as "the shot heard round the world"?
5. Identify one anthology that contains the poem in item 4.
6. What was the Edict of Nantes? Who revoked it? Briefly explain how revoking the Edict of Nantes affected the Huguenots.
7. What does the pH scale measure? What does a pH of 7 mean?
8. With what movement in art is Mary Cassatt associated? In what country was she born?
9. Name two famous works by composer Aaron Copland.
10. Name two inventors or scientists associated with the development of photography, and state their contributions.

OTHER LIBRARY RESOURCES

MICROFORMS

Microforms are tiny photographs of printed pages that are stored on filmstrips **(microfilm)** or cards **(microfiche)**.

Library materials that you are likely to find on microforms include newspapers and those magazines used often for reference, like *Newsweek* and *Time.* Microforms require special reading projectors to restore their tiny images to normal size and project them onto a lighted screen. Reading projectors are not difficult to operate, although you will probably need a demonstration.

THE VERTICAL FILE

The **vertical file** is a collection of news clippings, magazine articles, photographs, pamphlets, and other brief material arranged alphabetically by subject.

The vertical file is a good source of up-to-date information on current events, science, and other changing fields. Most libraries keep a vertical file in a cabinet in or near the reference section.

NONPRINT MATERIAL

In addition to printed material and microforms, many libraries contain **nonprint material** such as filmstrips, videocassettes, phonograph records, and tapes. Consult a member of the library staff for information on how to locate and use this material.

REVIEW

CHAPTER 34–35 RESOURCES

CHAPTER 34 THE DICTIONARY AND THE THESAURUS

Using a Dictionary (pages 659–664). Examine the following dictionary entry, and then answer the questions that follow it.

> **dul·cet** (dul′sit) ***adj.*** [ME. ***doucet*** < OFr., dim. of ***douz,*** sweet < L. ***dulcis,*** sweet < ? IE. base ****dl̥ku-,*** sweet, whence Gr. *glykys*] **1.** soothing or pleasant to hear; sweet-sounding; melodious **2.** [Archaic] sweet to taste or smell —***n.*** an organ stop like the dulciana, but one octave higher in pitch —**dul′cet·ly** ***adv.***
>
> *Webster's New World Dictionary, Second College Edition*

1. What does *dulcet* mean in this phrase: "her *dulcet* tones"?
(a) sweet-tasting **(b)** melodious **(c)** organ stop **(d)** high in pitch

2. The word *dulcet* should be
(a) hypenated after the *l* **(c)** pronounced with a *u* as in *rule*
(b) stressed in the last syllable **(d)** Choices *a–c* are all correct.

3. The word *dulcet* should be used
(a) as an adjective only **(c)** as a noun or an adjective only
(b) as a noun only **(d)** as a noun, an adjective, or an adverb

4. The word *dulcet* is related to the word for "sweet" in
(a) Old French **(b)** Latin **(c)** Greek **(d)** Choices *a–c* are all correct.

Using a Thesaurus (pages 665–666). Select the answer that best completes the following item.

5. All thesauruses include
(a) synonyms for every entry word **(c)** an index of every entry word
(b) antonyms for every entry word **(d)** Both *a* and *c* are correct.

Answers: **1.** b; **2.** a; **3.** c; **4.** d; **5.** a

CHAPTER 35 THE LIBRARY

Using the Library (pages 667–679). Select the answer that best completes each of the following items.

1. To find a catalog card for the novel *The Last of the Mohicans,* look in
(a) the Author/Title Index under *T* **(c)** the Subject Index under *M*
(b) the Author/Title Index under *L* **(d)** Both *b* and *c* are correct.

2. Nonfiction books are arranged on library shelves
(a) alphabetically by title **(c)** by the Library of Congress System only
(b) by call number **(d)** alphabetically by author's last name

3. To learn in which magazines articles about the economy appeared, consult
(a) the *Social Sciences Index* **(c)** the *Biography Index*
(b) the *New York Times Index* **(d)** the vertical file

4. To find out last year's Tony Award winner for Best Musical, consult
(a) the *Readers' Guide to Periodical Literature* **(c)** an encyclopedia
(b) the *Oxford Companion to American History* **(d)** an almanac

5. To read about the life of astronaut Sally Ride, consult
(a) *Books in Print* **(c)** the *Humanities Index*
(b) *Bartlett's Familiar Quotations* **(d)** *Who's Who*

Answers: **1.** b; **2.** b; **3.** a; **4.** d; **5.** d

INDEX

A

B

C

D

E

F

G

H

I

N

O

P

Q

R

S

T

U

V

W

Y